Diary of a
Court Reporter

To Veta & John Support -

Thank you for your Linda

Diary of a Court Reporter

What goes on behind the scenes in the Halls of Justice

READ SHOCKING TRUE COURT TRIALS AND
SEE IMPORTANT DETAILS JURIES WEREN'T ALLOWED
TO HEAR . . . CONDENSED FOR EASY READING

Roommate murder trial
Shaken Quadruplet Baby Syndrome
Captured foreign abductor of an American citizen
Car wash murders

Linda L. Russo, RPR
with George B. Blake

To order additional copies of this book, contact:
Xlibris Corporation
1-888-795-4274
www.Xlibris.com
Orders@Xlibris.com
43523

Contents

FOREWORD

Everything in this book actually happened—in the courtrooms across the country and in the judges chambers associated with these courts. Whether or not the incidents described in each trial were true was up to a jury to decide. You may have different opinions, especially when you read what the juries weren't allowed to hear. Even though the private discussions between judges and attorneys are kept from the juries, they aren't kept from the reader in this book. You will be "joining" them in the judges' chambers and "eavesdropping" on them in their "asides" during the trials to help you form what might possibly be a different reaction than the jury's.

As you involve yourself in the courtroom style of the various attorneys, you might feel that these courtroom scenes are copied after your favorite movie or television courtroom drama. Actually, it's the other way around. The TV and motion picture trial procedures always have copied the way the U.S. courts have operated for many, many years. You will feel strangely comfortable and familiar with the REAL trial action.

Although the co-author has transcribed many hundreds of trials, we sifted out the numerous boring cases from these exciting trials presented here.

All records of courtroom procedures (except where defense or security related) are a matter of public record and available in their entirety at a steep cost, to all interested parties. In this book, however, in most cases we have altered locations, dates and names of persons involved in each trial so that we don't "open old wounds" of innocent persons or expose witnesses or participants to any possible future harassments. They suffered enough hardships doing their civic duties and we don't want to put them out any further. They know who they and if they wish to identify themselves to their friends, that is their choice.

We would be very remiss if we didn't compliment:

THE JUDGES—In each trial, the sitting judges displayed an incredible amount of professionalism, oftentimes in the face of unexpected tough legal challenges. They showed by their knowledge and acuity that they were truly qualified to judge trial cases.

THE PROSECUTORS—In all the trials considered for this book, the prosecuting attorneys: The United States Attorney's Office, the District Attorneys and Assistant D.A.s really did their homework and assembled a plethora of evidence that was hard to dispute by anyone or any jury. Our hats off to these trial attorneys.

THE PUBLIC DEFENDERS—We found it amazing the thorough and professional job these persons did in defending their clients all without the incentive of reaping high court fees as their counterparts might receive. Even when the defendant "appeared" guilty from the start, the Public Defenders gave them every benefit of the doubt and did their best to free them. We salute the Public Defenders of America.

As the reader gets into each case, he or she will notice that we have eliminated a lot of repetition that normally occurs in a trial, and we summarized many areas that seemed redundant or had already been thoroughly discussed. Hopefully, this will make your reading experience flow more pleasantly.

All trials began with the Judge (The Court) greeting and identifying the participants, welcoming the jurors, followed by a reading of the charges by the Court Clerk and the judge's instructions to the juries. In this book we have eliminated these preliminaries except where they might add to the courtroom atmosphere.

Linda L. Russo

George B. Blake

CHAPTER ONE

THE ROOMMATE MURDER TRIAL

Dear Diary:

This case was especially brutal when it came to viewing the exhibits and hearing the gory details. I noticed several of the jurors wince from time to time, and I have to admit I winced a few times myself.

First Day, December 28, 2006.

THE JUDGE (THE COURT) MADE HIS OPENING REMARKS AND ASKED THE CLERK OF THE COURT TO READ THE INDICTMENT AGAINST THE DEFENDANT, WHICH HE DID AS FOLLOWS.

State of Arizona versus Robert Tenny

Indictment: Second-degree murder.

The grand jury of Maricopa County, Arizona, accuse Robert Tenny, on this 20th day of June, 2004, charging that in Maricopa County, Arizona Robert Tenny, on or about the 14th day of January, 2004, without premeditation, intentionally caused the death of Garrett Daniel or knowing that his conduct would cause death or serious physical injury, caused the death of Garrett Daniel, in violation of Arizona law. The State of Arizona further alleges that the offense charged in this count is a dangerous offense because the offense involved the discharge, use, or threatening exhibition of a knife, a deadly weapon or dangerous instrument, and/or the intentional or knowing infliction of serious physical injury upon Garrett Daniel, in violation of Arizona law.

(NEXT, THE JUDGE GAVE THE JURY VERY LENGTHY INSTRUCTIONS ABOUT THE COURT PROCEDURES, THEIR DUTIES AND RESPONSIBILITIES, AND THE FAIRNESS THEY MUST SHOW THE DEFENDANT. HE INCLUDED THESE RULES ON WHAT IS AND IS NOT TO BE CONSIDERED AS EVIDENCE.)

1. You are to determine the facts only from the testimony of witnesses and from exhibits received in evidence.
2. Ordinarily, statements or arguments made by the lawyers in the case are not evidence. Their purpose is to help you understand the evidence and law. However, if the lawyers for both parties agree or stipulate that some particular fact is true, you should accept it as the truth.
3. By itself, a question is not evidence. A question can only be used to give meaning to a witness' answer.
4. If a lawyer objects to a question and I do not allow the witness to answer, you must not try to guess what the answer might have been. You must also not try to guess the reason why the lawyer objected in the first place.
5. At times during the trial, testimony or exhibits will be offered as evidence but I might not allow them to become evidence. Since they never become evidence, you must not consider them.
6. At times I may order some evidence to be stricken from the record. Then it is no longer evidence and you must not consider it for any purpose.

(THE JUDGE ALSO ADMONISHED THEM AGAINST DISCUSSING THE TRIAL WITH ANYONE—EVEN AMONG THEMSELVES. NOW THE CASE WAS READY TO PROCEED HE CALLED ON THE PROSECUTING ATTORNEY, MR. LEV, TO MAKE HIS OPENING STATEMENT.)

MR. LEV: May it please the Court, defense counsel, ladies and gentlemen of the jury, as you know, I'm Noel Lev, Deputy County Attorney. It is my obligation to bring the evidence to you. I'm what is otherwise called the State. And my burden is to prove to you the facts and the elements beyond a reasonable doubt.

In order to do that, we start with the presumption that the defendant, Robert Tenny, is innocent. And then, I then must present the evidence for your consideration, and then you decide after all of the evidence is in and the judge has read you the final instructions whether I have proven this case to that standard. I ask you to hold me to that standard. My burden is to prove beyond a reasonable doubt that Robert Tenny intended or knew he would cause the death of Garrett Daniels, that this death occurred on 14 January, 2004, between 12:00 and 1:00 p.m., and that the victim, Garrett Daniel, was stabbed to death. At the time of death, Garrett Daniels was age 43. The instrument of death was a knife. And that is the aspect of the allegation in the charge murder in the second degree, a charge of dangerous, which is the knife. The knife in this case was a single-edged knife that one can find in a kitchen. There were ten stab wounds to the body of Garrett Daniel, several were fatal, and these were to the chest and the neck. Now, while the time of death and the date of death was January 14, 2004, between 12 and one p.m., the body was not actually found until January 27, 2004. The location of the body when found was 250 feet north of Carefree Highway on 14th Street. This was a dirt road. And the body was 20 feet east of the side shoulder on 14th Street. The body was dragged to the spot where it was found. There was no shirt on the body. There was no evidence of any kind of theft, because there was a checkbook, wallet and keys found on the body of Garrett Daniel. Included was a receipt from Motel 6 for January 13, 2004. Garrett Daniel had been dead a couple of weeks by its appearance. Mummification of the hands, maggot infestation, dried appearance. He had no shirt; he had pants, socks, underwear and a belt. And an autopsy was performed by Dr. Buch on Wednesday, January 29, 2004. There were 10 separate knife wounds; one in the forehead, three in the left front neck; left chest above the nipple; left inner forearm just below the elbow; left outside forearm between the elbow and the wrist; left upper biceps. These stab wounds caused incised wounds of the heart, right and left lungs, esophagus, the left jugular vein and the left subclavian artery. There were also rib fractures, secondary to the stab wounds with regard to the amount of force used. There was also postmortem, that is after death, trauma to the right and left leg and the right and left shoulder. Dr. Piak identified the body as Garrett Daniel by a positive match on the dental records.

Garrett Daniel and defendant Tenny had been living together since on or before 2002 in Phoenix. They moved to that address at about that time. Domestic violence was observed between Robert Tenny as the aggressor and Garrett Daniel, and this was observed in December of 2003, particularly in Christmas of 2003. A guest, Cori Crel, had come over there who knew them through the years, and made the observations that at about that time Robert Tenny threatened Garrett Daniel with a knife This was in the house of Garrett Daniel and Robert Tenny, again, where the Crels were the guests. On January 13, 2004, Garrett Daniel came to work and was observed to be haggard looking, and he talked to co-worker Cori Crel, the same person who, with her husband, was a guest, to make the observations in December, just before Christmas of 2003. Okay, we are on January 13 of '04. He came to work at the insurance place shown. He told her he didn't go home all weekend as he and Robert Tenny were not getting along and Garrett was moving out and leaving Bob Tenny. Garrett told another neighbor, Kim Floy, who lives across the street, on January 10th that he was staying at a Motel 6 as Bob was in one of his moods, and he had it and was moving out. He told her he would sell his one-half share of the house or have Bob buy him out, but he wouldn't just sign over the house to Bob. They were joint tenants on the deed. Garrett Daniel stayed at Motel 6 on January 10, 2004, perhaps a day or so before, perhaps a day or so after, because the bill on

January 10 was $99 and something. And he stayed also on January 13, 2004. The bill was $33. He may have stayed in his car on January 12, 2004. He charged these bills to his American Express card. In addition to the house having joint title between Garrett Daniel and Bob Tenny, also Bob Tenny's 1996 black Jaguar was also in a joint title with Garrett Daniel. Garrett Daniel had an income. The State will prove that a split-up of Garrett Daniel leaving Bob Tenny would have resulted in the loss of the relationship, the house, the car, his income. The sequence of events that lead up to the death and immediately followed the death of Garrett Daniel are as follows. Garrett Daniel was last seen on Tuesday, January 13, 2004, when he left his place of employment at Schol Insurance and went home for lunch. This was between noon and 12:15 pm. Daniel never returned to work and has not been seen or heard from since until his body was discovered on January 27, 2004. That same afternoon, perhaps 3:00 or 3:10 pm, something right in that close time frame, Bob Tenny called Garrett Daniel's place of work and spoke with his co-worker, Cori Crel, who knew both of them and was familiar with the voice of Bob Tenny. Bob Tenny told Cori that Garrett Daniel would not be back to work because he had been in an accident and he needed to get checked out. Bob Tenny was last seen by Jackie Lesp at approximately 12:50 pm. She saw Bob Tenny driving Garrett Daniel's red convertible Sunbird out of the front driveway of their residence. He left southbound on 28th Street, he drove by her, she was driving northbound, and he was in the vehicle by himself, in Garrett Daniel's red Sunbird. Both Cori and Jackie attempted numerous times after the 14th to contact either of the missing men, but were unsuccessful. Cori in particular made several phone calls to the residence. No response. They could not locate Garrett Daniel's car. On January 19, 2004, Garrett Daniel's vehicle was located at 23rd Street and Flower after a phone-in by an apartment complex. It was found abandoned a mere one-half mile from the residence of Garrett Daniel/Bob Tenny. Due to the vehicle having been legally parked and no apparent break-in or anything noted and no stolen vehicle report, the officer did not think a whole lot about it until later when the missing person's detail, asked the officer to go back and look further. He did, on the 21st, and he saw in the inside, blood on the seats and mud on all four wheels, wheel wells and fenders. And one of the witnesses, Cori, will testify that Garrett Daniel never allowed his red Pontiac Sunbird to be anything other than in an immaculately clean condition. In the road near where the body was dumped was dirt. And on January 13th, 2004, there was a big rain, a lesser rain the next day, and the roads would have been muddy. Phoenix P.D. served a search warrant on the home of Daniel and Tenny. The search revealed several rooms with blood splatter on the floor and walls, there was also an indication that a pool of blood had been cleaned up in the kitchen. There were no indications of any type of forced entry into the house.

On January 21, 2004, Jeff Kin, being a board member of HID, that's Housing For the Independently Disabled of which Robert Tenny was executive director, received a letter on the 21st postmarked January 17, 2004 from New York without a return address. It was from Robert Tenny. It was a typed letter that was his formal resignation as executive director. It listed the reasons as a culmination of personal disappointments and economic stress leave me no choice but to step aside. No one had ever been told prior thereto that that was what he was going to do. A neighbor, Walter Weiss, a next-door neighbor of the Daniel/Tenny residence, had seen the black Jaguar parked in the front driveway late in the afternoon of January 14, 2004, between 12 noon and 1:00 p.m. He observed Garrett Daniel's red colored convertible parked in the rear driveway. He felt this was not normal as Garrett usually parked his car in the front driveway, and Bob Tenny parked his black Jaguar to the rear. He also was aware that Garrett Daniel normally came home for lunch at his residence around this time. When Mr. Weiss returned to his home that same day approximately between 5:00 and 5:30 p.m., he observed Bob Tenny's black Jaguar in the front driveway but the red convertible was not present. He noticed the Jaguar had remained parked in the driveway. He received a handwritten letter from Robert Tenny on 1/17/2004. It was postmarked New York City 1/14/04. It said to Walter Weiss that he had gone to visit his family. He had been trying to call Garrett on the phone but had received no answer. He indicated to Mr. Weiss, tell Garrett to answer the phone and check on Louise, the cat. Mr. Weiss observed in his interview that it was unusual for Mr. Tenny to write a letter, as he knew Walter's phone number and could have called. The cat would have been there about a week by the time he got the letter. Robert Tenny's separate American Express card allowed the police to note through the business records that he purchased an air line ticket on United Airlines on 1/15 of '04, the day after the murder. It was purchased by phone at about 6:40 a.m, because it was an electronic ticket. The flight left Phoenix the same morning at 7:35 a.m. It went via Denver to New York City on United. Bob Tenny remained for two days at the Hotel JFK, and then he left this country on British Airways to London. He stayed in London about a day or so, and then the credit card transaction showed that he got a ticket from London to South Africa. Garrett Daniel worked at Schol Insurance Company. The receptionist there, Doris Giff, stated that Garrett Daniel left work on Tuesday, January 14, 2004, between 12:00 noon and 12:15 p.m. He told Doris that he was going to lunch, and she observed that when he left by himself he would be eating lunch at home. That's the last time she ever saw him or heard from him, Garrett Daniel.

Cori Crel, also a co-worker at Schol Insurance, she's the one that saw the argument just prior to Christmas of 2003 that I already described. She said that after this incident she and her husband avoided going to Garrett's home. Cori said that Garrett Daniel did not come into work on Monday, January 13th, until after the lunch hour. He looked terrible. He didn't appear to have gotten much sleep over the weekend. She asked him if he was all right. He told her he didn't go home Friday night because Bob and he were not getting along. Garrett told her he spent the weekend in a hotel.

He was late for work on Tuesday the 14th. He didn't arrive until 9:15 or 9:30. He again looked horrible as though he had not been sleeping, according to Cori. Cori left work to meet her husband for lunch approximately 11:45 a.m. and never saw Garrett Daniel after that. However, when Garrett did not return from lunch, she became concerned. She didn't think there was anything seriously wrong until she received the telephone call later that afternoon from Bob Tenny around 3:10 p.m. She answered telephone at Schol Insurance. Bob Tenny told her that Garrett would not be back. She asked him what he was talking about, and he said Garrett was in an accident and they wanted to get him checked out. She never understood what he meant by that. She tried numerous times that same day, the 14th, and the next few days to get ahold of Garrett or Bob, but could not locate either of them. There was just the answering machine. Jackie Lesp was another neighbor of Garrett Daniel and Bob Tenny. She lives in the house directly across from Garrett and has known Bob and Garrett for approximately five years. She last talked with Garrett Daniel on Sunday, January 12, 2004, approximately eight P.M. Garrett came to her house and talked for a couple of hours. He wanted to spend that night at her house, but she made an excuse about her kids having to get up early for school. On Tuesday, January 14th, as I mentioned before, at 1:50 p.m. she observed Bob Tenny backing out of the front driveway of their house in Garrett Daniel's red convertible. Garrett Daniel was not in it. He drove southbound past Jackie. She did not see Garrett's car again, but the next morning she saw his black Jaguar parked in the front driveway of their house, and she observed that was unusual because Garrett's car was almost always parked in the rear.

Kim Floy is another neighbor. She said she spoke by telephone with Garrett Daniel on the evening of Friday, January 10th, at approximately 7:30 p.m. Garrett told her that Bob was in one of his bad moods and that he, Garrett, had not gone home after work, that rather he had gone to a hotel. He told her he was going to move out on Bob. His plans were to sell the house and split the profits with Bob. While talking with Garrett on the 10th, Kim made arrangements for her and her husband to meet Garrett at his house the next morning. She wanted to get a sewing machine back she had loaned to Garrett and Bob. She went to his house at 10:30 a.m. on the 11th. Garrett was sitting in his car in front of the house. As soon as Kim and her husband pulled up, Garrett jumped out of his car, went over to the sewing machine sitting on the front lawn, and with the help of Kim's husband he put it in their car. Then he told them he had to go. He got in his car and left. That was the last time she saw or spoke with Garrett Daniel. She observed he seemed to be very nervous and afraid that day.

On February 5th, 2004, a search warrant was served at the home of Garrett Daniel and Bob Tenny by the Sheriff's Office. They noted that a knob on the door between the living room and the kitchen had blood on it, a throw rug had some blood on it, and there was a hair being held on a knob by the blood. Several areas on the floor and walls of the bathroom, hallway, living room and rear patio were found to contain blood drops or spatter. Spatter is if blood hits something, it leaves a certain pattern. Blood was found on the kitchen cabinets and on the toe kicks beneath the cabinets. Blood was also found in the back of the rear yard on a covered pathway that leads into a rear garage. Blood swab samples were taken from numerous areas. Luminol testing was completed. The Luminol will produce a chemical reaction. If there's blood there, even if it's been mopped up, it will produce a reaction, and it looks like a turquoise glow. This was all over the floors. It also indicated possible wiping patterns, such as with a mop. It was on the floors of the master bedroom, hallway, living room and kitchen. There were barefoot impressions to the west edge of the patio.

Garrett Daniel had socks on when his body was found.

The car was also impounded and it was also gone through. There was blood on the back seat, there was blood on a front buckle in the passenger front seat, there was blood on one edge of the passenger front seat like wipes and smears, and these were all tested. On Monday, March 3rd, 2004, Garrett Daniel's mother, Phyllis, contacted the Sheriff's Office because she had received a phone call at 7:30 a.m. in the morning from Bob Tenny who identified himself by name. She also recognized his voice, as she had spoken to him many times in the past. And he told her he had been on vacation overseas and was asking her what is going on. At the time Bob Tenny suddenly departed Phoenix, he was a citizen of South Africa and Canada. His folks live in Canada. The State will show beyond a reasonable doubt that Robert Tenny intended or knew he would cause the death of Garrett Daniel that occurred on January 14, 2004, between 12:00 and 1:00 p.m., at which time Garrett Daniel was stabbed to death by Robert Tenny. After which Robert Tenny took the body of Garrett Daniel in the red convertible sometime during the evening hours and dumped the body. Immediately after the death the State will show he simply went to work in his regular clothes. And the location where the body was dumped was relatively remote, and that he came back and parked the car within a half mile of the house. And that he suddenly departed Phoenix, Arizona, to South Africa via New York and London. And based upon these facts, together with admission to Cori Crel that Garrett Daniel was not coming back, that he had been involved in an accident, he had to be checked out, these will be the proof the State will provide to you over and during the course of this trial, which will come in through physical evidence, which will come in through testimonial evidence, including officers that did the search and seizure, collected the evidence, including the experts with regard to the blood testing, the Luminol, the DNA testing, all of which will present to you for your determination which ultimately is, the State has proven the case beyond a reasonable doubt.

Thank you for your attention. Your Honor; defense.

(AT THIS POINT THE COURT CALLED UPON THE DEFENSE, PUBLIC DEFENDER, MR. SCHRE, TO GIVE HIS OPENING STATEMENT.)

MR. SCHRE: Thank you, Judge.

Good afternoon, ladies and gentlemen of the jury. I'm now going to give you Robert's opening statement. I'd like you to pay close attention in this case to one thing. The one thing I'd like you to pay close attention to is time, because it's a very important factor in this case. What you're going to find out through the evidence is that from the time Garrett Daniel left his work at about 12:30 on January 14, 2004, until the time that Robert Tenny took a plane to Denver and then New York on the morning of January 15, 2004, not a great deal of time elapsed. It wasn't a time frame that expanded a millennium. Instead, it was a very, very short time frame.

Now, at the time Robert left for New York and then South Africa, he wasn't acting out of the ordinary. He wasn't acting unusual for Robert Tenny. You see, Robert Tenny was born in South Africa in 1966. When he was 18 years old, at the snap of a finger he left South Africa. He left that country with nothing more than the clothes on his back. He didn't bring big amounts of luggage over to North America, he didn't bring cars over, he didn't bring much over but the clothes on his back. And he went to Canada. He arrived in Canada about 1983. When he got to Canada, he started a life for himself; he started a life in the advertising field. He's worked his way up the ladder in advertising in Canada, and then his job wasn't going so great, so at the snap of a finger, once again, Robert Tenny all of a sudden left Canada with nothing more than the clothes on his back. He didn't take possessions, he didn't take cars or anything like that, and he went off to Hawaii. Just like when he left for Canada and he didn't know anybody in Canada, he went to Hawaii. He didn't know anybody in Hawaii and he started a life for himself. What he started doing there was working for a jet ski company. He was doing okay in the jet ski company in Hawaii. He was in Hawaii for about a year, then in 1998 Robert Tenny met Garrett Daniel. Garrett Daniel had come to Hawaii on vacation and they developed a relationship while Garrett was in Hawaii for a brief period of time. And at the snap of his fingers, Robert Tenny once again got up and left a place that he was living in. He left Hawaii at the snap of his fingers and moved with Garrett Daniel to Indiana. They lived there from about 1998 to 1999. When they were in Indiana, they lived as a couple. They had a relationship, and Robert worked a little here, a little there, remodeling homes, things like that. And then at the snap of a finger once again, Robert packed up with Garrett and he moved to Phoenix, Arizona. Just like in Hawaii, Robert didn't know anybody when he moved to Indiana, and just like in Indiana, Robert didn't know anybody when he moved to Phoenix, Arizona. He lived in Phoenix, Arizona, for about five years. He lived with Garrett Daniel, they got a home together, and Robert when they first moved here worked for quite sometime at remodeling that home. Once that was done, Robert formed his own business, he formed Homes For The Independently Disabled. He did this through his own research and his own ingenuity. What the purpose of the Homes For The Independently Disabled was, was to get people who were disabled who were credit risks, and to find them housing that they could own. So some of these people had bad credit, so Robert formed this business, and it was going okay. And he was proud of what he was doing. He was having some success finding disabled people homes. And then some years went by and Robert and Garrett's relationship went sour. Like every relationship, they had their ups and downs. But what happened was, over the years they were fighting a little too much. They weren't getting along. They weren't being faithful to each other, and so Robert decided at the snap of a fingers once again to move on. He decided to move on for three reasons. The first reason that Robert left Arizona was because his relationship with Garrett was going nowhere. The second reason that Robert left the state of Arizona was because there were some problems at his company, Homes For The Independently Disabled, and he was a little frustrated with the problems. He wasn't making as much money as he wanted to make. The business wasn't run as smoothly, so he decided to leave the business. The third reason that Robert decided to leave Arizona for South Africa is because Robert wasn't a citizen of the United States. Robert was having immigration problems. Things were not going well with immigration.

Instead of dealing with a failing relationship, a failing business, and problems with immigration, Robert decided at the snap of his fingers to go to South Africa, visit with family and start his life over again, just like he did when he went to Canada, Hawaii and Phoenix. This is the evidence that you're going to hear during the course of this trial. At the end of this trial, I am confident when you pay attention to the time factors in this case, that you will find Robert Tenny not guilty. Thank you.

(AFTER THESE LENGTHY OPENING STATEMENTS, THE COURT CALLED FOR A LUNCH RECESS AND AGAIN ADMONISHED THE JURORS NOT TO DISCUSS THE CASE. THE COURT DISCUSSED THE UPCOMING PROCEEDINGS WITH THE ATTORNEYS, OUT OF THE PRESENCE OF THE JURY, TO BE SURE THINGS WOULD RUN SMOOTHLY.)

THE COURT: Anything we have to cover? Any issues?

MR. SCHRE: I don't think so.

THE COURT: Mr. Lev, anything we have to cover?

MR. LEV: No, Your Honor.

THE COURT: Do you have your witnesses lined up for 1:30?

MR. LEV: Yes. I will be candid with the Court, I have Detective Brue here who, I anticipate that based upon past experience, it will take two, two and a half hours. So I have three witnesses, the person who discovered the body, the initial deputy on the scene, and Detective Brue.

THE COURT: I always ask this, is there anything that the parties can stipulate to, any areas at all that might warrant a stipulation?

MR. Lev: I will think about it. I can't think of any at the moment. Nothing for today that I'm aware of. Perhaps something will come along.

THE COURT: All right. We will see you back here then.

(A luncheon recess was taken.)

AFTERNOON SESSION

THE COURT: The record will reflect the presence of the jury, counsel, and the defendant. Mr. Lev, you may call your first witness.

THE PROSECUTOR THEN CALLED UPON A HOMEOWNER WHO LIVED IN THE DESOLATE AREA WHERE GARRETT DANIEL'S BODY WAS FOUND. HE DESCRIBED HOW A NEIGHBOR LADY ON HORSEBACK ASKED HIM TO COME WITH HER TO CHECK OUT SOMETHING SHE STUMBLED ON IN THE DESERT . . . A BODY OR A MANNEQUIN. THE HOMEOWNER THEN ACCOMPANIED HER TO THE AREA—ABOUT 900 FEET AWAY—AND DISCOVERED GARRETT DANIEL'S BODY UNDER SOME BRUSH AND VEGETATION. THE PROSECUTOR DESCRIBED THE LOCATION, THE CONDITION OF THE ROADS LEADING TO THE BODY, AND DESPITE SEVERAL OBJECTIONS FROM THE DEFENSE (OVERRULED) THIS LINE OF QUESTIONING CONTINUED)

BY MR. LEV:
Q. Did you go where she suggested you check?
A. Yes. I walked south of our property where there's a large desert tree. Underneath the tree is where I was told they thought there was either a mannequin or body. I could see there was some brush covering something. I probably came within probably five to six feet from the body. I looked at it and I could tell it wasn't a mannequin. I could see lividity, which is whenever a body has been sitting

for a period of time, the blood pools. In this case the body was laying on its back. I could see a dark line where the blood from the body had pooled, so I could tell—

THE COURT: What is the objection?

MR. SCHRE: I object that he's giving expert testimony. There's no foundation that he's qualified to give this testimony.

THE COURT: The testimony, he said there was lividity, he said he observed there was blood pooling. I think a lay person can observe when blood's pooling. I'm going to overrule the objection. Ask your next question.

BY MR. Lev:
Q. You were saying?
A. I was a paramedic approximately six years prior to that date.
Q. You have seen this before?
A. Yes, sir. That's one of the things as a paramedic that we would look for which would be a sign of death, irreversible death, biological death, something that you cannot resuscitate, to bring anybody back, when you see that. Once I noticed that, I backed away without disturbing anything and we called the Sheriff's Office.
Q. Did you see whether or not the body was covered with brush?
A. Yes, sir. Branches had been pulled over the top of it.
Q. Was the brush in such a way that it that shaded the body?
A. Yes. It blocked the view from the street. This was the day after my son's birthday party. My son's birthday is January 21st, we celebrated his two year birthday on the 26th, so the day before was when we had a birthday party, approximately 50 to 60 people came to my house. You couldn't see anything from the street. It wasn't until I came off of the road from the east side that I could even spot anything.
Q. So the body was well concealed?
A. Yes, sir.

(AFTER THIS, THE WITNESS IDENTIFIED PHOTOS OF THE AREA AND THE APPROXIMATE TEMPERATURES AND WEATHER CONDITIONS AT THAT TIME OF YEAR. IT HAPPENED TO BE VERY COOL—AND RAINY—WITH MUDDY, UNPAVED ROADS, AND COLD, BARE—EVEN ICY—GROUNDS THROUGHOUT THE NEIGHBORHOOD. IN HIS CROSS-EXAMINATION, THE DEFENSE DISCUSSED THE TYPE OF CLAY DIRT IN THIS AREA AND WHETHER IT LOOKED LIKE THE CLAY PICTURED

ON A RED PONTIAC SUNBIRD CONVERTIBLE, A PHOTO OF WHICH
WAS ADMITTED TO EVIDENCE. THE WITNESS AGREED THAT IT DID.
AFTER A LENGTHY CROSS-EXAMINATION WHICH ESTABLISHED
THAT THE MONTH OF JANUARY HAD BEEN A PARTICULARLY WET
MONTH, THE NEXT WITNESS WAS CALLED: A DEPUTY SHERIFF.
PROSECUTOR LEV BEGAN THE QUESTIONING:)

BY MR. LEV:
Q. Were you on duty on January 27, 2004?
A. Yes, I was.
Q. Did you go to the vicinity of the Cave Creek area?
A. Yes, I did.
Q. For what purpose?
A. I was dispatched there by radio in reference to a possible body found in
that area.
Q. Who did you meet?
A. A subject who identified himself as Mr. Franz.
Q. Okay. So you met Mr. Franz. About what time of the day was it?
A. It was about 5:45 in the evening.
Q. And where did you go after you met him?
A. I spoke with him briefly and he showed me the area of his concern. I looked
in that area.
Q. What did you find?
A. I couldn't see much of anything because of the brush and the shadows that
were made during that time of the day. I didn't approach very closely.
Q. What did you believe it to be for purposes of your being there?
A. A deceased person.
Q. And what did you do next?
A. At that point, I secured the crime scene, taped it off and notified my
supervisor.
Q. Subsequent to that, did members of the homicide detail come out?
A. Yes, they did.

(THE WITNESS THEN IDENTIFIED PHOTOS OF THE AREA WHERE
THE BODY WAS FOUND. IN THE CROSS-EXAMINATION, THE DEFENSE
TRIED TO ESTABLISH THAT SINCE THE BODY DIDN'T GIVE OFF A
FOUL ODOR, IT MUST HAVE BEEN NEWLY DECEASED—AT A TIME
WHEN THE DEFENDANT WAS OUT OF THE COUNTRY.)

BY MR. SCHRE:
Q. And on this occasion you were purposefully trying to smell the body, right?
A. Trying to see if there was an odor of decay.

Q. You took several whiffs?
A. Yes.
Q. You didn't smell anything, did you?
A. I could not smell anything.
Q. You were specifically looking for that odor, and you didn't smell it, right?
A. That's correct.
Q. And one reason why you may not be able to smell the odor of decay is if the body hasn't been there for very long, correct?
A. That's one possibility, yes.
Q. That it was just put there recently, and that's why you couldn't smell it?
A. That's correct.

(ON HIS REDIRECT EXAMINATION, THE PROSECUTOR TRIED TO NAIL DOWN THE THOUGHT THAT THE BODY WOULDN'T HAVE HAD AN OVERWHELMINGLY FOUL ODOR BECAUSE IT HAD BEEN EXPOSED TO THE COLD WEATHER—AS IN COLD STORAGE IN A MORGUE—AND THE WITNESS AGREED THAT THE GROUND AND WEATHER HAD BEEN PARTICULARLY COLD. THIS MANEUVER SEEMED TO QUASH THE DEFENSE'S STRATEGY THAT THE BODY WAS NEWLY DECEASED.

THE NEXT WITNESS CALLED WAS A SHERIFF'S DETECTIVE WHO VERIFIED NUMEROUS PHOTOGRAPHS OF THE SCENE WHERE THE BODY WAS DISCOVERED. THE GRAPHIC PHOTOS SHOWED GARRETT DANIEL'S BODY AS IT LAY HIDDEN UNDER TUMBLEWEED AND OTHER VEGETATION, WITH ONLY A PART OF THE ARM AND ELBOW EXPOSED. ANOTHER PHOTO SHOWED GARRETT DANIEL'S CHECKBOOK WHICH HAD BEEN FOUND ON A PATH LEADING TO THE BODY. NOW THE PROSECUTOR WANTED TO DISMISS ANY DOUBTS ABOUT HOW LONG THE BODY HAD BEEN THERE, AND IT GOT A LITTLE GRUESOME.)

BY MR. LEV:
Q. First of all, have you seen dead bodies before?
A. Yes.
Q. Have you seen decomposition?
A. Yes.
Q. Have you seen maggots on dead bodies?
A. Yes.
Q. So I will rephrase it. What did you notice about the body and decomposition?
A. There was decomposition of the body. There was insect infestation about the head area. I would say that from what I saw, that the victim could have been dead from several days to several weeks.

(NOW THE QUESTIONING MOVED FROM THE BODY RECOVERY AREA TO THE ALLEGED MURDER SCENE AS THE DETECTIVE IDENTIFIED THE HOME THAT GARRETT DANIEL AND ROBERT TENNY SHARED. THE PROSECUTOR CONTINUED:)

Q. Now, preparatory to the next series of questions, was blood spatter found in the house?

A. Yes.

Q. I have all the specific photographs, but to your recollection, the blood spatter was generally where?

A. I'd say the majority of it was in the kitchen and living room areas.

Q. Now, was there blood spots visible to the naked eye?

A. There were areas of blood droplets, there were also areas of spatter on the walls.

Q. Is this another area of the blood spatter?

A. Yes. That would be the front living room area looking back towards the hallway.

(THE PROSECUTOR AND THE DETECTIVE CONTINUED TO IDENTIFY MANY PHOTOS OF BLOOD SPATTER THROUGHOUT MUCH OF THE HOUSE, INCLUDING THE CARPETING, KITCHEN, BATHROOM, BEDROOM, EVEN ON THE REAR PATIO AND POOL AREA. THEN THE PROSECUTOR ADDED:)

Q. Let me ask you this. Are you familiar with homicide scenes where there's been stabbings?

A. Yes.

Q. You're familiar there were ten stab wounds?

A. Yes.

Q. You went to the autopsy?

A. Yes.

Q. You did a supplement on your own on the autopsy; is that correct?

A. Correct.

Q. When the knife is plunged into a living body and pulled out again, what happens?

A. The first plunge will pick up some blood from the body. Each subsequent plunge will pick up more blood. As the knife is forced in and drawn back out, you can get some cast-off blood that will go in the direction that the arm is moving. If I'm stabbing this way and pulling back, you can get some cast-off blood back on this wall. Some may drop down because of the weight toward the floor, some may be up high.

Q. What about the person being stabbed, bleeding, does the blood drop, and with the force have gravity, does it tend to drop down?

A. It can, yes.

Q. And if the person is moving around, from here to there, does the blood spatter and drop?

A. That's another factor. The human body itself can cast off blood, depending on how much movement is going on by the victim.

Q. In addition, though, if the person's literally moving from one room to another, for example.

A. There can be quite a bit of blood.

(MORE PHOTOS WERE PRESENTED INTO EVIDENCE.)

Q. Were you there when there was Luminol testing done?

A. Yes.

Q. And just briefly, what is Luminol?

A. Luminol's is a chemical that reacts with blood, and under certain lighting conditions it can be photographed as it's usually done in dark and special photography used to photograph it.

Q. Can you tell a smear pattern with Luminol?

A. Smear and wiping, yes.

Q. With that, let me show these to you and ask you, is this an example of the Luminol testing done by the Sheriff's Department on that date in this house, and if that's indeed Luminol?

A. That's Luminol testing with the lights out, completely dark, and special photography to photograph that chemical reaction with the Luminol in the blood.

Q. Let me ask you this. Can one mop, and blood not be evident to the eyes but still have enough left to get a Luminol reaction?

A. Yes.

(ADDITIONAL PHOTOS OF LUMINOL TREATED BLOOD SPOTS WERE PLACED INTO EVIDENCE. NEXT, THE WITNESS IDENTIFIED PHOTOS OF A BLACK 1989 FOUR-DOOR JAGUAR CAR, REGISTERED TO BOTH GARRETT DANIEL AND ROBERT TENNY, PARKED IN THE DRIVEWAY IN FRONT OF THE SUSPECT'S HOME. NEXT THE PROSECUTOR SWITCHED GEARS AND ENTERED INTO EVIDENCE A TYPED LETTER OF RESIGNATION ALLEGEDLY WRITTEN BY ROBERT TENNY, QUITTING HIS JOB IMMEDIATELY. THE LETTER WAS POSTMARKED FROM NEW YORK CITY. NEXT HE TRIED TO INTRODUCE A MONEY ORDER RECEIPT THAT WAS GIVEN TO HIM BY A MS. CHARL, BUT IT

MET WITH VEHEMENT OBJECTIONS FROM THE DEFENSE COUNSEL. SENSING A LONG, DRAWN OUT DEBATE, THE COURT DISMISSED THE JURY UNTIL THE NEXT DAY. THE FOLLOWING PROCEEDINGS WERE HELD OUT OF THE PRESENCE OF THE JURY:)

MR. SCHRE: Understand this is a money order receipt from Sherry Charl who is listed as a witness in this case, and that she claims that on January 14, 2004, at about three in the afternoon, two in the afternoon, she went to see Mr. Tenny in his office and she gave him that money order at that time. And Ms. Charl can come in here and I have no objection to her testifying about seeing Mr. Tenny on the 14th, if she saw him, and the observations she made that day. But I think admitting the money order receipt into evidence is a little—it's not relevant. It doesn't add anything to the case. She can testify she saw Mr. Tenny, she went there to make him a payment, but the money order receipt is not dated on the 14th of January.

THE COURT: I understand what you're saying.

MR. SCHRE: What it leads into is Ms. Charl, I believe, needs to be instructed before she takes the witness stand tomorrow because I think she is a fire cracker ready to go off. I believe she wants to testify about Mr. Tenny being involved in a long involved fraud scheme where any money she ever gave him for the payment of her home through him did not go into HID's bank account, rather went into his pocket, and she lost her home because of that, and there were eight or ten or fifteen other people who were customers who never had their payments made to their account. Just from her attitude, I think she is going to want to get on the witness stand and want to testify to that. She is also going to want to tell the jury about how she got the news media involved in this and that was the only way the mortgage company didn't start evicting people. I think she needs to be instructed before she gets on the stand because I believe she has some anger that she wants to communicate to the jurors.

THE COURT: Mr. Lev.

MR. LEV: No problem. I'm glad that Mr. Schre brought this out. I was unaware that she had this kind of a repressed desire to do all of this. So I will instruct her. I'm only interested in the 14th and her being there for a limited time for what she saw.

THE COURT: Do you think, Mr. Lev, do you think I need to talk to the witness, or do you think you're going to be able to handle this?

MR. LEV: If I get any feeling of a problem, I will be glad to make that request in Mr. Schre's presence.

THE COURT: I need you to impress upon her the parameters. The reasons she is being called to testify is simply this meeting on the 14th and not all the other ancillary things, which really are not relevant to the case, and may be inflammatory.

MR. LEV: I will tell her to listen to my specific questions and give me specific answers. If she sounds like she's about to go off, I will try to make a halt and do sort of an alert.

MR. SCHRE: I'm not attacking her character. She appeared to be a nice lady to me, but it seemed like she had some things that she wanted to communicate in court.

THE COURT: Okay. I'd be careful, maybe the types of questions I asked her also so you didn't open that door.

MR. SCHRE: Right.

THE COURT: Okay. Anything else we need to cover before tomorrow? Is ten o'clock—I didn't ask either of the attorneys, hopefully you can cover your other matters. Is there anything else that you were covering, Mr. SCHRE?

MR. SCHRE: No, Judge.

(THAT ENDED THE FIRST DAY'S SESSION.)

Second Day—December 29, 2006

(THE SESSION OPENED WITH THE PUBLIC DEFENDER CROSS-EXAMINING DETECTIVE BRU, WHO HAD COMPLETED HIS DIRECT TESTIMONY AT THE END OF THE PREVIOUS DAY.)

BY MR. SCHRE:
Q. Detective Bru, do you eat red meat?
A. Occasionally, yes.

MR. LEV: Objection. Irrelevant.

MR. SCHRE: I'm leading up to the relevance here.

THE COURT: He can answer that.

THE WITNESS: Occasionally.

BY MR. SCHRE:

Q. Do you own a refrigerator?

A. Yes.

Q. Have you ever left meat, let's say hamburger meat, in your refrigerator for a week without cooking it?

A. Usually in the freezer, not in the refrigerator.

Q. Well, have you ever come across meat in the refrigerator that's been there a little too long?

MR. LEV: I think that this is an irrelevant line of questioning.

THE COURT: I'm going to sustain the objection. Let's move on.

MR. SCHRE: All right.

BY MR. SCHRE:

Q. Detective Bru, there are many different factors that can affect the odor of decomposition in the body, correct?

A. That's correct.

Q. You do a lot of cases with bodies out in the desert, correct?

A. I'm familiar with quite a few of them, yes.

Q. One factor is heat?

A. Correct.

Q. Heat can speed up the rate of decay?

A. Yes.

Q. Heat can affect the smell of decay, correct?

A. It can speed up or slow down the decomposition, depending on the heat. The decomposition is what affects the smell.

Q. But there's other things besides the rate of decomposition that can affect the smell, correct?

A. As in?

Q. For example, water can affect the odor of decomposition coming from a body?

A. It can slow down the decomposition.

Q. But water can cause its own smells when it's mixed with the decomposing body.

MR. LEV: Object to this line of questioning. I don't believe this witness is qualified, nor has the foundation been laid that he's some kind of an expert on decomposition of bodies over and above his experience as a homicide detective.

THE COURT: He can answer if he can. If it's outside of his area of expertise, he can say so.

THE WITNESS: I don't know that. I know that water can slow down decomposition, moisture.

BY MR. SCHRE:

Q. But you don't have any idea how it can affect the smell?

A. I don't know what the combination of the mixture, how it affects it.

Q. Humidity can affect the rate of decomposition, correct?

A. True. Moisture and humidity will slow it down, yes.

(THE PUBLIC DEFENDER ASCERTAINED THE WEATHER CONDITIONS IN THE AREA THAT THE BODY WAS FOUND TO TRY TO ESTABLISH THAT THE BODY HAD BEEN PLACED THERE RECENTLY WHEN ROBERT TENNY WAS OUT OF THE COUNTRY, AND THAT IS WHY IT HADN'T HAD TIME TO DECOMPOSE AND SMELL FOUL. ABRUPTLY, HE CHANGED HIS LINE OF QUESTIONING OF DETECTIVE BRU AS FOLLOWS:)

Q. Now, you did collect evidence during the course of your investigation in this case that Robert Tenny attempted to contact people and authorities in Phoenix, or in Arizona, in relation to Garrett Daniel's death, correct?

A. In Phoenix I know of one attempt to contact.

Q. That was a letter to Officer Tim Camp of the Sheriff's Office, correct?

A. Lieutenant Camp was the public information officer at the time.

Q. And you also know through your investigation that Mr. Tenny attempted to contact Mrs. Daniel?

A. Yes. That was in her residence which is in southern Arizona by phone.

Q. Tell me whether you, during the course of this investigation, examined Garrett Daniel's red car.

A. No, I did not. That was done by the Police Department.

Q. There was no blood in the photos you reviewed of the red car in relation to the trunk?

A. Not that I recall.

Q. And the trunk of the red car was quite messy?

A. There was a lot of personal items packed in there, if I recall.

Q. Now, this is the wallet you found on the body of Garrett Daniel?

A. Yes.

Q. What was in that wallet?

A. There was a driver's license, a social security card, numerous credit cards belonging to the deceased. Also, one credit card belonging to the defendant. There was also some personal business cards, and things like that.

Q. There was no money in that wallet, was there?

A. No.

Q. And you have no idea whether or not the person who murdered Garrett Daniel took money out of that wallet, do you?
A. No, I don't.
Q. And you don't know if any jewelry was taken from Garrett Daniel when he was killed, do you?
A. No.

(NOW THE PUBLIC DEFENDER QUESTIONED ABOUT THE CONDITION OF THE DANIEL/TENNY HOUSE.)

Q. You weren't the first person to go to that house and investigate, were you?
A. No.
Q. Earlier in the week prior to Garrett Daniel's body being found in the desert, the Phoenix Police Department was there, correct?
A. That's correct.
Q. And Detective McEl lead the investigation?
A. That's correct, the missing persons detail.
Q. And prior to McEl going to the Tenny/Daniel house, other police officers went there earlier in the week, correct?
A. Some patrol officers did. I don't know if they went inside or not. I don't recall.
Q. Did you ever speak with these patrol officers that had gone to the Daniel/Tenny house prior to Detective McEl?
A. No.
Q. Even before those patrol officers, other people went into the Tenny/Daniel home and conducted a search after the disappearance of Garrett Daniel?
A. Yes.
Q. And you did interview some of those people?
A. Yes.
Q. One person was Cori Crel?
A. Yes.
Q. Another person was Jackie Lesp?
A. Yes.
Q. And during the course of your investigation in this case, you obtained phone records of the Tenny/Daniel home, correct?
A. That's correct.
Q. And you found that on January 17, 2004, a phone call was made from the Daniel/Tenny home?
A. I believe so, yes.
Q. And later on in your investigation you found that Cori Crel made that phone call, correct?
A. Correct.

Q. Now, let's talk a little more about the Tenny/Daniel home. Is it fair to say when you began your investigation of that home, there was quite a bit of blood that you observed?

A. Yes.

(NOW THE PUBLIC DEFENDER HAD DETECTIVE BRU DESCRIBE MANY OF THE PLACES THAT BLOOD WAS FOUND IN THE HOUSE AND PATIO, AND HOW IT WAS PRETTY OBSERVABLE "WITH THE NAKED EYE." HE CONTINUED:)

Q. And from your testimony yesterday, you alluded to a belief that Mr. Daniel was traveling through the house as he was being stabbed. That's your theory as to why you found blood in various parts of the house?

A. That's one possibility, yes.

Q. Besides the blood that you found that was visible to the naked eye, you believe you found evidence that the blood was cleaned up through your Luminol testing?

A. Detective or I.D. Tech Serp did the Luminol testing. He's trained in that. And it was his opinion that there was an attempt to clean up some of the blood based on his testing with the Luminol.

Q. Did you find any signs of forced entry into the home?

A. There was a broken window on the rear patio that was taped over with cardboard.

Q. You said there was a broken window on the back patio?

A. Yes, next to the double French doors that lead between the kitchen and the patio, just to the west of there, there's a single window that was broken. It had cardboard taped over it.

(NOW THE PUBLIC DEFENDER INTRODUCED A SERIES OF PHOTOGRAPHS OF THE BROKEN WINDOW, INCLUDING THE CARDBOARD THAT WAS TAPED OVER IT WITH DUCT TAPE, AS THE QUESTIONING CONTINUED:)

Q. And it would be pretty easy to get in through that window, correct?

A. Probably, yes. It's a means of entry. But usually if somebody would burglarize the house, they wouldn't take the time to put the duct tape and cardboard back up.

(THWARTED IN HIS ATTEMPT TO IMPLY THAT AN INTRUDING BURGLAR MIGHT HAVE BEEN INVOLVED IN THE MURDER SCENE, HE SWITCHED HIS QUESTIONING TO THE LETTERS ROBERT TENNY WROTE TO VARIOUS PEOPLE THAT SUPPOSEDLY ESTABLISHED HE WAS FAR AWAY WHEN THE CORPSE WAS FOUND. HE DISCUSSED LETTERS WRITTEN TO THE SHERIFF'S OFFICE AND TO HIS NEXT

DOOR NEIGHBOR THAT BORE POSTMARKS FROM NEW YORK CITY ON THE 17TH OF JANUARY. THE CORPSE WAS DISCOVERED ON THE 27TH OF JANUARY. THE CROSS-EXAMINATION CONTINUED.)

Q. Now, did you also obtain charge card records in this case?
A. Yes.
Q. And from these charge card records you found that Mr. Tenny had purchased an airplane ticket out of Phoenix on January 15th, 2004?
A. That's correct.
Q. You obtained charge card records dating back to 2002?
A. I'd have to review the records, but that would probably be fair to say.
Q. You just didn't get them for January of '04?
A. No, there was quite a few records that were obtained.

(THEY WENT INTO A LENGTHY DISCUSSION ABOUT ADMITTING THE AMERICAN EXPRESS CARD RECEIPTS INTO EVIDENCE, AND THE COURT DETERMINED THAT THEY WOULD BE ENTERED LATER ON WHEN THE CREDIT CARD COMPANY'S REPRESENTATIVE TOOK THE STAND. NOW THE PUBLIC DEFENDER RETURNED TO THE RED CAR OWNED BY THE DECEASED, GARRETT DANIEL, THAT HAD BEEN FOUND ABANDONED SEVERAL MILES FROM HIS HOME.)

Q. And Robert Tenny's fingerprints were never found in Garrett Daniel's red car?
A. Not to my knowledge, no.
Q. And there was an area on that red car on the seat that had blood on it, correct?
A. There was a rear seat that had blood, and part of the front passenger seat.
Q. And in neither of these spots was Robert Tenny's fingerprints found?
A. To my knowledge they didn't find any usable prints on the car at all.
Q. And there was no physical evidence that was taken from the car that showed during the week of, let's say January 14th through January 28th, there was no physical evidence obtained from the car that could show Robert Tenny had been in that car?
A. That's correct.

(NOW THEY WENT BACK AND FORTH ON THE ART OF FINGERPRINTING AND THE FACT THAT APPARENTLY NO ONE TESTED THE BLOODY FINGERPRINTS IN THE HOUSE TO SEE IF THEY BELONGED TO ROBERT Tenny. NOW THE PUBLIC DEFENDER RETURNED TO HIS PREVIOUS SUGGESTION THAT A BURGLAR WAS INVOLVED IN THE MURDER.)

Q. From your investigation at the house, could you tell whether or not any items were missing from the house?
A. No, I couldn't.

Q. So you have no idea whether or not when this murder was committed there was also a robbery or a burglary where possessions were taken?

A. To my knowledge from neighbor interviews, friends and family interviews, nobody has mentioned anything being missing from the house to me.

Q. Nobody went into any specifics about jewelry or money?

A. None of the friends, neighbors, or family, no.

Q. And it could be missing, but you don't have any idea because the only person that knew about the contents of the house in specific detail were Mr. Daniel and Mr. Tenny?

A. That's correct.

(NOW THE DISTRICT ATTORNEY TOOK HIS TURN AT REDIRECT EXAMINATION, WITH A MINOR "BUMP IN THE ROAD.")

BY MR. LEV:

Q. With regard to the cash or lack of cash in Garrett Daniel's wallet, did you notice in the invoices from ABC Market as well as Motel 6 that right about that time he was charging?

A. It appeared so, yes.

Q. With regard to the calls made from the Tenny home by Cori Crel?

A. I believe it was a long distance toll. She called one of the family members of Mr. Daniel trying to find out where he was at.

Q. And there was another phone call with regard to some scheduled thing with a travel agency somewhere in Mexico?

A. There was a trip to Mexico planned for February.

Q. And who was supposed to be there?

MR. SCHRE: I'm going to object. This is hearsay.

MR. LEV: He's opened the door.

MR. SCHRE: I haven't opened the door to anything. I made a question about were phone calls made from the house. When we get into contents of phone calls or even why phone calls were made, we are getting into the hearsay evidence.

THE COURT: I'm going to sustain the objection.

MR. LEV: Thank you, Your Honor.

Q. With regard to the blood all over the place, then, this was a very bloody scene; is that correct?

A. One of the bloodiest that I have seen, yes.

Q. Based upon what you're saying, the victim, Garrett Daniel, possibly was maybe even crawling around in a wounded state?

A. I believe that's possible, yes.

Q. A person can bleed even after he's physically immobile from stab wounds out of shock, or whatever?

A. That's true.

Q. There were drops even outside?

A. Yes.

Q. In several rooms?

A. Correct.

Q. Concentrating where?

A. I'd say the main concentration was the—most of the concentration was in the kitchen. The second would probably be in the living room.

Q. With regard to that issue, has it been your experience that if, let's hypothetically say there was, someone broke in and stabbed Garrett Daniel, do they sort of stick around and swab the place?

A. To my experience that's never happened, a random killing where someone would stay and clean up.

Q. Do they stick around and tape the window up?

A. No.

Q. In your experience, does someone who breaks into a house go and find cardboard that just happens to fit and duct tapes the window?

A. Eight years as a detective I have never seen it.

(THE DISTRICT ATTORNEY NOW DISCUSSED THE BROKEN WINDOW AND THE FACT THAT THERE WERE NO GLASS SPLINTERS, JUST A LARGE BROKEN PIECE NEATLY LEANING AGAINST AN OUTER WALL. THE BURGLARY BREAKING AND ENTERING IDEA WAS SLOWLY BEING QUASHED.)

Q. Now, let me see the question about him contacting people. Based upon your investigation, did he make even one single phone contact until he attempted to contact Phyllis Daniel, Garrett's mother, on 3/3 of '04?

A. That was the first, to my knowledge, and to my knowledge the only phone contact.

Q. His two letters had no return address, 1/17/04, letters postmarked from New York to a Mr. Kin, and the other was postmarked the same date to the neighbor?

A. Yes. Mr. Weiss.

Q. With this plea to "feed the cat" and he gets it about a week later?

A. Correct.

(NOW THE DISTRICT ATTORNEY RETURNED TO A DISCUSSION OF FINGERPRINTS, AND MORE SPECIFICALLY FINGERPRINTS IN GARRETT DANIEL'S CAR, AND THE BLOODSTAINS FOUND THERE.)

Q. Can a person wipe prints down?

A. That's true.

Q. Or are some people nonsecretors and they don't even leave prints?

A. That's true.

Q. And then it depends on the surface, et cetera, et cetera; is that true?

A. Surface, weather conditions, things like that, yes.

Q. So I take it, it wasn't Robert Tenny that bled in that red Pontiac, it was Garrett Daniel?

A. By the DNA testing, that's true.

Q. I take it, it wasn't Robert Tenny that bled all over the house, it was Garrett Daniel?

A. By the DNA testing, that's true.

(NEXT, MR. KIN WAS CALLED TO THE STAND. HE WAS A DIRECTOR OF THE ORGANIZATION THAT ROBERT TENNY HEADED, AN ORGANIZATION DEDICATED TO FINDING AFFORDABLE HOUSING FOR INDEPENDENT DISABLED PERSONS. HE KNEW BOTH ROBERT TENNY AND GARRETT DANIEL QUITE WELL. IT WAS TO MR. KIN THAT ROBERT TENNY MAILED A LETTER FROM NEW YORK CITY SUBMITTING HIS UNEXPECTED RESIGNATION.)

Q. With regard to the events of January 14, 2004, did you ever see Bob Tenny after that?

A. No, I did not.

Q. Did you ever see Garrett Daniel after that?

A. No, I did not.

Q. Were you ever told by Mr. Tenny prior to departing that he was going to resign from the agency?

A. No.

Q. Did you have any information, knowledge of the disappearance of Bob Tenny?

A. No.

Q. Did his departure leave certain operating problems with the agency that you observed?

A. Yes.

Q. Such as?

A. At the very least—

(AT THIS TIME THE PUBLIC DEFENDER OBJECTED TO THE DIRECTION THESE QUESTIONS WERE HEADING. AFTER BOTH ATTORNEYS APPROACHED THE BENCH AND DISCUSSED THE SITUATION OUT OF THE HEARING OF THE COURT REPORTER AND THE JURY, THE COURT OVERRULED THE OBJECTION, AND THE TESTIMONY CONTINUED. THE DISTRICT ATTORNEY ESTABLISHED THAT NO ONE AT THE AGENCY EXPECTED THE RESIGNATION, AND SOME OF ITS CLIENTS WERE LEFT OUT IN THE COLD. NEXT THE DISTRICT ATTORNEY ESTABLISHED THAT MR. KIN RECEIVED THE LETTER OF RESIGNATION, AND THEY VERIFIED THE POSTMARK OF THE LETTER DATED JANUARY 17TH.)

Q. Is this the letter?
A. That is the letter.
Q. It says "resignation of executive director," is that Bob Tenny?
A. Yes.
Q. And he's asking for formal resignation from the board of directors?
A. Yes.
Q. You had no information, knowledge?
A. No.
Q. He gives as a reason, a culmination of personal disappointments and economic stress leave me with no choice but to step aside?
A. Yes.
Q. Were you aware of any economic stress, or any personal disappointments with him?
A. No, I was not.
Q. On the assumption that he departed Phoenix, Arizona, at 7:30 a.m. on United Airlines to New York, arrived in New York on the 15th of January, 2004, you received no phone call?
A. No, sir.
Q. This is not airmail, correct?
A. That's correct.
Q. So a certain passage of time between, let's say, January 14th and January 21st occurred, is that so?
A. Yes.
Q. It's about seven days?
A. Yes.
Q. In the interim, was there anybody until this letter was received, anybody that could operate this business?
A. No, sir.
Q. And these were independently disabled people that this company dealt with?
A. Yes.

Q. And nobody there at the agency to service them?
A. A part-time secretary.
Q. That's it?
A. Yes.

(NOW THE PUBLIC DEFENDER BEGAN HIS CROSS-EXAMINATION:)

Q. Mr. Kin, you first became concerned about Mr. Tenny's whereabouts on January 16, 2004, correct?
A. Yes.
Q. And that's because you he had not been into work for several days, correct?
A. That's correct.
Q. You also had some communication with people that Garrett Daniel worked for?
A. Yes.
Q. So you contacted the police on January 16, 2004, and you filed a missing person's report?
A. Yes.
Q. And when you contacted the police, you met them at Mr. Tenny's home, correct?
A. Yes, I did.
Q. And there were two police officers?
A. Yes.
Q. And they reported to you that there was nothing out of the ordinary in the home?
A. I don't know if they went in, but I know that they did look at the property and they said that there was nothing out of the ordinary. They spoke to me briefly and said everything seems to be in order. And then we talked for a few more minutes, and then they left.
Q. You socialized with Mr. Tenny?
A. I saw Mr. Tenny and Mr. Daniel socially occasionally, yes.
Q. And you never personally witnessed a physical altercation between Mr. Tenny and Mr. Daniel?
A. No, I did not.

MR. LEV: Objection. Irrelevant without a point in time.

THE COURT: Well, he's already answered it. Ask your next question.

Q. And you wouldn't characterize yourself as close with Mr. Tenny, would you?
A. I would not.

Q. And were you familiar with how much money Mr. Tenny was supposed to earn each year as an employee of his agency?

A. No, I wasn't.

Q. And you weren't familiar with whether or not he was actually making the money he was supposed to make? Let's say the salary was supposed to be $29,000.

MR. LEV: Objection to defense counsel testifying to this witness.

THE COURT: Sustained.

MR. LEV: Move to strike.

THE COURT: It will be stricken from the record.

(THE PUBLIC DEFENDER TRIED TO DETERMINE HOW MUCH MR. KIN KNEW ABOUT ROBERT TENNY'S EMPLOYMENT—WHICH SEEMED VERY SPARSE—AND HE ALSO ESTABLISHED THAT GARRETT DANIEL WAS A MEMBER OF THE BOARD OF DIRECTORS OF ROBERT TENNY'S AGENCY. THE DISTRICT ATTORNEY IN HIS REDIRECT EXAMINATION TRIED TO CLEAR UP A FEW POINTS THAT MIGHT HAVE BEEN CONFUSING.)

Q. Mr. Kin, did Mr. Tenny ever complain to you about the amount of money he was making, or any other economic stress that he mentioned in his letter postmarked January 17, 2004?

A. No, sir.

Q. Mr. Daniel was also a member of the board?

A. That's my understanding.

Q. In what capacity was he associated with the company?

A. I believe that he was secretary treasurer.

Q. And do you have any idea whether or not he made anything at all?

A. I don't believe that he was a paid employee at all.

(THE NEXT WITNESS CALLED WAS AN EMPLOYEE OF THE INSURANCE FIRM WHERE GARRETT DANIEL WORKED, A MS. DORIS GIFF. SHE DESCRIBED WHAT HE DID AT WORK AND ALSO STATED THAT SHE KNEW THE DEFENDANT, AND BEGAN TO DISCUSS BOTH OF THEIR ACTIVITIES BEFORE JANUARY 14, 2004. AT THIS POINT, THE PUBLIC DEFENDER SHOWED HIS PROFESSIONALISM AND HIS DEDICATION TO HIS CLIENT BY REQUESTING A PAUSE IN THE PROCEEDINGS AND A PRIVATE MEETING ABOUT HER TESTIMONY. THE COURT AGREED, AND ADJOURNED UNTIL AFTER LUNCH, AND MET WITH THE TWO

ATTORNEYS AND MS. GIFF. THE FOLLOWING PROCEEDINGS WERE
HELD OUT OF THE PRESENCE OF THE JURY:)

THE COURT: Everybody can be seated. Mr. Lev, go ahead.

MR. LEV: Let me just ask the questions of the witness and it will be a better way
for the Judge to assess whether to allow them.

THE COURT: So this is in the form of an offer of proof?

MR. LEV: Yes.

THE COURT: Go ahead.

Q. Doris, with regard to your knowledge of Garrett Daniel, had you had an
opportunity in the past to see him when he came in?

A. Yes.

Q. And did you see whether or not he had any bruising or injury on his body from
time to time?

A. Yes, I did.

Q. What did you see, and when did you see it?

A. Prior to Christmas of '04, so it would have been '03. Probably a week or so after
Christmas he had come back. He had bruises to his face. He's come in after that
over the year with cuts, stitches on his forehead, a fat lip, stitches on his cheek,
black eyes, he'd wear glasses that were tinted so no one would notice, but it was
pretty obvious.

Q. Did you notice whether Mr. Daniel had a problem ambulating? Did he fall down
and smash himself all the time?

A. No, I didn't.

Q. Did he ever indicate to you what or who was the cause of these injuries?

A. Yes.

Q. Particularly in regard to, let's say December of 2003.

A. He had said he was in a fight with Bob.

Q. Were you aware of whether he had ever moved away from the residence from
time to time?

A. Yes. He had moved out and lived with another co-worker. He lived with her for
several months.

Q. What about close to the time particularly, say, the weekend or the few days
before his disappearance?

A. He was living in a motel or a hotel. He was staying out of the house. He had
moved out again.

Q. What did he tell you about that relative to Bob Tenny?

A. He said they were not going out. He had moved out, he was not going back to the house. He said that they had broken up, basically.

Q. Did he express to you any concerns he had about Bob Tenny immediately prior to his disappearance?

A. No. Garrett moved out; Bob stayed at the house.

Q. And you know that because Garrett told you?

A. Yes. He told me he was not living at the house, he was staying elsewhere.

Q. I think I see in the report, were there at least two occasions that you know of when he moved out from Bob Tenny to live elsewhere?

A. Yes.

Q. One you said was—

MR. SCHRE: Can I make my objection now. We are getting into—

MR. LEV: Excuse me, I haven't made my offer of proof yet. You will have all the information before you—

THE COURT: How many more questions do you have?

MR. LEV: A couple.

THE COURT: Why don't you let him ask a couple of questions. If you want to ask any questions, you'll be able to do that and make your objection specifically.

BY MR. LEV:

Q. On the assumption that you were aware that he stayed elsewhere a couple of times with co-workers or something like that, when and who?

A. After they had been in a fight after Christmas of '02, he moved out for three months, or two months.

Q. And the next time?

A. Right prior to him disappearing he had moved out, probably a week or two before that. He was staying, at least I know he was staying in a hotel. He had told me that.

Q. All right.

MR. LEV: That's the offer of proof.

THE COURT: Do you want to ask this witness any questions?

MR. SCHRE: Before I even ask her any questions, I have an objection. This evidence is not—

THE COURT: There seems to be at least three parts from this evidence. Number one, the witness's observations of various bruises, et cetera, the statement that the decedent was moving out of the house, and also the statement that the decedent was living in a motel at the time that the witness spoke to him, or on or about the 14th of January. Specifically, is your objection to all those things or just part of those things?

MR. SCHRE: I will make my individual objections.

THE COURT: Go ahead.

MR. SCHRE: First of all, the observation of bruises, what the State is attempting to do is say Bob has a general character for violence, that he always beats Garrett. Number one, in the 404(B) motion, that they didn't notice that Doris Giff was going to testify about Bob's general character for violence. Even if they did notice that, it's inadmissible, but it's general and it's vague. We don't know if those bruises were caused by Bob or not. She has no personal knowledge of it. She noticed no specific action of misconduct. The Court has already said that the State can bring in two or three different specific acts of misconduct because they have precluded the State from bringing in general acts of misconduct in our 404(B) motion and acts that are—they want to bring in solely based on hearsay and speculation, rather than what somebody actually observed. So as far as number one goes, I think it's highly prejudicial, it's not probative. There are no facts to support those bruises. We have no eyewitnesses to it. I'm asking the Court—

THE COURT: Wait a minute. You have no eyewitnesses to the bruises? This is the eye witness. What are you talking about?

MR. SCHRE: We have eye witnesses to the bruises, we do not have eyewitnesses to the cause of the bruises. So I'm asking the Court to preclude that first set.

THE COURT: Why don't you go ahead for the next.

MR. SCHRE: Moving out, first of all—

THE COURT: Isn't that already coming in, the fact that the decedent told somebody that he was moving out or he was leaving the defendant, isn't that already coming into evidence pursuant to a prior ruling?

MR. SCHRE: It is coming in, but I think we need some limiting instructions on how it should come in. Moving out because of fear of Bob, without any foundation as to what the fear was based on, what it's alluding to, without any facts that during that week prior to Garrett's death, or two weeks prior to his death, Bob was making specific threats. But no witness can testify about any specific threats, and they can't get into Garrett's state of mind. One of the witnesses, I believe, is going to be Ms. Cori Crel. She's going to say Garrett said Bob was in one of his moods again. When we use those words, Bob's in one of his moods again, it brings in character evidence that's inadmissible, that Bob is this moody violent guy. That's what it's trying to show the jury. So I believe she should be allowed to testify Garrett said he's moving out, but with Bob's mood, that should be precluded as character evidence. There are many different reasons why Garrett could have been moving out: Financial conditions, seeking new jobs, there's all kinds of different reasons. Maybe Bob wanted Garrett to move out because Garrett was unfaithful, something like that. Maybe Garrett wanted to move out to be with someone else. But, Bob's in one of his moods, gets into general character evidence, and I ask that the witness be not allowed to talk about Bob's mood again.

THE COURT: What about the living in the motel, that the decedent was living in a motel?

MR. SCHRE: There's no doubt the decedent stayed in the motel.

THE COURT: I think that's coming in through the receipts, anyway.

MR. SCHRE: Right. There's no doubt he said he's moving out, but staying in a motel doesn't mean he was already moved out. After he stayed in the motel, apparently the testimony is going to be from Ms. Giff here Garrett went home to his house for lunch. So he's staying in a hotel because he's moving out, but he's going back to the house to eat lunch.

THE COURT: Okay. Are you saying you don't want either of these things, that he went back to the house to eat lunch or that he was living in the motel?

MR. SCHRE: It can come in that he went back to the house to eat lunch, but to try to attribute it to Bob and Bob's moods—

THE COURT: I don't disagree with that part, and the testimony from Ms. Giff that the decedent's said he was moving out of the house but not the specifics of why. I think we have already covered that. I don't think it falls under any hearsay exception at this point. What about the bruises? Mr. Lev, how do you believe that those come in, her observations of bruises?

MR. LEV: There's a rule of law. It's all probative. We are talking about the reason that Garrett Daniel moved out. So we already have some other testimony with regard to observations about their interactions in the Christmas time area which she is aware of. Now she is testifying that she sees bruises upon him, okay, about the same time that Cori Crel makes these observations in their house about the fight, and then he's moving, went away from home. He isn't moving away from the house, he's moving away from Bob Tenny. That's an important probative factor, and that's an exception on state of mind, and it is inextricably involved as to him moving out. To the extent of his concerns about Bob Tenny, I realize you've got to be limited, but it also goes to, again, his state of mind, moving out, why does he go to a motel. He wants to sanitize it in such a way that I can't even—you know, he doesn't even want me to even inferentially touch Bob Tenny when the touchstone to this thing is Garrett Daniel moving away from Bob Tenny. He has bruises, so we have physical proof with her testimony, coupled with the other, and that the victim's telling her he's moving away from Bob Tenny and that he's moving into a motel. So I realize you're going to make some relation here, but I would like you to consider that this is inextricably intertwined, and that it is probative, and I would ask that you rule accordingly.

THE COURT: Anything else, Mr. Schre?

MR. SCHRE: Judge, first of all, we don't have anyone that's witnessed the cause of these bruises. I think this witness has testified around Christmas time there were the bruises, yet after Christmas Garrett and Bob go to the Rose Bowl together in California. I don't think this witness will testify the week before Garrett was last seen alive he had bruises on him, and I don't have a specific date that he has the bruises. I believe that Cori's date with the knife is a different date. I just say it's general character evidence. It's more prejudicial than it is probative. The State's already going to bring in specific instances that were witnessed by witnesses.

THE COURT: Here's what we're going to do. Number one, Ms. Giff can testify as to the moving out of the house, that the decedent's told her that, not the specifics of why and about Bob's moods. Do you understand that, Ms. Giff?

THE WITNESS: Yes.

THE COURT: Also, that she can testify that the decedent was living in the motel at the time, and not particularly the reasons why or anything like that.

THE WITNESS: Okay.

THE COURT: And, also, I'm going to preclude any—because of the attenuation in time to the death of the decedent, I'm going to preclude her testimony of the appearances of the bruises. However, the State may reurge that on either rebuttal or possibly asking on cross-examination should the defendant take the stand and testify to something that alludes to that that may be relevant to those bruises. Let's take our lunch break.

MR. LEV: Can I ask one question?

THE COURT: Yes.

MR. LEV: You said she can testify about him moving out of the house, moving away from Bob Tenny. Can I bring that up that that's who he's moving away from?

THE COURT: He moved out of the house away, and you object to that, correct?

MR. SCHRE: To phrasing it, away from Bob Tenny. I don't think we have a foundational waiver that he's moving out to get away from Bob Tenny.

THE WITNESS: If he wasn't afraid of him, he wouldn't have moved out.

THE COURT: Hold on, ma'am.

THE WITNESS: Okay.

THE COURT: I'm going to let her testify that he was moving out of the house away from Bob Tenny, not why, as far as any bruising, et cetera, things like that. Do you understand that?

THE WITNESS: Yes.

THE COURT: All right, we are at recess.

AFTERNOON SESSION

THE COURT: When we left off, Ms. Giff, you were on the stand. You had been sworn in. Go ahead, Mr. Lev.

BY MR. LEV:
Q. Shortly prior to January 14, 2004, state whether or not Garrett Daniel gave you any information about moving out and where he went to?
A. He told me that he wasn't living at his house any more. He had moved out and was living in a motel.

Q. And did he give you any indication as to anything about Bob Tenny?

A. He told me they had broken up.

Q. Now, on Monday, January 13th, 2004, did Garrett Daniel come into work?

A. He came in late in the morning.

Q. Okay. So then Tuesday the 14th, could you explain the events of that day with relation to Garrett Daniel?

A. I came in on the front desk at 12:00 to do the phones, and shortly after that he came up and said he was going to lunch.

Q. Do you know where he went for lunch?

A. Usually, unless he was going out with someone, he'd go to his house and eat lunch there and come back.

Q. Did he ever return from lunch?

A. No, he did not.

Q. Did you expect him back from lunch?

A. Yes, we did.

Q. Was there any contact in any way, shape, or form from Garrett Daniel to you after he left for lunch?

A. No, there was not.

MR. LEV: That's all I have.

THE COURT: Mr. Schre.

Q. Ms. Giff, you were good friends with Garrett Daniel?

A. Yes, I was.

Q. And he left for lunch around 12:15?

A. Yes.

MR. SCHRE: I have no further questions.

MR. LEV: Could I ask one additional question?

THE COURT: Go ahead.

Q. Is your office very far from Garrett Daniel's home?

A. It's 28 blocks.

Q. Okay. So how long did it take—

A. Five to seven minutes. We've gone there for lunch before. Five to seven minutes to his home.

Q. Do you know what kind of car he left in?

A. He left in his car. It's a convertible red Sunbird.

MR. LEV: Thank you.

THE COURT: Thank you, ma'am. Mr. Lev, call your next witness, please.

(THE NEXT WITNESS WAS THE MOTHER OF THE DECEASED GARRETT DANIEL. SHE TESTIFIED THAT SHE KNEW ROBERT TENNY AND THAT HER SON HAD LIVED WITH HIM. SHE SAID ROBERT TENNY HAD VISITED HER HOME SEVERAL TIMES WHILE THE TWO MEN WERE LIVING TOGETHER. THE DISTRICT ATTORNEY CONTINUED:)

BY MR. LEV:

Q. Did there come a point where Bob Tenny was no longer welcome at your place?

A. Yes, I'd say within the last year before Garrett's death.

Q. In that period of time, did he attempt to call you up and socially have conversations with you?

A. No.

Q. However, after the disappearance of your son, did you in fact, receive a couple of calls from Bob Tenny?

A. Yes.

Q. Did you expect the calls?

A. No.

Q. Did the calls occur some period of time after the disappearance of your son?

A. Within a few months, I don't recall.

Q. On this call on March 3rd of 2004, did Bob Tenny identify himself?

A. Yes, he did.

Q. And what did he ask you, or tell you?

A. I was so taken back, and he said, "This is Bob." And I said, "Where are you?" And he said, "Well, I took a little time off and I'm overseas." And with that, I hung up. I said, "Well, good for you," I guess is what I said, and I hung up.

Q. All right. Then was there one other time that he called you?

A. Yes.

Q. And was that on April 21st, 2004?

A. Approximately.

Q. Some months after the disappearance of your son?

A. Yes.

Q. Okay. Did you recognize his voice that time?

A. Yes, I did.

Q. Did he tell you it was him?

A. I don't know. I handed the phone to my husband.

Q. Did you expect that call?

A. No.

Q. So you just handed the phone off to your husband?

A. I didn't want to talk to Mr. Tenny.

(NEXT THE PUBLIC DEFENDER CROSS-EXAMINED THE MURDER VICTIM'S MOTHER. SHE SAID SHE ONLY OCCASIONALLY VISITED HER SON AT HIS HOME, AND THAT HE DIDN'T WEAR JEWELRY EXCEPT A WRISTWATCH. THE CROSS-EXAMINE CONTINUED:)

BY MR. SCHRE:

Q. When Mr. Tenny called you on March 3rd of 2004, is it fair to say that you were scared when he called you?

A. Yes, very much so.

Q. Were you nervous?

A. Of course.

Q. Okay. And you didn't take notes about what he said that day, did you?

A. Why I—no, I didn't take notes.

MR. SCHRE: I have no further questions.

THE COURT: Redirect.

Q. Mrs. Daniel, after that call, did you immediately call the Sheriff's Office and report this to them?

A. Yes, I did.

(NOW THE DISTRICT ATTORNEY CALLED ON SHERRI CHARL, A DISABLED BENEFICIARY OF ROBERT TENNY'S AGENCY. SHE TESTIFIED SHE KNEW ROBERT TENNY QUITE WELL, EVEN KNOWING THAT HE DROVE A BLACK JAGUAR AND SEEING IT PARKED EVERY TIME SHE VISITED HIS OFFICE TO MAKE RENT PAYMENTS.)

BY MR. LEV:

Q. Do you recall going there, going there on Tuesday, January 14th, 2004, to make a payment?

A. Yes.

Q. And what was the purpose of the payment?

A. It was for that month's house payment.

Q. Did you usually go there directly?

A. Yes.

Q. And about what time did you arrive at the agency office?

A. It was in the afternoon that day. I want to say it was 2:00 or 2:30, around there.

Q. Did you expect to see Mr. Tenny there?

A. Yes.

Q. And when you arrived, did you see his black colored Jaguar?
A. No.
Q. What did you see?
A. There was a red convertible that was parked in the spot that he normally parked in.
Q. When you went into the office, what was he doing?
A. When I went in, he didn't see me at first because he was on the phone talking, and so I waited there because I didn't want to disrupt him.
Q. Did you finally go into his office?
A. Yeah. He waved me in and I went in, and he was still on the phone and was finishing his phone call.
Q. Did you make any observations about his demeanor, how he was acting?
A. He was not acting like he normally acted.
Q. How do you mean?
A. Preoccupied. That day he was just trying to rush me along. He didn't want to be bothered with anything, and I basically just assumed he was having a bad day and I would end up speaking with him another time over the issues, because I wasn't getting anywhere that day.
Q. Did you ever hear the phone ring while you were there?
A. Yeah. There were a couple of calls that came in.
Q. Do you have knowledge about those calls?
A. One of them. He had said that he would have to take them out and show them a house when he got back, that he was going away.
Q. Did he ever talk to you about that?
A. No.
Q. Did he ever say that he was going to leave the next day?
A. He didn't say when. He just said he was going to be going.
Q. Okay. Now, with regard to seeing him on the 14th after 2:30, do you recall when you left?
A. About an hour, maybe a little longer than that.

(THE DISTRICT ATTORNEY CONTINUED TO ESTABLISH WITHOUT A DOUBT THAT ROBERT TENNY WAS IN HIS OFFICE ON TUESDAY, JANUARY 14TH 2004, AFTER 2:30 P.M., WITH A RED CONVERTIBLE CAR IN HIS USUAL PARKING SPACE. THE PUBLIC DEFENDER THEN BEGAN THE CROSS-EXAMINATION, ESTABLISHING THAT MS. CHARL'S VISIT WAS UNEXPECTED, WITHOUT A PRIOR APPOINTMENT, AND POSSIBLY WAS INTRUSIVE ON ROBERT TENNY'S NORMAL DAILY SCHEDULE. THE PUBLIC DEFENDER ALSO ESTABLISHED THAT MS. CHARL DID NOT SEE ANY BLOOD OR SCRAPES ON MR. TENNY OR ON HIS CLOTHING. THE PUBLIC DEFENDER ALSO ESTABLISHED THAT MR.

TENNY WAS NOT SOCIAL ON A PERSONAL BASIS WITH MS. CHARL AND THEREFORE WOULD NEVER DISCUSS HIS TRAVEL PLANS WITH HER, AND NOW WANTED TO CAST DOUBT ON THE RED CONVERTIBLE SHE SUPPOSEDLY SAW IN ROBERT TENNY'S PARKING SPACE.)

BY MR. SCHRE:

Q. Now, you just told us that when you came to the agency that day, January 14th you saw a different car parked in Mr. Tenny's parking spot?

A. Uh-huh (indicates affirmatively).

Q. Now, isn't it true that you saw media accounts of Mr. Tenny and Mr. Daniel's disappearance?

A. After that, yeah.

Q. On the television, they had pictures of Mr. Daniel's red vehicle; isn't that correct?

A. Yes.

Q. And you watched those news accounts, correct?

A. Yes.

Q. In fact, you even kept some paper clippings of their disappearance, correct?

A. Yes.

Q. And you were very interested in what happened because you knew Mr. Tenny, right?

A. Yeah. That wasn't the only reason I did it. I was interested in what happened.

Q. And you saw this picture of the red vehicle on the television?

A. Yes.

Q. And then you told the police that it was a red vehicle you saw in that spot, right?

A. Yeah.

(NOW THE DISTRICT ATTORNEY ON HIS REDIRECT EXAMINATION ATTEMPTED TO REPAIR ANY DAMAGE TO HIS CASE.)

BY MR. LEV:

Q. Sherri, the media coverage didn't start until late January, right?

A. Right.

Q. You remember independently that red car on January 14th?

A. Yes.

Q. And you previously had left a note at the agency office that you were coming in on the 14th?

A. Uh-huh (indicates affirmatively).

Q. You had been coming in every month from what, since—

A. Since August.

Q. And you had to make your payment somehow or another to keep your house?

A. Yes.

Q. Nevertheless, when you came in, he was short with you?

A. Real gruff. I tried to discuss a problem I was having a couple of times with him in between the phone calls, but that's really where he was short. It wasn't that he wanted me to quickly leave and get out of the office. He was just more short in discussing the things that I wanted to bring to his attention.

Q. Did you sense that he was preoccupied?

A. Yes.

Q. Did you observe whether he made any phone calls out?

A. I really don't know if he did or not. He didn't in front of me. A couple of times he walked into a couple of the other rooms that were there, and I know there were phones in the other rooms, but I don't know.

Q. This could have been between, for example, 2:50 and 3:10 p.m. that he could have made these calls?

A. Could have.

Q. And so he didn't discuss that business with you about leaving and going to South Africa the next day?

A. No.

(THE NEXT WITNESS CALLED WAS CORRI CREL, WHO WORKED AT THE SAME INSURANCE AGENCY THAT GARRETT DANIEL DID. AS THE DISTRICT ATTORNEY DISCUSSED HER NORMAL BUSINESS ROUTINE, HE WAS INTERRUPTED BY THE PUBLIC DEFENDER.)

THE COURT: Mr. Schre, do you have an objection?

MR. SCHRE: Judge, I'm objecting—it seems like this witness is going to testify to things she didn't have personal knowledge of.

THE COURT: I don't know what—these questions seem preliminary in nature. If we get to that point and she says she doesn't have personal knowledge of some significant things, why don't you object. Please continue.

MR. LEV: Thank you, Your Honor.

Q. And did you know Garrett Daniel?

A. Yes.

Q. How did you know him?

A. He was a co-worker and friend.

Q. How long did you know him prior to January 14 of 2004?

A. Since October, 2002.

Q. In the time frame of December, 2003, preceding January 14th of '04, did you have an occasion, you and your husband, to go over one or more times to their house?

A. Yes.

Q. Did you make any observations about their interaction?

A. We had gone the very first time for dinner. They had invited us to dinner, and I would say the first time we went there it was a pleasant evening. The last visit we had was approximately December 21st, I know, before Christmas Eve.

Q. What did you observe about the interaction between Bob Tenny and Garrett Daniel at that dinner meeting?

A. It was not a good evening.

Q. Explain.

A. They had some kind of a disagreement over some letter, and both had drank a lot. There was some interaction in the kitchen over some letter, and I guess Bob Tenny did pull a knife and was kind of swinging it around. There was some exchange of some sort or other. I don't remember specifically what was exchanged. But I did hear Garrett saying, "Put that thing away."

Q. Did you hear an altercation?

A. Yes. Bob was in the kitchen fixing, or getting ready to fix something to eat, and he had pulled the utensil out, maybe because of the noise that it made, you know, shuffling in the drawer, pulled it out of the drawer. I don't know, I mean, I'm just kind of visualizing what I heard. And because they were fussing at each other, Garrett—

Q. What do you mean fussing? Did they have words?

A. Yeah.

Q. Where was this location?

A. In the kitchen. Garrett was on one side of the island where I could see him, and Bob was on the other side where he was more in my blind side where I could not see him from my vantage point.

Q. What did you see of Garrett's—how was he reacting to this?

A. Well, he was turning kind of red and they were having words, just commotion, just—I don't know, more of a physical commotion where I didn't know what the content was, other than it just made me feel like we needed to get out of there.

Q. Did you just suddenly leave?

A. Pretty quickly.

Q. Did you ever go back?

A. Not until after Garrett was gone.

(NOW CORRI DISCUSSED HOW SHE AND HER HUSBAND TRIED TO TAPER OFF SOCIALIZING WITH THE TWO MEN BECAUSE IT WAS AN UNCOMFORTABLE SITUATION. SHE ALSO MENTIONED THAT

GARRETT DANIEL HAD ASKED HER AND HER HUSBAND TO COME TO HIS HOUSE ON FRIDAY BECAUSE HE DIDN'T WANT TO SPEND TIME ALONE WITH ROBERT TENNY. WHEN THEY DECLINED THE INVITATION, GARRETT SPENT THE WEEKEND IN A MOTEL, HIS LAST WEEKEND ON EARTH. NOW THE DISTRICT ATTORNEY GOT MORE SPECIFIC ABOUT THE EVENTS OF JANUARY 14TH, 2004.)

Q. All right. Did you see him Tuesday, the 14th of January, 2004?

A. Yes.

Q. When did you first see him?

A. It was later in the morning. I went out in the back to smoke a cigarette, and Garrett was there and we started to talk, and that was approximately 11 o'clock or so.

Q. How did he look that day?

A. Pretty bad. He was distraught. He wanted me to go to lunch with him, and I couldn't because I had already made other plans with my husband, and we just kind of chatted outside while we were smoking a cigarette. And I said, Garrett, you really don't look good, you know, what's going on? And I said this lady called this morning and said that she had the apartment that you inquired about and it will be ready by the 16th. And he said, yeah. He said, I've been looking for an apartment. I said that's good. It will be nice to get out of the situation. I think it was the first time Garrett openly admitted that he was into a bad relationship and a bad situation and, you know, he was crying. And I just kind of felt bad because I didn't go to lunch with him.

Q. Do you recall what time he went to lunch?

A. Maybe five until twelve.

Q. Did you ever see Garrett Daniel again?

A. No.

Q. Did you receive a phone call from Bob Tenny later that afternoon?

A. Yes.

Q. What time was it that you received this call?

A. It was approximately ten until three.

Q. What did you say when you answered the phone?

A. I answered it as Schol Insurance. And I guess Bob Tenny said, "Corri?" And I said "yes." And he said, "Garrett won't be back."

Q. How did he say it?

A. "Garrett won't be back." It was just a real final statement. It was just kind of a matter of fact. And I said "What do you mean?" And he said, "He won't be back." And I said, "What do you mean?" "Oh, he's been in a car accident." And I said, "Oh, okay. Where? What? How is he? Where is he?" "Oh, he's fine. They're going to take him to get him checked." And that was it.

Q. Did he ever talk to you again after that?

A. No.

Q. When did Garrett usually come back from lunch?

A. Pretty much on time, give or take ten minutes.

Q. After 1:00 did you notice he hadn't come back?

A. Not immediately, no.

Q. Did you become concerned at some point in time before this phone call from Bob Tenny?

A. Yes, because I had a couple of phone calls for him and I could not locate Garrett.

Q. After the call from Bob Tenny, did you become concerned?

A. Yes.

Q. What did you do? Did you make any calls?

A. I talked to the personnel manager and I said that something just did not seem right. I just did not feel comfortable about the call that I had just taken. I personally called Garrett's house several times from the office: Three, four, five times, whatever, between 3:00 or 3:15 until I went home. And then again from the house, you know, trying to call his house, trying to see if we could find out what happened.

Q. Did you make any inquiries as to calling any hospitals to see if—

A. Yes, we did that night, because we couldn't get any answer at his home, so I called. I don't remember how many hospitals I called. It might have been three or four, the main ones here, and they had not had anything that had been checked in, or been in and out in terms of emergency room situations.

Q. So at the end of that night, did you have any idea of what had become of Garrett Daniel?

A. No, not then.

Q. And the next day, this is Wednesday, the 15th?

A. I tried to call the police. I don't know exactly when. We were told that, number one, it was too soon, and it would have to be a relative making this call as to a missing person. And I think not much else went on that day other than we did drive by their house to see if he was there.

Q. Did you see a car?

A. Yes, I saw Bob Tenny's car. The Jaguar, parked in the front.

Q. Did you see Garrett Daniel's car?

A. No.

Q. What kind of car did he drive?

A. A red car with a white top. A convertible.

Q. Is that the car you usually saw him drive in?

A. Garrett's car used to be in the front of their house 99 percent of the time.

Q. Did you ever go into that house after that?

A. Yes, the following Wednesday, January 15th.

Q. And when you went in, how did you go in? Did you go in by yourself or with someone else?

A. With their neighbor, Jackie. We did go the first time without entering the premises, and that was just walking around the yard and trying to see if there was any kind of movement in the house.

Q. What day was that?

A. It would have been Wednesday evening that we walked around the house to see if there was any kind of activity.

Q. Was there?

A. No, absolutely none. No lights; no movement. We just walked around the backyard. We never went in the house that day.

Q. Was the black Jag still in the driveway?

A. Yes.

Q. So the next day, Thursday, you went into the house?

A. Right.

Q. For what reason?

A. We were trying to make sure if Garrett wasn't in there hurt or otherwise, and we didn't find him there. There seemed to be a lot of things missing.

Q. What was missing?

A. Clothes.

Q. Whose clothes?

A. It could have been either. There was hardly any clothes left. It appeared his guitar was missing, which is really what we were looking for, his guitar. We thought, well, if Garrett took off, you know, he would take his guitar with him. That was kind of his prized possession. The guitar wasn't there, so that didn't give us any more clues.

Q. Was his car there?

A. His car, no.

Q. And you say most of the clothes were gone?

A. Uh-huh (indicates affirmatively). The reason why we realized the clothes were gone was there was a chair when you walked in on the right side of the bedroom, and it had a fairly high pile of clothes hangers. And so that's when we realized all the hangers are here and there is nothing in the closet.

Q. Did you go through drawers, anything?

A. We were looking for Garrett's mom's phone number. We were trying to look for something that would give us phone numbers or some kind of a clue where both would be gone, Bob and Garrett, because we kind of hoped they were gone together at the time.

Q. What time were you in the house?

A. It had to be after work in the afternoon around 4:30.

Q. If there were tiny little blood drops on the floor, would you have likely seen them with the kind of lighting they had?

A. No. We weren't looking for that.

Q. What were you looking for?

A. Any kind of paperwork that would give us a clue, you know, if they had gone together, or what would have happened, and primarily, Garrett mom's phone number.

Q. Did you call her?

A. Yes, I believe I called her from the house.

Q. How did you come in?

A. The back door. The back of the house had like a garage door. And on the left side of the garage door, there was a big window, and the window had been busted and was still busted.

Q. When did you know the window had been busted?

A. I guess before Christmas when we were there, that window was already busted.

Q. And did one of the—either Garrett Daniel or Bob Tenny tell you?

A. Uh-huh (indicates affirmatively). When we were there that last time, we were there around Christmas. The blind was kind of waving in the window, and I said what happened to the window. And Garrett said the window had been broken.

Q. So it was already broken, and you knew that?

A. Yes.

(THEY DISCUSSED THE BROKEN WINDOW AND ITS CARDBOARD COVERING. CORRI SAID SHE STEPPED IN THROUGH THIS WINDOW, THEN REPLACED THE CARDBOARD WHEN SHE LEFT. THERE WAS NO GLASS ON THE FLOOR AROUND THE WINDOW. CORRI FURTHER TESTIFIED THAT ON THIS VISIT SHE COLLECTED MAIL THAT WAS GARRETT'S, AND TOOK IT BACK TO HER MANAGER WHO WAS KEEPING HIS OFFICE ITEMS FOR HIM. THE DISTRICT ATTORNEY CONTINUED:)

Q. When you made an observation when you first came in, did it appear as though there was any ransacking as though a burglar had gone in looking for anything, drawers pulled out, stuff strewn about, anything like that?

A. No, it wasn't as neat as they usually keep it, because of the hangers thrown about. It was lived in, but not spic and span, I guess.

Q. So other than that?

A. Right, I mean, it wasn't like somebody came in and just trashed the place. It didn't look like that. But it didn't look right either, because it usually used to be kept very clean.

Q. Did you come back again?

A. Uh-huh (indicates affirmatively), one or two days later. It was just with the consent of Garrett's mom in order to preserve some things, get anything that was Garrett's that was personal.

Q. Did you bring out a deed?

A. Yes.

Q. And do you recall who was on the deed?

A. I think both of them were.

Q. Garrett Daniel and Bob Tenny?

A. Yes.

Q. Okay. So what did you do the next time? How did you get in?

A. The second time the neighbor had a key and we got in the front door.

Q. I take it when you went in the first time, you just didn't walk through the door. You went through that window, correct?

A. That's correct.

Q. The door was locked?

A. Right.

Q. Were all the doors locked as far as you knew?

A. Yes.

Q. The second time you came, was the door locked?

A. Yes, but Jackie had a front door key.

Q. And so what did you see when you went in?

A. Not much different than the first time. It was the way we had left it, other than we spent, you know, more of a lengthy amount of time collecting things. We went through the drawer where the computer was, and picked up documents and whatever seemed to us at the time that was important.

Q. Relating to who?

A. Garrett primarily.

Q. Corri, do you recollect whether Garrett Daniel owned a cat?

A. Yes.

Q. Was the cat in the house when you went in the first time on the 17th of January?

A. Yes. We actually looked for the cat.

Q. And share with the jury what you did.

A. The cat was in one of the back bedrooms. It was kind of a skittish cat to begin with, but he was hiding and then we found him. And eventually Jackie took the cat out of there so she could care for it.

Q. Other than that, did it appear that any water dishes had been set out or anything for the cat?

A. There was no food left and very little water left.

Q. This is the 17th, a couple of days after the 14th?

A. Right.

(NOW THE PUBLIC DEFENDER CROSS-EXAMINED MS. CORRI CREL, AND BEGAN BY RECAPPING THE TESTIMONY SHE HAD JUST GIVEN. SHE

ADMITTED THE PHONE CALL ON JANUARY 14TH FROM ROBERT TENNY WAS VERY ALARMING TO HER, AND THAT IS WHY SHE TRIED TO TRACK GARRETT DANIEL DOWN AND WHY SHE WENT TO HIS HOME. NOW THE PUBLIC DEFENDER POINTED OUT SEVERAL INCONSISTENCIES IN THE DATES SHE GAVE IN COURT AND THE DATE SHE GAVE ON AFFIDAVITS MANY MONTHS PREVIOUSLY. SHE STUCK TO HER GUNS THAT THE DATES SHE GAVE TODAY WERE THE CORRECT DATES.)

BY MR. SCHRE:

Q. Now, when you went into that house, you were looking for evidence of a crime?

A. No. Looking for anything that would give a clue.

Q. You were suspicious Garrett may have been hurt?

A. Right.

Q. And you went in there and you were looking for his guitar, correct?

A. When we didn't find him.

Q. So you looked carefully enough through the house to find that his prized possession, his guitar, was gone?

A. Right.

Q. And you looked through paperwork when you went in the house?

A. One of the times, yes.

Q. You looked closely enough at stickies to make phone calls to the numbers that were on the stickies, correct?

A. Yes.

Q. And on the second time you went to the house, you even took documents out of the house?

A. Yes. We just kind of sifted through bills on the counter, mail that had come through.

Q. And the bills and papers were on the counter tops, correct? You looked at the counter tops?

A. Yeah.

Q. When you were looking through that house, you never saw any blood?

A. We weren't looking for blood.

Q. But you were looking for something when you went through the house, and you didn't see any blood?

A. I didn't see any that I looked for, no.

Q. You knew that Bob had trouble with immigration?

A. I knew he had difficulties obtaining a green card.

Q. You even noticed in Bob's kitchen a business card from an immigration lawyer?

A. Yes.

Q. And Bob talked to you in the past about his immigration problems, correct?

A. Some.

Q. And in the middle of December of '03, Bob gave your husband about ten CDs, correct?

A. Ten CDs.

Q. When Bob gave your husband these CDs, it made you think he was going away, he was giving his stuff away, correct?

A. I think my comment was, gee, that's a lot of CDs. And he said, I won't be needing these any more. Bob gave those to my husband.

Q. You thought that meant because he was leaving, right?

A. I don't think that I consciously thought that. I thought it was odd to be giving ten CDs away and making the comment he wasn't going to be needing those any more.

Q. In a previous transcript, you talked about Garrett's mood on the last day you saw him, January 14th, 2004, correct?

A. Yes.

Q. And on that morning when you had interaction with Garrett, he even snapped at you, didn't he?

A. Yes.

Q. In fact, he said "screw you," to you, correct?

A. I don't remember word for word, other than he did get pretty snappy, yes.

(THE DISTRICT ATTORNEY ON HIS REDIRECT EXAMINATION ESTABLISHED THAT ROBERT TENNY NEVER MENTIONED TO HER ANY DIFFICULTY WITH THE I.N.S. ABOUT HIS IMMIGRATION STATUS AND TROUBLE GETTING A GREEN CARD, EXCEPT THAT HE NEEDED TO BE EVALUATED EVERY SO OFTEN, UNLIKE IT IS WITH A GREEN CARD. HE NEVER EXPRESSED CONCERN THAT HE WOULD BE THROWN OUT OF THE COUNTRY. NEXT THE DISTRICT ATTORNEY ESTABLISHED THAT SHE HADN'T SEEN ANY BLOOD IN THE HOUSE BECAUSE SHE DIDN'T LOOK FOR ANY, AND DIDN'T HAVE A FLASHLIGHT. AS FAR AS THE TEN CDS BOB GAVE HER HUSBAND, BOB SPECIFICALLY SAID HE WON'T NEED THESE ANY MORE. FINALLY, CORRI CREL'S TESTIMONY CONCLUDED, AND THE PROSECUTION CALLED ITS NEXT WITNESS, MR. WEISS, THE NEXT-DOOR NEIGHBOR TO THE DANIEL/TENNY HOME. MR. WEISS STATED THAT GARRETT DANIEL FREQUENTLY CAME HOME FOR LUNCH DRIVING HIS RED PONTIAC, AS HE HAD ON JANUARY 14TH, BUT HE NEVER SAW THE RED PONTIAC AGAIN. THE BLACK JAGUAR WAS NOW PARKED IN ITS PLACE. NOW A LETTER MR. WEISS RECEIVED FROM ROBERT TENNY TOOK CENTER STAGE.)

Q. Do you know whether or not Bob Tenny had your phone number?

A. Yes, he did.

Q. Did he ever call you?

A. No, sir.

Q. Do you know if Garrett had a cat?

A. Yes, he did have a cat.

Q. Do you recognize this letter?

A. The handwriting. I received this letter, but I also know there was no return address on it.

Q. This was a letter from who?

A. From Bob Tenny.

Q. And did you give that letter to the police department after you got it?

A. That's right.

Q. When did you receive it, if you recall?

A. It was about a week or two later.

Q. And it says, "Have gone to visit family for a while, and have been trying to contact Garrett by phone. Please check in on the cat. And tell Garrett to answer the phone," correct?

A. Right, correct.

Q. And this you get a week or two after he disappeared; is that so?

A. About two weeks after.

Q. And it's postmarked 17 January from New York, is that what it looks like?

A. Right.

Q. Just sent a letter, regular mail?

A. Regular mail.

Q. So do you know how long it took to get to you?

A. About four days.

Q. You've taken care of that cat before, haven't you?

A. No, sir, I haven't.

Q. You haven't?

A. A neighbor across the street took care of the cat.

Q. I mean, do you have any idea whether that cat could have lasted seven days without food or water until you got this letter?

A. No, sir, I don't.

Q. After you got the letter, did you ever look in on the cat?

A. No, sir, I didn't.

Q. Mr. Weiss, prior to Bob Tenny's disappearance, did he ever tell you he was leaving?

A. Not that I recall, no.

MR. LEV: That's all I have. Thank you.

(WHEREUPON, THE PUBLIC DEFENDER BEGAN HIS CROSS-EXAMINATION.)

BY MR. SCHRE:
Q. Mr. Weiss, did Bob Tenny ever tell you he had your telephone number memorized?
A. No, but I know he had the phone number.
Q. Bob and Garrett were your neighbors for several years?
A. Correct.
Q. And you had a key to their house?
A. No, sir, I didn't.
Q. Now, did you share a recyclable bin with Bob and Garrett?
A. No, we didn't share a recycle bin. We each had one, but they parked it in my driveway.
Q. So the recyclable bins were in your driveway?
A. That's right.
Q. Shortly after Bob and Garrett first moved into your neighborhood, you had a confrontation with Garrett that Garrett was taking the recyclables and putting them in a plastic bag and tying it up?
A. Right.
Q. And you told him, hey, this is against city regulations, the recyclables have to be put in the recyclable bin, washed out, and not in a plastic bag, correct?
A. Correct.
Q. You know that Garrett Daniel disappeared, or you never saw him again after January 14th, 2004, right?
A. No, sir, I didn't.
Q. But on January 15, 2004, you went out to your recyclable bin and you put something in there, right?
A. Correct.
Q. When you put something in there, you noticed it was empty?
A. Right.
Q. And then on January 16th you went out to the recyclable bins again, didn't you?
A. Right.
Q. When you went out there, you noticed there was a bag in the recyclable bins that was tied up just the way Garrett Daniel tied it up, correct?
A. Correct.

(NOW THE DISTRICT ATTORNEY CONDUCTED HIS REDIRECT EXAMINATION, AS THE LAST INTERVIEW OF THE DAY'S SESSION.)

BY MR. LEV:

Q. So you didn't even have a key to Garrett Daniel's and Bob Tenny's house?

A. No, sir, I didn't.

Q. Yet you get this letter to look in on his cat?

A. Right.

Q. You have no idea who put that stuff in the recycle bin? You didn't see anybody?

A. I don't know.

Q. Somewhere close to the street?

A. No. They were on the back of my carport.

Q. You don't know who put anything in there?

A. I don't know.

Q. And you certainly didn't see Garrett Daniel around your property from and after January 14, 2004, did you?

A. No, sir.

Q. Or Bob Tenny?

A. No, sir.

Q. In fact, did you see any activity in that house after that Tuesday day, January 14th of 2004?

A. I didn't notice anything.

(WITH THAT, THE COURT RECESSED UNTIL THE FOLLOWING MORNING.)

Third Day, January 3, 2007

MORNING SESSION

(THE JURORS WERE GIVEN THE NEW YEAR HOLIDAY OFF, AND THE TRIAL RESUMED ON THE FIRST MONDAY OF THE NEW YEAR. THE FIRST WITNESS WAS ELIZABETH DUR, OFFICE MANAGER AT THE SAME INSURANCE AGENCY WHERE GARRETT DANIEL WORKED. SHE TESTIFIED THAT GARRETT NORMALLY WENT TO LUNCH AT 12:00 NOON AND RETURNED ONE HOUR LATER. SHE KNEW OF HIS RED CONVERTIBLE, AND STATED THAT HE LEFT EVERYTHING IN HIS OFFICE AS IF HE PLANNED TO RETURN AFTER LUNCH. THE PUBLIC DEFENDER CROSS-EXAMINED MS. DUR AND BROUGHT OUT THE FACT THAT GARRETT DANIEL WAS UNHAPPY WITH THE SALARY HE WAS RECEIVING AS A COMPUTER PROGRAMMER AND MAY HAVE BEEN LOOKING FOR ANOTHER JOB. THERE WAS NO REDIRECT EXAMINATION. THE NEXT WITNESS WAS POLICE OFFICER MCCAUL OF

THE PHOENIX POLICE DEPARTMENT WHO WAS CALLED ON JANUARY 19, 2004, TO CHECK ON AN ILLEGALLY PARKED CAR THAT HAD BEEN THERE FOR SEVERAL DAYS. THE LOCATION WAS APPROXIMATELY ONE MILE FROM THE DANIEL/TENNY HOME. HE MERELY SHONE HIS FLASHLIGHT IN THE CAR AND DETERMINED THAT IT WAS LOCKED AND HADN'T BEEN TAMPERED WITH. THE CAR WAS A RED PONTIAC SUNBIRD, REGISTERED TO GARRETT DANIEL. TWO DAYS LATER HE WAS ASKED BY HIS SUPERIORS TO GO BACK AND CHECK IT OUT AGAIN. THE QUESTIONING BY THE DISTRICT ATTORNEY CONTINUED:)

Q. Was it in the same location?
A. It had been in the same location, yes.
Q. Did it appear anything had been tampered with?
A. No. It appeared pretty much the same.
Q. Did you take somewhat of a closer look at it this time?
A. Yes.
Q. For what reason?
A. The detective specifically asked me to check around the trunk and see if I could smell any foul odors.
Q. Did you?
A. I did not.
Q. Did you check other things about the car?
A. Yes.
Q. What did you check?
A. I checked in and around the seats a little bit, not thorough, and just gave the exterior of the vehicle a better look as well.
Q. What did you see?
A. I noticed that the wheel wells and the tires had a large amount of dry mud on them.
Q. What else, if anything, did you notice about the car?
A. After examining closer the exterior of the vehicle, I noticed what I believed to be some dried blood droplets on the convertible top. I also, from the outside of the vehicle, saw somewhat I believed again to be dry blood on the passenger side seat belt buckle, front passenger side seat. I believe there was a blue shirt or sweater in the back that I thought may have had some dry bloodstains on it as well.
Q. So as a result of seeing these things, what did you do?
A. I called the detective back, advised him of what I had seen, and he told me to remain with the vehicle, as it was going to be impounded as evidence.
Q. Did a wrecker come?
A. It did. I personally drove behind the tow truck and wheeled it into the secured area in the basement.

Q. With regard to the mud, did you look for such things back on the 19th when you first came?

A. No, I did not.

Q. The second time you specifically looked because you were asked to check it out?

A. Correct.

Q. Did you ever go into the vehicle yourself?

A. No, I did not.

Q. And did you look once again to see whether there was any tampering of the car on the 21st?

A. I did.

Q. What did you see?

A. It had remained unchanged from the 19th.

MR. LEV: That's all I have. Thank you.

(THE PUBLIC DEFENDER DECLINED TO CROSS-EXAMINE OFFICER MCCAUL. HE WAS EXCUSED. THEN BOTH LAWYERS APPROACHED THE BENCH AND THE COURT GAVE THE JURORS A 15 MINUTE RECESS. THE FOLLOWING PROCEEDINGS WERE HELD OUT OF THE PRESENCE OF THE JURY:)

MR. LEV: Your Honor, Detective Bru, I was going to call him back for extra foundation. So he's here, he'll fill in. He's not going to take as long.

THE COURT: Have you got enough to fill up this afternoon?

MR. LEV: Well, probably, because I think the one like Serp has a half hour. He's a criminalist. Dr. Buch, she's got a half hour. She's the Medical Examiner. It might take a little bit longer. It will be pretty well filled. Even if it isn't, we are still going to finish by tomorrow morning.

THE COURT: All right. I ask that you both try to get the jury instructions, or any jury instructions that you might have.

MR. LEV: I only have one, Your Honor, and it will be here today.

THE COURT: Mr. Schre, I haven't received yours yet. Can you get them to me by tomorrow morning at least?

MR. SCHRE: Yes, Judge.

THE COURT: If you have anything special. If you don't have anything special, then I guess you really don't have to submit them. I'll do my usual ones. And then the forms of verdict, unless you had some special ones.

MR. SCHRE: Judge, if I have anything, I will get it to you by tomorrow morning. At this time I have not thought of any special jury instructions that we are requesting, besides reasonable doubt and those kind of instructions.

THE COURT: All right. Okay, so we will see you back here in about 15 minutes.

(THE JURY RETURNED AFTER A 15 MINUTE RECESS. THE DISTRICT ATTORNEY CALLED A STATE CRIMINALIST, SHANNON GUL. SHE SAID HER JOB WAS TO SCIENTIFICALLY EXAMINE EVIDENCE AND PRESENT HER FINDINGS IN COURT. SHE SAID SHE HAD EXAMINED APPROXIMATELY 100 CASES SO FAR FROM ALL OVER THE STATE. THEY DISCUSSED HER ABILITIES AND TRAINING, INCLUDING GATHERING EVIDENCE FOR DNA ANALYSIS, WHICH SHE DID ON GARRETT DANIEL'S RED CONVERTIBLE. THE PUBLIC DEFENDER DECLINED TO CROSS-EXAMINE HER.NEXT THE DISTRICT ATTORNEY CALLED MR. SCOTT MELN, ANOTHER CRIMINALIST FOR THE STATE, WHO SPECIALIZES IN DNA ANALYSIS. HE EXPLAINED THE PROCESS OF EXTRACTING DNA FROM BLOODSTAINS. HE SAID HE HAD THE KNOWN DNA FROM BOTH GARRETT DANIEL AND ROBERT TENNY FOR THE PURPOSE OF MATCHING HIS SAMPLES FROM THE RED SUNBIRD CONVERTIBLE. HE DESCRIBED THE VARIOUS SAMPLES THAT MATCHED GARRETT DANIEL'S BLOOD PROFILE WITH A CHANCE OF ERROR BEING ONE IN EVERY 87 QUADRILLION . . . IN OTHER WORDS, WITH SCIENTIFIC CERTAINTY.IN THE CROSS-EXAMINATION, THE PUBLIC DEFENDER ASKED MR. MILN IF HE ALSO TESTED ROBERT TENNY'S BLOOD, AND HE RESPONDED, "YES." HE ASKED IF IT MATCHED ANY OF THE SAMPLES FROM THE RED CONVERTIBLE HE HAD TESTED, AND MR. MILN SAID IT DID NOT. NO FURTHER QUESTIONS. NEXT, DETECTIVE BRU WAS RECALLED TO THE STAND. HE GAVE A LENGTHY DISSERTATION ABOUT THE PROCESSING OF CLUES IN HIS DEPARTMENT. THEN HE IDENTIFIED VARIOUS SAMPLES SHOWN TO HIM:)

A.   They were from the red Sunbird from the seat cushion areas. One was collected from the rear seat cushion, one was collected from the passenger side front seat cushion. This one from the front right passenger seat, on the upper left shoulder area of the seat.

Q. When criminalist Jim Serp was testing the blood item evidence in the home, were you there?

A. Yes. He did the actual preliminary testing of the stains and the collection of the stains. It was done in my presence, under my jurisdiction.

Q. Are blood items impounded generally in the freezer?

A. That's correct.

Q. When you ship blood items for analysis, what precautions do you take to assure there is no further degradation, assuming there had been some?

A. We have freezers that the items with blood and bloodstains are kept in those freezers until they're transferred to the property room.

Q. In any event, they go from freezer to freezer?

A. That's correct.

Q. Detective Bru, was there an answering machine tape from the Tenny/Daniel home originally obtained by Detective McElva and then turned over to you?

A. Yes. It's a cassette tape of the voice mail from the Tenny/Daniel home.

(WITH THIS, THE DISTRICT ATTORNEY CONCLUDED HIS QUESTIONING OF DETECTIVE BRU, AND THE PUBLIC DEFENDER DECLINED TO CROSS-EXAMINE HIM. THE COURT THEN RECESSED UNTIL THE AFTERNOON SESSION.)

AFTERNOON SESSION

(THE DISTRICT ATTORNEY NEXT CALLED CRIME LAB ANALYST JAMES SERP. AFTER ESTABLISHING HIS RATHER REMARKABLE CREDENTIALS, HE GOT TO THE NITTY-GRITTY:)

Q. What does a crime lab analyst do? What do you do?

A. Generally, duties of the crime lab analyst are to assist the investigating officers at scenes of crimes. That assistance consists of photographing the crime scene and all evidence collected therein, assisting and advising in the collection of evidence, chemical processing for various types of evidence, including blood and blood that was not clearly visible to the eye, latent prints, dusting for fingerprints and collection of evidence, returning to the laboratory and processing for latent prints and various other physical and biological evidence.

Q. Did you have an opportunity to participate in the home investigation of a decedent, Garrett Daniel, in relation to one, Bob Tenny?

A. Yes, I did.

Q. When did you go to that address?

A. That was February 5th of 2004.

Q. And what did you do there?

A. My function was to assist in the execution of a search warrant, to photo document the condition of the house and any evidence that we collected, and also to search for blood.

Q. Would you give an explanation to the jury of the exterior layout of the house with regard to any vehicles you may have seen, carports, exterior pool, patio, walkways, et cetera?

A. Certainly. It's a two bedroom, single-story house. There was a carport on the south side of the house, and in the carport there was a Jaguar, four door sedan, black in color. There was a covered patio on the west side of the back of the house, as well as a swimming pool, a pool pump. A utility shed was located southwest of the yard, and a carport in the northwest corner of the yard.

Q. Was the focus of your investigation the interior of the house?

A. Yes, it was.

Q. Could you describe generally the interior of the house, the layout?

A. The interior entrance door opens up into the living room. To the immediate left is a archway or doorway to a dining room. To the front in the living room on the west wall is a fireplace, a doorway to the patio, and a doorway to the kitchen. There's a hallway to the right of the living room, and the hallway has doors to the master bedroom, a spare bedroom—

PUBLIC DEFENDER: Objection. If we could have the record reflect that this witness I believe is reading from his report, and I believe this is improper refreshing his recollection, if the record could note that.

MR. LEV: I don't believe the record would be correct if it noted that. If there could be an inquiry made of Mr. Serp, I would be glad to do it.

THE COURT: All right.

BY MR. LEV:

Q. Have you been reading from notes so far?

A. No, sir.

Q. If you need to refresh your recollection for accuracy, might that be necessary from time to time?

A. Certainly.

Q. And, if so, could you indicate when you're doing it, simply look down, refresh your memory, look back up and testify?

A. Yes.

Q. Has defense counsel been accurate in its assessment of your testimony so far?

A. As to a brief three lines that I read to refresh my memory as to the color of the Jaguar and the exact location of the residence, but as to the direction of the interior of the residence, that was not the case.

MR. LEV: Your ruling, Your Honor?

THE COURT: Public Defender?

PUBLIC DEFENDER: Your Honor, I wasn't talking about the last three sentences. It seemed throughout the testimony that he was looking down and reading from a report.

THE COURT: Well, he said he wasn't. If you have any evidence to the contrary, I'll be glad to hear it. But, Mr. Serp, if you need to refresh your memory, if you could state for the record that at the time that you are refreshing your memory from the report, all right?

THE WITNESS: Certainly.

THE COURT: Thank you. Go ahead.

MR. LEV: Thank you, Your Honor.

Q. So why were you going in as a crime scene analyst and actually analyzing, going in there as part of the search?

A. For two reasons. One, it was that the Sheriff's Office per se had not executed a search warrant upon that residence, so we had not searched it prior to. And, also, there was information that there was visible blood within the residence, and that we needed to deal with that.

Q. Were you present, Mr. Serp, when these photographs were taken of the various areas within the house?

A. Yes. In fact, I took those photographs.

(NOW THE CRIME LAB ANALYST IDENTIFIED NUMEROUS PHOTOS OF BLOOD SPLATTER HE HAD TAKEN. HE TESTIFIED THAT THERE WAS NOT A LOT OF LIGHT IN THE HOUSE AND THAT IS WHY HE USED A FLASHLIGHT AND A FLASH CAMERA. HE SAID THE BLOOD SPOTS WERE NOT PARTICULARLY OBVIOUS IF YOU WEREN'T FOCUSED ON FINDING THEM. THEN HE IDENTIFIED PHOTOS OF BLOOD SPOTS ON THE TILE FLOOR, A LIVING ROOM STOOL, WHITE SHAG CARPET, KITCHEN DOOR, KITCHEN ISLAND, BLINDS, CABINETS,

BATHROOM, PATIO DOORS, BACKYARD WALKWAY. HE INDICATED THAT AN EFFORT HAD BEEN MADE TO ELIMINATE SOME OF THE BLOODSTAINS. THE DISTRICT ATTORNEY CONTINUED:)

Q. Did you do Luminol testing?

A. Yes, I did. That was the second chemical test that I did.

Q. What was the first?

A. The first chemical test I did was called a phenolphthalein test.

Q. As a result of the phenolphthalein test, did you find positive results?

A. Yes, in each and every one of these blood sites.

Q. Where you got a positive reaction, did you swab the area to, say, save as an item of evidence?

A. There were samples taken. We did not swab every single blood droplet or stain that we found.

Q. What was the second type of test that you did?

A. The second type of test is called Luminol. It's a chemical test, also a presumptive for latent blood, that is, blood that has either been washed away, wiped away, or is not readily visible because of the surfaces.

Q. This is Exhibit 94. Would you share with the jury what it is that they're seeing on the floor?

A. Luminol is sprayed on all surfaces, floors, ceilings, walls and all furnishings. In the presence of blood, it will produce a luminescence. The color is blue-white in appearance. And this light is very weak, but it is capable of being photographed. What we are looking at here is a photo of the living room floor. You see the stool in the middle of the living room floor, the reaction area is blue-white. And in the upper center of the photograph is the open kitchen door. The blue-white reactions extend from the door to the bottom of the photograph.

Q. What is a white pattern?

A. A white pattern would be any pattern that results from mechanical distribution of the stain, wiping it with a rag, mop, your hand, whatever it might be.

Q. Is there anything about this white pattern that is indicative of some particular mechanism, mop, towel, whatever?

A. It could be interpreted as a mop wipe.

(THEY CONTINUED THROUGH MANY MORE PHOTOGRAPHS THAT SHOWED THE BLUE-WHITE GLOW OF LUMINOL TESTED AREAS WHERE ATTEMPTS HAD BEEN MADE TO WIPE UP THE BLOOD SPOTS.)

Q. Did you find a trail of blood in wipe pattern from some part of the house to another part of the house?

A. Yes.

Q. And did it start?

A. I couldn't actually determine its exact starting point, but there was a continuous band of reaction with Luminol from the foot of the bed in the master bedroom through the doorway down the hall to the kitchen door, through the kitchen, around the kitchen island and into the dining room, and out on the patio walkway.

(WHEN THE DISTRICT ATTORNEY COMPLETED THE IDENTIFICATION AND FLOW OF THE BLOOD SPOT PATTERN, THE PUBLIC DEFENDER CROSS-EXAMINED MR. SERP.)

Q. You have just been telling us about the blood that you saw in certain areas, correct?

A. Yes.

Q. And that blood was visible to you when you got there?

A. It was.

Q. And some of it stood out, right?

A. Well, again, it stood out because I was looking for it, and a lot of it was on my hands and knees with the flashlight.

Q. But often times you didn't use any tools to look at the blood, isn't that right? You just looked at it with your naked eye?

A. And a flashlight, yes.

Q. And you saw there was blood in the patio area. I think we saw a picture of that?

A. Yes.

Q. And that was observable to you, wasn't it, without enhancement?

A. Yes. But, again, there was no light out there. It required a flashlight.

Q. You also saw some blood on the shag carpet, correct?

A. Yes.

Q. That was pretty obvious to you?

A. Because I was looking for it.

Q. And while you were in the house, you didn't look for any hair samples, did you?

A. No.

Q. And you didn't look for any fingerprints, did you?

A. No.

Q. You found a barefoot impression on the patio?

A. Yes.

Q. You didn't compare that with anybody, did you?

A. No.

Q. I'd like to talk to you a little bit about the testing procedures. You told us that the first one you used was the phenolphthalein?

A. Yes.

Q. That shows the presumptive presence of blood?

A. That's correct.

Q. But it's not a positive confirmation of blood, is it? It reacts with other things besides blood?

A. Yes.

Q. It reacts to certain plant materials, also certain chemicals, right?

A. Yes.

Q. Then you talked about Luminol. That was the second test that you did, correct?

A. That's correct.

Q. And that's also a preliminary test for blood?

A. Yes.

Q. Which means that you always have to do another test to confirm that blood is actually what was observed with the Luminol?

A. Yes.

Q. And that also only indicates the possible presence of blood?

A. That's correct.

Q. In fact, you need a confirmatory test to find out if it's even human blood, right, because it may be animal blood?

A. Yes. The Luminol and phenolphthalein are not specific for only human blood.

Q. Right. So you need to do further tests, correct?

A. Yes.

Q. And with Luminol it's also impossible to tell how long blood has been there or how long a substance has been there; isn't that correct?

A. That's correct.

Q. And you also mentioned the words "false positives." Would you explain what a false positive is?

A. A false positive with any chemical test is a reaction that is similar to the reaction one would expect when testing a known substance. However, it is a reaction from another substance.

Q. So with false positives, something may look like blood when, in fact, it's something else?

A. That can be, yes.

Q. And, for example, some false positive with Luminol might be met at surfaces such as iron, that could give a false positive?

A. Yes.

Q. Also with cleansers containing an iron base substance, that could be a false positive, correct?

A. Yes.

Q. Rust can be a false positive?

A. Again that's iron, yes.

Q. And any oxidizing agents can give you a false positive?

A. Yes.

Q. Bleach and dish washing detergents can give you a false positive for Luminol?

A. Many cleaners that contain oxidizers.

Q. Many cleaners such as Comet?

A. Yes.

Q. And even a simple penny could give you a false positive when you're talking about Luminol, correct?

A. Yes. Copper and copper alloys are known false positives.

Q. So basically, Luminol is a possible indicator for blood and it's not positive, correct?

A. It is a presumptive test, yes.

Q. You also talked about wipes and drips that you found throughout the house?

A. That's correct.

Q. You didn't find any mops in the house to test, did you?

A. No, we didn't.

Q. You didn't find any rags in the house, did you?

A. I don't believe so.

Q. So you didn't find anything that could be attributed to this wiping motion, did you?

A. No.

(THE PUBLIC DEFENDER DID A CREDIBLE JOB OF CASTING DOUBT ON THE VERACITY OF THE ANALYST'S BLOOD TESTS, AND THE DISTRICT ATTORNEY HAD A DIFFICULT CHORE GETTING THE BLOODSTAIN IDENTIFICATION BACK ON TRACK ON HIS REDIRECT EXAMINATION.)

Q. So the blood was visible to you because sometimes you were down on your hands and knees with a flashlight?

A. Yes.

Q. Does that include, for example, like the shag carpet as far as illuminating?

A. Yes.

Q. The shag carpet is white?

A. Yes.

Q. But was there much of a pattern on it that would be particularly visible?

A. No. The difficulty with the shag was that it has a lot of shadows associated with the shag fibers.

Q. And the phenolphthalein, was that the presumptive test you used to decide which amongst the many items to actually impound for future testing?

A. No. The phenolphthalein was used as a screening to examine tests that were presumed by visual examination that they could be blood. Phenolphthalein gave a further confirmation of the visual examination. Samples were selected from various areas of bloodstains.

Q. There were 19 total samples taken and impounded; is that correct?

A. Those are the total that were taken by me. There were some knives taken, and the door handle obviously was taken.

Q. Questions were asked about other things that could make a false positive. And with regard to the Luminol testing, did this appear to be more consistent with a blood pattern than something else, such as vegetable juice or cleansers, whatever was asked during cross-examination?

A. In addition to the reaction, the area of reaction was indicative of a mechanical wiping of blood. As I said, there were blood spots, undiluted and diluted blood spots on either side of this white pattern, if you will.

Q. What does diluted and undiluted mean?

A. Well, diluted blood would be any variation, weakening of the blood concentration so that when the blood droplet dried, you would have a ring of blood around the outside of the droplet, or the circle, and what appeared to be a void in the middle, whereas undiluted blood would dry as a discrete droplet. that was essentially red all the way through.

Q. You said you found no mops in the house or rags. Are such items particularly difficult to dispose of?

A. No.

(WHEREUPON, A 15 MINUTE BREAK WAS TAKEN. NEXT THE DISTRICT ATTORNEY QUESTIONED A DETECTIVE FROM THE MISSING PERSONS BUREAU WHO TESTIFIED SHE EXAMINED ALL ACCIDENT REPORTS AND DIDN'T FIND THE NAME OF GARRETT DANIEL. THE NEXT WITNESS WAS A FORENSIC PATHOLOGIST WHO WORKED FOR THE MEDICAL EXAMINER'S OFFICE, DR. ANN BUCH. AFTER SHE RELATED HER QUALIFICATIONS AND EXPERIENCE, SHE STATED SHE PERFORMED THE AUTOPSY ON GARRETT DANIEL IN THE PRESENCE OF DETECTIVE BRUE. THE EXAMINATION CONTINUED:)

Q. What did you determine to be the cause of death?

A. I certified the death as, the cause of death as multiple stab wounds.

Q. And the manner of death?

A. Homicide.

Q. And did Dr. Piak do some forensic dental examination to make absolutely sure that the body was that of Garrett Daniel?

A. Yes, he did.

Q. What was your knowledge with regard to finding of the body in the sense of where, and any particulars?

A. I knew that the decedent was found unresponsive in the Cave Creek area covered by brush.

Q. In that regard, there has been testimony elicited that it rained on or about January 15th, or the 14th, 2004, in the Cave Creek area, that it was a significant rain, that it was cold, it didn't snow but the elevation in Cave Creek is a thousand or so feet.

MR. SCHRE: I'm going to object. Maybe we could have a limiting instruction on this, that it's a hypothetical, and that the jury determines what the evidence is.

THE COURT: Well, it's not a hypothetical. He's stating what he believes the evidence has shown so far.

Ladies and gentlemen of the jury, you are, as I said in the preliminary instructions and I will state in the final instructions, you are the triers of the fact. If you remember something different than what Mr. Lev is saying, then please take that into account, if you say he's misstating the evidence, Mr. Schre.

MR. SCHRE: That wasn't my objection.

THE COURT: Well, then, your objection is overruled. Please continue, Mr. Lev.

MR. LEV: Thank you, Your Honor.

BY MR. LEV:
Q. So when you first did your physical examination of the body, what did you see when the body was taken out of the bag?
A. What I saw was a decomposing Caucasian male. The postmortem stiffening of the body was absent. Lividity, or settling of the blood was present but fixed, meaning it wasn't changeable. There was early decomposition changes present, including maggot infestation. The face was red-green and discolored with subcutaneous gas formation and skin slippage, or the skin was actually falling off the surface. There was drying of the hands and feet, early mummification we call it. And there was also maggots involving the face and in the stab wounds.
Q. Was there also maggot infestation, for example, in the extremities, such as the ears?
A. Yes. There were maggot holes, we call them actually chew areas, on the ears.
Q. And are maggots fly larvae that eat flesh?
A. Yes.
Q. So, now, at this point, what was the pathologic diagnoses?
A. The first diagnosis was that of multiple stab wounds. There were incisions or stab wounds of the heart, the right and left lungs, the esophagus, left jugular vein and the left subclavian artery.

Q. Were there rib fractures?

A. Yes, there were.

Q. In order to produce a rib fracture in this type of body, does it require a certain amount of force?

A. Somewhat. It's harder to cut through a bone than it is a skin. Skin is fairly easy to cut through, but bone requires more force.

Q. Were they associated with the stab wounds, the rib fractures?

A. Yes.

Q. Could you now explain the various wounds into Garrett Daniel's anatomy?

A. There was a stab wound to the top of the head near the hairline. It was superficial but didn't enter the skull. There were also three stab wounds to the side of the neck. One entered the deeper structures and actually incised the left jugular vein, on the side of the neck, and also the left subclavian artery.

Q. The jugular vein carries blood to where?

A. Carries blood away from the brain.

Q. Is it a major artery?

A. It's a major vein, yes.

Q. And if it's opened up, as in the stab wound, would a lot of blood come out?

A. Yes.

(NOW DR. BUCH WAS ASKED TO IDENTIFY THE STAB WOUNDS IN A NUMBER OF PHOTOGRAPHS SHE TOOK IN THE MORGUE. SHE SAID THE DEPTH OF THE TEN STABS WAS FROM ONE-EIGHTH INCH TO FOUR AND ONE-HALF INCHES. STAB WOUNDS WERE SHOWN IN GARRETT DANIEL'S ARMS, CHEST, ARM MUSCLES, HEART, LUNG, AND NECK. SHE CLAIMED HE WAS STABBED WITH A SINGLE-EDGE BLADE KNIFE. THE DISTRICT ATTORNEY CONTINUED:)

Q. Now, on this photograph, could that be what they call a defensive wound?

A. Yes, that's consistent with a defensive wound. Classically, we'd call defensive wounds any kind of injury on the arm where the arms or legs are raised to defend the more vital areas.

Q. Do you have an opinion with regard to a time of death?

A. It comes down to estimating time of death rather than giving an exact time. It's very dependent on environmental temperatures, the conditions the body is left in, full sun or not, trauma or not, how heavily they're clothed, whether they're covered. A lot of variables. Mr. Daniel has evidence of some decomposition changes. How long does that take? Is there any idea of how cool it was? Do we have any range of environmental temperatures during that period for the previous two or three weeks prior to death, or when he's found?

Q. Cold.

A. Cold?

Q. If I recall the testimony to the extent of not quite knowing whether the water tanks for the horses glazed over with ice or not.

A. That's pretty cold. The reason that matters is, that approaches our cooler temperatures. When you start getting into the temperatures where you have ice forming on water, or there's snow, and then if the body is shaded, that also creates a lower temperature for it. In my opinion—I got him on January 27th. With the changes I saw, he's at least a week.

Q. Would it be consistent or inconsistent if the time of death was indicated as being January 14, 2004, at between 12:00 and 1:00 p.m.

A. That would make it 13 days prior to him being discovered. And there's nothing to say that it's inconsistent with that.

Q. And in his particular case, was cold and is cold an important factor in keeping the body preserved, relative to there being no more decomposition than you saw?

A. Yes.

Q. Does rain or moisture have some affect on decomposition?

A. Rain cools the body quicker and keeps the environmental temperature lower. It's cloudy, usually. It's overcast. That will lower the environmental temperature which will help preserve it a little bit longer.

Q. And you saw one of these photos with some kind of shrub over the body. Is that kind of the shade you're talking about?

A. Yes. Anything to keep direct sun from striking the body.

Q. How about the cold ground relative to the body?

A. That's also helpful in preserving it.

Q. When you preserve a body in the Medical Examiner's Office prior to the autopsy, what is the temperature in the holding cooler?

A. In the holding cooler it's around 34 degrees.

Q. What does that 34 degrees do?

A. It lowers their body temperature quickly. You just have to lower it so the body isn't too warm.

Q. Does it assist in also, how shall I say, reducing or even eliminating decompositional odors, body decay odors?

A. Yes.

Q. What produces these odors? Let's go the other extreme and say it's a hot day and the sun is on the body and you know the body is getting, let's say it's summer, what produces the odors?

A. The body forms methane gas, like the smell of rotten eggs, and that sort of thing, the putrid fraction on the inside and the bowel, and that makes the body swell and bloat. Whereas when you cool it, the bacteria slows down and are unable to produce the gas.

Q. Again, did the appearance of the body, is that consistent with what you saw, consistent with a potential date being on or about January 14, 2004?

A. There's nothing inconsistent with that.

MR. LEV: That's all I have.

THE COURT: Mr. Schre.

CROSS-EXAMINATION

BY MR. SCHRE:

Q. From the evidence that you have seen, there would be nothing inconsistent with the time of death being, let's say 10:00 in the evening on January 18, 2004, correct?

A. That would be nine days.

Q. Yes.

A. And the time is irrelevant to me because nine days versus eight days, I can't tell the difference.

Q. Now, your estimate of over a week is based on a body being out in the desert, partially clothed, when it's cold out, and there's brush covering part of the body, correct?

A. Yes.

Q. And if a body was in the passenger compartment of a car for some time, that could change your estimate of the time of death, correct?

A. Yes. It depends on how long it was, for one hour, five minutes or three days. If he was stored in there three days and then put in the desert, he might look a little more decomposed than he is.

Q. The reason that storing a body in a car can increase the rate of decay is if the windows of the car act like a magnifying glass?

A. Yes, that's correct.

Q. What happens is, the temperature inside the car becomes like a greenhouse, correct?

A. It can.

Q. After examining the body, you found that the chest wall was positive for ethanol .06 grams?

A. Yes.

Q. What does that mean?

A. In a body such as this that's decomposed, probably not much. The body forms alcohol when it decomposes and bloats, and you can get up to .06 to .08, and it does not mean that the person was drinking prior to that. We can't say that they maybe didn't have one drink, but it's probably not significant. It's definitely below the legal limit.

Q. So this person could have been drinking before the time of death?

A. Maybe one. Not much, not with this amount of decomposition. It's most consistent with just a decomposed body and no drinking.

Q. But you can't rule out from that ethanol figure that you obtained that this person was drinking prior to the time of death?

A. I can't tell.

Q. Thank you.

(THE DISTRICT ATTORNEY BEGAN HIS REDIRECT EXAMINATION BY TRYING TO ESTABLISH THAT THE ENVIRONMENT THAT THE BODY HAD BEEN IN, OR MIGHT HAVE BEEN IN, COULD PRESERVE IT LONGER ON THAT COLD JANUARY 14TH DAY IN 2004. THE RESULTS OF THE TESTIMONY WERE FAIRLY INCONCLUSIVE BECAUSE DR. BUCH STILL COULD NOT PIN DOWN THE TIME OF DEATH OTHER THAN "A WEEK OR LONGER." NOW THE JUDGE RECESSED THE COURT UNTIL THE FOLLOWING MORNING. THE FOLLOWING CONVERSATION TOOK PLACE AFTER THE JURY HAD GONE HOME:)

THE COURT: How many witnesses do you have tomorrow?

MR. LEV: Three: Detective McElva, the American Express custodian of records, and United Airlines.

THE COURT: And you think that will finish up by noon?

MR. LEV: Yes, Your Honor.

THE COURT: Do you have your witnesses lined up for the afternoon?

MR. SCHRE: Yes, Judge.

THE COURT: How long do you think they're going to take?

MR. SCHRE: I think in the afternoon at the most I would take two hours.

THE COURT: So, do you want to put off closing arguments until Wednesday?

MR. SCHRE: I'm fine with putting it off until Wednesday, and we can settle jury instructions after the close of evidence.

THE COURT: It doesn't sound like it's going to be a lengthy process.

MR. SCHRE: Right.

THE COURT: All right. You may or may not have some rebuttal witnesses?

MR. LEV: Correct.

THE COURT: We will see you back here at 10:00.

MR. SCHRE: I think there's one other issue maybe we can take up now. I know earlier in the day Detective Bru had testified about an answering machine tape or a voice mail tape, and that Detective McElva was going to further go into that. And I'm going to make an objection of that tape as not being relevant.

THE COURT: I don't know what is on the tape. Do you know?

MR. SCHRE: I have listened to the tape.

THE COURT: What is on it?

MR. SCHRE: It begins, to my understanding, on January 15, 2004, and it has people calling about Garrett Daniel and his job interviews. It has people calling wanting to talk to Mr. Tenny leaving him messages. It has Garrett's mother calling concerned about him. The tape, it's a voice message tape that goes about a week long of messages.

THE COURT: Why don't you think it's relevant?

MR. SCHRE: I don't think that there's anything in there that tends to make a fact of consequences more likely or less likely in this case, and it would be without that evidence. And aside from that relevance aspect, many of the people that are on the tape we don't know who they are. They're just leaving messages and they say a name, and I don't know who that person particularly is. I haven't been able to find out.

THE COURT: Well, let me hear from Mr. Lev.

MR. LEV: Your Honor, the probative value is that the defendant, and it's in evidence, sent a letter to Mr. Weiss, and in the letter to Mr. Weiss he's telling Mr. Weiss to tell Mr. Daniel to answer the phone, as though Mr. Daniel wasn't answering. And, of course, this voice mail recording is devoid of any call from Mr. Tenny. To anyone. And, therefore, it is probative to show he, in fact, did not call. So his suggestion to Mr. Weiss, the reasonable inference being that he did call telling Mr. Daniel to answer the phone is probative to show that he never ever made any attempt to call that house.

THE COURT: It seems, Mr. Schre, that the centerpiece of your defense is, at least one of the centerpieces, is the time frame. And this phone call seems to go to the time frame, so I think it's probative in regard.

I don't see where the prejudice outweighs the probative value at this point, so I'm going to allow it. If I hear something on it that I think is prejudicial or not relevant, then let's object at that time. If there's something significant on there that you think is prejudicial, then let me know about it. Otherwise, we will see you tomorrow.

Fourth Day, January 4, 2007

MORNING SESSION

(THE SESSION BEGAN WITH THE DISTRICT ATTORNEY EXAMINING THE RECORDS CUSTODIAN FOR AMERICAN EXPRESS CHARGE CARDS. HE TESTIFIED THAT THE DECEASED GARRETT DANIEL CHARGED A MOTEL ROOM IN PHOENIX ON JANUARY 8TH, 9TH AND 10TH, 2004, AND AGAIN ON JANUARY 13TH, THE NIGHT BEFORE HIS MURDER. HIS CHARGE RECEIPTS ALSO INCLUDED VARIOUS RESTAURANT CHARGES ON THESE DATES. THEN HE SHOWED HIS RECORDS FOR ROBERT TENNY, THE DEFENDANT, AS THE DISTRICT ATTORNEY CONTINUED:)

BY MR. LEV:
Q. With regard to Robert Tenny, is there a charge on January 15, 2004, for airline tickets?
A. Yes there is.
Q. What airlines?
A. I have one for British Airways, and one for United Airlines.
Q. United Airlines, does the record show where the ticket was purchased?
A. From Phoenix, for $486.
Q. And are there charges on January 16, 2004, for New York?
A. There's one charge here at the Hilton Hotel, J.F.K, 1/16/04 for $173.97.
Q. Are there charges also on the 17th in New York?
A. There's another charge from the Hilton Hotel J.F.K. for $6.44. Another one for $14.45.
Q. Is there a charge for British Airways?
A. Yes, there is, for $1,378 from J.F.K. to London to Johannesburg.
Q. What is the date of the purchase?
A. Transaction date is 1/15/04.
Q. Were there further charges in South Africa subsequent to 1/15/04?
A. There's a number of charges from South Africa.

(AT THIS POINT THE AMERICAN EXPRESS CUSTODIAN ITEMIZED A NUMBER OF CHARGES AT VARIOUS HOTELS AND RESTAURANTS IN SOUTH AFRICA, INCLUDING A $684 RENTAL CAR CHARGE. THE

CROSS-EXAMINATION MERELY ESTABLISHED THAT ROBERT TENNY WAS AUTHORIZED TO USE THIS CREDIT CARD. THE NEXT WITNESS WAS A SUPERVISOR FROM UNITED AIRLINES PHOENIX OFFICE. SHE SHOWED PROOF THAT ROBERT TENNY PURCHASED AIRLINE TICKETS ON THE NIGHT OF JANUARY 14TH AT 11:46 P.M., USING AN AMERICAN EXPRESS CREDIT CARD AND ORDERED OVER THE TELEPHONE FROM HIS HOME. THE FLIGHT LEFT PHOENIX THE FOLLOWING MORNING, JANUARY 15TH, AT 7:35 A.M., AND ROBERT TENNY CHECKED IN AT 6:43 A.M. THE PUBLIC DEFENDER HAD NO CROSS-EXAMINATION.

THE NEXT WITNESS CALLED WAS DETECTIVE MCELVA WHO TESTIFIED THAT HE AND SIX OTHER INVESTIGATORS WENT TO THE DANIEL/TENNY HOUSE ON JANUARY 21, 2004. THEY OBTAINED A TAPE OF THE VOICE MAIL IN THE HOME, AMONG OTHER THINGS. THE DISTRICT ATTORNEY ASKED:)

Q. With regard to that tape, did you hear on the tape anyone announcing themselves as Bob Tenny for anyone?
A. No, I did not.
Q. Anyone announcing themself as Garrett Daniel for anyone?
A. No, I did not.
Q. As part of your investigation, was a letter turned over to you from Jeffrey Kin, one of the directors of the agency, purporting to be a letter from Robert Tenny?
A. Yes.

(AT THIS POINT, THE PUBLIC DEFENDER TOOK OVER THE CROSS-EXAMINATION. HE ESTABLISHED THAT THE DETECTIVES WENT INSIDE THE HOME ON JANUARY 21, 2004, SEARCHING FOR EVIDENCE. AFTER THEY FOUND BLOOD IN THE HOME, THEY DISCONTINUED THEIR SEARCH UNTIL THEY RECEIVED A SEARCH WARRANT.

DETECTIVE MCELVA STATED THAT HE IMPOUNDED A MOP FROM A STORAGE SHED, A BUCKET, SOME BLOODY TILES, AND SEVERAL DRINKING TUMBLERS TO CHECK FOR FINGERPRINTS. THE DETECTIVE ALSO RECEIVED TWO DIFFERENT LETTERS WRITTEN BY ROBERT TENNY: ONE FOR MR. JEFF KIN POSTMARKED JANUARY 17TH, 2004, AND ONE FOR NEIGHBOR MR. WEISS. HE TESTIFIED THAT MR. WEISS ALSO HEARD AN ARGUMENT IN THE BACKYARD OF THE DANIEL/TENNY HOME ON JANUARY 14, 2004, BETWEEN NOON AND 1:00 P.M., BUT COULDN'T PIN DOWN WHAT WAS SAID

AND BY WHOM. AFTER THIS, THE DETECTIVE ISSUED A MISSING PERSONS BULLETIN. WHEN GARRETT DANIEL'S BODY WAS FOUND ON JANUARY 27, 2004, HE DROPPED THE MISSING PERSONS SEARCH. THEY BRIEFLY DISCUSSED THE TELEPHONE VOICE MAIL TAPE, BUT IT WAS INCONCLUSIVE.

AT THIS POINT, THE STATE RESTED ITS CASE, THE COURT CALLED FOR AN EARLY LUNCH RECESS. WHEREUPON, THE FOLLOWING PROCEEDINGS WERE HELD OUT OF THE PRESENCE OF THE JURY:)

THE COURT: Before you do your Rule 20 motion, (dismissal of charges) Mr. Schre, do we need to put anything on the record reference the agreement on the tape. I don't know if it was somewhat a stipulation, but if you want to put anything on the record that will be fine. If you don't feel it's necessary, that's also fine, Mr. Lev?

MR. LEV: We just made an arrangement. The stipulation was what Detective McElva testified to. There were a number of calls, and so forth and so on.

THE COURT: Mr. Schre, was that your understanding?

MR. SCHRE: That's my understanding. I just want to make sure, I don't believe the tape was admitted into evidence.

MR. LEV: No.

MR. SCHRE: I just want to make sure it doesn't go back to the jury.

THE COURT: It won't. They wouldn't have a tape recorder, anyway.

MR. SCHRE: Okay.

THE COURT: Everybody can sit down except Mr. Schre. Do you want to make your Rule 20 motion at this time? Or you can wait. You can make it actually twice, but I will leave it to you.

MR. SCHRE: I will make my Rule 20 motion now, Judge. And I'm going to ask the Court for a directed verdict because there was no substantial evidence that can support a conviction in this case. I think reasonable jurors would not differ about this evidence.

There's no confession, there's no murder weapon, there's no substantiation of a time of death.

For that reason, I ask that the Court grant my Rule 20 motion.

THE COURT: The Court finds that there is substantial evidence and that this case can go to the jury.

It is ordered denying the defendant's motion for a directed verdict of acquittal pursuant to Rule 20.

Mr. Schre, you'll start up, I hope I was correct in saying that you think we will finish with the testimony today?

MR. SCHRE: Yes, Judge. I need a few minutes maybe before we break, maybe I can have a few minutes to speak with Mr. Tenny. And when I'm done, Mr. Lev and myself can go back to your chambers and tell you what is going to happen this afternoon as far as witnesses go.

THE COURT: Okay, that's fine.

MR. SCHRE: I also do have jury instructions. They were supposed to be submitted earlier this morning, but they ran them over to me at this desk instead of to your office.

THE COURT: Okay. You can bring them back there when you go back.

MR. SCHRE: That's fine, Judge.

AFTERNOON SESSION

(AT THIS TIME THE PUBLIC DEFENDER TOOK OVER AND CALLED THE DEFENDANT ROBERT TENNY TO TAKE THE STAND. HE WAS DULY SWORN, AND THE PUBLIC DEFENDER CONTINUED:)

Q. Where are you from?
A. I was born in Capetown, South Africa, January the 22nd, 1966.Q. Now, you knew Garrett Daniel?
A. I did.
Q. And how did you meet Garrett Daniel?
A. I met Garrett in Hawaii in April of 1998 socially.
Q. What were you doing in Hawaii?
A. I was living there temporarily, and I was operating a jet ski water sports program.

Q. And did you develop a relationship with Garrett while he was in Hawaii?

A. I knew him for approximately one week in Hawaii, then I departed Hawaii for Florida on a business trip. I was planning to extend my jet ski interest in Florida. And then I met up with him in Pittsburgh. He invited me to Pittsburgh. From Pittsburgh, he invited me to his home in Indiana.

Q. When you say you met up with him in Pittsburgh, what was the purpose of going to Pittsburgh?

A. The way the airplane flight worked, he suggested instead of going directly to Florida, I could meet him in Pittsburgh and stay with him in the hotel. So we had a rendezvous there.

Q. How long was your rendezvous in Pittsburgh?

A. Two days. From there, we went to Indiana upon invitation.

Q. Had you ever been to Indiana before?

A. No, I had not. I was looking forward to that.

Q. And how long did you stay in Indiana?

A. I never left Indiana until I came to Phoenix.

Q. Why didn't you leave Indiana?

A. My friendship with Garrett began at that point and he asked me to stay in Indiana, and I ended up staying there.

Q. Did you stay at Garrett's home?

A. Yes.

Q. Now, prior to going to Indiana, you were in Hawaii, correct?

A. Correct.

Q. And before that, you were where?

A. I was in Toronto, Canada.

Q. How long were you in Canada for?

A. Eleven, twelve years.

Q. What did you do in Canada?

A. I was an advertising executive.

Q. And why did you leave Canada?

A. Personal reasons. I guess the best way to describe it is the well had dried up. I just felt I had enough of Toronto, and as you put it, snapped my fingers and made a choice to leave. I was not doing particularly well at the end of the 12 year period, so I sold my house and car and decided to do the trip to Hawaii.

Q. Did you have any family in Canada?

A. I do.

Q. Now, prior to moving to Canada, where did you live?

A. Capetown, South Africa.

Q. And how old were you when you left South Africa?

A. Eighteen.

Q. And why did you leave South Africa?

A. As a student, as a graduate, I had choices to make about my destiny, and those days politics in that country was not conducive to a solid future. I was faced with military choices. I preferred to go to Canada where my father lived.

Q. All right. Now, what year did you arrive in Hawaii again?

A. 1997.

Q. How long were you in Indiana?

A. A year.

Q. And what did you do when you lived in Indiana?

A. I worked on Garrett's house.

Q. When you say worked on his house, could you elaborate for me?

A. I painted his house for him inside and out, I added some wall dividers between the kitchen and the dining room. We did some carpentry there. I also did some roofing for another building company that he knew of that he introduced me to in the region, so I worked on other properties as well.

Q. Besides Garrett when you moved to Indiana, did you know anybody there?

A. No.

Q. When you moved to Hawaii, did you know anyone there?

A. No.

Q. Now, you said your father lived in Canada. When you moved there, besides your father did you know anyone in Canada?

A. No.

Q. And what about your sister and mother?

A. Well, they followed me to Canada.

Q. So they were back in South Africa when you went to Canada?

A. Right.

Q. And when you moved to Phoenix, besides Garrett, did you know anybody here?

A. No.

Q. How did it happen that you and Garrett moved to Phoenix?

A. Garrett knew that his time and offers as a computer consultant was limited, so he had choices to make himself. It was my understanding he would move to Hawaii. By meeting him, I thought it would be an opportunity not only to develop the relationship and friendship, but also to get back to Hawaii to the jet ski, which is what I wanted to do. But, in the course of that first year, Garrett decided that it was too expensive in Hawaii, and he chose to move to Phoenix. So it was his choice to select Phoenix as his destination, and I went with him.

Q. And you went with him because you were having a relationship?

A. Yes.

Q. And when you went to Canada from South Africa, what did you bring with you?

A. The clothes in my suitcase.

Q. When you went from Canada to Hawaii, what did you bring with you?

A. Just a suitcase of clothing.

Q. And when you went to Pittsburgh, and then Indiana from Hawaii, what did you bring with you?

A. Clothing that I might have accumulated along the way, but I was traveling very light at that time.

Q. When you went from Indiana to Arizona, what did you bring with you?

A. A U-Haul truck of mostly Garrett's possessions.

Q. And then how long were you in Arizona before you left?

A. Six years.

Q. And after those six years in Arizona, where did you go to?

A. I went to South Africa.

Q. And what did you bring with you when you went to South Africa?

A. A suitcase of clothing.

Q. All right. Now, are you a citizen of the United States?

A. No.

Q. Tell me about your immigration status in this country.

A. I have established an annually renewable work visa through the Canadian/U.S. Trade Act. So it is a privileged executive visa for specialized technical work. My job in Phoenix as a nonprofit executive will qualify for that status, but it was only renewable on an annual basis and only good for approximately four or five renewals, at which point you're obligated to apply for permanent resident status.

Q. Did you have any problems with that visa?

A. The lawyers that I retained explained that the job profile, although it was good for a temporary, was not qualifiable on a permanent resident status. I wasn't going to be able to live here permanently and do that job.

Q. How did you feel about that problem?

A. You know, it was a stumbling block that I never got over. The only way around that is through the labor board, and then they advertise your job in the newspaper. If somebody comes forward and takes it, that's it. So I realized the time was running out.

Q. Now, can you tell me about your job?

A. It was a nonprofit housing organization that I founded here in Phoenix designed to help people with disabilities and subsidize them through government grants in obtaining housing for them and their families.

Q. How did you found it?

A. I did a lot of networking in the computer community. I felt there was a market for somebody to get up and do something for people in wheelchairs, so we held a public forum at the City Hall and invited various disabled interest groups to come forward and speak on the issue of housing and the shortage thereof, and it was from that point we moved forward and established the company.

Q. When you say "we," was it just you?

A. Three foundling members, and Garrett Daniel was one of them, and I believe another friend of his from his insurance company was involved.

Q. Was it your brainchild?

A. Yes.

Q. Now, what year did you start the agency?

A. The incorporation of the agency was April 3rd, 2000.

Q. And when the agency was incorporated, was there a salary that was decided upon that would be paid to you?

A. We did pass a resolution to the effect that I would earn a salary. I was the only one to earn a salary.

Q. What was your salary—

A. At that time it was $29,000.

Q. Now, was your salary at the agency supposed to increase over the years?

A. I think that was the decision that was commensurate upon performance, so if the monies were forthcoming and available, we would. We had one other resolution passed by the group to increase it to $39,000. I think that came down to '02.

Q. And was your salary ever increased to $39,000?

A. I drew down one year at $39,000. I believe that was '02.

Q. What about in 2003?

A. I drew $33,000.

Q. How did you feel about that?

A. I was disappointed.

Q. Why were you disappointed?

A. I didn't meet my goal.

Q. And describe to me the effort you put into your agency. What did you do?

A. Everything. I did the job of five people. It's a very complicated juggling of various acts being an executive, being a social worker, and being a construction expert, government liase, HUD specialist, a number of different ingredients that go into that job profile.

Q. How many hours a week would you say you put into your work?

A. Thirty-five, forty.

Q. Were those hard hours?

A. Yes, they were consistent.

Q. Did you work hard?

A. Every day I was at the office at nine and I was never out of there until five. I went home once or twice a week for lunch.

Q. When you mentioned going home once or twice a week for lunch, who would you see when you went home for lunch?

A. If Garrett was home, I would see Garrett. Maybe the neighbors.

Q. Was Garrett in the habit of going home for lunch?

A. He more often went home.

Q. You knew he went home for lunch?

A. I knew he went to the house more often than I did. He drove around town a lot more on his lunch breaks than I did. I think his office job was such that come lunch he would get out of there. Mine was quite often on the road because of the real estate. So I was always out there on the road and I didn't need to go home at lunch.

Q. Now, what lead up to your resignation for the agency? What was the culmination?

A. I think my personal relationship with Garrett was the reason I left on the 15th of January of '04. That would have been the first decision to call at 11:30 at night and book an airplane flight.

Q. Was there more to it than just your relationship with Garrett?

A. Well, the U.S. Immigration status weighed very heavily on me. It was also very expensive. The lawyers and trips to Canada, to get the passports organized, I just—it seemed to be an ongoing battle and not enough funds to do it.

Q. Was there also some disappoint over your salary?

A. And the third element was the job, and it was limited in its scope. It was limited in its scope and needed a lot more board member participation.

Q. Did Garrett know about your plans to resign from the agency?

A. I told him that we either did something about establishing a trust foundation and increasing the budget, or I wouldn't go on with it year to year without fulfilling those goals.

Q. On January 14, 2004, did Garrett know about your immediate plans to leave the agency?

A. He knew that I was going to make an announcement at the next board meeting on the 22nd.

Q. And how did he know that?

A. I told him. We discussed it a number of times as we discussed his work. If we had communication between us, it was to do with our work. That was one area that we didn't fail one another on.

Q. Did Garrett know on January 14, 2004, you were leaving Arizona?

A. I don't think I told him I was going to book an airplane flight and leave that day. We went to L.A. for New Year, we went to the Rose Bowl and we had a miserable Christmas. He didn't buy me any gift and it was very strained. We were not getting along on a personal level.

Q. So you didn't tell him actually when you left on the 14th?

A. I told him coming back that I was definitely packing it in.

Q. Did he know a specific date?

A. No.

Q. Now, tell me about the process for you resigning your position at the agency, what needed to be done?

A. You just write a letter and resign, formally put it in notice. Most people do it for two weeks, but that's because they're on a paycheck.

Q. Did you do that?

A. I wrote a letter. I typed up a letter on the computer at the house.

Q. How did you write the letter?

A. I didn't have a printing machine at the house. It's difficult not to have a printer at home, so I printed the letter out of a New York Kinko's.

Q. Who did you send the letter to?

A. To Jeff Kin. I sent it to Jeff Kin because Jeff Kin was the other serious contender as management of the company. He was a landlord and he was a nonprofit housing executive himself, and if anybody could run the show on the big picture, it was him.

Q. Now, in your job for the agency, did you work with Linda Hernand?

A. Linda Hernand was a HUD approved appraiser. She was appointed by a bank, a Scottsdale bank that I had negotiated a line of mortgages with. And, yes, we worked together on two occasions.

Q. Prior to January 14, 2004, did you have an appraisal set for that day with Linda Hernand?

A. Apparently so, yes.

Q. Do you remember that?

A. I remembered it and it didn't bother me. I stayed home that morning. I was not well that day. I did not feel well on Tuesday the 14th, and I stayed home. I probably called down to the office and did not receive a response from the voluntary receptionist who was supposed to be at the front desk. If she'd been there, I would have been able to get a hold of Linda Hernand's phone number and I would have made a call to her from my home to cancel and/or postpone the appointment to let her know that I wouldn't be there.

However, it wasn't a vital meeting. This was not a vital appointment. She was able to handle the HUD house appraisal herself. She didn't have to have my presence there.

Q. On January 14, 2004, did you ever go into the office?

A. I might have. I really don't remember. I thought I stayed home all day long, but it's possible that I went to the office that afternoon. I'm saying that only because Sherry Charl has been here to testify that I was at the office, and if she says I was at the office then maybe I did go into the office that afternoon. But, however, I know I would have driven my own car.

Q. Do you remember the last time you saw Sherry Charl?

A. I saw Sherry Charl the week previous. I believe it was the Friday the 10th. She came to the office unannounced and she left a check for her rental property, and I gave her a receipt that I believe was dated for that day, on the 10th.

Q. Have you ever driven Garrett Daniel'—

A. I was driving Garrett Daniel's car all of that week. Mine was in servicing.

Q. So you have driven Garrett's car before?

A. Frequently.

Q. Have you ever driven Garrett in his car?

A. Oh, yeah. That week I drove Garrett to and from work every day while my car was in service.

Q. And was it just that week while your car was in service, or is it something you have done over the years?

A. That's the arrangement we have. We jockey one another around town when it's car pooling.

Q. Now, this American Express credit card, can you explain whose name is on that card to me?

A. My name is on that card as well as the agency.

Q. Can you tell me who was liable for the payment on that card?

A. It's my understanding that on an American Express corporate card, the corporation is responsible as the primary applicant. But the individual whose name appears on the credit card is also responsible or liable for payments on the card.

Q. How long did you have that American Express card for?

A. Several years.

Q. Can you tell me what your practice was over the several years you had the American Express card? In using it, as far as purchases, were they personal or strictly business?

A. Both.

Q. How extensive was your personal?

A. More so than business.

Q. And where would the bills for the American Express card be sent?

A. To the house, which was the formal agency of record.

Q. Did the American Express card bills ever go unpaid?

A. No.

Q. Now, did you use that American Express card when you purchased your plane ticket to New York and when you stayed in New York?

A. I did.

Q. Did you use it to fly to London and South Africa, did you use it there?

A. Yes.

Q. Now, when you got to South Africa, did you continue to use the American Express card?

A. Yes.

Q. And when you were in South Africa, did any of your bills become past-due?

A. No.

Q. Did you attempt to use your American Express card at some point in time and were unable to?

A. Correct.

Q. Can you tell me what happened?

A. On arrival in Johannesburg, I obtained a developing consultant's position with a group there, Ambers, in a full profit environment. And Avis Rent-A-Car and I had a contract with them. They arrived at the door asking for their car to be returned. They asked me to surrender the keys to the Avis car. I asked them why, and they said that the American Express card was now no longer valid, and that the account had been closed and I was to surrender the car to them. And upon questioning them as to the surrender of the car, they said that it had had been reported as stolen. So I assume that Garrett phoned in upon my resignation.

MR. LEV: Objection. Calls for speculation.

THE COURT: Sustained.

BY MR. SCHRE:

Q. Were you able to straighten out your American Express problems in South Africa at the American Express agency there?

A. No.

Q. Now, let's talk about your Jaguar. Where did you usually park that?

A. I parked it in both the front and the back of the house, either in the front carport or the back garage.

Q. Now, since we're talking about cars, can you tell me if Garrett had any habit when he backed his car out of the driveway?

A. No.

Q. You don't know about a honking habit?

A. No, I have never heard him honk the car.

Q. Now, on January 14, 2004, what car did you drive on that date?

A. I drove both Garrett's red car and I drove my black Jaguar on the 14th.

Q. Can you explain that?

A. Okay. Garrett came home for lunch. As I explained, I wasn't well and I stayed at home that day. Garrett came home for lunch and he was in the kitchen for quite some time before he came into the bedroom, and I was still sleeping. He went into the closet. He brought a lot of clothes with him.

I point out to the jury that I had not seen Garrett since the Saturday. It's now Tuesday and he had not resided by night at the house since Thursday of the previous week, so I hadn't seen Garrett for five days.

Q. Can you explain my question of driving the cars on that date?

A. One of the rules that I have in the house is that if you are going to load boxes and hangers of clothing and suitcases and things into one of the cars in the carport out front, that's one of the rules, you may not do that. Only because there were very sensitive bougainvilleas that I have trained up and over out there, and we have had problems with damaged plants out front, so it's a very narrow drive. If you want to load the car up, you use the garage out back. So I believe I got the keys to Garrett's car and I think I drove—I know I drove his car around the alley.

Q. And what did you do with it in the alley?

A. I parked it in the back garage.

Q. What did you do with your car?

A. I believe I drove it to the carport. If I didn't drive it to the carport, he drove it to the carport.

Q. Okay.

A. We swapped cars around.

Q. When did Garrett come home that day?

A. Approximately noon.

Q. And why did he come home?

A. For lunch.

Q. And what time did he leave?

A. Approximately an hour after that.

Q. And where was Garrett going?

A. He told me he was going for a job interview.

MR. LEV: Objection. Hearsay.

THE COURT: Sustained.

BY MR. SCHRE:

Q. Now, did you call Corri Crel on January 14, 2004?

A. I did.

Q. And why did you call Corri Crel?

A. I was requested to call her.

Q. Who requested that you call her?

A. Garrett requested.

Q. Why did Garrett request that you call her?

A. He told me that he was—

MR. LEV: Objection. Hearsay.

THE COURT: Sustained.

MR. SCHRE: Judge, it goes to—

THE COURT: Sustained. Ask the next question.

BY MR. SCHRE:

Q. When you called Corri, what did you tell her?

A. I said Garrett won't be coming back this afternoon. She asked me why, and I said he's had an accident and they're going to take him to be checked out.

Q. Why did you tell Corri that?

A. Well, Garrett was going off for a job interview and he asked me to tell them that he won't be back.

MR. LEV: Objection. Hearsay.

THE COURT: Sustained.

MR. LEV: Move to strike.

THE COURT: The jury is to disregard the last answer.

MR. SCHRE: Can I make an offer of proof later, Judge?

THE COURT: No. Ask your next question.

BY MR. SCHRE:

Q. Can you describe Garrett's mood on January 14, 2004?

A. Aloof.

Q. Can you tell me, are you familiar with Garrett's clothing? The types of clothing he used to wear?

A. Yes.

Q. And can you tell me how many pairs of tan pants Garrett owned?

A. Half a dozen.

Q. Now, how long did you live in what we have described as the Tenny/Daniel residence?

A. Six years.

Q. And when you moved into that house, what condition was it in?

A. Well, it needed a complete renovation.

Q. And so how did you renovate it?

A. I took nine months off to do just that. I ripped out the kitchen, reworked the bathrooms, laid the tiles throughout the house, stuccoed the exterior, added on the kitchen, installed a fireplace, reworked the dining room, built closets, all in those nine months.

Q. Now, whose name was on the deed to the house?

A. Garrett applied for the mortgage on the property, and he took ownership of the house initially. At the time of my departure, my name was also on the house.

Q. Can you tell me at the time of your departure what the fair market value of your home was?

A. About $110,000.

Q. Can you tell me how much was owed on the house at the time of your departure?

A. About 95, 99.

Q. The Jaguar, who owned that?

A. I did and Garrett did. He also had ownership on the car.

Q. And who had a note on the Jaguar?

A. It was rolled into the mortgage on the house.

Q. How was your interest in the house going to be handled after you left for South Africa?

A. Communication difficulties as they were between Garrett and myself, the understanding was that I would provide him with a quitclaim deed and/or he would provide me with a quitclaim deed if at any point in time we agreed to separate our interests in the property. There was no value in the house, so it wasn't as if there was any profit to be had out of the house. All the equity had been withdrawn from the house, so either the property had to be sold or the property had to be turned over to one or the other owner.

Q. Now, did you have cleaning utensils in the house?

A. Yes.

Q. Let's say, for example, to clean the floor?

A. Yes.

Q. What did you use to clean the floor?

A. We used a broom, a broad commercial styled broom, we had a commercial style yellow bucket for the mop, and we had a mop to clean and wash the floors.

Q. Did you have cleaners?

A. Several.

Q. Where did you keep those?

A. Either in the storage shed at the bottom of the garden or in the laundry area in the house, or under the kitchen sink.

Q. Now, after you left Phoenix on January 15, 2004, did you have contact or did you attempt to contact anyone in Phoenix?

A. I telephoned Garrett. I was concerned about this cat. I telephoned, I would not call him at his office, but I phoned him from New York, I believe, if not, Denver, to tell him that I wasn't going to be around and he was to look after the cat. But I wasn't sure that I would catch up with him. He hadn't been there for five days, so I didn't leave a message.

Q. How many times did you telephone him? Was it only once?

A. I probably tried two or three times. As I say, I didn't leave any messages, so there's no record of that.

Q. Did you attempt to communicate with people in Phoenix other than by telephone?

A. I wrote letters.

Q. Who did you write a letter to?

A. I sent a resignation letter to Jeff Kin, I sent a letter to the neighbors requesting that they look out for the cat. I thought they had keys to the house.

Q. Which neighbor are you talking about?

A. Walter Weiss.

Q. Bringing up Mr. Weiss, could you tell me what his telephone number is?

A. No.

Q. Did you ever memorize his telephone number?

A. No. That was the problem. You know, I didn't—it occurred to me that I left the cat behind once I got on the plane. I mean, I left food and everything for the cat, but I was concerned that Garrett would be gone for another five days and that somebody should come in and look out for the cat. It wasn't unusual for Walter to come and do irrigation with me at the house. I thought he had keys to the property.

Q. Now, after you were in South Africa, did you attempt to contact anybody in Phoenix, or in Arizona?

A. Not until March.

Q. Who did you attempt to contact in March?

A. I contacted a lawyer in Phoenix. His name is Mink.

Q. Did you contact anybody else in Phoenix?

A. I contacted a detective, Tim Camp.

Q. How did you contact him?

A. By telephone.

Q. Did you speak with him on the telephone?

A. No.

Q. How many times did you call him?

A. Two or three times.

Q. And how did you get Detective Camp's name?

A. It was provided to me through lawyer Mink and recited to me from newspaper articles that had appeared in the Phoenix newspaper.

Q. And is that how you found out about Garrett?

A. I found out about Garrett's death from my mother.

Q. Now, in addition to people in Phoenix, did you try to contact anybody else in Arizona after you found out about Garrett?

A. I tried to reach his mother.

Q. Did you speak with her?

A. Very briefly.

Q. Why did you try to reach his mother?

A. To offer my condolences.

Q. Now, how did you feel when you heard what happened to Garrett?

A. I was devastated.

Q. Now, let's go back to when you left Phoenix. How did you get to the airport?

A. When I left Phoenix?

Q. Yes.

A. I took an airport shuttle.

Q. And about what time did you leave for the airport?

A. Early in the morning.

Q. Do you remember the time?

A. It was at dawn, 5:00.

Q. All right. And when you left for the airport, did you still have access to the Jaguar?

A. Yes.

Q. And what did you do with the keys to the Jaguar?

A. I left them in the house in the ashtray there.

Q. When did you make your reservations to fly to New York, on what day?

A. Tuesday night.

Q. You heard Corri talk about an incident with you and Garrett in your home when she was visiting. Do you remember that incident?

A. No, I do not.

Q. Okay. And can you say whether or not there was actually an argument between you?

A. Garrett and I could be quite abrasive with one another. The tempo of our conversations were quite sharp, and I think to visitors it might have been a little offensive. Even the language sometimes used was not always kosher. She might have found it abrupt. But beyond that, no.

Q. Now, can you describe to me what happened in your house at night with the lights, I mean, when you weren't home?

A. I usually kept a dimmer on and usually exterior lights if it's at night. That's assuming that I'm returning to the property.

Q. Were you at your house on the night of the 14th?

A. Yes.

Q. Did you go anyplace?

A. I don't believe so.

Q. Can you characterize for the jury the main reasons, very briefly, that you left Phoenix?

A. In a nutshell, I would say my relationship with Garrett had reached a point where we had irreconcilable differences on a personal level. I was faced with U.S. Immigration, and that was a very serious decision to make, qualify or no qualify. And the job itself had reached its full potential. I was done; my term was done. There wasn't any more growing to do at the agency.

Q. How did you feel about the way you left the agency when you left it?

A. I was delighted. I thought it was in tiptop shape, very auditable and had some good people there.

Q. There wasn't anyone to step into your position?

A. No. That was for the board to do. That was their job.

Q. Now, what did you—where did you work at when you went to Africa? What kind of jobs?

A. I was employed by Ambers Development, a residential housing developer in Johannesburg.

Q. Now, when you went to South Africa, you said your parents or your mother and sister now lived in Canada, did you know anybody in Africa?

A. Not initially. I went to see an uncle, my mother's family, and I visited a lot of friends back in Capetown, both business, former business associates of my father and school friends that I had in Capetown.

Q. When you left South Africa, you said you had previously left for certain political reasons?

A. Yes.

Q. Why in 2004 did you go back to Africa, given that you left for political reasons?

A. I would underline "political," because the environment was conducive to change in that part of the world and was now approved, not only by the U.S., but by the United Nations as being a visitable country. They have completely dismantled the former regime.

Q. The house that you left, you saw some slides of a broken window?

A. Yes.

Q. Can you tell me, did you help clean up that broken window?

A. Yes.

Q. What happened when you were cleaning up the broken window?

A. Well, Garrett broke that window, and I wasn't there when he broke the window. But he broke the window. I can give you a date.

Q. What date?

A. The 28th of December, '03.

Q. What happened when you were cleaning up the broken window?

A. Well, it's a very big window. It's two and a half feet by five feet. It's a custom-sized window that I had made up by Home Depot. It's a very thin sheet. It's not shatter proof. And there were big shards of glass on this window. So I had to—I removed it immediately. We were leaving for San Diego the next day and we would be gone for a week, so I had a security problem and I was more concerned about the window than Garrett's damage. I mean, he hurt himself on that window. He cut himself on that window.

Q. Okay.

A. So I removed that glass window and I knocked off all the glass, and it was all out on the patio. And I transported that glass in black plastic bags to the back of the garage area. Out there is the garbage, the big black garbage containers in the alley. And one of the plastic bags broke with the big shards of glass at the end of that garage, so I called Garrett to come and help me pick up the shards of glass and transport them over into a wheelbarrow and then out into the alley. And I know he cut himself on his hand out there.

MR. SCHRE: I have no further questions.

THE COURT: Cross-examination.

MR. LEV: Thank you, Your Honor.

CROSS-EXAMINATION

BY MR. LEV:
Q. I show you this letter. You mentioned writing several letters; do you recall?
A. That's correct.
Q. Is this your signature and did you write this to a Tim Camp?
A. Yes, sir.
Q. So you recognize it's all your handwriting?
A. That is my letter.
Q. And this was postmarked from South Africa, correct?
A. Yeah.
Q. And the date of the letter is on it, correct?
A. I believe so.
Q. Mr. Tenny, this letter of your resignation which you postmarked from New York on January 17, 2004, indicates a culmination of personal disappointments and economic stress, correct?
A. Correct.
Q. And you had written that letter to Jeff Kin, correct?
A. Correct.
Q. And you had never told him prior that you were leaving?
A. I probably mentioned it in passing, but not at a formal level.
Q. Okay, we'll go with Jeff Kin's memory, is that okay?
A. All right.
Q. So as far as the evidence goes, and you were here listening to it, he was never told previously that you were going to leave the agency, correct?
A. Formally he was not told.
Q. And, furthermore, when you left the agency, you charged your United Airlines flight on their card, and then you charged your flight on British Airways to London, and on to South Africa also on their card?
A. That is correct.

Q. This is according to you, when you knew you were leaving the agency; is that right?

A. That's correct.

Q. Now, exactly what time did you order the ticket on United Airlines to leave Phoenix?

A. It's purported to have been at 11:45 on the 14th.

Q. And you just decided to pick up and leave, so you left your nice Jag in the front; is that right?

A. Our Jag, yes.

Q. And you're the one who drove it?

A. I drive it.

Q. And then you have this problem with your bougainvilleas?

A. On the left and right of that car, yes.

Q. However, there's a space that one can go with regard to your bougainvilleas; is that correct?

A. If you chose to break the rules, yes.

Q. Your rule?

A. My rule.

Q. When your rule is broken, you get real upset, don't you, Mr. Tenny?

A. No.

Q. Particularly if Garrett Daniel breaks it; isn't that so?

A. I would object.

Q. Isn't that so?

A. I would object to that.

Q. Are you refusing to answer?

A. No. No, sir.

Q. Just answer whatever way you wish to answer.

MR. SCHRE: I'm going to object that this is argumentative. The question was answered. He said no, I don't get upset when the bougainvilleas are broken.

THE COURT: I think his answer was he would object. Ask your next question.

BY MR. LEV:

Q. Anyway, you left the Jag, you left this nice little house that you spent nine months of your personal time renovating, correct?

A. Correct.

Q. And you just dropped it; is that so?

A. I left the house.

Q. And you claim you slept there that night?

A. On the 14th, that's correct.

Q. Where did you sleep?

A. I probably laid back on the sofa or my bed.

Q. And that's after you cleaned up, correct?

A. Cleaned up?

Q. Yes. All the blood.

A. No.

Q. And, in any event, here's a photo of the bed, and that doesn't look particularly slept in, does it, that bed?

A. That's not the state of the bed I left.

Q. And I don't believe that there's any evidence that anyone else was in the house?

A. That bed was not in that condition when I left.

Q. How about this photo, you claim you could have been in the bed, you could have been on the sofa, they don't look particularly like they had been slept in, do they?

A. No.

Q. And then, Mr. Tenny, again, you're leaving this nice house, you're just kind of going to pick up and leave with a suitcase of clothes; is that so?

A. Correct.

Q. After nine months of putting your personal time in it, right?

A. After six years.

Q. Yes, and nine exclusive months; is that what I understood you took time off?

A. Renovating the house, that was an ongoing renovation project.

Q. It cost a lot of money?

A. It did.

Q. You're the one who incurred the expenses because you wanted to renovate it?

A. We incurred a lot of expenses.

Q. You're the one who did it?

A. We both worked on the house.

Q. I thought you were the one—you testified that you—

A. I was the primary—

THE COURT: Hold on. We can only have one person talking.

Q. You, Mr. Tenny, testified that you were the one who did all the work. Did I hear wrong?

A. I did most of the major renovation, physical renovation on that house.

Q. And you have a nice backyard pool; is that so?

A. That's correct.

Q. And your walkway goes to that rear carport; is that so?

A. That's correct.

Q. All these are your renovations; is that so?
A. That's correct.
Q. And you just walked away from it?
A. Yes.
Q. You wrote another letter. You wrote another letter to Mr. Weiss also from New York postmarked January 17, 2004, correct?
A. Correct.
Q. And in this you say you went to visit family. Is that what it says?
A. Correct.
Q. So you didn't go for a job. You went for a visit, according to your letter, to Mr. Weiss; is that what it says?
A. In connection with Mr. Weiss.
Q. Is that what it says, Mr. Tenny?
A. I make reference to family.
Q. Is that what it says?

THE COURT: Hold it. Mr. Tenny, if he asks you a yes or no question, you have to answer yes or no. Mr. Schre will get a chance when he gets redirect. If he thinks you need to explain something, then he will ask you the proper question. Go ahead.

THE DEFENDANT: Could you ask the question again?

BY MR. LEV:
Q. Does it say in the letter in your handwriting to Mr. Weiss, went to visit family for a while?
A. It does.
Q. Furthermore, you said you were trying to contact Garrett by phone, correct?
A. Yes.
Q. Now, could you tell us all when and what time you made contact or tried to make contact with Garrett?
A. I believe I tried to make contact with Garrett from the New York hotel when I arrived there, which would have been on Friday night on the 15th and probably the next night, the 16th.
Q. What time?
A. I cannot tell you what time.
Q. Well, you can tell me whether it's day or night?
A. It was night.
Q. What time at night?
A. Anywhere from 5:00 p.m. through 10:00 p.m.
Q. Fine, Mr. Tenny. And you heard Detective McElva—by the way, did you get ahold of Garrett?
A. No.

Q. And did you announce yourself?

A. No.

Q. Are you going to be one of the hang-ups?

A. I don't understand that question.

Q. Did you call and hang up?

A. If Garrett doesn't answer the phone, I wouldn't leave a message.

Q. Detective McElva said that the hang-up on Thursday, 1/16/04, was 1:11 Phoenix time, which would be 3:11 a.m. New York time, so I take it this isn't you; am I correct?

A. Probably not.

Q. And then there was no other hang-ups until Saturday, January 25th, 2004, Phoenix time 9:29 a.m. So I take it, Mr. Tenny, you never called Garrett by phone at the house?

A. Incorrect.

Q. Mr. Tenny, according to the deeds on your home, there is no Jaguar listed as part of any of the mortgage process, so when you say that the Jaguar is rolled into this, there is absolutely no document confirming that. Are you aware of that?

A. I wasn't aware of that.

Q. Furthermore, you indicated that the balance due with regard to the mortgage was something in the neighborhood of $96,000, is that what you said?

A. I believe the house had appraised for over 100, but certainly up—when they did the pool appraisal, it would have been well into the high 90s.

Q. Well, on 5/3/04 on the notice of trustee sale, the original principle was listed as $46,900, not $96,000. Are you aware of that?

A. That would have been on the first mortgage. There were three.

Q. This was the trustees sale in May, Mr. Tenny. Wouldn't they roll it all up, unless you don't really know those things but I thought you were aware of that, being in realty. Don't they roll it all up in the trustee sale, all the value?

A. It depends who's doing the appraisal. Was that a HUD appraisal?

Q. This is the trustee's sale. Do you want to see it? Do you see the date here, May 30th of '04. Do you see the amount? What does it say there?

A. $46,900. That was approximately the value of the first bond that was placed on the property in 1998.

Q. I'm assuming it was sold by HUD, was it not?

A. I cannot answer that.

Q. In any event, the documents speak for themselves, would you agree?

A. If that's what they sold the house for, then I would agree.

Q. No, that was the principle balance. Do you recall my question, Mr. Tenny? Do you recall my question?

A. I did hear your question, but I tried to explain to you the financing on the house.

Q. Now, assuming that that's all that was remaining, and you claim the value was $106,000, there's considerably more equity in it than what you're testifying to, wouldn't you agree?

A. I would not agree.

Q. One of the reasons that you left is, according to you, that you weren't getting along with Garrett, correct?

A. Correct.

Q. Irreconcilable differences, correct?

A. Correct.

Q. Did you know that Garrett was leaving you?

A. No.

Q. Did you know that he wasn't going to sign over his one half interest to you?

A. No.

Q. And you wanted that one half interest, didn't you?

A. No.

Q. Well, according to the deed and according to your testimony, you're a joint tenant on the property, correct?

A. I am.

Q. As far as the ownership on a joint tenancy deed, you get it if Garrett Daniel is eliminated off, correct?

A. That would be correct.

Q. But he wouldn't sign over his half interest to you, would he?

A. I didn't ask him for it.

Q. And when he left you, there must have been a serious reason for him to be gone for, you said something like five days?

A. I didn't think it was a serious reason.

Q. You didn't?

A. There were personal reasons. Garrett had his personal reasons.

Q. And they weren't serious?

A. No.

Q. As a matter of fact, we have receipts at the Motel 6 for the 10th, we have testimony that he tried to stay at somebody's house on the 12th, we have evidence that he stayed in a Motel 6 on the 13th. You recall that evidence?

A. I do.

Q. So he had to get away from you, correct?

A. Incorrect.

Q. Because, I mean, he's half owner of that house, and used to be the whole owner, correct?

A. He was part owner on the house.

Q. And if he is leaving that house, Mr. Tenny, isn't he leaving you?

A. For the weekend.

Q. When he left, he left you and went elsewhere, correct?

A. I didn't know that.

Q. If he goes to a Motel 6, he's away from that house?

A. I didn't know he was at Motel 6.

Q. You didn't know? You knew he was away?

A. He might have been away at Motel 6. I didn't know for certain where he was.

Q. You knew he was away?

A. He had not been back to the house. I knew he was away.

Q. For five days he left you, correct?

A. He left the house.

Q. And you?

A. And me.

Q. Because why? Because he could not stand you any more?

A. I really don't know why, his personal reasons.

Q. With regard to the letter that you wrote to the County Sheriff's Office on March 19, 2004, one of the reasons you wrote it and a primary reason why you wrote it is, you requested a release of personal property and requested that the Sheriff's Office provide you a release so you could go forward on the probate of the house, correct?

A. That is correct.

Q. But you knew that if you didn't go forward pretty soon, they would put up a trustee's deed of sale for the house for abandonment?

A. Correct.

Q. So you had to make your move?

A. That's correct.

Q. So that was the primary reason of writing it?

A. That is correct.

Q. And then you added this other stuff in, in a letter to him. You claim that attorney Wink read you by telephone information publicized in newspaper articles on January 24th and January 31st, as you write there, is that so?

A. That's correct.

Q. But you don't write Tim Camp until 19 March of '04, right?

A. That's correct.

Q. So we are in, there's January and then there's February, and then there's March, correct?

A. There are a number of dates there.

Q. Now, as you already stated, the primary reason that you wrote him was to obtain release of the estate, correct?

A. Correct.

Q. So it was important for you with regard to that house?

A. At this point in time it was.

Q. Because you wouldn't do this if it wasn't worth it to you, would you have?

A. It was my responsibility as part owner on the property to do something about it, given that Garrett was no longer alive.

Q. Now, you say, "as planned, my schedule was a departure from Phoenix," you wrote that to Mr. Camp of the Sheriff's Office?

A. I did.

Q. And that was to create an alibi, wasn't it?

A. No.

Q. Because no one, Mr. Tenny, who has testified in this court had any inkling that you were leaving Phoenix, much less resigning your position at the agency, is that what you heard in testimony?

A. Correct.

Q. So your plan was in your head, correct?

A. Correct.

Q. And your plan came to fruition as far as thinking about going away on January 14, 2004, after your encounter with Garrett Daniel at your home between 12:00 and 1:00 p.m. that day; is that correct?

A. Partially correct.

Q. That's when you had the plan in mind, right?

A. The plan was in place at that time.

Q. Only you knew about it?

A. That's correct.

Q. And then you said, "to New York for a brief stay."

A. In New York, yes.

Q. One day?

A. Two days.

Q. Two days. And you pretty much stayed at the J.F.K. hotel at the airport, didn't you?

A. That's correct.

Q. And so that was just brief enough to wait for your British Airways flight to London?

A. Yes. I also visited the South African consulate.

Q. Also, to give you time, Mr. Tenny, to devise these couple of letters, one to Jeffrey Kin with regard to your the agency resignation?

A. I wrote that from—

Q. And two to Mr. Weiss, both postmarked 17 January, as part of your alibi, wasn't it?

A. No, it wasn't. It was not.

Q. Do you know what an alibi is, Mr. Tenny?

A. Yes.

Q. What is an alibi?

A. Well, an alibi is a witness—

MR. SCHRE: I'm going to object to the relevance of this.

THE COURT: I'm going to sustain that. Ask the next question, please.

BY MR. LEV:

Q. Then you went on to say, "to New York for a brief stay." And then, "I traveled to London, England, and onto South Africa for a visit." Right?

A. Correct.

Q. That's what you wrote. "And will depart for Canada within the week."

A. Correct.

Q. Correct. Now, you wrote this in March, didn't you, Mr. Tenny?

A. Yes.

Q. And yet you have just testified that you, while in South Africa, got a job with some kind of a development company called Ambers in Johannesburg?

A. That's correct.

Q. And then you say, "A possible stop over in Germany is planned."

A. That's correct.

Q. So, actually, what you're telling Lieutenant Camp is that, well, you were just briefly in South Africa, then you're going to go to Canada and maybe on the way you'll visit Germany. That's what you said?

A. Almost correct.

Q. And then your next line is, "My resignation from the agency coincides with my decision to leave Phoenix and my partner, Garrett Daniel." How is he your partner?

A. In every way. Business, because he was involved in the Board of Directors, he's a partner in the house, and he's a personal partner—was a personal.

Q. He was the treasurer of your agency?

A. Secretary treasure.

Q. But he was never a business partner?

A. No.

Q. Anyway, your decision claims it was based on three factors and had culminated over a period of six months; is that so?

A. Correct.

Q. And yet you and Garrett on New Years went to San Diego, saw the Rose Bowl, and things like that; is that correct?

A. That's correct.

Q. So, now, you claimed your U.S.A. visa to work was temporary but it was renewable?

A. Possibly renewable in '04.

Q. But you were never on the verge of being deported, were you?

A. No, not yet.

Q. It was just a temporary visa that you had to renew, correct?
A. I had to return to the Canadian border and have special approval to do that. It wasn't just a matter of going to the airport and getting a stamp, it was a work permit.
Q. What does Canada have to do with it, since your a—
A. I also have residency in Canada.
Q. But you're a resident of South Africa?
A. I'm a citizen of South Africa.
Q. And you're not a citizen of Canada, are you?
A. I have citizenship in Canada.
Q. You have dual citizenship? Well, let's say, Mr. Tenny, that according to you, since this visa was temporary, you could have applied for a permanent visa, correct?
A. I could have.
Q. You were here, you had a home, a Jaguar automobile, correct?
A. Correct.
Q. You were executive director of the agency?
A. And that was the problem.
Q. And you were making income?
A. Some.
Q. And all of this qualifies you to stay in the United States?
A. No, it does not.
Q. Really?
A. I'm sorry, but it doesn't.
Q. Well, you could have applied for a permanent visa; is that so?
A. I wouldn't have been approved. The lawyer advised me of that.
Q. The lawyer advised you?

MR. LEV: I move to strike. Its hearsay.

THE COURT: Sustained. It will be stricken.

BY MR. LEV:
Q. You were not on the verge of being deported?
A. No.
Q. Then your next thing was, the corporate government budgets were cut and personal income reduced. According to your testimony, you got a raise some years before, it went down a little bit, but it never was what you started out with, which is something like $29,000, correct?
A. Yes.
Q. So this is for the disabled you were working, this was your brainchild; is that so?
A. Yes.

Q. And you just, when you left, you didn't tell them, these disabled people you were leaving, did you?

A. I didn't have to.

Q. You just left, you didn't have to tell them, you just let them fend for themselves, like Ms. Sherry Charl; is that right?

A. I told the Board of Directors that I was leaving.

Q. Well, let me see, I think Jeffrey Kin testified he didn't have a clue, and I think that Bill Mill testified and he didn't have a clue. Do you recall that testimony?

A. I do.

Q. In any event, your income had not been reduced in the year or so prior to your departure, correct?

A. It had been reduced.

Q. In a year or so prior to your departure?

A. That's correct.

Q. From what to what?

A. It came down from 39 to 33.

Q. You said that that was sometime before?

A. That was in the fiscal year '03.

Q. And then your next thing was, "Garrett Daniel and my personal and professional relationship was strained;" is that so?

A. Yes.

Q. So you weren't getting along with Garrett Daniel?

A. No.

Q. Garrett Daniel wasn't getting along with you?

A. No.

Q. And it was very strained?

A. Yes.

Q. So strained that you put it down as one of the three reasons for you leaving the country, to go all the way around from Phoenix, Arizona, back down to Johannesburg, South Africa; is that so?

A. Yes.

Q. There are other airports in South Africa other than Johannesburg, correct?

A. Capetown has one.

Q. But Johannesburg is pretty far around the horn, it's way down to the south of Africa, and even somewhat south within South Africa, correct?

A. That's correct.

Q. A long ways from Phoenix, Arizona?

A. A long way.

Q. You claim here that Garrett was aware of your departure and was not too supportive; is that so?

A. That's correct.

Q. So on January 14, 2004, he came home for lunch. He didn't expect to see you there, did he?

A. My car was outside.

Q. But he wouldn't have expected you to be home?

A. When he walked through the door, he knew I was there.

Q. But he wouldn't necessarily have expected you from the time he left work, would he?

A. Probably not.

Q. Because you didn't oftentimes come home for lunch?

A. Once a week.

Q. But, in any event, there you were?

A. Correct.

Q. And you and he got into an argument?

A. No, we didn't.

Q. And the argument lead to a lot more, didn't it?

MR. SCHRE: Objection. He said there was no argument.

THE COURT: This is cross-examination. The objection is overruled. The witness can answer.

THE WITNESS: No.

BY MR. LEV:

Q. Now, you cooked. You have used the kitchen in the past?

A. Yes.

Q. You have used knives in the past?

A. Yes.

Q. There are single-edged knives in the kitchen?

A. Yes.

Q. Some of which will penetrate four and a half inches?

A. Yes.

Q. And the knives are easily accessible to you; are they not?

A. Yes.

Q. And you have used them, correct?

A. To cook, yes.

Q. Mr. Tenny, according to the evidence there was a lot of blood in your house when the detectives came later?

A. I didn't see any.

Q. After you cleaned it up, you didn't think—

A. I didn't clean up anything.

Q. You said that you had a commercial mop, and so forth, that you cleaned up with, correct?

A. There were cleaning utensils in the house.

Q. And you're the one who cleaned?

A. We both cleaned.

Q. You said that you had chemicals?

A. There were chemicals.

Q. But the best type of application for the saltillo tile on your kitchen floor is nothing more than vinegar; isn't that so?

A. We never used vinegar on the tiles.

Q. Nor did you use any cleansing compounds either?

A. We did.

Q. Because if you used a cleansing compound, it would remove the glaze that you so carefully put on to preserve it?

A. That is correct.

Q. If you put on a cleansing compound, then you would have had to have reglazed it?

A. From time to time, yes.

Q. Are you suggesting by the letter the window incident that you were talking about, about Garrett cutting himself on the glass, that it spread all of this blood all on the floor over the house here, as I have just gone through in these exhibits?

A. I can't tell you exactly what amounts of blood versus that blue stuff, you know. I think that blue stuff is all cleaning fluids, but there was some blood spillage in the house when Garrett cut himself.

Q. And all those blood drops?

A. That did transpire.

Q. That's from Garrett back in December of '03 cutting himself?

A. That's correct.

Q. All of these blood drops?

A. In the house, yes.

Q. So he just walked through the house dripping blood; is that so?

A. I wasn't there.

Q. He just walked through the house dripping blood?

A. I would assume so.

Q. You are so fastidious that you didn't notice it in an attempt to clean it up?

A. He told me about it.

Q. After all, it was on the cabinet, it was on the floor, it was on the island, and so forth. And, you saw the exhibits, this is all from Garrett cutting himself back in December of '03, is that so?

A. Some of it might be.

Q. And you didn't bother to clean it up?

A. He had cleaned it up when I returned to the house that day.

Q. Garrett Daniel came home for lunch, Mr. Tenny, not to clean up the floors; isn't that so?

A. That was—this was a weekend that this incident happened.

Q. I'm talking about January 14, 2004.

A. We didn't clean house on the 14th.

Q. In any event, if you claim that he cleaned all those blood drops off, they just kept staying there all the way through January until the detectives went in and found it, correct?

A. Two weeks, yes.

Q. And then the blood drops go out the double doors from the kitchen to the patio; is that right?

A. I never saw them.

Q. And then from that you can access to this walkway going back to the rear carport, is that so?

A. That's correct.

Q. So, for example, if one were to take a body that was stabbed to death in the house, you could move it through the double doors in the back through this pathway here, and that goes directly to the carport in the back, does it not?

A. No.

Q. It doesn't go to the carport?

A. There's a path that goes around the swimming pool from the house to the carport.

Q. You're right-handed, are you not?

A. Yes.

Q. And you're six feet tall?

A. Yes.

Q. You weigh 170 pounds?

A. Yes.

Q. Whereas Garrett is about five foot nine?

A. Yes.

Q. And he weighs 140 pounds or less, correct?

A. I'm not sure of his weight.

Q. So you're bigger than him?

A. I'm bigger than Garrett.

Q. Now, Exhibit 12, these stab wounds here, Mr. Tenny, are they not consistent, if your right-handed and they're on the left side, is that not consistent with a right-handed person?

A. I don't know.

MR. SCHRE: I'm going to object. This witness does not have the expertise to testify in this area.

THE COURT: Sustained. Please ask your next question.

BY MR. LEV:
Q. Well, if you did it, Mr. Tenny, you would know, wouldn't you?
A. I don't know anything about it.
Q. You don't?
A. No.
Q. You don't even know the sequence of the stab wounds? A. I have heard testimony in this courtroom. I don't know about sequences. There are various numbers that were provided. I don't know about sequences.
Q. Well, you traveled so light when you left for South Africa that all you took was some clothes and a suitcase?
A. That's correct.
Q. And you left behind your Jaguar?

THE COURT: Hold on. Mr. Lev, I hate to interrupt you, but I think we need to take a break. Let's take until 25 'till.

(Whereupon, a the following proceedings were held out of the presence of the jury:)

THE COURT: Mr. Schre, do you wish to make a record on the issue concerning Ms. Crel's testimony regarding the statement, or the statement regarding the phone call? You said you wanted to make an offer of proof.

MR. SCHRE: Yes, I do, Judge. I want to make an argument. Ms. Crel testified that on January 14, 2004, at approximately 2:50 to 3:00 in the afternoon, Mr. Tenny had called up, he said Garrett wouldn't be back, that he had been in an accident, they're taking him to the hospital.

Mr. Tenny chose to testify in this case, and he does not disagree with the statement that Ms. Crel said he made to her. He got up to the stand and gave the statement very similar to hers, and agreed that he called up.

What Mr. Tenny also attempted to testify to but there was a hearsay objection, is the reason why he was making the phone call. One of the things that the jury is going to want to know in this case is why Mr. Tenny would call Corri Crel up and tell her that Garrett Daniel was in an accident, that no accident had taken place whatsoever.

And Mr. Tenny was attempting to tell the jury the reason he had called her up and said that Mr. Daniel had been in an accident, and Mr. Daniel asked him to call up and make an excuse for him not going into work later that afternoon because he was going to a job interview. And there had been people that had testified previously that Mr. Daniel was looking for a job. I think that this is an exception to the hearsay rule.

THE COURT: Which exception?

MR. SCHRE: It goes to Mr. Tenny's state of—it explains his state of mind in telling Ms. Crel that Garrett Daniel has been in an accident, and, Garrett told me he's looking for a job isn't offered for the truth of the matter asserted because Garrett was actually going to look for a job. What it's offered for is Mr. Tenny's state of mind as to why he would call Ms. Crel and give that statement.

THE COURT: Isn't the hearsay exception to the declarant's state of mind rather than to Mr. Tenny's state of mind?

MR. SCHRE: I think it can go to Mr. Tenny's state of mind.

THE COURT: You show me a case where it goes to Mr. Tenny's state of mind rather than the declarant's, and then maybe I'll reconsider my ruling. I'm looking at all the cases and I haven't seen one case, and I'm looking at the rules and the rules don't say that.

MR. SCHRE: It goes for more than the state of mind. We are not offering that statement, Garrett said he's looking for a job, for the truth of the matter asserted, that Garrett actually said that. We are offering it to explain Mr. Tenny's actions in making the phone call.

THE COURT: But while you're not offering it for the truth of the matter, it certainly is being offered for the truth of the matter that he told him that and that he acted upon that. My ruling stands unless you can show me something different. Anything else before we resume? I'm going to take a break.

(Whereupon, a recess was taken, after which the following proceedings were held in the presence of the jury:)

THE COURT: Mr. Tenny, would you please resume the witness stand. Go ahead, Mr. Lev.

MR. LEV: Thank you, Your Honor.

BY MR. LEV:

Q. Mr. Tenny, you testified that you tried to contact Garrett Daniel on, I believe, January 16 and 17 of '04. Was that your testimony?

A. I telephoned the house, that is correct.

Q. Now, let's go back to the letter to Lieutenant Camp of March. It says here, "it was my intention to keep in contact with Garrett by telephone." Is that what it says?

A. That's correct.

Q. And then down here it says, "I tried to reach him at home by telephone two or three times mid February with no results." Is that what it says?

A. I—

Q. Is that what it says?

A. That's what it says.

Q. Thank you. Now, remember I asked you of that alibi and so forth before, correct?

A. Yes.

Q. And you claimed that somebody read you some newspaper articles, correct?

A. Yes.

Q. Now you're telling Lieutenant Camp, and you know they're investigating the homicide?

A. At this point I'm aware of it.

Q. And you knew it back then, didn't you, because you asked Lieutenant Camp to release your stuff, didn't you?

A. At that point in time, yes.

Q. In any event, you claim in this letter that Garrett had been murdered by multiple stab wounds in the Phoenix desert. That's what it says?

A. Someone told me that.

Q. So in this letter you're trying to suggest that Garrett Daniel was stabbed to death in the desert, is that why you put that down there?

A. Someone told me that.

Q. In any event, that would sort of shift it off from the house out to the desert as far as you putting it in the letter, right?

A. I was never aware that the house was—I'm not sure about the house, but it was my impression that the desert had played a role in it. His body was found in a desert.

Q. Well, you wrote what you wrote, didn't you?

A. I wrote that.

Q. Yes. So, did you think, Mr. Tenny, that by writing this letter and the other letters that you could somehow or another actually get away with it by suggesting you just coincidentally left?

A. No.

Q. Now, you went so far in the letter here, "I need stress to you that I know nothing of the events leading to Garrett's death." You stress that in your letter because that's why you wrote it there, correct?

A. I wrote that.

Q. And I take it you were hoping that Lieutenant Camp of the Sheriff's Office who was investigating the homicide that you figured maybe he'll think, well, you must know nothing about it, so that's it for you?

A. Yes.

Q. Then you claimed you last saw him on January 15th noon. Is that what it says here?

A. I was incorrect about that time.

Q. Then you go on to say, it was my understanding he had been to work that morning and was home for lunch. I had not reported to work that day as my resignation was definite and my plan to move on was firm. Garrett returned to work at about one p.m. and that was the last I saw of him. That's what you wrote?

A. Correct.

Q. By writing that there, did you not inform Lieutenant Camp that, first of all, when you testified you said the reason you stayed home that day was you were sick, but you wrote in the letter back in March that your plan to move on was firm; is that correct?

A. That's what I was sick about, yes.

Q. By that time you had not even made reservations, and you're going all the way to South Africa, correct? But when you put this down there, Mr. Tenny, what you had said was, Garrett Daniel came home at noon, and the last you saw of him was one p.m. Therefore, Mr. Tenny, that was the time of his death; was it not?

A. Absolutely not.

Q. And then it wasn't enough to say, "I need stress to you that I know nothing of the events," you had to repeat this on the next page where you say, "I am unaware of the circumstances, location or persons responsible for this horrible crime." So you had to repeat that, and you did, correct?

A. I wrote that.

Q. And did you think that Lieutenant Camp somehow might think, well, if he wrote this, that's all he knows?

A. Yes.

Q. So to that extent, it was what you call, if I may ask this again, an alibi, correct?

A. I'm not sure about the definition of the word "alibi."

Q. And then you go on to say, "For me this is a tragedy of the worst kind, and if I feel badly it is that Garrett's demises happened so close to my resignation and departure from Phoenix." You were a little concerned that it might be suspicious; were you not?

A. He wasn't missing at that time, and I was concerned.

Q. Because you ought to know, huh, Mr. Tenny?

A. I was informed.

Q. You ought to know, correct?

A. I was informed.

Q. Because you last saw him, right, about one p.m. that day, correct?

A. That was the last time I saw him.

Q. And that's the last time you saw him alive, correct?

A. Correct.

Q. But, in fact, you saw him again when you took his body to the desert; isn't that so?

A. That is not correct.

Q. And then you went and wrote this letter to Lieutenant Camp, with the ending paragraph, "Enclosed is a request for property release. Please contact the attorney with your input. Clearance is required." That's your last paragraph in this letter; is that so?

A. That's correct.

Q. Again, that was your primary concern?

A. That's correct.

Q. Now, the evidence is that you were seen in this red car at 12:40 p.m. on January 14, 2004, backing out of the driveway of yours and Garrett Daniel's house.

A. I have explained that.

Q. That's easy to see that car, it's bright red, it's a convertible, it's easy to see, isn't it?

A. That's Garrett car.

Q. And you were driving it?

A. Around the block.

Q. You claimed that you were driving it because the Jaguar was in service; is that so?

A. No.

Q. You didn't just testify to that?

A. No, I did not.

Q. Well, assuming that you did, assuming you testified to that, Mr. Tenny, I show you a portion of Exhibit 201. This is a summary of the account on American Express, which documents came in through the American Express custodian of records. I want to point out to you, sir, that your Jaguar was serviced on December 13, 2003, and it cost you $504.54 which you charged with the American Express card. That being the case, the Jaguar was not in service such that you had to use Garrett Daniel's car, and as you testified, actually took him to work all that week and used his car?

A. The car was in service twice that season. That Scottsdale Jaguar was, we serviced the car before Christmas and there was an additional problem, and I had the car serviced at a different garage. And I had it done as I reported it that week. That bill was paid out of my personal checking account, which you also have records for.

Q. Well, then, there was another little notice with regard to Scottsdale Jaguar on December 27th. Do you see that?

A. On the 27th, yes.

Q. In any event, Mr. Tenny, the Jaguar was not in service?

A. The Jaguar was in service.

Q. Well, if that's so, Mr. Tenny, then why is that Jaguar sitting right there?

A. Because I believe Garrett and I picked the car up together from the other service center, which is not Scottsdale Jaguar, and it wasn't an American Express charge. We picked the car up on either the Thursday and/or I believe Friday the 10th, Friday the 10th of January, '03.

Q. And Friday—

A. And that was the week the car was in servicing, additional servicing.

Q. And you testified, Mr. Tenny, that you hadn't seen Garrett for five days, which included the 10th, and he stayed at a Motel 6?

A. That evening he took off, and he took off to Motel 6 on Friday the 10th. That's apparently Motel 6.

Q. So the Jaguar being in the driveway from that period of time then, there was absolutely no reason for you to have used this '99 Pontiac of Garrett's on January 14th, was there?

A. Other than to move the car around to the back of the house so he could move his clothes, there wasn't any reason.

Q. But you testified that you drove him to work in that red Pontiac. Did you forget?

A. Not on the 14th I didn't testify to that. I didn't drive Garrett to work on the 14th.

Q. That's right, you didn't. And when you took that car on January 14, 2004, wasn't that another part of your alibi so that you could go to work where you were seen by Ms. Charl, and she specifically saw in your parking place on the 14th in the afternoon, at about 2:30 or so this red Pontiac convertible?

A. I believe Ms. Charl is mistaken on that account. If I was at the office on the 14th, I would have gone to the office in the Jag.

Q. But you did hear her testify?

A. She testified. I believe she is mistaken.

Q. I see. And I take it that this red sort of is a bright red, is it not?

A. Yes.

Q. Would you say it would be a little hard to misstate that color for your black Jaguar?

A. I agree.

Q. So perhaps she wasn't mistaken?

A. She was mistaken.

Q. I see. But you did drive it away from the front of the house about 12:50 p.m. as seen by the neighbors, didn't you?

A. I drove around the block.

Q. As a matter of fact, nobody saw that, that I'm aware of, are you, aware of anyone seeing that?

A. No.

Q. Now, when you made your arrangements to leave for South Africa at 11:46 p.m. on January 14, 2004, you had taken care of business by then; had you not?

A. I'm not sure what you mean by "business."

Q. Well, you swabbed up the blood, correct?

A. No.

Q. And then you transported Garrett Daniel's body out to the desert in his red Pontiac?

A. Absolutely not.

Q. Well, there was blood found in it; do you recall that testimony?

A. I have seen the evidence.

Q. And it came back DNA Garrett Daniel?

A. I know nothing about that.

Q. Well, you heard it?

A. I heard it in this court.

Q. And then, by the way, how did you know, Mr. Tenny, to go to 14th Street in Carefree? Had you been out there on some kind of an appraisal?

A. I don't know the area at all. I believe Kim Floy lives up there.

Q. So you do know somebody up there?

A. I don't know Kim Floy very well.

Q. You have heard the testimony that it rained on or about the 14th, it was cold, et cetera, correct?

A. I have heard that.

Q. Now, you also heard the testimony that a Motel 6 receipt was found on the person of Garrett Daniel for 1/13 of '04, do you remember that?

A. I have also heard that.

Q. And testimony was, there was blood in the car, also there was mud in the car, that a witness testified was never usually on there. Do you see that?

A. I see that.

Q. Well, I mean, is your alley muddy, Mr. Tenny?

A. Yes.

Q. When you drove down, it's going to get all of that mud?

A. If it really did rain, yes. There's a very large pool on our alley, so I could see that.

Q. Well, you certainly wouldn't take your Jaguar down that alley if it was that muddy, would you?

A. We did that on Tuesday the 14th at noon.

Q. And you wouldn't allow your Jaguar to get all muddy like that, would you?

A. Was my Jaguar muddy that day? You have the photographs. I don't know, sir.

Q. Let's assume that it wasn't, because the photographs speak for themselves. What about that?

A. I don't know. You might be correct about the desert and the mud. I think that's logical.

Q. In any event, this particular car was only parked, oh, not more than a mile away. That isn't a very difficult hike for you, is it, a mile away from your house?

A. That's a long walk. I'm not a walker. I'm not a Phoenix walker.

Q. Well, this is winter, and so forth. It's not too far for you, is it? You can walk a mile, can't you?

A. I can walk a mile.

Q. I assume that if you drove the car in the carport, the carport's not muddy, is it?

A. The carport could be muddy if the alley is muddy.

Q. Well, then, I suppose that explains how the mud got on the floor then?

A. I don't know how the mud got on the floor.

Q. Are you saying you got the mud on the car?

A. I'm saying I don't know how the mud got on the floor.

Q. Was there mud in the alley?

A. There could have been mud in our alley at the house.

Q. Could have been?

A. If it had rained. I don't recall.

Q. The question is, did you get mud on the car?

A. I don't recall.

Q. How did the blood get on the right front passenger seat?

A. I have no idea.

Q. How did the blood get on the belt buckle?

A. I have no idea.

Q. How did the blood get on the rear, going past into the rear seat?

A. I don't know.

Q. And then do you have any idea how the blood spot got up on the—

A. No, sir.

Q. —convertible top? Now, in my prior cross-examination of you, there was a question to you about where he stayed, and you claim you didn't know that it was Motel 6. Do you remember saying that?

A. I knew that he had frequently over the years that I knew him, and particularly the last six months, he had spent a lot of time away from the house.

Q. I will ask you the question again, Mr. Tenny.

A. All right.

Q. Do you recall telling me on cross-examination earlier that you had no knowledge it was a Motel 6?

A. I wasn't 100 percent as to whether it was a Motel 6.

Q. I didn't ask you that. I said do you remember telling me that?

A. You and I have questions on this issue, and I have said I didn't know where he was staying.

Q. All right. Now, I will get back to the letter again which was written in March of '04. Did you not specifically put down there it was either or both Motel 6 or Travelodge? You put that down there; did you not?

A. Yes, I did.

Q. So you knew that he stayed at a Motel 6 or you wouldn't have written that?

A. I knew he was at a hotel. I believe he told me.

Q. A Motel 6 receipt for Garrett Daniel was found in the trunk of his car, according to the testimony, and on the Motel 6 receipt was some blood. That particular one showed for 1/10 of '04. And since it was in the trunk, had you already handled his body, Mr. Tenny?

A. I don't know anything about that.

Q. And then did you sort of rub some blood on this receipt and stick it in the trunk?

A. I don't know anything about that.

Q. Yet you tell Lieutenant Camp that it was a Motel 6 or Travelodge?

A. Garrett told me he was staying at a motel, and I knew that he frequented Motel 6 and he frequented Travelodge over the months and years that I knew him.

Q. Well, in the American Express documents in evidence, there is not one reference to a Travelodge that I recollect. How about that, Mr. Tenny?

A. Garrett rarely used his American Express.

Q. But you used it a lot; is that so?

A. I used mine.

Q. A lot?

A. Yes.

Q. For thousands?

A. Yes.

Q. Particularly those large amounts were airline flights?

A. That's correct.

Q. Just when you needed it; is that correct?

A. It's very convenient to have an American Express.

Q. Now, we have heard your testimony about the blood and so forth. Crime scene analyst Jim Serpa of the Sheriff's Office indicated that the blood evidence went all the way from the master bedroom through the dining room, into the kitchen, I guess the front room, and then back into the dining room. Do you recall that testimony?

A. I do recall his testimony.

Q. And he testified that he's an expert, he's testified a lot with regard to blood evidence. Do you recall that?

A. Yes.

Q. And you, Mr. Tenny, said that when Garrett Daniel came home you were in the master bedroom; do you remember saying that?

A. I believe I was in the bedroom sleeping.

Q. And this is where the blood trail starts, according to Mr. Serpa.

A. I heard the testimony.

Q. You left Capetown, let's see, you were born January 22, 1966. You left Capetown at age 18?

A. That's correct.

Q. Because you didn't want to get involved with military service, correct?

A. Yes.

Q. And therefore you went to Canada?

A. That's correct.

Q. And that was a convenient country for you to go to?

A. I have relatives there.

Q. Well, I mean, then if you went to Canada, the government of South Africa couldn't involve you in military service; is that so?

A. That's correct.

Q. So you didn't just pop-up and leave. You actually had a reason to leave, correct? Isn't that correct?

A. There were serious riots in Capetown that week.

Q. So you had a real reason to leave Capetown at age 18 because you didn't want to get involved in all that, did you?

A. That's correct.

Q. Then when you went to Hawaii with your jet ski service, you had a reason to leave, and that was with Garrett Daniel; is that right?

A. When I left where?

Q. Hawaii.

A. I left to go to Florida. That was my motivation. I was going to Florida.

Q. You left with Garrett Daniel?

A. I left on separate flights. I met him a week later in Pittsburgh.

Q. And it says, my notes say that, I met Garrett and moved to Indiana. I thought I heard correctly that you met Garrett in Hawaii. Did I hear wrong?

A. I met Garrett in Hawaii.

Q. And you moved to Indiana where he was at, correct?

A. That's correct.

Q. And you worked on his house?

A. That's correct.

Q. This is going from an advertising executive in Canada and Toronto to jet ski service in Hawaii to working on his house in Indiana; is that so?

A. That's quite correct.

Q. But you also did roofing for a building company?

A. Yes.

Q. Because Garrett lived there?

A. Yes.

Q. You wanted to be with Garrett?

A. Yes.

Q. Garrett was supporting you?

A. Yes.

Q. Well, then, you were in Indiana, and the only reason you moved was because Garrett chose Phoenix, correct?

A. Yes.

Q. So in each case, Mr. Tenny, your move was motivated for a specific reason, because you don't just pop-up and leave. You leave for some particularized reason, correct?

A. Yes.

Q. And the particularized reason that you left Phoenix, Arizona, on January 15, 2004, at approximately 7:30 in the morning was because Garrett Daniel was dead; is that correct?

A. That is not correct.

Q. And your relationship was at an end; is that correct?

A. The relationship was coming to a close.

Q. And you couldn't take that relationship coming to an end, not getting his half of the house, and you decided that that was it; is that so?

A. That is not so.

Q. You left behind the house, Jaguar, and all you had was a suitcase full of clothes?

A. That's correct.

Q. However, when you moved from Toronto, Canada, to Hawaii, you sold the house and the cars, correct?

A. Those prior six months to previous leaving, yes, I did, but I was single.

Q. But in this case you didn't bother selling the Jaguar?

A. Everything was tied to Garrett. Garrett had authority to do as he pleased and agree or not agree as to the disposition of our property.

Q. And you didn't care for that at all, did you?

A. I couldn't cooperate with Garrett. It was best that I go away and give him time to brood on his own.

Q. So you couldn't take that, that Garrett wouldn't go along with everything that you demanded, correct?

A. Incorrect.

Q. In any event, you didn't try to sell your Jaguar, correct?

A. Correct.

Q. And you didn't try to sell your half interest out to Garrett before you left in the house; is that so?

A. Correct.

Q. And you just left the agency with documents, and you never left any access to the computer or anything, did you?

A. Incorrect.

Q. As a matter of fact, Jeff Kin, he had his own business. He wasn't about to also take over the agency. And you knew that, didn't you?

A. I thought he would.

Q. And, nevertheless, Bill Mill came in and he said that there was nothing in order, and he had to get a computer expert and all of that; do you recall that testimony?

A. Particularly he needed help, yes.

Q. And you just left. You never notified any of these handicapped people that you were leaving, correct?

A. I might have mentioned it in passing. Formally, no.

Q. Certainly not to Ms. Charl. You never mentioned it to her on the 14th?

A. No.

Q. And they came to your office to make payments on their mortgages?

A. That was the procedure.

Q. And then when you left Indiana to come to Phoenix, well, you had a U-Haul full of possessions, right?

A. That's correct.

Q. Now, you know, from South Africa, you lived in Canada; is that so? Are you aware there's no such thing as a labor board advertising your position in a company you started and somebody bidding on it, and just maybe getting it out from under? You understand it doesn't work that way here, don't you?

A. It does work that way.

Q. What labor board?

A. It could be the Department of Labor.

Q. Where?

A. It's, I believe it's a state run organization. So I was advised by my legal counsel.

Q. I see. But you founded your agency?

A. Yes.

Q. And the government grants you got were federal government grants, correct?

A. They were city of Phoenix grants.

Q. And the reason that you founded it was you felt there was a market and, therefore, you could put yourself in as a paid position and you founded the company. It was a niche situation; is that correct?

A. It worked well.

Q. And Garrett was secretary treasurer?

A. That's correct.

Q. And since you weren't getting along with Garrett, that certainly made it even more untenable, correct?

A. That's correct.

Q. And you knew Garrett went home for lunch, generally speaking?

A. He would come home. I knew he was at the house occasionally, perhaps two to three times per week.

Q. And so you knew he would probably be home for lunch at the noon hour on Tuesday, January 14, 2004?

A. Not necessarily.

Q. But, in any event, he did come home, because that was his regular pattern?

A. It wasn't his regular pattern, nope, particularly because he had been staying away from the house.

Q. At some point in time there was an argument out on the patio between you and Garrett?

A. We had conversations, but very scant conversations.

Q. And you were out in the pool area talking loudly?

A. I believe Garrett went out to the car to put his clothes in there.

Q. But, as a matter of fact, the clothes that left that house were your clothes when you went to South Africa, correct?

A. No, that was later on.

Q. But you saw the photographs of Garrett's car and there's no clothes in there. There was a few?

A. Those are Garrett's clothes.

Q. There's no clothes in the interior of the car, and there's a few odds and ends in the trunk, which there actually is a picture of; do you recall that evidence?

A. Yes.

Q. So certainly not a bunch of clothes coming out of the house into his car. It just isn't there, is it?

A. I don't quite follow your question.

Q. There's none of Garrett's clothes in his car, is there?

A. Those are all—those were all Garrett's. When he left the house, he left with his clothes.

Q. When you left the house, you left with your clothes?

A. That's correct.

Q. But what is left in the house are his clothes; is that so?

A. Both of our clothes.

Q. You also testified that you were going to make the announcement of your leaving your agency at the next board session, but the next board session wasn't until late January, correct?

A. Yes. If I had remained in the city, I would have resigned.

Q. As you say, you just accelerated your departure?

A. Yes.

Q. Because of the situation with you and Garrett on January 14, 2004?

A. No, not necessarily to do with the 14th and work, no.

Q. Now, if you had such plans, Mr. Tenny, to leave, and they were all set according to your letter to the Lieutenant at the Sheriff's Department, in that letter you wouldn't have made an appointment with Linda Hernand on the 13th?

A. I don't know when we set that meeting up.

Q. You heard the testimony with Jeff Kin that you looked at your calendar?

A. If I set it on the 13th, I probably had intentions to be there. But I wasn't feeling well on the 14th.

Q. And you weren't feeling well because of the situation with you and Garrett Daniel; is that correct?

A. No. It was more due to the fact that I had to go to work, and I was sick about the work.

Q. But you already said in the letter to the Lieutenant in March, it had nothing to do with not feeling well, just that you already had your plans set so you didn't go to work at the agency on the 14th. Do you remember writing that?

A. I wrote that in hindsight. I wrote the letter in March.

Q. And then you left all the agency keys in your Jaguar on the floor?

A. They were mostly spare keys.

Q. Well, it seems like they were necessary because you heard the testimony that they were requested to—

A. I think what they were requesting was the other key, which was the front door key to the office.

Q. Did you hear the testimony that some 17 keys were requested to be returned that came from the floorboard of your Jaguar?

A. Well, there would have been duplicates at the office.

Q. Apparently they didn't find them because you just left suddenly, correct?

A. There were duplicates of keys everywhere. I had a road set and I had sets at the office in a drawer. We kept keys there.

Q. But you recall them just laying on the floorboard of your Jaguar?

A. That's where the keys always were in the car.

Q. And then going back to our earlier comment about your car being in service, you said that you drove Garrett's car while your car was in service all that week, and that you drove Garrett to work. Do you recall saying that in your direct examination not very long ago?

A. I do.

Q. And yet your car was not only not in service—

A. It was in service.

Q. —but it had come back earlier in the week, according to your later testimony. And we don't see any American Express charges about your car, do we?

A. My testimony was as follows. There was a car service which took place in December, and the charge for that appears on the American Express. There was additional service conducted at a separate garage in Phoenix, not Scottsdale, it was a Phoenix garage. And that was on the week of the 6th of January through Friday the 10th of January.

Q. Which garage?

A. I do not recall the name. It was the first visit.

Q. Where was it located?

A. Perhaps 17th Street and Camelback. Around there.

Q. If I suggest to you there's no garage there?

A. You will find the payment in my checking records, which you have.

Q. You testified that most of your payments were by American Express?

A. Some, not all. It depends on the means and methods and source and use.

Q. Well, in any event, your Jaguar was in the driveway from and after January 14, 2004, because it was observed by your neighbor, Mr. Weiss. Do you recall that?

A. I left the Jag there.

Q. If you claim that you used your Jaguar to go to work, but still we have a witness saying otherwise, that she saw that red Pontiac at work, correct?

A. If I went to work on the 14th.

Q. The only reason that you went to work, because you said twice, one, you weren't feeling well and, two, in the letter to the Lieutenant that you had already sent your resignation so you didn't go to work yet. You went to work—

A. I don't believe. I'm not sure that I went to work on that date.

Q. Did you go to work to access the Internet?

A. I don't have Internet set up at the—there was no Internet set up at that office.

Q. Ms. Charl said that she observed you doing—

A. We never worked on the Internet at all.

Q. In any event, you went there to sort of cover things so nobody would be suspicious?

A. I don't recall being at the office that day.

Q. Is that where you called Corri?

A. No. I thought I called her from the house.

Q. Well, yes, but you called her between either 2:50 or 3:10?

A. Correct.

Q. And you were at the office at that time?

A. I can't be sure.

Q. According to your direct testimony, you said Garrett brought clothes into the house, not take them out?

A. He brought laundry back into the house.

Q. And in your letter to the Lieutenant you say that Garrett left back for work, correct?

A. That's a broad word, "work."

Q. But we all know according to the witnesses testimony he never went back to work?

A. He told me he was going for a job interview.

Q. Well, he didn't go for that either because he couldn't, could he?

A. I don't know.

Q. Well, I mean, you wouldn't permit him, would you?

A. He left the house in his car.

Q. No, he didn't. Did he, Mr. Tenny?

A. He did.

Q. No one saw that, but they did see you in his car at 12:50 p.m. Do you remember the testimony?

A. I drove around the block, that's correct. He packed his car up with clothes.

Q. Another witness said they saw you at your work about 2:30 with his car parked in your space. Do you recall that testimony?

A. At the office?

Q. Yes.

A. Sherry Charl I believe is very mistaken.

Q. You're right and she's wrong, correct?

A. Well—

Q. Is that correct?

A. My testimony is, I do not recall going to the office that day. But if somebody saw me going to the office, I must have been at the office. But if I was at the office, sir, it wasn't in Garrett's car. It was in the Jaguar.

Q. How about Corri Crel's testimony? You're right; she's wrong, correct? There was never the incident of you flashing a knife to Garrett Daniel, correct?

A. No.

Q. And you're going to stick by this window broken thing of 1/28/03?

A. There's a receipt for it.

Q. That's when it was broken?

A. That's the day we replaced the replacement sheet of glass.

Q. What was the date it was broken?

A. On the 28th.

Q. You're going to stick with that, right?

A. I am.

Q. Now, Garrett cut himself up, and all this glass, I take it, he went to the hospital and had it taken care of?

A. I don't know. I wasn't at the house when this happened.

Q. Then how would you possibly know, Mr. Tenny?

A. I left the house at 10:30 that day and I returned at approximately four o'clock and the window was broken. And upon questioning, Garrett said he had broken the window and that he had hurt himself.

Q. As a point of fact, you had broken the window; do you recall that?

A. No.

Q. And you wish to deny that?

A. I didn't break the window.

Q. Well, one thing you know, Garrett was wearing tan pants the day of January 14, 2004?

A. Probably.

Q. And, well, you saw it in the pictures when they recovered the body, didn't you?

A. I saw what he was wearing in the photographs.

Q. Tan pants?

A. He was wearing tan pants, yes.

Q. What kind of a shirt?

A. Was he wearing a shirt?

Q. When he came home for lunch.

A. I don't know what kind of shirt he was wearing.

Q. And then after doing all that renovation at the house, you just up and leave it. All that, tile on the outside, stucco, the fireplace, the kitchen, taking nine months off and putting in six years of your time, you just left it?

A. Yeah, I took a trip.

Q. That's because of what happened between you and Garrett, right?

A. Nothing happened between Garrett and I.

Q. One thing you said on direct examination, one of the reasons you claim you left Phoenix is that you and Garrett had irreconcilable differences on a personal level.

A. We were not communicating.

Q. Irreconcilable?

A. I believe so.

Q. Do you remember using that word?

A. Yes.

Q. You know what it means?

A. No compromise.

Q. Can't ever get back together?

A. I think so.

Q. Irreconcilable doesn't mean that, does it?

A. I'm not sure what the word means. I never use it.

Q. But you chose to use that word.

A. I used it.

Q. And you're articulate; are you not?

A. I can't say I've used the word in writing before.

Q. Now, you just testified about that broken window that you didn't have a clue that Garrett Daniel had cut himself, and yet you testified on direct that you helped clean it up and that's where you saw that he cut himself?

A. I testified to the fact that Garrett cleaned his own blood spots up from the house.

Q. That's not what you testified to. So if you're changing it, that's okay, Mr. Tenny.

A. Would you repeat what your statement was?

Q. You testified that you helped Garrett clean up the broken glass.

A. That's correct.

Q. That it was on 12/28/03 when it occurred, right?

A. That was December the 28th, that's correct.

Q. So you were aware, according to your testimony, that he cut himself and that's how the blood got all over the house?

A. That's correct. Some of it.

Q. And the rest of it got there through other means, I take it?

A. I don't know.

MR. LEV: That's all I have, Your Honor.

THE COURT: Redirect.

REDIRECT EXAMINATION

BY MR. SCHRE:

Q. Mr. Tenny, when you left South Africa when you were 18 years old, it was for political reasons, correct?

A. That was one of the motivating factors for leaving.

Q. And there were political reasons why you did not want to go into the military?

A. Very much so.

Q. Those political reasons dealt with homosexuality?

A. That, too.

Q. They dealt with how homosexuals were treated in South Africa in the military?

A. Yes.

Q. Did that climate change when you returned to South Africa?

A. They have a brand new constitution, and freedom of sexual expression is written into the first ten constitutional points.

Q. Now, in March of 2004, you made attempts to contact Detective Tim Camp by phone?

A. Yes.

Q. And did you ever speak with him by phone?

A. I never got through to him on the phone, no. He had an answering machine.

Q. And so then you wrote a letter?

A. And I wrote a letter about two or three days after first receiving his name and phone number.

Q. And you received his name and phone number from whom?

A. A lawyer, Mink.

Q. And prior to contacting Detective Camp, you were read newspaper articles about this case, or about Mr. Daniel?

A. I was dictated newspaper articles by lawyer Mink over the telephone.

Q. And when you were dictated those newspaper articles, you learned that the Sheriff's Office was interested in you?

A. They were interested in contacting me.

Q. And you wrote the letter to Mr. Camp to explain, given that they were interested in you, that you did not have anything to do with Garrett Daniel's disappearance?

A. It was less to do with—I would rephrase that and I would suggest that I was trying to communicate with Mr. Camp as to anything that I might have known about Garrett before my departure.

Q. And did the newspaper article tell you where Garrett Daniel was found?

A. Someone told me.

Q. Okay. Now, you testified about moving Garrett's car around to the back?

A. Uh-huh.

Q. Because of the bougainvilleas, correct?

A. Yes.

Q. Do you know when Garrett left that day about what time he left your house?

A. About an hour after he arrived. I would say 1:00, 1:15.

Q. Did you move that car around to the back of your house right before Garrett left, or was it sometime before?

A. I think it was before Garrett left.

Q. What car did Garrett leave in?

A. He left in his car.

Q. I want a time frame. We know you said Garrett left around 1:00, 1:15, somewhere around that time frame. Was it right away when you moved the car, or was it—

A. Garrett was probably home half an hour before I moved the car. I don't know if I moved both cars, but I know I drove his car. So I think, you know, he probably had lunch in the kitchen and then got into the closet and started to move clothes, and I said, well, I'm going to move the cars around.

Q. How much time did you spend drafting the letter to Mr. Weiss?

A. Mr. Weiss, I just scribbled a note.

Q. How much thought did you put into that note?

A. I was just worried about the cat. I was trying to tell him that I would be away for a while and Garrett had not been there for a while, somebody ought to know that the house was empty and that the cat was over there.

Q. And when you said that you wrote the letter to Mr. Weiss because Garrett had not been there for a while, did you think that because you could not get ahold of Garrett by phone?

A. No. I wrote the letter with the understanding that Garrett had left the house with his clothes and was probably gone for another five days. So I wrote the letter with the understanding that Garrett was moving a long way and where he was spending time away from the house. He was noncommittal as to where he was going and how long he would be gone, so I couldn't tell.

Q. But you did try to contact Garrett by telephone?

A. And I did phone in once or twice from New York to see if he came home that night.

Q. Did anybody answer the phone?

A. No.

Q. And did you leave a message?

A. No.

Q. Do you know the exact time you phoned in?

A. No.

Q. Do you know the exact day that you phoned in?

A. From New York it would have been the Wednesday night and/or the Thursday.

Q. Are you sure about the date?

A. Well, I was only in New York for two days. I didn't call from oversees until later on.

Q. When you called from overseas, did you speak with anyone?

A. Nobody. I didn't get any answers at the house.

Q. And did you leave a voice mail message?

A. No.

Q. And when no one answered the phone after you left Phoenix, did you ever leave voice mail messages?

A. I don't think I ever left a voice mail message at the house, and I wasn't in the habit of calling Garrett at his office.

Q. When you called, did you want to speak to Garrett directly?

A. Yes.

Q. Now, when you went to New York, where did you plan on going from there?

A. I was going to London and from London to Johannesburg.

Q. And did you have plans on staying in South Africa?

A. I wasn't sure. I thought I might come back to Phoenix. I was not sure.

Q. What about this talk of Canada?

A. And that became an issue after the reports of Garrett's death. I thought I might come back to Phoenix. Unfortunately, I didn't have funding to do that. I didn't have the airline tickets to do that. I was invited to Germany, but I didn't take that trip either. I thought I would go visit family up in Canada. I was a little nervous and unnerved by the whole experience, and I wasn't settled in Capetown yet. I did have this consulting contract in Johannesburg. It was a short term study. I left Johannesburg and went to Capetown. I was in a guest house, a bed and breakfast, and I just wasn't sure about the future.

Q. About what time did you first find out that Garrett had been found in the desert?

A. Well, I found out from, my mother told me that Garrett was dead.

Q. About when?

A. I believe it was February the 23rd.

Q. And why did you wait until March 3rd?

A. There wasn't any need to phone in. We speak once every six weeks, once every couple of months. If I take a trip or go somewhere, I will let them know where I am. But not on a daily basis.

Q. Meaning your mother?

A. My mother and/or my sister.

Q. Why did you wait until March 3rd to call Arizona?

A. Well, on the 23rd of February, I phoned my mother who informed me of Garrett's death, and she said to call my sister in Vancouver. And my sister told me in a little more detail about Garrett's death. I cannot recall the telephone conversation, but she did tell me that she was in contact with Corri Crel at Garrett's office, and she had phoned in to find out where I was on my birthday.

Q. When did you call your sister?

A. I believe it was February the 23rd.

Q. Why did you wait until March 3rd to phone Arizona?

A. Because I asked my sister to ask Corri to obtain newspaper articles so that I could get a better understanding of what was going on in Phoenix. There was talk about missing persons, there was talk about Garrett's death, and I didn't really know what was going on. So I thought the best thing to do was to get ahold of newspaper articles. She wasn't able to get them. Corri would not work with her.

Q. Tell me how many different loans were taken out on yours and Garrett's home?

A. There were three loans on the house. The first was for $46,500. That was Garrett's mortgage. The second was for about $70,000. Pardon me, an additional $30,000, which was for the car and some of the rehabilitation, as in renovations on the house.

Q. Now, who was your sponsor for your visa? Did you have a sponsor?

A. Garrett. My legal sponsor in the U.S.A. was Garrett Daniel.

Q. And were you communicating with Garrett around the time that he left?

A. At what level?

Q. Okay. Well, you never did obtain a green card, did you?

A. No.

Q. How did you feel about your immigration status?

A. I felt I had worked very hard for a place in the community, that it wasn't forthcoming without considerably more effort, the financial hiring of lawyers to do this immigration thing. I felt I was a little bit, a little hurt by the whole experience. It was a rainbow that I didn't want to chase any more.

Q. Did you feel like you were having a lot of trouble dealing with immigration?

A. Yes, it was a constant nagging thing on me to comply with the rules and regulations and go on with work. It was constant.

Q. Have you ever lived anywhere where there didn't have knives in the kitchen?

A. No.

Q. Now, let's clarify something. You had talked about the window that was broken earlier?

A. Yes.

Q. Were you there when it was broken?

A. At the time of breakage I was not there.

Q. Now, were you there when Garrett was cleaning up?

A. There was a mop and a bucket in the kitchen that day, but I didn't see blood in the kitchen. I really didn't see blood in the kitchen. I did see some evidence of it on the way off to the bathroom. There were just a few little spots on the floor. Really, there wasn't much. And I didn't fuss and bother over this whole thing with Garrett. I was so angry with him on account of the glass. I had to go out, buy a glass window, we had a security issue going off to L.A. the next day. I just didn't want to talk about it with him.

Q. Was there a time that day when you observed Garrett getting cut?

A. No, I didn't see that. Well, there was—he nicked his hand on the garage area out at the back of the house when we were moving those shards of glass. It was almost nighttime.

Q. When you wrote your letters back to Phoenix, were you looking at a calendar to figure out what particular day you had left Phoenix?

A. I resorted to a calendar to try and recall my exact departure date because I don't think I kept the airline ticket. I thought I had left on the 15th and/or the 16th. According to my letter, I had made mistakes on quoting dates in that letter.

Q. Now, you said the morning of the 14th you didn't go into work because you felt sick?

A. Yes.

Q. And you felt sick because you knew your relationship with Garrett was coming to an end?

A. I was very disappointed that Garrett was on one of his stay-away-from-the-house phases. So he had been gone for four days, and I didn't know where he was. He didn't tell me where he was. I had no telephone number to reach him if I had to reach him for work. I would have had to call him at the office, and he asked me not to call him at the office. I just felt that we were not going—I mean, I spent a lot of money on the San Diego trip, but we were going nowhere on the friendship. Our friendship was not where it should be.

Q. When was the next board meeting of your agency, if at all, in January?

A. Well, it was slated for the 22nd of January.

Q. And did you have some feelings about attending that board meeting?

A. I didn't want to be there.

Q. Why didn't you want to be there?

A. Because I knew that I was going to go through another year of planning and presenting to a group of board members that were not going to fulfill any of the goals and objectives that I had set, and I really didn't want to do another full year, and that I would resign at that meeting.

Q. You owned a Jaguar for a couple of years?

A. Yes.

Q. And is the Jaguar a reliable car?

A. It works out. Yes, it's all right.

Q. But?

A. It's not unreliable.

Q. Did you have to take it to the shop?

A. Once or twice a year.

Q. Okay. And did you pay for things in any other way when you lived in Phoenix by American Express?

A. I also had a Master Card, and by check.

Q. How about Garrett, how did he pay for things?

A. In addition to those methods of payment that I just quoted, he also had a Discover Card, I know that. I would assume very similar avenues of payment.

Q. Mr. Lev had asked you questions about a letter and a knowledge of a Motel 6. And I'm referring to that letter to Tim Camp.

A. Yes.

Q. Were you familiar with Garrett's habits when he didn't stay at home? When he went other places, were you familiar with where he went to?

A. No. That was absolutely off balance, out of bounds.

Q. But my question to you is, how would you come up with Motel 6?

A. Because when I asked him, I'd say, Garrett, where have you been? He would say, at a motel. I'd say, what do you mean a motel? He'd say, well, it's a Motel

6, or Travelodge. So that's how he would brush it off. But he wouldn't tell me where it was or who he was with. It was off limits. It wasn't mine to ask him.

Q. The five days that Garrett was gone or so, in the middle of January?

A. Yes.

Q. Did Garrett specifically tell you where he went to?

A. Absolutely not.

Q. Now, back when you moved from Indiana to Phoenix, Arizona, what was your relationship to Garrett?

A. Those were better times. They were—we were good friends. Garrett and I were good friends in those days.

Q. Were you more than friends in those days?

A. Yes.

Q. And because you were more than friends with him, was that why you came with him to Arizona?

A. Yes, it was very much a motivating thing.

Q. When you moved from Indiana to Arizona, there was a U-Haul that was brought out here, right?

A. Yes.

Q. Whose stuff was that, for the most part?

A. Garrett's.

Q. And in the house here in Phoenix, the furniture, that type of stuff, who owned most of it?

A. Well, once we got to Phoenix and I started to produce, I would say 50 percent of that was my furniture, if not, more.

Q. And how expensive would it have been to take that to South Africa?

A. I looked into it and it would have been—it was a luxury. It was not feasible. I didn't really want to do that.

Q. Was there a typical type of pants that Garrett would wear to work?

A. Those beige pants he wore often. That was the uniform he wore to work, the pants. He usually had different shirts.

Q. Why did you decide to stay in South Africa?

A. Frankly, I was stranded because of the way the American Express people and the ruckus that they caused there, so initially I was not in a position to get on an airplane and come back to deal with Phoenix and/or move to Canada, even though I had planned to go on. Shortly after I wrote the letter to Tim Camp, I came by a good position in a real estate agency in a development division in Capetown, and I stayed with them for about nine months. And that got me started on credit in South Africa, and I stayed.

Q. Thank you.

THE COURT: All right, any other questions by the jury? Will counsel approach the bench, please.

(Discussion at bench, and then the following proceedings continued in open court:)

THE COURT: The question is, Mr. Tenny, the window, it was testified it was broken on December 28th. Was this the date and time for the Rose Bowl trip to L.A?

THE DEFENDANT: It was the day preceding our departure for the Rose Bowl parade.

THE COURT: Thank you.

Anything else, Mr. Schre?

MR. SCHRE: No, Judge. At this time the defense rests.

THE COURT: Ladies and gentlemen, we're going to recess now. If we could start up tomorrow at 10:30. My understanding is, Mr. Lev has some short rebuttal, which we will take up at 10:30, and then I'm going to settle the final instructions with the lawyers after that. So my sense is that we will have the closing arguments at 1:30 tomorrow. And then, as I said, the jury will get the case tomorrow afternoon. All right, so we will be at recess. Have a good evening.

(Whereupon, the following proceedings were held out of the presence of the jury:)

THE COURT: Everybody can sit down. Mr. Schre, you can stand up or sit down.

MR. SCHRE: That's fine, Judge. I just wanted to reurge my motion on allowing Mr. Tenny to testify about why he made the phone call to Corri Crel, and I'd like to recall him for that purpose.

It's my argument that he cannot get a fair trial without presenting a complete defense, which he's allowed to do under the Arizona and United States Constitution, and a complete defense includes when the State makes allegations that he made a phone call, which he's admitted on the stand he made, a phone call that is going to be used in argument as incriminating evidence against him, he should be allowed under the Constitution to explain his state of mind in making that phone call, why he made that phone call.

And if the Court wants, we can give a limiting instruction that this statement from Mr. Tenny, that which is that he made the phone call because Garrett had asked him to, because Garrett said he was going on a job interview, and give Schol Insurance

Company, Garrett's work, an explanation as to why he would not be in that afternoon. If the Court wants to let him do that, we can give the jury a limiting instruction that they not take Garrett's statement for the truth of the matter asserted, that he was looking for a job interview that afternoon.

Our purpose in offering the phone call into evidence or the reason for making the phone call, which is, Garrett told Robert to make it because, I'm going to a job interview, is to explain why Robert would make a phone call that the jury is going to see is highly unusual. And if we can't explain that, they're going to want to convict on that phone call alone, and he's not going to be able to get a fair trial. That's why I want to recall him so he can give an explanation as to that phone call. And that's the only thing that I want to recall him for is the explanation as to the phone call. And I think that when he makes that phone call, there is a state of mind, and I'm asking to bring in Garrett's statement to explain Robert's state of mind, not for whether or not Garrett's statements are true or not.

THE COURT: I asked before whether or not you have any case law that says under that exception to the hearsay, since you're looking at the nondeclarant's state of mind, that's the exception, whether you have any cases. I will give you until tomorrow if you can give me some cases on that.

MR. SCHRE: I'm asking to bring it in, and the catch-all exception, too, and also under his right to present a complete defense.

THE COURT: Well, under the catch-all exception, it has to have some basis for the truthfulness. Just because Mr. Tenny isn't getting on the stand and saying it, I don't think that's enough under the catch-all. I mean, that's how I read it. Mr. Lev, do you want to respond at all?

MR. LEV: It has to have an indicia of reliability. That isn't it. Furthermore, it is for the purpose, it's obviously for the truth of the matter, otherwise they wouldn't bother with it. And that's to, of course, give some explanation or excuse or something why he made this call. And so, no, it shouldn't be allowed to come in. I don't see it as any kind of exception.

THE COURT: Well, if you have some case law on that, show me something. I really will reconsider my ruling tomorrow if you have something to show me.

MR. SCHRE: Yes, Judge.

THE COURT: So tomorrow you're going to have supposedly some rebuttal, maybe somebody from I.N.S., and somebody else? Ms. Crel?

MR. LEV: Yes.

THE COURT: And also, do you see any surrebuttal?

MR. SCHRE: I'm not certain as to what Ms. Crel is going to testify about.

THE COURT: Well, I guess I don't know either. Maybe you can talk about that. I just don't want any cumulative testimony.

MR. LEV: Rebuttal is what was brought up with his testimony, it has to do with the glass breakage and the incidents, both of which he denied, saying it's just a misunderstanding.

THE COURT: Okay.

MR. SCHRE: Meaning the incident as to the phone call?

MR. LEV: No. Meaning the incident as to what she actually heard.

THE COURT: Why don't we do this. Why don't you make an offer of proof as to what the rebuttal is, and then Mr. Schre and I will be able to ascertain whether or not it's a legitimate rebuttal.

MR. LEV: The glass breakage occurred before December 21, 2003. Garrett told her that Bob Tenny, in fact, broke the glass, that the incident with regard to him threatening Garrett Daniel with a knife, it wasn't some kind of misunderstanding, that it actually occurred. This is rebuttal. And the actual words that he used with regard to his call to her on 1/14.

THE COURT: Let me stop you on that point. Mr. Tenny first said he didn't recall it, and then he denied it. Let's say he denied it happened. Just for argument's sake, what is she saying other than, well, the same thing she said before?

MR. LEV: He didn't just say that, Your Honor. He said, oh, no, it was a misunderstanding. Or, we were just using words, and that was it. No physical threats. That's the rebuttal.

THE COURT: On that, I'm not inclined to, on that point. What about the glass? That she would testify that the glass incident happened rather than on December 28th it happened on December 21st?

MR. LEV: When she came to visit on the 21st, it was already broken, and Garrett Daniel told her that it occurred and that Bob Tenny broke it.

THE COURT: I guess she can testify as to what she observed on the 21st. Under what hearsay exception will she testify what Garrett Daniel told her?

MR. LEV: It's impeachment.

THE COURT: Mr. Schre?

MR. SCHRE: Judge, it's a hearsay exception because Ms. Crel never observed the glass being broken. She's coming into court and testifying about what Garrett—

THE COURT: Well, I understood that he said she would testify that on December 21st she observed that the glass was broken.

MR. SCHRE: I have no problem with her testifying to that, that it was on the 21st the glass was broken. I believe she already testified to that in the cross-examination, she said on the 21st the glass was broken. As far as to Garrett telling her how the glass was broken, it's hearsay. And she is not the one that—she can't impeach him because she doesn't truly know if it happened, and I don't see it as a hearsay exception.

THE COURT: Mr. Lev, I'm willing to let her testify that she observed on December 21st that the glass was broken, not to the hearsay of Mr. Daniel or what I think is the cumulative thing about the other point. What about the I.N.S. official? You don't know what that person is going to say yet?

MR. LEV: Not exactly, but I don't think he had all those problems he's claiming.

THE COURT: All right. Well, I will let you work it out. I'm not sure either of those things are going to make or break this case for anybody. But it's your case, and you run the case like you think you should run it.

We will either start arguments tomorrow morning if you don't have anything else or we will start at 1:30. Okay?

MR. LEV: Yes, Your Honor.

MR. SCHRE: Yes, Judge.

THE COURT: See you tomorrow.

Fifth Day, January 5, 2007

MORNING SESSION

(THE TRIAL STARTED WITH REBUTTAL TESTIMONY CONDUCTED BY THE DISTRICT ATTORNEY, MR. LEV. HE CALLED UPON AN AGENT FROM THE IMMIGRATION AND NATURALIZATION SERVICE WITH REGARD TO STATEMENTS MADE BY ROBERT TENNY ON HIS VISA SITUATION. MR. LEV ALSO PLANNED TO CALL BACK CORRI CREL TO CLARIFY THE BROKEN WINDOW GLASS SITUATION. IT WAS GOING TO BE A DIRE DAY FOR THE DEFENDANT. FIRST THE I.N.S. AGENT TOOK THE STAND. AFTER ESTABLISHING HIS CREDENTIALS, THE TESTIMONY CONTINUED:)

BY MR. LEV:

Q. What did you find out about his original citizenship?

A. Basically, sir, I ran checks of our I.N.S. databases, and I found no record that existed of Mr. Tenny having entered the United States to work or reside here in the United States.

Q. Does that include annual renewals?

A. Yes, sir.

Q. In other words, never has he applied for an annual renewal?

A. That's correct.

Q. And you checked the national database?

A. Yes, sir.

Q. Where did you further check to see where he originated from to this country?

A. I contacted Canadian immigration to find out his actual country of birth, and I was told by a Canadian immigration supervisor that I spoke to yesterday, and they told me that Mr. Tenny had entered Canada from South Africa, and that he was a naturalized Canadian citizen. And that occurred on April 30 of 1993.

Q. Now, if one becomes a naturalized Canadian citizen, is there a requirement to visit the United States, to have a visa to visit the U.S?

A. No, sir. Canadians are exempt the passport or visa requirement to enter, to visit temporarily the United States.

Q. And the temporary is how long?

A. It depends on their length of visit. It could be anywhere from a month to several months, as long as the trip is of a temporary nature, but it's not to reside or to work in the United States. If a Canadian citizen intended to come to the United States for employment or to reside permanently, there would be a requirement to have authorization from I.N.S. But to visit on a temporary nature for varying lengths of time, as long as it was temporary and the intent was not to reside or work in the United States, there would be no requirement to show a passport or have any prior authorization.

Q. Mr. Tenny testified yesterday and indicated that he came from Canada into the U.S. to Hawaii, stayed for a period in Hawaii, then went to Indiana, stayed in Indiana for a while, then went to Arizona, has resided in Arizona since, for about six years. Can a Canadian citizen come in like that and just sort of get lost?

A. Yes, it has been known to happen, but that person would still be residing without any authorization here in the United States.

(NOW THE PUBLIC DEFENDER CROSS-EXAMINED THE I.N.S. AGENT ABOUT THE CHANGES IN THE IMMIGRATION LAWS WITH THE PASSING OF NAFTA (NORTH AMERICAN FREE TRADE AGREEMENT) WHERE PERSONS CAN ENTER THE COUNTRY FOR EMPLOYMENT PURPOSES. BUT THE DISTRICT ATTORNEY IN HIS REDIRECT EXAMINATION ESTABLISHED THAT WHEN ROBERT TENNY ENTERED THE UNITED STATES IN THE EARLY NINETIES, NAFTA DIDN'T EXIST AT THAT TIME. NOW CORRI CREL, THE FRIEND AND CO-WORKER OF GARRETT DANIEL, TOOK THE STAND AGAIN TO DISCUSS THE BROKEN WINDOWPANE. THE DISTRICT ATTORNEY TOOK CHARGE:)

Q. Corri, do you recall when you were testifying earlier about the window in the rear of the house that you knew had been broken out?

A. Yes.

Q. When did you see this window having been broken out?

A. The first we knew about it was on December 21st.

Q. And how did you know about it, that it was broken then?

A. The blind was swinging, and I had asked what had happened to the window.

Q. Now, in regard to that, did you see any cuts on Garrett Daniel's hands as though he might have picked the glass and cut his hands?

A. No, none.

MR. LEV: That's all I have.

THE COURT: Cross-examination. Mr. Schre, do you have any questions?

BY MR. SCHRE:

Q. Ms. Crel, how do you remember you were at Garrett Daniel's house on December 21st, which is well over three years from today?

A. Because we had been invited over there for Christmas. We had plans for Christmas Eve, Christmas Day, and we left Phoenix, Arizona, on the 26th for a ten day trip.

MR. SCHRE: I have no further questions, Judge.

MR. LEV: That ends the State's rebuttal case against the defendant, Robert Tenny.

THE COURT: Ladies and gentlemen, I hate to do this to you, I know you just sat down but there's a legal issue that we need to take up briefly. And my sense is the following. We will take this up, it will take us about 15 minutes to complete it, then you'll come back. We will settle the instructions with the attorneys, so it doesn't break up the closing arguments, rather than do it piecemeal this morning, and then this afternoon we would start closing arguments. So if you would give us 15 minutes, indulge us. You don't have to sit back in the jury room if you want to go outside, just be back here at ten after, if you would. Thank you.

(Whereupon, the following proceedings were held out of the presence of the jury:)

THE COURT: Mr. Lev, could you take some time and look at that.

MR. LEV: Well, here's my observation, if I may. I don't read this that the defendant can testify that Garrett Daniel said this, that, and the other. At most, and just accepting these cases and I'm not sure that the law supports it, but just accepting it because I didn't do any research against it, it would be, it seems to me, limited to Garrett Daniel told me to call. Period. Not that he said that I had to say blah, blah, blah, blah, blah. And I think the Court's made some observations and read some law on the subject already with regard to that portion.

It would be limited to Garrett Daniel told me to call the office at most, not anything else, because at all the rest of it would go for the fruit of the matter because, after all, in the context of this case, the whole purpose of what Mr. Tenny is suggesting in the call is, well, I said to Corri Crel that Mr. Daniel wouldn't be back but Garrett made me do it.

But he wants to go on to say that Garrett made me say that because he wanted to cover about his job interview which is, of course, the facts of the case are that the Schol manager there had been asked by Garrett Daniel whether he could go make some interview. I don't know that the interview was particularly scheduled for that day, but he had already asked him.

But, anyway, I think it's disingenuous to say that he's not offering it for the truth of the matter, and it certainly is hearsay to ask to have him testify Garrett Daniel made me say this, that, and the other. So, that's about the best I can do. I'm just going to have to defer to the Court reviewing this. I don't have that much to offer on a scholarly level.

THE COURT: Public Defender, do you want to add anything?

PUBLIC DEFENDER: If we allow Mr. Tenny to testify just that Garrett told him to call, I think that the jury may draw inferences from that, that, well, why did he tell him to call? Is it because he was doing something to him, or whatever. I just think that they may draw Impermissible inferences of why Garrett told him to call. I think it adds to the testimony. I think it completes the picture for the jury of why he would say there's been an accident and can't come back. I have nothing further.

THE COURT: I think it's a close question, but given the seriousness of the case, I am inclined to let at least Mr. Tenny testify that, in fact, Mr. Daniel told him that he should call. I think the details of it are hearsay, and in this case I don't think there is any indicia of reliability. But I do believe, as Mr. Schre pointed out, the defendant has the right to at least tell his story, albeit I don't think he can say anything of hearsay. So when the jury comes back, Mr. Schre, you can ask him why he made the call and he can testify that Garrett Daniel told him to make the call. I suppose if Mr. Lev wants to cross-examine him on that point, he can. And that's my ruling. You're not to go into anything concerning his immigration status. Mr. Schre, I think that goes without saying.

MR. SCHRE: When I recall him, I understand that. I want to make sure we have this clear. I can simply recall him to ask him why did he call Corri on that date, and I presume he's going to say I called her because Garrett told me to. Can I go any further than that?

THE COURT: No.

MR. SCHRE: One other thing I wanted to make sure of because I don't want to go around your ruling.

THE COURT: I wouldn't want you to either.

MR. SCHRE: I like to play it safe. We did have Kim Floy testify that on the 14th, or prior to the 14th, she had a telephone conversation with Mr. Daniel, and that Mr. Daniel had told her he had a job interview on Tuesday. We also had other people talk about Garrett's search for another job.

THE COURT: I wouldn't limit your argument if you want to submit it to the jury that, I mean, those are inferences that any attorney can make in closing argument.

MR. SCHRE: I just wanted to make sure.

THE COURT: Why don't we bring the jury in.

MR. LEV: Your Honor, if the defendant exceeds the scope of your ruling, I will just preadvise you, you don't have to say anything about it. I will motion to strike it.

(THE RECESS CONCLUDED, THE JURY RETURNED, AND THE PUBLIC DEFENDER RECALLED HIS DEFENDANT, ROBERT TENNY. HE ASKED WHY HE HAD CALLED CORRI CREL ON JANUARY 14, 2004, TO TELL HER THAT GARRETT DANIEL WAS IN AN ACCIDENT. TENNY REPLIED THAT GARRETT DANIEL TOLD HIM TO. THE PUBLIC DEFENDER HAD NO FURTHER QUESTIONS. NOW THE DISTRICT ATTORNEY AGAIN CROSS-EXAMINED THE DEFENDANT:)

BY MR. LEV:
Q. But, Mr. Tenny, you knew at that time Garrett Daniel was dead and couldn't have told you to, could he?
A. That is not true.

MR. LEV: Thank you.

THE COURT: You could step down, sir.

THE COURT: All right. Ladies and gentlemen, when you come back at 1:15, first I will read you the final instructions, then the attorney's will have an opportunity to make their closing arguments to you. Thank you very much.

AFTERNOON SESSION

THE COURT: The record will reflect the presence of counsel and the defendant. Late this morning the Court got a request for media coverage for the closing arguments. Mr. Schre, why don't you go ahead and tell me your position.

MR. SCHRE: Judge, I'm going to object to the cameras in the courtroom. I think that what they're going to tend to do is to distract the jury from their job, which is, to listen to the attorneys and to deliberate on the evidence. And I just think that the cameras are going to have a strong impact on the jurors while they're sitting out here in the courtroom during deliberations and when they're back in the jury room deliberating.

I think you can't get it out of their head that the case they're taking part in is going to be on television, and I think it's going to impact Mr. Tenny getting a fair trial. I'm going to ask that the Court preclude the cameras from the courtroom.

THE COURT: Mr. Lev, do you have a position?

MR. LEV: No objection.

THE COURT: Looking at the rule, that the Court should give due consideration to the privacy rights of witnesses and parties. I don't think the privacy rights of witnesses are going to be relevant here because we have had all the testimony. If the Court would grant permission, it would strictly forbid coverage of jurors in a manner that would permit recognition of the jurors by the public. Based upon that, the Court's going to permit, at least for the closing arguments in this case, the media coverage.

(Whereupon, the following proceedings were held in the presence of the jury:)

THE COURT: Ladies and gentlemen, before we get started, you can't help but notice that there is a camera now in the courtroom. Please don't be concerned with the camera. The media has a right to be in the courtroom, and the Court has permitted it for this part of the proceedings.

The court rules require that the proceedings be photographed in such a way that no juror can be photographed, just so you understand that. And please don't be concerned with the camera. Please pay attention to both the attorneys closing arguments rather than pay attention to the camera. I think that that's easy enough to do. That said, you have been provided with copies of the final instructions. What I am going to do is read to you all but the last page of the final instructions. After I read those to you, the attorneys are going to have an opportunity to make their final arguments to you, and then I will read the final page to you.

(AT THIS POINT THE JUDGE (THE COURT) READ VERY LENGTHY INSTRUCTIONS TO THE JURY, AGAIN, ABOUT THEIR DUTIES AND RESPONSIBILITIES, AND THAT TO AGREE TO A CONVICTION THEY MUST BE BEYOND A REASONABLE DOUBT. THEN HE CALLED UPON THE DISTRICT ATTORNEY TO MAKE HIS CLOSING ARGUMENT.)

MR. LEV: May it please the Court, defense counsel, ladies and gentlemen of the jury, you are the judges of the facts. That means that you have the power the same as the judge in this case, the difference being that you judge the facts.

Now, the most important element with regard to the case against Robert Tenny for the murder of Garrett Daniel is the element of second-degree murder, which you have heard in all of these instructions already. But just to reiterate, the crime of second-degree murder requires one of the following.

1. The defendant intentionally caused the death of another person; or

2 Either one, the defendant caused the death of another person by conduct which he knew would cause death or serious physical injury.

What is intent? Intentionally, or with intent to, means that a defendant's objective is to cause that result or engage in that conduct. Ten stab wounds equals the intent to kill. Garrett Daniel received ten stab wounds in his body. Cleaning up a crime scene equals intent to hide evidence. Taking a body 20 miles away to dump in the desert equals intent to conceal the body from discovery. Ordering a ticket to New York at 11:30 p.m. on the night of the murder, the day of the murder, January 14, 2004, for a flight out in the early morning hours of 7:30 a.m, thence to London and South Africa equals the intent to flee the crime.

Running away, hiding, or concealing evidence, as is covered by the instruction, that you may consider any evidence of defendant's running away, hiding or concealing evidence together with all the other evidence in the case.

Running away, hiding, or concealing evidence of a crime that's been committed does not itself prove guilt, but coupled with other evidence it does prove guilt. Ordering a plane flight the day of the murder and flying out to South Africa via New York and London without prior notice to anyone equals running away. Not telling anyone you're in South Africa for three months equals hiding.

Cleaning up a crime scene and disposing of the evidence, being the knife, mop and bucket used to clean up the blood, hiding the body in the desert under brush 20 miles to the north of their house, parking the car, which is Garrett Daniel's red Pontiac, which transported his body to the dump site, and then parking it a mere mile from their house within relatively easy walking distance equals concealing evidence. Ladies and gentlemen, Robert Tenny in this case needed time to flee the crime. Other acts, evidence of other acts, the acts of the defendant, has been admitted. You are not to consider this evidence for character, but you can consider the evidence as it relates to the defendant's motive, opportunity, intent, preparation, plan, knowledge, identity, or absence of mistake or accident. The defendant was seen to previously assault the victim with a knife on 12/21/03 by Corri Crel with her husband present. The defendant was viewed as the aggressor. This was done in front of them in the kitchen area in the victim and defendant's home.

In this case the defendant testified as to every move he made in moving from place to place, being South Africa to Canada, Canada to Hawaii, Hawaii to Indiana to Phoenix to New York, New York to London, and back to South Africa. He made every move after a careful consideration of the situation.

Age 18, South Africa to Canada. Escape military service. He gave you the reasons in his redirect. He did not move until the opportunity arose. He planned and prepared every major action like he planned these house renovations. By the way, when he moved from Canada, you know, he took several months to dispose of his property, sell things before he moved to Hawaii. He very carefully planned everything that he did.

When he devoted himself to a project, be it a house renovation in Indiana, he devoted himself fully. That's all he did. When he first, after he was met by Garrett Daniel in Hawaii, he moved to Indiana after Garrett went back to Indiana, renovated Garrett Daniel's house, totally devoted himself to it.

Apparently, only in Canada had he accumulated property by which he needed to plan ahead to dispose of it, which took him some months before he made that move. When he devoted himself to these activities, such as house renovation, it was to the exclusion of all other activities.

For example, he testified how his agency for the independently disabled, was his brainchild. It was a niche that he saw he could make money at. And he did it, he founded it, became executive director. The man, he was goal oriented wherever he went and whatever he did. And he was goal oriented to make as much money as he could. He thought ahead, he was very knowledgeable. For example, he was very knowledgeable with regard to house renovations. Back here in Phoenix when he followed Garrett down here, he devoted nine months exclusively to just remodeling that house to Bob Tenny's specifications and tastes. You saw these pictures. Very nice home, would you say? Nice pastel colors. Nice saltillo tile, nice white tile in the kitchen, nice pool, et cetera, in the sort of a pueblo look. He was very knowledgeable with regard to saltillo tile, for example, and knew how you need to glaze it, and how he talked about using chemicals, and so forth, in order to clean it. The very particularized thing about even when he talked about a piece of glass. Very, very particular kind of a person as he described himself in his knowledge and in how he prepared all of these things, neat and orderly.

Now, he testified there were rules, Bob Tenny's rules of the house. Now, ladies and gentlemen, that wasn't in the end Garrett Daniel's house. That was the House of Tenny, created by the very hands of Bob Tenny. He had put his time and his sweat and equity into that house to make it just the kind of house he wanted. Garrett Daniel was not allowed to break the Bob Tenny rules. For example, this is winter. Bougainvilleas usually die in the winter. They dry up. They can be cut back. Bougainvilleas are prolific, but Bob Tenny testified that Garrett Daniel on that particular day couldn't even take some clothes out to put in his car because it might harm the bougainvilleas which he so carefully nurtured. Garrett Daniel was not allowed to break a Bob Tenny rule. That took precedence over the person of Garrett Daniel, according to the testimony of Bob Tenny which you heard yesterday. Bob Tenny testified he did not like the fact that Garrett Daniel had been absent from the house for five days, that there were differences between them which were irreconcilable.

He knew that Garrett Daniel was making every attempt to break the relationship with him, to get away from him, to move away from the very house that originally was deeded to him, and that he subsequently put Bob Tenny on as a joint tenant, Garrett Daniel was trying to flee that house, his own house. But it was no longer his house. It was the House of Tenny.

Well, Bob Tenny couldn't understand that kind of conduct from Garrett Daniel, because Garrett Daniel was no longer obeying the rules. He wanted to abandon Bob Tenny. He wouldn't be willing to sell his half interest in that house or give his half interest in that house to Bob Tenny. And that was the House of Tenny. And he was leaving him in this relationship. So, by January 14, 2004, Bob Tenny knew that it was the usual habit of Garrett Daniel to come home for lunch. And this day he happened to come home for lunch as was his usual habit. And who was there to meet him? Who was there to meet him who normally didn't come to that house for lunch? Bob Tenny took that opportunity to murder Garrett Daniel then and there.

He had motive and he had the intent to kill. His anger was reflected in the ten stab wounds, far more than necessary to kill. There were several fatal wounds, according to Dr. Buch. This was no accident or mistake. He wanted Garrett Daniel dead because Garrett Daniel was leaving him for good. And, as I said, he wouldn't deed over his one half share in a joint tenancy deed, so there was no more use for Garrett Daniel in that relationship. And in order to end that relationship on his terms and perhaps in an effort to get his joint tenancy full ownership on the house, Bob Tenny murdered Garrett Daniel then and there shortly after 12 p.m. on January 14, 2004, at the House of Tenny. Circumstantial evidence is the proof of a fact or facts from which you may find another fact. The law makes no distinction between direct and circumstantial evidence. It is for you to determine the importance to be given to the evidence, regardless of whether it is direct or circumstantial.

Now, you may think that this is just a circumstantial evidence case. It is not. There is a great deal of direct evidence here, direct evidence that points the finger irrevocably and finally at the person of Robert Tenny, the defendant in this case, as the murderer of Garrett Daniel at the time and place I've stated. What is direct evidence, you may ask. What witnesses saw, heard, or otherwise observed an event. Allow me to outline. Eye witness Doris Giff at Schol Insurance Company, seeing Garrett Daniel leave at noon for lunch and never seeing him again. Eye witness Jackie Lesp seeing the defendant driving Garrett Daniel's red Pontiac, backing out of their property at 12:50 p.m. on January 14, 2004. Only Bob Tenny was in the car, not Garrett Daniel. And it went up the street. Eye witness Walter Weiss, the next-door neighbor, seeing Garrett Daniel's car during the noon hour. Also seeing the black Jaguar. But, thereafter, in the afternoon, never seeing the red Pontiac of Garrett Daniel, but seeing the black Jaguar remain parked where he saw it at the noon hour. In addition, Mr. Weiss overheard an argument coming from the backyard of the House of Tenny on January 14, 2004, between 12:00 and 1:00 p.m. Eye witness Weiss lived just next door. Sherry Charl, a customer of Bob Tenny's agency, saw the defendant at work the afternoon of January 14, 2004, at his office. She specifically saw that bright red Pontiac convertible parked in the spot that she knew Bob Tenny normally parked his black Jaguar. He even told her during their conference that he, Bob Tenny, had borrowed his roommate's car that day, that he was preoccupied. The witness who directly heard Bob Tenny call between 2:50 and 3:10 p.m, Corri Crel, and knowing Bob Tenny's voice, and Bob Tenny telling her that Garrett is not coming back with a very ominous tone, a tone of finality, and further to add that he had been in an accident and they were taking him to the hospital.

The defendant was also a direct witness. In both the letter to Lieutenant Camp in March of '04 and in his testimony yesterday, admitted this important fact. He was at the house on January 14, 2004, between 12:00 and 1:00 p.m. when Garrett Daniel showed up about noon. And, furthermore, that he saw Garrett Daniel alive for the last time at about 1:00 p.m. And, furthermore, that in the letter to Lieutenant Camp, that he last saw Garrett Daniel leaving for work at 1:00 p.m.

Inasmuch as there was blood all over the house per the expert testimony of Mr. Serp, the crime scene analyst, including a Luminol test which you saw, inasmuch as Garrett Daniel was never seen or heard from again following going home over the noon hour on January 14, 2004, inasmuch as the defendant admitted that he was there when Garrett Daniel came home, then I submit, Robert Tenny has admitted to you that he murdered Garrett Daniel then and there, and the admission is in conjunction with all of the evidence. It is both direct and circumstantial.

Proof of this fact is based upon proof of all the other facts, that it was known that Garrett Daniel was going to his home for lunch, that he left in his red Pontiac, that he arrived there. Not only Mr. Weiss saw him, but Robert Tenny admitted that he came in. And, finally, the defendant calling Corri Crel between 2:50 and 3:10 p.m. that same day stating that Garrett Daniel will not be back. If you take all of that together, the direct and circumstantial evidence, you have, ladies and gentlemen, the admission by Bob Tenny that he is the murderer of Garrett Daniel.

Circumstantial evidence, that would include Garrett's state of mind regarding whether he no longer could take the relationship between he and Robert Tenny, being so much that he had to be gone for apparently five days, Motel 6, Friday, Saturday. He tried to stay with Jackie Lesp but she made up excuses, and so he slept in his car. This is a man that's, supposedly that's his house, but it was the House of Tenny. Then on the 13th, Monday, Motel 6, him saying to Jackie Lesp on January 12th that he's leaving Bob Tenny, Garrett Daniel telling Corri in the afternoon of January 13, 2004, he was leaving Bob, staying away from the house all weekend, saying that he and Bob not getting along all goes to his state of mind.

Her observations that when Garrett came in, I think he came in part of the day on the 13th, and he came in later in the morning on the 14th, he looked terrible. He said he was moving out of the house leaving Bob. He was looking for an apartment.

Kimberly Floy saw Garrett Daniel at ten a.m. on 1/11/04, and that was with regard to the sewing machine, it was on the lawn even though they had it in the house for years. Quick as that machine got loaded, Garrett Daniel takes off in his car and he looked fearful. And he told her on January 10, 2004, he was staying at Motel 6 to get away from Bob and he was moving out of the house.

The defendant was seen in Garrett Daniel's red car at 12:50 p.m. driving off without Garrett Daniel. The car later is found with Garrett Daniel's blood in it when it was finally discovered by the police. That was the car used to transport Garrett Daniel's body to the desert. It was then parked a mile away or so, away from the house, and it was locked. It was not broken into, and there were no keys around. And there was mud on the wheel wells, and the underbody from the muddy road near where Garrett's body was dumped on the day that it rained, there was mud there. And the type of mud was a sticky clay type mud, very much stuck to the wheel wells of the red Pontiac and the underbody. Bob Tenny testified: Where did you stay the night before you left? He said, the house. So the red car is parked where? Not very far away when it was found.

Then you saw that there was blood all through the house, and some of the blood came back to DNA to Garrett Daniel. There was no forced entry in the house. There appeared to be swipe marks suggestive of an attempt to clean up the blood. No mop or bucket was found in the house, no bloody knife. Furthermore, blood in the car came back by DNA testing to Garrett Daniel.

These facts show the murder was committed in the house, and Garrett's car was used to transport the body to the desert 20 miles away. Bob Tenny was in the house at the time of death. Bob Tenny had the red car, was seen in the red car. That red car was used to transport the body.

Garrett's car was never seen again. The house was abandoned as far as Mr. Weiss saw after January 14, 2004. If Bob Tenny stayed in that house the night of January 14, 2004, like he said, Corri Crel called that place several times because she got this terrible news that Garrett Daniel wouldn't be back and there was an accident. She called the house, there was no answer.

Further circumstantial evidence: The body was dumped 20 miles away in a remote location and covered with brush. Bob Tenny testified that he traveled light with only a suitcase of clothes. Thereby he abandoned his house, his car, his position as executive director which he founded, to go to the land of opportunity, South Africa, where, of course, there was no job waiting, in which he got no job and where he went the limit on his American Express card and couldn't charge any more after a little bit of charges, including Avis Rent-A-Car in South Africa. And the only job that he testified he ever got was some short consulting job in Johannesburg.

Consider such things as the witness' ability and opportunity to observe, their manner and memory while testifying, any motive or prejudice the witness might have, or any inconsistent statements they may have made. Let's look at them briefly.

Sherry Charl, customer of the defendant saw him on the 14th, saw the red car there, heard him say he borrowed the roommate's car. Corri Crel saw the fight on December 21, 2003. She also saw that window had already been broken out. She also saw that Garrett Daniel had no cuts on him per the testimony of Tenny. And he told her he was leaving Bob Tenny.

Kim Floy. Garrett Daniel told her he was leaving Bob Tenny, that he stayed in the Motel 6. We have her observations of his fear, getting away on that day that the sewing machine was picked up. She remembers that he might have had an appointment later in the day on the 14th to see someone from the temp agency. He never kept that because he had been murdered over the noon hour.

And, furthermore, in the letter to Lieutenant Camp, the defendant specifically stated that he saw Garrett Daniel leave for work. Keep that in mind, that he saw Garrett Daniel leave for work at one p.m. Doris Giff saw Garrett Daniel leave for lunch and never saw him again. And the gist of the testimony was he was expected back from lunch at work, no matter what. Maybe he did have an appointment with an agency just to see if he could get some more work. But he was due back, as was his regular pattern, to work after lunch.

Jackie Lesp saw him on 1/12/04. Garrett told her he was leaving Bob. That's the woman he asked to stay in the house. She lives across the street. She sees Bob Tenny driving the red Pontiac, backing out of the driveway at 12:50 p.m. that day. And she never saw Garrett's car after that.

All of these witnesses, you should consider their credibility. How about the firefighter who found the body, Jerry Franz. He testified that during that period of time it was cold, rain, about how it had just a slight rain the day before the body was discovered on the 27th, that when he went to the body, it was covered with brush. Officer McCaul, he first saw the car after the apartment complex called and reported it on January 19th of '04. He went up, didn't see anything unusual, it was night. Since the door was locked and it didn't seem to be broken into or the column cracked, or any of that. It wasn't entered. Keep in mind, this is a trained police officer. Now, a trained police officer has a little bit more ability to see blood and see other things if they're looking for it than a civilian, such as Corri Crel or Jackie Lesp going in the house looking around to see if there's anything amiss, or something else they might find. When he went back, Officer McCaul specifically was instructed to look carefully, and he did. It was at night and he used his flashlight. And what did he see? Blood in the car, blood in the passenger seat shoulder, blood on the buckle, some kind of a shirt that had some blood on it in the back seat. He also noted at that time that there was mud on the wheel wells. Having run the plates, it came back to Garrett Daniel.

The guy who took over as executive director of the agency testified that it was in disarray, couldn't get it in the computer to do normal business, he had to get some kind of a specialist to get in there. Walter Weiss, the neighbor who made the observations about the car and heard the argument in the noon hour, Detective Bru who did the crime scene, impounded the evidence along with Jim Serp, who is an expert. With regard to credibility of witnesses, you should determine the credibility of all the witnesses.

Bob Tenny. This is the person who told you of all the effort and expense he went to with regard to his immigration status and visa. And you just heard the I.N.S. special agent testify to you that there was never any transaction, any record that he made any such applications, did anything about a visa. All the record showed was that he became a Canadian citizen. That allowed him to cross into the U.S. border without any visa or anything, and he was never heard from again.

Bob Tenny, who testified to you with regard to the glass being broken in the back specifically on December 28, 2003, whereas Corri Crel testified it was December 21, 2003. Bob Tenny testified to you that to justify and explain the blood in the house, that it came from Garrett Daniel's handling the glass and picking it up and then getting a bloody hand and somehow or another that spreads the blood into the house. Even though it was all over the house, goes out of his way to try to explain away this kind of forensic fact.

Bob Tenny who tells you that, well, he had reached his goals and he moved on. Never told a soul, not one customer, not any of the other board of directors, nobody, because he didn't just move away to resign, he was fleeing the murder.

Bob Tenny who testified to you that surely Sherry Charl must be wrong if she testified she saw him in the office that day with the red car.

Consider all of these things in making your assessment of the credibility of witnesses because that is the stuff of which you must decide a case, people testifying before you as well as forensic evidence. What about Dr. Buch? She went over all the wounds with regard to the autopsy, and she gave you an opinion as to the time of death. And it could have certainly been even passed January 14, 2004, with regard to the level of co-decomposition of the body in relation to the temperature, shade, and other factors.

Jim Serp, the crime scene analyst with regard to his expertise in seeing blood spatter, blood drops, doing the phenolphthalein presumptive test and the Luminol presumptive test.

Now, you have seen these photographs, you have seen them more than once, but I would like to just emphasize with regard to the Luminol test and the extent of the blood. Do you remember his sketch, and the blood went from the master bedroom through the front room, kitchen, back around the dining room. You remember that sketch. Keep in mind that Garrett Daniel was stabbed ten times: Heart, lungs. It's a lot of blood.

Ladies and gentlemen, what is your duty in this case? It's to determine the facts in the case, by determining what actually happened, by the evidence produced in this court. Now, what is the burden of proof of the State? As you heard, beyond a reasonable doubt. Hold me to that standard. However, proof beyond a reasonable doubt is proof that leaves you firmly convinced of the defendant's guilt. But there are very few things in this world that we know with absolute certainty, and in criminal cases the law does not require proof that overcomes every doubt. But if, based on your consideration of the evidence, you are firmly convinced that the defendant is guilty of the crime charged, you must find him guilty. On the other hand, if you think that the State has failed to produce that level of proof, then find him not guilty.

Let me make a few observations. What was Bob Tenny likely to gain by certain actions he took from and after the murder? Well, if he moved Garrett Daniel's car from the front of the house, it would seem that Garrett Daniel is no longer in the house. He needed time, you see, to flee the crime.

If he called Corri Crel at 2:50 or 3:10 p.m., and said Garrett will not be back, then nobody is going to go over to the house looking for him, because he further added, they took him to the hospital. It was crucial that nobody come looking for Garrett Daniel. His car is not there, he's not there. If he calls and says that at that time, nobody is going to think to look in the house, because the body is still there. Now, in order to cover himself after the murder, what is he going to do with the car? He takes it to work. Did he expect Sherry Charl? No. She just happened to drop in. But she made that observation. And then he had to dispose of the body and clean the place up.

Well, it's a 20 mile drive out to the 14th Street location. He had to swab up the place as best he could, dispose of the knife, the mop, the bucket. It takes time. And then when he completed business, that's when he arranged for the tickets, at 11:46 p.m. at night for a 7:30 a.m. flight. He needed time to flee the crime. And that time was obtained by him because nobody saw a body, nobody saw a car, nobody is going to come in the house. And then he can make his escape, his escape to South Africa. A very quick escape. And the only reasonable linkage between his escape to South Africa was the murder of Garrett Daniel shortly after noon on January 14, 2004. The evidence all points to, be it direct or circumstantial, to Robert Tenny.

Ladies and gentlemen, if you feel that the evidence is such that the State has proven its case beyond a reasonable doubt, then you must find the defendant, Robert Tenny, guilty of murder in the second degree of Garrett Daniel. And if the evidence has shown that a dangerous instrument, to wit, a knife, was used to cause the death of Garrett Daniel, you must return a verdict along with guilty of murder in the second degree of the allegation of dangerous, which would be included in your jury verdict form.

Now, ladies and gentlemen, the defense will have an opportunity to present their argument whereas I must have an opportunity to focus in on certain aspects of the defense close because the State has the burden of proof at all times beyond a reasonable doubt. And at this point you have not reached a decision. The defendant is still presumed innocent until you retire, until you retire to the jury room and you collectively decide this case, only then can you start making real decisions. So I ask you to withhold any decision on your part until all of this comes to pass. In the meantime, I thank you for your attention and patience in listening to my closing argument.

(NOW THE COURT CALLED FOR A BRIEF RECESS OF ABOUT
TEN MINUTES WHILE THE PUBLIC DEFENDER PREPARED HIS
EXHIBITS FOR HIS CLOSING ARGUMENT. THE COURT BADE HIM TO
PROCEED:)

MR. SCHRE: Thank you, Judge. Good afternoon, ladies and gentlemen of the jury.
Now it is the time for Robert Tenny's closing argument. And to start his closing
argument I'm going to give you a roadmap of where we're going to go in this closing
argument and what the evidence is going to be. And my roadmap is pretty simple.
It boils this case down into approximately four general categories. The first stop
on this map is the stop to a destination called reasonable doubt. I'm going explain
to you what a reasonable doubt is all about.

The second place that we're going to go is to three different time lines in this case.
The first time line and the second time line are the State's time lines. They are the
time lines of the alleged attack. And the second time line of the State is the alleged
attack, cleanup and departure.

And the final time line that I'm going to take you through is the time line of the
defense, that is, the time line of innocence. Once we are done with the time lines,
we're going to go into the second big area in this case and I'll categorize that or call
that stop on the roadmap the major issues area and the major characters area. We're
going to address the major issues in the case.

Our final destination as we go down this roadmap is going to be reasonable doubt
once again. The reason we're going to stop and start with reasonable doubt is because
reasonable doubt is one of the cornerstones of a free country that we live in. And
reasonable doubt is a standard that's been applied in criminal cases in this country
for over 200 years. And it's a standard of proof that separates our country from
other countries like, let's say France, where you are guilty until you prove yourself
innocent.

But it doesn't work that way in this country. There's a presumption of innocence.
And when Robert Tenny walked before you last week on the first day of this case,
he was presumed innocent, and it is the State's burden to prove him guilty. And
reasonable doubt is a very important standard because in criminal cases, unlike civil
cases, the standard is firmly convinced, no real possibility of innocence. That equals
guilt beyond a reasonable doubt.

Now, let me go through this chart a little more. The bottom ends of the standard
ladder is, I don't know one way other another. Some of you may be there at this
point in time. If you are there, then you're not up here, and the State hasn't met

their burden. Some of you may be at clear and convincing evidence, and that's not reasonable doubt. Now, I'd like to go into the first time line with you. And that time line I've called the attack event, according to the State. And basically what we have in that time line is a total time period of 35 minutes when this attack allegedly occurred. And the first point we go to on the time line is Garrett Daniel leaving work. And Doris Giff testified that Garrett left work somewhere after 12:00. Okay. We don't know the exact minute, but we know it was 12:00 or after, as lunch started at 12, or usually started at 12 at Garrett's work.

And the next point on the time line after Garrett leaves work is his drive home. We know from different witnesses that it takes some time to go from his office to the Tenny/Daniel home. I think Doris Giff said it takes five to seven minutes. Another witness said it takes ten to fifteen minutes. The bottom line is, it takes between five and fifteen minutes to go from Garrett's work to home.

And our next point on that time line, because lines have different points on them, is when Jackie Lesp sees the car leaving the Tenny/Daniel home at 12:50, and the car is the red Sunbird. And this point in the time line is going to intermingle with some other points I'm going to make later, but my argument to you is that when Jackie Lesp testified, she testified first upon direct examination from the prosecution pretty clearly that she did not see at 12:50 in the afternoon on January 14, 2004, she did not see who was driving the red Pontiac Sunbird. And she was asked quite a few questions about her ability to observe who was driving that Sunbird by the State. She didn't know. She didn't see their face. She couldn't tell who it was. She couldn't tell if it was Bob, she couldn't tell if it was Garrett. And then upon cross-examination, once again, Ms. Lesp was quite clear, that she could not see who was driving that Sunbird at 12:50 in the afternoon on January 14, 2004.

Under the State's theory of Garrett being stabbed ten times in this first time line, it wasn't just ten quick stabs. The State has showed you this map that was diagrammed and drawn by Mr. Serp where allegedly there's this trail of blood where Garrett is being followed around the house and he's being stabbed at different points in the house. And Mr. Serp could not tell you where the first point was of this alleged stabbing, but what he could tell you was there was blood in the bedroom, and there was blood in the living room, and there was blood in the kitchen, and there was blood in the bathroom, and there was blood on the hallway. And the State's theory or thesis in this case is that it wasn't just a bunch of stabs at one point, but that Garrett was running and being chased around this house and being stabbed. And that takes some time. And in this time line, we have a lot of different things that have to be done in 35 minutes, and if you buy into this 35 minute time line when the State says Garrett was murdered, there's some other problems.

Now, the State's arguing to you that Mr. Tenny went to work after 12:50, that he was the one that was driving the red Sunbird at that time, and that Sherry Charl saw him at work. Mr. Tenny has told you otherwise, and that's not how he remembered it.

But the State's thesis that on the 14th Mr. Tenny saw Ms. Charl at his work actually casts reasonable doubt on their theory that Mr. Daniel was killed in the 35 minute time line. And the reason it casts reasonable doubt is because if Bob Tenny went to work at 12:50, then prior to driving off at 12:50 he had to wash up, clean up, take a bath, change his clothes. And the reason for this is that Detective Bru describes the crime scene in his testimony as one of the bloodiest he had ever seen. And Mr. Serp describes the crime scene from all this alleged accurate Luminol testing as a very bloody crime scene. Detective McElva describes the crime scene as being bloody. And if somebody is running around a house and chasing another person and stabbing them ten times and there's blood drops and there's blood spatters and there's blood spray, what is going to happen is, this attacker who is stabbing is going to get blood on them and they're going to have to clean up that blood from their body, and they're going to have to clean up, they're going to have to change their clothes. And so that all is sucked into this 35 minute time line, and it's not reasonable. And that's my argument to you. The 35 minute time line, that we have some reasonable doubt there. And if Mr. Tenny actually did go into work and Ms. Charl saw him there, and we are talking about this 35 minute time frame that he had to clean up the area and he had to clean up, and the bottom line is what Ms. Charl said was she looked at him, she remembered he was wearing Dockers, she remembered he was wearing a button-up shirt, and she didn't say that he was dirty. She spent over an hour with him from about 2:30 to 3:40. His hair wasn't messed up, his clothes were not ripped, he had no blood on his pants, no blood on his shirt, anything to that affect. So that's the first time line in this case, the time line of attack which casts a reasonable doubt on the State's theory of the case.

Our second time line is the time line for the attack, the clean up and departure, according to the State. And when we get into that time line, we have it beginning at approximately, let's just give the State a few minutes and say it starts at 12:10 because Garrett Daniel drove home for lunch at 12:10 in the afternoon, and then it must end at 6:40 a.m. January 15, 2004, because that's when Mr. Tenny, clearly from the testimony of the United Airlines person, is in the airport actually doing his ticket purchase. And between 12:15 on the one day, and 6:40 the next day, we have approximately 18 hours and 28 minutes. And in between this time line we must have had the attack, the clean up, and the departure. What I'm going to do now is go through some of the stops on that time line, and some of them overlap with the State's first time line.

And the first point on the time line is Garrett leaving work about 12:10 to 12:15. The second point is, Garrett gets home. Bob and Garrett allegedly argue. And then, next, Garrett is chased around the house and he's stabbed ten times. After that, Bob has blood on him. Bob has to clean up this blood evidence that's allegedly on him. And we are talking once again about the blood, one of the bloodiest crime scenes Detective Bru had ever seen. And then Bob drives the red car away at 12:50. Well, is it reasonable to think that in that—that's our 35 minute time frame once again from the first time line—is it reasonable to think that this house was cleaned up in those 35 minutes, this supposed bloodiest, one of bloodiest crime scenes Detective Bru had ever seen? Was it cleaned up in those first 35 minutes? That is not reasonable. So after 12:50 Bob's driven the car away, he's not at the house. Instead, it's the State's theory he went to work. And at 2:50, in the afternoon, actually 2:30, Sherry Charl shows up at work and Bob isn't just walking in the door supposedly when she shows up at his office. Bob is there and he's got papers on his desk. It looks like he's working.

We believe what Sherry Charl said happened on January 14, 2004, between 2:30 in the afternoon and 3:40. If you had just committed a murder and were planning on getting out of the country and just fleeing from the scene of this alleged murder that you were alleged to have committed, why would you waste time discussing or arguing with someone over whether or not the company was liable for the heating bill of the residence or the heating problem or repairs with the residence. And, here's another thing. Why is Mr. Tenny, why is Robert going to drive Garrett Daniel's car to work if that's such an unusual thing for him to do? Why is he going to draw attention to himself by doing that when he can just put the car in the back, there's a place in the back to put the car where no one sees it. Why not drive his Jaguar? He usually drives his Jaguar.

But the next stop on the time line is, Bob has to go back to the house sometime after 3:40. That's the next point. The reason why is allegedly there's Garrett's body in the house, and Bob has to take care of that body. So somewhere after 3:40 Bob takes the time to drive back to the house, and supposedly in that time frame he does quite a few different things. He cleans up one of the bloodiest crime scenes that Detective Bru has ever seen. And, in addition to that, he, at 11:46 in the evening, calls and makes his reservations to fly to New York, and he calls United Airlines in Los Angeles. And just from common sense, when we are thinking about this time line, we know when we call up the airlines you don't snap your fingers and two seconds later you got your flight booked. You usually get a recording and you're on hold, and then someone comes on and they're looking through the computer, and then you have to give them your credit card information and you have to give them your name, and different things like that. And it takes a little bit. And that is done around 11 something in the evening on the 14th. And, also, there's another point in the time line during that whole time frame. Bob allegedly has to drag Garrett's body out of the house, and he has to go by the pool and down the walkway and into the carport and put that body, not in the front seat, but maneuver it in the back seat. And that takes some time. And then sometime after 11, unless before 11 he goes out when things are more visible, when roads are more traveled, he has to go out sometime after 11 and drive the 20 miles to Cave Creek.

Once again, there's more time on the time line at that point because it takes time to drive out there, and once he's out there he's got to take that body, and bodies are not light, and he has to pull it out of the car, pull it out of the back seat, and not just dump it once he gets out of the back seat, but that this body was actually dragged to the location.

And then there's some more time on that time line at that point because the body has to be camouflaged, or covered up, and you can see in the pictures how that body is covered up. It wasn't just dumped. Rather, there was somebody who took some time and they did cover it up. And then once this body is covered up, there's another point on the time line. Got to drive back the 20 miles to Phoenix, and what do you do there? Park the car, get out, and walk home a mile and a half, or something like that.

And that's another point on the time line, walking home. And once you're home, from the State's theory, clothes got to be packed up and shoved into suitcases, and then you're not going to the airport in a car that you own. So what do you have to do at this point on the time line? Call up and arrange for transportation to the airport. And once you arrange for that transportation to the airport, you have to wait for that transportation. That's a point on the time line.

And then one other thing I forgot as far as points go on the time line, the State's theory is that this house was cleaned up. Their theory about this Luminol testing, that it's admitted that there are inaccuracies in it, shows this big trail of blood and this big great clean up job from one of the bloodiest crime scenes Detective Bru had ever seen.

Part of the State's theory is there were no mops or buckets in the house. Therefore, mops and buckets had to be disposed of and rags and whatever was used to clean up this bloodiest crime scene. That's another point, waiting for the transportation, then the drive to the airport, 20, 30 minutes, something like that, to the airport. And the airport shuttle is taken, and different people get dropped off along the way. And into the airport, and carrying some luggage, and then waiting in line at an airport to buy a ticket at 6:40 in the morning. That's pretty much where the time line stops as to the State's theory of attack. Even though the plane that Mr. Tenny leaves on, and we do agree that he did leave on a plane on January 15, 2004, that plane doesn't leave until 7:35 in the morning.

The bottom line is, he had to be to the check-out window at 6:43. And what I submit to you is, with all the different acts that had to be done on January 14th, as far as the State's theory of attack, clean-up and departure go, there isn't enough time as far as reasonable doubt goes.

There's no dispute that Bob Tenny did not get to the airport with any red Sunbird or any Jaguar. If you just committed this murder and you're going to go to the airport and you're fleeing the country at a moment's notice, why aren't you just going to drive the Jaguar up to the front of the airport and just walk into the airport and leave that Jaguar there and fly off to New York City? Why are you going to take time to put your Jaguar in the back, which is just another little step on the time line. Why are you going to call an airport shuttle? Why aren't you going to abandon your Jaguar right there in the parking structure, walk out to the elevators, take them up to the ticket counter?

Now, what I am going to do next is, I'm going to go to the time line of innocence, and I have a chart here to assist me. This is the Tenny/Daniel time line of innocence and it starts on January 13, 2004. And I think it's pretty clear that Garrett Daniel was staying in a hotel at that time. It is pretty clear that both Robert and Garrett had decided to end their relationship. And Robert testified that during their Rose Bowl trip to California that he had talked with Garrett about ending the relationship and resigning from his agency. And Robert told you that he and Garrett were not getting along, really weren't communicating, so Garrett was staying in the Motel 6 on January 13th. There's a receipt in evidence to show that. But Robert also told you that it was Garrett's habit over the course of their relationship to stay in hotels from time to time, to go off, disappear from time to time where he wouldn't see him for days. I think you could gather from Robert's testimony that he really didn't approve of that. And that was a sore point in their relationship. The next stop which is also on the State's time line is, Daniel goes home for lunch at 12:15, and the next stop, some of these are things the State wants to establish, and they have established them. We are not really arguing with them. It's pretty clear around 12:15 Garrett Daniel went home for lunch. But here's something that's a problem with Daniel going home for lunch at 12:15, and Daniel leaving Mr. Tenny and hasn't been home for five days. And there's reasons why he's not going home, but if you're so bothered by going home and it's your habit, and everyone in the world, the people you work with, your lover, know that you go home for lunch pretty routinely, and you don't want to be anywhere near your lover, why are you going home for lunch at 12:15 to your house that you want to stay away from?

The next stop on the time line is January 15, 2004, Robert Tenny leaves on a plane for New York City. We are not denying that. Robert got up on the stand and told you, I left for New York City. He told you he left for New York City for three reasons, he had immigration problems which is clearly established by the evidence. He had personal problems with Garrett Daniel, which is clearly shown by the evidence. He had planned on leaving Garrett; Garrett had planned on leaving him, they weren't getting along, they weren't communicating. And he had some disappointments with work. He was supposed to be drawing $39,000, he worked pretty hard being the supervisor, being the real estate agent, the HUD liaison, the city liaison, and he wasn't getting as much money as the goals he set so he was frustrated. And when you put all these three things together, he's not really in this country legally, and he's contacted lawyers about his immigration problems and has not had any success.

Well, that leads into our immigration gentleman here today. He did say that you could come here under NAFTA, or be here under NAFTA working a little different than you could through just his immigration office. But there were three reasons that Robert left on January 15, 2004, when he left. As he told you and as we talked to you about in our opening statements, it wasn't unusual and it hasn't been unusual for Robert to get up and go. There's various things in life that have prodded him to leave a specific place.

He left South Africa not to avoid military service per se, it isn't a negative reason why he didn't want to go into the military. He didn't want to go into the military in a country that discriminated against homosexuals. They were all treated badly in the military. So he left. He didn't have much but the clothes on his back. When he went to Canada, his father was living there, his father wasn't living with his mother. That's the only person he knew in Canada, but he flew off to Canada and he didn't tell you about selling any or having any possessions, or how long an event he planned to go to Canada, that it was like months or years. And then when he was in Canada, and it is pretty clear that Robert is a hard-working, ambitious guy. He said he worked as an advertising executive, and you can determine if it sounds credible or not. When he had this brainchild to get disabled people homes and get them to rent homes, and different things like that, and be a construction supervisor and a city liaison, and different things like that. He didn't tell you that he had any contacts in Hawaii, that he had a job in Hawaii, that he even made plane reservations for Hawaii months in advance. He started selling off his stuff when his advertising executive job was going down the tubes. And once we get to Hawaii, Robert leaves suddenly again. And there's different reasons why you leave places. And he left Hawaii. He had a jet ski business he was working in, and he met Garrett Daniel and they connected. And he was going to go to Florida for a brief time, but all of a sudden he's off to Pittsburgh for a liaison with Garrett Daniel. The next thing you know, he never goes back to Hawaii, is in Indiana living with Garrett. He was there and didn't have any connections in Indiana, didn't know anyone besides Garrett, and he was just there working on houses, working on Garrett's house, doing some roofing because he had a relationship. And he was in Indiana for a relationship. And then he came to Phoenix for a relationship. He didn't know anybody, didn't have a job here in Phoenix. But that gets into the three things. The relationship pretty much deteriorates, it's gone. What keeps him in Phoenix? He didn't have a relationship any more. Should he be here? The only reason he came here was Garrett, so I'll leave again, I'll go back to South Africa, contact, visit relatives, I'll try to decide what I want to do with my life. But that gets us to the next stop on the time line. And this is a very important point on the time line. January 15, 2004, at 5:30 in the evening. And that's the approximate time of Corri and Jackie's search of the Tenny/Daniel home. This search is very, very important because it goes towards innocence. They went in the house looking for clues, and they looked in closets, they looked through drawers, and when I talk about their looking, their looking is not only on January 15, 2004, but the second time they go to the house, which is Wednesday, January 17, 2004, they were looking for clues where Garrett and Robert had gone, what might have happened to Garrett.

They noticed there was an expired passport, they noticed there was no address book, they noticed a phone number for some travel agency on a sticky. They found Mrs. Daniel's home phone number that first time. They noticed that clothes were missing on both times. But these two women from their testimony did a pretty thorough search of that house. They noticed a guitar was missing, Garrett's favorite guitar. They noticed a number of things. When you're noticing all those things, that means you're paying attention to details and you're looking.

And Mr. Lev has talked about the police noticed blood on a car because they're trained investigators. Well, the bottom line is, these women went into that house for one reason and one reason only. These women were suspicious of something. And when you're suspicious of something, you pay close attention to what you're looking at, the environment you're in.

And Jackie Lesp is a housekeeper and she had her own housekeeping business at one point in time. Housekeepers pay very close attention to dirt and filth, and different things like that. The bottom line is, Corri didn't see any blood and Jackie didn't see any blood. The both of those women when they get on the witness stand, they have biases. Witnesses come into this court with biases. Mr. Tenny has biases, we will concede that, because he's charged with a crime. Everyone has biases. Corri and Jackie have biases because they were friends of Garrett Daniel, and they were suspicious about something that happened to Garrett Daniel, and they bring their biases into the courtroom. And people with biases can possibly favor one side over the other and be more receptive to one side or the other. They say they weren't looking for any blood, but the bottom line is, they were looking very closely in that house and neither of them saw any blood, not on January 15, 2004, and not on January 17, 2004. And that was a house that was described by Detective Bru, or the crime scene, as one of bloodiest he had ever seen.

When we talk about that crime scene, you have seen some pictures of it and you have seen what can be obvious or not obvious. The bottom line, in one of those pictures that Mr. Lev has showed you, there's a doorknob and there is a big blotch of blood on that doorknob, and there are these blinds. And there is blood splatter all over the blind. And in those pictures you can see blood smears on the counters and there are blood drops on walls and there are blood drops and blood spatter on doors, and there is blood drops and blood spatter on the tile. And what that issue shows is that prior to the 17th of January, 2004, Garrett Daniel was not murdered in that house. And it's not our position and not our argument that a murder did not occur in that house. The blood evidence that they found makes it pretty clear that at some point in time Garrett Daniel was murdered in that house. It was not prior to January 17, 2004.

Now, when we are talking about this time line of innocence and Garrett Daniel being alive after January 17, 2004, the important issue that leads us down the road to reasonable doubt is January 15, 2004, at 7:35 in the morning. That's what we are interested in, was Garrett Daniel alive or dead at that time? What I submit to you is, Mr. Weiss is a key witness to show that Garrett Daniel was alive after January 15, 2004, at 5:30 in the evening.

If you remember, Mr. Weiss's testimony, when Garrett Daniel first moved into that house in 1998 or 1999, he had a little confrontation with Mr. Daniel. And that meeting was over the recyclable bins. It was over, Mr. Daniel was putting garbage bags in the recyclable bins. That's against the city code. He was tying it up a particular way, and Mr. Weiss confronted him and said it's against the city code. And Mr. Weiss remembered that, and on January 15, 2004, in the evening, Walter Weiss went out to those recyclable bins, and he went out there and there was nothing in them. They shared a recyclable bin. And then, as Mr. Weiss told you, January 16, 2004, in the evening he goes out to the shared recyclable bins and he notices a bag tied the way Garrett Daniel ties the bags. And that is evidence that on January 15th—after January 15, 2004, at 7:35 in the morning Garrett Daniel was still alive while Robert Tenny was on a plane to New York City. And that's evidence of innocence. And what it establishes is reasonable doubt for you that this man is guilty of the crime he's charged with.

Now, the State brought up some issues with Mr. Weiss. Well, could somebody else put trash in that recyclable bin. Well, yeah, someone could, but the bottom line is, why is somebody else going to? It's Walter Weiss' recyclable bin, and just putting trash in it out of the blue and tying it up in a bag the way Garrett Daniel particularly tied it up in the bag, why would somebody else be doing that? And you heard a lot of evidence about how neat and clean and particular Garrett Daniel was with the garbage bag, or with his house, or with his car, never have mud on his car, never leave the house untidy. And I ask you to think about these garbage bags.

Now, another important date, January 17, 2004. Mr. Robert Tenny sends a resignation letter to his agency. He sent the resignation letter that he typed up prior to leaving. He did have plans that week to leave. He was fed up with his relationship, his immigration status, and how things were going back at work, so he sent the letter to Jeff Kin who was on the Board of Directors. And he sent the letter to Jeff Kin and he also had told Garrett previously, I am leaving. I'm leaving because of my frustration with my life. I'm resigning.

Mr. Tenny was not chained to his agency. He didn't have a ball and chain that stuck him with it. It is legal in this country to walk away from a job any time you want, and simply because you walk away from a job does not mean you're guilty of a crime. It's legal in this country to leave a lover any time you want, and that doesn't mean you're guilty of a crime.

It's legal to pull up stakes and go away in this country any time you want, but Mr. Tenny did send his resignation letter. This resignation letter and the letter to Walter Weiss are very important because the State's position, one of their bits of evidence is Mr. Tenny was hiding. Well, if you're hiding, you don't let everyone know you're in New York City by sending a letter resigning from your job. If you're hiding, you don't send a letter to the neighbor asking them to feed the cat. Why would you send a letter to the neighbor asking them to feed the cat if you've committed a murder and you're hiding out from the law? Why would you even send a letter?

But now we take those two dates and the letters, and we put them next to the credit card transactions. And the bottom line is, everybody knows it's common sense that if you go into Macy's in New York City and charge something, your credit card receipt or bill will be sent to your house and it will say Macy's charge, New York City. And you're not hiding from anyone when you're using your credit card. That goes where the bills go, back to your house.

If you write a letter with a postmark from South Africa to the Sheriff's Department, Officer Tim Camp, the bottom line is, people are going to know that you're in South Africa. And if you call up someone's mother and talk to them, and Mr. Tenny said he called up to give his condolences, if you do that, the bottom line is people are going to know that you're still alive and that you're someplace.

So, the letters received on January 21st, the resignation letter and the cat letter are very important, and the State makes a big deal out of, he could have called Mr. Weiss. Well, Mr. Tenny did not have Mr. Weiss' phone number memorized. He told you that. And I think it's pretty common sense to think you may not have someone's phone number memorized, many of you may have plenty of friends, plenty of neighbors whose phone numbers you have written down at your house but you don't have their phone numbers memorized.

Now, the letter to Mr. Weiss, what does it show? Mr. Tenny said he was in a hurry, he wrote off a quick letter from New York. The purpose of his letter for the most part, he wanted the cat fed. When he left, he didn't know that Garrett Daniel wasn't going to be around. He said he called the house a couple of times and he didn't leave any messages on the voice mail, but he did hang up. And hang-ups sometimes show up on voice mails, or if you hang up before a certain number of rings they don't show up on voice mails. And Mr. Tenny wanted the cat fed. That was one of the purposes of his letter.

If you murdered someone and you go off to New York City or South Africa simply because you have murdered someone, why are you going to be concerned about feeding the cat and write a letter to feed the cat? It didn't make any sense that you do that.

Now, January 21, 2004, blood is found by Detective McElva in the Tenny/Daniel home. That date is significant because we do know from the blood in the home that Garrett Daniel was stabbed, was dead by January 21, 2004. In fact, I will submit to you that we are not contesting that there was blood in the car. There was clearly blood in the red Sunbird. The DNA tested it and it was blood.

We are not arguing to you that Mr. Daniel's body was not transported out to the desert in some other car. It's pretty clear that the amount of blood in that back seat and the amount of blood in that car, that body was transported out to the desert in the red Sunbird and we won't tell you anything differently.

Our argument to you is that the body was not transported out to the desert in the red Sunbird on January 14, 2004. Our argument is that sometime after January 15, 2004, at 7:35 in the morning, and sometime around January 19, 2004, when the car of Mr. Daniel is first spotted illegally parked by an apartment complex, our argument to you is, between that time frame but after Mr. Weiss checks the recyclables, Garrett Daniel was murdered in his own home in the Tenny/Daniel home. Well, we have another situation around the 17th or 18th of January, 2004. In that situation is Mr. Jeff Kin, because Mr. Tenny didn't come into work, Mr. Kin gets concerned and he contacts the police department. And officers go over to the home around the 18th. Our problem is, we don't know who those police officers are. We didn't have anyone who came in here and told you who those police officers are. This is one of our problems.

We do have a faulty investigation because there should have been a thorough search, and those police officers should have been found and they should have been questioned to tell you what they observed when they went out to the Tenny/Daniel home. And what they observed could have been, I submit to you, evidence of innocence, that there was no blood in there and Mr. Daniel was not murdered yet.

Now, March 3rd, 2004, goes down our time line. What prompted Mr. Tenny to make that phone call on that date? Well, he told you from his own words he did find out that Garrett Daniel had been murdered through his mother and his sister. They were told certain circumstances of the crime which were related to Mr. Tenny. And Mr. Tenny's knowledge of the crime comes from two things, that, as the State was trying to point out to you, he had knowledge of the crime, therefore he must have done it. Secondhand information from sister or mom in Canada who he contacted when he was in South Africa, and he's not incredibly close with his family, but he calls them every month or two months. They relate the information to him, but he also, once he found that out, contacted an attorney Mink to handle things for him here in the United States.

Think about this. With the great rains, isn't that blood going to be washed away and not stay in the ground? If that mud is so sticky when it's wet, Mr. Franz knows there was rain throughout the period but he just remembers particular dates, at any time on January 15, 16, 17, 18, 19, and 20, that car could have got the sticky mud on it from driving down the dirt road that was wet when Detective Bru showed up there on the 27th of January and the 28th. And if it was so wet when this body was supposedly dragged from the road to the location in the tumbleweeds, why wouldn't the body be full of sticky mud? I mean, it's dragged from the roadway. And so those are just some issues I wanted to bring up about the car. But there's no doubt that that's Garrett blood in the car, and there's no doubt that the car transported Garrett's body there.

Bob admitted that he drove the car that day sometime after Garrett came home, not at 12:50. That's when Garrett left. But he drove it to move it around to the back to load it up so my bougainvilleas would not get messed up, and that's how we did things in the house. Even though you're moving at a moment's notice, when you take care of a house you still don't want to get it messed up.

That's the first thing with the car. There's a second issue with the car. There's been a big issue made of Garrett keeping his car immaculate. They had Kim Floy testify to that, who also testified she's never even been inside of Garrett's car. They had Corri testify to it and Jackie, and different people, and they had these people testify about the condition of the car just before Garrett disappeared. But here's the bottom line. Mr. Franz testified, there were these great rains between the 13th and 14th of January. And he also says that pretty much throughout the later part of that month or the middle of that month it did rain, and that the roadway there is like a creek, it takes a while to dry. It's a dirt roadway although, where the body was at up in the brush, it doesn't stay as wet. It all drains down. And when you see the pictures from the 27th, and apparently there was some sprinkle on the 26th, Detective Bru remembers that because he watched the Super Bowl on the 26th. And he remembers the rain. Even from the pictures, it looks wet on the 26th. It looks like there was quite a bit of rain for quite a bit of time.

While we're talking about the rain, there's a problem with the State's theory of the case. Mr. Tenny testified there was a broken window and I came home, I didn't see how Garrett broke the window and I didn't see him cut himself or anything, even though I thought he cut himself. He's testified he didn't know how the blood got there. Garrett was cleaning up when he came home to the broken window, and he testified he did see Garrett cut his hand when they were putting the glass from the wheelbarrow out in the dumpster. So he was giving you explanations from the blood, from what he has observed or seen or known. If there were great rains on the 13th and 14th, the State has brought out all this evidence that out on the patio there's barefoot impressions in blood, and blood drops and blood drips, and a blood trail around the pool through the hallway up to the carport.

Let's get into the value of the house. One of the State's arguments is Robert Tenny's motive for allegedly committing this murder is to get the house. Garrett supposedly wasn't going to sign the house over to him and wasn't going to give up his interest in the house. The State brought in some documents from the recorder. After I had done my direct examination of Mr. Tenny and questioned him about the deeds and, oh, there's this deed from HUD I had, it's only worth $42,000. You're saying that you weren't going to get anything out of the house because it was appraised at 105 and you only owed 90.

But later on Mr. Tenny was shown that same packet presented by the State about his ownership interest in the house and about the deeds to the house, and you can look at that packet from the recorder's office and it's pretty clear that Mr. Tenny was correct in saying that more was owed on that house than the $42,000 on the original deed because there's a deed from the pool company in that packet, and that pool is a pretty nice pool with a waterfall, and it doesn't look like a cheap pool. It's a nice pool, and there was a deed on the house. So that goes towards that house not being worth much of anything and Robert Tenny not having as a motive to murder Garrett Daniel getting all that money out of that house, because there wasn't much to get out of that house after a broker's fee is paid. And, as Mr. Tenny told you, there wasn't much for the Jaguar either. The Jaguar was tied in with the house and refinanced with it.

Now, I've pretty much finished my final time line of innocence, and I'm going to go into my third stop on my roadmap. And that third stop is some of the major issues that have been raised and some of the witnesses. And I have mentioned some of these major issues and witnesses already on my time line, but I will start with one major issue.

The State's made this big, big production as far as the time of death occurring January 14, 2004. And one of the ways they are attempting to establish the death occurred on that date is through the car, the red Sunbird. And there are several ways they're trying to do that through the car. Robert is driving away. Robert heard all the testimony in this case. He's been sitting here. Right there.

The next major issue is time of death. And Dr. Buch did say that January 14, 2004, between 12:30 and 1:00, or 12:15 and 1:00 was not inconsistent with the time of death. When she was asked if it was consistent, she would not say that it was consistent with the time of death. Her wording was, it's not inconsistent with the time of death. She also said the 15th wasn't inconsistent with the time of death, and the 16th, the 17th, and the 18th, and the 19th. Dr. Buch's estimation was somewhere more than a week. She was basing her estimation for the most part on facts that were given to her that the body was killed on this date, this time, when it was about this weather, not that it was in a car as it possibly could have been for two or three days, not that it was in a heated house someplace else for two or three days. She was basing her estimate on a particular thing. And she didn't know the weather condition. She was given those weather conditions.

When we talk about the time of death, there were some issues raised about the odor of decay. Dr. Buch told you something about the odor of decay, maybe that you don't smell it when it's 40, or between 30 and 40 degrees when you're in the cooler like they have at the morgue. But the bottom line is, the hotter it gets, the greater the odor of decay gets. The longer the body is out there, the greater the odor of decay, the stronger. The State's theory of the case is the reason for that is odor of decay increases over time, weather conditions, heat. And you can use common sense to think about that. The 14th to the 27th is approximately two weeks. And as a hypothetical, I give to you that you could think about your own human experiences, you can, even in the cold refrigerator, have meat, and when it's been there two weeks it starts to smell if it's hamburger meat or something that's put in there to defrost. When things get wet, you cut the grass in January it's wet and cold, you smell a certain smell from the grass. And so there are things like time that can affect the odor of decay.

Just because it's cold outside doesn't mean that there is going to be no odor of decay. Mr. Franz didn't smell an odor of decay. Detective Bru could not remember smelling an odor of decay. He said maybe a little when he moved the body. And Dr. Buch didn't tell you that she smelled any odor of decay.

Now, Sherry Charl, and I already went through this once before on the time line of innocence. Mr. Tenny says he doesn't remember being there. Sherry gives a description of how he was there, and Mr. Tenny thinks Ms. Charl was incorrect, that the week before he was shuttling Garrett, and they did over the course of years and from time to time shuttle each other around because they were a couple, they did give each other rides to work, rides to different places, and he thinks around that time his car was in the shop.

And the State pointed out, hey, it's not on your American Express bill. And what he said is, hey, you got my check records, too. I believe I paid for it by check. And I have other credit cards. But Mr. Tenny believes it was the week before that she saw him there, and he remembered something about her coming in the week before with two money orders to pay her rent.

But Ms. Charl also told you, and this could affect her memory as far as the car goes, she told you that she did save newspaper clippings of this event because it's an event where she knew the characters. She knew Mr. Tenny and she heard about it in the newspaper, and she saw it on television, and she saw the car on television. And when she contacted the detectives and talked to them, that could influence what she thought she saw or perceived, either as far as the day goes or whose car was at the agency on the day that she was there.

As far as the State's argument that his leaving his job is evidence of guilt, Mr. Tenny told you he really didn't want to go to that board meeting. Garrett was on the board. He wanted to get out of here. He wanted to leave for three reasons: Immigration, relationship, and disappointment with the job, and didn't want to deal with the board and give them explanations.

Let's talk about Garrett's attitude, and what's going on with Garrett. Well, he's staying in hotels. They talk about, well, Garrett wouldn't leave at this time from the house because Garrett was so meticulous and timely, and everything else. But the bottom line is, on January 13, 2004, and supposedly Garrett had not seen Robert for quite sometime, he was staying away from him. And if you're not seeing someone and you're staying away from him, why are you going to be all frazzled?

On January 13, 2004, Garrett didn't go into work in the morning. He didn't come in until 1:00. And there was some note on his supervisor's desk with Comp time. And then on January 14, 2004, Garrett came into work at ten, and Ms. Crel talked about Garrett was talking about Robert and he's going to leave him, he's getting his apartment. But she also said that he lost his patience with her and he said something to her. There were other things going on with Garrett as far as being timely and everything else. He was described as coming into work on the 14th by Corri as looking disheveled, but on the 13th and 12th he didn't have anything to do with Robert and wasn't around him. Ms. Floy said that he sounded up-beat when she talked to him on the telephone on the 10th. So on the 10th he's up-beat, the 11th he's frazzled. As far as that goes, we know Garrett was also looking for a job. He hadn't had a raise in five years.

Kim Floy said when she talked to Garrett on the 10th, he told her that he had a job interview on Tuesday, January 14th. Now, there is this phone call to Corri that the State wants to use as evidence of guilt. And Robert told you he made that phone call, he didn't deny making that phone call. He didn't say, like, I didn't make that phone call. He told you, I made that phone call and I made that phone call because Garrett asked me to make that phone call. And Garrett asked him to call his work and say he wouldn't be coming in, making excuses. You can infer from the evidence, why did Garrett ask him to do that? Garrett could have been going to a ball game or, as he told Kim, he could have been going to a job interview. There's a lot of different reasons why Garrett could have told him to make that phone call. So there were a lot of things that were going into Garrett's attitude and how he was feeling, and one of them was, he was breaking up with Bob.

I'm going to briefly talk about Bob. And just, very briefly, I have already told you of the immigration problems that he testified to, personal problems, job disappointment, explanations as to why he was leaving. I missed something. That's the Luminol testing. The Luminol testing, Detective Serp admits that gives many false positives, cleaning detergents can give it, cleansers can give it, anything with iron can give false positives for Luminol testing. And Luminol testing with iron and false positives, you got to think about the substance they were testing: Saltillo tile. And saltillo tile comes from the earth, it's made of clay, and the earth is riddled with iron. So that's one problem with it.

And there's another explanation, Bob's explanation. He doesn't know what happened. He knows Garrett did cut himself and Corri said, I didn't see any cuts, and there's a dispute about the date. You can look in the American Express records that have been submitted into evidence, and it's very clear in the American Express records that on December 30, 2003, I believe at Home Depot or a glass shop, a piece of glass was purchased. And Corri could be wrong on the date, Bob could be wrong on the date, but the date is not a big issue.

How do you remember a date for an incident that happened well over two years ago as far as when did I purchase a window or not purchase a window, when you don't think about it for over two years? I covered Luminol testing. When we were talking about Luminol testing, Garrett could have cleaned up, it could be a false positive. Whoever committed the murder could have wiped stuff up to get the body in the car and not have blood all over. Whoever did commit this murder could have known Garrett, could have been a friend, it could have been a relative, it could have been someone that he met at Motel 6. There are many different explanations that go to reasonable doubt. The State's argument is a burglar wouldn't clean up. We don't know if it was someone that knew Garrett or didn't know Garrett. And that does sound rational that a burglar wouldn't clean up, but we also have false positives with Luminol testing.

My next issue is the State's economic approach to this case, and we have a crime scene full of evidence, the Tenny/Daniel home. We have a car that is just full of evidence, the red Sunbird. Let me give you an example of evidence. In the red Sunbird, the State has pointed out in their closing statement about this Motel 6 receipt that they showed you a slide of that has blood on it, that they propose to you was put in the trunk by someone. Well, first of all, if you hold something and stick it in the trunk, there could be fingerprints. They didn't tell you on this bloody piece of paper that they ever made any efforts to get fingerprints off a bloody piece of paper that was supposedly handled by the killer.

We live in an advanced society where you can feed fingerprints into computers and get matches on them, and that you can do DNA testing on all sorts of things. And what did we hear about the fingerprint testing on the car? We had the detective testify she wasn't there when the fingerprint testing on the car was done. She was there when the inventory was done, but if somebody was touching that belt buckle where there's blood on it and touching that seat where there's blood on it, there's a possibility of fingerprints. And this goes towards reasonable doubt. And if they're touching the trunk of a car, opening it up and closing it, and it's wet, you can get in the mud or the dirt or the whatever on the car, the fingerprints. It's an economic approach of not looking for other possible suspects.

Let's go further with this economical approach. You had your officers testifying, or the chemist testifying, we talked with the detectives, we make the final decision but we only test certain items of evidence. They make decisions on what to test and what not to test, but if you have someone charged with a crime like murder, you should test everything.

Charging someone with a crime like murder, and doing an investigation into the murder should not only be an investigation to find out who the true killer is, but it should be an investigation to find out who the killer isn't. It should be an innocence project. There should be DNA testing. Who cares if the lab is backlogged for a year. And if there's only two labs in the country that does DNA testing, we should go to that lab, not take an economical approach when someone is charged with murder, and do the proper DNA testing, do whatever we can to find out whether or not the person did it, whether or not there's any evidence. There's hair on the door, there's a hair on the floor, there's a hair in the blood. And when we talk about the economical approach and the State says no bucket, no mop found in the house, everything was disposed of, but there is a bucket. And Detective McElva told you that with the Squeegee, those were found in the garage, and there's a mop found in the garage. And if these are items supposedly that a mop and a bucket that Mr. Serp saw patterns that showed the blood was cleaned up, why aren't we testing that mop and that bucket?

Blood is water soluble. If the mop is dry, if they're left not touched, there should be blood in the mop. And the mop should be tested, and we should see that this Luminol testing is accurate, and we should see that the mop wasn't used to clean up the blood. And because they haven't done that, I submit to you that that's evidence of reasonable doubt and evidence of innocence.

One final point, or one of the points I'd like to make about the witnesses and this window incident, that's used as an attack on Robert's credibility. No cuts. Well, we did have slides shown to you of Mr. Daniel. And even at one point in the slides, as the State was questioning Dr. Buch about the stabs and injuries, they went down to the hand, and they had asked Dr. Buch if that was a stab, or something to that effect, and she said that was a scrape or something. I don't know what that is. And that's just something within this realm of reasonable doubt and the realm of possibility as maybe it was caused by Garrett getting cut on the window. There are many possibilities.

When we were speaking of Corri, the State brought up this motive as an issue saying because of motive Robert Tenny did this, and they talk about what they characterize as a knife waving incident. But what you got out of Corri is, she never saw a knife, she never heard the word "knife" yelled out. Corri heard Robert was in the kitchen, Garrett went in there, she heard an argument and Robert said, hey, I may have been arguing with him. I've spoken to him abrasively in the past, I may have raised my voice, but I don't remember an incident with a knife. And Corri said she heard some silverware in the drawer and Robert was cooking in the kitchen. Corri was there with her husband and they were being entertained, but she didn't see a knife. She never heard the word "knife," and she didn't run out of there and call the police and say officer, this man just used a knife against another man. But the State has characterized it as a knife assault. And you need to weigh the evidence, each and every bit of evidence, when you're making that determination in your jury room.

Now, the pictures I'm going to go over one last time. You got to look at the pictures, and some blood isn't obvious in them and some is incredibly obvious when you look at those pictures. And I don't remember if I mentioned this, but the clothing, the State tried to establish that January 14, 2004, was the date of death because the clothing of Garrett Daniel on that day when he left work or was seen by other people on that date, matched the clothing that was found at the scene where the body was found. There's just one problem with this. Robert testified Garrett had about six pairs of khaki pants, Dockers, whatever you want to call them. And Detective Redd testified that there were two pairs of those types of pants, tannish pants, found in the vehicle when it was searched. And Garrett had been characterized for his work outfit as pretty much wearing tan pants. In fact, Sherry Charl described Robert as wearing khaki Dockers on the day that she last saw him. So there's nothing unusual about khaki pants, and no one, when the State asked the questions, could tell you about a blue shirt that was found in the back. And Robert said it's not his shirt, and no one told you that this blue shirt covering up the blood was Robert's size. So that's just one issue to think about on the clothing.

They characterize Robert as a planner and a plotter, that he planned and plotted how he was going to fix up that house, the particular things he was going to do, and his brainchild of HID. And that he was precise in planning and plotting. Well, if he's so precise as being a planner and plotter, why is he going to be messy? The person alleged to have done this is messy, blood all over the place. If he's a planner and a plotter, why is he going to leave at the last moment? Why isn't he going to let everyone know months in advance, I'm leaving around this time. But there is no evidence that he's a planner or a plotter. And if that's his character, this is going to be done differently, and I submit to you he didn't do it.

Now, the State also talked about he went to South Africa and he only had a consulting job for a couple of months, but he talked to you about going to South Africa and trying in the real estate business for profit what he did here in Phoenix in making some money. He did say my intentions were not to stay in South Africa, I was going to visit some family, I wasn't sure what I was going to do with my life. But then he got into that real estate job there and he decided to stay. And things had changed in South Africa since he had left, because now when you're a homosexual your protected under the Constitution, sexual preference is protected in South Africa now unlike when he left when he was 18.

My reasonable doubt chart here shows three propositions. The first is, Robert murdered Garrett. And that's what the State would like you to believe. The second one is blank. The third one is Robert did not murder Garrett. And that's what I submit to you. That's what our side submits to you, and what you see in criminal cases is that the sides are usually at two great extremes.

And the way our law exists in this country is that it's set up to protect the innocent from being convicted when you, the jury, are not certain of what happened, when you're not convinced beyond a reasonable doubt. And this area of number two, this is the middle ground. And this area belongs to the defense. It's the realm of possibility. Unless you're up here, you can't convict Robert Tenny.

And there's some things that I will concede to you, move you up past our extreme of number three. You can argue that you go up this ladder up the chart because Robert left somewhat at the last moment, at the drop of a dime, and we have given you explanations as to why that's not completely out of his character. And he left his work, and it just happens around the time Garrett is last seen alive Robert did disappear and go to South Africa.

However, there's things that move you away from the State's extreme and down into this realm of possibility. And I've already talked about many of these things. I gave you my time line of innocence with Corri and Jackie. I gave you my time line of innocence that included Walter Weiss and his observations after 7:35 in the morning on January 15, 2004, meeting at the trash can on the 15th and the recyclable bin on the 16th.

There are some other things that move you down the extreme, down into this realm of uncertainty, that belongs to the defense. And there they are, lack of a confession, lack of any physical evidence whatsoever that links Robert Tenny to the murder of Garrett Daniel, lack of any eyewitnesses that link Robert Tenny to the murder of Garrett Daniel, lack of any weapon that links Robert Tenny to the murder of Garrett Daniel. And the State will argue to you they had knives in the kitchen, and so that's evidence because it was a single blade wound ten times to Garrett Daniel. However, as Robert's told you and what is common sense is, everybody has knives in their kitchen.

Down into the realm of uncertainty, the realm of possibility, lack of a time of death. Dr. Buch couldn't give you a time of death. Lack of thorough investigation. The State's economic approach to the case. And we have three years for them to do that thorough investigation. And I submit to you lack of a motive, because the point the State has raised about getting money from a house that didn't really have any money in it is not a valid point.

I'm done with my closing statement at this time. But since I don't get to talk to you again, I'm going to ask you to think about the two extremes. I'm going to ask you to think about this area that belongs to the defense, the realm of uncertainty, of probability.

Each of you will go back to the jury room and you will be at a different position on my reasonable doubt chart. And one of your jobs as jurors is to talk about the evidence, debate the evidence, and listen to the other jurors and deliberate. And some of you may change your mind during deliberation based on what the other jurors have told you. And that's okay. That's what happens in a jury room. Just because everyone else in the jury room thinks it but you're not convinced, you can't vote for guilty just because you watched them and you believe they're convinced, even if you're not convinced in your heart. And the bottom line is, you can't watch someone else go over that line. You got to do it yourself. And I am confident when you go back in that jury room and after you deliberate, you will find Robert Tenny not guilty. Thank you.

THE COURT: Ladies and gentlemen, I know I told you earlier that we would be done today, the case would go to the jury. Obviously, we are not. Mr. Lev still has an opportunity to make his rebuttal argument. I don't know how long it will take, but I would assume that it would take us past the 5:00 hour.

What I'm going to do is ask you to come back tomorrow at 10:30. At that time Mr. Lev will have an opportunity to make his rebuttal argument to you.

I'm sorry for any inconvenience this has caused you. Please don't hold it against either of the parties.

Court's at recess.

Day Six January 6, 2007
MORNING SESSION

(THE DISTRICT ATTORNEY BEGAN HIS REBUTTAL ARGUMENT BY FIRST APOLOGIZING IF IT RUNS FOR 45 MINUTES OR SO, AND THEN HE TRIED TO PUT THE CONCEPT OF REASONABLE DOUBT UNDER A DIFFERENT MICROSCOPE:)

MR. LEV: The American Justice System was established for protection of the entire community. If a defendant commits murder, he is to be held accountable.

The concept of reasonable doubt was not intended for a defendant to confuse the jury by concealing and hiding evidence, or misstating facts or providing false evidence, and then to use such tactics to escape accountability under the noxious cloud of confusion. That is not reasonable doubt.

Doubt, if any, must be based on reason, not some imaginary or semantically created illogic founded upon misrepresentation, contrary to evidence and common sense.

In this, as with any criminal trial, absolute certainty is not required. The only burden is to prove the defendant guilty. The defendant is already presumed innocent, and you have been so instructed. He's presumed innocent until such time as the State proves him guilty. The only purpose the law allows closing arguments by attorneys is to assist you in understanding the evidence. It is not a forum to misstate the evidence or misrepresent evidence, or confuse you for the purpose of sowing doubt.

But, as you are the judges of the facts, you are expected to be able to sort out the actual evidence produced in this court by witnesses and physical evidence from mere argument by attorneys. The defendant testified before you in this court. Your jury instruction is clear that you must evaluate the defendant's testimony the same as any other witness. In this regard, you are to judge the credibility of the defendant's testimony.

Here it is the defendant who is on trial for murder. He suddenly left Phoenix the early morning hours of January 15, 2004, which was soon after Garrett Daniel's death, or shall I put it this way, which was soon after Garrett Daniel was last seen with the defendant and heard at their home between 12:00 and 1:00 p.m. on January 14, 2004. The State contends that Garrett Daniel was murdered at that home, and the scene of the crime was altered by attempts to clean up the blood evidence. The body was concealed from discovery by dumping it in the desert 20 miles away under the cover of brush. And, in these regards, you may consider running away, hiding, and concealing evidence of a defendant after a crime has been committed. These facts, coupled with the other evidence, does in this case prove the guilt of the defendant.

Therefore, as the defendant is on trial for murder, and where there is evidence that he attempted to conceal the body from discovery, and that he made a sudden and unannounced departure in the early morning hours from Phoenix to another state and out of this jurisdiction, and he did that following the complete disappearance of Garrett Daniel who was last seen in the house between twelve and one p.m. with the defendant, Tenny, then I submit it is reasonable to conclude that Garrett Daniel was killed on January 14, 2004, between twelve and one p.m. by the defendant, Robert Tenny.

The actual evidence: Garrett Daniel came to his home on January 14, 2004, at 12:00 to 12:15 p.m. He came in his red Pontiac, and he parked it in the front of the house. He went into the house. He was never seen again. In the house at this time was defendant, Tenny. The situation between the two was that Garrett was attempting to get away from the defendant and was splitting up. The relationship was at an end. It became so tenuous in that last weekend that he actually lived away from what was his own home. The defendant had prior assaulted Garrett, and Garrett was the victim and the defendant was the aggressor, according to Corri Crel. Garrett was described as a mild and gentle person. The defendant, Tenny's, prior act around Christmas time, December 21, 2003, was viewed as aggressive.

Thus, when Garrett went into the house at that time on January 14, 2004, at about 12:15 p.m., I submit that the lamb went into the lion's den, and Garrett Daniel did not come out alive. He came out dead. And he was transported by defendant Tenny, who had Garrett's car, he had Garrett's car keys, and he drove the body to the desert and dumped it. Garrett's car was never broken into and it was found parked on the street relatively close to his home locked and secured. Garrett's blood at the crime scene had been wiped in an attempt to conceal the evidence. As the photos show, the concealment was adequate to the discernment of lay persons, such as Corri Crel, Jackie Lesp, and even a couple of the police that went in just to look around before the missing persons investigation really took off. These actions, moving Garrett's car at 12:50 p.m. from the front of the house witnessed by Jackie Lesp who admitted on the stand that she, in fact, saw defendant Tenny alone, dressed in his usual business attire, driving it away.

Defendant Tenny continued the keeping of Garrett Daniel's red car as seen by Sherry Charl at 2:30 p.m. the same day. The defendant's call to Corri at Garrett's place of employment at either 2:50 p.m. or 3:10 p.m. that same day, January 14th, when he said that Garrett won't be back, and further said that he got in an accident and they are taking him to the hospital before mopping up the blood in the residence, taking the body out in Garrett's car where only defendant Tenny had the keys, and taking the body to a remote site 20 miles north in the desert. Parking Garrett's car a mile away on a residential street, securing the car to look as though it was merely parked there, and as the officer saw both on the 19th and the 21st, it was locked and was secured and hadn't been broken into, you may conclude that Tenny had the keys.

The defendant ordering tickets at 11:46 p.m. on January 14th by phone to United Airlines, not to the local ticketing office but to the L.A. office, providing only a phone number and not an address, and then leaving on the first flight out the following morning to New York at 7:30 a.m., had to get to New York to get on British Airways to make the connection to South Africa via London. Hiding in South Africa on and after January 17, 2004, two continents away from the United States.

With regard to some of the evidence, this is a covered patio, and if it rained on the 14th the blood didn't wash away because the patio is covered, including the barefoot print. This continues, the covered patio, to the rear garage area, carport area. There is no evident blood. Just looking as a lay person, you're not going to see blood evident, including this knob, when you don't go through the door and touch the knob.

The counter, there's no blood evident. The wall where the spatter was against and including the blinds, there is no blood evident. And even outside, if you were out in the back patio, there is no blood particularly evident. It's already been described to you by Jim Serp and even Detective McElva that you have to be looking for it because these were small bloodstains.

Now, this was a bloody scene, according to Detective Brue and according to Jim Serp, because the Luminol showed how bloody it was. It was fairly well cleaned up. Bob Tenny had a lot of hours to do this after 3:50 p.m. and did a fairly decent job.

However, when you do the Luminol, you can see this was indeed a bloody scene because this was a vicious murder. Ten stab wounds, over and over and over into the body of Garrett Daniel.

(NOW THE DISTRICT ATTORNEY DESCRIBED AGAIN ALL THE PHOTOS SHOWING THE TRAIL OF BLOOD THROUGH THE HOUSE.)

MR. LEV: Now, a comment was made about the time it takes. How long does it take to do ten stab wounds. That's for you to decide. How long does it take to go in a small house, and undoubtedly it wasn't slow motion since Garrett Daniel was being stabbed, how long does it take to go through a small house, and then how long would it take to quickly wash up, throw on a pair of pants and a shirt, get in Garrett Daniel's car and, being Bob Tenny, drive off so that car is no longer there, to indicate perhaps Garrett Daniel might still be alive. How long does it take? It doesn't take 35 minutes, does it? Does it take 15 minutes? Twenty minutes? How long does it take to stab a person ten times? How long is a minute?

Starting now. Fifteen seconds. Thirty seconds. Forty-five seconds. One minute. Thirty-five times that. How far could I have gone in one minute? How much could Bob Tenny have done in up to 35 minutes? There was corroborating evidence 1/14/04 between twelve and one p.m. the defendant Tenny was at the house when Garrett arrived. 1/14/04, at 2:50 or 3:10 p.m. defendant Tenny called Corri and stated, Garrett won't be back, in a very ominous tone. 1/14/04 after Garrett left for lunch, he was never seen again. There is no historical evidence of his living existence thereafter.

1/14/04, Corri called the house after the call by defendant Tenny some time later in the day, and no one answered the phone.

1/14/04, the defendant ordered his ticket to New York at 11:46 p.m. by telephone.

1/15/04, when the defendant arrived at New York, he purchased the British Airways ticket.

1/17/04, the defendant sent two alibi letters without return addresses to Jeff Kin and to Walter Weiss.

The letter to Walter Weiss, who didn't have a key to the house, who didn't appear to be particularly close to these people, although he lived next door. The letter simply said, Walter, have gone to visit family for a while. His family, of course, lived in Canada. Have been trying to contact Garrett by phone. However, as you recall, the phone log showed no call by Bob Tenny. This was on the 17th.

The phone log, according to Detective McElva who listened to it, said on the 16th there was a hang up, which would have been 3:11 a.m. New York time. And we already know from the testimony of Bob Tenny that he indicated that wasn't the time, if he supposedly called. And the only other hang up was on January 25th of 2004 at 9:29 a.m. local time, also a hang up.

I submit to you there was no phone call by Tenny, and this letter was simply a process to create an alibi. He went on to say, after having said everything, trying to contact Garrett by phone. No answer. Please check on Louise, the cat, and tell Garrett to answer the phone. Bob.

Now, again, Mr. Weiss had no key and had no obligation or whatever to look after a cat who apparently was left unattended. No food; no water. With a sudden departure of the defendant, Robert Tenny.

Now, the other letter also postdated from New York with no return address on January 17, 2004, was directed to members of the board of his agency in care of Jeff Kin. This is all it said:

Resignation of executive director. Please accept this letter as my formal resignation from the Board of Directors. And this is the only reasons provided: A culmination of personal disappointments and economic stress leave me with no choice but to step aside. I do hope you find a replacement quickly so the good work can continue.

Sincerely, Bob Tenny.

Now, that was mailed, I submit, as an attempt to create a cover, an alibi.

January 27, 2004, Garrett's body was found in the desert.

January 29, 2004, the autopsy performed by Dr. Buch confirmed ten stab wounds, three of which were fatal.

On January 14, 2004, it was a Tuesday. As I described to you before with regard to the concept of time to kill, how long would that take? And to wash and change clothes. Between 12:15 p.m. and the time he got in Garrett's car at 12:50 was 35 minutes. I suggest that's way in excess time to do these deeds.

12:50 p.m. the defendant was seen driving away in Garrett Daniel's car without Garrett. And it was Garrett who drove it there. January 15, 2004, Wednesday, Corri came to their house. She didn't go in. She came with her husband, walked around, saw no one there. Also, Walter Weiss noted that there was no activity or lights on after 1/15 of '04. On January 17, 2004, it was a Friday. Corri and Jackie Lesp did go into the house that day. Some items were out of place, there were hangers piled up.

January 20, 2004, was a Monday. Again, Corri and Jackie Lesp went into the house. There were no changes from January 17, 2004. Other dates were given to you yesterday, these dates were inaccurate. These were the actual dates. The missing persons investigation commenced on or about January 21, 2004, and continued on until January 27, 2004, when Garrett Daniel's body was found in the desert.

Initially when the police officers went into the house, they noted nothing particularly obvious. Detective McElva then went into the house and he began looking as an experienced detective of some 20 plus years with the department, and looking closely. And he did see some blood evidence, so he drew a search warrant.

Ladies and gentlemen, it was argued to you yesterday that with regard to Dr. Buch's estimation of the time of death, there's no contest that the murder occurred at the house, and there's no contest that Garrett Daniel's car was used to transport the body in the desert. So it was argued to you that as long as Bob Tenny was gone from the scene, which was by the 15th, then it was okay for you to consider that the murder had occurred after January 16, 2004. That was the logic presented, and what I would call a theory. And, by the way, with regard to theories, I care for evidence. That's what you are to decide.

He said one U.S. visa to work was temporary. We already know that's false testimony by the special agent. He had never done any such thing. Then he says, government budgets were cut and personal income reduced. No evidence, no testimony by any of the agency's Board of Directors who were here.

And then, finally, Garrett Daniel and my personal and professional relationship was strained. I don't know what he means by professional relationship to Garrett. But

I suggest to you that wasn't the only reason that he left Phoenix suddenly. It was certainly strained since, I submit, he just murdered Garrett Daniel.

Again, Bob Tenny said he had to renew this visa yearly, this work visa, and he went to Canada to do it. No record. The special agent of the U.S. Department of Immigration and Naturalization Service testified before you just a couple of days ago and stated that Tenny never applied for any work visa. There's no record whatsoever. As a matter of fact, based thereon and on the defendant's comment yesterday, Tenny was in the United States illegally. Therefore, there was no expense that he had to incur with immigration attorneys. And he produced no evidence, even though it was argued to you that he had to go up to Canada and do this NAFTA stamp on his passport. Not a bit of evidence. Just a statement. Just because Bob Tenny says it, do you have to believe it? You don't have to believe the testimony of witnesses that are not credible.

And that is the instruction to you. And the defendant's testimony is no different from any other witness. Therefore, the entire immigration excuse was false. The entire factor of leaving due to not making enough money or goals of the board members not sufficiently participating was not proved. Government budgets cut and personal income reduced, not proved. Take those away and what do you have? The only reason that he left the United States suddenly was the irreconcilable differences that he had with Garrett Daniel, and they were irreconcilable because once he murdered Garrett Daniel, you could not reconcile any difference.

He also tried to explain away the blood evidence in the house by suggesting that on December 28, 2003, Garrett Daniel broke the window and then picked up the glass and then spattered blood through the house. Well, as a matter of fact, that's contrary to the observations of Corri Crel who stated specifically that she knew exactly the date she went over there when she was invited by them, it was December 21, 2003. It was before Christmas. The window had already been broken and she saw no cuts whatsoever on the hands of Garrett Daniel.

The Jaguar that he claimed was in service, he spent $504.34 on December 13, 2003. Now, I remember that he threw back to me, well, you have my checking account. Well, Mr. Tenny, I don't have to do anything for you. It wasn't in service. It had been fixed a long time ago.

Now, let's continue on. There was a comment made about glass being purchased as though it's for the back window on December 30, 2003. Guess what, folks? I don't know what the glass was for, but it was in Indio, California. And it was for $113.47. I don't know what glass was purchased there, but then it goes on, a charge in Temple City, and then at San Diego. Do you remember the trip for New Years?

So one has to be careful to separate out the actual evidence from any arguments made in an attempt to confuse you.

Now, to go on, the plane tickets which he actually purchased from United Airlines on 1/15 of '04 through the agency's American Express card, which he claimed in testimony that he knew he was going to leave, and yet he takes the corporate card, makes personal expenses, the agency would be the primary obligor, and that would be to whom the bills would be sent or payment expected.

Is this the act of a responsible person to which and who should be worthy of your belief in his testimony and denying his guilt on the repeated questions of whether he killed Garrett Daniel? His inconsistent statements that have absolutely no backing in evidence. The only evidence presented is defendant's denial that he murdered the victim. Do you believe him? You have got to remember that Garrett Daniel came to that house at about 12:15 p.m. on the 14th. Bob Tenny was inside. He came in his car. Garrett Daniel was never seen again.

But the defendant, Tenny, then drove that red car out, and he continued his life. But Garrett Daniel didn't. And you know that he was murdered because his body was found in the desert on the 27th stabbed to death.

Again, Robert Tenny's testimony must be judged like any other witness. You must assess his credibility. Do you believe him. Your duty is to determine what the facts are in the case by determining what actually happened. And you determine this by evidence produced in court. And that's only the testimony of the witnesses and exhibits introduced in court.

Now, proof beyond a reasonable doubt should leave you firmly convinced of the defendant's guilt. There are very few things in this world that we know with absolute certainty, and in criminal cases the law does not require proof that overcomes every doubt. If, based on your consideration of the evidence, you are firmly convinced that the defendant is guilty of the crime charged, you must find him guilty. Thank you.

(NOW THE COURT FURTHER INSTRUCTED THE JURY AS TO THEIR OBLIGATIONS AND DUTIES TO CONSIDER ONLY THE EVIDENCE—AND THIS CONTINUED FOR QUITE A WHILE. THEY WERE INSTRUCTED TO ELECT ONE MEMBER OF THE JURY AS THE "PRESIDING JUROR" OR "FOREPERSON" WHO WOULD PRESENT THE FINAL VERDICT IN COURT. A BAILIFF WAS SWORN IN TO SUPERVISE THE JURY, AND THEY LEFT THE COURTROOM TO DELIBERATE. IN A SURPRISINGLY SHORT PERIOD OF TIME AFTER THE LUNCHEON

RECESS, THE JURY HAD REACHED A UNANIMOUS VERDICT. THE COURT WAS QUICKLY CALLED BACK IN SESSION:)

THE COURT: The record will reflect the presence of the jury, counsel, and the defendant. Has the jury reached a verdict?

MR. WALK: Yes, we have.

THE COURT: Mr. Walk, will you hand all forms of verdict to the bailiff. The clerk may now read and record the verdict.

THE CLERK: We, the jury, duly empanelled and sworn in the above entitled action, upon our oaths, do find the defendant guilty of second-degree murder. We further do find this offense to be a dangerous offense.

Foreperson, Roger Walk.

Is this your true verdict, so say you one and all?

THE JURY PANEL: Yes.

THE COURT: Mr. Schre, do you wish to poll the jury?

MR. SCHRE: Yes, I do, Judge.

THE COURT: Members of the Jury, you will each be asked a question by the clerk. Simply answer it yes or no.

(NOW THE CLERK OF THE COURT ASKED EACH OF THE EIGHT JURY MEMBERS IF THIS WAS THEIR OWN VERDICT. THEY ALL ANSWERED "YES.")

THE COURT: Ladies and gentlemen of the jury, I want to thank you for giving up two weeks of your lives to participate in this. I hope you found this an interesting experience, and I know you know it was an important function, important experience that you just had.

(Whereupon, the following proceedings were held out of the presence of the jury:)

THE COURT: Mr. Schre, my inclination is to set sentencing more than 30 days out, given the gravity of the defense and the range of sentencing, so each party can either put on aggravation or mitigation, whatever they see fit. Is any date, for example in March, good with you?

MR. SCHRE: Any date in March is fine, Judge. I don't have much in March at this point.

THE COURT: How about March 2nd, does that work for both of you?

MR. LEV: Okay.

MR. SCHRE: The 2nd is fine, Judge.

THE COURT: How about if we set this at 9:00 rather than on the 8:30 calendar.

MR. LEV: That's fine, Judge. If I'm in trial, I will ask the other judge to call you.

THE COURT: The defendant is remanded to custody pending sentence. There will be no bond situation.

Court's at recess.

MR. SCHRE: There is one thing for the sentencing date of March 2nd, Judge. If there's going to be either aggravation witnesses or mitigation witnesses, can we have a deadline to list those witnesses and what documents might be used?

THE COURT: How much time, ten days before—

MR. SCHRE: That sounds fine with me.

THE COURT: Can you do that, Mr. Lev?

MR. LEV: Yes, Your Honor.

THE COURT: We will just say that any witnesses that are going to appear or speak at the aggravation/mitigation should be disclosed within ten days. My usual practice is to just have them speak rather than have them sworn in.

If either party wants to cross-examine and have them sworn in, I'll accommodate them.

MR. LEV: Does that include witnesses over and above victims, if any witnesses were to appear?

THE COURT: Yes. But I would imagine, Mr. Schre, if the victims wish to say something, you're not going to put them on the stand and cross-examine them.

MR. SCHRE: I don't think so, Judge.

THE COURT: All right. Thank you.

(Whereupon, the matter was concluded.)

SENTENCING, MARCH 2, 2007
MORNING SESSION

(THE JUDGE, THE DISTRICT ATTORNEY AND THE PUBLIC DEFENDER MET IN COURT AT 9:00 A.M., ALONG WITH ROBERT TENNY AND A NUMBER OF WITNESSES TO DISCUSS THINGS THAT DIDN'T GET INTO THE ACTUAL TRIAL—TO TRY TO SWAY THE JUDGE'S FINAL SENTENCING DECISION. NONE OF THE WITNESSES WERE TO BE SWORN IN, AND IT WAS AN INFORMAL, CASUAL HEARING. THE FIRST WITNESS CALLED BY THE STATE WAS JACKIE LESP, THE NEIGHBOR OF GARRETT DANIEL AND ROBERT TENNY, WHO TESTIFIED THAT SHE OFTEN SAW ROBERT TENNY ATTACK GARRETT DANIEL, ONCE WITH A STEEL PIPE, ANOTHER TIME WITH A HUGE BOULDER, ANOTHER TIME WITH A LAMP. ONCE WHEN SHE WENT INTO THEIR HOUSE TO FIND OUT WHAT THE RUCKUS WAS, ROBERT TENNY CAME TOWARD HER WITH A LARGE LETTER OPENER, WANTING TO STAB HER. UNDER CROSS-EXAMINATION SHE SAID THAT ROBERT TENNY DRANK A LOT, AND WHEN HE DID, HE WOULD JUST "LOSE IT" AND ACT STRANGELY—NOT MAKE ANY SENSE.

THE NEXT WITNESS, CORRI CREL, SAID SHE OBSERVED MANY CUTS AND BRUISES ON GARRETT DANIEL. IN ONE INSTANCE IN THE TENNY/DANIEL HOME, SHE HEARD BOTH MEN ARGUING, AND TENNY PULLED OUT A KNIFE AND SAID, "ONE OF THESE DAYS I'M GOING TO PUT IT THROUGH YOU." ANOTHER TIME AFTER THE TWO LOVERS QUARRELED, ROBERT TENNY HAD GARRETT DANIEL'S PET DOG PUT TO SLEEP.

THE NEXT WITNESS, DORIS GIFF, WHO WORKED WITH GARRETT DANIEL FOR ABOUT FIVE YEARS, SAID SHE OFTEN HAD LUNCH WITH HIM, AND HE ADMITTED THAT HE HAD BEEN BEATEN UP AND BRUISED 40 OR 50 TIMES OVER THE YEARS BY ROBERT TENNY.

THE NEXT WITNESS WAS DETECTIVE BRU WHO MENTIONED THREE PRIOR POLICE DEPARTMENT REPORTS OF AGGRAVATED ASSAULT BY ROBERT TENNY ON GARRETT DANIEL, ONE OF WHICH WAS SO SEVERE THAT GARRETT REQUIRED HOSPITALIZATION AND HAD TO HAVE HIS SPLEEN REMOVED. THAT PARTICULAR FIGHT WAS OVER A DISPUTE WHEN ROBERT TENNY INSISTED ON BEING A JOINT TENANT ON THE REAL ESTATE PROPERTY OWNED BY GARRETT DANIEL—THEIR HOUSE. GARRETT FINALLY RELENTED AND SIGNED OVER HALF OF HIS PROPERTY TO ROBERT TENNY.

IN ANOTHER ALTERCATION, GARRETT DANIEL HAD RECEIVED MEDICAL CARE FOR 10 STITCHES TO HIS HEAD, A CONCUSSION, AND THREE BROKEN RIBS IN FEBRUARY, 2002, BUT THE TWO MEN SUBSEQUENTLY RECONCILED. AFTER MORE DISCUSSIONS ABOUT OTHER MISTREATMENTS, THE DISTRICT ATTORNEY CONCLUDED HIS ARGUMENTS WITH:)

MR. LEV: Bob Tenny had a habit of extreme violence against Garrett Daniel, and this time he took it to the ultimate end and stabbed him multiple times and killed him, which is also consistent with what he did before. It wasn't that Bob Tenny just hit Garrett Daniel. It was repeated blows, constant and horrific type of injuries, and unrelenting in his aggressive, dominant role.

He's been convicted of second-degree murder, and the aggravated term is 22 years. And I stand here and urge the Court to give him 22 years. And I believe that all of the statements by all of the interested parties would be in agreement. I leave it up to the Court's discretion. Thank you.

THE COURT: Mr. Schre, how would you like to proceed? Do I take it you're not going to call any witnesses?

MR. SCHRE: Mr. Tenny would like to address the Court first.

THE COURT: Before you make your statement?

MR. SCHRE: Yes, Judge.

THE COURT: All right. Mr. Tenny?

THE DEFENDANT: Your Honor, I was not prepared for the witnesses who came today, and I had no idea that we would be discussing violence between Garrett Daniel and myself. I think it's very unfair for the Court to hear everything through the eyes of other people and not hear it through the eyes of either Garrett or myself.

THE COURT: How is the Court going to hear it from Garrett?

THE DEFENDANT: Well, they have never interviewed me, Your Honor.

THE COURT: How is Mr. Daniel going to testify?

THE DEFENDANT: He's not here to do that.

THE COURT: Please proceed.

THE DEFENDANT: If Garrett were in this courtroom, he would put a stop to a great deal of this, and he would also tell you that I didn't kill him. And he would find some other story to tell the Court about how he actually died.

As far as that's concerned, if you'll permit me to read a nine page letter that I have already written.

THE COURT: I have read the letter.

THE DEFENDANT: I'd like the Court and all the witnesses to hear some of that.

THE COURT: That's fine.

THE DEFENDANT: Garrett has been painted and portrayed by prosecutor Lev as a meek and mild person, and I have been portrayed as a violent individual who is constantly being horrific with Garrett Daniel, and it's not true.

Detective Bru has never spoken to me. I have never met that man. Nobody has come to me here in jail, I'm in jail a year, to discuss this case at all. I have never been interviewed as to violence issues.

I will admit to the Court that there were three or four instances along the way that Garrett and I came to blows. We came to confrontations. We had fights. We did not have 50 or 60 fights, as one of the witnesses said. That's impossible over a six year relationship. Garrett would long since have left. She talks about him having slept in motels, and I would like to add he also slept at steam baths, he also had outside relationships, he had outside affairs. His reports to his friends and family and staff have been utilized and construed as strictly Bob's violence, when indeed many of

Garrett's disheveled appearances at the office and conversations with respect to me and our relationship is because he was having an affair, or he was having something else in his life at Motel 6 or at a hotel.

Violence was a two-way street with Garrett. When I met Garrett, he introduced me to alcohol. Garrett was a drinker, and we started to drink heavily. He drank spirits, and that had a lot to do with our relationship.

I was hospitalized. Garrett's mother took me to a hospital, that the prosecution would not address to the Court. They have never interviewed me. They don't know that my front teeth are missing as a result of a confrontation with Garrett Daniel. This was a violent relationship on occasion, but it was a two-way street. It wasn't just Bob the aggressor and Garrett the meek and mild.

The only reports that had been brought to the Court are from Garrett's friends and Garrett's relatives and Garrett's association. My defense has not brought anybody. We haven't brought up my hospitalization and the many incidences where I was a victim of Garrett's alcoholic abuse, physical alcoholic abuse.

Ms. Corri Crel talks about a dog and how I apparently had been violent with Garrett on the night of Sasha's death. Well, I'll tell you something. Garrett sat on that sofa while Sasha was going through the throws of death. She was my kid. She was with me for 16 years, and I had to carry that poor dog to the hospital in the middle of the night and put her away. And Garrett sat on that sofa and he folded his arms and he wouldn't do a thing to help me. That's the kind of person Garrett Daniel was. That's the kind of abuse.

This spleen incident is nonsense. I had nothing to do with Garrett's spleen. There was an incident around that time, and I will admit that we came to blows, but it was to do with a deed on this property.

Bru says that I threatened Garrett. Garrett seduced me into coming into the city. Garrett brought me to Phoenix. He brought me to Phoenix on the promise that we would purchase a property. We purchased property. We put it in his name. I worked free, sweat equity for three months on that property.

And the deal was, you give me half the house and I'll work for it and we will build equity in the house and we will start a life together here. And that's how we got the Jaguar, too. What they don't want to know about was that Garrett would take off on the steam baths and go sleep there on nights like that. And that's violence for you, it's not just Bob beating up Garrett. There were confrontations and there were relationship issues that transpired.

At no time in the previous three years since the tragic killing of Garrett Daniel have I ever been questioned, interviewed or interrogated by the police detectives. My appearance in court once charged for second-degree murder of Garrett Daniel was the only direct contact the District Attorney or the investigating officers have ever had with myself.

The Court must record my statement now. I did not murder Garrett Daniel, nor was I involved in his disappearance from his regular work, nor his death.

I have been wrongfully charged of this crime and wrongfully convicted. A verdict of guilty of the described crime has been handed down by a jury. I must appeal this verdict and sentence that you, Your Honor, will hand down in this court today. I'm appealing the conviction.

Much evidence was presented by the District Attorney's office, and also much evidence was not presented by the District Attorney's office. My defense attorney, if you will permit me, Mr. Schre, also failed to bring to light many questions, some evidence and relative witnesses. This case is not over yet.

The facts: Over 30 witnesses appeared for the District Attorney and were cross-questioned by the defense. Not one person pointed a finger at me and identified me as a killer. Not even police detectives have done so. Only the District Attorney himself has accused me of a murder. And he so scientifically and calculatingly and rudely waited until after the defense had rested its case to do so.

The D.A.'s rebuttal was not a rebuttal but an opening statement. He stood there in this court and told the jury that I had laid in waiting at my house for the victim. How I had, like a lion, killed a lamb, how I had preyed upon Garrett, how I had controlled, manipulated, and overpowered Garrett's financial affairs, his home affairs, and his life in general. How I had stabbed Garrett ten times. Your Honor, the tale that this prosecutor has used to seduce the jury's confidence is not only immoral, it is unjust. Mr. Lev's witch hunt has utilized every possible detail about my being, and he has twisted these details to suit his goal. I told the Court that Garrett had cut himself breaking a large two and a half by five foot window in the kitchen, that it happened on or before the 28th of December, the date on the replacement sheet of glass purchase receipt, that he had bled considerably in the house and out in the patio, that I had not seen the incident but that I had returned to the house and assisted him in removing the broken glass out back to dispose of.

That Garrett had mopped, swept, and washed the floors after the incident, and that we had gone to San Diego thereafter. The D.A. has chosen to ignore this truth. Instead, the D.A. claims that the invisible blue-black luminous infralight they use to detect blood patterns was attributed to a murder, that the D.A. refused to note the receipt for the glass window located in the kitchen, they refused to acknowledge the photos provided to show that the window was boarded up. The detective's acknowledgment that chemicals and cleaning fluids might have contributed to the patterns in the house.

The D.A. did not show the jury alleged countertop and floor tile samples taken from the house. Why? Because there are no blood patterns as described by the District Attorney. It is all an illusion, a luminary infra blue light photographed by detectives who sprayed that house artificially with agents.

This is not a murder scene. This was Garrett's instigation, broken window accident, and Mr. Lev knows that fact.

Additional appeal facts, Your Honor, my defense attorney failed to produce my Phoenix glass company retail clerk's receipt that was available by summons to prove that it was purchased, and that exact size of the window, and what the exact size of the windowpane was.

I told the Court, the District Attorney and the detectives in this courtroom that on the 14th of January, at the alleged lunch hour of his death, that Garrett had been at the house for approximately one hour, and that he left the property and was on his way to a job interview.

My defense attorney failed to locate and summons to court the interviewee Garrett was appointed with that day.

The Court was presented with no character witnesses, neither clients nor officials from the city, HUD, or the accounting firms that regularly audited my financial integrity did not appear in court.

The Court was shown a photograph of a bloodstained Motel 6 receipt found in his car. However, the prosecutor failed to declare that Garrett spent four nights at Motel 6 prior to his alleged disappearance.

Detectives did not investigate telephone calls made from or received from the motel. Who was he with?

The fact that he had a life insurance policy recently drawn up with a stranger's name on it as a beneficiary, who was the beneficiary? The detectives mentioned it in their police report as a possible lead, in that that person's name was also on the registry at the Motel 6.

Was Garrett having an affair with somebody? Had they made up a policy together? A big question not even my attorney wants to address and did not investigate on my behalf. How much was it worth, this policy? A million? Did anybody collect on that?

Some additional facts to prove innocence. No factual evidence puts Garrett's death to our house. No weapons were presented. No time of death was established. No witnesses accused me of a murder or identified me as such. No forensics experts analyzed before this court findings at the house that implicated me specifically. No forensic evidence indicated, recognized or implicated myself in Garrett Daniel's car found in Phoenix, or Garrett Daniel's body found in the desert, or the alleged crime scene at the house. No solid proof exists that I murdered Garrett, only circumstantially suggestive maniacally manipulated and imponderable, immeasurable evidence is available.

Untruths told by a prosecutor who is desperate to cover his police department's failure to interview the suspect, and their ignorance as to the glass window, facts, immigration facts and the fact that not one member of my family in Canada was ever contacted by the police department. Yet the media broadcast my alleged disappearance to all the public. What kind of a detective goes looking for a missing person but fails to call the man's mother?

The fact that I wrote to the detectives from South Africa upon learning of Garrett Daniel's demise, the fact that the letter was not read out in full by the defense to the jury, the fact that I left the care of my share in the house, cars, furnishings to Garrett's care, the fact that after his death I requested the detectives release our property to the care of one attorney, Mink, here in Phoenix.

Lawyer Mink was never summoned to this court. The fact that I contacted Garrett's mother who so well remembers hanging up the phone on me, but who in court under oath failed to recall that I telephoned her and spoke to Garrett's stepfather and briefly asked him, do you need me for the estate settlement? Is everything all right? And he replied, everything is taken care of.

The fact that his family, not I, are the recipients of my half of the house, of my Jaguar automobile, Garrett's red sports mobile, my half of all of our household furnishings of considerable value. That they, not I, are recipients of over $55,000 in insurance policies payable to me.

I'm sorry about your grief. I, too, Phyllis, have suffered and always will suffer. Keep the money and property. Perhaps it will ease your suffering, but remember this moment in time. I did not kill your son.

I was your son's lover, soul mate and partner. Our six years together did not end in murder. Only separation. How soulless a family and community it is that, that would convict me of Garrett's death, but to this day not one of you has ever declared whether Garrett's body was buried or cremated, whether Garrett has a headstone on his grave, or even where he is buried.

Your Honor, I am weak. I am without hope. Sentence me, you must. But please support me in my appeal for justice. Support me if I motion for executive clemency. Please, if there is any hope, it is in you, sir, and the judicial system.

I did not commit this crime and I need you to report that for the record.

Thank you for hearing me. This has been my only peace of mind.

THE COURT: Anything else, Mr. Tenny?

THE DEFENDANT: No.

THE COURT: Mr. Schre?

(NOW THE PUBLIC DEFENDER ASKED THE COURT FOR A MITIGATED SENTENCE, AND PROCEEDED TO RECAP ALL THE CIRCUMSTANTIAL EVIDENCE IN THIS CASE THAT COULD BE TIED TO ANYONE. HE ARGUED THAT ROBERT TENNY WASN'T CRUEL, HEINOUS OR DEPRAVED, AND HE ATTEMPTED TO FIND FAULT WITH MANY OF THE WITNESSES' TESTIMONY. HE EVEN INTIMATED THAT THE DEFENDANT HAD SOME MENTAL HEALTH PROBLEMS, AND THAT HIS HOMOSEXUALITY WOULD CAUSE HIM TO BE THE VICTIM OF VIOLENCE IN PRISON—ANOTHER MITIGATING FACTOR.

THE PUBLIC DEFENDER DEVOTED QUITE A LOT OF TIME TRYING TO CONVINCE THE COURT TO BE LENIENT WITH HIS CLIENT, AND WHEN HE HAD FINISHED, THE JUDGE TOOK OVER:)

THE COURT: All right. Mr. Schre, do you want to come forward with your client.

MR. SCHRE: Yes, Judge.

THE COURT: Mr. Tenny, from all accounts, Garrett Daniel was a slight, gentle man. He was a good worker, he was for a period of time at least your friend, your lover, and he was a good son to his mother. He helped support you for all intents and purposes, and you returned his friendship and his companionship this way.

You physically and mentally abused him, because the Court has been presented evidence of that by at least four different people. And I think that it is apparent that over the course of your relationship that's what you did.

On January 14, 2004, you brutally murdered him by stabbing him ten times as he apparently tried to crawl away from you in the house that you shared with him. One can only imagine the fear and pain you inflicted upon him.

After the murder, you tried to clean up the scene, obtained a plane ticket to London, and called Mr. Daniel's place of work to tell them he had been in an accident and would not be returning to work.

Next you put his body in his car and drove out to the desert in North Phoenix and there dumped his body and covered it with brush.

Thereafter you fled first to London and then to South Africa where you were located, then extradited back to Arizona.

You left Mr. Daniel in the desert and let his mother and his friends agonize over his whereabouts for two weeks before someone fortuitously found his body in the desert.

You have shown no remorse throughout these proceedings. The jury had little problem convicting you on the overwhelming circumstantial evidence that was presented. Mr. Tenny, this was an evil crime, dispassionate, calculating and cold-blooded.

I have considered the aggravating and mitigating circumstances. The mitigating circumstances being that you have the lack of prior felony convictions. The aggravating circumstances being, number one, the cruel manner of death. There were ten stab wounds, and there is evidence that Mr. Daniel was alive at least after the first stab wound because he had a defensive wound on his hands. It was apparent from the crime scene that no doubt he suffered at your hands.

Number two, the affect on the next of kin, as I stated earlier, the two weeks without knowing, Ms. Daniel, where her only child was, the emotional loss and the affect on her.

Next, the prior incidents of domestic violence and assaults that you perpetrated on Mr. Daniel.

And, finally, your lack of remorse. Mr. Tenny, you have shown more remorse today about the death of your dog than you did about Mr. Daniel's death, and that is very apparent to everybody in this courtroom.

Based upon that, the Court having weighed the aggravating and mitigating circumstances, the Court finds that an aggravated sentence is appropriate in this case.

It is ordered sentencing the defendant to the aggravated term of 22 calendar years in the Department of Corrections, with credit for 410 days of presentence incarceration.

Mr. Tenny, I need to tell you, you do have a right of appeal. You must file the notice of appeal within 20 days of today's date.

If you cannot afford a lawyer or the transcripts, they will be provided for you free of charge.

Please sign off on your appeal rights.

The Court does not believe the sentence is excessive, and declines to make a finding of that and send anything to the board of executive clemency.

Mr. Schre, there is a request for extradition costs. Do you have a position on that?

MR. SCHRE: Judge, I know that Mr. Tenny did not fight extradition. He voluntarily came back here. And I just object to the cost, that he has no likelihood of paying that back at all.

THE COURT: Notwithstanding that, I'm going to order the extradition costs be paid by Mr. Tenny at the rate of $100 a month, beginning four months subsequent to his release from the Department of Corrections.

Anything else?

MR. SCHRE: No, Judge.

THE COURT: Court's at recess.

CHAPTER TWO

SHAKEN "QUADRUPLET BABY" SYNDROME

TRIAL DATES SEPTEMBER 27-OCTOBER 28, 2006

DEAR DIARY:

THIS PARTICULAR CASE INVOLVED SUCH UNBELIEVABLE ABUSE OF FOUR INNOCENT BABIES THAT WE WANT TO GET THROUGH IT AS QUICKLY AS POSSIBLE. SO WE'LL CUT IT AS CONCISELY AS WE CAN AND ELIMINATE REFERENCE TO THE DAYS OF THE TRIAL. HOPEFULLY, THIS WILL ALLOW THE READERS, AND OURSELVES, TO BE ABLE TO SLEEP AT NIGHT. WE ALWAYS ALTER THE NAMES OF THE PEOPLE INVOLVED IN THESE TRIALS. IN THIS TRIAL, BOTH PARENTS OF THE QUADRUPLETS WERE TRIED AT THE SAME TIME: ELIZABETH WHIT, WITH HER LAWYERS NORMAN KAT AND JAY LOOM, AND THE FATHER ANTHONY PERE, WITH HIS LAWYERS WES PETERS AND EMMET RONA OF THE PUBLIC DEFENDER'S OFFICE. PROSECUTING THE CASE IS KAREN CONNOR, DEPUTY COUNTY ATTORNEY. SHE STARTED THE PROCEEDINGS WITH HER OPENING STATEMENT:

MS. CONNOR: Good morning, everybody. On April 5th of 2005, three-month-old Mario Pere was taken to Children's Hospital and he was in critical condition. He had bruises on his back, he had bruises on his arms, and bruises on his chest. His head was swollen. These were injuries caused by somebody picking Mario up and violently shaking him. Four days later, on April 9th, Kayla, Nathan and Jake Pere were admitted at the Hospital. They, too, had serious injuries as a result of physical abuse.

Now, we are starting back when the injuries were discovered. What I'm going to do right now is take you back a year prior to that and go through that full year, because those are the witnesses that are going to be coming to testify as to the contacts they had with Elizabeth Whit and Anthony Pere during that time period, and also it will take you through the prebirth of these babies, the birth, and then the after-birth and what their situation was during this time period. So let's go back to April of 2004 because that's when Elizabeth Whit and Anthony Pere first meet.

Now, I should stop here for a minute and tell you a little bit about Elizabeth Whit. At this time back in April of 2004 she was 23 years old. She had a six-year-old daughter, and her name was Rica. She had Down's Syndrome. Rica and Elizabeth lived with Elizabeth's mother, Anita Whit. You'll be hearing Anita Whit testify during this case. Anthony Pere at this time back in April of 2004 was 21 years old. Here's our time line. We're going to start in April of 2004 when Elizabeth and Tony meet. A couple of months later in June, Elizabeth became pregnant.

Now, Elizabeth had some mental health issues at that time. She was on disability and was receiving social security for her mental health disability. She was diagnosed as being bipolar or manic depressive. She was also collecting social security for her six-year-old daughter who has Down's Syndrome.

After she became pregnant, she moved in with Anthony Pere into a small apartment. Now, this apartment that you're going to hear about during the trial was a one bedroom apartment. It had one small bedroom which was connected to a living room area that flowed into a kitchen. That was it. And it had one small bathroom.

In September and October of 2004, Elizabeth Whit was receiving prenatal care. Now, here we have a single mother—a single mother with a six-year-old already, and she has just found out that she is going to have four babies. She is going to need a lot of help and a lot of support. The staff met with her about evaluating her situation, and they set her up with an organization called Care which had social workers and medical workers to help Elizabeth through this time period and help her eventually when the children were born. These Care workers gave her a case manager to coordinate all the different activities that were going on, social activities, to get her involved with certain organizations with different issues. They talked to her about her home situation, how small that apartment was and how she could do things to try and get out of her apartment and how they could help her get into a new house, a bigger space for these children that were coming into her life. They referred to her about her mental health issues. They expressed how important it was for her to take care of herself in order for the babies to be taken care of.

They provided her with nurses, medical nurses to come to the home and help with the children, help if she had any questions in caring for the children. They took up collections, diapers, formula, car seats, bassinets, cribs, and there was even a citizen that donated a car to them, to Anthony and Elizabeth. They set her up with various different organizations, with churches, and one specifically which is a support group that comes to the home and helps out with the children and helps out with any issues that are involved. And they set up a fund for Elizabeth for her children, for cash donations from the public which the community supported. So that was all going on, those conversations were going on back in October of 2004.

Now, in December, Elizabeth has a brother named Rik. He is 17 years old. He was 17 at the time. And he moved into the same apartment, the small apartment that I have described to you. He moved in to help care for the six-year-old Rica while Elizabeth was going to be busy with the four babies. He moved in and his purpose was to help his sister out in caring for Rica.

In the latter part of December of 2004, Anita, Elizabeth's mother, moved in the apartment. The purpose for her moving in was to help care for the babies that were going to be born any time January or February. So in December of 2004 we have four adults and a six-year-old in that small apartment.

January 9th, 2005, Mario, Kayla, Nathan and Jake were born, and they were born about eight weeks premature. They were born healthy. They stayed in the hospital until the end of January until when they were ready to be discharged. Kayla was the first one to be ready to leave. At the time Kayla was discharged, the doctors sent each one of these children home on monitors to assist Elizabeth and Anthony so they didn't have to worry about the babies breathing or monitoring their vital signs. And so when they were discharged, instructions were given to both Elizabeth and Anthony on the monitors, how they work. If there was any problem at all, the monitors would go off and they would be able to take care of that child.

The next day Mario and Nathan were ready to be discharged, and they in fact were discharged on that day. And then Jake finally on February 4th, he was ready to go home and he was discharged. Now, during this time, in the month of February, Elizabeth had her mom there helping her with the babies. Tony was working up until February 28th when he lost his job. She had Rik in the home helping her with the six-year-old Rica. And she had the Care social workers and nurses visiting the home, talking to her about services. And you will hear that over and over again Elizabeth Whit refused services. From the time period when the babies were at home when they were discharged from the hospital, and in the first part of March these babies grew, they were healthy, they were being cared for by Elizabeth, Tony and Anita. And then we get to the beginning of March. And at that time Elizabeth's mother moved out of the apartment around March 7th. At that time Elizabeth Whit and Tony Pere became the sole primary caretakers of these four babies. And when I'm talking about sole primary care takers, I'm talking about Anthony Pere is in the house full-time, he's not working any longer. Elizabeth Whit is in the house full-time, she is not working. Every day they are feeding these babies; every day they are changing these babies' diapers; every day they are bathing these babies. There's no one else. They are the main people that has the care, custody and control of these babies during March 7th in the time the injuries are discovered.

Now, on March 22, keep in mind this is before the abuse is discovered in April. On March 22, Mario has been running a fever for three days, and Elizabeth and Tony, his parents, bring him into Children's Hospital. And what do they tell the doctor? They don't tell the doctor about the pain that Mario has been enduring during this time period. They don't tell the doctor about Mario crying when he's being picked up or when a diaper is being changed. What they tell the doctor is that Mario's had a fever for a couple of days. And that's it. There's no history that the doctors are given of anything else wrong with Mario except for his head is swollen and he has a fever. The doctors who rely on the history from the parents start treating Mario, and they take and they start treating him, and they tell Elizabeth and Tony these are symptoms of spinal meningitis, we're going to treat him for spinal meningitis, we're going to treat him maybe to see if he has a viral infection and whether or not he has pneumonia. He's not being treated for child abuse injures at this time. There was an x-ray that was taken at that time which showed that Mario had a broken collar bone, but the doctors missed it. So Mario is in the hospital on March 22nd and he's being treated for spinal meningitis, and he's under medication for spinal meningitis. Between March 22 and March 30 he's under the care of nurses, he's being fed, he's growing, he's getting better. He's actually doing really well. And on March 30th Mario is taken over to a medical facility where nurses give him the remaining antibiotics that he's taking. And he stays there until the medication is gone, until he's finished with the medication. And he comes home on April 3rd.

April 3rd is a Friday, and he comes home that Friday night. Now, let's back up for a minute and talk about the day between April 3rd and April 5th when he's admitted for injuries. He comes home Friday night, April 3rd. The next day Anita Whit comes to the apartment for a visit. Anita now is working and she has her own apartment, and she visits regularly the babies and her daughter Elizabeth.

On April 4th Anita sees Mario home from the hospital and he's looking fine, he looks good, and she takes Rica, the six-year-old, and she takes her to her own apartment for the night. And this is April 4th, the Saturday. She leaves the apartment and she goes to her apartment. The next day on April 5th, the afternoon, early evening hours, Anita comes back to the apartment to drop Rica off, and she discovers Mario in his bassinet in critical condition. He's lethargic, he's unresponsive to anything, his head is swollen, and they rush him to the emergency room. That evening he's admitted to Children's Hospital, and the doctors look at Mario, they look at his condition and they will tell you that Mario's brain was severely damaged. Mario will not be normal. Also on April 5th the police were called, Child Protective Services was called. Child Protective Services took the other children at that time and placed them in the custody of the grandma, Anita Whit. On April 8th, Child Protective Services and Care case workers went over to see how Anita was doing, and they went to check on the three babies. And at that time when they were evaluating the babies in Anita's home, they made a decision that these babies needed to be physically examined by doctors. And so the next day they brought these three babies in to be examined, and at that time they discovered that all three babies had also suffered from child abuse, from physical abuse. They had all been picked up and violently shaken. They had broken ribs, broken bones, and head injuries. I'm going to run through briefly what injuries we are talking about to each child.

Mario Pere on April 5th, 2005, had significant local bruising to the brain. He had acute subdural hematoma, bleeding on the brain. Acute means recent. He had retinal hemorrhage, which is the bleeding in the back of the eyes that you have with shaken injuries. Count 2, he had chronic subdural effusion, which is bleeding on the brain. He had left and right skull fractures. He had rib fractures, multiple rib fractures. And he had a clavicle fracture, a broken right collar bone. In his upper right arm he had a humerus fracture, a broken upper right arm.

Kayla, on April 9 of 2005, had bruising to the brain, she had bilateral subdural hematoma, bleeding on both sides of the brain, she had multiple skull fractures, multiple rib fractures, fractures of the left arm and left leg. And these fractures are fractures that occur in joints, wrists, elbows, knees, ankles, so when you're shaking the baby, those are the things that are going to be swinging back and forth and that's where you get the fractures. She also had retinal hemorrhage, which is the bleeding in the back of the eye that's consistent with the shaken baby injuries, she had a second episode of bruising on the brain, the fracture of the right femur or broken right leg. She had a fractured broken right clavicle, collar bone.

Nathan on April 9, 2005, had a subdural fluid collection on the brain, skull fracture, multiple rib fractures, fractures of both legs and right arm, a fractured left humerus. And Jake, shear injury to the brain, which is the tearing inside of the brain, he had chronic bilateral subdural hematoma, bleeding on both sides of the brain, multiple skull fractures, multiple rib fractures, fractures of both legs. He also had a second episode of shear injury to the brain, tearing inside of the brain, and a second episode of subdural hematoma, bleeding on both sides of the brain. You heard the judge last week tell you that Counts 11 through 14 were counts against both Elizabeth Whit and Anthony Pere, and they were counts that say that the two defendants failed to protect these babies, as well as failing to get medical treatment for the babies. They failed to protect Mario, they failed to protect Kayla, they failed to protect Nathan, and they failed to protect Jake. And at no time did they bring these children into the doctor and tell the doctor that these children were in pain, or these children couldn't move without screaming.

Now, the pediatric neurosurgeon that treated Mario at Children's Hospital will come in and tell you about the injuries to Mario's brain. He will tell you that these injuries were non-accidental, that these injuries were serious. He will describe the mechanism used to cause these type of injuries, and he will tell you about the symptoms that Mario would have displayed after being inflicted by these injuries. He will also talk to you about the timing of these injuries. And he will tell you that the timing of these injuries occurred when Mario was in the care, custody and control of his parents, Elizabeth Whit and Anthony Pere.

The pediatric orthopedic surgeon is going to talk about Mario's bones and where his bones were fractured and how many times they were broken and how many bones were broken. He will talk about the mechanism, how these bones were fractured, what caused these bones to be fractured. He will also talk about the timing of these fractures. And he will tell you that these fractures occurred in the same time period when Elizabeth Whit and Anthony Pere had the sole care, custody and control of Mario. And he will talk to you about the symptoms that a baby would display upon being inflicted with these injuries.

Now, a child abuse expert evaluated Kayla, Nathan and Jake on April 9th of 2005, and she assessed their injuries and treated them for their injuries. She will talk to you about her assessment of these children, she will talk to you about this trauma that was inflicted was serious, it was not accidental. She will talk to you about what shaken baby syndrome is, she will talk about the symptoms that these children would have displayed upon being inflicted with these injuries, and she will also talk to you about the timing.

The chief of pediatric neurosurgery treated Kayla, Nathan and Jake for their head injuries. He will talk to you about those head injuries, that they're not accidental. He will talk to you about the mechanism for those brain injuries, and he will talk to you about the timing. He will talk to you about the symptoms that these babies would have displayed. And then finally Kayla, Nathan and Jake's orthopedic surgeon will talk to you about their bones and their fractures, talk to you about the number of fractures, talk to you about the mechanism, again, the timing and the symptoms.

During the course prior to the babies' birth, during the birth and after the birth, obviously the medical workers and the social care workers were concerned with the stress level in that small apartment, and they were concerned that Elizabeth Whit know how to deal with the stress. Four babies alone is going to put a lot of stress on anybody. I mean, one baby alone is stressful. You multiply that by four, and you add in the other factors that Elizabeth Whit had to deal with. During the course of the birth and after birth, the social workers sat down with Elizabeth and they talked to her and they asked, is there anything we can do, here are some suggestions, let us know how we can help. One of the questions put forth to Elizabeth was, how are you going to deal with stress? What do you do to handle stress? And this was a conversation that occurred after the babies were born. This was Elizabeth's response to that individual: I get so stressed, I lock myself in the bathroom and hold one of the babies. On April 5th, the night that Mario was admitted to Children's Hospital when the abuse was discovered, he was there in critical condition. No one knew whether or not he was going to live or die. They were working frantically to save him. There were nurses there, there were police at the hospital, and Elizabeth made some statements that maybe will help you get to know what her thought processes were that night when her child lay there in the hospital in critical condition, and while her other three children were at home also in serious condition. One statement she made she said, I've got my hands full. She told someone there that she was diagnosed as manic depressive bipolar. She also said she had not taken her antidepressants for two days. She made the statement to a police officer, I always wanted to be a police officer, bust people and kick in doors. And she made the statement that night, the television and the paper are going to be busy with me and my children now.

Now, during the course of this night, there was some point in early morning hours of April 6th Mario had been admitted, Child Protection Service was called, and we are now into the early morning hours on April 6th. And during the early morning hours there was a point in time where Elizabeth Whit and Anthony Pere were together in a room at Children's Hospital. And in the next room, which was separated by one of those curtains that are pulled down in the middle of the room, in the next room was a mother who was there trying to get some rest because she was there with her child. And this mother overheard a conversation that Elizabeth had on the phone with Anita Whit, the grandmother. After that conversation ended, this mother overheard Elizabeth Whit make a statement.

And this was the final statement that night made by Elizabeth to Tony, on that night or early morning hours of April 6th. "I think I shook it too hard this time. I may have broke its back." Now, during the course of this trial you're going to hear from several doctors describing these injuries. And you're going to hear testimony that during the course of from March 7th to April 5th, that Elizabeth Whit and Tony

Pere were the only care-givers to these babies. You will hear from the doctors that this abuse and injuries occurred during this time frame.

Now, I'm not talking about injuries, incidental injuries from surgeries or from medical procedures. I'm not talking about those types of injuries. I'm talking about the actual violent nature of these injuries. The violence that occurred to these children occurred only when Elizabeth and Tony had sole care and custody of these babies, Mario and Kayla and Nathan and Jake. They suffered terribly during this time period. They suffered terribly. Their parents, their mother and their father, did nothing for them.

When they brought Kayla in at the end of March to the doctor, they reported to the doctor she has a cold, nothing more. Nothing about the crying and the pain that these babies had to have been displaying because of these injuries. They did nothing. At the end of the trial I will ask you to hold them accountable for what they did to these babies. Thank you.

THE COURT: Who is going to make the next opening statement, Mr. Kat?

MR. KAT: I will, Your Honor.

Good morning, ladies and gentlemen, Your Honor, counsel. Karen Connor would have you believe that Elizabeth Whit is some kind of monster, that she intentionally hurt her children and she didn't protect them. She is no monster. You're going to find she is a loving, caring, kind person. She is a family person. She is a wife, she is a sister, she's been a mother for eight years.

When she was 17, she gave birth to Rica, her first daughter. Rica was born with Down's Syndrome. You will find that meant she was of limited capability. She was in diapers until she was the age of four. It required a lot of hard work and a lot of patience. But Elizabeth was there for her daughter. She raised Rica. Rica's father wasn't in the picture, and she did it alone, and she raised a happy and healthy child. One day she met Anthony. They fell in love. Soon thereafter a miracle happened. One day Elizabeth found out she was pregnant. The birth of Rica was difficult. She thought she was never going to have children again. She found out she was pregnant, and the miracle continued, because it wasn't just one child, not two, it was four. She was going to have quadruplets.

This was a joyous time. But this miracle turned tragic, as we all know, because on April 5th, 2005, what happened to Elizabeth can only be described as the beginning of a mother's worse nightmare. Picture the scene. It's a Sunday afternoon, she's home, it's spring time. The family's visiting her. She's in the living room talking with her mom. There's a lot of excitement in the air. One of the babies, Mario, had just gotten home from the hospital where he had been for two weeks. A lot of people are coming and going. Everyone wants to see them. There was a lot of people in the house. While she was talking with her mom, she hears a frantic voice come from the back room. Elizabeth, come quick, there's something wrong with Mario. But Mario just got back from the hospital, the doctor said he was fine. She goes in, and when she gets in, she sees there is something seriously wrong with her son. Mario was just lying there, he's not responsive. He looks lethargic, he's not breathing right, his color is purple and his head was swollen. All of a sudden she realizes, we have to get him back to the hospital now. She yells for Tony, Tony get the car, call the pediatrician have him meet us at the hospital. Someone find Rik. Where is mom? Mom, you have got to watch the other kids, we have to get the baby back to the hospital now. They pick him up and they put him in the car, and they rush over to the nearest hospital emergency room. This is the same hospital they just brought Mario to two weeks earlier. They're met by Dr. Berg. Dr. Berg, we don't know what's wrong with this child. All I know is he's dying. Dr. Berg is emotional. All he knows is we have to get this child to someone that can help him immediately.

They call for a helicopter and Air Evac'd little Mario over to Children's Hospital. Elizabeth and Tony get in the car and rush over to Children's Hospital. When they get there, that nightmare continues because they're told, yes, your child is dying. Your baby's in critical condition. But this time it's not meningitis like we thought two weeks earlier. No, your child has been hurt and somebody's seriously hurt him. At that point, with no information, no evidence, no witnesses, fingers start pointing. And they automatically start pointing at the parents with no basis. The police are called, and the first thing the police do is separate the parents. They take Elizabeth and Tony and separate them and place them into two small rooms. For the next three hours while Elizabeth is being held in police custody so she can be interrogated, she cries over and over, let me see my baby; what is going on with my baby; why can't I see my baby.

The doctors had no problem with Elizabeth going to see her child. The police officers said no, we don't want you to, you're going to stay here and you're going to wait and you're going to be interrogated. It was a long night that April 5th. At the end of that night, actually the early morning hours of April 6th, Tony and Elizabeth went home. They knew the condition of baby Mario, they knew he would survive, but they knew he would be permanently disabled. When they got home, that nightmare continued. They came home to an empty house. They didn't know the night before when they rushed out that they should stop and kiss their children goodbye because they would never be home again.

By this time Child Protection Service had been called, and just like the police, without any information, without any evidence, they start pointing fingers. We have to get the children away from the parents. And they take the other three babies and take Rica. Even though there was no sign of anything wrong with any of the children, they take them away from the parents and give them over to Anita Whit. Doesn't matter that every single person in this world that had access to the children before that night continued to have access, they just make sure that the parents didn't have access.

After they were taken away from the parents, they were injured again, all three babies. Not Mario, because he's in the hospital. Jake, Nathan, Kayla, they were all injured again after they were taken away from the parents. You're going to see that. Elizabeth's nightmare didn't end. It continued. Because on April 9th, her other three babies were brought to the hospital where it was determined that they had an injury of similar nature and of similar timing as little baby Mario. Now she stands before you, she is accused of some of the most heinous crimes imaginable, that she intentionally hurt her own children. She, alongside her husband Tony, they're accused of knowing about it and doing nothing.

One thing we don't have here is direct evidence. There's no contesting that. There's no eyewitness that will tell you, I saw this happen, I saw anybody hurt. These charges, there's no fingerprints or blood or DNA, nothing of that sort. So the question is, how do you solve a case like this? How do you begin to investigate it? You know the children are injured, what do you do? Well, you're going to learn from the investigators in this case, there's a methodology to be found. What we need to do is find out who had access when all the injuries were inflicted. It makes sense, if you weren't there when they were hurt, you couldn't have been the ones that hurt them. You figure out who had access. You get your list and you investigate them thoroughly. You leave no stone unturned. What you're going to find out is, that was far from the case here. It wasn't a thorough investigation. Critical evidence was missed, critical witnesses were not interviewed.

Step one in this investigation, method. We try to find out when the injuries were inflicted. You need to get a time-line. That's the first step. How do you go about doing that? First, you have to identify all the injuries. What you're going to learn is, each injury contains different information, tells you something different about when it may have happened, the nature of it, how it was caused. If you miss something, if you miss a particular injury, you might be missing something critical.

How do you go about identifying the injuries? You look to the information that the doctor's have gathered, and it's two types of information. There's clinical information and there's diagnostic. By clinical, I mean observations, symptoms, events. When did things happen? Diagnostic, I'm talking about testing. I'm talking about things such as x-rays, you could see if there are fractures, you could see how long they have been healing for.

I'm also talking about things such as CT scans. It's like an x-ray of the brain, layer by layer by layer. It let's you look inside of the brain. You can see if there's bleeding, you can see if there's blood build-ups, whether or not the fluid is being drained out of the head normally. When this information was first gathered by the doctors, they're doing it for purposes of treatment, diagnoses, to find out what is wrong with these children, how are they injured, how can we fix it. But then, the information is looked at from a different perspective. That is called a forensic perspective. Now you're looking at it to try and determine the time frames.

Now, one thing you're going to see, and it's obvious from the State's case, is that it's really hard to get narrow time frames. No doctor, no expert can look at a CT scan or x-ray and tell you that your injury occurred on April 5th at four o'clock a.m. Don't work that way. What you get is time range. They will look at an x-ray and tell you judging by the healing this injury was inflicted anywhere between seven and ten days ago, up to as much as three weeks. If you look at the indictment and charges against Ms. Whit, you get dates such as between March 9th and April 2nd, between March 15th and March 30th. Sometimes, however, individual injuries can suggest a narrow time frame. These are called acute injuries. Fresh. Recent. And sometimes you can narrow those down to about two or three days. That's why it's critical. Find out all the injuries. If you miss something with that kind of information, you might be missing something critical. The next step in our process is try to find out who had access when the injuries were inflicted. That's important. Another thing that the diagnostic information tells us, in addition to timing it tells you about the severity of the injuries. What type of injuries are we looking at. You're going to find out there are broken bones, and then again there are broken bones. There are different types. Some of the worse types of broken bones are called displaced fractures. Picture, if you will, a pen or piece of chalk and you snap it. That break, it's an obvious break. That's a displaced fracture. Most of these fractures here are of a much less severe type. For instance, some of the long bone fractures. You can picture an onion. It has different layers. Picture one of those layers peeling away a little bit. That's a nondisplaced fracture that we see in a lot of the bones of these children.

So we determine who had access, and we identify all of them. Again, you can't miss somebody. Whoever was there, whoever possibly could have hurt these children when the injuries were inflicted, that's the investigation, that's what you need to determine who had access during each and every injury time frame. You figure out every single time these children were hurt. If it's multiple occasions, you have to figure out each and every time and then figure out who was there each and every time. Which leads us to the third step. Once you have that list, you investigate these people, and again you have got to be exhaustive. You can't just focus on one person. You can't focus on two, not without any other information, not without any direct evidence. You've got to check them all out and investigate everybody. And what you could do is, first of all, you can rule out those that didn't have access. Again, if you weren't there to hurt them, you couldn't have hurt them. When you have your list, you investigate everybody that had access during every injury time frame. This is very important. This is the investigation method that needs to be done.

You're going to find that it wasn't followed thoroughly here. Some of these steps were missed, and it wasn't thorough. What we need to do is apply the method to this case. We need to take a look at the information, take a look at the diagnostic, and apply it to our method. And what we know is really the information that the events started on March 22, 2005. Because on that date, on March 22nd, the parents noticed that Mario was running a fever. Did they fail to protect? What they did was, they rushed him to the emergency room at Valley Hospital and they said, doctor, our child is running a fever, please can you examine him? They didn't know what was wrong. What they did is Air-Evac'd him by helicopter to Children's Hospital, and there he was admitted to rule out meningitis. What is meningitis? It's a bacterial infection of the brain. The doctors were not sure what was going on, so they admitted him. The next two days, on the 23rd and 24th of March, 2005, the parents took their other children into the doctor even though they weren't showing any signs of injury, no signs of illness. They brought Kayla, Nathan and Jake to the doctors to be checked out following little Mario's visit in the hospital the day before. They were fine. The doctors gave them the authorization, they were all fine. Mario was still at Children's Hospital. He was admitted there and he stayed there until he was discharged. Nobody knew he was injured. And you're going to find out that he was injured at that time. It wasn't meningitis. He comes home on the 3rd. We know that the night of April 5th he was rushed to the emergency room by his parents, and there he was Air-Evac'd by helicopter to the Children's Hospital and he was readmitted. This time they got it right. It wasn't meningitis. He was injured. He was admitted, and as we mentioned, a few days later on the 9th, the other three children Nathan, Jake and Kayla were brought to the hospital. There it was discovered that they were injured as well. These are the clinical events. This is the information we need to gather to determine our time frames. That's the clinical. I also mentioned there is diagnostic testing that's done. That's what happened in this case. We know that when Mario was admitted to the hospital on April 5th they took an x-ray, they took CT scans of this child. What is showed on April 5th, what those tests showed is, yes, Mario was injured. He had all these broken bones. But they were old. They were already healing at that time. And the doctor's will tell you that on April 5th they were at least seven to ten days old. Think about this. For the past two weeks he was in the hospital every single day. We don't think the injuries happened in the hospital. Doesn't make sense. It happened before. So we take a look at the x-ray that was taken on March 22nd when he was first brought into the hospital. They did a chest x-ray. The doctors missed something critical. That x-ray showed that there was a clavicle fracture. He had a broken arm, and the rib fractures were there. They were missed by the doctors. And we know that while he was in Children's Hospital being examined by nurses and doctors, he had those fractures. We also know that they were relatively recent. You can tell by the March 22nd x-ray that those rib fractures were new. They weren't there for very long, yet those doctors didn't see it. They had no clue this child was injured. They're examining him day in and day out, and they had no idea. Well, we also know that when the other three children were brought in on the 9th they were given CT scans then given x-rays. They revealed information about the timing of the injuries, that they had similar injuries. It seems as though they all happened during the same time, if not the same day. That's it. We have gone through the clinical, we have gone through x-rays, the CT scans, the diagnostic. That's a world of information that we need to look at. First it's gathered for diagnoses and treatment to see what has happened, what is wrong with the children. Then it's looked at from a forensic standpoint. And what we use that for is to try and get our time frames.

Now, remember what we are doing. We have identified the injuries, now we're trying to figure out the time frames when they could have happened. We know the first time frame was somewhere between March 9th and March 22nd of 2005. March 22nd was the cut-off date. That's the day Mario was brought into the hospital. We know he wasn't injured after that. That's the first time frame. It's pretty wide. There's a second time frame. This time frame is somewhere between April 3rd and April 5th, 2005. That's the weekend that Mario came home from the hospital. We know from all these injuries over here, from Nathan, Jake, Mario and Kayla. The second time frame, this is questionable. It's not clear whether or not he was actually hurt during this weekend. Yes, he was rushed back to the hospital in a deteriorated state. He wasn't responsive; he had a brain injury. But it's not clear whether that brain injury was just a reaggravation of the earlier brain injury. He may have been rebleeding, it may have been that the head reached the point of critical mass.

What happens, the brain is bathed in cerebrospinal fluid, then that drains. Sometimes the child is injured. That drainage is blocked off. The fluid has nowhere to go and it builds. Sometimes it reaches a critical mass and the head starts to swell. It's not clear if that's what happened to Mario, but we will consider that a time frame. That's the third time frame. This is critical. This was the one that was missed by the State's investigators. This is one that's not in the indictment.

So how do we know they were injured? All three babies were injured between April 7 and 9. How do we know that? We look at the diagnostic, the events, the testing.

Let's look at the events. We know on April 5th Mario was rushed to the hospital. Child Protection Service stepped in. That was on April 6th, the early morning hours. Detective Shor, one of the investigators in this case and a Child Protective Services specialist, Irma Veg, the two of them went to Elizabeth's home to check, specifically to check on the other three babies to see how they were doing. And they're both going to tell you, both Detective Shor and the specialist will tell you the children were all fine. They checked the babies out, they were fine. No need to go to a doctor, no need to rush to a hospital. But then they were taken out of the parents' care and given over to Anita Whit, and other people had access as well, except the parents. Two days later, on April 8, 2005, we have had a social worker and a nurse. They went to the house again to check on the babies, except this time the babies are injured. They see that Kayla's head is now enlarged. Her head is swollen. They also see that Nathan and Jake are in pain at this point. You're going to hear that Jake let out a scream. He was hurt. Two days earlier he was fine when they took them from the parents. Now they're hurt.

What is interesting at that point is the nurse didn't rush him to the emergency room even though Kayla's head is large. They say it's okay, we can wait until tomorrow. We will bring him to the doctor tomorrow. So they come back to the house and bring them to the hospital where all three babies are examined. When they went back there the next day, Kayla's head is enlarged. It grew overnight. And still the other children are in pain. You're going to hear from Dr. Farl, when she examined the babies they were in pain. She didn't notice the extreme pain that they were in just the day before. It seems to have lessened. Now, they're not screaming like they were the day before. So they're admitted to the hospital and examined by the doctor, and on April 11th another doctor examined the children. When he saw the children, the pain was gone. They were now fine. No signs of pain. None whatsoever. So what we know is that when Detective Shor and the case worker took the children from the parents, they were fine. We know there were no signs of pain, no signs of injury. That two days later when everyone else still had access to them during this time frame, they became injured. And what you're going to hear from the State's own experts is that this pain wasn't directly related to the fractures that they had. That pain goes away relatively quick. If they show any signs of pain at all, it's only for a day or two. The fractures don't hurt after that. By this time these fractures were old, very old, more than a week. They had been reinjured. Somebody else hurt them during this time period. This information was either overlooked or missed by the State's investigation. On that day Kayla's head had been swollen. She had a fluid build-up that needed to be drained immediately. When she was brought into the hospital on the 9th, they immediately drained that fluid build-up.

The next day, on April 10th, they did a CT scan of Kayla's head. It revealed that the fluid collections had been drained. But that CT scan contained critical information that was missed, just as they missed that x-ray on the 22nd. This is missed by the doctors as well. That CT scan showed acute blood. Fresh; recent. There will be expert testimony from the State's own witness that what that acute blood meant is that Kayla sustained a violent injury within three days of April 10th. Three days of April 10th. The only thing we know about that time period is the parents weren't there. That CT scan is hard evidence, and you can't contest the fact that there is fresh blood on that. I said it was missed. So when was it discovered? Well, that CT scan is more than a year and a half ago, when it was missed. The information about this acute blood wasn't discovered until three months ago during the defense's investigation. The State was there, their investigator, the County Attorney was there. He looked at that CT scan and he said, that's fresh blood, that's an acute injury, a violent injury. It happened within three days of April 10th. Dr. Rekat was giving his opinion based solely on the medical. He didn't know who had access. He didn't know if this opinion was important or not. It turns out it was very important. As we said, the parents weren't there.

After Dr. Rekat gave that opinion, he got a little visit from this woman right here, Deputy County Attorney Karen Connor, and the State's lead investigator, Sue Lind. They went to see Dr. Rekat again, this time they didn't record their conversations as they had done previously, and they said, Doctor, I know this opinion that there's acute blood on that scan, that's trouble to us because the parents didn't have access. They weren't there. So could you go check that opinion again? Could you take another look at that CT scan? And do you know what happened after that? Dr. Rekat wrote a letter and sent it to myself and to my partner, Mr. Loom. This letter says, I have rechecked the CT scans. I made a mistake. There's no fresh blood anywhere. I was wrong. He tries to explain it by saying he was thinking of another case.

This is that CT scan, ladies and gentlemen. After we got that letter, Mr. Loom and myself went to go back to see Dr. Rekat and we showed him the CT scan and said, Doctor, isn't that acute blood? Yeah. Yeah. He acknowledged that what he had said originally, this was the truth, this was acute blood. This letter that the County Attorney's Office asked him to write, all wrong. False. There was acute blood. It was trouble to the State's case. What else is trouble is the State has no direct evidence. What did you hear this morning? What are they going to show you about who injured these children? Well, the State's critical witnesses is that mother who overheard that statement, that statement that was just left on there for you. What you didn't hear about this person, well, the State is relying on a convicted criminal. She is a liar, she is a thief, and she was angry at Elizabeth.

Let's talk about what happened on that night of April 5th. Elizabeth and Tony, they were in police custody. She is yelling over and over, let me see my baby. She's crying. She's there for hours. She's questioned. At the end of the night, her and Tony go back to the room. These rooms that they were placed in are sleeping rooms where some of the patients mothers and fathers sleep when they're visiting their children.

You're going to hear that that witness hadn't slept in four days. When she heard the statement—she wanted one of these rooms really bad, she reserved it, and she was mad because the police said, no, you can't use it. We want to hold the parents there so they can be questioned. That didn't sit well with her.

About four o'clock in the morning they finally give her the room and she fell asleep for the first time in days. And after about ten minutes of sleeping, she was woken up by crying, by the noise from the next room where Elizabeth and Tony were, and she got mad. They were disturbing her sleep. Didn't matter that fingers were pointing at her, no, she wanted to sleep. She got mad. Words were exchanged, and she left that room angry and came up with this statement so critical to the State's case. We will show you at trial that that statement is not reliable.

So what else does the State have? What evidence are you going to see in this case to tell you who hurt these children? They're going to make a big deal about Elizabeth's mental health background. Do you know what her mental health background is? Years before her children were even conceived, she thought she needed some counseling. She went and got it for a couple of months, and she was done. The other time she was five years old, her father had been abusive to her mom, abandoned the family and they got her some counseling. That's it. Total. You will not hear one single doctor come in here and tell you she has any kind of mental health problem at all. You won't hear any doctor tell you she needs counseling, she needs medication. Nobody is even going to tell you what these alleged illnesses are. You're not going to hear any of that, and you're not going to hear anybody tell you she is a threat.

Do you know what else is missing from the State's case? Motive. Why? Why would anybody want to hurt these children, these beautiful babies? You will not hear any evidence that Elizabeth ever mistreated these children. All you're going to hear is that she was loving, she was kind to them, she cared. Nobody is going to tell you different.

You are going to hear from social workers who are going to say that Elizabeth wasn't interested in the services we had to offer. They weren't interested. That's the evidence the State's going to show you here. And ask yourself when you're hearing this, what is this telling me about who injured these children, because that's the issue here, who hurt the children?

Let's take a look at the living arrangements. It's a small apartment, trying to imply it's a breeding ground for stress. You're going to hear eight people living in a one-bedroom apartment. Let's put it in perspective. You had Anthony and Elizabeth in the bedroom. Their six-year-old daughter Rica slept next to them on the side bed. The four babies, and these were premature infants, they were lined up in bassinets. The only other person in the house was Rik who slept alone in the living room. Yeah, it's eight people, but four of them don't move. Four of them just lie in the bassinets. If people are of limited income, you're going to hear this wasn't unusual, this was normal. So, again, what other evidence will you hear? They will try to make a big deal about the donations. Elizabeth was interested in donations. One of the public relation persons in the hospital put the idea in her head. Okay, they got cribs and diapers, and they got booties, some people gave money. Do you know how much money they got? They got about $5,000. That's it. You're going to hear that Elizabeth and Tony wanted to use that money to buy a house when they got bigger and they needed the room. That's the evidence. By the way, you're not going to hear any evidence at all that can tie down that Elizabeth and Tony was alone with the children when they got hurt. Ms. Connor keeps saying the sole caregivers. You know other people were there, other people babysat, other people cared for the children.

When she said sole caregivers, yeah, they were the parents, they were there almost all the time. As far as the investigation, a glaring example of the lack of thoroughness and lack of professionalism is the execution of the search of Elizabeth and Tony's home. The County Attorney's Office got a search warrant and they went there. They went to this one bedroom apartment to search it. You would think they found something.

Let's take a look at what they took out of that residence. Well, they took diapers, unopened packages of diapers. Why? They took a bumper sticker, they took photos, they took videotapes of things like Gomer Pyle, they did take metal rods and metal poles, and when asked why they said, well, medical personnel told us some of these injuries may have been inflicted by a blunt instrument. You think maybe they did some kind of testing on these instruments. Nothing. They didn't check it for fingerprints, they didn't check it for blood, they didn't even bring it to the doctor's to see if it was consistent with the injuries. Shipped it off in a box and gave it to the County Attorney's Office. But there was something else. There was a calendar taken. This calendar was taken because it had scheduling dates of doctors appointments, which is ironic because the State is charging and is going to be alleging Elizabeth and Tony failed to keep doctors appointments, failed to go to the doctor. Well, this calendar that had information about that vanished after it was given over to the County Attorney's Office. Gone without explanation. Nothing else is gone. They still got the diapers, they still have that bumper sticker, but that calendar with that information, that's gone. That's the investigation that was done in this case. And they charged them with failing to protect their children, failing to go to the doctor. These children were only born just a couple of months before they were all hospitalized.

So what I'd like to do now is go over the events of the short lifetime. Let's go back to January of 2006. We know the children were born on the 9th, four beautiful, babies, and because they were premature they had to stay in the hospital for the better part of that month. On the 31st Nathan, Kayla, Mario came home. A whirlwind of joy and attention. Just a couple of days after that, on February 3rd, little Kayla had a problem with her breathing. It's called a period of apnea, which is normal for premature infants. Did the parents fail to protect? They brought her to the doctor to get the medication she needed.

The next day Jake came home. Now he joins his brothers and sister. It's a joyous time. Then the next two days the parents bring their other children to be checked out, they bring in Mario, Nathan and Jake, and they also bring in Rica. They didn't bring in Kayla because two days earlier she had been there. Everybody is fine. They're not just fine, they're thriving, thriving under Elizabeth's care. Then on February 8th another miracle happened in this case.

You have to understand the situation here. It's late at night, Elizabeth's working, someone's got to take care of these kids at night. Elizabeth did that. While everyone else slept, she took care of them. She would sleep during the day. All the State witnesses are going to say we kept calling her during the day. She was sleeping. We are concerned. She slept during the day because she took care of the children at night. But on this particular night, thank goodness Elizabeth was there. She noticed Nathan wasn't breathing and he had turned blue. Did she fail to protect? What she did is, she yelled, call 911, get the paramedics here. And she picked up her child and she laid Nathan on the floor and she gave him CPR. She breathed life back into her baby and she saved his life. The paramedic comes up, there was no need, everything was fine, and they left. Elizabeth saved her son's life. Now, it was around this time that all the social workers and nurses kept coming by the house, and among all these visits we know they came by on the 11th, the 17th, the 19th, and they came by on the 26th. And each and every time when they saw the children, the children were fine. Again, the babies weren't injured, they weren't being neglected, they were thriving while Elizabeth and Tony took care of them. No concerns at all.

On February 27th they bring Nathan and Jake to the doctor to be circumcised. While they're there, they're given thorough examinations by the doctor. Again, thriving. Everything is fine. A couple of days later, they bring in the other boy, Mario, to the doctor on March 2nd for his circumcision. He's checked out. He's fine. Just a week after that, on the 10th, they stopped sending the nurses because their job was done. There was nothing left for them to do. The babies were fine; they were home. Elizabeth and Tony were doing a wonderful job.

You're going to hear there were no signs of pain, no signs of illness. These babies were not crying. Ms. Connor kept saying they didn't tell the doctors that the babies were crying. They weren't crying. There were no signs of pain. We're going to get into that in a second. But we know that for the next two weeks everything is fine, until the 22nd when Mario is running a fever. Do they fail to protect? They take their son to the emergency room and he's admitted to the hospital. Their doctors got it wrong. But, think about it. He's sitting in the hospital with broken ribs, a fractured skull, brain injuries, and the doctors don't know, and they're looking for something because they don't know what is wrong with this child. And every single day, on the 22nd, the 23rd, the 24th, day after day, shift after shift, doctor after doctor and nurse after nurse, this child was examined. And even though he had all these injures, they said he's fine, he's a happy baby, he's cooing, he's healthy, he's gaining weight. There's no indication there was anything wrong. When the other two children were brought in on the 23rd and 24th, they were fine. When Mario was discharged, again, day after day, shift after shift he's being examined, and the doctors and nurses don't see anything. None of the doctors are being charged with failing to protect. No, they want you to believe that the parents should have known, the parents must have known. Well, you're going to hear from various experts in this case. In fact, the State's going to call a lot of doctors, and over and over again you're going to be told this is abuse, these injuries were inflicted. Nobody's contesting that. Ask yourself, why am I hearing this over and over again? What is it telling me about who injured them? And through these experts—first of all, you're going to hear from Dr. Rekat. His opinion is, the parents had to know, it was so obvious. There would be so many signs of pain, you couldn't miss it.

You're also going to hear from some of the State's other witnesses. They're going to tell you, no, you can miss these things because these are really, really young boys. They don't talk, and they can't tell you, I hurt here, my arm's broken. All they do is cry. If they're in pain, they cry. They cry just as they do when they're hungry, they cry just as they do when they're wet and need to be changed. And then, as the doctor will tell you, the pain goes away in just a couple of days. So if you weren't there to see them injured, you might not know. The doctors didn't know.

Well, how do we know what happened in this case? Rik was there every single day. He lived there. He didn't know. He's not being charged. He never heard the babies crying in pain. He fed them, he moved them, he played with them. He had no idea they were hurt. This was a shock to everybody.

We are still left with the question though, okay, they were hurt. Who did it? Who injured these children? If it wasn't the parents, who did it? Got to look back to that methodology, that investigation method that we talked about. Remember, you gather the information. We know what the injuries are, we have established the time frames, now determine who had access, who could have hurt the children. Who was there? Who had access to them?

Well, let's look at the picture of the immediate family, if we can. We have Anthony and Elizabeth, Elizabeth's mom Anita, Anita's boyfriend Bob. We also know that Rica, Elizabeth's six-year-old daughter, was in the house. They had access. We know that Anthony's family came by. Besides his parents, he had a brother, he had a sister, they came by. We know friends came by. And there were a lot of others. They were very popular. Social workers, nurses, everyone's dropping in and out. A lot of people have access. The second time frame between the hospital stays, almost everybody still had access that had it the first time, except now we know that Mario's parents didn't come by that weekend so we can cross them off the list. Again, if you weren't there, you couldn't have hurt them. But everybody else was still there. The families, the friends. We know they were there. But now we look at this critical time frame, the one that was missed by the State between April 7th and April 9th. Who had access? Well, Tony's parents didn't come by. Tony's brother didn't come by. We can scratch them off the list. The parents weren't there, thanks to Child Protective Services, and they're jumping to conclusions. They weren't there to hurt their children during this critical time frame. These people were. Remember the last step in that methodology, investigate these people. Well, you're going to learn that these people were barely investigated, if at all. What is the State going to be able to tell you about Anita's background, about Bob's background, about Rik, about Rica, about Anthony's other family members? They didn't even bother interviewing these people. They knew about them. On April 10th Rik was interviewed by the police. He told them that a woman named Anne cared for the children, and they could have easily found out that her 12-year-old daughter had access at the same time, but nobody bothered to investigate them at all. Nobody bothered to interview them. Why? All I know is they were focusing on the parents. And there are certain things you need to keep in mind. We are not talking about people that had to be left with the children for hours. The doctors are going to tell you these injuries took seconds. Seconds. Enough time for you to go to the bathroom and come back, the babies could have been hurt.

You're also going to hear that they could have been knocked unconscious. They all had skull fractures, their heads were banged against something when they were injured. And it's common to go into unconsciousness, which could have been confused with sleep. You have to understand how little these children were, how easily they could have been mishandled. They were premature. They were tiny, really small. They grew a little bit after that, but they were still small around the time they were injured. These are Elizabeth's children. They're not just quads. These are her babies. Her babies. This is the last chance I have to speak to you directly. At the end of this case my co-counsel, Mr. Loom, is going to show you how the evidence supports every single thing I told you here today. I'm going to ask something of you. The Judge has already told you the procedure in this case. The State goes first, then we go. They call their witnesses, they question them and we cross-examine them. A lot of the critical points are going to be brought out during cross-examination, so please listen very, very carefully to the questions we ask when we are cross-examining their witnesses. At the end of this evidence, Mr. Loom will ask you to render a fair verdict, to be just. And I'm asking the same thing. Please be thorough. Be exhaustive. Come back with a verdict of not guilty, and finally end this prosecution nightmare that Elizabeth has been experiencing since her child was taken away.

THE COURT: All right, this is the time for defendant's argument on behalf of Mr. Pere. Mr. Peters?

MR. PETERS: Thank you, Your Honor. My opening statement is going to be relatively brief. The reason it's going to be briefer than the other statements is because Tony Pere is only charged with four of the counts in the indictment. If you look at the indictment, the charges are intentionally failing to protect each of the quadruplets. You have to look at this case and look through the emotion of this case. It's very emotional. It's very tragic to look at children hooked up to IV, oxygen masks, things going into their noses. You need to look past the emotion.

What are the facts in this case? Certain things are not disputed. We know when they were born. We know when they got out of the hospital. We also know when certain people came to visit them. We know that social workers came to the apartment. You'll hear from the social workers who went to the apartment.

You'll hear one of the social workers talk about when they went. On one occasion the children were being fed. Elizabeth had one of the children and was feeding that child, and Tony had two of the children and was somehow feeding both of them at the same time. The social worker will tell you how proud Tony seemed that he had figured out a way that he could feed two of the children at the same time, and how proud he seemed of his children and how well he seemed to be bonding with the children. So we know that the social workers went to the home. We know that these social workers are trained professionals. Some of them were nurses, some of them were just other social workers, but they're trained. They're trained to look for signs of injury or abuse. None were found on any of the children during any of these visits. Another thing you need to be careful and look for is, Tony is charged with failing to protect and failing to seek medical attention for his children. Look very carefully all the appointments that Tony and Elizabeth took these children to. They took them in February for shots. They took the boys to be circumcised in March. I'd like to draw your attention specifically to the March 23rd and 24th visits. On March 23, Nathan and Kayla were seen by Dr. Berg. Dr. Berg is an older gentleman. He's been a doctor for many years. He will tell you about the type of medical exam he gives. He examined these children many different times, and he will describe to you when he gives a medical exam, he gives a complete medical exam. He will talk to you about this frog position he puts the children in where he has them spread their legs and pushes their legs back almost over the head to see whether or not there's any problem with range of motion, or anything like that.

Dr. Berg will tell you he gave this frog test to the children each of the times he saw them, specifically on March 23rd and 24th when he saw the other three children. By this time Mario was in Children's Hospital being treated for what turned out not to be meningitis but to be abuse. But Dr. Berg will tell you he gave the other three children this test. He didn't see any type of injury, he didn't see any type of inability in their range of motion. And he is a trained medical professional. Under law, he's required to report any suspected abuse, as are all of the doctors and nurses who treated these children. If they saw any evidence of abuse, they are under obligation to immediately notify CPS so that an investigation could be done. None of that was ever done in this case. None of the people who came in contact with any of these quadruplets ever suspected abuse up until the time Mario was readmitted to Children's Hospital on April 5th. That's clearly the first time abuse is suspected. And I mention the dates where Kayla, Nathan and Jake were seen by Dr. Berg. Mario during this entire time frame was in Children's Hospital from March 22nd through about April 3rd. He was seen by doctor after doctor. You will hear other doctors who treated him. He was seen by nurses constantly, especially when he was in Children's Hospital. What is the evidence as far as the exact time frames? First of all, who abused them. Secondly, we don't know based upon the evidence whether or not Tony was home at the time of this alleged abuse, whether or not he was sleeping, whether or not he was in another room outside, anything. You'll hear no evidence about specifically when these injuries occurred and how Tony could have protected them in any way. When he saw on March 22nd when Mario was sick, he and Elizabeth took Mario to Valley Emergency, and then again on April 5th when it became obvious that Mario was in distress, he again rushed his child immediately to the emergency room where he was then Air-Evac'd to Children's Hospital.

So look through the emotion in this case, look for the evidence, look specifically for the evidence of whether or not Tony was aware of any of these injuries and whether or not Tony did anything other than provide immediate access to doctors.

As soon as he was aware of anything, any problem with the children, he immediately took them to a hospital.

If you look through all the evidence, you're going to see that the State simply does not have the evidence against Tony Pere. At the end of the case, we will ask you to look back through all of the evidence and find Tony Pere not guilty because the State doesn't have any evidence that Tony either failed to protect any of these children or, secondly, that he did anything to prevent them from getting immediate medical attention. Thank you.

THE COURT: Thank you, Mr. Peters.

Counsel, I understand that there's a motion that needs to be heard outside the presence of the jury before we begin testimony. Is that accurate?

MR. LOOM: Yes.

THE COURT: I think probably the easiest thing is to take the noon recess early. We will stand at recess. I will ask counsel and the court reporter to remain.

(Whereupon, the following proceedings were held out of the presence of the jury:)

THE COURT: Defense counsel have requested an opportunity to make a motion. Please proceed.

MR. LOOM: During the State's opening, Ms. Connor told them that during the period when the children were injured that Elizabeth Whit was diagnosed with having a mental health problem. She specifically said she was diagnosed at that time with bipolar disorder and manic depression. We haven't seen one witness disclosed to us that is going to say that. There are no witnesses on the witness list, no doctors, there was no one. And not only is there no one who can say that, there's absolutely no evidence that that's true specifically at that time. And, based on that, we think that this jury has been tainted and that we have a problem in this case.

THE COURT: What is your note or recollection with respect to what was said precisely, Mr. Loom?

MR. LOOM: That she said Elizabeth Whit had mental health issues at that time. This is when she was referring to the time that the children were injured. And she said that Elizabeth Whit was diagnosed at that time with bipolar disorder, manic depression.

THE COURT: And the time referred to is?

MR. LOOM: The time that was referred to is when the injuries were discovered. We have no evidence of that at all.

THE COURT: Mr. Rona or Mr. Peters, do you wish to be heard?

MR. RONA: Are you moving for a mistrial?

MR. LOOM: Yes.

MR. RONA: We join in that motion.

THE COURT: Ms. Connor.

MS. CONNOR: Any statements that he referred to in my opening statement regarding Elizabeth Whit's mental health issue comes from Elizabeth Whit's own mouth to witnesses in this case. As far as my saying that Elizabeth Whit was diagnosed as bipolar or manic depressive at the time of the children's injuries, I don't recall ever saying that. And there's no evidence that she was diagnosed on that day or around that time period, and I don't believe I said it. If I did, it was just a misstatement. Any of the statements that I referred to regarding her mental health are statements that Elizabeth Whit told various case workers, various nurses and police officers. There was nothing that I said in opening statement that in any way, shape or form said that anyone had diagnosed her, and I'm certain I didn't use that word.

THE COURT: Mr. Loom, anything further?

MR. LOOM: Just to clarify, if any statement that Elizabeth Whit made as to her own mental health, she was referring to periods years before as far as when she had a problem when she sought counseling.

THE COURT: I'm going to deny the motion without prejudice.

(NOW THE PARADE OF WITNESSES BEGAN: DOCTORS, NURSES, POLICE, SOCIAL WORKERS, FRIENDS, RELATIVES. THE GRAPHIC DESCRIPTIONS AND COPIES OF X-RAYS AND MRI SCANS SHOWING THE BABIES INJURIES ARE JUST TOO AWFUL TO OUTLINE HERE. EVEN MY CO-AUTHOR IS BECOMING DEPRESSED AND WANTS TO GET THROUGH THIS CHAPTER AS QUICKLY AS POSSIBLE. WHEN I REPORTED THIS TRIAL, IT WAS SO DEPRESSING THAT I CRIED MYSELF TO SLEEP EVERY NIGHT. SO WE'LL ONLY HIGHLIGHT A FEW OF THE WITNESSES. WE HOPE YOU DEAR READERS WILL UNDERSTAND.

IT'S SAFE TO SAY THAT THE FOUR DEFENSE ATTORNEYS WANTED TO CAST DOUBT THAT ELIZABETH AND ANTHONY WERE THE PERPETRATORS AND THAT POSSIBLY SOMEONE ELSE CAUSED THE INJURIES, SOMEONE LIKE HER DOWN'S SYNDROME DAUGHTER, HER BROTHER, HER MOTHER'S BOYFRIEND, HER BABY SITTER, THE GRANDPARENTS . . . EVEN THE NURSES AT THE HOSPITAL. HERE'S ONE EXCERPT THAT SUBTLY SUGGESTS THAT SOMEONE ELSE WAS GUILTY. IT WAS DURING THE QUESTIONING OF ELIZABETH WHIT'S MOTHER, ANITA)

Q. Could you describe Rica for us, please?
A. I could talk about Rica for hours. A physical description?
   Rica is an eight-year-old child with Down's Syndrome.
Q. What is her temperament?
A. Typical Down's. I don't quite know how to answer that. Rica is sweet and loving, as Down's people are. Rica has stubborn streaks, as Down's Syndrome children do. Rica is intelligent for a Down's Syndrome child.
Q. Can you tell us whether or not Rica was ever allowed to hold the babies?
A. Not alone. Not allowed alone, no.

(THEN THE PROSECUTOR ATTEMPTED TO CAPITALIZE ON THE MANIC DEPRESSIVE DIAGNOSIS OF ELIZABETH, SUGGESTING THAT SHE WAS UNDER TREMENDOUS STRESS LIVING IN A TINY ONE BEDROOM, ONE BATH APARTMENT WITH HER BOYFRIEND ANTHONY, HER DAUGHTER RICA, HER MOTHER, HER BROTHER RIK, AND FOUR INFANTS . . . NINE PEOPLE IN A 700 SQUARE FOOT APARTMENT, HARDLY LARGE ENOUGH FOR ONE COUPLE. REFERRING BACK TO THE DEFENSE'S OPENING STATEMENT ABOUT ELIZABETH REVIVING HER BABY NATHAN, ANITA THE GRANDMOTHER DESCRIBED IT THIS WAY IN ANSWER TO THE PROSECUTOR'S QUESTIONING)

Q. At some point in time when you were living in the apartment, do you recall any incidents involving the apnea monitor with Nathan?
A. We had an incident with one of the monitors. The incident was with Nathan. The monitor didn't go off, and my daughter happened to, thank God, be in the right place at the right time. And she looked down and Nathan was not breathing and there was no monitor alarm at all.
Q. She called the paramedics?
A. Yes, she did.
Q. When the paramedics arrived, she was just getting ready to do CPR?
A. Yes.

Q. When the paramedics arrived, Nathan was fine?

A. Not that instantly, but she saved Nathan's life. The paramedics made certain that, as they were leaving the house, they complimented her many times for her quick action.

Q. Did Elizabeth call 911 immediately?

A. Yes.

Q. Do you recall making a prior statement during the grand jury testimony that she was just getting ready to perform CPR when the paramedics arrived?

A. Well, I don't remember every little thing like that. I don't know at what stages she was doing with the child when the paramedics came in. There was a lot of excitement.

Q. You didn't see what actually she was doing?

A. I know she was holding the child. I don't know CPR. I know every intention was to revive this child.

(AT ANOTHER TIME WHEN GRANDMOTHER ANITA'S BOYFRIEND, BOB, WAS ON THE STAND, THE DEFENSE TRIED TO INTIMATE THAT SOMEONE ELSE SUCH AS RICA, THE DOWN'S DAUGHTER, WAS THE GUILTY PERSON.)

Q. Bob, when you were in the home during the month of February and March, did you ever see Rica interact with the babies?

A. Yes.

Q. Describe how she would interact with the babies.

A. She would touch them.

Q. Did she ever pick them up?

A. Not that I recall.

Q. Was she supervised around the babies when you were in the home?

A. Well, there was times I think that she went to the bathroom. I don't think anybody followed her to the bathroom.

CROSS-EXAMINATION
BY MR. KAT:

Q. You mentioned that she would go to the bathroom occasionally?

A. Yes, sir.

Q. Where was the bathroom located in the house?

A. It was off the bedroom.

Q. How far was the bathroom in connection with the bassinets where the babies slept?

A. Maybe four feet.

Q. Is that the only bathroom in the house?

A. Yes, sir.

Q. Was Rica free to go to the bathroom on her own?

A. Yes, sir.

Q. When you would go there, sometimes you would socialize in the other areas of the house?

A. Most times in the home people would sit in the kitchen or in the carport area by the door.

Q. You can't see in the bedroom where the babies are from those areas?

A. No.

Q. There were other people in the house besides Elizabeth and Tony, right?

A. Yes.

Q. Who else would be in the house at the times you were there?

A. Anita her mother, Rik her brother, and at times there would be family and friends there.

Q. Did you ever meet Anne?

A. Yes.

Q. During the months of February and March, do you know if Anne ever cared for the babies?

A. Yes, I do.

Q. Does Anne have a daughter?

A. Yes.

Q. What is her name?

A. Suzie.

Q. How old is Suzie?

A. I'm not real sure. I think she's 12.

Q. Would she ever come with Anne to the house?

A. All the time.

Q. Did Suzie go and use the bathroom on her own?

A. Yes.

Q. Did Anne?

A. Yes, sir.

Q. Were there times that you're aware of, where she could have been left alone with the children?

A. Yes.

Q. Are there times when Anita, the grandmother, could have been left alone with the children?

A. Yes.

Q. Rica?

A. If she was going to the bathroom, yeah, there's a possibility she could have been. She was free to—nobody put a restriction on her where she could and couldn't go.

Q. How about Rik, the brother?

A. Him, too.

Q. There are other family members that could have been alone in that bedroom with the children. When I say alone, I'm referring to a period of seconds.

A. Anybody who would come in the home was free to go as they pleased.

(AFTER MORE LENGTHY INTERROGATIONS BY BOTH SIDES, THE PROSECUTION HAD ITS CHANCE TO DROP A BOMBSHELL. ON THE NIGHT OF APRIL 5TH, WHEN THE PARENTS BROUGHT BABY MARIO TO THE HOSPITAL FOR THE SECOND TIME AND HE WAS SUBSEQUENTLY HELICOPTERED TO ANOTHER HOSPITAL, THEY SOON JOINED HIM IN A SORT OF "PARENTS WAITING ROOM." IT WAS QUICKLY OBVIOUS TO THE ATTENDANTS THAT THE INFANT HAD SUFFERED MULTIPLE INJURIES AND THE POLICE AND STATE SOCIAL WORKERS WERE CALLED IN, ESPECIALLY AFTER THEY LEARNED THERE WERE THREE MORE INFANTS AT HOME. WHILE ELIZABETH AND ANTHONY WERE IN THIS "WAITING ROOM" UNDER POLICE GUARD, ANOTHER PERSON, MS. SHAND, WAS IN AN ADJACENT ROOM AND OVERHEARD THE QUADRUPLET PARENTS CONVERSATION. THE PROSECUTOR'S QUESTIONING OF MS. SHAND ON THE STAND EXPOSED IT:)

Q. What did you hear this voice say?

A. She said, "I think I messed up this time. I think I shook it too hard. I may have broke its back."

Q. Was there any other voice that you heard after you heard that statement?

A. Yes. I heard a male's voice.

Q. What did the male's voice say?

A. "Shut up. Don't talk like that."

(THERE WERE DOZENS OF OBJECTIONS, SIDEBARS AND CONFERENCES REGARDING THE ADMISSABILITY OF ANY OF THIS WITNESS' STATEMENTS. THE DEFENSE BROUGHT OUT HER PRIOR PETTY CRIMINAL CONVICTIONS TO IMPUNE HER VERACITY. SHE HELD HER GROUND ABOUT WHAT SHE HEARD AT THE HOSPITAL, AND IT WAS OBVIOUS THE JURY WAS IMPRESSED. AMID A FLURRY OF DEFENSE OBJECTIONS TO NEARLY EVERY QUESTION THE PROSECUTION ASKED, THE STATE FINALLY RESTED ITS CASE, AND NOW THE DEFENSE BROUGHT IN THEIR WITNESSES. THEY BEGAN THEIR DIRECT EXAMINATIONS OF DOCTORS, NURSES, SOCIAL WORKERS, POLICE IN AN ATTEMPT TO SHIFT THE BLAME TO AN UNKNOWN CULPRIT. A LARGE NUMBER OF WITNESSES TESTIFIED THAT THEY HADN'T NOTICED ANY INJURIES TO BABY MARIO BEFORE APRIL 5TH, AND HADN'T HAD ANY CONTACT WITH THE OTHER THREE INFANTS

| Linda L. Russo, RPR with George B. Blake

UNTIL APRIL 9TH. A SURPRISING AND CONFLICTING TESTIMONY WAS GIVEN BY THE GRANDMOTHER ANITA WHIT. AFTER VEHEMENTLY DENYING THAT HER DOWN'S SYNDROME GRANDDAUGHTER RICA HAD EVER BEEN ALONE WITH THE QUADS, SHE NOW ADMITTED UNDER INTENSE QUESTIONING "I DO KNOW THERE WERE TIMES THAT RICA WAS ALONE IN THE ROOM WITH THE BABIES AND SHE ALSO PLAYED WITH THEM OUTSIDE OF THEIR BASSINETTES." THIS ADDED MORE FUEL TO THE DEFENSE'S CONTENTION THAT MAYBE SOMEONE ELSE CAUSED THE INJURIES OTHER THAN THE PARENTS. ANTHONY PERE'S LAWYER NOW ASKED FOR A JUDGMENT OF ACQUITTAL BASED ON A LACK OF SUBSTANTIAL EVIDENCE, BUT THE COURT DENIED IT. THE DEFENSE'S QUESTIONING FURTHER BROUGHT OUT THE FACT THAT AMONG OTHER THINGS THE POLICE AND COUNTY ATTORNEY NEVER BOTHERED TO QUESTION THE BABYSITTER ANNE OR HER 12-YEAR-OLD DAUGHTER SUZIE, EVEN THOUGH THEY VISITED THE INFANTS AS OFTEN AS THREE TIMES A WEEK, AND OFTEN CARED FOR THEM ALONE. IN ONE BENCH CONFERENCE THE COURT WOULDN'T PERMIT TESTIMONY THAT THE QUADS' MOTHER ELIZABETH HAD USED ILLEGAL DRUGS IN THE PAST AS CONFIRMED BY ANITA, HER MOTHER. AFTER MORE LENGTHY QUESTIONING OVER SEVERAL DAYS, THE DEFENSE RESTED. LONG CLOSING ARGUMENTS WERE THEN MADE BY BOTH SIDES. WE'LL SKIP THESE BECAUSE BASICALLY ALL OF IT IS REPETITION OF THEIR OPENING STATEMENTS COVERED IN THE FIRST PART OF THIS CHAPTER. HOWEVER, IT SHOULD BE NOTED THAT BOTH DEFENSE ATTORNEYS HAMMERED AGAIN AND AGAIN ON WHAT THEY CALLED THE SHODDY WORK DONE BY THE POLICE AND THE CRIMINAL INVESTIGATORS IN NOT CHECKING INTO THE PARTS THE OTHER FAMILY FRIENDS MIGHT HAVE PLAYED IN THIS TRAGEDY. THEY BROUGHT UP THE NAMES OF NOT ONLY ANNE THE BABYSITTER AND HER DAUGHTER, BUT ALSO HER BROTHER RIK, DAUGHTER RICA, TONY'S FAMILY, AND A HOST OF OTHER PERSONS WHO HAD ACCESS TO THE QUADS, OFTEN IN PRIVACY OUT OF SIGHT OF THE PARENTS. THEY DID A COMMENDABLE JOB OF TRYING TO INSTILL DOUBT IN THE MINDS OF THE JURORS THAT MAYBE ELIZABETH AND TONY WERE MERELY VICTIMS OF AMATEURISH POLICE WORK. BUT WERE THEY ABLE TO SOLIDIFY THEIR DEFENSE ON THIS DOUBT? WOULD THE JURY RETURN A NOT GUILTY VERDICT? THE TENSION MOUNTED AS BOTH SIDES RESTED THEIR CASES. AFTER ADDITIONAL LENGTHY INSTRUCTIONS FROM THE JUDGE, THE JURY RECESSED TO CONSIDER THE CHARGES. WITHIN A VERY SHORT TIME, THEY RETURNED A VERDICT: ELIZABETH WAS

GUILTY OF ALL COUNTS OF CHILD ABUSE, AND TONY WAS GUILTY OF ALL COUNTS OF NOT PROVIDING FOR THE SAFE CARE OF HIS CHILDREN.)

MONTHS LATER THE SENTENCINGS WERE HELD. THE FATHER, ANTHONY, WAS SENTENCED TO FIVE YEARS IN PRISON AND FIVE YEARS PROBATION FOR HIS NEGLECT OF THE WELFARE OF HIS QUADRUPLETS. THE MOTHER, ELIZABETH WHIT, ACCUSED OF THE HEINOUS CRIME OF SHAKEN BABY SYNDROME AGAINST HER FOUR INFANTS, WILL NOT EXPERIENCE FREEDOM FOR A LONG TIME, IF EVER. SHE WAS SENTENCED TO 83 YEARS IN PRISON. MEANWHILE, HER FOUR INFANTS ARE SEVERELY HANDICAPPED. MY CO-AUTHOR AND I ARE HAPPY TO QUICKLY MOVE TO THE NEXT COURT CASE IN THE FOLLOWING CHAPTER.

CHAPTER THREE

CAPTURED FOREIGN ABDUCTOR OF AN AMERICAN CITIZEN TRIAL

DEAR DIARY:

THIS TRIAL MADE ME PROUD TO BE AN AMERICAN. OUR JUSTICE DEPARTMENT NEVER GAVE UP PURSUING, CAPTURING AND BRINGING TO TRIAL A MAN WHO ALLEGEDLY KIDNAPPED AN INNOCENT AMERICAN OVERSEAS WORKER MORE THAN 13 YEARS BEFORE. I GUESS THERE IS NO STATUTE OF LIMITATIONS WHEN IT COMES TO PROSECUTING TERRORISTS. I LIKE THAT. EACH OF THE FOUR ALLEGED TERRORISTS WAS CAPTURED AND TRIED IN SEPARATE TRIALS. THIS IS THE TRIAL OF JUST ONE OF THEM.

FIRST DAY, SEPTEMBER 4, 2005, MORNING SESSION

PROCEEDINGS

THE CLERK: This is United States of America versus Artur Tchibass. Laura Ingers and Jennifer Evy for the government. David Bo for the defendant.

THE COURT: Thank you. We will bring the jury in. I'm going to give some short preliminary instructions to them. We have a brief summary of the conspiracy matter, and then go forward with the opening statements.

(Jury in.)

THE COURT: Ladies and gentlemen, good morning. Thank you for getting here early. We're going to have you sworn to be the jurors in this case.

(The Jury Is Sworn.)

THE COURT: Ladies and gentlemen, by your oath you're now sworn to be the official jury in this case, and we're going to proceed with the trial.

NOW THE JUDGE EXPLAINED THE DUTIES AND RESPONSIBILITIES OF THE JURY IN A RATHER LENGTHY STATEMENT. THEN HE DESCRIBED THE CONTENTS OF THE INDICTMENT.

The indictment, ladies and gentlemen, recites the United States of America and it refers to four people in the indictment, one of them being Mr. Tchibass. And the grand jury has charged a conspiracy to commit hostage taking, actual hostage taking and aiding and abetting. There are two counts in the indictment. The first count is the conspiracy to commit hostage taking that refers to the Front For The Liberation of the Enclave of Cabinda-Military Position. That was a paramilitary organization. It's objective was to promote the independence of the province of Cabinda from the country of Angola.

And Mr. Artur Tchibass, along with three other defendants, are alleged to be members of that group. And that back in 1992 within the nations of Angola, Zaire and elsewhere, these defendants conspired together with others to do an offense against the United States. That was to seize unlawfully and detain, and threaten to continue to detain one, Brent Swane, who is an American, who was employed by Petrol Helicopter, Incorporated, an American corporation, in order to compel Chevron Overseas Petrol, which is related to the Helicopter company, to do certain acts as a condition for the release of Brent Swane.

And they include in their allegations that he was seized in October, 1992, and that Mr. Tchibass, along with others, negotiated conditions for the release of Brent Swane at various times through 1992. Count Two indicates that Mr. Tchibass and others did knowingly and willfully and actually seize and detain Brent Swane, again, to meet certain demands, including the supply of vehicles and equipment to the Front For The Liberation of the Enclave of Cabinda. So the first count is a conspiracy count, and the second count is what they call a substantive count, the actual hostage taking count. So it's two counts in the indictment, two charges. A person may become a member of the conspiracy even if that person agrees to play only a minor part, as long as that person understands the unlawful nature of the plan and voluntarily and intentionally joins it. So even if a defendant is not part of the agreement at the very start, he can become a member of a conspiracy later if the government proves that he intentionally joined the agreement. But, again, mere presence at the scene of the agreement or of the crime, or merely being with the other participants, does not show that a defendant knowingly joined in the agreement. So, the second thing that must be shown is that the defendant was part of the conspiracy. Third, the government must show that one of the people involved in the conspiracy did something for the purpose of carrying out the conspiracy. This "something" is referred to legally as an overt act. The government must show one of the people involved in the conspiracy did one of the overt acts listed in the indictment in order to carry out the conspiracy. That person need not have been the defendant, so long as it was one of the conspirators. In order to find the defendant guilty you must all agree on at least one overt act that was done by one of the coconspirators.

In summary, a conspiracy is a kind of partnership in crime. In this case for the defendant to be convicted of the crime of conspiracy, the government must prove three things beyond a reasonable doubt. First, during the charged time period, there was an agreement to commit the offense of hostage taking. Second, that the defendant intentionally joined in that agreement at some point. Third, that one of the people involved in the conspiracy did one of the overt acts that was charged in the indictment. In Count Two, the defendant is charged with actual hostage taking. It's against federal law for any person outside the United States to seize or detain or threaten to detain a national of the United States in order to compel a third person or organization to do, or abstain from doing, any explicit or implicit condition for the release of the person detained. It is equally unlawful for a person to commit that crime by causing it to be committed or by aiding and abetting its commission. In this case, the defendant is charged with causing and aiding and abetting the hostage taking. And, finally, the defendant acted intentionally and deliberately and knowingly, and not because of accident, mistake, or inadvertence.

Ladies and gentlemen, every defendant in a criminal case is presumed to be innocent. This presumption of innocence remains with the defendant throughout the trial unless and until he is proven guilty beyond a reasonable doubt. The burden is on the government to prove the defendant guilty beyond a reasonable doubt. If you find at the end of the case that the government has proven beyond a reasonable doubt every element of any of the offenses with which Mr. Tchibass is charged, it is your duty to find him guilty as to that offense. On the other hand, if you find that the government has failed to prove any element of the offense beyond a reasonable doubt, as to the defendant, then you must find the defendant not guilty as to that offense.

(AGAIN THE JUDGE WENT INTO LENGTHY DETAIL ABOUT WHAT THE JURY MUST AND MUST NOT TAKE INTO CONSIDERATION AS THE TRIAL PROGRESSES. NOW HE CALLED UPON ONE OF THE U.S. PROSECUTORS TO MAKE HER OPENING STATEMENT.)

MS. EVY: Thank you, Your Honor. Good morning, ladies and gentlemen. My name is Jennifer Evy. And I along with Laura Ingers are the prosecutors representing the United States in this case. This statement is the government's first opportunity to present an overview. It is our opportunity to give you a preview of what we expect the evidence will be. This case is about the kidnapping of a 31 year old American citizen in the country of Angola in October of 1992. This case is about his 61 days of captivity in the jungles of Africa, miles from anywhere he knew, under the constant control and supervision of dozens of armed captors.

This case is about the efforts to negotiate, the efforts to come to a resolution that would ensure his safe and speedy return to his family and friends in the United States. This case began on October 19th, 1992, almost 13 years ago. Ladies and gentlemen, the government submits that there were three phases to this hostage taking. All were carefully planned and carried out by the defendant's group and by the defendant himself. Phase one of the hostage taking involves the initial capture of Brent Swane. The evidence will show that early in the morning of October 19th, 1992, Mr. Brent Swane, who was working as an airplane mechanic for a company called Petrol Helicopters, Incorporated, or PHI, was on his way to work. He left his residence in a place called Malongo, and he was traveling by Jeep on a road to the airport where he worked as a fixed wing helicopter and aircraft mechanic. You'll hear, ladies and gentlemen, that Cabinda is an area within Angola that is rich in natural resources, and where companies such as Chevron Overseas Petrol, Incorporated, had been involved in oil exploration activities for years. You will hear also that there were a number of insurgency groups operating in the country of Angola and attempting to catch the attention and catch the ear of the authorities in Angola to address issues of autonomy and issues of economic development for the province of Cabinda, which is a province within the country of Angola. One of the insurgency groups that you will hear much about during this trial is a group called the Front For The Liberation of the Enclave of Cabinda, Military Position. It will also be referred to as FLEC-PM.

The evidence will show that on the morning of October 19th, 1992, Brent Swane's Jeep was ambushed by at least eight or nine armed men in military fatigues armed with assault rifles. You'll hear that these men told Mr. Swane that they wanted him for his government, and that they were members of this group called FLEC-PM. The evidence will show that at least one of these men pointed his rifle at Mr. Swane's head, forced him from the driver's seat, accompanied him with others into the car, drove the car a distance, forced Mr. Swane out of the vehicle, took everything of value, and then forced Mr. Swane off the road into the bush to begin a very long trek into the jungle. According to Mr. Swane, who you'll hear from very shortly, in his opinion this was a very carefully organized operation. Mr. Swane will tell you how he trekked for hours through the bush, to the jungle, to a base camp.

Phase two of this hostage taking, ladies and gentlemen, the evidence will show the efforts that were made by the United States Department of State, as well as representatives of Mr. Swane's employer and of Chevron Overseas Petrol, Incorporated, to ensure the safety, the well-being, and the quick release of Mr. Swane. You'll hear from Roy Whitak, who is a State Department Political Officer serving in the United States Embassy in Kinshasa, Zaire, and that this was the primary location, where members of the FLEC-PM group came to address the United States representatives.

You'll hear from Mr. Whitak that on October 26th, 1992, a full week after Mr. Swane had been abducted, a representative of FLEC-PM came to the United States Embassy, advised embassy personnel on that date that his group had taken an American. This representative, Mr. Whitak will testify was named Major Zulu. Major Zulu demanded to meet with representatives of Chevron as a precondition for Mr. Swane's release. You'll also hear from Mr. Whitak that Major Zulu presented several demand letters on that day. The first to the president of Chevron. The second to the president of the United States. The third, to the members of Congress. So these letters demonstrate that the group had claimed responsibility for this act of hostage taking. A very well planned, well organized first visit to the embassy by FLEC-PM.

You'll also hear that on the next day, October 27th, 1992, the defendant, Artur Tchibass, came to the United States Embassy in Zaire with Major Zulu and with a third representative of FLEC-PM. You'll hear that these representatives presented documents of introduction, one of which establishes the defendant as the Secretary of Exterior Relations or Foreign Affairs for the organization FLEC-PM. You'll hear, and the evidence will establish, that the defendant was the representative of the delegation who came to the embassy who did all the talking. You'll hear that he again reiterated the demand to meet with representatives of Chevron Overseas Petrol, Incorporated, as a precondition for the release of Brent Swane. The evidence will establish that FLEC-PM's agenda was set well in advance, and very specific. The testimony will show that eventually the defendant and his colleagues did succeed in getting representatives of Chevron and PHI to meet with them. Witnesses will establish that throughout this process, these meetings at the State Department, the negotiations with Chevron representatives and PHI representatives, at no time did the defendant shy away from or disavow the hostage taking and continued detention of Brent Swane.

You'll hear from Chevron representative Sydney Anders and Scott Taylo who headed up the negotiation team for Chevron. You'll hear from them about the nine meetings that they held with the defendant and the other FLEC delegation negotiators. During the course of November of 1992 into December of 1992, during which the defendant Major Tchibass, as he has been referred to in documentation, continued to present and negotiate the demands of his group. The evidence will show that the primary demand made by Mr. Tchibass on behalf of FLEC-PM was that Chevron provide military equipment for 2,000 soldiers of his organization, or alternatively, money for that purpose. These were demands that Chevron could not and would not agree to. You'll hear from Gary Web, who is a representative from Petrol Helicopters, Inc., the employer of Mr. Swane. You'll hear from Simon Adams who was employed by a company called Control Risk, Incorporated. This is a company that was hired by Chevron to assist in the negotiations for the safe release and return of Brent Swane. The evidence also includes an audio tape recording made by Brent while he remained in captivity. You'll hear that early in the process, early into the time when Mr. Swane was abducted, the State Department asked the representatives of FLEC-PM for proof that he was alive and well, as they attempted to find a resolution to this situation. Mr. Whitak will testify that embassy personnel gave representatives of FLEC-PM a camera to use and to bring back the film to demonstrate what can be termed proof of life photographs. You'll see as evidence that many of the photographs show the defendant was in the camp that Mr. Swane was held in. Several of the photographs will show the defendant and the other members of the FLEC-PM negotiating team actually in pictures with Mr. Swane.

Phase three of the hostage taking, ladies and gentlemen, involves the release of Mr. Brent Swane. The evidence will show that on December 18th, 1992, on the 61st day of his captivity, Brent Swane was released by his captors after there was a full settlement negotiated by the defendant and members of the FLEC-PM negotiating team after those demands were settled with the Chevron negotiators. You'll hear that those terms included that Chevron agreed to provide an assortment of equipment, vehicles and provisions to FLEC-PM with a fair market value that totaled approximately one half million dollars.

You'll hear that the defendant was there at the release of Brent Swane, that he was accompanying Brent Swane out of the jungle. You'll hear all about the circumstances of the release. The defendant is charged with hostage taking as well as conspiracy to commit hostage taking. Those culpable for hostage taking include not only the people that abduct an individual, but also those who are involved in the continued detention of that individual in order to compel a third party to do something or not do something in exchange for the release of that person. The evidence will clearly show that he was responsible under law for the continued detention of Brent Swane until specific demands that were made by FLEC-PM with the defendant as their spokesman were met by Chevron. The evidence will show that the defendant was a full member of this conspiracy which involved other members of FLEC-PM to take Mr. Swane hostage, continue to detain Mr. Swane until those demands were met. The evidence will show that the defendant was fully participating in the continuing detention of Mr. Swane. He demonstrated control over the conditions set for the release of Mr. Swane and he participated in the release of Mr. Swane on December 18th, 1992, all according to FLEC-PM plan and design. At the conclusion of the evidence, Ms. Ingers on behalf of the government, will have the opportunity to address you again. She will ask you that you evaluate very carefully everything you have seen and heard in the trial and she will ask that you return a verdict of guilty against this defendant to the two charges of the indictment: Conspiracy to commit hostage taking, as well as the hostage taking of Brent Swane. Thank you very much.

THE COURT: Thank you, Ms. Evy. Ladies and gentlemen, the Court's going to recognize Mr. David Bo on behalf of Mr. Tchibass at this time.

MR. BO: Thank you, Your Honor.

Good morning, ladies and gentlemen of the jury. Mr. Tchibass did not plan in the abduction of Brent Swane. He didn't participate in the abduction of Brent Swane. He didn't even know about the abduction of Brent Swane until after it occurred. He is completely innocent of these charges. The evidence is going to show, in fact the Government made a big deal about the fact that this is a case about Brent Swane being abducted. It's not. The issue in this case is what role did Mr. Tchibass play in that abduction. And the issue in this case and what the evidence will show is that what Mr. Tchibass tried to do was do all he could to make sure that Brent Swane was released as quickly and as safely as possible.

This is how Mr. Tchibass got involved in this case. You're going to hear evidence that Brent Swane was abducted on October 19th. At that time, the people who abducted him was a group called the FLEC-PM. That was a group that Mr. Tchibass did not belong to. What you're going to hear is that he was approached by representatives of the FLEC-PM and they told him, we have a problem. Some of the members of our group have abducted this American oil worker, Mr. Swane. And the first words out of Mr. Tchibass' mouth was, you need to release that person right away. Now, the question is why is it that these people approached Mr. Tchibass. You're going to hear that Mr. Tchibass was, in fact, born and raised in Cabinda, an enclave of Angola, and that the Cabindans have been seeking their independence from Angola for a number of years. Some of the people who sought independence from Angola resorted to means such as hostage taking. Well, Mr. Tchibass was not one of these people. You're going to hear that Mr. Tchibass was a well known diplomat in the Kinshasa area where the negotiations in this case occurred. You're going to hear that Mr. Tchibass was well known to the United States Embassy before this incident and long after this incident. And that Mr. Tchibass realized that what these people had done was a nightmare for the cause that he does fervently believe in, and that is the freedom of the Cabindan people. But by taking an American hostage he realized that they would lose the good faith of the United States if Brent Swane were to be harmed or if he was continued to be held. And that was the situation that he found himself in. The person who actually first approached Mr. Tchibass was a man named Mr. Luemba. You're going to hear a lot about Mr. Luemba because he's actually the head of this particular faction of the FLEC-PM. What you're going to hear is that when Mr. Luemba spoke to Mr. Tchibass, he said, listen, there's a faction of our group that have taken Mr. Swane hostage. We don't know what we should do. Mr. Tchibass said immediately, you have to contact the United States Embassy. No harm can come to Mr. Swane. And that's what they did. And initially they sent Mr. Zulu to the United States Embassy. That was the visit that happened on October 26th. You will hear that Mr. Zulu did not go to the United States Embassy, unlike what Ms. Evy just told you, with a list of demands saying these are the things we need to have. But rather, he was trying to talk to the United States Embassy to explain what happened. What Mr. Tchibass was hoping to do, is to make sure that the U.S. Embassy would monitor the situation to make sure that Brent Swane would not be harmed.

And that's what happened in this case. And you're going to hear that Mr. Tchibass did become the spokesperson for this organization, not because he agreed with their goal, the continued detention of Brent Swane, but rather he felt that if he didn't intervene that some harm would come to Brent Swane, and that would cause a greet deal of harm to their cause for the freedom of Cabinda. You're going to know that he didn't agree, he didn't conspire, he didn't threaten to detain Mr. Swane. You're going to see at the very first meeting, Mr. Tchibass doesn't even refer to himself as a member of the organization. He doesn't even know the people who have abducted Mr. Swane.

He was afraid that the military people, if they didn't get their demands met, that some harm must come to Brent Swane. And he did not want that to happen. And you're going to hear that during the negotiations, Mr. Tchibass repeatedly told the people from Chevron, look, I'm stuck in the middle of this situation. I have people out here who I don't even know who have abducted this U.S. citizen, they're not going to release him unless we give them something. He can't just say I want them to release him, I don't agree for him to be continued to be held, they're not going to do that. And so there was a negotiation period that occurred and eventually, after ten meetings, Mr. Swane was in fact released. I submit to you the evidence will show that he was released in large part because of the efforts of Mr. Tchibass, and he was not harmed because of the efforts of Mr. Tchibass.

Ladies and gentlemen, you're going to hear that Mr. Tchibass had quite an uphill battle during this incident because not only did he have to convince the Chevron authorities that he really was acting in good faith trying to get Brent Swane released, but he also had to convince Brent Swane's abductors that he was legitimate, that he was trying to actually help their cause as well. You're going to hear that he had a difficult time doing that.

The reason why he had a difficult time doing that is because they had never met Mr. Tchibass before. They were somewhat suspect of Mr. Tchibass. In fact, you're going to hear about a meeting when the photographs of Mr. Swane were taken with Mr. Tchibass on November 22nd of 1992. That was a meeting where Mr. Tchibass went into the bush to meet with the abductors to try to explain to them that what they did was completely wrong, that they had to release Brent Swane right away. Now, how else will you know that Mr. Tchibass was not part of the abductors but rather was somebody that was trying to work towards Mr. Swane's freedom? You're going to hear that Mr. Tchibass insisted, insisted on being with Brent Swane at the time of his release because he was concerned that there might be some harm when Mr. Swane was released.

Ladies and gentlemen, you're also going to hear that the government knows full well that Mr. Tchibass was not part of the captors. You're going to hear that Mr. Tchibass regularly met with U.S. officials after this incident. He apologized for this incident, and again he repeatedly said that it was wrong, they should not have done what they did. He didn't agree to abduct Brent Swane. He didn't conspire with anyone to plan this abduction or Mr. Swane's continued detention. This case is not about Brent Swane being abducted. And you know the government knows that because I suspect they're going to start their case by putting Mr. Swane on and talking about the terrible things that happened to him. Terrible things did happen to Brent Swane. Being abducted at gunpoint is a terrible thing. Being marched out into the jungle is a terrible thing. But don't be swayed by that and don't be fooled by that, because that's not what's at issue in this case. What is at issue in this case is what was Mr. Tchibass' role in this incident. And what is at issue in this case was Mr. Tchibass a participant in the abduction, was he planning the abduction, was he in any way in agreement with the continued detention of Mr. Swane.

The evidence will show conclusively that Mr. Tchibass' only motivation in this case was to make sure that Brent Swane got released safely. Now, it's true that his motivation may not have been solely for Brent Swane's release safely. In fact, his real concern was that he knew that if something happened to Brent Swane, that the Cabindan cause would be hurt, devastated, if something were to happen to an American citizen.

And at the end of this case, I'm going to come back and ask you to return the only just verdict in this case, and that's a verdict of not guilty on both charges.

(AFTER THESE OPENING STATEMENTS, THE JUDGE CALLED FOR A SHORT RECESS AND THE JURY WAS LED OUT OF THE COURTROOM. THE FOLLOWING DISCUSSION TOOK PLACE OUT OF THE PRESENCE OF THE JURY.)

MR. BO: Your Honor, I do have just one preliminary matter.

THE COURT: Sure.

MR. BO: It has to do with the government's reference to the testimony of Mr. Swane's wife. I don't see where that evidence is relevant. There are also some other issues concerning the government's exhibit list, concerning Mr. Swane's journal, which I don't think is relevant.

THE COURT: The government has some concerns about his journal, too, so we'll talk about that.

MS. INGERS: No, our concern is not with the journal, Your Honor. It's with some note he made in a retyped version of that journal. The journal itself the government is going to be offering in evidence. I mean, it's his record, it's his present sense impression of what he was observing and what he was experiencing at the time. It's clearly his then-recorded recollection. And it's clearly admissible as substantive evidence, and the government intends to so move it.

MR. BO: I'm just flagging the Court that we will be objecting to that.

THE COURT: I will look at the rules. What is your major concern with it?

MR. BO: It's completely irrelevant. There may be some coconspirator statements in there, but we are talking about a 30 to 40 page document that talks about digging latrines, panning for gold, stuff that is completely irrelevant to the case.

MS. INGERS: The government submits that the conditions of detention are absolutely relevant to this case.

MR. BO: Your Honor, the conditions of detention are not at all relevant to a hostage taking case.

THE COURT: I will have to hear argument on that. We will see what conditions are relevant or not.

(A SHORT TIME LATER, THE JURY WAS BROUGHT IN AND THE JUDGE ADDRESSED THEM:)

THE COURT: We're ready with the trial. This will be the beginning of the evidentiary phase of the government's case.

MS. INGERS: The government calls Brent Swane.

(NOW BRENT SWANE, THE GOVERNMENT'S FIRST WITNESS IS SWORN IN. HE ANSWERS THAT HE IS 44 YEARS OLD AND IDENTIFIES HIS EDUCATION, MARITAL STATUS AND HIS JOB AS AN AIRCRAFT MECHANIC FOR PETROL HELICOPTERS, INC. (PHI) BOTH IN THE U.S. AND THE PROVINCE OF CABINDA, ANGOLA, AFRICA. HE IDENTIFIED ON A MAP WHERE CABINDA, ANGOLA, WAS LOCATED. IT CONTINUED:)

BY MS. INGERS:
Q. I'm pointing on the map to an area that says "Cabinda," what is that?
A. The city of Cabinda.
Q. So there's the province of Cabinda, and there's a city as well?
A. That's correct.
Q. Right up here is handwritten something called "Malongo," what is that?
A. That's an oil field base that we stayed at.
Q. What kind of a facility was that? You said you stayed there. Describe it for us.
A. It had residential quarters as well as industrial buildings for supporting their off-shore oil.
Q. Were there off-shore oil facilities in the water off that coast?
A. Yes.
Q. And what were the lighting conditions, the exterior lighting in the facility?
A. It was fairly well lit.
Q. And you say it was residential. How many people lived there?
A. Approximately 300.
Q. Where were those people from?
A. All over the world.
Q. And were there additional people who worked there but didn't live there?
A. A few local personnel.

Q. Now, in 1992, what kind of work schedule did you have?

A. I worked a 28 day on, 28 day off schedule.

Q. And when you were 28 days off, where did you go?

A. Home.

Q. Where was home?

A. To central Florida.

Q. And when you were on, 28 days on, what was your work schedule like?

A. It was approximately 6:00 in the morning until 7:00 or 8:00 p.m.

Q. And who did the work when you weren't there, that is, in the 28 days that you were off?

A. Another mechanic worked an opposite schedule that I had.

Q. What specifically was your job in that period of time?

A. I was an aircraft mechanic on a King Air twin engine turbo prop, fixed wing aircraft.

Q. Where was that King Air kept?

A. It was kept at the Cabinda airport in Cabinda City.

Q. And you lived up in Malongo?

A. Yes.

Q. And how did you get to the air field?

A. Traveled back and forth by pickup truck.

Q. Every day?

A. Every day.

Q. Now, in those six years from 1986 to October, 1992, did you travel about much in the country in the area of Cabinda?

A. Most of my travels were from Malongo to the Airport.

Q. Did you ever go inland?

A. No.

Q. And what, if any, safety concerns did you have?

A. People walking on the roads sometimes were a safety concern. You didn't want to hit them.

Q. What about safety as to you?

A. I felt secure.

Q. Between October 19 and December 17, 1992, where were you?

A. I was in the bush.

Q. And what generally were the circumstances that had you there?

A. I had been abducted and taken back into the bush.

Q. And what person or group of persons held you in the bush?

A. FLEC-PM.

(NOW THE PROSECUTOR EXHIBITED LETTERS THAT HE WROTE FROM HIS JUNGLE CAPTIVITY. AS HE DESCRIBED THESE LETTERS,

THE PUBLIC DEFENDER, MR. BO, ASKED TO APPROACH THE BENCH OUT OF THE HEARING OF THE JURY.)

MR. BO: Your Honor, our objection is that these letters are not at all relevant and they're very prejudicial as they relate to the condition of his health, what type of medical treatment that he's seeking. There's no exception I can think of under hearsay rules that would permit the government to introduce this evidence, even if they could find under an exception to the hearsay rules, it's more prejudicial than probative to any material fact in this case.

THE COURT: Where does this go to proving his hostage taking and conspiracy to hold him as a hostage?

MS. INGERS: On a number of grounds. One is that indeed he was being held hostage, that he was being detained against his will. The government has to show that he was in fact held hostage, that he couldn't walk out, and that he was held under conditions of confinement and restraint. And these records as well as his testimony go to that. The conditions of his health are also relevant because they're part and parcel of the story of what this victim suffered as to conditions of privation. Defense counsel has stated that his defense is going to include some claim that his client tried to help the victim, and these records make it absolutely clear that there was no amelioration of the conditions in which Mr. Swane was kept. And the government is entitled to present that.

MR. BO: No, they're not, Your Honor. It's completely irrelevant. They can elicit testimony, did you feel that you were free to leave, I suspect that his testimony would be, no, I did not feel that I was free to leave. In fact, we are not even disputing that he was being held and that he wasn't free to leave.

MS. INGERS: There are also reflections in there about who was holding him hostage and about why he was being held hostage. The government is entitled to present that.

THE COURT: Does he recall this on his own?

MS. INGERS: Some he recalls, some he doesn't recall in detail, and we want to have him describe how it is he was marched through the bush, and understand where he was being held, and what his captors said and did. And to the extent he cannot remember specifically times and distances and directions, those contemporaneous records, it's present sense impression, which is the principle hearsay exception, and also past recollection recorded.

MR. BO: Under the government's theory, if the FLEC had abducted him and put him in the Four Seasons Hotel—

THE COURT: As opposed to them saying they put him in a palace and he was treated beautifully.

MS. INGERS: Your Honor, the conditions are significant.

THE COURT: I understand that. Do you have any case law? I looked at the rule of present sense impression, and past recollection recorded, and there's no foundation of past recollection recorded. Present sense is more like, I just saw a guy go through a red light and I made a note of that. Some of this may be present sense, some of it's got to be also looked at as, one, relevancy; and, two, balancing whether it's probative or not.

I don't see anything that is relevant. I think some of this maybe, to show that he's being held, they won't let him go, that he needed to leave because of health situations, and he was still being detained, which go to some of the elements. But just the general, putting in of all the letters that he sent and all the comments of how he felt about the insects and what it is to be a hostage, I don't think they're relevant.

MS. INGERS: Your Honor, the Court and defense counsel raised a moment ago the issue, what if he had been kept at the Four Seasons. In fact, these inure arguably to the benefit of the defendant in that they don't show that he was tortured. They show that he was not beaten, that he was not threatened to be killed. The jury is entitled to know the circumstances under which this victim was held and what his understanding of what his circumstance was.

THE COURT: The facts at issue, whether or not he's been detained as a hostage against his will, and if he can't remember about certain items, and he testified he can't remember, then you may be able to get things in under past recollection recorded that go to that issue, or if his present sense impressions, where he takes immediate note about something that's happened and is relevant to the issues in the case, it may be admissible. But I don't think it's admissible to put every letter he wrote in and every statement about everything he's feeling and his general state of health, et cetera, unless it's relevant. I don't see it. He can testify this letter, or this letter I gave to so-and-so, and then you bring the next witness to show that they received these letters. But I don't think that makes it admissible as to the content of the letters. The fact that they're written is fine. You identify them as to what was sent to whom, but the fact that a diary, that some kind of bug that gets in his skin he doesn't like, that the ants are all over the place. There's a lot here that has nothing to do with the facts of the case.

MS. INGERS: He talks about where he's traveled to. He describes the camp he's in. He talks about who his captors are. And that's surely squarely within the ambit of what the jury is entitled to.

THE COURT: He can't testify to this?

MS. INGERS: He certainly can as to some. But, Your Honor, these other witnesses are going to testify that they received these.

THE COURT: I'm not forbidding them coming in as I said, but you're going to have to get me some law to show me how they're coming in—letters written while he's in captivity about everything in the world not relating to the issue that is before this Court.

MS. EVY: Your Honor, the testimony is going to show that the State Department asked for proof of life, proof of continuing fairly good health. And in response to that, the FLEC delegation brought letters that he had written that demonstrate that he was alive and relatively well during the period that they were negotiating for him. That's the content that's in these letters to go to the doctor, to his employer, even to his wife.

THE COURT: I think the fact that he wrote letters as a hostage I think is all right, but I just don't think you can put everything in every letter involved before the jury. All those other comments he said, all of his reflections about everything. You can show through other people the letters were received, you can show that he was in reasonably good health, that he was alive, that's fine. I don't think everything he's written in a period of months, also present sense impressions are relevant to the issues in the case.

MS. INGERS: Your Honor, I would like to offer the first one at this time, because that's the proof of life. That's the first letter. He was directed by the conspirators to write this letter, and he wrote it at their instruction. It's the letter that was delivered on the 26th of October at the embassy by this defendant's coconspirator and codefendant.

MR. BO: Your Honor, proof of life is not an issue in this case.

MS. INGERS: Your Honor, the government still has to prove all of the elements of the offense. And the fact that he was detained, the fact that there were negotiations, the fact that the demands were made, that whole process is part and parcel of the government's case.

THE COURT: Referring to a two page written ink letter dated 10/25/1992. This was written at the direction of his captors?

MS. INGERS: Yes.

THE COURT: That's why he wrote it and it was delivered?

MS. INGERS: Yes.

THE COURT: I have reviewed the letter. It's talking about the abduction and his arrival at camp, and his being held in camp. I will admit that with the government's promise to be connected up, and his recollection will be that he was directed to write this letter regarding his capture to show that obviously he was a hostage.

MR. BO: I would ask for the government to redact everything other than that information in the letter.

(NOW A LENGTHY DISCUSSION ENSUED AT THE BENCH CONCERNING WHAT LETTERS AND WHAT PARTS OF LETTERS WERE ADMISSABLE EVIDENCE. FINALLY A JUROR SIGNALED TO THE COURT THAT HE HAD TO ANSWER NATURE'S CALL, AND THE JUDGE QUICKLY CONCLUDED THE BENCH CONFERENCE AND CALLED FOR A LUNCHEON RECESS.)

AFTERNOON SESSION

THE COURT: All right, ladies and gentlemen, we're ready to go for the afternoon session. The government's going to continue the questioning of Mr. Swane.

MS. INGERS: Thank you, Your Honor.

BY MS. INGERS:
Q. Mr. Swane, I asked you before about the first of nine of the letters that you identified, when did you write these letters? During what general period?
A. October 19th through December 18th, 1992.
Q. Now, I also want to show you Government's Exhibit 2 and ask you to identify that for us.
A. That's the journal that I wrote while I was in captivity.
Q. What type of information is in that journal?
A. What had happened, living conditions.

(AGAIN THE PUBLIC DEFENDER OBJECTED TO THE CONTENTS OF ANY LETTER OR DIARY BEING READ TO THE JURY. ANOTHER BENCH CONFERENCE WAS CALLED, AND THE JURY, BY NOW, WAS BECOMING RESTLESS. THE BENCH CONFERENCE CENTERED AROUND WHETHER THESE LETTERS WERE BEING OFFERED AS PRESENT RECOLLECTION, PAST RECOLLECTION OR PRESENT SENSE IMPRESSION, AND THE DISCUSSION OF THEIR LEGALITY BECAME MIND-NUMBING. THE PUBLIC DEFENDER HUNG ON TENACIOUSLY.)

MR. BO: My concern, Your Honor, is that after every question we will be coming up here having a bench conference and grinding to a halt.

THE COURT: I don't think that's necessary. I think the government is going to ask him if the details are not fresh in his mind, would it help him if he reviewed the details of the dates of captivity. He can read it over and say, yes, and put that aside and then testify as to whether he can recall that.

MR. BO: Well, Your Honor, I guess what I'm asking is to preclude the government from listing what his day-to-day details of what he did, whether or not he was panning for gold or building a latrine, or anything that doesn't relate directly to the nature of his captivity or his abduction or the negotiations wouldn't be relevant.

THE COURT: I think not to undermine my earlier rulings about not letting in the other letters or anything else, but I do think it is some relevance for the government to show that he was a captive, that he was being held against his will, and what he was doing there. Was he just sitting there all day or was he trying to escape? I don't know what the government's going to elicit. I certainly don't want to sit around and listen to his concerns about going to the bathroom somewhere, but I think they have a right to show what happened to him, that he was not free to leave and that it's not something that he had any choice in.

MS. INGERS: Your Honor, I will say to the Court at this time we are going to be somewhat detailed about the first few days of his captivity. We hope the defense counsel is not going to continue to grind our case to a halt with these, with—

THE COURT: I'm going to allow you to describe his days of capture and what have you, for the first couple of days that he got to this camp. I think that's appropriate to show he was a hostage and where he was taken and where he was held. He can show that.

MR. BO: I ask the Court to note our continuing objection, and I'll object to anything I think is objectionable.

THE COURT: That's fine. We will allow the defendant to refresh his recollection.

(End of bench conference.)

(NOW THE PROSECUTOR BROUGHT OUT A LENGTHY SERIES OF PHOTOGRAPHS TAKEN OF THE CAPTIVE AND HIS ABDUCTORS IN THE JUNGLE. HE HAD A CAMERA IN HIS CARRY BAG THAT WENT WITH HIM WHEN HE WAS KIDNAPPED AND WAS ABLE TO PHOTOGRAPH HIS SURROUNDINGS. THE PROSECUTOR GOT DOWN TO THE CHRONOLOGY OF THE KIDNAPPING:)

Q. Mr. Swane, I want to take you back to the day that you were abducted, October 19th, 1992. Would you tell us how your day began?

A. Pretty much like any other day at work.

Q. And when you say just like any other day, what does that mean? What time did you get up?

A. Normal routine was get up between 5:00 and 5:30.

Q. And what did you do once you got up to get your work day going?

A. Picked up a lunch at the mess hall, got into the truck with some ice and prepared to depart to camp.

Q. And what time did you leave?

A. Approximately 6:00.

Q. What were the weather conditions?

A. It was raining.

Q. Now, when you left, in what kind of vehicle did you go?

A. Pickup truck.

Q. Was there anything on that, any markings on that truck?

A. It was a basic white pickup truck with a camper top on the back.

Q. And who went with you in that truck that day?

A. No one.

Q. Was that usual?

A. Yes.

Q. And approximately how long was the drive from Malongo down to the air field at Cabinda City?

A. Approximately 45 minutes.

Q. And did something in particular happen to cause you to stop your vehicle?

A. Yes. There was some vehicles in the road, a bus and a truck.

Q. Had you seen any people at around that location?

A. Yes, I had. Some military shortly before I got to that location.

Q. And when you got to the bus, what happened?

A. Several people came out of the grass with guns and were shooting, held me at gunpoint.

Q. What happened when these military men firing guns came out, what did you do?
A. I brought the truck to a complete stop. Put my hands over my head.
Q. Did you stay in the truck or get out?
A. I stayed in the truck.
Q. Do you remember anything particular, any particular type of firearm that was held by any one or more of the men?
A. There was two men in front with automatic weapons, one man on the right side with a grenade launcher.
Q. What did they do?
A. They got into the truck, two of them on the right-hand side, one on the left-hand side.
Q. Did you recognize these men?
A. No.
Q. Did you recognize the uniforms that they were in?
A. I recognized them as military camouflage.
Q. And when they got in the vehicle, what did they do?
A. They turned the vehicle around and departed the main road.
Q. Who was driving, you or one of the men?
A. One of the men.
Q. Now, when the men got into the truck, what if anything did they do with regard to you?
A. They just kind of sandwiched me into the middle of the seat.
Q. Did they speak to you or say anything?
A. They were speaking to themselves but not to me.
Q. And did they look for any identification of who you were?
A. Yes, by looking at the name badge on my shirt.
Q. And your Angolan driver's license?
A. That's right.
Q. When they looked at the name on your shirt, did they do anything else?
A. Yes. They compared it to a piece of paper.
Q. Did you see what was written on that piece of paper?
A. Four names: Schumach, Carr, Bull and, Swane.
Q. And do you know who Carr, Bull and Schumach are?
A. Fellow co-workers.
Q. Where did they work?
A. They worked on the helicopters in Malongo.
Q. Now, did you ask questions of these men?
A. I tried to ask all the questions I could.
Q. And what was their response?
A. They seemed to be speaking with each other but nothing that I could understand.
Q. And what language is the language spoken in Angola?
A. Mostly Portuguese.

Q. Did you at the time understand Portuguese?

A. A little bit.

Q. Now, what happened when the vehicle turned around, where did it go?

A. They turned it around. They didn't go very far, maybe 100 yards or so, and took a right off of the road.

Q. Is that inland or toward the coast?

A. Inland.

Q. How far did they drive inland?

A. The best I can recall approximately five miles.

Q. And then what?

A. They stripped everything out of my pockets, took my watch, cleaned out the truck of anything that was in it.

Q. And about how many men were with you at this time?

A. Three. The three that were in the truck.

Q. And at some point did you go somewhere?

A. Yes.

Q. And how did you travel?

A. Traveling was by foot.

Q. And what was the kind of terrain that you were traveling over?

A. Initially it was grassy terrain.

Q. And when you were walking through that terrain, about how many people were there with you?

A. It started out with three, and then the numbers increased up to 24.

Q. So the other people joined you later?

A. A little later, yes.

Q. Are you depicted in this photograph?

A. Yes, I am.

Q. Who is directly behind you?

A. It's an Angolan policeman.

Q. What was he doing there?

A. He appeared to be in the same situation I was in.

Q. And had you seen him before he joined you in the bush here?

A. No.

Q. And how long did you travel until your next stop?

A. A couple of hours.

Q. What, if anything, had been told to you by this time about who these people were and why they had taken you?

A. One man had mentioned he was FLEC, not FAPLA.

Q. He was FLEC, not FAPLA?

A. Correct.

Q. At that time had you ever heard of FLEC before?

A. Not to my knowledge, no.

Q. Had you ever heard of FAPLA before?

A. Yes.

Q. What was FAPLA?

A. The Angolan military.

Q. How did you feel when you heard this man tell you that we're not FAPLA, we're FLEC?

A. Scared.

Q. Why?

A. Because it wasn't the military that I was used to being around.

Q. Now, did anyone in this group tell you why they wanted you?

A. I remember asking several questions, but to say exactly what they was after, I wasn't sure at that time.

Q. What had happened to the Angolan policeman?

A. I'm not real sure. He had been taken away from the group where I was at.

Q. When he was taken away, did you see or hear anything in particular?

A. Yes. They took him back the way that we had walked up to this resting point. There was a lot of hollering going on, some gunfire, and then the FLEC members came back.

Q. And what was going through your mind about what had happened to the Angolan policeman?

A. I assumed they may have shot him.

Q. Now, another picture of you. What does this picture show you doing?

A. Pointing at my left foot.

Q. What had happened?

A. I had a cut on my left ankle, and it indicated day one.

Q. What did you mean by it indicated day one?

A. By the one finger it was the first day.

Q. Were you aware that somebody was taking your picture?

A. Yes.

Q. For whom was that "one" to indicate day one intended?

A. Anybody that would see that photograph.

Q. Now, at some point did you stop and rest and eat?

A. Yes, we did.

Q. Now, what kind of place was this that you were at?

A. It appeared to be a camp of some sort.

Q. After you ate, what happened?

A. They picked up everything in the camp and scattered leaves and sticks back so it looked like no one was ever there.

Q. And did you do anything in particular?

A. Yes, I did.

Q. What was that?

A. I left a cigarette butt in the crotch of a tree.

Q. Why did you do that?

A. In hopes someone might find the trail.

Q. At some point did you hear something that drew your attention?

A. Yes, I did.

Q. What is it you heard?

A. A helicopter.

Q. When you heard it land, did you have any idea where it was landing?

A. Yes. In Malongo.

Q. Malongo, the very place that you started out for that morning?

A. Yes.

Q. How close were you?

A. Approximately three miles.

Q. How long did you continue walking?

A. Until 11 p.m. that evening.

Q. And at some point that night did the pace at which you were traveling change?

A. Yes. They sped the pace up.

Q. Did you know why?

A. The best I can recall at this time was because we were in what would be their enemy territory.

Q. What do you mean by their enemy? The Angolan military?

A. Yes, that it might be the last time I ever saw it.

Q. Did you make camp that night?

A. Yes.

Q. Was this an established camp or did it have to be set up?

A. It was set up.

Q. And who was present with you in that camp?

A. The FLEC members.

Q. On the next day, the second day of your captivity, what time did you get up?

A. The best I can recall about 6:00.

Q. How generally did you spend the second day?

A. We walked and made another camp.

Q. The next day, what happened after you woke up? The third day?

A. I woke up, they had breakfast, then we packed up again.

Q. Now, by this time had you been told anything about where you were going or who you were going to see?

A. They had indicated that I would be going to see their leader.

Q. And did they say when you'd meet him?

A. It was going to be a walk of another two or three days.

Q. What was your reaction on hearing that?

A. That I wanted to get there as soon as we could.

Q. On the fourth day, when you got up in the morning, did you hear anything in particular?

A. Yes.

Q. What was that?

A. A radio broadcast.

Q. And what was it? Did you understand any of it?

A. I understood some of it.

Q. And what is it that you heard?

A. UNITA, Brent Swane, FLEC, and Cabinda.

Q. What's UNITA?

A. A rebel group in Angola.

Q. And what was your reaction on hearing those four terms in this Portuguese radio broadcast?

A. Again, very scared.

Q. What happened that day? Did you travel or did you stay?

A. We stayed there most of the day.

Q. And at some point did you then move on?

A. Yes. That evening we traveled basically south.

Q. Did you stop that night?

A. Yes, it was very late that night we stopped.

Q. The next morning, day five, did you move on to yet another location?

A. Yes.

Q. Now what, if anything, happened right after you entered the camp?

A. They had a ceremony.

Q. What kind of ceremony?

A. It appeared to be a presentation of hostage.

Q. What after this military ceremony did you do?

A. I wrote a letter.

Q. And how is it that you came to write a letter?

A. They told me to.

Q. Who is "they"?

A. FLEC.

Q. What did they tell you about what you should say in this letter?

A. They told me that I should write to the U.S. Embassy.

Q. Did they tell you why, Mr. Swane?

A. So they could work on a release for myself.

Q. Would you please read the letter.

A. "I have finally arrived at FLEC base camp. It has been a long hike. I am in fair health. Insect bites, scratches, bruises, typical jungle rash. My feet are tired but I could go another day and I'd be in good shape. I am told I am not in Angola but in the country of Cabinda."

Q. Who had told you that?

A. FLEC.

Q. Continue reading.

A. "So far I have been fed well from barbecued banana to sardine soup, and the porkypine is mighty tasty. "We have rested well during the day and hiked mostly at night, three to four hours. Last night's was six hours. I know where the bat shits in the woods."

Q. Now, if you look at the third line up where you wrote "last night was six hours," there's an extra "S" after the "was." What does that mean?

A. That last night we had hiked south six hours.

Q. Why didn't you just say we hiked south six hours?

A. I was trying to disclose my location without actually saying it.

Q. The next line is, "until then it was," and then there's a "never" is broken up by some space, "more than four." What does that mean?

A. That prior to that, we had been hiking northeast.

Q. So the "NE" means northeast?

A. Northeast, yes.

Q. The last line about the bat, does that mean anything in particular?

A. Yes.

Q. What?

A. The fruit bats that hang out in Malongo during the day would depart Malongo in a northeasterly direction.

Q. Was that also a kind of a code?

A. Yes.

Q. Would you continue reading?

A. "Though it may not seem it, my mind is almost at ease. I look at this as one hell of a camping trip. I am free to do as I please within, of course, camp. One scratch with infection has been looked at by camp medical officer, treated with hydrogen peroxide, and an ointment. Basically, I am being treated as well as could be expected. I know the meaning of severe depression. "I certainly hope that an agreement can be reached soon."

Q. What lead you to believe that there was anything about an agreement that might happen?

A. From the members of FLEC.

Q. Continue reading.

A. "I certainly hope that an agreement can be reached soon. I fear that this could be a long hitch. New Hampshire has a pretty license plate."

Q. What is New Hampshire's license plate?

A. It has a slogan: Live free or die.

Q. Continue.

A. "And I hope my options stay favorable. I guess I have been lucky. My travel bag has made the trip as well as the rest that's missing from the truck. I assume you found it, five miles out on the left. I take it communication may be slow, as I understand this will go through Kinshasa. I'm sure my wife is in contact. Please tell her I love her. Will be home soon? I only hope. "Wish I could have written neater or more, but we just arrived one hour ago. Hunger and tiredness is sloppiness. Hope to hear from you soon. Having a great time. Wish you were here."

Q. Mr. Swane, what assurance, if any, did you have that this letter would not be read by the people who held you captive?

A. None.

Q. Did you see any of your captors read this letter?

A. Yes.

Q. Who?

A. Agostino.

Q. Did you see him do anything with regard to the letter?

A. Read it and translate it for other FLEC members.

Q. Was Agostino one of the FLEC men?

A. Yes.

Q. And did you have in mind as you wrote this letter that it also might be read by your captors?

A. Yes.

Q. Mr. Swane, what did you do with this letter after you wrote it?

A. I gave it to FLEC members.

Q. And do you know what happened to it?

A. To the best of my knowledge it was taken to the U.S. Embassy.

(NOW THE PROSECUTOR SHOWED PHOTOS OF THE BASE CAMP MR. SWANE WAS HELD IN, THE LOCATION OF OUTDOOR TABLES AND A FLAGPOLE IN THE MIDST OF THICK JUNGLE BRUSH. THEY SHOWED THE DAILY RAISING OF THE FLEC FLAG.)

Q. Approximately how long did you stay at this base camp?

A. Six weeks.

Q. Who traveled from the first base camp to the second base camp with you?

A. Members of FLEC.

Q. Do you remember any of their names?

A. Agostino would have been one of them.

Q. Who was in charge at these camps?

A. Francisco Rodrigue.

Q. Now, did you at some point come to learn the names of people who were among your captors and their roles in FLEC-PM?

A. Yes.

Q. Who gave this to you?

A. Agostino.

Q. And what was it that he was trying to tell you about FLEC?

A. Telling me what their organization was, what their names were.

Q. For what purpose?

A. I'm not sure. I mean, I was trying to learn the names of FLEC and their positions in hopes that I could possibly take this list out with me when I was released.

MS. INGERS: Your Honor, at this time I offer into evidence this list.

MR. BO: May we approach, Your Honor?

THE COURT: All right.

(AGAIN A LENGTHY DISCUSSION AT THE BENCH ENSUED, AND LATER IN THE PRESENCE OF THE JURY REGARDING THE AUTHENTICITY OF WHO WAS WHO ON VARIOUS LISTS AND PHOTOGRAPHS OF FLEC KIDNAPPERS AND THEIR RANKINGS IN THE ORGANIZATION. IT BECAME RATHER COMPLICATED, BUT THESE FACTS WERE ACCEPTED BY THE COURT AS THE PROSECUTOR CONTINUED:)

Q. Mr. Swane, I want you to tell us what this information is.

A. The organization of FLEC.

Q. And looking at the first line, what's the name with the title "President?"

A. Jose Luemb.

Q. And underneath that, "General Secretary"?

A. Bent Bembo.

Q. And underneath it, "A" what does that mean?

A. President Members.

Q. And how is it that you knew to write "President Members"?

A. By discussing the organization of FLEC with Agostino.

Q. Did you and Agostino discuss what was on this piece of paper?

A. Yes.

Q. And after the name "Artur Tchibass," it says "Major." What does that mean?

A. That he was a major member.

Q. And where did you get that term associated with Artur Tchibass?

A. From Agostino.

Q. And underneath there's another name, what's that name?

A. Mauricio Amado Nzul.

Q. Right next to it is a name, what's that?

A. Alfredo Nhumb, Lieutenant Colonel.

Q. And right next to it?

A. Francisco Rodrigue.

Q. On the reverse of that particular sheet of paper there's a series of names all associated with the title Captain. And underneath there's another series of names under the title Lieutenants. The first one, what is that?

A. Agostino C. Manuel.

(AFTER IDENTIFYING MANY MORE NAMES OF SOLDIERS IN THE FLEC REVOLUTIONARY MOVEMENT, THE PROSECUTION TURNED TO PHOTOS OF THE CAMPSITE WHERE MR. SWANE WAS DETAINED.)

Q. Now, I want to show you a few pictures of the second camp. Did you take these photos of the camp?

A. Yes.

Q. I'd like to draw your attention to the sort of a series of slabs. What are those?

A. Tables with benches.

Q. And what were those used for?

A. Eating.

Q. Photo number 22, what's that?

A. Sleeping area.

Q. So you shared your sleeping quarters with your captors?

A. Yes.

Q. Mr. Swane, you testified earlier about that first letter you wrote out on October 23rd. Did you get anything back from the U.S. Embassy?

A. Yes, I did. A care package. There was several items in it for healthcare, some books, medicines.

Q. How did you receive it?

A. From one of the FLEC members.

Q. Did you have an opportunity to send something back out?

A. Yes.

Q. And what was that?

A. There was letters and a tape recording.

Q. What was on this tape recording?

A. Me talking to the U.S. Embassy.

Q. All right. Before I get to the tape recording—

MR. BO: Your Honor, may we approach?

THE COURT: All right.

(Bench conference on the record.)

MR. BO: I apologize for interrupting this time, but I'm objecting to the admission of this audiotaped statement that Mr. Swane made, the same objection as far as the letters that he sent out. I don't believe it's relevant to any issue, and extraordinarily prejudicial. So at this point I want to put on the record that as Mr. Swane read the letter, the first letter that he wrote out, he became quite emotional obviously when he was reading that letter. My fear is that this can be unduly prejudicial to Mr. Tchibass for him to have to relive the moments of his captivity, and certainly to hear it in his voice at the time the captivity happened. I don't think it's relevant at all. To the extent it's relevant, certainly its prejudicial value far outweighs any probative value.

(THE PUBLIC DEFENDER AND THE PROSECUTOR WENT BACK AND FORTH OVER THE EFFICACY OF SUBMITTING THE TAPE RECORDINGS AND OTHER LETTERS MR. SWANE WROTE, INCLUDING HIS JOURNAL. FINALLY THE EXASPERATED PROSECUTOR MADE HER FINAL PLEA TO THE JUDGE.)

MS. INGERS: Your Honor, we've been precluded from offering the journal. We've been precluded from offering the letters, except for one. And the government submits that this is squarely something that the jury is entitled to hear, and it's not cumulative.

THE COURT: It seems to me that they should be allowed to hear them. I'll overrule the objection for the following reasons. One, it seems to me it's a product that was made at the request of his captors to prove that he was a hostage, and that he was alive, and negotiations therefore would be worthwhile to go through. And, secondly, that he is continuing to be a hostage, and that their intention was to keep him until they worked out some type of negotiation. The contents obviously could be extremely inflammatory. You have to be careful if something comes out that it seems to be far more prejudicial than probative. And that if he made it at their direction, and they listened to it and they had him continue with it, it seems to me it could be used against them as an admission basically that they were keeping him as a hostage and that they intended to. And this is one of the evidences of that. So I'm going to allow it in on that basis against this defendant as part of the conspiracy and subject to connecting it up with this defendant to the whole conspiracy. I think that they have a right to play the tape at this time. So I'll overrule the objection. If I hear something that's inappropriate, I'll strike it.

(End of bench conference.)

THE COURT: All right, I've overruled the objection to allow further testimony about this tape recording and the playing of the tape as may be appropriate.

MS. Ingers: Your Honor, at this time I move into evidence the letter that the witness has just described.

THE COURT: All right. Over objection it's allowed.

BY MS. INGERS:

Q. Again Mr. Swane, I'm just going to ask you to read the first part of that: Embassy of the United States, Kinshasa and the date. Would you please read the second paragraph?

A. "The men who have come to us from FLEC-PM, the organization that is holding you, tell us that they, too, are working for your release and that they are doing their best to treat you well. I trust this is so, and that your personal relations with them are as good as could be expected."

Q. And the last paragraph?

A. "Haven't time to send you more, but we are working to get you home and hope to see you soon."

Q. Now when you read "soon," what did you understand that "soon" to mean?

A. A few days.

Q. Did your captors, just as they read the mail that you sent out, did they read the mail that you received?

A. In some cases, yes.

Q. And did they examine the contents of the care package?

A. Yes.

Q. Where did that tape recorder come from; do you know?

A. As best I can recall from the U.S. Embassy.

Q. And how is it that you came to make a tape recording?

A. FLEC asked me to.

Q. And were they present when you made the tape recording?

A. Yes.

Q. And what, if anything, did they say about what you should say on that tape recording?

A. They told me a few things that I should say so that people would hear my voice and know I was still alive.

Q. What time of day was it when you made this?

A. I believe it was in the morning.

Q. Are there breaks in the tape?

A. Yes, there are.

Q. And why is it that there were breaks in the tape?

A. Because there was certain things they wanted me to say.

(AUDIOTAPE PLAYED. DURING THE PLAYING, BRENT SWANE BECAME VISIBLY EMOTIONAL AND THE COURT CALLED A SHORT RECESS. JURY IS OUT.)

THE COURT: Mr. Swane, try to get composed again. On the record, Mr. Swane obviously reacted to this tape recording and broke down.

MR. BO: Your Honor, at this time on behalf of Mr. Tchibass we will be moving for a mistrial. Your Honor, Mr. Swane understandably was unbelievably emotional during the playing of that tape. My observation was that he was openly sobbing through the major portions of that tape. Our position is this, that the issue in this case is not whether or not Mr. Swane was in fact abducted. There's no dispute about that. The question is, what was Mr. Tchibass' role in that abduction. Playing that tape before this jury and before Mr. Swane, the government knew or should have known that there was going to be a very powerful reaction on behalf of Mr. Swane. That, in fact, has happened in this case.

My fear is that the jurors will think because Mr. Swane was treated so poorly, that now ten years after the event, that still brings back very, very powerful emotions for him, that they'll convict not on the evidence but rather the emotional impact that this has had on Mr. Swane.

The evidence of playing this tape in front of this witness was so powerful that there's just no way that Mr. Tchibass at this point can get a fair trial. So at this point we will be moving for a mistrial.

THE COURT: All right, thank you. Does the government want to respond?

MS. INGERS: Yes, Your Honor. First, I would note that in the government's view, defense counsel has overstated the reaction of the witness. There was no audible sound. While he appeared to be very somber and weeping at some points, it was quiet. It was not distracting to the jury. It didn't appear to distract from their listening to the tape, which is the purpose for playing the tape. It's of course understandable that someone who went through any traumatic experience would have a severe reaction. That doesn't mean that the government can't present the testimony of that witness in an orderly and proper fashion. It was certainly not extraordinarily inflammatory.

The government is entitled, as the Court recognized in ruling as to the admissibility of the tape, that the government is entitled to put on its case with the best available relevant evidence, which this is. And it certainly is not any basis for a mistrial in this case.

THE COURT: All right. The Court's going to deny the motion at this time. I will note for the record the Court did notice Mr. Swane was teary, that he used a handkerchief and put his head into his hands. He did not heave, sigh, make any audible noises. His body was not shaking and moving around in tremendous distress, but he sat quietly, put his head down, became somewhat red in the face, was obviously upset. And the jury could see that, but it was no wildly emotional scene whatsoever in the courtroom. I'll certainly inform the jury they should not be swayed by emotion, but by whatever the evidence is in the case. And that we will stick to the issues as to what Mr. Tchibass' role was in this matter, and what was the situation with Mr. Swane vis-a-vis FLEC and Mr. Tchibass' role in that. And I'll also advise the jury at this time to make sure that they're not being overly impacted by any of the emotion Mr. Swane may be legitimately showing.

But I do not think it rose at all to the level where there needs to be a mistrial in the case, that they can't fairly try the issues in an impartial fashion, listening to the evidence. The tape really did show, it seemed to the Court, at least the first part of the tape, that his captors were directing him what to say, and that they listened to the tape, were very careful. You could hear them getting him ready to make the tape. And I think it's very relevant to the fact that there was a continuing intent to keep him a hostage until they got their negotiations satisfactorily completed from their point of view by getting the equipment and supplies that they were demanding in this matter. And the government has to prove this continuing intent to keep him as a hostage. All right, if we can come back, we'll try to finish up with some more testimony and bring the jury in.

(Jury in.)

THE COURT: Ladies and gentlemen, we're ready to resume back to the direct testimony of Mr. Swane. Ladies and gentlemen, you may have noticed that Mr. Swane was upset by the playing of this tape. That's understandable. But you as jurors have to set aside emotion and listen to the evidence impartially and fairly, and not make any judgment based upon sympathy, favoritism or emotion, but only upon the evidence and the facts that you find have been proven by the government beyond a reasonable doubt. So don't be swayed by any emotion or any such feelings in this case. All right, let's continue on.

(AGAIN, MORE LETTERS TO AND FROM THE CAPTORS, AND TO AND FROM MR. SWANE WERE ADMITTED INTO EVIDENCE, ALONG WITH MANY PHOTOS OF THE FLEC MEMBERS FROM THE PRESIDENT OF THE REBEL GROUP ON DOWN TO THE GROUND SOLDIERS. NOW THE SEQUENCE OF LETTERS NEARED HIS RELEASE DATE:)

Q. Now, at some point did you learn that you were going to be released?
A. Yes, I did.
Q. How was it that you learned that?
A. By Bent coming in as well as a letter.
Q. And who was that letter from?
A. From Gary Web.

Q. Who was Gary Web?

A. He was the foreign supervisor for Petrol Helicopters.

Q. Is that the letter you were referring to just now?

A. That's the letter that I remember.

Q. And what is the date of that?

A. 13 December.

Q. The date is 13 December '92; is that correct?

A. That's correct.

Q. Would you read the last paragraph?

A. "Ultimately, Major Bent will accompany you to a point where you will meet with us."

Q. And would you tell us what happened on Monday the 17th of December?

A. Well, the first thing on Monday, I got up but then they had a ceremony for my release.

Q. And did you receive some items at that ceremony?

A. Yes, I did.

Q. Now, this first one is a document. I'm going to read it quickly. It's headed "Front of Liberation of the Enclave of Cabinda, F-L-E-C Military Position, Certificate of Nationality. We members of Central Committee of FLEC-PM, legal representatives of Cabindan people in war, we have freely decided by the present certificate to confer on Mr. Brent Swane, American citizen, the nationality of Cabindan citizen, assuming that he has lived and experienced the misery of Cabindan fighters during his two months of stay in bush.

"For the future generations that will have upper hand in Cabinda when it will enjoy its freedom, will pray them to consider Mr. Brent Swane a genuine Cabindan citizen with no differences with those Cabindans origin in rights and privileges.

"We freely deliver to him the present certificate which testifies it is worthwhile to him to have the merits above mentioned.

"Victoria Base. December 17, 1992. Cabinda."

I'm turning over to the reverse of it. What was your understanding of what this was?

A. That it was a passport.

Q. Whose picture is that?

A. Mine.

Q. And was this given to you also on that occasion?

A. Yes.

Q. Again, for the record, I'm going to read it.

"Today is December 17, 1992. In the bush of Cabinda, King Base. It's the departure of Mr. Brent Swane.

"We are deeply convinced that Mr. Brent Swane carry a lively sense of our goodness.

"We assure to Mr. Brent Swane that in our minds will live a deep and positive impression after the two months you stayed over in our bush.

"We're sure that Mr. Brent Swane, America and Americans will have a clear and real idea as to the regards to the struggle of Cabindan people.

"After six years of work in Cabinda, Mr. Brent Swane knows to what extent Cabindan people has been undergoing a life in harshness. We'd not like Mr. Brent Swane to consider the two months you stayed in our bush as a period of captivity. Please think it over deeply. Consider our other people's impressions and you will discover what does it mean.

"In our opinion, all the time has a deep sense and it's just meaningful. Please Mr. Brent Swane, don't forget to witness about everything you've lived, side-by-side with Cabindan fighters. Cheers to Mr. Brent Swane, thank you."

THE COURT: Ladies and gentlemen, it's 5:00. We have been here since 8:00 this morning. We're going to recess the trial for today and come back tomorrow morning.

SECOND DAY, SEPTEMBER 5, 2005, MORNING SESSION

BY MS. INGERS:
Q. Can you tell us a little bit about that ceremony, what happened in the ceremony.
A. As best I can recall there was some pouring of whiskey on the ground for the blood lost of the brothers. And there was one of the FLEC members, Lourenc, did a clown act, an entertainment type of thing.
Q. When you were finally, on the 17th of December, 1992, about to be actually released from your captivity, by what means of transportation did you leave that base camp?
A. We left on foot. We walked out to a location, from what they told me, we crossed the border into Zaire and stopped at a waiting point.
Q. Who did you see at that release point?
A. I remember several FLEC members going out with me, and a Zaire representative.
Q. Did the Zaire representative give you anything?
A. Yes, he did. A letter from Gary Webe.

Q. What generally does that letter consist of?

A. That the bearer is a Zaire government official, and he's going to hand me this letter so I know who he is.

THE COURT: Would you just identify Gary Webe for the record again, please, sir?

THE WITNESS: Gary Webe was my supervisor. He was the main representative for Petrol Helicopters Foreign Department.

THE COURT: All right.

BY MS. INGERS:

Q. When you received this letter, did you in fact go with the Zairian representative?

A. Yes.

Q. Did you get in that truck where you met the Zairian official?

A. Yes.

Q. Where did he take you?

A. To a place in Moanda, Zaire.

Q. When you arrived in Moanda who, if anyone, did you meet?

A. I met with Gary Webe and Scott Taylo.

Q. Who was Scott Taylo?

A. A Chevron representative.

Q. And what happened between you and them and the people who brought you down to Moanda in those vehicles?

A. Gary Webe went with me in another pickup truck and left the area.

Q. And where did you go from Moanda?

A. We departed Moanda in the morning, arriving in Kinshasa that same morning. Departed that evening for London, and then the next day arrived in Atlanta.

Q. And from Atlanta, did you meet anyone in Atlanta?

A. Yes. My wife.

Q. Where did you go from Atlanta?

A. To the Tulane University in New Orleans.

Q. Why did you go there?

A. Medical attention.

Q. Mr. Swane, after you were released on the 18th of December, 1992, after two months in captivity, did you ever go back to Cabinda?

A. Yes, I did.

Q. About how long after you were released from captivity did you go back?

A. The best I can recall I went back in November, 1993.

Q. You went back to work?

A. Yes.

Q. And for how long did you continue working in Cabinda?
A. I worked there until March of 2004.
Q. Why did you go back?
A. I liked the job, I liked the schedule, the money was good.
After being released, I wanted to get my life back to normal as quickly as I could.
Q. Kind of like getting back on a horse after you've been thrown?
A. Exactly.
Q. Mr. Swane, how, if at all, did the way that you lived and worked in Malongo and Cabinda City Airport change after you went back?

THE COURT: I'm sorry?

MR. BO: Objection.

THE COURT: Why don't you come to the bench. I don't know what the relevance of that is.

(Bench conference on the record.)

MS. INGERS: Your Honor, the jury knows and was going to know certainly that he went back, and in order to fairly assess the credibility and sincerity of his testimony here today, we believe that the jury is entitled to know what it is that caused him to be comfortable going back to that place. In addition, there were additional security measures. There were two things that happened. One is, he didn't drive that road anymore. The second thing is that the company put in other security measures. I don't think he knows about the security measures, but he can talk, he can say that although he went back, he didn't—he took a helicopter to the airport. He didn't drive.

THE COURT: What relevance is that?

MS. INGERS: It goes to—

MR. BO: It goes to proof of life.

MS. INGERS: It seems extraordinary that someone who had gone through this experience would go back and put himself in the same harm's way. And the fact is, he didn't—he went back, but he didn't put himself in harm's way.

THE COURT: I'm going to sustain the objection. If he gets into it in cross, you can come back to it. That he wasn't upset by this kidnapping, it didn't mean anything to him, he certainly can bring it up again. I'll sustain it now.

MS. INGERS: Thank you.

(End of bench conference.)

THE COURT: I'll sustain the objection. You can go with another question.

MS. INGERS: No further questions.

THE COURT: Thank you. Are you ready for cross?

MR. BO: Yes, sir.

THE COURT: All right. We will subject Mr. Swane to cross at this time.

MR. BO: Thank you, Your Honor.

(THE PUBLIC DEFENDER TOOK OVER THE CROSS-EXAMINATION AND STARTED WITH A RE-IDENTIFYING OF THE PEOPLE IN THE NUMEROUS PHOTOGRAPHS ENTERED AS EVIDENCE. WHEN THE FBI INTERVIEWED MR. SWANE FOUR WEEKS AFTER HIS RELEASE (JANUARY 7, 1993) THEY ASKED HIM TO WRITE ON THE BACK OF EACH PHOTOGRAPH THE IDENTITIES OF THE PERSON IN THE PHOTOS. A FEW OF THE PEOPLE HE COULDN'T IDENTIFY THEN, AND COULDN'T NOW, EITHER. MR. BO TOOK A RISKY CHANCE BY HAVING THE DEFENDANT STAND UP AND ASKING IF MR. SWANE RECOGNIZED HIM. HE SAID HE DIDN'T RECOGNIZE HIM, BUT DID REMEMBER HEARING HIS NAME AND SEEING IT ON HIS "CERTIFICATE OF NATIONALITY." THE TESTIMONY CONTINUED:)

Q. Now, I want to clear up a couple of things you said yesterday. You testified that after your abduction you noticed that there had been a second individual that was also abducted, correct?
A. That's right.
Q. This was an Angolan police officer; is that your understanding?
A. To the best of my knowledge he was an Angolan police officer, yes.
Q. Now, you testified that after his release there was some hollering and some gunfire; is that correct?
A. That's right.
Q. Just so that we're clear, you now know that the Angolan police officer wasn't shot, right?
A. No.

MS. INGERS: Objection. The basis of his knowledge.

THE COURT: I think it's a fair question. I'll overrule it. If he knows or doesn't know he can answer. It's all right.

THE WITNESS: I don't know if that Angolan policeman is alive today, no.

BY MR. BO:
Q. Well, sir, you certainly knew after your release that he was alive, correct?
A. No.
Q. Sir, didn't the Angolan police officer say some things about his abduction that you knew were not true?

MS. INGERS: Objection.

THE COURT: Why don't you come to the bench and we will talk about whether he knows or doesn't know.

(Bench conference on the record.)

MS. INGERS: Outside the scope and lack of relevance.

THE COURT: It's not outside the scope because I assume from the impression of his earlier testimony he gave he was killed.

MS. INGERS: It goes to his state of mind while he was in captivity.

THE COURT: I understand that, but I'm a bit worried—

MR. BO: It's completely misleading to the jury.

THE COURT: It's certainly state of mind, it terrified him, and that's fine. He didn't feel he could leave because he could be shot.

But you shouldn't leave the jury with the impression that he was executed if he wasn't.

MS. INGERS: The question, I think, should be did he personally see or talk to that man afterwards. Because if he didn't, he only has it through hearsay.

MR. BO: Whether or not he has it through hearsay, he knows.

THE COURT: If he knows through some method, if he can answer that whether it's true or not, I don't know. But if he has knowledge of it, he should be permitted to answer that. I don't know what he knows.

MR. BO: Your Honor, I know he knows because he wrote in his journal about some misstatements that he made during his captivity. I hope that he will answer truthfully when I ask a question.

THE COURT: I'm going to allow it.

MS. INGERS: For the record, the government is not contesting the fact that the Angolan remained alive.

(End of bench conference.)

THE COURT: I'll overrule the objection.

BY MR. BO:
Q. Mr. Swane, isn't it true that you know that the Angolan police officer was, in fact, released alive?
A. I don't know that he was.
Q. Let me ask it a little more specifically. Didn't you learn after your release and after the Angolan police officer's release that he had said that he had been blindfolded during the course of his abduction?
A. I learned that an Angolan policeman had been released from them, but I'm not sure if it was the same one that I saw.
Q. Well, sir, didn't you have some problems with the fact that he had said that he had been blindfolded, and that you had been blindfolded as well?
A. I was not blindfolded, no.
Q. Okay. Now, you testified that the first night, I believe either the first or the second night, you heard a gunshot in the middle of the night, correct?
A. That's right.
Q. Isn't it true that the next morning you found out what that gunshot was all about?
A. Yes.
Q. It had nothing to do with anyone getting hurt, right?
A. Only a porcupine.
Q. A porcupine which they served you for breakfast, right?
A. Exactly.

MR. BO: Your Honor, I have no additional questions of Mr. Swane.

THE COURT: Thank you, sir. Redirect, if the government wishes it.

MS. INGERS: Briefly, Your Honor.

REDIRECT EXAMINATION

BY MS. INGERS:

Q. Now, Mr. Swane, you testified that Tiburci and his group came into the camp the day before Thanksgiving?

A. Yes.

Q. When Tiburci came in, who of his group were you most interested in talking to?

A. Tiburci.

Q. And why was that?

A. He's the top man.

Q. Now, when you got out from captivity, did the people who had been involved in the negotiations over your release talk to you about the negotiations?

A. A little bit.

Q. And did you hear names of people that you understood to have been involved on the FLEC side of those negotiations?

A. Yes.

Q. And was there a name you heard that puzzled you a little bit?

A. Yes.

Q. What was that name?

A. Tchibass.

Q. And what was it that puzzled you about the fact that the people you were released to, your friends and colleagues, were talking about a Tchibass?

A. It puzzled me that they hadn't been talking with Tiburci.

Q. Did you draw any conclusions about the fact that they were talking about Tchibass, but you had been focused on Tiburci?

A. I'm not sure if I came to any final conclusion other than Tiburci being the president and possibly I had gotten the two names with T's confused.

Q. And, sir, in the entire time that you were held captive by FLEC-PM, did you ever see any member of FLEC-PM dressed up in a suit with a tie?

A. No.

MS. INGERS: Thank you. Nothing further.

THE COURT: Thank you, sir. You're free to step down.

(Witness excused.)

MS. INGERS: The next witness is Francoise Ker.

(MS. KER IS A TRANSLATOR/INTERPRETOR WORKING WITH THE FBI. SHE DESCRIBED HER IMPRESSIVE QUALIFICATIONS FOR THE JOB AS AN EXPERT TRANSLATOR.)

MS. INGERS: Your Honor, at this time I tender the witness as an expert in the translation of French to English and English to French for the purpose of authenticating translations of documents relevant to this case. They're in those languages.

THE COURT: Ladies and gentlemen, I'm going to admit the testimony of Ms. Ker as an expert translator in the area of French and documents and languages and the oral language of French to English. I'll just give you a brief advice as to expert witnesses. Ordinarily the Rules of Evidence do not permit witnesses to testify as their opinions or inclusions about something. Witnesses testify on their personal knowledge and what they have seen, they have heard, et cetera. But there's an exception to the rule for expert witnesses, and experts are allowed to give their opinions or conclusions because they have become experts in some art or science or calling or profession. They may give their opinions and conclusions and the reasons for their opinions and conclusions. So, in this case, I'm going to permit Ms. Ker to testify as an expert. You're not bound by the expert's opinion. If you find the opinion is not based upon sufficient experience, education, or the reasons for the opinion you don't believe are sound, or it's outweighed by other evidence, you can partially or completely disregard the opinion. But you give it the weight you think it deserves along with all the other evidence. But I'm going to allow Ms. Ker to testify as an expert translator in the area in which she has specially been trained. All right.

(NOW THE PROSECUTOR HAD MS. KER IDENTIFY 24 DIFFERENT DOCUMENTS THAT SHE TRANSLATED FROM FRENCH INTO ENGLISH. IT SEEMED THAT THE LANGUAGES SPOKEN IN CABINDA PROVINCE WERE BOTH FRENCH AND PORTUGESE. THE NEXT WITNESS WAS A MR. ACEITUN, A PORTUGESE TRANSLATOR WITH THE FBI WHO IDENTIFIED ALL THE DOCUMENTS HE HAD TRANSLATED FROM PORTUGESE INTO ENGLISH. THE COURT ALSO ADMITTED HIM AS AN EXPERT WITNESS. HE ACCOMPANIED THE JUSTICE DEPARTMENT LAWYERS TO PORTUGAL WHEN THE PORTUGESE POLICE WERE INTERVIEWING PORTUGESE-SPEAKING WITNESSES TO THE ABDUCTION. HIS TASK WAS TO INTERPRET FOR THE AMERICANS WHAT THE PORTUGESE WITNESSES WERE TELLING THE AUTHORITIES. THE NEXT WITNESS WAS ROY WHITAKE, A U.S. FOREIGN SERVICE OFFICER.)

BY MS. EVY:

Q. Can you state your full name for the record, please?

A. Roy L. Whitake.

Q. What is your occupation, sir?

A. I'm a Foreign Service Officer.

Q. Mr. Whitake, in October of 1992, where were you posted?

A. I was posted in Kinshasa, what was then known as Zaire, what is now known as the Congo.

Q. Can you please tell the jury where the post was in Zaire?

A. Yes. Kinshasa, which is just across the river from Brazzaville.

Q. What job did you have at that posting?

A. I was political officer at the embassy.

Q. What did that entail?

A. That entailed primarily following domestic events in Zaire, also to some extent following regional events, Zaire's relationship both with the United States and with other countries in the region.

Q. Mr. Whitake, are you familiar with a group called FLEC-PM?

A. Yes, I am.

Q. When did you first learn about that organization?

A. That was in October of 1992.

Q. And are you familiar with the circumstances of the abduction of an American citizen named Brent Swane?

A. Yes, I am.

Q. When was Mr. Swane abducted?

A. He was abducted on October the 19th.

Q. And how did you learn of that abduction?

A. We first learned about that when Chevron contacted our embassy in Paris, and we received a copy of that at Embassy Kinshasa.

Q. Were kidnappings common in Angola or Zaire at that time?

A. They were certainly taking place. In Cabinda, there had been Portuguese and French citizens abducted.

Q. Ever an American?

A. Up to that date, no.

Q. So what, if anything, did you do when you heard about the abduction of Mr. Swane?

A. Well, we immediately tried to get as much information as we could.

Q. After trying to get that information, did there come a time when you met representatives of this organization called FLEC-PM?

A. Yes. On October 26th one of the members of FLEC-PM came to the embassy.

Q. Do you remember his name?

A. Yes. There were three majors, and one was a Major Zulu.

Q. Mr. Whitake, can you describe what happened when Major Zulu came to the embassy on October 26th, 1992?

A. The major asked to see someone in the political section, and said that he had information on the abduction of Mr. Swane. He saw my supervisor, and later on saw me as well. And during this visit he gave us several items, one of those was a letter Mr. Swane had written in the jungle. He also gave us letters which were addressed to the Chevron corporation, a letter addressed to the President of the United States, and a letter addressed to the U.S. Congress.

Q. I'm going to hand you what's been marked as Government's Exhibit 7c and ask if you have ever seen that before?

A. Yes, I have. This is the letter addressed by FLEC-PM to the President of Chevron Overseas Petrol in California.

Q. And this is a letter sent by whom?

A. This was sent by the president of FLEC Military Position, FLEC-PM, Mr. Jose Tiburci Zinga Luemb.

Q. Had you ever heard of Mr. Tiburci Luemb before?

A. At that time I don't believe I had, no.

Q. And if I may, can I ask you to read the first paragraph of this letter for the record?

A. "The Central Committee of the Liberation Front of the Enclave Military Position," I'm sorry—

MR. BO: Objection, Your Honor. Can we approach?

THE COURT: Sure.

(Bench conference on the record.)

MR. BO: The government's been doing this throughout the trial so far, having the witnesses read the exhibits. The exhibits speak for themselves. I don't think there's any reason why any witness should be reading the exhibit itself.

THE COURT: It's overruled, the objection. I think that the exhibit that's put in evidence can be reviewed by a witness to introduce it to the jury. To let the jury wait until they get back to the trial two or three weeks later don't help. I'm going to allow it. I don't think it's prejudicial or unfair as long as they read what it says.

MR. BO: The concern is what words they emphasize or de-emphasize. I haven't seen that happen yet, but I do have that concern.

THE COURT: I'll watch if they get dramatic.

(End of bench conference.)

THE COURT: We can go ahead. I think there was a question to you to read the first paragraph of the letter for the record.

THE WITNESS: "The Central Committee of the Liberation Front of the Enclave-Military Position, has the honor to inform the management of the Chevron multinational that on October 19, 1992, their Armed Forces had made prisoner Mr. Brent Swane of American nationality in their operational zones."

BY MS. EVY:
Q. And is this letter dated?
A. The letter is dated 23 October, 1992.
Q. Thank you, sir. I'll show you now what's been marked as Government's Exhibit 7d and ask if you've ever seen this before?
A. This is a letter from FLEC-PM addressed to Their Excellencies, the members of Congress of the United States of America.
Q. And is there a signature at the end of the document?
A. It's also from the president of FLEC-PM, Jose Tiburci Zinga Luemb.
Q. Mr. Whitake, I'm going to turn your attention to the first paragraph and ask if you can please read that to the jury.
A. It says "The Central Counsel for the Front for the Liberation of the Enclave of Cabinda has the honor to inform the American Congress that its armed forces took prisoner, in its operational zones on 19 October, 1992, an American citizen, an employee of the Multinational Chevron operating in Cabinda."
Q. Thank you.

THE COURT: We will take our lunch recess at this time, ladies and gentlemen.

(A luncheon recess was taken.)

A F T E R N O O N S E S S I O N

(Jury in.)

THE COURT: Ladies and gentlemen, we are ready to get going again at this time with the continuation of the testimony of Mr. Whitake, who had begun his testimony before lunch.

MS. EVY: Thank you, Your Honor.

BY MS. EVY:

Q. Mr. Whitake, I'm going to show you this government exhibit and ask if you have seen this before?

A. Yes, I have. This is a letter from FLEC-PM addressed to His Excellence, Mr. George Bush, President of the United States.

Q. And who has signed that letter?

A. This was also signed by the president of FLEC-PM, Mr. Jose Tiburci Zinga Luemb. This is one of the letters that Major Zulu brought to the embassy and to me on October 26th, 1992.

Q. Now, Mr. Whitake, I'd like to direct your attention to the first paragraph and ask if you would please read that for the members of the jury?

A. Yes. "At a time when humanity is going through a period of unexpected transformation and upheaval for the re-establishment of justice and the installation of peace in the world, the Central Counsel of FLEC-PM has the honor to inform his Excellency, the President of the United States of America, that on 19 October 1992, Mr. Brent Swane of American nationality was taken prisoner by the freedom fighters of Cabinda who struggle unceasingly for the liberation of their territory."

Q. Thank you. If I can direct your attention to paragraph six, can you please read that.

A. Yes. "The arrest of an American citizen by the combatants for liberty is not an anti-American act, but is simply in order to attract the attention of humanity in general, and the United States in particular to the situation of the Cabindan people and the harmful role played by multinational Chevron in the genocide of the Cabindan people. It is for this reason that the Central Council of FLEC-PM solicits the intervention of his Excellency, the President of the United States, so that a just solution may be found returning to the Cabindan people their rights."

Q. Thank you. Now, Mr. Whitake, as to the letters to President Bush and the letter to Congress, did you do anything in particular with those documents when they were presented to you?

A. As a matter of standard procedure we took the documents, made Xerox copies of them and kept them, but we then returned the original letters to Major Zulu.

Q. Why did you return the originals?

A. We did not feel it was appropriate under the circumstances to forward those either to the U.S. Congress or to the U.S. President.

Q. Why was that?

A. At that point we considered them a terrorist organization, and we did not feel it was appropriate that we should facilitate any messages between a terrorist group and American authorities.

Q. Did you eventually accept them?

A. Much later. Later in the discussions with FLEC-PM we ascertained, we determined that accepting them might actually help us in obtaining the release of Mr. Swane. So at that point later in the discussions we did accept them.

Q. Okay. After the meetings with Major Zulu on October 26th, 1992, what happened then?

A. The next day, Major Zulu came in with two of his colleagues, Major Bent and Major Tchibass. They presented their identification in terms of badges and letters, and they insisted on a meeting with Chevron to be facilitated by the embassy.

Q. Had you ever seen any of these representatives of FLEC-PM before?

A. Only Major Zulu who had been in the day before. But Major Tchibass and Major Bent, no.

Q. I'm going to show you what's been marked as Government's Exhibit Number 8a and ask you if you've ever seen that before?

A. Yes. These are copies of the identification cards that Majors Tchibass and Bent brought into the embassy and gave to us.

Q. What, if anything, did you do with them?

A. Again, our standard operating procedure was to take these, make Xerox copies of them, and give the originals back. We then sent copies, as we sent copies of everything we received from FLEC, back to the Department of State.

Q. Now I'm going to show you what's been marked as Exhibit 10a and ask if you've ever seen Exhibit 10a before?

A. Yes, I have. These are orders issued by the President of FLEC, Jose Tiburci, authorizing a number of people to represent FLEC-PM. I found in Third World countries that organizations, other than those directly linked to the government, generally try to cover themselves in as extensive documentation as they can, letters of introduction, badges of identification, and so forth. It's a way I think of creating an image of legitimacy.

Q. Mr. Whitake, what was the primary purpose for the United States Embassy to receive this delegation?

A. We had only one concern, and that was the life and well-being of an American citizen, Brent Swane.

Q. Did the FLEC representatives return at another time to the embassy?

A. Yes, they did, some three days later on October 30th.

Q. And for what reason did they return?

A. On the 27th they had asked, insisted really, on a meeting with Chevron. During the three intervening days, we were in communication with Chevron as regards such a meeting, but at the same time we were preparing a package for Brent Swane: Medicines, American style foods, clothing, things that he might need in the jungle. And finally we wanted some proof that he was still alive, so we gave a camera to FLEC-PM so that they could take a photograph of Mr. Swane and bring the photographs back to us. We gave FLEC-PM those things on the 30th. Major Zulu came back to see us on November the 3rd, three days later.

Q. And what, if anything, happened during that meeting with Major Zulu?

A. Well, a number of things. First of all, they gave us photographs showing Mr. Swane in the jungle. They brought us an audiotape that they allowed Mr. Swane to prepare also in the jungle. They brought us several letters from Mr. Swane. But in terms of the meeting that was to be held with Chevron, they also brought back a fairly significant change in their position.

Q. Can you explain that?

A. Yes. At the beginning, the understanding between them and us was that Brent Swane would be released, and that upon his release there would then be a meeting with Chevron. So that the release of Swane would either be prior to or simultaneous with the meeting with Chevron. But when they came back on November 3rd, they brought back a letter changing that position and saying that Brent Swane would only be released after the meeting with Chevron.

Q. Now, I'm going to show you Exhibit 5 and ask if you can identify that?

A. Yes. This is the audiotape prepared by Brent Swane and brought back to us at the embassy by FLEC-PM on November 3rd.

Q. And based on what you heard in that audiotape, what did you think about the situation with Mr. Swane at that point?

A. We had always been concerned about his health. For those who have been in Africa, especially in a place like Zaire. It's a very rough place to live. He was in captivity. He had no control over his food, medicine, et cetera, so we had been concerned from the beginning. But based on what we heard in this audiotape, discussions of his medical conditions, for example, we were increasingly concerned about how well he was.

Q. So as a result of that concern what, if anything, was done at the embassy to send him anything?

A. Two things were done. First of all, we continued our insistence that FLEC-PM release him. Second of all, we prepared a new care package.

Q. And did the care package include items to address the health issue?

A. Yes, it did. In fact, we brought our U.S. Embassy doctor into this, and our doctor along with the representatives of FLEC selected some medicine which would address some of the specific health problems that he was suffering: Skin problems, gastric problems, stomach problems.

Q. And Mr. Zulu accepted those?

A. Yes, he did.

Q. Now, when was the next time that you saw FLEC-PM representatives?

A. The next time was two days later when all three, Major Tchibass, Major Bent and Major Zulu all came to the U.S. Embassy.

Q. What was the purpose of that visit?

A. The purpose was to agree to a November 9 meeting that Chevron International had proposed.

Q. From your experience on October 27th and November 5th, can you describe the respective roles of the three individuals who came as a group at that time?

A. At first, we had no way of knowing who was more equal than others, but it soon became obvious for both linguistic reasons and I think because he had greater authority within the group, Major Tchibass began to take a leading role and continued to take a leading role.

Q. Was there a consistent request or demand made by the members of the delegation as they visited you at the embassy?

A. Yes, of course. The first meeting was for the meeting with Chevron, but as it moved into substance they began to suggest specific demands. And over time it came out, probably their underlying theme was that they were a political military group with emphasis on military. And that what they wanted most from Chevron was funding to arm and equip a fairly large number of FLEC-PM troops. I believe the number was 2,000 troops.

Q. By this time what, if anything, was Chevron doing to make progress in this situation?

A. Chevron was exploring all possibilities with FLEC-PM. But, again, there was a major discrepancy between FLEC-PM's initial position and its later position. Its initial position being that Brent Swane would be released before any detailed talks took place. The later position was of course that Brent Swane would continue to be held while these discussions took place.

Q. Did they return to the embassy after November 5th?

A. They came back on November 13th.

Q. And what was the purpose in coming back?

A. They wanted to advise us of what they considered an impasse with the negotiations with Chevron.

Q. Did they explain to you what the nature of the impasse was?

A. We already had a very good idea because, of course, we had been communicating very closely with Chevron. But I think the key difficulty was that Chevron was insisting on limiting any aid that it give to FLEC to humanitarian goods, and that these humanitarian goods if they were to be delivered, would be delivered through charitable organizations. At the same time, FLEC-PM was continuing to insist on money payments specifically for the purchase of arms.

Q. And which among the FLEC delegation did most of the communicating?

A. By this time in the talks Major Tchibass was definitely taking the dominant role.

Q. Mr. Whitake, did the delegation say anything more about Mr. Swane on that day, if you remember?

A. Well, we always talked about Mr. Swane's health and his emotional state. Those are questions we always brought up, as we did at this meeting. And at the time we gave a letter and another care package for Mr. Swane.

Q. More specifically, however, did they say anything about who was going to be responsible for what would occur with Mr. Swane?

A. Yes. They complained that Chevron had not paid attention to them, that Chevron was drawing out the negotiations, and therefore they said it was Chevron who had ultimate responsibility for Mr. Swane's health and well-being.

Q. Mr. Whitake, did you hear from the FLEC-PM representatives after that date?

A. Yes, we did, but a long time had passed. We had another meeting with Major Zulu on November 26th in which he delivered some more letters from Brent Swane to his wife, to Gary Webe, and to Dr. Dumon, our embassy doctor, outlining many of the medical problems that Brent Swane was having.

Q. Finally, Exhibit Number 7. Have you ever seen those before?

A. These are letters from FLEC-PM to the president of Chevron Overseas Petrol on November 26th.

Q. Mr. Whitake, if you may, can you read the fourth paragraph for the jury.

MR. BO: Your Honor, for the record, we're going to be renewing our objection made earlier at the bench conference concerning the reading of documents.

THE COURT: All right. I'm overruling that objection, and allow the witness to identify the document and to read the particular parts that the government points out to bring it to the jury's attention, because the jury will have all this eventually to read in any event. Go ahead.

MS. EVY: Thank you.

Q. Mr. Whitake, can you read the fifth paragraph of this letter?

A. Okay. "The Central Committee of FLEC-PM that met during a special assembly on November 19-22 in the liberated territories, informs Mr. President that the basis for the negotiations remains the demands that was presented by its delegation during the first round of negotiations in Kinshasa. The members of the delegation of FLEC-PM remains unchanged."

Q. Thank you. Did you have any sense at that time when or if talks would resume between FLEC-PM representatives and Chevron representatives?

A. We were becoming extremely concerned. It had been well over a month, five weeks, going on six weeks I guess and there had been no movement. We had had expressions of disappointment by FLEC. There were also indications from Chevron that the talks were not going well, so we were extremely concerned.

Q. Did you ever discuss with FLEC-PM representatives what your concerns were with the continuing hostage taking?

A. Yes, absolutely. Every time we saw them. One of the significant meetings, came on November 27th. Major Zulu came to see me and indicated probably for the first time that there might be some flexibility in FLEC-PM's position. At the same time, however, he was still pushing for the maximal FLEC position, which was money for armaments. And his reasoning was that this had to be done for the release of Brent Swane. That, yes, it might very well violate American laws, but that some laws after all had to be circumvented. I immediately responded that this might be the case in some countries, but in the United States we expected laws to be implemented. I emphasized that Chevron was restricted by limitations of American law, that it could not simply give everything that FLEC-PM asked, and that if FLEC-PM expected to gain anything at all from these negotiations, they would have to modify their demands, and that there would have to be assurances that Brent Swane would be released in the very near future.

Over the next three weeks we did see at least that FLEC-PM and Chevron were talking more or less on the same wavelength, that they were talking in realistic terms. Rather than simply stating and restating maximal positions, they were stating positions that actually could be acted on, and talking about details of, for example, delivery of goods. It was a realistic discussion after that, even though it continued for almost another month.

Q. Mr. Whitake, were you involved in the release of Brent Swane from captivity?
A. Not actually on the day he was released, no. I had to handle a Congressman's visit, so the embassy sent its Consulate Officer to the border to help in his release.
Q. And did you see Mr. Swane after he had been released?
A. Yes, I did. It was just before Christmas, and we had a kind of combination Christmas/congratulations-on-being-free party.
Q. How did he look to you at that time?
A. Tired, haggard. You could see that he had had some skin condition. On the other hand, he looked like a very happy man to be free.
Q. Did the embassy continue to meet with FLEC-PM representatives after he was released?
A. Yes, we did.
Q. Did those representatives include Major Tchibass?
A. Yes. Now, I wasn't involved in many of the ongoing talks. Occasionally I would see them briefly, but the embassy did, in fact, continue to see them.
Q. Why would the embassy continue to see them after that?
A. Because we wanted to gauge not so much the success of the settlement that was made between Chevron and FLEC. We wanted to see the extent to which FLEC was satisfied with the outcome of the negotiations. Because we had seen their capacity for striking at an American citizen before. We were afraid that if FLEC were dissatisfied with the settlement and what was actually delivered, they might once again try to strike at an American citizen or American interests. And as the U.S. Embassy, it was our obligation to gauge the extent to which that might actually be a possibility.

Q. Now, Mr. Whitake, is there anyone in the courtroom today that you recognize as having been in Kinshasa, Zaire in October, November, December, of 1992?

A. You know, it's been 13 years and people change, but I believe I recognize Major Tchibass.

Q. Can you please indicate to the ladies and gentlemen of the jury who you're talking about?

A. This person right here.

THE COURT: All right. He's identified Mr. Tchibass.

MS. EVY: Thank you, Your Honor.

THE COURT: Thank you.

MS. EVY: That's all our questions.

CROSS-EXAMINATION
BY MR. BO:

Q. Mr. Whitake, your testimony today is that it was your opinion during your contacts in 1992 that Mr. Tchibass was the leader of the delegation; is that correct?

A. That's correct.

Q. Now, it's fair to say that prior to October 26th you had never heard of Mr. Tchibass before, correct?

A. That's correct.

Q. You hadn't heard of the FLEC-PM before, correct?

A. That's correct.

Q. Now, you testified that when Mr. Zulu appeared on the 26th he was alone, correct?

A. Yes, that's right.

Q. You said that he had some demands, correct?

A. Yes.

Q. It wasn't until the 27th when Mr. Tchibass first appeared; is that correct?

A. That's right.

Q. And, in fact, when Mr. Tchibass first appeared, he had some direct conversations with you, correct?

A. That's right.

Q. And at that point it was your understanding that if Chevron were to agree to a meeting, then Brent Swane would be released; is that correct?

A. The reverse is true, yes. First the agreement, then the release, then the meeting.

Q. But that changed, right?

A. That changed.

Q. Initially the agreement was that once there was an agreement as to a meeting had been guaranteed, then Mr. Swane would be released, correct?

A. That's correct.

Q. And that turned out not to be true, right?

A. When they changed position, yes, they continued to hold Mr. Swane.

Q. The October 30th meeting was a meeting with Mr. Zulu; is that correct?

A. That's right.

Q. And that wasn't a meeting in which Mr. Bent appeared?

A. That's correct.

Q. And it wasn't a meeting where Mr. Tchibass appeared, correct?

A. That's correct.

Q. In fact, that was a meeting I believe where Mr. Zulu obtained the camera and a care package that was taken to Mr. Swane?

A. That's correct.

Q. In fact, during the course of that meeting, Mr. Zulu said that he would try and contact Mr. Bent concerning Mr. Swane's release, correct?

MS. EVY: Objection, Your Honor.

THE COURT: Why don't you come up.

(Bench conference on the record.)

THE COURT: The question was during the course of the meeting Mr. Zulu said he would try and contact Mr. Bent concerning Mr. Swane's release.

MS. EVY: Yes, Your Honor. The fact that the meeting occurred is certainly indirect. The fact that Mr. Zulu, Major Zulu, brought, visited, and accepted a care package is in the record. But the additional conversation that's being elicited by defense counsel is outside the scope, and it's hearsay, and it's just inappropriate.

MR. BO: Your Honor, one, it's relevant because it's going to show that Mr. Bent was the one that was the lead person as far as this delegation was concerned.

Two, that Mr. Tchibass was not the person that Mr. Zulu believed he needed to contact in order to get Mr. Swane released.

MS. EVY: I believe it's way beyond the scope of direct.

THE COURT: Well, he can make it. I'm going to overrule, I will allow it. But I do think as a coconspirator's statement, it can come in.

(End of bench conference.)

THE COURT: The objection is overruled. You can ask that question again.

MR. BO: Thank you, Your Honor.

BY MR. BO:

Q. Sir, at the October 30th meeting, didn't Mr. Zulu tell you that he would contact Mr. Bent concerning Mr. Swane's release?

A. He may have done so.

Q. He did not mention that he would contact Mr. Tchibass concerning his release, correct?

A. I don't recall specifically what he said.

Q. Mr. Whitake, I'd ask you to take a moment to review this document. Does that document refresh your recollection as to whether or not Mr. Zulu said he would contact Mr. Bent concerning Mr. Swane's release?

A. I think what he says in full is that he would contact Major Bent who was still in Kinshasa, the implication being that Tchibass perhaps at some point was not there.

Q. I'm asking you, does that tell you who he would contact?

A. Yes.

Q. And nowhere did he say that he would contact Mr. Tchibass?

A. I think the emphasis is on who he could contact in Kinshasa, which was Major Bent.

Q. Now, Mr. Zulu also appeared back in the embassy on November 3rd, correct?

A. That's right.

Q. And that was when he returned with the audiotape for Mr. Swane?

A. Yes.

Q. And, in fact, by November 3rd it had become apparent to you that Mr. Zulu and Mr. Tchibass, and Mr. Bent didn't have the authority that they claimed that they had had in earlier meetings; is that correct?

A. That's correct.

Q. And, in fact, it was clear that Mr. Zulu was only serving as a messenger; is that correct?

A. Yes.

Q. In fact, that was somewhat frustrating because up until then you thought that Mr. Zulu, Mr. Bent, Mr. Tchibass may have had the authority to release Mr. Swane, they certainly presented themselves as though they did; is that correct?

A. Yes.

Q. And it was clear by November 3rd, that they didn't have that authority; is that correct?

A. They by themselves did not have that authority, yes.

Q. Now, Mr. Whitake, earlier you testified that it was your impression that Mr. Tchibass was the leader of the delegation of the FLEC; is that correct?

A. Yes, that's correct.

Q. Well, isn't it true that on November 5th of 1992 you sent a cable to the State Department in which you identified Major Bent as the delegation chief?

A. That's true, yes, I do know the document.

Q. Okay. Now you met with Mr. Zulu a total of eight times?

A. That's right.

Q. And you met with Mr. Bent four times; is that correct?

A. Yes, I suppose.

Q. Those meetings were face-to-face meetings with Mr. Zulu and Mr. Bent; is that correct?

A. That's correct.

Q. Just for completion, you also had a number of face-to-face meetings with Mr. Tchibass?

A. Three times, four times, five I guess it is.

MR. BO: I have no further questions of Mr. Whitake.

REDIRECT EXAMINATION
BY MS. EVY:

Q. Why are you so certain about the identification of Mr. Tchibass?

A. For two reasons, I think. Number one, he clearly was delegation chief or what have you, he clearly took the leading role. He was the dominant personality. And I have to say about him he has a certain charisma, a certain flair. He's the sort of person you remember.

MS. EVY: Nothing further.

(Witness excused.)

MS. EVY: Your Honor, the government calls Gary Webe.

(MR. WEBE DESCRIBED HIS POSITION AS MR. SWANE'S BOSS AT THE HELICOPTER FIRM. HE WAS BASED IN LOUISIANA AND CONTROLLED THE COMPANY'S OPERATIONS IN TEN OTHER COUNTRIES BESIDES ANGOLA. MS. EVY CONTINUED:)

Q. Before October, 1992, were there any security concerns for PHI employees operating in Malongo?

A. There were occasional incursions into the Malongo compound area by small mortar attacks, things like that, but we didn't have any concerns for security from an abduction standpoint.

Q. Where did PH employees live in relation to where they worked?

A. They all lived within the Malongo compound. There was a dormitory type situation. Their living quarters, the messing, food facilities, and the heliport location were all within several blocks of each other.

Q. So how would most people get from their residences to their job site?

A. They either walked or rode bicycles.

Q. Were there any off-sites that people had to go to off the compound?

A. The King Air airplane that I mentioned earlier was housed and maintained at Cabinda airport, which is in downtown Cabinda, approximately 30 miles from the Malongo compound.

Q. Mr. Webe, was there a regular time for a PH employees to commute to and from their jobs?

A. Our normal operating hours were sunrise to sunset, seven days a week. They worked 28 days continuous sunrise to sunset, every day of the week.

Q. The people who had to work at the Cabinda airport, how did they get to work?

A. They drove by a pickup or a vehicle supplied by Chevron between the Malongo compound and the Cabinda airport, and that generally took place between six and seven each morning, and back to the compound at roughly between five and six each evening.

Q. Now, jumping ahead, after Mr. Swane was released, did you have occasion to talk to him about the circumstances of his abduction?

A. Yes.

Q. And in that context did he tell you about a list that he saw?

A. Yes. He mentioned a list that had the names of several other PHI employees and as well as his own on it. That list contained his opposite. Remember we talked about a 28 and 28 work cycle, so that when Brent wasn't there, his opposite was there working. His name was on the list as well as several other PHI maintenance personnel.

Q. Was there anything else in common among the four names on the list?

A. They were the only ones of the staff that were allowed to leave the compound driving.

Q. When did you first learn that Brent Swane had been abducted?

A. I received a call from PHI's on-site manager in Malongo.

Q. Had you heard anything about where the abduction had occurred?

A. Yes. I was told that it was approximately halfway between the work site and Cabinda town.

Q. What did you do after you heard about the kidnapping?

A. I immediately went to my office. This was about 3:00 in the morning. I started informing the appropriate company officials, and then shortly thereafter I informed Brent's wife, Barbara.

Q. When did you first learn who was responsible for the abduction?

A. Around the end of October, the start of November, we received letters through the U.S. Embassy from Brent that told us in the letter who his abductors were.

Q. What did you think of the contents?

A. Well, first of all, I was surprised who Brent claims in his letter who they were. Secondly, I found interesting a number of places where Brent tries to give us little hints or signals that absolutely confirm that it was him writing the letter. It was kind of a read-between-the-lines type of thing.

Q. What did you do when you received the letter?

A. We started forming a crisis management negotiating team comprised of myself, Scott Taylo of Chevron, and Simon Adams from a company called Control Risk, and we also provided Mrs. Swane a fax machine so that in the event we received additional correspondence we could get it to her as quick as possible.

Q. Now, you went to Africa. Approximately when did that happen?

A. About the first week of November of '92.

Q. And why did that happen at that time?

A. It became apparent then through some of the communications that we were getting through the embassy that we had the opportunity to sit down and talk with FLEC directly in the hopes that we could ascertain Brent's release.

Q. And did you travel there alone?

A. No. The gentlemen I mentioned earlier, we went together to Kinshasa.

Q. And among the three of you, who was to take the lead in whatever communications occurred with the FLEC people?

A. Scott Taylo, the Chevron security gentleman, took the lead, and it was basically a unanimous decision that he do so. Everybody that worked within the Malongo compound was considered to be Chevron.

Q. Do you recall when you had the first negotiation session with anyone from FLEC-PM?

A. Yeah. It was about the 8th or 9th of November.

Q. And how many people represented the FLEC delegation?

A. Just three.

Q. Do you remember their names?

A. They all carried the title of Major. There was a Major Bent, Major Zulu, and a Major Tchibass.

Q. And did you have subsequent meetings with these three representatives of FLEC-PM?

A. There were approximately ten total meetings.

Q. And based on your observations at those meetings, can you describe the role of each of those FLEC individuals at the meeting?

A. Tchibass was the General and frequent spokesperson who did all the primary talking. Major Zulu was primarily an observer from our perspective and a notetaker, and although we all kind of agreed that Major Bent was the one in charge because of the way they would conduct their side discussions when they weren't directly negotiating.

Q. But the primary person speaking to you on their behalf was whom?

A. Major Tchibass did all the primary speaking as the negotiator.

Q. Did Major Tchibass speaking on behalf of the delegation ever attempt to distance himself from the abduction of Brent Swane?

A. No. As a matter of fact, they all took full claim and credit.

Q. At the end of the first meeting, was there an agreement as to when Mr. Swane would be released from captivity?

A. No, although it was our hope that there would be. The primary reason that we agreed to meet on the first meeting because of some of the correspondence that they, FLEC had sent, saying that the meeting would create the situation to allow for the release of Brent.

Q. So why have a second meeting?

A. Because no conclusions were reached. Initially also there were a number of demands that were beyond anybody's ability to respond to.

Q. What sort of demands were those?

A. The initial requirement had a large amount of military or paramilitary equipment, guns, weapons, vehicles that they were claiming as a condition of release.

Q. Did the Chevron negotiating team keep a written record of what was going on at these negotiation sessions?

A. Yes. It was done in each session. Our note-taker was Simon Adams. And in the evening after each session we would collectively go over the notes and make sure that we all had the same clear understanding of what had transpired that day. We used those notes then as a means of corresponding back to our respective companies to ensure that we all had the same information available.

Q. And were the negotiation sessions with FLEC delegation tape recorded?

A. No, they were not.

Q. Why not?

A. The FLEC negotiating team would not allow the tape recorder.

Q. Do you remember anything specific that Major Tchibass said concerning when Mr. Swane would be released?

A. I do specifically remember being approached after we had come to an agreement where Major Tchibass mentioned to me that he had really expected a large sum of money to be able to obtain the release of Brent. That was his original expectation.

Q. Did Major Tchibass, Major Zulu, and Major Bent attend each of those meetings?

A. Yes, they did.

Q. Were you present when Brent Swane was eventually released?

A. Yes, I was. It was in a remote location. Outside of a small town called Moanda, Zaire.

Q. Can you describe what your experience was at that release?

A. Scott Taylo, the Chevron security gentleman, and myself went out several miles east of the city at a dirt road intersection and met up with two vehicles. Shortly after that Brent Swane emerged from one of the vehicles, and we met in the middle of the road and left.

Q. What were you concentrating on when all of this happened?

A. Just to confirm that Brent was the first face that I saw, and that we wouldn't be hindered in any way in trying to depart.

Q. How long did you stay in the area?

A. Approximately 20 minutes from the time that we arrived there until the time we departed with Brent. We took him back to a Chevron facility just north of Moanda, Zaire, got cleaned up, did some medical examinations, took him back that same morning to Kinshasa, Zaire, and the following evening departed for Europe.

(NOW THE PROSECUTOR ASKED MR. WEBE TO IDENTIFY A NUMBER OF LETTERS HE HAD SENT TO BRENT SWANE, ALONG WITH A NUMBER OF LETTERS HE HAD RECEIVED FROM THE HOSTAGE. HE ALSO WAS ASKED TO IDENTIFY PERSONS IN A SERIES OF PHOTOGRAPHS. HE COULD EASILY IDENTIFY BRENT, AND ALSO TWO OF THE NEGOTIATORS FOR FLEC, BUT HE COULDN'T RECALL THEIR NAMES. SHE CONTINUED:)

Q. Now, Mr. Webe, was there a time after Brent was released that he returned to Angola?

A. Yes. He returned approximately a year and a half after his release, back to the same exact job he had before.

Q. And whose idea was it to send him back initially?

A. His.

Q. Did PHI revise any security procedures? Were there any operational changes made at the Cabinda facilities that you're aware of?

A. Yeah. No one was any longer allowed to drive between the two work locations, that's the Malongo base and Cabinda town itself. They flew by helicopter or by boat, but no driving on the roads.

MS. EVY: Nothing further, Your Honor.

THE COURT: All right. Thank you.

MR. BO: May we approach?

THE COURT: Sure.

(Bench conference on the record.)

MR. BO: Your Honor, I am going do ask that we conclude the testimony today. We did receive about ten pages as to this witness that we have not been provided with before today. Mr. Tchibass hasn't seen that material. It's important that some of the testimony that this witness has testified to relates to some instances I would like to have the opportunity to talk with Mr. Tchibass about to conduct my cross-examination of this witness. It's now 4:15. I understand—

THE COURT: It's the weekend.

MR. BO: But this is a problem the government knew about and they chose to proceed in this fashion. I don't think Mr. Tchibass should be held responsible.

MS. EVY: Your Honor, first of all, as we told the Court earlier, this witness is among those who is not a local witness and he has been here since the start of trial. We would agree to a brief recess perhaps, but this witness has plans to go home, and we don't think it would be fair for the witness to have to stay over the weekend simply because defense counsel needs some extra time to look at the material.

MS. INGERS: Which is not voluminous.

THE COURT: You just got that today?

MR. BO: Yes, Your Honor. And more important, Your Honor, I got material as to other witnesses yesterday.

THE COURT: Well, what I'm going to do is take a recess and try to have you look at it now and finish it up, because we won't get back until Monday afternoon, and there's no sense in keeping him if we can give you 15 or 20 minutes to look at the material, come back for a half hour or 45 minutes to finish the cross-examination.

MR. BO: Your Honor, if we can make the interpreters available, that's fine.

THE COURT: Thank you.

(End of bench conference.)

THE COURT: Ladies and gentlemen, we're going to ask you to stay a little bit longer this evening, because if we don't finish the cross this evening the witness will have to come back on Monday afternoon and he's from out of town. He'd have to fly all the way back, it's very difficult to do that. So if we just spend a few more minutes this evening we could probably finish it up. What I'm going to do is take a few minutes break so you can refresh yourselves a little bit, then we will come back and finish up the cross-examination.

(Jury out.)

THE COURT: Mr. Tchibass will need an interpreter for a few minutes to go through some documents, if one of you wouldn't mind staying for a few minutes to work on this.

Marshal, would you let him work on the documents so he can talk to his counsel about these documents that they haven't reviewed yet. Thank you.

We will take a short break until about 4:30 or so.

(Recess taken)

THE COURT: Bring the jury back and we will be ready to go.

MR. BO: Your Honor, we're not finished. We still have four pages to go and—

THE COURT: Oh, I understood you had finished. You still have four more pages to go?

MR. BO: Four more pages of this document and two pages of another document.

MS. INGERS: Your Honor, it was available last night, as I indicated before. We cleared the building and neglected to turn it over. Mr. Bo didn't remind us and we didn't realize it until it was very late last night.

THE COURT: All right. We're going to give you another few minutes to try to finish that up. For the jury's sake I don't want to be too much later.

(Recess taken)

THE COURT: Let's get the jury, please.

MR. BO: While the jury is coming in, I think I can just put this on the record. There's some references by Mr. Webe about some notes and statements that he took that he did not turn over to the FBI. The government has informed me that they don't have those notes. I'm assuming that that would not be producible material.

THE COURT: If they don't have it, yes. Thank you for putting that on the record.

(Jury in.)

THE COURT: All right. Ladies and gentlemen, thank you for your patience. We will go forward with the cross of Mr. Webe.

MR. BO: Thank you, Your Honor.

CROSS-EXAMINATION
BY MR. BO:

Q. Now, Mr. Webe, you were present at all ten of the negotiation sessions in this case; is that correct?

A. Correct.

Q. Mr. Bent appeared to be the leader of the delegation, correct?

A. Yes.

Q. In fact, it would be fair to say that he was the one that was in charge of the delegation, correct?

A. I don't know that for a fact.

Q. Didn't you, in fact, tell members of the FBI on February 28th of 1993 that Mr. Bent was the leader of the delegation?

A. No.

Q. Sir, on February 28th—well, sir, isn't it also true that the other members of the delegation acquiesced to Mr. Bent; that was your assessment?

A. Yes.

Q. Now, you testified on direct examination about a conversation that you had with Mr. Tchibass. Do you remember that?

A. Yes.

Q. In that testimony you testified that you had a conversation with Mr. Tchibass after the negotiation sessions, correct?

A. Correct.

Q. And your testimony today was that during that conversation, Mr. Tchibass said that he thought he was going to get a lot of money based on the Brent Swane incident, correct?

A. Correct.

Q. Now, sir, during your interview with the FBI, do you ever mention that conversation that you had with Mr. Tchibass?

A. I don't recall.

Q. Would you like a chance to review the document?

A. Sure.

Q. I'd ask you to take a look at the February 28th document, and nowhere is that incident referenced, is it?

A. No, sir. It is referenced.

Q. But, in fact, there is a reference about a conversation that you did have with some FLEC representatives after the release of Mr. Swane, correct?

A. Yes.

Q. And the FLEC representative told you that Brent Swane would be eventually released because it was bad for the FLEC to have Mr. Swane, correct?

A. No.

Q. They feared for his health, correct?

A. That he was a burden and they feared for his health.

Q. Okay. Now, you also on the 28th told the FBI, did you not, that you believed that the negotiators were "honorable men"?

A. Yes.

Q. And just so that I'm clear, is it your testimony that you told the FBI about the meeting that you had with Mr. Tchibass in which you mentioned the money, and that that somehow didn't get into the report, or is it that that's something that you're just telling us for the first time today?

A. No. It's right here in your document.

Q. It's your testimony that the conversation that you say you had with Mr. Tchibass in which Mr. Tchibass said that he thought that he was going to get a lot of money for Mr. Swane's abduction is in that report?

A. Correct.

Q. Can you point to me exactly where in that report where you see that language?

A. The last two lines of the last paragraph of the first page.

Q. Can you read those last two lines?

A. "After agreement had been reached, they were going to ask for $10 million for Swane."

Q. And you're attributing that to Mr. Tchibass?

A. Yes.

Q. You didn't say Mr. Tchibass, right?

A. No. The term "they" was used.

MR. BO: Okay. No further questions, Your Honor.

THE COURT: All right. How about some redirect, then? Any redirect?

MS. EVY: Very briefly, Your Honor.

THE COURT: Thank you.

BY MS. EVY:

Q. Mr. Webe, did the FBI show you a copy of this report of the interviews that they had with you?

A. Not that I recall.

Q. And did they ask you at any time to endorse the language that was used?

A. No, ma'am.

MS. EVY: Thank you. No further questions.

THE COURT: All right. You're free to go then, sir. Thank you.

(Witness excused.)

THE COURT: Ladies and gentlemen, that's going to conclude our session today.

THIRD DAY, SEPTEMBER 8, 2005, MORNING SESSION

(THE FOLLOWING PROCEEDINGS TOOK PLACE OUT OF THE PRESENCE OF THE JURY, AND IT'S A GOOD THING. THE DISCUSSION WAS SO FILLED WITH LEGALISE AND PREVIOUS COURT RULINGS THAT IT SURELY WOULD HAVE PUT THE ENTIRE JURY TO SLEEP. THE DISCUSSION CENTERED AROUND THE ADMISSABILITY OF HOSTAGE NEGOTIATION SESSION RECORDS AND NOTES. THE PUBLIC DEFENDER ARGUED LONG AND HARD THAT THESE NOTES TAKEN BY A CHEVRON EMPLOYEE WHO TRANSLATED THEM FROM THE FRENCH LANGUAGE INTO ENGLISH FOR THE AMERICAN NEGOTIATORS WAS NOT A RECOGNIZED INDEPENDENT TRANSLATION EXPERT AND SHOULD NOT BE INTRODUCED IN COURT. THEIR DISCUSSION— OFTEN HEATED—COVERED A WHOPPING 77 PAGES OF COURT REPORTING, BUT IN THE END THE COURT CITED A NUMBER OF PREVIOUS TRIALS WHERE SUCH MEMORANDA WERE ADMISSABLE, AND HE OVERRULED THE OBJECTION, ADMITTING THAT THE COURT SHOULD INSTRUCT THE JURY HOW THEY SHOULD TREAT THESE NOTES. THE JURY WAS THEN BROUGHT IN, AND THE PROSECUTOR CALLED SIMON ADAMS, ONE OF THE HOSTAGE NEGOTIATORS FOR CONTROL RISK GROUP, A BRITISH COMPANY THAT IS CALLED UPON AFTER A KIDNAP OR ABDUCTION HAS TAKEN PLACE. HE DESCRIBED HIS PRIOR EXPERIENCES WITH THE BRITISH ARMY SPECIAL FORCES UNIT INVOLVED IN HOSTAGE RESCUE SITUATIONS AND PERSONAL SECURITY FOR DIPLOMATS, AND OVER 1,000 KIDNAPPINGS AND EXTORTIONS. THE PROSECUTOR CONTINUED:)

Q. What was your role?

A. My role was to provide them with advice designed to obtain the freedom of Brent Swane.

Q. And how was it that you were going to achieve that freedom?

A. Well, generally speaking, when you have an abduction or a kidnap, you will have some demands being made for the release of that person.

Q. How is it that you prepared by way of understanding who your opposites would be?

A. Well, we have an information service in London whose job it is to research the methodology used by different groups worldwide. Plus one would then seek information from Chevron's own experience in working in Africa of what previous incidents may have occurred, and you can learn about the objectives and methods of the abductors.

Q. And what, if anything, did you learn about the individuals who would be participating in this meeting that had been set up for November 9th?

A. We learned from experience, I suppose. We didn't know them individually beforehand. They announced their identities in writing, the credentials for the people attending the meeting to represent FLEC: Bent, Tchibass and Zulu.

Q. I'm showing you the English translation of that document. I'm going to read it into the record. We, the undersigned, the Central Committee for the Front for the Liberation—

MR. BO: Objection, Your Honor. There's no reason why the government needs to read the documents.

MS. INGERS: It's brief.

THE COURT: You don't need to read it. You can point out whatever you want to because it's already in evidence.

BY MS. INGERS:

Q. Would you tell us what the titles are attributed to the three people with whom you were to meet?

A. Bent is described as Secretary General, Tchibass is described as Foreign Affairs Secretary, and Zulu is Information and Press Secretary.

Q. What is the significance of the first paragraph describing the individual people?

A. It's an attempt to show authority has been granted to these individuals to carry out policy on behalf of FLEC.

Q. And it's signed by a person bearing what position?

A. The president, whose name is Tiburci.

Q. Based on your experience with negotiations with persons claiming to be holding hostages, what did you take from the presentation of those credentials?

A. It's an indication of an organization which is seeking to be taken seriously.

Q. And what did that mean to you as you thought of the plans for the negotiations?

A. This was going to be a politically sensitive case, much more so than an average criminal one. Therefore, likely to be more complicated.

Q. And to be clear, what were your team's objectives as you went into these negotiations?

A. The objective was to obtain the safe release of Brent Swane in as short a period as possible without endangering the interest of the company.

Q. And how many negotiation sessions did there turn out to be?

A. Nine.

Q. And did you attend every one?

A. Yes.

Q. Now, in the course of those nine meetings, were records kept?

A. Yes.

Q. In what form?

A. Written form.

Q. And what generally was recorded in these written records?

A. The content of the conversations between FLEC-PM and Chevron.

Q. And did the three FLEC-PM representatives remain constant throughout the nine negotiation sessions?

A. Yes.

Q. And of the three, was there any one that was the principal spokesman?

A. Tchibass.

Q. And were the proceedings electronically recorded?

A. No.

Q. Why not?

A. Well, we thought that the members of FLEC-PM would seek to search the building to see if anybody planted any recording devices, which is hardly conducive to developing a compatible relationship with them. We thought they would become suspicious if they found such devices.

Q. And how is it that Mr. Taylo came to write notes of what was said during the course of the first and second meetings?

A. He wrote the notes because it was important to have records of what had been said. It's a standard Control Risk's procedure.

Q. What happened to those notes and to what use were they put after the conclusion of meeting one and meeting two?

A. Well, you then study the content of the meeting to work out what you're going to do next.

Q. Who studied the content?

A. The team, which is basically Webe, Taylo and myself.

Q. And to what extent did you rely, if at all, on those two handwritten notes in order to review what had transpired at those meetings?

A. This was the only record, so therefore to a great extent.

Q. Now, the first meeting was November 9th, the second was the next day, November 10th, and the third on November 12th; is that correct?

A. Yeah.

Q. Then why is it that beginning the third meeting you started typing up a record of what had transpired?

A. Well, we wanted to get better organized, and obviously it's much better to have a typewritten record rather than somebody's handwriting.

Q. And on what were those typescripts based?

A. On the handwritten notes that we kept of the meeting.

Q. And did you also on occasion make notes of other observations?

A. Occasionally to provide additional information about the mood of the meeting. It might be useful.

Q. And how important was it in your professional view to that process that the records be accurate?

A. It is important because you may need to refer back to meetings that took place, say, two months ago, and you need to have a record to remember what decisions had been made and what had been said.

Q. Did you and your team review each of those records as they were developed?

A. Yes.

Q. And did you have an opportunity at that time to assess whether they were, in fact, accurate based on your immediate experience, immediate past experience?

A. Yes.

MS. INGERS: Your Honor, at this time I'm going to offer Government's exhibits on bases that have been previously stated to the Court.

MR. BO: The same objection, Your Honor.

THE COURT: Preserving the objection, I'm going to allow at this time the notes of the negotiating session between the parties, overruling the objection.

BY MS. INGERS:

Q. I've handed you what's marked as Government's Exhibit. What is it?

A. It's a list of demands.

Q. Tell us about how this document related to how the discussion proceeded in the first meeting.

A. Well, it became an exchange of views from one side to the other, with Tchibass basically pressing for concessions by Chevron. And Syd Anders would respond, and this is where his historical knowledge was absolutely vital. He was able to rebut many of the claims made by Tchibass from his own personal knowledge of the history of the company inside Zaire and Angola.

Q. So is it fair to say that the first part of the meeting constituted a kind of a discussion of history and politics?

A. Yes. And also the demands and what Chevron would consider and what they wouldn't.

Q. All right. And specifically under the heading Expectations of the People of Cabinda, would you tell us what they are?

A. Well, there's the political objectives of FLEC, which basically means to take over Cabinda and run it on behalf of the Cabindans, and then there's both material and financial demands made, as well as demands for educational support and medical support. And finally they wanted some military equipment to be provided for 2,000 people. So it's a genuine mixture of different things. So the first problems Chevron had to deal with was how to sort out what was possible and what was not.

Q. So is it fair to say that the demands were categorized under these headings, a political set of demands, social demands, and then military?

A. Yes.

Q. Now, I'd like to focus on the last one of these, the military category. If you can read for us what the two sentences say.

A. Military: Provide complete equipment for 2,000 people. Chevron must agree to assist the Cabindans on a permanent basis for equipment and financial aid.

Q. And were you able to respond as to these categories of demands?

A. Yes, some of them. For instance, military was turned down completely, and some sort of political support was offered in terms of bringing the Cabindans case to the attention of the Angola and American governments.

Q. And as to the social issues, what, if anything, was decided at that first meeting?

A. Attention was drawn to the fact that Chevron was already providing philanthropic and medical support throughout Cabinda.

Q. And at the end there is a paragraph that refers to the hostage Brent Swane, and what did that provide for?

A. As soon as satisfaction is obtained on the social demands, Mr. Swane will be delivered in the hands of Jesse Jackson or former President Jimmy Carter.

Q. Was that discussed at that first meeting to any conclusion?

A. I think we excluded the involvement of Messers Jackson and Carter.

Q. And why was that?

A. Because you don't want publicity, and also they're unnecessary.

Q. Now, what were the two sides understandings at the conclusion of that first meeting about the circumstances under which Brent Swane would be released?

A. Basically, it would be a stand-off and an agreement to meet again.

Q. Was it agreed that you would meet again?

A. Yes.

Q. And what generally occurred in the second and third meetings?

A. A continuation of the same process, but becoming more and more clear.

Q. And who was it who spoke in these three meetings for the FLEC-PM side?

A. Tchibass.

Q. And what do you recall about the fact that photographs of Swane were produced?

A. I remember being glad that they did so because it gave us more evidence of his state of health. It also indicated that the FLEC understood the business of kidnap negotiations. They volunteered to provide the proof of life without any request from us, which indicated that they had experience in these sorts of things.

Q. And did you at that time in that period receive any other proof of life of Mr. Swane?

A. Yes, we had a letter we received on the first day, and subsequently we got other letters, too.

Q. I see that there's a fairly long break between the third and the fourth negotiation sessions. What is it that lead to that break?

A. Basically, the position would have been where neither side could make any alterations to their position, which allowed the FLEC to return to discuss with their own leadership what they were going to do next.

Q. And what was the impasse over?

A. It would have been over financial demands and military, because I remember the FLEC insisted either they had military or they had financial, and they were told they weren't going to have either. So that meant they had to go think about that, while at the same time trying to convey a threatening impression to the company.

Q. A third of the way down the page, would you read this, please?

A. "We must have financial assistance. There can be no release of Brent Swane without financial assistance."

Q. Who said that?

A. Tchibass.

Q. Now, what is it that Tchibass and his comrades had to do after the third meeting, after the impasse?

A. They had to meet up with Tiburci and have a discussion about what they were going to do or give the appearance of having referred to higher authority, although they also claimed authority themselves. In conversation they said "we are senior."

Q. When you say "we," who are you referring to?

A. Bent, Tchibass, and Zulu.

Q. Who was the principal spokesman?

A. Tchibass.

Q. By the way, when Tchibass introduced himself, did he use any title?

A. Major.

Q. And were the other two introduced by any title?

A. Major.

Q. Did Tchibass talk about any military background he had?

A. I don't recall. We did see pictures of him in military uniform.

MR. BO: Your Honor, may we approach?

THE COURT: Sure.

(Bench conference on the record.)

MR. BO: This witness has referred to Mr. Tchibass throughout his testimony as "Tchibass." I would ask for him to refer to him politely as Mr. Tchibass, as he has referred to other members of the Chevron negotiating team.

MS. INGERS: Or "Major Tchibass" as he knew him then.

THE COURT: All right.

MR. BO: That's fine, too, but "Tchibass" is inappropriate.

THE COURT: All right, thank you.

(End of bench conference.)

THE COURT: You knew him as Major Tchibass or Mr. Tchibass?

THE WITNESS: Major.

THE COURT: Refer to him as Major Tchibass, then.

BY MS. INGERS:

Q. And when Major Tchibass came to the negotiation sessions, did he wear military uniform?

A. No.

Q. What did he wear?

A. Shirt, trousers.

Q. Why did your side not just go in and rescue Brent Swane?

A. We don't have the jurisdiction to do law enforcement activity anywhere in the world for a start. Secondly, we are advisors as opposed to being implementors. And thirdly it's an absurd question. In order to rescue somebody, you need to know where they are. If they're being hidden in the jungle, they're holding somebody in a remote place where you don't know where they are. Because if you did, you would go and rescue them. It's safer to be released without rescue attempts because there are many hostages who get killed by law enforcement seeking to rescue them. So on the basis of which is safest, it's much safer to be released.

Q. And the end of that maybe two week, two and a half week period between November 12 and November 29, how was it that you learned that negotiations were to resume?

A. We were notified by the American Embassy.

Q. And with whom did your side meet on that occasion, that fourth meeting?

A. The same three.

Q. And how did that round of meetings go.

A. More progress started to be made because our side suggested substituting different things for cash.

Q. Such as?

A. Medical supplies, food, equipment.

Q. Why was your side concerned about giving cash to FLEC-PM?

A. Well, quite apart from being against American law, it would be very threatening to Chevron's position with the Angola government.

Q. In what way?

A. The Angolan president wrote a letter to Chevron saying that they were not permitted to make any payments of cash to FLEC, although they were prepared for humanitarian concessions, which is a clear tip that there is a loophole there through which we would be able to negotiate a settlement as long as it wasn't cash and it wasn't military. And if they had paid cash, then they may have lost their entire operations in Cabinda. So the threat, political threat, was if you displease us, we, the government, will confiscate your operation.

Q. And were there any other additional concerns that your side had about any use to which cash might be put?

A. Yes. It might be used for military operations.

Q. And would you describe for us the dynamics of the discussion that Major Tchibass had about the relationship between military and financial?

A. Well, he wanted one or the other, and he insisted on that until he was persuaded to start talking about alternatives to cash. But one must remember that Tchibass didn't just stick straight away to one simple straightforward path. He was constantly going back to the beginning and starting with the original demands.

Q. And at some point were the lists of items as to which an agreement was being reached, as substitutes for cash, at some point was that memorialized?

A. Yes, a list of equipment and nonmilitary materials.

Q. And what generally were the parameters of the hammered out agreement?

A. Some effort to draw the government's attention to the Cabindan claims. Not that that they would be able to influence these, but they could at least draw it to the government's attention. There would be no military, no finance, that there would be a donation of aid to a charity for the relief of Cabindan refugees, there would be medical and other sorts of support, there would be scholarships for certain Cabindans, to be organized in the future, and then there was a list of equipment.

Q. And once this agreement was handed over by you to Major Tchibass and others of FLEC-PM, what did you do?

A. Personally I went home.

Q. I want to ask you some questions based on your experience in the course of those nine negotiation sessions specifically about Major Tchibass. What was your assessment of his ability to frame and present the issues for his side?

A. He was—

MR. BO: Objection, Your Honor. It's not relevant.

THE COURT: It's overruled. I think it's relevant. It goes to motive. Go ahead.

THE WITNESS: I thought he knew exactly what he was doing and operated very effectively on behalf of his beliefs and organization.

Q. How articulately was he able to present his side?

A. Very much so, and always seeking to gain extra advantages whenever possible.

Q. Did you observe him in any way at any time disassociate himself from Majors Bent and Zulu?

A. No.

Q. Did you ever observe him in any way disassociate himself from those other FLEC-PM members who were actually holding Brent Swane in captivity?

A. No.

Q. Did you ever observe him in any way express any view about the captivity of Brent Swane that was at variance with the position of his comrades?

MR. BO: Objection, Your Honor. Leading.

THE COURT: It's overruled. Go ahead, he can answer the question based upon his observations whether or not he saw any disassociation.

THE WITNESS: No.

Q. And were you able to make any assessment based on your professional experience of Major Tchibass' negotiating skills?

A. Yes. I thought he was good. He's persistent, intelligent, and inventive.

Q. Inventive?

A. Yes.

Q. What do you mean by that?

A. Well, he became a pass master at slipping in extra demands when you thought everything was finished.

Q. And to what extent was he able to respond to any changes that were proposed by your side?

A. I got the impression that before he would make a decision of that nature, he would talk to his two colleagues as opposed to doing it just by himself. But, nevertheless, he was an important part of that trio.

Q. What about his reference to "We have been sent by a political committee," going back to our military colleagues, what based on your experience is the role that's played by negotiators references to having to go back and talk?

A. They tended to go both ways. Sometimes they would claim they had complete authority themselves, and other times they would imply there was somebody else to whom they had to refer.

Q. By way of another example, on the bottom of page 8 there's a reference again by Tchibass, correct?

A. Yes.

Q. "We understand from the first day that military assistance we would not receive. We believe that for him to be liberated, Chevron must find a solution to the financial assistance problem, in order not to block progress." And who is referred to as "him" to be liberated?

A. Brent Swane.

Q. Going on, "You should consider Brent Swane as an incident because Mr. Anders . . ."—

MR. BO: Objection, Your Honor. If the government wants to read what's on the page, they can read what's on the page. As far as a dramatic reading—

THE COURT: All right, just read it.

BY MS. INGERS:

Q. " . . . because Mr. Anders is a businessman." Now, to whom was Tchibass directing his remarks in this meeting?

A. To Mr. Anders, and through him to Chevron.

Q. And then a little further down there's another reference to "The military are only interested in weapons." And what was the significance to you as a negotiator of this emphasis on the interest in weapons?

A. Well, it's quite a common demand. I don't see a huge amount of significance apart from the fact that it's unlikely that Chevron is going to agree to such a demand, something which I suspect Tchibass and his colleagues knew from the start.

Q. And, again, at the bottom of page 10, Tchibass, "When we go back to get Brent Swane, we must give good news to the military. We must not make them angry to push them more than what they have done." What, based on your experience in hostage negotiations, was the effect of this kind of statement?

A. It's a threat. It's dressed up in nice language trying to blame somebody else, but it is a clear threat.

Q. And it's specifically a threat to what?

A. To the life of Brent Swane.

Q. And did your side on the negotiating table take it as such at the time?

A. Yes. I mean, it's there all the time, every day.

MS. INGERS: At this time, Your Honor, this might be a good stopping point.

THE COURT: All right, ladies and gentlemen. Tomorrow morning we'll get a full day and get some real work done. I appreciate your patience with us today. We will be back to continue finishing the testimony of the witness, and then ready to proceed.

(Jury out.)

FOURTH DAY, SEPTEMBER 9, 2005
MORNING SESSION

THE COURT: Good morning, counsel. We're ready to proceed. I understand there may be a preliminary matter before we bring the jury out?

MR. BO: That's correct, Your Honor. Your Honor, this morning I received information that an individual by the name of Martins Lieta was interviewed by the government. I don't know when that interview occurred. I do know that Mr. Lieta is from Portugal, was flown in by the government for the purposes of this trial and is scheduled to depart today. I'm in the process of having him subpoenaed as a defense witness. More important, Your Honor, it's my understanding from a very, very brief conversation that I had with Mr. Lieta this morning that he has provided information to the government concerning Mr. Tchibass' involvement in a 2003 hostage taking incident in which Mr. Lieta, who owns a construction company in Portugal, had some workers abducted by some other group.

In any event, Mr. Tchibass interceded in that case exactly in the same way that he interceded in this case, that even though he was not a participant of the group that actually held the hostages, he secured the hostages release.

I can't give the Court any more information about that because I haven't had a chance to speak with Mr. Tchibass about it, but Mr. Lieta asked me if I had received his declaration concerning these events, which I would suggest would mean that he gave some type of statement to the government concerning this incident.

There are a couple of things. One is, we're going to have him under subpoena as a potential defense witness. I need to talk with him, and I want to make sure that he does not depart the country this afternoon.

Two, I am making a request for Mr. Lieta's statement that he gave to the government, and any other instances that the government is aware of, either through discussions with Mr. Lieta or anybody else where Mr. Tchibass did just as we say he did in this case is interceded on behalf of others to negotiate the release of hostages.

Mr. Lieta is somebody who is not unfamiliar to me because Mr. Tchibass had told me about him, but we did not have any information as far as exactly where he was, how to contact him, what information he may have that would be relevant in this case.

I received an e-mail about 2:00 this morning from somebody in Paris telling me that Mr. Lieta was in fact here in town, and I was only able to reach him this morning.

THE COURT: Thank you. What about this Portuguese person, from the government's point of view?

MS. INGERS: Your Honor, the government had, as the Court knows and as counsel knows, filed motions indicating that we had intention to introduce evidence of a number of other hostage taking incidents.

Mr. Lieta will not be testifying for the government. Any testimony he may have is not relevant to this case. And the government would object to him being presented by the defendant. Now, if he wants to testify as a character witness to the extent he can, that's another matter.

It's my understanding that he was in telephone contact with the defendant over recent months. So it's hard to understand how the defendant didn't know how to reach him. The fact is, he is here. I believe he is scheduled to leave later today. If defense counsel wants to make arrangements to have him held over for the limited purpose for which he can testify, then obviously—

THE COURT: I thought the government's position is that he was not involved in a similar type of hostage situation, but intervened to help get someone out.

MS. INGERS: No. It was indeed a hostage situation. And it's the government's understanding that Mr. Lieta did play a role in the release of the hostages who were being held by Major Tchibass' group.

THE COURT: Do you have some type of a statement from him?

MS. INGERS: Mr. Lieta is in possession of his own declaration that was made to the Portuguese authorities. It's not a declaration, it's really a police interview. And we do have it, and in our view it simply does not contain pertinent material.

THE COURT: He's here now and staying here in town? Mr. Bo, do you know where he is?

MR. BO: I do, Your Honor.

THE COURT: So you can reach him all right? I don't want him to leave town and have to go through some battle to get him back here.

MR. BO: That's right, Your Honor. We know where he is. And when I left the office this morning, I left instructions for him to be subpoenaed. The only concern, Your Honor, I have is that his understanding of Mr. Tchibass' role is very different than what the government has just represented. My understanding from what he told me this morning was that some other faction or some other group was holding some of his workers, and that Mr. Tchibass interceded on his behalf in order to get those workers out. And he was very happy to have Mr. Tchibass' assistance in that matter, which is completely consistent with our theory as to what Mr. Tchibass was doing in this case as well.

THE COURT: All right. I think you better grab him and see. The government says they don't have any material on him. I don't know if he has his own declaration, you can look at that.

MR. BO: Well, I guess one of my concerns is that if the declaration is in Portuguese, which I suspect that it probably is, it may take me at least overnight to try to find somebody that can interpret it for me.

THE COURT: All right.

MS. INGERS: The government will be happy to provide a translation of it to the extent we have it. But, again, the government will strenuously object to that witness testifying about any matter that is not directly relevant to this case.

THE COURT: We will have to hear that, as to whether it's relevant or not.

All right. We'll have the jury out and continue with the direct examination of Mr. Adams. Mr. Adams, when you refer to Mr. Tchibass, either call him Mr. Tchibass or Major Tchibass, not just by his last name.

(Jury in.)

THE COURT: All right, ladies and gentlemen, we are ready to resume the trial. We are ready to continue with the direct testimony offered by the government of Mr. Adams at this time.

CONTINUING DIRECT EXAMINATION
BY MS. INGERS:

Q. Mr. Adams, yesterday in discussing the negotiation sessions you testified about threats made by Major Tchibass regarding Brent Swane. I'd like to show you some excerpts from a couple of sessions, and ask you about some of the statements the defendant made there. Looking to the negotiation session of the third meeting, November 12. There is a reference to 15 years spent fighting, and then it says, Major Tchibass says, "but we have never attacked Chevron. If you make an analysis of Cabinda, Chevron should reach an agreement or Chevron ceases to exist in Cabinda." And then it says, "We are not blackmailers, but we ask Chevron to understand our situation." The second excerpt from that same session establishes that it is Major Tchibass speaking. And then there is a statement that, "At the present time we will not harm Chevron, but this is not a permanent guarantee. In the future, we may decide to change our views. If Chevron decides not to change its position, this would be a disaster to Chevron. We are convinced that Cabinda has a significant impact on Chevron's business."

The record of the fourth negotiation session that occurred after the two week break and in which Major Tchibass refers to "our agreement is that our intention is not to kill Swane." With regard to those statements, Mr. Adams, could you tell us to what extent you perceived these as actual threats to Chevron?

A. Well, the first two were threats to the physical installations that Chevron had in Cabinda.
Q. And what role did that play in your conduct of the negotiations, that those threats had been made?
A. Well, it's something you take into account, and there's nothing unusual about this.

d in this case, they did so by presenting you with a letter; is that correct?

h. The letter wasn't the important thing. The important thing was that they ved Swane was alive.

ay. Now, I want to talk a little bit about the nature of the negotiations in this e. The interpreter in this case was a man by the name of George Fensi?

s.

d Mr. Fensi was an employee of Chevron?

rtainly.

r, isn't it true that Mr. Fensi was a very important part of the decision making ocess?

ell, do tell me how.

sn't it true that Mr. Fensi was the person who would be responsible for eceiving the names of the people that would potentially get the scholarships rom Chevron?

Yes. After Swane was released they would then refer to George Fensi and provide the names for the scholarships. That doesn't make him part of the decision making process.

Well, it doesn't make him just solely an interpreter in these negotiations?

After Swane's release, it's totally different.

Now, you have testified that Mr. Tchibass was pressing during the negotiations, that he was constantly coming back and reiterating positions, correct?

Yes.

In this particular relationship you noted in your journal that the FLEC representatives were acting in a friendly manner, correct?

They were friendly enough, yeah.

Now, those notes that Mr. Taylo took on the first and second meeting weren't shown to the FLEC representatives; is that correct?

Certainly not.

Okay. So no FLEC representative was ever able to say, wait a minute, that's not exactly what I said, or you've misinterpreted what I had said; is that correct?

No. Why should we give it to them?

Q. So even though it appears to be a translation of what was said, it's really what Mr. Taylo and what you and Mr. Fensi understood was said that day, correct?

A. Correct.

Q. There was no input at all from the FLEC representatives whether or not it was, in fact, accurate?

A. No, none at all.

Q. I want to show you what's been marked and introduced into evidence. If you look at the last sentence in that exhibit, what Mr. Tchibass says is that they had to take Swane to gain Chevron's attention. They are not against Chevron, correct?

A. Yes.

Q. In what respect?

A. Kidnappers usually try and extract concessions based upon th[e]
of the person that they're holding. In this case, they're not onl[y]
life of the person, they're also threatening the installations an[d]
the company, which is basically inside Cabinda and dominate[d]
So they could have taken violent action against the installation

Q. Now, I'm referring you to the fifth negotiation meeting on N
and looking at the last paragraph on that page, on a somewhat
again, a statement by Major Tchibass. In what way, Mr. Adams, d[id]
of authority and of rank indicate to you the ability of Major Tc
two companions to engage in substantive negotiations?

A. Well, they were authorized to do so right at the beginning. Ther[e]
credentials which they presented. And here they are reinfo[rced]
claiming—by stating their seniority in the organization. On the o[ther]
sometimes use it tactically to refer back to their president. On th[e]
when it suits them, they have the authority to take positions.

Q. In fact, ultimately did these three men, whose spokesman was Ma[jor]
take a position to reach a negotiated agreement for the freedo[m]
Swane?

A. Yes.

MS. INGERS: Nothing further, Your Honor.

THE COURT: Okay. All right, ladies and gentlemen, we will have
examination by Mr. Bo at this time.

MR. BO: Thank you.

CROSS-EXAMINATION
BY MR. BO:

Q. I want to talk a little bit about the credentials that FLEC representatives pr[esented]
to you at the beginning of the negotiation session. Would you have neg[otiated]
with any negotiator if you did not believe they had the authority fro[m the]
captors to release the hostage?

A. We would have negotiated with anybody that could prove that they had [contact]
with them alive.

Q. And so it was important that the people that you're negotiating with demon[strated]
to you that they were in fact connected with the people who had Mr. Swa[ne;]
that correct?

A. Yes. They'd have to prove that, otherwise we wouldn't start negotiating [with]
them.

Q. And when he's referring to "they," he is referring to the people who are holding Mr. Swane, correct?

A. Yes.

Q. So his first statement he refers to the captors as "they;" is that correct?

A. Yes.

Q. Now, I'd like to direct your attention to the last page. Referring to the captors, Mr. Tchibass states they are looking for Chevron for political help; is that correct?

A. Yes.

Q. So, again, he's referring to the captors in a third person; is that correct?

A. Yes.

Q. Now, showing you Government's Exhibit, meeting number three, that meeting happened on November 12th; is that correct?

A. Yep.

Q. It would be fair to say that this is Mr. Tchibass who is speaking at that point?

A. Yes.

Q. It reads that, "We are seeking a solution acceptable to both parties. We also have concessions to make, but we cannot go back to our military colleagues without a compromise." That's words that Mr. Tchibass spoke that day, correct?

A. Right.

Q. And, in fact, that's when Mr. Tchibass made the following statement. "Brent Swane is not in the hands of the political faction, but in the hands of the military men. This is a touchy business. Therefore, we are trying to find a point in the middle to satisfy both parties". Did he make that statement?

A. That's correct.

Q. In the last sentence, Mr. Tchibass said, "We are mandated to make an agreement with Chevron to liberate Brent Swane;" is that correct?

A. Yes.

Q. And then what he said was, "When we go back to get Brent Swane, we must have good news to the military. We must not make them angry to push them to do more than what they have already done." Is that what he said?

A. Yes.

Q. Now, directing your attention to the colloquy that begins with, "We want to make trips to the U.S." The person who appears to be stating that is Mr. Tchibass, correct?

A. Yes.

Q. So it's about Mr. Tchibass wanting to come to the United States; is that correct?

A. That's correct.

Q. In fact, that was actually part of the demands that were being negotiated during these sessions, that there would be four tickets paid for by Chevron, for four representatives of the FLEC to come to the United States, correct?

A. Yeah.

Q. And if you look at the top of page 17, Mr. Tchibass states, "We will advise our people and they will decide. We don't believe that this is a good position for you. We have tried to limit the problem." Did he make that statement?

A. Certainly.

Q. Okay. And by the way, all these statements that we've reviewed so far occurred prior to or on November 12th, correct?

A. Yes.

Q. And it's your understanding that the negotiators went back to the people in the bush to have some further consultation; is that correct?

A. Yes.

Q. Now I want to show you the notes from the December 4th meeting, a meeting that occurred after there was consultation with the captors, correct?

A. Right.

Q. Now I want to refer you to page 12 of Government's Exhibit, there appears to be someone speaking, for the record, Mr. Tchibass?

A. Yes.

Q. And at that point he states, if we press so hard on social immaterials, not the military equipment, there's an impasse. The assistance required is not only material but also political. You should be aware that the list was given to us. We should be able to go back and say look what we have negotiated, correct?

A. Yes.

Q. And the second to last sentence states "We are asking for U.S. 2.5M." I'm assuming that's 2.5 million dollars?

A. Yes.

Q. And then Mr. Tchibass states, "We need a compromise. We need to find a consensus. We are happy with the political side. We need enough to convince our Central Committee. We need a realistic offer." Did he, in fact, make that statement?

A. Yes.

Q. And it would be fair to say that prior to the negotiation sessions, the negotiators know what the parameters of what they can negotiate away, correct?

A. Yes.

Q. Didn't Chevron tell you that you could only make these concessions, but you couldn't go any further than that?

A. Yes.

Q. So, they were the ones that were telling you what things were not negotiable?

A. Yes.

Q. And even though there needs to be some flexibility as far as negotiations as far as the give and take, there are certain things that each side would say we cannot do that, correct?

A. Absolutely.

Q. For example, like giving military assistance, or direct financial assistance?

A. Yes.

Q. Now, you testified yesterday that negotiators sometimes say, "we don't have the authority, we've got to check it out with somebody else," correct?

A. Yes.

Q. And so when they say we need to go check it out with somebody else, they in fact need to get the authority before they're able to go forward with the negotiation; is that correct?

A. Yes.

Q. And, in fact, FLEC had sent two letters to Chevron prior to the Brent Swane incident; is that correct?

A. Correct.

Q. And both of those letters were signed by Mr. Luemb; is that correct?

A. Yeah.

Q. Mr. Tchibass' name doesn't appear on any of the letters; is that correct?

A. No.

Q. In fact, his name doesn't appear even on the October 23rd letter when the FLEC announced that they are the people responsible for having taken Mr. Swane; is that correct?

A. As far as I recall, yes.

Q. In fact, the first time that you saw Mr. Tchibass' name on any official document was when he presented his credentials at the first negotiation; is that correct?

A. Yes.

MR. BO: Your Honor, I have no further questions of Mr. Adams.

THE COURT: All right, thank you, sir. The government has some redirect questions?

REDIRECT EXAMINATION
BY MS. INGERS:

Q. Now, you were shown several remarks made by Major Tchibass about the military group and the military demands that were among the wish list presented initially by FLEC negotiators. You also stated, I believe, that right from the beginning as far as your side was concerned, the military equipment aspect of equipping 2,000 men was not on the table.

A. Yes.

Q. Based on your observations in those nine negotiating sessions, what was your assessment of why Major Tchibass kept coming back to the military aspect of their demands?

MR. BO: Objection, Your Honor. It's not relevant.

THE COURT: Overruled. Go ahead.

THE WITNESS: Well, Mr. Tchibass came back to things over and over again. Even when they had been agreed, he'd still come back and start again. So I presume it's one of the things that he was hoping to get out of Chevron, but he probably realized that he wouldn't get it.

MR. BO: Objection, Your Honor. Can we approach?

THE COURT: All right.

(Bench conference on the record.)

MR. BO: Your Honor, I think not only is it not relevant, but also it goes in the thought process of Mr. Tchibass. How does he know what Mr. Tchibass' thought process was?

THE COURT: All right.

(End of bench conference.)

THE COURT: We're going to strike the last comment about what Mr. Tchibass probably realized, speculating what he was thinking about.

BY MS. INGERS:
Q. If Brent Swane had not been taken captive by Major Tchibass' group, would you have flown to Kinshasa and sat down with Major Tchibass and his group at those negotiating sessions?
A. No.
Q. In terms of the cordiality, the friendliness of the proceedings, did Major Tchibass' group have anything that you and your side wanted?
A. Brent Swane.
Q. Was Major Tchibass' role as spokesman for his side, who had at times to refer to his colleagues and people not present in the sessions, any different from that of the spokesman on your side, Syd Anders or Scott Taylo?
A. Not really.
Q. And as for the issue of a statement made by Major Tchibass to the effect that we were asking for $2.5 million and need agreement available to our Central Committee, what does it say that the listed people are?
A. They're members of the Executive Branch of the Central Committee.
Q. And finally with respect to efforts to distance himself from the military side, could you tell us what kind of clothing Major Tchibass was wearing?
A. Military combat clothing.

MS. INGERS: Nothing further, Your Honor.

(Witness excused.)

MS. LEVY: Your Honor, the government calls Syd Anders.

(NOW MR. ANDERS TOOK THE STAND. HE STATED, THOUGH HE IS RETIRED NOW, HE WAS THE CHEVRON VICE PRESIDENT WHO REPRESENTED THE CORPORATION IN THE NEGOTIATING SESSIONS. HE DESCRIBED THE CHEVRON FACILITIES IN ANGOLA AND THE FINANCIAL ARRANGEMENT THEY HAD WITH THE ANGOLA GOVERNMENT, WHEREBY THE ANGOLA GOVERNMENT RECEIVED ROYALTIES FROM THE CRUDE OIL PRODUCTION, AND TAXES PAID ON THE PROFIT. IN ADDITION, HE STATED CHEVRON ESTABLISHED A MEDICAL CLINIC IN THE TOWN OF CABINDA, IMPROVED THE HOSPITAL FACILITIES, UPGRADED THE LOCAL AIRPORT, ESTABLISHED LOCAL SCHOOLS, IMPROVED ROADS, UPGRADED THE ELECTRICAL SYSTEM, AND SUPPLIED THE AREA'S NATURAL GAS FOR FREE. IN OTHER WORDS, CHEVRON WAS A VERY GOOD NEIGHBOR. MR. ANDERS IDENTIFIED LETTERS TO AND FROM FLEC AND CHEVRON, AND ALSO IDENTIFIED THE MEMBERS OF HIS NEGOTIATING TEAM AND THE THREE FLEC TEAM MEMBERS: MAJORS TCHIBASS, BENT AND ZULU. HE ALSO REITERATED THE DEMANDS THAT FLEC MADE IN ORDER TO RANSOM MR. SWANE. THE PROSECUTOR, MS. EVY, CONTINUED:)

Q. Did Major Tchibass ever disassociate himself from the kidnapping of Brent Swane?
A. No.
Q. Did he ever link Brent Swane's release to the satisfaction of certain demands?

MR. BO: Objection, Your Honor. Leading.

THE COURT: All right, it's overruled. Just try to move the case along.

BY MS. EVY:
Q. You can answer the question.
A. Yes, he did.
Q. When you mentioned the demand for military equipment proposed by Major Tchibass, what was your reaction?
A. Well, it was something that we just could not entertain at all.

Q. And how did Major Tchibass respond to your stating that that was not possible?

A. He was very upset with that position because he told us that he would have to go back to the bush and try to explain to the military arm of FLEC what our position was, and he wasn't relishing the thought of doing that.

Q. You made a reference to the Central Committee early in your testimony. What was your understanding of Major Tchibass' relationship to that Central Committee?

A. That he was reporting to it.

Q. Did you return to Kinshasa at another time while Mr. Swane was still being held hostage?

A. I did.

Q. And had there been any progress in the negotiations in that interim period?

A. They had, our team had worked with the FLEC people in determining the total demand package. We had costed out the total amount of that demand package.

Q. Mr. Anders, I'm going to show you Government's Exhibit and ask if you've ever seen that before?

A. Yes. It's a list of the equipment demands that has a cost estimate associated with it.

Q. Mr. Anders, who was responsible for that document that's in front of you?

A. I believe that Scott Taylo, the man on our team, did most of the leg work for this.

Q. Now Mr. Anders, the prices that are listed, what do they represent?

A. The estimated cost of acquisition of this equipment in Kinshasa.

Q. And what was the approximate total cost of supplying all of the equipment demanded?

A. One and three-quarter million dollars.

Q. Was Chevron prepared to buy all of that equipment for FLEC-PM at that time?

A. No.

Q. Why not?

A. We felt that just yielding to this demand was a very bad precedent, that it was excessive, that we could do something by way of reaching agreement, but this was much, much too high. That if we were to yield to this type of demand, that it would only encourage other similar actions.

Q. And do you remember what the final cost of the items was that was actually provided?

A. It was approximately half a million dollars.

Q. How did you get the cost down from two and a half million, to $500,000?

A. By a lot of give and take in negotiating sessions.

Q. Mr. Anders, did you have any follow-up conversations with representatives of the government of Angola after Mr. Swane was released?

A. I did go to Luanda to speak with the government. I did follow through on the promise that we would discuss this matter with the Angolan government and stress upon them the need to deal with the problem so that this type of thing would not happen in the future.

(THE GOVERNMENT HAD NO FURTHER QUESTIONS, AND THE PUBLIC DEFENDER BEGAN HIS CROSS-EXAMINATION OF MR. ANDERS:)

Q. It would be fair to say that Mr. Tchibass was the lead spokesperson on behalf of the FLEC representatives; is that correct?

A. That's correct.

Q. Now, the first time that you met with Mr. Tchibass was on November 9th, is that correct, the first negotiation session?

A. Yes.

Q. And at that time Mr. Tchibass presented you with some documentation that showed that he was there on behalf of the FLEC; is that correct?

A. That's right.

Q. Isn't it a fact that they told you repeatedly that they would need to get clearance from the military people as far as any negotiations that they agreed to; is that correct?

A. They were fearful that the military would not agree to much of a compromise.

Q. In fact, they told you, did they not, that they were using their efforts to try to convince the military people that they should be releasing Mr. Swane; is that correct?

A. Well, they said that, yes.

Q. Okay. And you had no reason to believe that was not true, right?

A. No.

Q. In fact, when Mr. Tchibass first spoke at the first meeting, he referred to the people who were holding Mr. Swane as "they;" is that correct?

A. He said that FLEC were.

Q. Well, he said that "they" were holding Mr. Swane, correct?

A. The FLEC were, yes.

Q. Now, I want to talk to you a little bit about what your understanding was of the organization of FLEC. You testified that you understood that there was a Central Committee, and I believe you testified that there was also a political group, correct?

A. That's what the FLEC team told us, yes.

Q. You testified that it was your understanding that the FLEC negotiators were reporting back to the Central Committee; is that correct?

A. That's what they told us.

Q. And just so we're clear, as the lead spokesperson, did you have complete decision making authority to strike a deal with the negotiators?

A. I did, yes.

Q. So, for example, if they had said we want $10 million for Brent Swane's release, you had the authority to say yes?

A. I wouldn't have said yes, no.

Q. Did you have the authority to say yes?

A. I think as a senior member of the organization I had authority to go very high, yes.

Q. But my question to you is that you did not have complete authority to make any decision that you wanted; is that correct?

A. Well, it's like anything else in a large company. I had certain responsibilities. And even though I had the authority, in all probability if the number had been extremely high, I would have said no.

Q. Were you given any directive as to what things you could negotiate and what things you could not?

A. We didn't know what was coming. We didn't know what their demands might be.

Q. But you certainly knew prior to the first negotiation session that if a demand was give us military aid, that you were not authorized to do that; is that correct?

A. That's right.

Q. And the same is true for direct cash payments; is that correct?

A. That's correct.

Q. Now, I believe you testified that Mr. Tchibass' conduct during the negotiations was relatively calm; is that correct?

A. Yes.

Q. And that was actually somewhat different than, for example, Mr. Bent's conduct at some of the meetings; is that correct?

A. There were times when Mr. Bent appeared to be agitated and would speak with his colleagues.

Q. But certainly during your discussions with Mr. Tchibass it appeared that he was trying to work towards some type of agreement; is that correct?

A. That's right.

Q. Just like you were trying to work towards some agreement; is that correct?

A. That's right.

Q. Didn't you testify that Mr. Tchibass was disappointed because he knew the Army would be upset?

A. Yes, that's what he said.

MR. BO: Your Honor, I have no further questions.

REDIRECT EXAMINATION
BY MS. EVY:

Q. Mr. Anders, what title did Mr. Tchibass present himself as having when he came to the negotiating sessions with you?
A. Major.
Q. Finally, Mr. Anders, you testified that you were the decision maker for the negotiating team; is that correct?
A. Yes.
Q. So you were authorized to reject demands that were too high as far as Chevron was concerned; is that correct?
A. Yes.

MS. EVY: No further questions.

THE COURT: Ladies and gentlemen, it's close to lunch.

(AT THIS POINT, THE JUDGE CALLED FOR A LUNCHEON RECESS, AND THE JURY DEPARTED THE COURTROOM. THEN A LENGTHY CONFERENCE WAS HELD AT THE BENCH REGARDING THE PROSECUTOR'S PLAN TO INTRODUCE A POLISH CITIZEN TO TESTIFY. IT SEEMS THIS POLISH MAN HAD BEEN KIDNAPPED BY FLEC FOUR YEARS AFTER BRENT SWANE HAD BEEN RELEASED. THIS POLISH MAN WORKED FOR A LUMBER COMPANY IN CABINDA PROVINCE, AND HE AND SEVERAL COMPANIONS WERE HELD IN THE SAME CAMP AS SWANE WAS FOR ABOUT ONE MONTH. THE LUMBER COMPANY'S ITALIAN OWNER OFFERED $120,000 FOR THE RELEASE OF THIS POLISH CITIZEN, AND HE WAS RELEASED. THE PROSECUTORS WANTED TO INTERROGATE HIM TO PROVE THAT MAJOR TCHIBASS WAS STILL INVOLVED WITH FLEC AND WITH KIDNAPPING FOUR YEARS LATER. THIS LENGTHY DISCUSSION OUT OF THE PRESENCE OF THE JURY COVERED 49 PAGES OF TRANSCRIPT, AS THE PUBLIC DEFENDER TRIED TO SUPPRESS THIS WITNESS AS BEING IMMATERIAL TO THE CASE. THE JUDGE EVENTUALLY OVERRULED HIS OBJECTION, AND THE POLISH EX-HOSTAGE WAS ALLOWED TO TAKE THE STAND OPENING THE AFTERNOON SESSION. THE MAN—MR. P. DIETRIC—EXPLAINED HIS CONFINEMENT IN THE BUSH AND THE FACT THAT HE CONTRACTED MALARIA WHILE THERE. WHEN HE WAS ASKED DURING THE CROSS-EXAMINATION IF HE EVER SAW MAJOR TCHIBASS IN PERSON, HE COULDN'T REMEMBER DOING SO. AFTER NUMEROUS BENCH CONFERENCES OVER SEEMINGLY TRIVIAL

POINTS, THE WITNESS WAS EXCUSED, AND RECESS WAS CALLED UNTIL THE FOLLOWING MORNING.)

FIFTH DAY, SEPTEMBER 10, 2005
MORNING SESSION

(THE DAY BEGAN WITH ANOTHER LENGTHY BENCH CONFERENCE OUT OF THE PRESENCE OF THE JURY.)

THE COURT: Mr. Bo.

MR. BO: Your Honor, there are actually two preliminary matters. The first one has to do with the testimony that's been elicited by Mr. Dietric concerning the Polish hostage-taking incident.

Your Honor, the testimony as established so far, was that there were members of the Italian timber company that were part of the negotiation team, the Polish Embassy that was also part of the negotiation team, and I believe there was a third party that escapes my mind at this point.

Your Honor, the government has been on notice of this particular instance, certainly since April of this year. We have no idea who those witnesses are. We don't know whether or not the government has had contact with them, but they certainly were in a position to be able to have contact with them. And the fact that they haven't presented those witnesses here in trial, I believe we should be entitled to a missing witness instruction as to that incident.

MS. INGERS: I believe his testimony was that his captors told him that the negotiation was being conducted by the president of the Italian timber company, and a Polish diplomat. As the Court, and defense counsel are aware, it's extremely hard and often impossible to obtain witnesses from other countries, particularly as we don't have the authority to serve process on them. We would oppose a missing witness instruction in particular because Dietric's testimony was elicited to show that the defendant was continuing to be associated with, as a full-fledged member of FLEC even while the organization continued its hostage-taking activities. There is no suggestion and the government won't imply that he was one of the negotiators.

THE COURT: Mr. Bo, you had a second matter. Is that about the other potential witness as of yesterday?

MR. BO: That's correct, Your Honor. I did meet with that witness last night and was able to speak with him. He doesn't understand English well enough that he could testify in a proceeding such as this. I called the Court Interpreter's office first thing this morning to make arrangements to have a Portuguese interpreter here. I have not heard back from them.

THE COURT: They may get someone here by two. What is the proffer of his testimony that's going to be relevant?

MR. BO: Well, Your Honor, it's actually quite interesting. It involves two instances, one in 1994 and one in 2003. And in both of those situations, there were Portuguese workers that were taken hostage in Cabinda, that Mr. Tchibass interceded and was able to secure the release of the hostages. And, in fact, the person that we intend to call is the person who was responsible for doing the negotiations on behalf of the company that the workers worked for.

So, in essence, this was the person that was kind of in Chevron's position in the Brent Swane incident. This person gives a very, very different characterization as to Mr. Tchibass' role and his intent and his motive in securing the release of these other hostages, which is identical to our defense in this case, and that is that he was an intervenor trying to get the hostage released, as opposed to a co-conspirator trying to keep the hostage detained.

THE COURT: All right. That is relevant for what reason? How is that admissible.

MR. BO: Our position is, it shows his intent and what his motivation was during the Brent Swane incident, which is exactly the flip side of what the government was trying to argue.

THE COURT: Suppose you had someone robbing a bank with a gang who has a certain MO. He's charged by the government in the bank robbery, and he comes in and he says, I want to bring in some people in two other robberies that my gang did but I didn't have anything to do with and I didn't want them to do, to show that I really wasn't involved in this third one, although I was there, they did it against my will; could he do that?

MR. BO: I think that in this case the real issue here is what Mr. Tchibass' intent was in this incident. How he acted in exactly the same situation would be extremely relevant as to what his motive and intent was in the first situation.

THE COURT: I'll look at it as we go forward. We're working to get your Portuguese interpreter here in time.

(Jury in.)

THE COURT: Good morning, ladies and gentlemen. We are ready to resume.

(ALAN TAYLO WAS THE GOVERNMENT'S FIRST WITNESS. HE DESCRIBED HIS POSITION AS THE GENERAL MANAGER OF GLOBAL SECURITY FOR CHEVRON'S GLOBAL OPERATIONS. HE OUTLINED HIS EXPERIENCE AND QUALIFICATIONS FOR THE POSITION. HE REPEATED MUCH OF THE TESTIMONY ALREADY GIVEN BY MR. ANDERS, MR. ADAMS AND MR. WEBE. MS. INGERS CONTINUED HER QUESTIONING:)

Q. How generally did the negotiations go over the course of those meetings with respect to these different ransom categories, beginning with the political category?

A. That was resolved fairly early on in the series of meetings where our negotiator did agree that Chevron would represent their issues to both the Angolan government and U.S. governments.

Q. So that one was pretty easily resolved, right?

A. Yes, it was.

Q. Now the second category is under the heading "social", correct?

A. Yes.

Q. And there appear to be two categories within that second category. One is immediate term and one is short term. Can you tell us how over the course of the nine sessions the first one of those was resolved?

A. We agreed that we would pay an amount in cash to be spent by a third party to buy medicines, food and clothing for Cabinda refugees outside of Cabinda, actually living in the southern part of Zaire.

Q. By the way, was there an organization that was already providing assistance to refugee groups in that area?

A. Yes, there was.

Q. What was it?

A. The United Nations High Commission For Refugees.

Q. What was the third party that you ultimately settled on to provide this assistance?

A. I believe when I left it, the UNHCR, the United Nations High Commission For Refugees, were going to provide, or purchase these items and deliver them to the villages. There was a problem with that, and somebody else then went to another third party to get these items delivered.

Q. But that issue was ultimately resolved in the course of the negotiations?

A. Yes, it was, and the items were delivered.

Q. The short term assistance identified in this initial demand, how was that resolved?

A. We agreed to provide some scholarships, I believe it was four scholarships, to FLEC nominated individuals to attend the university in Kinshasa. And also I know towards the end, additional medical items were substituted for some materials that we had agreed to.

Q. And what about that last item, helping FLEC-PM representatives travel to the United States?

A. FLEC-PM requested air tickets to the United States.

Q. Were those provided ultimately?

A. We provided four air tickets to the United States.

Q. And the final category, military, provide complete equipment for 2,000 people. Chevron must agree to assist the Cabindans on a permanent basis for equipment and financial aid, was that provided?

A. That was not provided and actually was the crux of why the negotiations took so long.

Q. Tell us about that process.

A. We quite clearly could not provide military equipment which could be used against people within the host country that we were working in. We also had fairly clear instructions from the president of Angola that was not something that he would support, and so we tried to convince FLEC to consider taking something as an alternative. Rather than having military equipment, would they take some form of materials.

Q. And was there any discussion of any other form of alternative to military equipment?

A. Yes, there was. Between getting them to agree not to proceed with their request for military equipment, they then wanted just a straight financial cash payment. And again we refused to give that and said no, knowing what that could well be used for. We said we'd have to give them materials.

Q. And ultimately who came up with a list of proposed material goods.

A. That list was prepared by FLEC-PM.

Q. And did your side have any problem with that shopping list?

A. Yes, we did. One in particular, they were looking for Motorola long range radios, communications equipment, and we classified those to be under the auspices of a military type equipment. So, we couldn't say yes to that.

Q. And what was your side's assessment of that total cost?

A. We believed that would cost in the range of $1.7 million.

Q. Was that acceptable to you all?

A. No, it was not.

Q. And as a result, was that shopping list modified?

A. Yes, it was.

Q. Now, throughout those nine negotiation sessions in the back and forth on these issues you've discussed, who is it who spoke for the FLEC-PM side?

A. Major Tchibass.

Q. Was there any particular issue that Major Tchibass most vigorously negotiated?

A. I think he vigorously negotiated throughout. Specifically, he wanted cash, after we had managed to persuade him that he could not have military equipment.

Q. And when you stated your position on it, was that the end of it?

A. No. It would come up over and over again.

Q. What was Major Tchibass' demeanor in bearing as he conducted these negotiations?

A. He at times could be quite forceful. He would raise his voice on occasions, he would bang the table on occasions, he would have arguments with his two representatives that were with him, talking over them, and would raise voices at times. He was determined. He was obviously passionate about his cause, quite often told us just how long he had been a member of FLEC-PM and just how much this all meant to him. Fifteen, sixteen years I can recall him saying he had been part of the movement. But he was determined, dogged, and was intent on getting financial assistance for the release of Swane.

Q. What is it that lead you to determine whether in fact he was a member himself of FLEC-PM?

A. Well, we had his credentials right at the very beginning which actually listed him as Major Tchibass. So that was the first evidence that he was part of the organization. His own verbal comments to us about his position, about his time with the movement. And then during one of my meetings when I was getting concerned about whether we could reach agreement on detail, I said now I'd like you to explain to me exactly, do you have the power of decision, or do you have to go back to a president, or do you have to go back to a council. And he said we are very senior people in this organization, we have the power to make a decision.

Q. Did you rely on that representation as you continued your negotiations?

A. I did. I had no doubt that these three gentleman, Major Tchibass leading them, could make a decision to finalize this negotiation.

Q. And did he at any time in the course of these negotiations attempt in any way to disassociate himself from Majors Bent, or Zulu, or indeed FLEC-PM?

A. At no time during these negotiations does he do so.

Q. Did he ever indicate he was reluctant to serve the role as chief spokesman in these hostage negotiations?

A. At no time did he show he was reluctant. In fact, the opposite. I think he was enthused by being the spokesman.

Q. And once the ransom terms were agreed on, who was responsible on your side for delivering it?

A. I was responsible for managing the delivery.

Q. And was it to be before or after Swane's release, or both?

A. Both.

Q. Showing you this delivery note listing items that were on that list that had been agreed for Swane's release, who signed that?

A. There are signatures of Major Artur Tchibass and Major Amado Zulu, and by Major Bent Antonio.

Q. Would you read through the items that are checked off here?

A. Item one, 100 35 millimeter camera films. Item two, two VHS format video camera. Three, 10 cassette players. Four, 100 video cassettes. Five, 100 audio cassettes. Six, four typewriter manuals. Seven, four typewriter, electronic. Eight, 100 electronic typewriter ribbons, cassettes. Nine, 20 manual typewriter ribbons. Ten, 1,000 reams of photocopy paper. Eleven, five 35 millimeter cameras. Twelve, one Toyota Landcruiser station wagon. Thirteen, four airline tickets: Kinshasa, Paris, New York, Washington and return.

Q. Were you present when Brent Swane was released?

A. Yes, I was.

Q. Would you tell us how that happened?

A. Yes. Both sides were quite naturally concerned for their own safety, and so we had to involve other people to assist us in this release. We asked for help from the Zairian authorities and we asked help from the United States Government. And a plan was put in place where Brent Swane would be driven to a coastal town called Moanda, and that he be driven there and released to me and Mr. Webe in the early hours of the morning, December the 18th.

Q. Describe how it happened.

A. Mr. Webe, myself and a government official from the United States sat close to the main Street in Moanda at about 3:00 in the morning, and we were in communication with the two vehicles that were traveling with Swane.

Q. How were you in communication?

A. We were in communication with our own radios. When Swane was about 30 minutes outside of Moanda, we received a call saying we are 30 minutes away. So we got ready to receive them. The two vehicles pulled up outside a restaurant that we had been sitting at with outside tables. We stepped on to the side of the road where the vehicles had pulled up. Swane got out. He and I exchanged very quick words, and then Mr. Webe took him under control and took him away to our company premises which weren't too far away. Then I acknowledged the FLEC representatives and thanked them for bringing Swane back.

Q. Who were the FLEC representatives who were present at the time that Swane was handed over to you?

A. The three that I had come to know during these negotiations: Zulu, Bent and Tchibass.

Q. Now, again, Majors Bent and Tchibass were not wearing their military uniforms when you met with them in the negotiation sessions?

A. No, they weren't. But this was right in the middle of Kinshasa, another country where our negotiations were taking place. I would not expect them to be in uniform in a major city of another country.

Q. Did you subsequently have contact with FLEC-PM after Swane was released, in connection with the delivery of the remaining ransom items?

A. Yes, I did.

Q. Specifically with who?

A. Different occasions I did meet with all four of them in January of the following year. When I say all four of them, I mean Major Tchibass, Major Bent, Major Zulu. But for the very first time they were very proud to introduce their president, President Tiburci. It was the first time I had met him.

Q. What was the occasion for that meeting?

A. The occasion was to finalize the items that were outstanding, and to work on achieving our end of the bargain as quickly as possible.

Q. In what kind of location did that particular meeting occur?

A. Well, because of who they are and what had happened, I chose the most public venue I could find in Kinshasa at that time. And that was the Intercontinental Hotel in a public restaurant.

Q. Did you, in fact all five of you, share a meal?

A. Yes, we did.

Q. Who hosted the meal?

A. I did.

Q. And in particular, Major Tchibass, how often approximately did you meet with him in addition to that one occasion in the course of finalizing the delivery of the ransom items?

A. Probably two or three times over the next few months.

Q. Now, did you observe any difference in Major Tchibass' appearance during that period after Brent Swane was released?

A. I remember clearly meeting him at the hotel that day, and being noticeably taken aback by their dress, which was they had brand new suits. They had brand new sunglasses, brand new shoes, leather briefcase. They looked exceptionally smart compared to the group I had been in discussions with in the previous two and a half months.

Q. By the way, Mr. Taylo, who to your knowledge was intended that those tickets were for, those airline tickets to the United States?

A. They were in the names of Zulu, Tchibass and Bent. I think we also got one for Tiburci.

Q. Do you know whether they actually traveled to the United States?

A. To my knowledge they never did.

Q. And did Chevron ever get the tickets back?

A. No, we did not.

Q. What is it you learned had happened to those tickets?

A. They had requested to return the tickets for cash.

Q. Who had requested?

A. Major Bent and Major Tchibass.

Q. Were they cashed in?

A. Yes, they were.

Q. Now, once all of the terms of the Swane ransom had been satisfied, did you continue to meet with any of the negotiators from FLEC-PM?

A. Yes, I did. I continued to meet specifically with Major Tchibass and at times Major Bent.

Q. And approximately how many times overall after the completion of the ransom delivery did you meet with Major Tchibass?

A. Between 1993 and about 2000, about 15 times in all.

Q. Now, Mr. Taylo, why in heaven's name were you continuing to meet with Major Tchibass after he and his organization had kidnapped one of your employees?

A. Well, first of all, Major Tchibass was in another country. He wasn't in the country where his Armed Forces were actually committing acts against people. He was in Zaire, whereas FLEC forces are down in Cabinda province.

Q. Why did that make a difference to you?

A. I wasn't in what I would refer to as a war zone. But the most important thing was that we had over 2,000 employees who were at risk from the separatist movement of FLEC, and it had come quite clear to us during our negotiations that one of the biggest items of support they required was a conduit between themselves and the Angolan government. So the more that I could achieve at least keeping up the lines of communication, the more I thought I would deflect their attacks away from our people to other areas.

Q. In what types of locations did you meet with Major Tchibass in Kinshasa?

A. Pretty difficult circumstances. He had an office in a broken down apartment block in one of the poorer areas of the city. The only way to get in to see him was to go through a rather dismal back alley, and then to go up some steps to what used to be an apartment but had been turned into an office.

Q. Whose office was it?

A. It was definitely Major Tchibass'.

Q. For what purpose?

A. For running and controlling most of the communications and directives between Cabinda and the FLEC representatives in Kinshasa.

Q. What matters did you talk to Major Tchibass about in those brief meetings?

A. Mainly courtesy discussions about how are you, can we help you, any messages you require, I'm on my way to Angola, I'm off to see the Minister of Interior in Angola, is there a message you'd like me to take there. So he felt that we were doing something rather than just idle gossip. And that would tend to be the type of discussion. On occasions I would ask him about incidents that had occurred in Cabinda province, and we would discuss those.

Q. Why was it of interest to you to talk to Major Tchibass about those incidents?

A. We had very significant physical security processes in place to protect our people down there from attack. I was very interested when these instances occurred to try and identify who was responsible, because that would help me in my understanding whether we needed to protect our people against these threats.

Q. And what was it that Major Tchibass could tell you about individual instances that would assist you in that?

A. He was cagey in a lot of occasions. I'm not surprised. He didn't really want to talk about operations. I wouldn't if I was commanding operations. But at times he did admit—

MR. BO: Objection, Your Honor. May we approach?

THE COURT: Do you mean his last remark there?

MR. BO: Yes.

THE COURT: All right. That's just speculation. We will strike the remark that he wouldn't if I was commanding operations. I'll strike that remark. Okay.

BY MS. INGERS:

Q. Now, Mr. Taylo, in late 1996, did you become aware of some non-Angolan employees of a timber or logging company having been taken hostage in Cabinda?

A. Yes, I was.

Q. Did you ever discuss that particular incident with the defendant?

A. Yes, I did.

Q. What did he tell you?

A. My specific question, because of the location of the incident, was to ask him whether FLEC were responsible.

Q. What is it that Major Tchibass told you in response to your inquiry?

A. Surprisingly he said yes, it was us.

Q. Why is it surprising?

A. Because he wasn't always so forthcoming, and so it was an occasion to remember. We used to try and identify who had been responsible for various incidents around the province of Cabinda. So to have him accept responsibility was unusual.

Q. And would you know why Major Tchibass would admit to you that his organization had committed another hostage-taking?

A. I think we were beginning to have a small amount of rapport between us, and it was these types of incidents that they knew would pressure the Angolan government in coming to the table. So he knew I would take that information back with me on my next meeting with the Angolan government.

Q. Because that was your purpose for being there?

A. Absolutely.

Q. And in that seven year period that you were meeting with him, did he at any time ever disassociate himself from FLEC?

A. He's never disassociated himself from FLEC with me.

Q. Did he ever disavow any of the actions of FLEC?

A. Never. He's actually been more a case of, there is nothing else left for us to do. The Angolan government will not negotiate, so we carry out these acts.

Q. Now, in your 15 or so meetings with Major Tchibass in that seven year period, did he ever apologize for holding Brent Swane captive?

A. I can't recall him apologizing.

Q. Did Major Tchibass in any way indicate to you that he had not been part of the taking and keeping hostage Brent Swane?

A. No, he did not.

Q. Mr. Taylo, I'd like you to look around the courtroom. Tell us if you see anybody here in this courtroom today who was present at the time you conducted these hostage negotiations.

A. Certainly. That's Major Tchibass.

THE COURT: The record will reflect the witness has identified Mr. Tchibass.

MS. INGERS: Nothing further.

CROSS-EXAMINATION
BY MR. BO:

Q. Mr. Taylo, I want to pick up where you just left off concerning whether or not Mr. Tchibass ever apologized for the Brent Swane incident. I'm showing you the notes that were typed up from the meeting of November 5th, correct?

A. Correct.

Q. It's fair to say that this is Mr. Tchibass speaking that's being recorded here, correct?

A. That is correct.

Q. And the second sentence reads "I have been asked to transmit our sincere apologies for the circumstances under which we have met and to thank Chevron for their willingness to meet with us". Does it not say that?

A. I think he saw the circumstance as unfortunate. I did not see that as a direct apology for taking Brent Swane.

Q. Do you understand the word "apology"?

A. I do.

Q. Do you see the word "apologies" in that statement?

A. I do.

Q. Now, I want to talk about this conversation that you had with Mr. Tchibass in 1996. You testified earlier that this was a conversation that related to the incident involving Mr. Dietric, the Polish hostage?

A. I don't know the name of the Polish hostage. I do know that they were timber workers and they were Polish.

Q. It's your testimony here today that Mr. Tchibass told you that the FLEC were responsible; is that correct?

A. That is correct.

Q. Just so that we're clear, it's your understanding of that conversation that happened over nine years ago was that you asked Mr. Tchibass who was responsible for the incident, correct?

A. I asked Major Tchibass if FLEC were responsible.

Q. And you certainly didn't ask him whether or not he was involved in the negotiation; is that correct?

A. I certainly did not ask him that.

Q. In fact, you have no evidence whatsoever from any source that Mr. Tchibass had any involvement in that?

A. Negotiations, absolutely not.

Q. Or the incident, correct?

A. Actual personal involvement, I have no evidence to that effect.

Q. Now, you testified earlier that at no time did Mr. Tchibass ever try to disassociate himself from the people who had taken Mr. Swane, correct?

A. At no time did he try to disassociate himself with FLEC, its ideals and objectives.

Q. Didn't he, in fact, repeatedly say that he wasn't part of the military, but that he was part of the political side of FLEC?

A. They all said they were part of the political side of FLEC when they're with us in Kinshasa. And then of course they go back into the jungle, put their uniforms on and their weapons on, and they're part of the military.

Q. Sir, I'm asking you what they told you during the meetings.

A. At the meetings they told us they were representing FLEC, the political faction.

Q. In fact, they repeatedly told you, whether or not you believed this, that the military people were the ones that were actually holding Mr. Swane; is that correct?

A. Yes.

Q. In fact, didn't they repeatedly tell you that they were having troubles convincing the military people that their demands were not appropriate?

A. They certainly mentioned that on a number of occasions.

Q. Now, you testified that during the course of the negotiations Mr. Tchibass would pound his fist on the table?

A. Yes.

Q. And you also said that he would sometimes get excited?

A. He would raise his voice on occasions, quite angrily at times.

Q. And it was clear that he was very passionate about his position; is that correct?

A. I think that comes out very clearly during all the meetings.

Q. In no way would you describe his conduct during the meetings as calm; is that correct?

A. Well, I think quite a lot of the discussions he was reasonably calm.

Q. Now, you testified that part of the demands that were made had to do with some airline tickets, correct?

A. That's correct.

Q. And those airline tickets, one of them was for Mr. Tchibass, correct?

A. That is correct.

Q. Those were tickets to come to the United States, correct?

A. That is correct.

Q. So at the time that that negotiation occurred, it appeared that they intended to come to the United States?

A. It certainly did.

Q. Didn't you advise the United States government not to issue visas—

MS. INGERS: Objection. Relevance. The issue is the tickets.

THE COURT: You will have to come up and tell me what the relevance is about it.

BY MR. BO:

Q. Didn't you advise the United States government—

THE COURT: She objected as to relevance of this issue. Tell me where the relevance is.

MR. BO: Certainly, Your Honor.

(Bench conference on the record.)

THE COURT: Where are you going with this?

MR. BO: The fact that they were unable to use the tickets because he recommended to the United States government that they not be issued a visa.

THE COURT: You're saying, counsel, the government opened the door because the tickets were never used, they were cashed in.

MR. BO: That that was some type of way to generate money.

MS. INGERS: Your Honor, as to his knowledge of why, the reason for the fact that the tickets weren't used is not relevant to the fact that they were not used. I guess if he knows that they were not given visas and therefore couldn't use them, we'd have no objection. But to inquire into who advised who about whether these visas should be issued, that's what is irrelevant. I have no objection to him asking—

MR. BO: The problem with that, Your Honor, is that it's suggested there may be some other party that had some reasons to why they didn't get the visa, or maybe they didn't get the visa because there were defects in the application.

MS. INGERS: That is irrelevant, that whole line of—

THE COURT: I agree with that. I think he can inquire whether or not he knows if they were able to get visas and use the tickets, or they could never use the tickets. There was a suggestion that they just cashed them in to get money. You have a right to address that.

(End of bench conference.)

BY MR. BO:
Q. The airline tickets were to go from Kinshasa to eventually the United States, correct?
A. That is correct.
Q. Do you know whether or not visas were ever issued to Mr. Tchibass so he could in fact use that airline ticket?
A. I do not know.
Q. Okay. Now, you testified that at some point those tickets were in fact cashed in, correct?
A. Yes, they were.
Q. During the course of the investigation, didn't it become clear that Mr. Bent was the leader of the negotiations?
A. Not Mr. Bent, but Major Tchibass. He was the person who was leading on all the discussions.
Q. So you're as clear about that as everything else you have testified to, correct?
A. I'm very clear on Tchibass being in the lead.
Q. Okay. Now, you testified that you had approximately 15 meetings with Mr. Tchibass.
A. Between 1992 and 2000.
Q. Those 15 meetings, all in Kinshasa?
A. No, they weren't. One was outside of the country with Major Tchibass, and that was in London.

Q. When did you have that meeting with Mr. Tchibass in London?

A. I believe it was the latter part of '93.

Q. And what were the circumstances of that meeting.

A. I received a telephone call out of the blue from the FLEC representative in Europe to say that these two were in London and would like to see me.

Q. Mr. Tchibass and who else?

A. Major Bent.

Q. And you readily received them, correct?

A. I met with them, yes.

Q. And then the remaining meetings happened in Kinshasa; is that correct?

A. All in Kinshasa.

Q. Mr. Tchibass had an office in Kinshasa; is that correct?

A. Yes, he did.

Q. And was there ever a time when you came to that office and you were refused admission?

A. There were times that I went to that office and there was nobody there.

Q. It's your testimony now that Mr. Tchibass told you in 1992 he had been a long-time member of FLEC-PM?

A. Yes.

Q. And when he said long-time member, what did you understand him to mean? A. I think I understood him to be a fully committed, active member of FLEC-PM by his actions during the negotiations, by the photographs of him in the bush, I thought he was an active member of FLEC and had been for some time, his own words 15 to 16 years.

Q. When is it that you got your information from Mr. Tchibass about the history of FLEC-PM?

A. We had the history of FLEC given to us at the beginning of our first meeting, a little bit about the reasons for taking Swane. We also had during our meetings the bit about that FLEC had been struggling for 15 to 16 years in their cause. And then the other detail that we discussed just now, about Tchibass' personal involvement, was during my post-meetings, post-incident.

MR. BO: I have no additional questions of Mr. Taylo.

THE COURT: Thank you. We will see if there's any redirect then.

MS. INGERS: Nothing further.

THE COURT: All right, Mr. Taylo, you're all finished. Thank you, sir. You're free to go.

(Witness excused.)

MS. EVY: The government calls Edward Montoot.

THE COURT: Before that witness comes in, I want to give a limiting instruction. Ladies and gentlemen, let me just talk to you a little bit about some of the evidence you've heard yesterday afternoon and today. You heard evidence from Mr. Dietric, the fellow from Poland, and from Mr. Taylo about a totally separate hostage-taking incident, not the one involving Brent Swane. This evidence that you heard, this is not a charge in the indictment. Now it's up to you whether or not to accept this evidence. This evidence came in for a limited reason. I'm going to explain that to you.

First, the defendant is not on trial for any of the acts that were not alleged in the indictment. Accordingly, don't consider it as evidence of this other hostage-taking as a substitute for the proof the defendant committed the crimes alleged in the indictment. Nor do you consider the evidence as proof the defendant has a criminal personality or he's a bad character. The evidence of this other similar act is admitted for a much more limited purpose.

Now, if you find the defendant participated in this other hostage-taking incident, you can consider it for the limited purpose of deciding the following. I'll repeat this at the end of the case for you, but you should be advised that whether the defendant had a motive to commit the offense charged in the indictment, it may be relevant to that, it may be relevant whether the circumstances of the other hostage-taking incident and the charged offenses are so similar that it is likely that the person who participated in the other incident also was involved in the charged offense.

And whether the evidence shows that the defendant had a specific plan to commit a series of crimes which are connected to one another. And finally whether the government has proved beyond a reasonable doubt the defendant acted knowingly and on purpose, and not because of mistake or accident.

So, if you conclude the defendant had such a motive or that the other hostage-taking was so similar to the charged offense, or that he had such a plan, then you can consider the existence of that motive or plan or the similarity of instances in helping you decide whether the government has proved beyond a reasonable doubt the defendant is the person who committed the offenses in the indictment.

Likewise, if you consider this other evidence, then you may use that evidence to help you decide whether the government has proved beyond a reasonable doubt the defendant acted knowingly and on purpose, and not by mistake or accident.

He has not been charged with any offense relating to this other hostage-taking incident. You're not to consider the evidence from this evidence to conclude the defendant has a bad character or criminal personality. The law does not allow you to convict the defendant simply because you believe he may have done some bad things, not specifically charged as a crime in this case.

The defendant's on trial for those crimes charged, and you may use the evidence of the other acts not charged only for the limited purpose of helping you decide whether the defendant is the person that committed the offenses charged in the indictment and whether the defendant, if he did commit the offenses charged in the indictment, did so knowingly and intentionally and not by accident or mistake. So, that's what it is, ladies and gentlemen. That other hostage incident was allowed in for a limited purpose, and it's up to you whether or not to accept that evidence or reject it. All right, we're going to go to the government's next witness at this time.

MS. EVY: The government calls Edward Montoot.

DIRECT EXAMINATION
BY MS. EVY:

Q. Good afternoon, sir. Can you state your full name for the record, please?
A. Yes. My name is Edward Wilson Montoot.
Q. What's your profession, sir?
A. I'm a special agent of the FBI.
Q. How long have you been a special agent with the FBI?
A. In excess of 16 years. And my current capacity is the Supervisory Agent of the Extraterritorial Squad at Washington Field Office.

THE COURT: Would you explain what you mean by "extraterritorial"?

THE WITNESS: The squad that I supervise investigates crimes that occurred against U.S. citizens outside the United States.

THE COURT: Thank you.

BY MS. EVY:
Q. Among the cases that you supervise, has your squad been working on the investigation into the abduction of Brent Swane in Angola in October, 1992?
A. Yes. In July of 2004 myself and a case agent traveled to the Democratic Republic of Congo to identify and arrest an individual who had been indicted in the kidnapping of Brent Swane.
Q. And that individual would be who?
A. Mr. Artur Tchibass.

Q. And when precisely did you first meet Mr. Tchibass?

A. I met Mr. Tchibass in July. I met him at the headquarters of the Democratic Republic of Congo's intelligence service building.

Q. Can you describe the circumstances of that meeting?

A. Myself and Special Agent Prout were waiting in a conference room at the Intelligence Bureau headquarters with language specialist Francoise Ker, and at approximately 5:30 in the afternoon an individual entered the conference room, and we stood up and we introduced ourselves, and an individual introduced himself as Mr. Tchibass.

Q. Did you arrest him immediately at that time?

A. No, we did not.

Q. Why not?

A. We weren't sure of the identity of the individual in front of us. The picture that we had was an old picture and one that wasn't of great quality, so we proceeded to ask him questions to make sure that the individual that we have indicted and wanted to arrest was the individual in front of us.

Q. Mr. Montoot, I'm showing you a Government's Exhibit and ask if you've ever seen that before?

A. Yes, I have. This is a Xerox copy of an identity card with a photograph on it, with personal data on it.

Q. And what precisely did you do with this document?

A. At that point, Agent Prout provided this to Mr. Tchibass and asked him was this in fact him, which at that time Mr. Tchibass replied, "Yes, that is me. If I had known that this was an important document to you, I could have brought it. I can go back to my residence if you want me to and obtain the original." At that time we said, "no, we just want to make sure because it doesn't look like you," and he kind of shrugged and laughed and stated, "well, that picture is an old picture. I now have a gray beard and a lot of time has passed."

Q. Mr. Montoot, I'm going to ask you to look around the courtroom and see if there's anyone here today who you saw in Kinshasa in July of 2004.

A. Yes. The gentleman just standing up now.

MS. EVY: May the record reflect the witness has identified the defendant?

THE COURT: Yes.

Q. Now, after he had identified himself to you on that date in Kinshasa, what if anything did you do?

A. After we were comfortable that Mr. Tchibass was the individual we were looking for, we identified ourselves as FBI agents and that we wanted to talk to him about the abduction of Brent Swane. But before we could discuss anything, he has rights under U.S. law—

MR. BO: Your Honor, may we approach?

THE COURT: Sure.

(Bench conference on the record.)

MR. BO: It appears the government's about to elicit the fact that he was about to assert his Fifth Amendment rights, which I don't think is appropriate.

MS. EVY: We have no intention of doing that, Your Honor.

THE COURT: Do you want to say I gave him the Miranda Warning?

MS. EVY: That's it.

The COURT: And then stop there?

MS. EVY: And that he was transported back to the United States.

MR. BO: I don't think that's relevant at all if he was given his Miranda Warnings—

THE COURT: I'll allow it. It's overruled. The jury will have no idea what happened to him. He could misunderstand what went on over there, so I'll allow it. Go ahead.

(End of bench conference.)

Q. Mr. Montoot, you were explaining?
A. At that point we told him we wanted to ask him questions about the abduction of Brent Swane. But before we got into those questions, under U.S. law there's certain rights that he's entitled to, and we presented him a document of Advisement of Rights written in French. The linguist who was sitting there read that to him, and at which point in time we started discussing what his rights were, and Mr. Tchibass asked us can he have an attorney.

MR. BO: Your Honor, may we approach?

THE COURT: Sure.

(Bench conference on the record.)

THE COURT: Where are you going to go with this?

MS. EVY: We are simply explaining the procedure he used for advising him of his rights. I will be happy—

MR. BO: It's completely irrelevant, Your Honor. Now we have a violation of the Sixth Amendment right.

THE COURT: Why don't we just have him move ahead.

MS. EVY: Very well.

THE COURT: The defendant is looking like he's trying to protect himself. He has the right to say he wants an attorney.

(End of bench conference.)

BY MS. EVY:
Q. Mr. Montoot, after he was advised of his rights was he ultimately taken out of Kinshasa?
A. Yes, he was.
Q. And who took him out of Kinshasa?
A. The Federal Bureau of Investigation, specifically myself and Agent Prout.
Q. Where did you take him?
A. We transported him here to the District of Columbia.

MS. EVY: Thank you. No further questions.

THE COURT: Any questions?

MR. BO: I have no questions.

THE COURT: Thank you. You're free to go, sir. Thank you.

(Witness excused.)

MS. INGERS: Your Honor, the government has no further witnesses or evidence at this time.

MR. BO: Your Honor, may we approach?

THE COURT: Sure.

(Bench conference on the record.)

(NOW THE ATTORNEYS FOR BOTH SIDES LAUNCHED AN EXTENSIVE BENCH CONFERENCE COVERING MANY ISSUES AND PRIOR COURT RULINGS. THE JUDGE DISMISSED THE JURY UNTIL 2:00 P.M. THAT AFTERNOON, BUT HE WAS A LITTLE OPTIMISTIC. THE PUBLIC DEFENDER MADE A MOTION FOR JUDGMENT OF ACQUITTAL ON MANY HIGHLY TECHNICAL GROUNDS, ALL OF WHICH WERE OVERRULED. THEN AFTER 23 PAGES OF COURT RECORDED COURT TESTIMONY, THE JUDGE CALLED UPON THE DEFENDANT, MAJOR TCHIBASS.)

THE COURT: Mr. Tchibass, let me talk to you for one minute and address you, if I may. You have a right to testify if you want to, as to relevant matters that are before the Court. And you have a right not to testify, not to say anything. And if you decide not to testify, there would be no suggestion of guilt drawn from the fact that you did not testify, and the jury can draw no inference of guilt from the fact that you decided not to testify. There is no obligation for you to testify, and you have an absolute right not to if you don't want to.

If you want to testify, you must understand the government then is allowed to cross-examine you after your direct testimony about any relevant matter that may have a bearing either on your actions in this case or that could affect your credibility or believability of your story by attacking you with other wrongs or other crimes they may have a basis to ask you about that they understand you have committed.

And so they're not restricted just to cross-examine you about whatever you say in your direct examination, but can go beyond that and cross-examine you about any information that they have in good faith that they know about, of other actions you have taken relating to FLEC and your activities in Angola or Cabinda or Zaire. So, you just have to be warned, once you start to testify you will not be able to refuse to answer a question, and that they can examine you about matters that you did not testify on direct that they know of. And you would be exposed to these other issues that they could raise. I just want to make sure you understand that. You do not have to testify, and no one can make you testify if you don't want to. The burden is always on the government in our system to prove you guilty beyond a reasonable doubt, and you have no obligation to offer any evidence. You're presumed to be innocent.

THE DEFENDANT: (Through the interpreter) Your Honor, I ask to please be allowed to speak with my attorney.

THE COURT: As much as he wants to. That's fine.

THE DEFENDANT: Thank you very much, Your Honor.

THE COURT: We're going to take a short break, and then we'll come back and see where we are about the testimony.

(Recess taken)

THE COURT: Let me take up first Mr. Tchibass' testimony. For the record, I took a recess while Mr. Tchibass asked to consult with Mr. Bo. And if you both want to come back to the podium and advise me about whether Mr. Tchibass is going to testify.

MR. BO: Thank you, Your Honor. For the record I did have a discussion with Mr. Tchibass, and as a result of those discussions, Mr. Tchibass would like to inform the Court that he's choosing not to testify in this case.

THE COURT: Mr. Tchibass, I know you had translated what your counsel just said. You've chosen not to testify, and as I explained to you, there would be no suggestion or inference made that you're guilty because you did not testify. But I want to make sure that that is your decision and that you do not feel that you had been forced not to testify in any way, and you have decided of your own free will not to testify.

THE DEFENDANT: It is I, myself, who have solemnly made this decision not to testify.

THE COURT: All right. Thank you, sir. We'll then continue on with the trial without your testimony.

(STILL OUT OF THE PRESENCE OF THE JURY, THE JUDGE AND THE VARIOUS ATTORNEYS AGAIN DISCUSSED THE NEXT WITNESS THE DEFENSE PLANNED TO CALL, AND AFTER AN ADDITIONAL 11 PAGES OF RECORDED BEHIND-THE-SCENES DISCUSSION, THE JUDGE SUSPECTED THAT IT WOULD BE A VERY DETAILED DISCUSSION AND DISMISSED THE JURY FOR THE DAY, TO REPORT BACK THE FOLLOWING MORNING. ONCE THE JURY DEPARTED, THE BENCH ARGUMENTS CARRIED ON FOR 25 MORE RECORDED PAGES OF TESTIMONY, CONSISTING MOSTLY OF THE PUBLIC DEFENDER'S CHALLENGES TO PREVIOUS STATEMENTS MADE ON THE STAND BY WITNESSES FOR THE GOVERNMENT. THEN THE JUDGE DISCUSSED THE INSTRUCTIONS HE PLANNED TO READ TO THE JURY, AND ALL THE LAWYERS GAVE THEIR INPUT.)

THE COURT: Let me look at the indictment for a minute. The indictment reads, the acts which are an offense against the United States, that is, to seize, detain, threaten to detain Brent Swane, that's the conspiracy part. I'm not sure there can be an argument made that he didn't know he was violating the laws of the United States when he kidnapped somebody. I mean, I don't think that with any relevance he could make that kind of argument.

MR. BO: Your Honor, I think actually it is very relevant. I don't see how it is that if your conduct occurs in a different country, how would you know that you're in fact violating the laws of the United States.

THE COURT: You're violating the United States' citizens rights. You must have some idea. The piracy statute here goes back to the 1790's.

MR. BO: It very well may be that you understand piracy in a situation where you're in international waters and international zones, but when you're in another sovereign country and you commit a criminal act doesn't necessarily mean that you know that that's going to find you culpable in some other sovereign country.

THE COURT: I don't think being aware of the fact that he knew it or not makes any difference. I don't see how that's a legal defense.

MR. BO: It seems to me that you have to know that you're violating a law that's applicable to you. "So the first thing that must be shown is the existence of an agreement." And we would be asking the Court to add the following language. "So the first thing that must be shown is the existence of an agreement to violate the laws of the United States."

MS. INGERS: We object, Your Honor. It's not standard. It's not the law.

THE COURT: All right, I'll consider that. I'm not convinced that that should be done, though, but I'll see if there's any basis for it when I get a chance to review it some more. But I don't see that he has to know he's violating any particular laws to be found guilty.

MR. BO: That's all I have concerning that instruction.

THE COURT: All right, thank you. Hostage-taking is Count Two. And then we go to aiding and abetting. This is the standard aiding and abetting. It does include a couple of the parentheticals that are in the standardized instruction, like mere physical presence is not sufficient, but if it's meant to help the commission of the crime, it may be. And the rest are just the standardized closing instructions.

What I have proposed to do is, once I finalize these instructions, I would give the first set, which are now 36 pages in length, the substantive ones first, and save the ones about selection of the foreperson and looking at the exhibits after closings are finished.

(Proceedings concluded.)

SIXTH DAY, SEPTEMBER 11, 2005

MORNING SESSION

(THE DAY STARTED OFF WITH ANOTHER LONG DISCUSSION OUT OF THE PRESENCE OF THE JURY. THE PUBLIC DEFENDER WANTED TO CALL AS A WITNESS A PORTUGESE BUSINESSMAN WHO HAD A SIMILAR KIDNAPPING OF AN EMPLOYEE BY FLEC SEVERAL YEARS AFTER THE BRENT SWANE INCIDENT. HE WAS PLANNING TO COMPLIMENT MAJOR TCHIBASS FOR THE HELP HE GAVE IN GETTING HIS EMPLOYEES FREEDOM, PICTURING THE MAJOR AS A HUMANITARIAN RATHER THAN A HOSTAGE TAKER. THE COURT OVERRULED THIS WITNESS' APPEARANCE, CITING NUMEROUS CASES. THEN THE PUBLIC DEFENDER MADE A MOTION FOR ACQUITTAL, AND THIS TOO WAS TURNED DOWN. THEN HE MADE A MOTION TO DISMISS THE CHARGES FOR VIOLATION OF A SPEEDY TRIAL, AND THAT WAS DENIED AS WELL. IT WASN'T A HAPPY DAY FOR MR. BO.

NEXT, THE JUDGE AND THE LAWYERS HASSLED OVER WHAT THE COURT'S CLOSING INSTRUCTIONS TO THE JURY WOULD BE. ALL THIS BEHIND-THE-SCENES ARGUING CONSUMED 34 PAGES OF THE COURT REPORTER'S RECORDS. FINALLY, THE JURY WAS CALLED IN.)

(Jury in.)

THE COURT: Thank you, ladies and gentlemen for your patience again. We've taken care of all our matters we had to deal with here. And good morning, and I appreciate your being here today. We are at the juncture of the case where all the evidence has now been prepared and submitted to you. So we are now at the final phase of the case. The case is now going to be submitted to you for a decision.

You're going to be listening to the closing arguments in a few minutes and my final instructions to you on the law that applies to the case and that you will follow in your deliberations. I'm going to break the instructions into two phases. I'm going to give you the substantive instructions at the beginning now, before you have the closing arguments so that you can listen to the closing arguments and have in your mind the law that applies. And then at the end of the closing arguments I'll give you about five minutes worth of instructions just governing your deliberations, how you go about your work.

And so I'm going to spend now about 20, 25 minutes giving you these instructions. I'm going to orally read them to you. You will additionally be given them in written form when you go back to deliberate, so you'll have them with you.

And then we will have the closing arguments. The government will go first in its closing, and then the defendant gives his closing, and then the government has a chance for a rebuttal argument at the end because they have the burden of proof, as I'll explain again to you, beyond a reasonable doubt.

So, ladies and gentlemen, some of these instructions that I give you will require you to listen carefully to what I have to say, and I'm going to ask you to do that. The instructions are meant to help you understand your role in this case and my role, and give you some guidance on judging the credibility, in other words, the believability of the witnesses, give you some instructions on what is evidence in the case and on your role as jurors. And finally we will give you instructions on the principles of law that you're going to apply, the definition of reasonable doubt, and then on the substantive offenses, the offenses that are charged and the elements of those offenses, that you will have to know and understand in order to review the evidence and find if the government's met their burden of proof as to proving each elements of these offenses beyond a reasonable doubt.

Your function as jurors is to determine what the facts are in this case. You are the sole judges of the facts. You alone decide the weight to give to the evidence presented during the trial. You decide the value of the evidence and the believability of the witnesses. You should determine the facts without prejudice, fear, sympathy, or favoritism. You should not be improperly influenced by anyone's race, ethnic origin or gender. Decide the case solely from a fair consideration of the evidence.

(THE COURT CONTINUED ITS INSTRUCTIONS TO THE JURY, COVERING ANOTHER 23 PAGES OF RECORDED TESTIMONY. NOW THE CLOSING ARGUMENTS TOOK CENTER STAGE.)

THE COURT: The Court will then recognize Ms. Ingers on behalf of the government for the closing arguments.

MS. INGERS: Thank you, Your Honor. This case is about, ladies and gentlemen, the violent deprivation of the liberty of an American citizen in a foreign country for the purpose of extorting a ransom from his employer, an American company. This case is about the role that one individual, this man, Artur Tchibass, played in the taking and keeping hostage that American citizen, and in maintaining him hostage while the details of the terms for his release were worked out, a release that happened only after a ransom of materials worth half a million dollars were actually paid.

Ladies and gentlemen, the case is about hostage taking. It's kidnap for ransom, outside the United States. Now, one advantage of a pretty short trial is that the evidence that you've heard and seen here is probably pretty fresh in your minds, and there are some basic facts that I want to talk about right away that nobody disputes. The defendant doesn't dispute, and they're very much part of the evidence that the government presented. This occurred in Cabinda on the 19th of October, 1992. And what occurred is the abduction of an American citizen: Brent Swane. That's undisputed.

It's also, ladies and gentlemen, having to do with the conspiracy charged in Count Two. So that's undisputed. The next undisputed thing is that the American citizen, Brent Swane, was held for two months in captivity. It's also undisputed that the people who took him hostage were members of an organization called FLEC-PM, the Front For The Liberation Of The Enclave Of Cabinda, Military Position.

He was held in captivity under armed guard until the early morning hours of December 18. Now, FLEC-PM claimed responsibility for this incident. That's undisputed. FLEC-PM demanded ransom for the release of Brent Swane, and that's undisputed. It's also undisputed that in the early days of November, three men, including the defendant, Artur Tchibass, came to Kinshasa in Zaire, next door to the province of Cabinda.

MR. BO: Objection, Your Honor. May we approach?

THE COURT: All right. Try to avoid these objections, if we can.

(Bench conference on the record.)

The COURT: What's undisputed?

MR. BO: It's not an accurate statement that Mr. Tchibass came to Kinshasa. It's suggesting that he was in Cabinda at the time of the abduction.

THE COURT: All right, you can say that there were three people that came, that appeared. All right.

(End of bench conference.)

MS. INGERS: That those three people, including the defendant, were in Kinshasa showing documents and credential of FLEC-PM, saying that they represented FLEC-PM, and demanding a meeting with Brent Swane's employer so that they could present demands. It's also undisputed that they did so. They had that meeting, they presented a letter of demand, you've seen it, and you'll have it back in the room when you go to deliberate.

Ladies and gentlemen, it's also undisputed that the terms that were haggled over the course of nine negotiating sessions were finally resolved. Ransom was paid, and Brent Swane was finally released. Now, the indictment you're going to have back in the deliberation room with you, charges two counts. The second one is hostage taking. And I want to say a couple of words about that before I talk about the evidence that you've heard and seen. As you heard the judge tell you, hostage taking isn't just the seizing, the taking of a person. It includes the holding of that person and keeping him in custody while demands are made to a third party. It's kind of a continuous act. You don't have to find that the defendant himself was present when Brent Swane was taken hostage. In addition, he's charged as an aider and abettor. All you have to find is that he knowingly associated himself with the hostage taking of Brent Swane, and participated in keeping him hostage until the ransom was paid.

Now, Count One was a conspiracy. That has to do with a plan, an agreement. The question is whether the defendant knowingly entered into that agreement, and that he and at least one of his coconspirators did one of the overt acts that are spelled out in the indictment, one of which we have already talked about.

The agreement here was quite simply to take and hold Brent Swane hostage, and threaten to keep him until the ransom was paid. The coconspirators, ladies and gentlemen, are all FLEC-PM members. Top to bottom, they were part of the hostage taking scheme. Four of them are named in the indictment. They're the people who were charged in the indictment. Only one of those is on trial here today: Mr. Tchibass.

The coconspirators, however, include everybody up and down the line that you've heard about, the people who took Brent Swane captive, the people who marched him back into the camps, the people who watched over him, the people who served as the couriers back and forth to Kinshasa. They're all part of that team. And, ladies and gentlemen, also part of that team were the people who went to the United States Embassy and to meet with Chevron to work out the terms for Brent Swane's release.

Ladies and gentlemen, you don't have to be in charge to be part of a conspiracy. You don't have to be a boss. You don't have to be a quarterback. Even the place kick holder is part of the team. And, ladies and gentlemen, while there's been much made in the course of the evidence that you have heard and the questioning back and forth about what was the job, what was the position that the defendant held in the course of all those negotiating sessions? Who had the higher rank? Was it Major Bent or was it Major Tchibass? That doesn't matter in this case, ladies and gentlemen. All that matters is asking whether this defendant was a part of the team. He didn't have to be the leader. Everyone who signed up to take and detain Brent Swane captive the way he was held was part of the team.

Next, FLEC-PM was a paramilitary organization. And it was an armed organization. The indictment alleges it, the evidence shows it. The objective of FLEC clearly stated in this case was to promote the independence of the Cabindan province from Angola. As for Jose Tiburci, the President of FLEC-PM, Mauricio Amad Zulu, Antonio Bent Bembe, and Artur Tchibass, the defendant here, they were all members of FLEC-PM.

Now, in counsel's opening statement, Mr. Bo suggested that the defendant was not a member of FLEC-PM until after Brent Swane was taken hostage. And I'd like you to think about the evidence as you consider that. The defendant's Cabinda ID card and which he, in fact, attested to the authenticity of by his own signature, bears a date, 5/5/90, ladies and gentlemen. 1990. That's over two years before Brent Swane was taken hostage.

And the profession attributed to the holder of this particular ID card, Artur Tchibass, "combatant." His profession is combatant. In addition, Scott Taylo said that the defendant was really proud of FLEC, and he talked about it in the meetings to discuss the ransom for Brent Swane. In addition, he held a military rank. He was a Major. He introduced himself as that, he was referred to as that, and that was not a Major in any other organization than the Military Position, PM, of FLEC.

Now, ladies and gentlemen, all you have to do in this case is find that the defendant was a member of FLEC-PM during the period of time charged in the indictment. That's what the indictment alleges. And the period charged in the indictment is October 19th until the time Swane was released. I submit to you, though, that it's abundantly clear from the evidence that the defendant was, in fact, a charter member of FLEC-PM before, during, and for long after Brent Swane's hostage taking.

Now, I want to talk about the hostage taking itself. What we know is that it was planned, it was clearly planned. You saw on the map annotated by the hostage, Brent Swane, that he was traveling his daily routine morning commute all alone in the company vehicle on the only road that went from Malongo to where he worked in Cabinda City.

He ran into a roadblock on a deserted stretch of that highway, and there were armed troops in wait. When they got in the car they checked his name against a piece of paper. And that piece of paper contained Brent Swane's name and the names of three other American guys who worked at Malongo and who Gary Webe told you were the four men who were authorized to leave Malongo. This was a plan.

They moved quickly. They went through a prearranged route. They traveled through tough territory. They traveled sometimes through hostile territory, often at night. And their stops were at established camps, transit camps. And when they finally got to the base camp, there was a military ceremony as they marched in to mark the occasion of the capture.

The fist thing that happens then is that Brent Swane is directed by his captors to write a letter, and he's told to explain where he is, and indeed he writes, "I have finally arrived at FLEC base camp." And then, ladies and gentlemen, after Brent Swane writes that letter, the next thing that happens for two months is a long wait for Brent Swane. And, by the way, ladies and gentlemen, Brent Swane testified that he was treated okay. And this case isn't about the maltreatment or abuse of the hostage. What this hostage was for his captors, was a valuable commodity. And there was no way they were going to hurt him. Think back to what Roy Whitake, the United States Embassy official said. Remember he was one of the earlier witnesses here. He worked in the U.S. Embassy in Kinshasa, and he told you that the first thing that happened by way of knowing about what happened to Brent Swane was that Mauricio Zulu on October 26th showed up and delivered FLEC-PM demand letters at the embassy. And, by the way, that's another overt act.

There were four letters that were delivered. One is the one from Brent Swane. Another one from Tiburci on FLEC-PM letterhead directed to Chevron, and a third one directed to the President of the United States. And the fourth one to Congress. And Roy Whitake told you that he was able to accept the letters from Swane and the letter to Chevron, but he couldn't accept the letters directed to the President and Congress because he wasn't permitted to accept such official correspondence from terrorist organizations.

Now, the next thing that happened, ladies and gentlemen, is that the very next day the defendant shows up again at the United States Embassy, and they're demanding by this time that they meet with Chevron. But at the very least, ladies and gentlemen, the defendant is part of this conspiracy as of October 27th, when he came to the United States Embassy together with his two potential fellow negotiators and demanded that meeting. And that's enough, ladies and gentlemen, that's enough.

On November 5, again, the defendant comes back to the U.S. Embassy, and at this time they make some progress. They agree to a meeting on November 9, and they take a care package for Swane. There is no indication, ladies and gentlemen, in the testimony of Roy Whitake that the defendant in any way suggested or indicated or presented himself as anything but a full-fledged member of FLEC-PM. He didn't say to Roy Whitake, I'm not with them. I'm here to just help out. I'm the good guy. I'm trying to broker some kind of arrangement. That's not what happened.

Now, Mr. Bo suggested that Mr. Tchibass was a well-known diplomat in Kinshasa at that time. But Roy Whitake told you that he didn't know Tchibass. And, indeed, when Mr. Bo asked him on cross-examination, Mr. Whitake said he never even heard of the defendant until he showed up on October 27th with Zulu and Bent. You also heard Roy Whitake tell you, ladies and gentlemen, of the three who he met with, it became the defendant who took the dominant role. He was the lead spokesman even with Roy Whitake. He was the one who had the more forceful personality, and he's the one who came forward as the leader in that group even though Major Bent outranked him in his civil capacity, and even though Major Bent was the one who spoke some English, and the defendant didn't.

Roy Whitake also identified the defendant for you, and when he was asked how it was that he could point out the defendant after the passage of so many years, he explained that he had a certain charisma, flare, and dominant personality. The defendant was memorable. The first three meetings, November 9, 10 and 12, that series of meetings is another overt act. And then there was a break. And then there was another series of three that were presided over by Scott Taylo. And then you had your final series of meetings that lead to the release of Brent Swane. Those are the overt acts that are charged in the indictment.

Ladies and gentlemen, you have 165 pages of meticulously kept records of what was said, of what happened in those negotiating meetings, and you're going to have them back in the room with you. Look at them carefully. Fifty percent of the statements made in those negotiating sessions were made by the defendant. He was the principal negotiator, he was the spokesman, he was the one who for his side drove the negotiations over the course of those nine meetings. And ask yourselves, ladies and gentlemen, where was he sitting at the table? He wasn't sitting at the head of the table with the Chevron people on one side and the FLEC-PM people on the other. He was sitting in the middle of the FLEC-PM side. He was one of the parties to the negotiation. He wasn't a mediator. From the very beginning he was the spokesman. He made it clear that he was a high member of FLEC-PM.

And you heard Simon Adams and Sydney Anders, and Webe and Taylo, all testified that they accepted him as he presented himself. And you also have the list of demands that was presented by the defendant. The core of their demands, provide complete equipment for 2,000 people. The defendant knew early on that the price tag for those demands was two and a half million dollars. And as the sessions went on, the negotiations really came down to, well, if we can't have all of those military goods, we want cash. And, of course, the U.S. side, as you heard through the witnesses, knew that if they got cash they'd just go out and buy the military stuff, so they said no, we will give you goods to substitute for cash. And there was another kind of a tone that the defendant took in those conversations. And the words were taken, you heard, by his opposite numbers as threats. "In the meantime, as long as there are no solutions, we must exist. We have spent 15 years fighting, but we have never attacked Chevron. Chevron should reach an agreement or Chevron ceases to exist in Cabinda." That, ladies and gentlemen, was a threat. Next, a statement of the defendant, "At the present time we will not harm Chevron, but this is not a permanent guarantee. In the future we may decide to change our views if Chevron decides not to change its position. This would be a disaster to Chevron." That's what the defendant said in those negotiating sessions, ladies and gentlemen. The defendant went into the bush with Bent and Zulu, and they met with the Central Committee on November 21st, and they were also there on the morning of the 22nd where they met Brent Swane. And in that one and a half days, the defendant was pretty much everywhere.

Now, ladies and gentlemen, ask yourselves, is that a man who is a stranger to FLEC-PM? Is that a guy who doesn't know the people that he's spending that day and a half with? And then, ladies and gentlemen, on the 17th of December in a ceremony in the bush at the base camp, the leadership of FLEC-PM, including Major Artur Tchibass, signed here a certificate of honorary membership of Cabindan citizen that's then presented to Brent Swane, just as he said.

The defendant then took Brent Swane to the release point and physically handed him over to Gary Webe and to Scott Taylo. And you heard both of them describe that. Ladies and gentlemen, the defendant was in this up to his ear lobes from start to finish as an aider and abettor of the initial taking of Brent Swane, and the holding of him in captivity, and in the conspiracy to take him and hold him.

Now, it has been suggested that Brent Swane was released in large part because of the efforts of the defendant, and you know that's absolutely not true. Ask yourselves whether the defendant went to the release point because he wanted to see that Brent Swane reached no harm. All they had received was the down-payment. If Brent Swane was hurt on the way out to the release point, there would be no more ransom payments out of that deal.

If the defendant were only involved with this as a neutral party, ladies and gentlemen, or just a good guy trying to bring two factions together for the sake of a kidnapped

Linda L. Russo, RPR with George B. Blake

victim, would he have shown up in military uniform in the camp? Wouldn't he have sat at the head of the table instead of on one side? Would he have signed all those documents as a full-fledged senior member of FLEC-PM? No. Even though the defendant is only charged, ladies and gentlemen, with the incident involving Brent Swane, you've heard in this courtroom testimony about another hostage-taking incident that occurred just about four years later. You heard from one of the hostages who had been taken in that incident, a Mr. Pyotr Dietric, and you saw a photograph that he brought to you.

And you heard, ladies and gentlemen, that the negotiations that were taking place for the release of the Polish hostages in Kinshasa. And ransom was paid. $120,000. And soon after, you heard when Scott Taylo was meeting with the defendant in his FLEC office in Kinshasa, Mr. Taylo made a point of asking pointblank to the defendant, was FLEC involved in the incident? And the defendant said yes. And he said it proudly.

If the defendant, ladies and gentlemen, had had an innocent altruistic role in the taking and holding hostage of Brent Swane in 1992, would he have remained a top leader in the same organization when it was doing the very same thing four years later? It is, at bottom, ladies and gentlemen, a kidnapping for ransom, the internal politics of a foreign country are not what this case is about. It's about the taking hostage of an American citizen, of a guy who was just minding his own business, and keeping him as a pawn in a ransom game. Don't let the fact that it happened in that foreign country get in the way.

Finally, I want to say there are five things I'd like to ask you to remember, quickly. One, hostage taking doesn't just mean taking a hostage. It means holding, continuing to detain a hostage. Keep that in mind as you're reviewing what the evidence shows about the defendant's involvement.

Second, you don't have to be the quarterback. Status, your role in the organization, isn't what determines whether you're a conspirator. The defendant didn't have to be the top guy, although the evidence shows he was one of the top guys.

Third, the significance of the records of the negotiating sessions is that they show the active role the defendant played.

Fourth, the defendant's claim that he was an uninvolved or neutral third party broker is just plain not borne out by the evidence. And finally, ladies and gentlemen, as I just said a minute ago, this is a straightforward serious crime of violence, kidnapping for ransom outside the U.S.

When you came into this courtroom last week, and as you came in every day, and as you prepare now to go into deliberations, nobody asked you to check your common sense at the door. You've had it with you as you've listened to the evidence, you've had it with you as you've seen the exhibits, and you're going to take it with you into what you're going to do now. Apply that common sense, keep it close to you as you consider the facts and apply the law.

And I submit to you, ladies and gentlemen, that at the end of that process the evidence will compel you to come out with the only possible verdict you can reach in this case. The defendant, Artur Tchibass, is guilty of hostage taking, and guilty of conspiracy to commit hostage taking, as he has been charged. Thank you.

THE COURT: Ladies and gentlemen, we're going to now turn to the defense's closing arguments. Mr. Bo will address you in this matter. Okay, Mr. Bo.

MR. BO: If there's no dispute about whether or not Brent Swane was abducted, why did the government spend so much time during its summation talking about it?

I submit to you the reason why they did is because they don't want you to focus on the evidence in this case. And the evidence in this case, ladies and gentlemen, is the testimony that you heard from the witness stand here and the exhibits that are going to be reviewed by you. And if you review those exhibits and you compare that to the testimony in this case, ladies and gentlemen, not only will there be a reasonable doubt in your mind about whether or not Mr. Tchibass was part of this conspiracy or whether or not Mr. Tchibass agreed to this hostage taking, there will be no doubt in your mind that he had absolutely nothing to do with the hostage taking, and that he certainly didn't agree with the goals. He was certainly not trying to further the goals of the hostage takers, and he certainly did not want to bring about the continued abduction being held of Mr. Swane.

Remember Mr. Taylo came up and testified yesterday about how Mr. Tchibass was pounding on the table, and that Mr. Tchibass was the hard-liner of the group, and that Mr. Tchibass was the one that seemed to be in control of all the situation? Well, ladies and gentlemen, you're going to have the transcripts of the notes from the Chevron people, and they're going to show you that Mr. Tchibass was the spokesperson. Mr. Tchibass was the person that was trying to work towards a resolution of this case. Remember what Mr. Anders said, that Mr. Tchibass was calm, that Mr. Tchibass was cordial, and that Mr. Tchibass was trying to work towards an agreement.

Ladies and gentlemen, one of the points that the government finished their closing argument on is about whether or not Mr. Tchibass is a neutral party in this. He's not a neutral party. He never has been. He never will be. He believes in the freedom of the Cabindan people, and he will fight for the freedom of the Cabindan people. But what he didn't believe in is in hostage taking.

And right at the very beginning you know what the problem Mr. Tchibass faces during the course of the negotiations. In fact, you'll see it repeatedly throughout the negotiations that Mr. Tchibass is saying this: I want Brent Swane released; we believe he should be released; we don't have control over his release. The people out in the bush, the people 12 hours away by car, are the people who abducted Mr. Swane. And I am here, in essence as their representative, but I want you to know something, that I'm also trying to work with my own people to explain to them what they did is a disaster, that this was the wrong thing for the cause. That, I share in their beliefs, in fact I'm a part of their group, but I don't share in the belief that you go and you abduct any citizen, let alone an American citizen. And that you have to understand, Mr. Taylo, Mr. Adams, Mr. Webe, that I'm trying to get this person released just as hard as you are. But I'm not in control of this situation. And those are what those statements say. He repeatedly referred to the fact that the military people were the people that were holding Mr. Swane, and that the military people had these outrageous demands, that they wanted to arm an army of 2,000, that they wanted $2.5 million, that they wanted Jessie Jackson and Jimmy Carter to participate in these negotiations.

Now, Mr. Tchibass knew that that wasn't reasonable, that that didn't make any sense whatsoever. But he knew that he had to give them something, because if he didn't come back to the military people with some type of resolution of this case, who knows what would happen to Brent Swane? And that was the position that he found himself in.

So what did he do? He acted. He said, yes, I am going to be a member of FLEC, and I do believe in the FLEC's cause, I do believe in the freedom of the Cabindan people from the Angolan government. I will serve as their spokesman, and I will work towards their goals. And that is the freedom of Cabinda, not towards some type of criminal enterprise of some hostage taking. So he wasn't a neutral party in this case, ladies and gentlemen. He was a full-fledged member of the FLEC.

Now, he knew that if he showed up with the Chevron people and said, do you know what, I'm not really part of this organization, and I just arrived here, but, you know what, I think I can get your guy released. Do you think that Chevron would have taken them seriously? Who did Chevron send to participate on their ends of the negotiations? A senior vice president. You need to know who the man is. You need to know who you're talking to. You need to know that the person you're talking to has the authority to make decisions. And that's why Mr. Tchibass held that position.

And he doesn't run away from that. He identified himself, Major Tchibass. He's part of FLEC. Just because he's part of the FLEC does not mean that he's part of the hostage taking.

And that's the fallacy of the government's case. That's what they're trying to sell you. They're trying to say because Mr. Tchibass was a member of FLEC, therefore you should find him guilty. But the law doesn't work that way. The law says that the government has to prove beyond a reasonable doubt that Mr. Tchibass intended to cause the kidnapping, or aided and abetted the hostage taking, that he sought to further the goals of the hostage taking, which is absolutely nothing of the case.

Now, ladies and gentlemen, remember, when Brent Swane was shown this photograph, they asked him, do you recognize these people? And sure enough, of course, he recognized himself, also recognized Mr. Luemb, and also was able to recognize Mr. Bent. Who is the one person that he wasn't able to recognize in this picture? Well, the only person that's remaining: Mr. Tchibass.

Now, does that strike you as somebody who is tightly involved in this organization, so tightly involved in this organization that he was well-known to Mr. Swane? Mr. Swane didn't know anything about Mr. Tchibass.

Now, I want to talk a little bit about the membership card that the government wants to make a big deal of showing Mr. Tchibass' alleged membership beginning in 1990.

Now, you remember when Mr. Taylo and Mr. Adams testified about how negotiations occur, one of the things you need to know is that the person that you're negotiating with really is the appropriate representative of the other side. Well, if Mr. Tchibass had shown up with a membership card saying that he had just been made a member of the FLEC a day or two before, or a week before, do you think that the Chevron negotiators, especially someone as savvy as Simon Adams, do you think he would have said, you know, wait a minute, should we really be talking with these people? Maybe you should bring us the people who really know what's going on. The government's just flat out wrong when it tries to argue to you that Mr. Tchibass was not known among the diplomatic community in Kinshasa. When Mr. Tchibass showed up at the embassy on the 27th, he specifically told Mr. Whitake that, listen, I am known. In fact, if you contact your embassy in Brazzaville, you will know that I am somebody that's part of the diplomatic community here. And Brazzaville and Kinshasa are right across the river from each other.

If you were just trying to extort money from Chevron, you would say, listen, we've got one of your workers, we're going to hold him, give us the money, we go away, you're going to be fine. Why would you bring in the United States government? It doesn't make any sense. You bring in the United States government if you think that you've got a problem. And that's what happened. There was a problem.

The people that were involved in the negotiation team knew that the military people of FLEC had done something wrong, and they didn't want to hurt the Cabindan cause. They wanted to make sure that the American Embassy knew exactly what was going on. The issue in this case is, what was Mr. Tchibass' intent during this whole incident. And his intent was trying to get Mr. Swane released. There was no criminal intent whatsoever. To this day, Mr. Tchibass thinks that because of his intervention, Mr. Swane is alive. Mr. Tchibass played a part in those negotiation sessions. Your job in a criminal case is to determine whether or not the government has proved to you beyond a reasonable doubt the allegations in the indictment. It's not a game. Your job is to evaluate the evidence. Your job is to evaluate what the government has presented based on the legal principles that apply in a criminal case.

Do you remember what Mr. Anders said about Mr. Tchibass' feelings, or how he appeared to feel about the way the process of negotiations were going? He was disappointed. Do you remember that word? That was a word that he used. And why was he disappointed, according to Mr. Anders? Because Mr. Tchibass knew that he was going back to the military people without probably an acceptable resolution to the military people. He was concerned about that.

But, do you know what, ladies and gentlemen. It appeared they did have some contact with the military people, and he was able to convince them to reduce their demands. In fact, you heard Mr. Tchibass wasn't even a leader of the delegation. It was Mr. Bent. Mr. Bent was the one armed with a weapon out in the bush. We know that Mr. Bent was the person that was in charge of that delegation, and that Mr. Bent was the one who was more excited than Mr. Tchibass during the course of those negotiations.

And, again, if you believe Mr. Anders that it was Mr. Tchibass who was the one who was trying to calmly negotiate out of this very difficult situation, and that Mr. Bent was the one who would oftentimes interject.

Ladies and gentlemen, again, in a criminal case before you can find a defendant guilty, you must be satisfied that the government has proven its case beyond a reasonable doubt. As the judge has already instructed you, that's an extraordinarily high standard. And the reason why that standard is so high is because the decision that you're being asked to make, if you're able to come to a consensus, is the most important decision that you will ever make. It's a decision that you're going to have to live with the rest of your life. And it certainly is a decision that Mr. Tchibass is going to have to live with for the rest of his life. And because of that, we make sure that before you're called upon to find somebody guilty, we require the government to have the absolute highest standard of proof. Because one day, it may be me, it may be you, it may be Ms. Ingers, and we want to make sure that before anybody in our criminal justice system is found guilty, that the government proves its case beyond a reasonable doubt.

Ladies and gentlemen, we are not disputing the fact that Mr. Tchibass was a member of team-FLEC. That's not the issue in this case. There's a different team involved here. The different team is the hostage-taking team. In order to be a member of what hostage-taking team, he has to agree with their goals. He has to somehow seek to further their goals. He has to wish that those goals were succeeded. He is not part of team hostage, ladies and gentlemen. Just because he's a member of team-FLEC doesn't mean he's a member of team hostage. Remember that, and don't fall for that.

What role did Mr. Tchibass play in Mr. Swane's negotiation or his release? He played an active role. He played an active role because he wanted to see Brent Swane's release, not because he wanted to see Brent Swane's continued detention. Was he neutral or was he biased? Of course he was biased. He believes in the freedom of the Cabindan people. But he also believed in Brent Swane's release.

It could have been very easy for Mr. Tchibass to say, you know what, we've got these third party people, they're out there, they're out in the bush. Mr. Swane is out in the bush. This is their demand. We're sticking to it, we're not changing. And you decide, Chevron, what happens to your employee. If he was that tough a negotiator, don't you think he would have done something like that? Or would he have been spending nine meetings trying to get some type of resolution? Nine meetings where he's repeatedly saying that Brent Swane is not in the hands of the political faction, but in the hands of the military men. You could see he's stuck in the middle and he's trying to get out. He's trying to find a solution.

Now, the last point that the government raised has to do with the crime of violence, that this is a dangerous thing. It is a dangerous thing, ladies and gentlemen. It's a terrible thing that happened to Brent Swane. But don't be swayed by that. Don't think just because a terrible thing happened to Brent Swane, and that Mr. Tchibass therefore is somehow responsible. Don't fall for that old lawyer's argument. It's a trick.

Look at the evidence. Evaluate the evidence. And if you do, and you apply the legal principles in this case, there's only one just verdict on both counts of this case. That's a verdict of not guilty as to Count One, and not guilty as to Count Two. Thank you.

THE COURT: Thank you, Mr. Bo. Ladies and gentlemen, I'm going to recognize the government for their rebuttal argument. Ladies and gentlemen, just recall, please, that arguments directed to you asking you to put yourself in somebody's shoes are not appropriate arguments. You have to look at this as a fair and impartial juror, not because of some personal feelings about the case one way or the other. All right.

MS. INGERS: Thank you, Your Honor. I want to respond to a few of the points that defense counsel made, ladies and gentlemen. Okay, the defendant was a member of FLEC-PM, but he just didn't go along with what all of his fellow FLEC-PM members were doing with respect to Mr. Swane, did he ever say so in any of those 165 pages of transcripts? If he was so all-fired concerned about Brent Swane, why didn't he have a side conversation with one of the American negotiators and say, look, I am trying to help you here, work with me. No. He was driving a hard bargain. It was a hard bargain over money, not over Brent Swane. It was over the ransom. As to his disappointment over the negotiations, of course, he was disappointed. He wasn't getting 2.5 million. It was a whole heck of a lot less than that.

Ladies and gentlemen, take the evidence, look at it carefully yourself. Look through those transcripts and make up your own minds about whether Artur Tchibass had a role in the conspiracy with which he's charged. And I submit to you that you can only come back with one verdict on both counts. And that's guilty. And I ask that you do so.

THE COURT: Thank you very much, Ms. Ingers.

(THE JUDGE NOW READ HIS FINAL THREE PAGES OF INSTRUCTIONS TO THE JURY AND EXPLAINED THAT THEIR VERDICT MUST BE UNANIMOUS. AND JUST AS HE WAS READY TO SEQUESTER THE JURY, GUESS WHAT?)

MR. BO: Your Honor, may we approach?

THE COURT: Sure. We're going to talk at the bench in one minute, but I'm going to send you back to get lunch and then I'm going to have the alternates back in a second.

(Bench conference on the record.)

MR. BO: Renewing my motion to strike juror number 7.

MS. INGERS: The government opposes it.

THE COURT: For the record, this is the gentleman who complained about the translation.

MR. BO: That's right.

THE COURT: That's juror number 7, Mr. Swiatkow, he's the gentleman who came to us earlier and said he got upset about challenging the accuracy of the interpretations, and then we decided to wait.

MS. INGERS: Your Honor, if he continued to be troubled by that issue, he had plenty of opportunity since the issue was first raised, to bring it to the Court's attention. He certainly showed he wasn't shy or reluctant to do so. I believe the Court even encouraged him to communicate with the Court if he felt he would have a problem. Not having done so, he is, I think, someone who has no issue with the evidence as he's heard it in this case, and can sit fairly to consider it.

MR. BO: Your Honor, we have 14 jurors in this case, 13 of whom expressed no interest, and certainly no personal animosity towards me. One of whom has. I don't see any prejudice by removing this juror, given the fact that we have two readily available alternate jurors who heard exactly the same evidence, that do not appear to have any particular personal problems with my conduct during the trial.

THE COURT: He did come and make a statement to my courtroom deputy, as we know, put on the record, and then he came in and talked about it and indicated that he could still continue in the case. We talked about it. I was concerned because if we went forward with more attacks against the interpreters he would be upset, but that really has not happened. He wasn't really imposing upon the accuracy of the translations or upon the credibility of the Chevron employees.

So, I'm going to deny your request. I don't see a basis that he should be stricken. At one point he said he was upset about Mr. Bo' challenge of the interpreter. When that didn't happen again, I don't think there was any concern. So I'm going to deny it. I don't see why he has to be replaced.

(End of bench conference.)

THE COURT: Ladies and gentlemen, we are ready to go. The only time you talk about the case is when the 12 of you are in the jury room and the door is closed. If somebody goes for a smoke break, the other 11 can no longer talk about the case. You only can talk when all 12 are together.

So, you're going to go with the Marshal. After lunch you will return to the jury room and begin your deliberations.

(Jury out.)

SEVENTH DAY, SEPTEMBER 12, 2005
MORNING SESSION

(THE DAY STARTED WITH SEVERAL WRITTEN QUESTIONS SUBMITTED BY THE JURY. AFTER A DISCUSSION WITH THE LAWYERS ON BOTH SIDES, THE JUDGE FIRMED-UP AN ACCEPTABLE ANSWER TO THEIR LEGAL QUESTIONS AND CALLED THE JURY IN. THEY WANTED EXTRA COPIES OF THE INSTRUCTIONS TO THE JURY AND ALSO WONDERED ABOUT THE CRIME OF CONSPIRACY IN COUNT ONE. THE JUDGE RESPONDED:)

THE COURT: In this case, the government has alleged that the defendant and his coconspirators committed eight overt acts in order to carry out the conspiracy. These are listed in the indictment. The government need not prove all of these overt acts were done, nor indeed that the defendant did any of them. But in order to find the defendant guilty, you all must agree on at least one overt act that was done by one of the coconspirators.

A conspiracy can be proved indirectly, by facts and circumstances which lead to a conclusion that a conspiracy existed. But it is up to the government to prove that such facts and circumstances existed and lead to that conclusion in this particular case.

In deciding whether an agreement existed, you may consider the acts and statements of all of the alleged participants. In deciding whether the defendant became a member of the conspiracy, you may consider only the acts and statements of this particular defendant.

A conspiracy is a kind of partnership in crime. In this case, for the defendant to be convicted of the crime of conspiracy, the government must prove three things beyond a reasonable doubt.

First, that during the charged time period there was an agreement to commit the offense of hostage taking. Second, that the defendant intentionally joined in that agreement. And, third, that one of the people involved in the conspiracy did one of the overt acts charged in the indictment.

So, ladies and gentlemen, reading your question we have, is that we must find Artur Tchibass responsible on all three parts on Count One. I don't want to emphasize any instruction over another. They're all to be taken as a whole, the entire group of instructions. But to try to answer your question is, the government, in the third part of the conspiracy instruction, the third element we just reviewed with you, must show that one of the people involved in the conspiracy did one of the overt acts listed in the indictment in order to carry out the conspiracy, and that person need not have been the defendant, so long as it was one of the conspirators.

(THE JURY RETURNED TO THEIR DELIBERATIONS AND ARRIVED AT A VERDICT BY 2:00 P.M. THAT DAY—A VERY QUICK VERDICT. THE JURY WAS BROUGHT BACK INTO THE COURTROOM.)

THE COURT: We received a note from you all saying you have reached a unanimous verdict on both counts. The foreperson, would you stand for a second, sir. Is that correct?

THE FOREPERSON: Yes.

THE COURT: Would you give the verdict form to my courtroom deputy and I'll return it to you after I make sure it's properly filled out and signed. For the record, the verdict is in a sealed envelope. Ladies and gentlemen, the courtroom deputy will ask the foreperson to deliver his verdict, and then we will ask if you agree with that verdict.

THE CLERK: Will the defendant please rise. Has the jury agreed upon a verdict?

THE FOREPERSON: Yes.

THE CLERK: What is your verdict as to Artur Tchibass on Count One as to the offense of conspiracy to commit hostage taking?

THE FOREPERSON: Guilty.

THE CLERK: What is your verdict as to Artur Tchibass on Count Two, as to the offense of hostage taking?

THE FOREPERSON: Guilty.

THE COURT: Thank you. You can be seated for one minute. Ladies and gentlemen, you heard the verdict announced of guilty in both counts, one to a count of conspiracy to commit hostage taking, and hostage taking in Count Two. Is that the verdict each and every one of you have agreed to unanimously?

THE JURY PANEL: Yes.

THE COURT: Would you like the jury polled, sir? MR.

BO: Yes, sir.

(THE COURTROOM DEPUTY ASKED EACH JUROR IF THEY AGREED WITH THE VERDICT, AND ALL RESPONDED "YES." AFTER COMPLEMENTING THE JURORS ON THEIR EFFORTS, THE JUDGE ANNOUNCED THE TRIAL HAD CONCLUDED.)

EIGHTH DAY, FEBRUARY 27, 2005
SENTENCING

(THE PUBLIC DEFENDER MADE A LAST STAB AT GETTING THE VERDICT OVERTURNED. HE STARTED THE DAY WITH AN EXTENSIVE ARGUMENT PLEADING MR. TCHIBASS' INNOCENCE. HE WAS FOLLOWED BY MS. INGERS WHO JUST AS VEHEMENTLY CALLED FOR STRICT SENTENCING. NEXT, BRENT SWANE MADE A BRIEF COMMENT THAT TERRORISTS WILL NEVER WIN. THEN THE PROSECUTOR AGAIN TOOK THE STAND AND GAVE HER RATIONALE AS TO WHY MR. TCHIBASS SHOULD GET THE MAXIMUM 24 YEAR PRISON SENTENCE. NOW MR. TCHIBASS MADE HIS PLEA:)

THE DEFENDANT: Your Honor, I wish to thank you for the possibility that you are affording me to be able to speak during this trial.

Your Honor, before I begin, I wish to, first of all, complete a duty that I have, it is to ask for Mr. Brent Swane's forgiveness for everything that happened to him in 1992. I wish to do this in my own name and I also wish to do this on behalf of the Cabindan people.

Your Honor, I know what freedom is, and I have known what freedom is since the age of five years because this is what the Cabindan people have been deprived of. I know what it means for somebody to be deprived of his freedom. I've been in prison now for 19 months and I really know what not having freedom is. I'm not in favor of this policy of depriving somebody of their freedom.

Your Honor, before I begin, I would like to tell you that I never participated in any way in the preparations nor in the execution of Mr. Brent Swane's kidnapping, because at that time I was not a part of that movement. And from the very first day when I went to the U.S. Embassy, I explained exactly that.

Your Honor, I'm not going to go into justifying here what the others did, but I would like to explain to you the reasons why I felt that I was forced, or that I had the obligation to participate in the negotiations.

From 1979, I came to the understanding that in order to achieve the freedom and independence of the Cabindan people, armed forces were not necessary, that in fact it could only be achieved diplomatically and through political means, and since that time, I chose to only post my efforts in the diplomatic and political sphere. I was somebody who was known, and I was quite used to being in diplomatic circles. And people were very much aware of my way of operating and of my aspirations for the Cabindan people.

Before I begin to speak about the negotiations themselves, I wish to give you a little bit of background in order that you can understand what the Cabindan people were facing in the year 1992. Cabindan used to be under the Portuguese protectorate, and in 1974 it became occupied, politically and militarily, by the Angolans. Cabinda does not have a common border with Portugal. Cabinda has two borders, one with the Democratic Congo Republic of Brazzaville. The reason for the occupation by Angola of Cabinda is because of its oil reserves. It is called the Kuwait of Africa. And this oil is being drawn by the Chevron company. There was absolutely no social, school or medical infrastructure in Cabinda in 1992.

In 1992, young Cabindans had only two choices before them: They could either join the occupation forces and fight against their own people, or they could go into the jungle and fight together for the liberty of Cabinda. That war had already caused the death of over 100,000 people in Cabinda. Four-fifths of the Cabindan population was living either like that, in the jungle, or in exile as refugees in the neighboring countries. And the youth that you saw in those photographs, Your Honor, are people that either came into the jungle very early on in their lives or were actually born in the jungle. And just to give you an idea of how important Cabinda is for Angola, Cabinda's resources represented 65 percent of Angola's domestic national product. There were 75,000 Cuban troops stationed in Angola and 70,500 in Cabinda. The population had no right even to food, and they imposed food restrictions just to make sure that the people would comply with all of the restrictions that were placed upon them. After having explained this panorama to you, Your Honor, I'd like to just tell you what I believed was possible, even after all of this suffering.

In 1988, I did not flinch at being able to sit at a round table with the Angolan authorities in order to discuss the situation with Cabinda, and I did so up until 1991. And all of the ministries, the foreign ministries, the U.S., the European, and the Africans, were aware of my role and my position in these situations with the Angolans. This is just to make you aware, Your Honor, that I am not a fanatic. I am a responsible man.

Your Honor, I'd like to now talk about Mr. Brent Swane's case, and what I'm going to say is my truth. From the very beginning when I was first informed of Mr. Brent

Swane's kidnapping, the first person who called me was my brother Tibusi. After I spoke with him at length about this issue, I told him that it was a huge mistake because it was going to be a strong blow against the freedom of the Cabindan people. I convinced him, Your Honor, I told him Mr. Brent Swane needs to be freed immediately. And in order to illustrate my belief and actions in getting Mr. Brent Swane freed immediately, I asked my brother Tibusi to avoid using any middlemen. It wasn't easy to convince my brother of this position. I told him, there's a need to go directly to the embassy, to reassure the embassy, to make it possible that there be direct communication between Mr. Brent Swane and his family, Chevron, and the embassy.

This, Your Honor, was my position from the very beginning of Mr. Brent Swane's kidnapping, and I don't believe that a bandit would have had that position. I love the Cabindan people and I love the Cabindan cause, but I didn't want other people to suffer because of the Cabindan problems. There had already been too many innocent victims. We went to the embassy, Your Honor, we presented ourselves there, and I believe that this gesture was a very strong one. And from the very first day, the embassy did not want to receive the people from FLEC-PM, and it was I, Your Honor, I was the one that reassured the American diplomats. I told them that they could verify my background, that I was well known by the Department of State, that I had already had contacts with American diplomats in Brazzaville, and that I was new in FLEC-PM. And they checked on this and they informed me 48 hours later that what I had said was correct.

Your Honor, we were all convinced that Mr. Brent Swane needed to be freed as soon as possible. My brother, Tibusi, had given me assurances that this would, in fact, take place. And in order to confirm this conviction, the U.S. diplomat who came here to testify said that in the first 11 days they were certain that Mr. Brent Swane would be freed immediately. But after that, we saw that complications arose. I was able to determine that my brother Tibusi did not really have control over the people on the ground.

We had a meeting with those people at the embassy who were in charge of this matter. We told them that they needed to suspend any negotiations and to allow us to go out into the field. Even though I'm a Cabindan Nationalist, I had never been in that part of the country. It was the first time I ever went into the jungle and met with my brother's people.

The photographs that you saw, the photographs that were presented by the prosecution in this case, were the photographs that were taken on that occasion when I first went into the jungle, and this was something that was known by the embassy. It wasn't something that I did in hiding when I went into the jungle.

And when we got to this wild area in the jungle, my brother had a position completely or extremely opposite to mine. This can be explained because he did not have the political or diplomatic viewpoints or exposure that I had as to how to achieve Cabindan freedom. It wasn't easy to convince them to change their position. And this is the work that we did for three days. It took that long in order to demonstrate to them and convince them that in order to achieve freedom for the Cabindan people, it wasn't going to be done by kidnapping people, and that we didn't need to have Chevron as an enemy, but rather, we needed to have them as our political ally. And we took steps to restructure the movement at that time.

The first day that I was there I had to deal with all of the officers and all the divergent viewpoints, and I knew that we'd never be able to reach an agreement. And we set up a provisional structure in order to be able to have a credible partner, and this bore fruit. When we went back to Kinshasa, the negotiations were not long. If it got more complicated within the first few hours of negotiation, Your Honor, it's because the first team wanted to act as a sort of police negotiator, but with Mr. Ander's arrival, things went quite rapidly. Your Honor, at the same time that we were negotiating with Chevron, we were in constant contact with the diplomats at the U.S. Embassy. And their message was quite clear to us: If you want the U.S. to assist the Cabindan people in achieving their freedom, you need to free Mr. Brent Swane immediately, and this advice was taken into account. Your Honor, had I had the authority to free Mr. Brent Swane, this would have taken place within the very first hour of his captivity. Of course, I was the spokesperson, of course I was an expert, but I did not have the power of decision. And all of the witnesses that came here said that Bent was the head of the delegation, and that always agreement had to be reached with Tibusi. Of course, it was explained here that I would have to withdraw, but it was an irresponsible attitude because there was a moral responsibility. I needed to be a realist in making sure that the Cabindan cause would go forward, and part of this was achieving Mr. Brent Swane's freedom.

Your Honor, I know that you have heard a lot of testimony, that a lot of proof has been presented here, that you saw the negotiators reports, but that does not really reflect the spirit of the negotiations as they took place. The atmosphere was quite relaxed. We spoke at length about political considerations that are not at all reflected in their reports. We talked with Mr. Anders about the future of Cabinda. We spoke about what the U.S. could do to help Cabinda, but at no time did I hear any mention of that here, nor did I see any of that in the reports.

Your Honor, I know that I am not of such a superior intelligence. However, I believe that I am wise enough to know that when we conducted the negotiations, it wasn't a matter of putting down figures and negotiating for Mr. Brent Swane as if he was a piece of merchandise. Mr. Anders acknowledged here that we acted responsibly, and this was also acknowledged by the embassy.

Your Honor, had I not behaved in this fashion, you must realize that I never would have had any access to the embassies of the United States, of European countries, or of African countries, had I behaved otherwise. I'm not going to cite here the names of all of the high level people, that wouldn't serve any purpose, but I'd like for you to know that I was always received very well, either by American diplomats, either those that actually lived in Africa, or those that came from New York, or Washington, as well as European diplomats. And I'm sure that if the prosecutors wished to do so, they would be able to verify that my reputation is quite good with all of these people in the different embassies of Europe and the U.S.

Your Honor, if Mr. Swane spent so much time in the jungle, it wasn't because we didn't want to free him, but rather that the negotiations were suspended for a certain period of time because the Chevron delegation sometimes needed to go back to work. Before I conclude, I'd like to say, Your Honor, I am not the person that has been described here. I love Cabinda greatly and I love people to have their freedom. I only had one concern in my mind, that this matter would be resolved and well. But in front of me, I had my brothers that did not have the same level of understanding that I did. I am a friend of the American people. I have always been received quite well in the U.S. diplomatic circles. I am one of the Cabindan diplomats that has always counted on the U.S. in order to obtain Cabindan freedom. I am well placed to know and state all the things that the U.S. has done directly and indirectly in order to assist the Cabindan people in obtaining their freedom. In this matter here, I did not have absolute power. I was a spokesman, of course, but there were bosses, there were heads that needed to be consulted with and who made the decisions. I personally wish to thank Mr. Scott from the U.S. Embassy, and Mr. Anders for their participation in resolving this matter. And in Mr. Anders place, I wish to thank him quite respectfully, because during the course of the negotiations, as well as during the time that he testified here, he always remained the same person.

Your Honor, I dare to believe that in a few statements I have been able to give you an outline and made you understand that I am a friend of people's liberties. And I ask Your Honor, as a man respectful of law, that you would take into consideration the circumstances, the ten-year-old circumstances.

I wish to address the man that you are, who has a heart beating like I do. On June 16th I will be 49 years old. I have been married to the same woman for 26 years. I have seven children who want to see me with them. In a few moments, Your Honor, you are going to make the decision over my life. You will be alone among men and God. And, Your Honor, I ask you to take the wisest decision possible in my regard, and I hope that you will allow me to continue, one day, with obtaining and working toward the obtainment of freedom for the Cabindan people and to share time with my loved ones.

Finally, I wish to say to you, Your Honor, I wish to give you my sincere thanks for your concerns for my health during the course of my incarceration here. I'd also like to thank and provide my greetings to all of your assistants. Once again, Your Honor, quite simply, thank you.

THE COURT: All right. We've had Mr. Tchibass' position in this matter. What concerns the Court, obviously, is that he was found, after a full trial here, to be part of a group as a leader of FLEC-PM, of armed, authorized insurrectionists to participate in a scheme to abduct and hold hostage and extort ransom for the release of an American citizen in the Angolan province of Cabinda.

Regardless of the merits of his political argument, he was found guilty by a federal jury here in this Court of hostage-taking, and in conspiracy to commit hostage-taking. The evidence was overwhelming and complete, both from Mr. Swane personally as well as from the negotiators who are present, as well as from other officers who investigated the case and the materials that were supplied, including all the exhibits. They clearly showed Mr. Tchibass' involvement. His position that he was a middleman trying to resolve a difficult situation seems to me to be nothing more than a shell game as old as the hills, where people wish to have deniability, who are the front spokesmen and negotiators for terrorist groups. They always take the position, "I didn't know what our military arm was doing. I wasn't aware of it, and I just tried to help release the fella. And that's why I spent several weeks trying to negotiate a lot of money and products for my people."

It really does not follow, in the Court's mind, that Mr. Tchibass was an innocent negotiator trying to help out Mr. Swane. That may be how he understands his position, but the trial indicated to the Court that even if he was not proven to be involved in the actual hostage-taking originally, that once it happened and he reported to the embassy, at no point did he disassociate himself or distance himself from the military wing.

He never spoke out against that publicly, which he was a key leader. He said he's number five in this organization. The government has asserted he actually benefited from the ransom that was paid. He appeared after the ransom was paid in what was described by Mr. Taylo as a fine new suit and carrying a new briefcase, that his prior stations he was attempting through these two months of negotiations to get his release, ring hallow to the Court because at any time he could have disclosed, perhaps even without making it public, where Mr. Swane was, since he visited the camp. He could have not demanded large sums of money and products, cars, and trucks, et cetera, but advocated strictly that he should be released. But he did not do so. The negotiations dragged on until Mr. Anders came, who had no more authority to pay these large settlements they demanded, made through thinly veiled threats concerning the well-being of Mr. Swane, and of Chevron's options in Cabinda. The record is clear on that point. The Court has some sympathies for Mr. Swane's situation, where he was originally grabbed by armed men and taken out into the jungle. Originally, as I recall the testimony, there was another individual with him, a local policeman who was also captive. After a few hours, that person was led away, there was a lot of shouting and then he heard gunshots. He never saw the policeman again. He reasonably understood that the policeman had been executed by the captors, and which then led him for the next almost 60 days to live in deadly fear that that would happen to him. It turned out, I believe the record shows, that the man was not executed, but Mr. Swane was not aware of that. He began his impact statement saying, "How would you feel if you were forced to wear a hat with a repaired bullet hole in it? That is, I was forced to wear a dead man's hat," and you can understand, from that brief statement the terror that he felt for those months, and that he still feels today. He has lost his employment, he has become debilitated, unable to work. His wife has gone through the same process of reliving this terror again with this trial, and now with the sentencing, and has also become ill as a result. And Mr. Swane finds himself unemployed for 12 years now after this kidnapping where his life, life as a young man, has essentially been taken away from him. It seems to the Court that the sentence that the Court has to impose is appropriate and should serve as a warning to those who will kidnap Americans abroad. In this day and age, obviously, we're very aware of these situations, and Mr. Swane had no opportunity to make a decision whether he should be part of this process, but was forcibly kidnapped at gunpoint and reasonably thought he would be murdered at any minute.

Mr. Tchibass clearly operated as the spokesperson to negotiate his release, clearly demanded substantial sums for his release, clearly was in control of the negotiating group, visited the camp, saw Mr. Swane, whether it's his first visit there or not, he was there, he knew about it, he worked with these people rather than disassociate himself. If his presentations are to be believed, he would not be part of this organization. He still remained with the organization after this. The government had other evidence, some of which came in at trial and some which they proffered from other kidnappings by armed individuals that Mr. Tchibass still worked with, and other negotiation releases of the hostages, that he then got back into the same game that he had in this case.

It seems to the Court that the sentence is entirely appropriate for the type of actions that occurred here in depriving Mr. Swane not only of his freedom for two months, but basically of his life. He and his wife have never lead a normal life again and it looks like they never will.

So it is appropriate for the Court to sentence Mr. Tchibass at the higher range of the guidelines, which I will do, and he would be in his '70s before he'll be released with this sentence. Based upon the convictions after trial by the jury and by the Sentencing Reform Act of 1984, it is the judgment of the Court that the defendant, Arthur Tchibass, will be committed to the custody of the Bureau of Prisons to be imprisoned for a term of 60 months on Count I, and a term of 293 months on Count II. Those counts shall run concurrently. That would be 24 years and five months.

The defendant does not have the ability to pay any fines and therefore I waive imposition of the fine. The defendant shall pay, however, a special assessment fee of $100 for each conviction, for a total of $200, due immediately, to be paid to the clerk of the Court of the United States District Court for the District of Columbia.

Additionally, Mr. and Mrs. Swane have submitted substantial losses, including a loss of employment, substantial medical fees, lost wages and other related expenses related to his imprisonment. And the defendant is ordered to make restitution in the amount of $303,000 to the hostage victim. This restitution will be taken from any wages that the defendant may earn in prison in accordance with the Bureau of Prisons financial responsibility program. Any portion not paid when he's released shall become a condition of his supervision.

And once Mr. Tchibass is released from prison, he'll be placed on supervised release, so that there's a continued accountability for a term of three years on Count I, five years on Count II, and they shall run concurrently. And once he's released, he has 72 hours to report to in person to the probation office in the district which he is released. All the general conditions of supervision adopted by the probation office shall apply, and the following special condition, that is: The defendant shall comply with the Immigration and Naturalization Service immigration process. If deported, the defendant shall not enter the United States without legal authorization during the period of supervision. Shall he receive permission to return to the United States, he shall report to the probation office in the area where he will reside within 72 hours of his return.

So, Mr. Tchibass, the sentence is a long sentence, but you have to take responsibility for what happened to Mr. Swane and his wife and to American citizens abroad who are subject to terrorism. You had a fair trial in a court of law here in the United States, and I hope it serves as notice to others who would harm American citizens abroad what will happen if you are apprehended.

You have the right to appeal this sentence. If you choose to appeal, you have ten days to appeal, and Mr. Bo will help you appeal once I enter judgment in this case. If you can't afford costs of the appeal, you can ask permission of the Court to appeal without costs. And also, you have the right to have counsel appointed for you to prosecute your appeal if you can't afford counsel. Mr. Bo can assist you on those matters. Are there any other counts to be dismissed by the Court?

MS. INGERS: No, Your Honor, there is not.

THE COURT: All right. That will be the sentence of the Court.

MR. BO: Your Honor, one additional matter.

THE COURT: All right.

MR. BO: I would ask that the Court, if the Court could in any way, expedite Mr. Tchibass' placing him in the Bureau of Prisons.

THE COURT: All right. I will ask that he'll be expedited to a federal institution appropriate, based upon his sentence and background and health conditions.

MR. BO: Thank you, Your Honor.

THE COURT: All right, we'll stand in recess. Thank you for your work in the case, counsel.

(proceedings adjourned.)

CHAPTER FOUR

THE CAR WASH MURDERS

Dear Diary:

This was one of the toughest trials I ever reported. The cast of characters was daunting due to its size and number of contradictions. I condensed it considerably in this chapter. I noticed at the end of the trial, the judge looked really tired, as did the attorneys. In fact, I was pretty dragged-out myself. I guess all trials can't be as cut-and-dried as we would wish.

TO HELP YOU BECOME FAMILIAR WITH SOME OF THE PARTICIPANTS IN THIS TRIAL, HERE IS THE CAST OF PRINCIPAL CHARACTERS:

AMY HOPP AND MICHAEL FRO—MURDER VICTIMS

RICHARD ROJA—DEFENDANT
TENISE ROJA—RICHARD'S SISTER
ANDY ARIA—RICHARD'S COUSIN
TONY MO—RICHARD'S FRIEND
MARY MUNGAR—TONY MO'S MOTHER
LOUIS CASTELL—RICHARD'S UNCLE
URSULA OCAN—LOUIS' FORMER GIRLFRIEND
STEPHANIE MARTIN (15 YEARS OLD)—LOUIS' GIRLFRIEND
ANGELA MARTIN—STEPHANIE'S OLDER SISTER
SANDRA MARTIN—LOUIS' SISTER (RICHARD'S AUNT)
MONICA MUNO—LOUIS' SISTER (RICHARD'S AUNT)

FIRST DAY, JANUARY 22, 2005
MORNING SESSION

(Whereupon, the following proceedings were held in the presence of the jury:)

THE COURT: Good morning, ladies and gentlemen. The record will reflect the presence of the jury, counsel, and the defendant. Ladies and gentlemen, the clerk will now read the charge.

THE CLERK: State of Arizona versus Richard Roja, number CR-99-12663. Indictment:

Count 1: Conspiracy to commit armed robbery, a dangerous offense.
Count 2: Armed robbery, a dangerous offense.
Count 3: Armed robbery, a dangerous offense.
Count 4: First-degree murder, a dangerous offense.
Count 5: First-degree murder, a dangerous offense.

Count 1: Richard Roja, on or about the 4th day of March, 2003, with the intent to promote or aid the commission of an offense, to wit: Armed robbery, agreed with one or more persons that at least one of them or another would engage in conduct constituting the offense of armed robbery.

Count 2: Richard Roja, on or about the 4th day of March, 2003, in the course of taking property of another from Michael Fro, and against his will, used threats or force against Michael Fro with the intent to coerce surrender of the property or to prevent resistance to Richard Roja's taking or retaining the property while he or an accomplice was armed with a deadly weapon or a simulated deadly weapon, or used or threatened to use a deadly weapon or dangerous instrument or a simulated deadly weapon, to wit: A handgun.

Count 3: Richard Roja, on or about the 4th day of March, 2003, in the course of taking property of another from Amy Hopp's person or immediate presence and against her will, used threats or force against Amy Hopp with the intent to coerce surrender of the property or to prevent resistance to Richard Roja's taking or retaining the property while he or an accomplice was armed with a deadly weapon or a simulated deadly weapon, or used or threatened to use a deadly weapon or dangerous instrument or a simulated deadly weapon, to wit: A handgun.

Count 4, Richard Roja, on or about the 4th day of March, 2003, intended or knowing that conduct would cause death, with premeditation caused the death of Michael Fro. Or, in the alternative, Richard Roja, on or about the 4th day of March,

2003, acting either alone or with one or more persons, committed or attempted to commit armed robbery, and in the course of and in furtherance of such offense or immediate flight from such offense, Richard Roja or another person caused the death of Michael Fro.

Count 5, Richard A. Roja, on or about the 4th day of March, 2003, intending or knowing that conduct would cause death, with premeditation caused the death of Amy Hopp. Or, in the alternative, Richard Roja, on or about the 4th day of March, 2003, acting either alone or with one or more other persons, committed or attempted to commit armed robbery, and in the course of and in furtherance of such offense, or immediate flight from such offense, Richard Roja or another person caused the death of Amy Hopp.

(AFTER THE CLERK READ THE INDICTMENT AND STATED THAT THE DEFENDANT ENTERED A PLEA OF NOT GUILTY, THE COURT READ ITS NORMAL LENGTHY ADMONITION TO THE JURY ABOUT THE DEFENDANT BEING PRESUMED INNOCENT UNLESS PROVEN OTHERWISE BEYOND A REASONABLE DOUBT, AND HE OUTLINED THEIR DUTIES AND OBLIGATIONS. THEN HE CALLED UPON THE COUNTY ATTORNEY TO MAKE HIS OPENING STATEMENT.)

Good morning, ladies and gentlemen. 3:55 a.m. on March 4th, 2003. Your name is Michael Fro. You're a 24-year-old young man in the prime of his life. You work for a limo company. You're at a car wash. You're a limo driver. That's what you do for your livelihood. So you're at the car wash in the off-hours, early morning hours to clean your vehicle. It's a Lincoln Town Car. You're with your girlfriend. Her name is Amy Hopp. She is 21 years old. You love her. She is effervescent; she is bubbly; she is enthusiastic. You're there with her, and you're cleaning the car. The car's been washed, it's damp, you got to wipe off the hood, get the water spots off the car. As you're leaning over the hood area, you hear a noise from behind you. You look up. When you look up, you see that man there, he's got a gun in his hand. It's a .45 caliber Sig Sauer Browning semi-automatic handgun. He's got it in his hands. He's pointing it at you. Give me the keys. What? Boom. The first shot by the ear. It hurts. You're in pain. You turn around, or you start to turn, the second shot. Boom. Back of the head near the right eye. You go down to the ground. You're in pain. He steps forward, shoots again. This shot is a through-and-through wound. You hear your girlfriend Amy, she screams. There's two guys next to Richard Roja: Andy Aria and his uncle, Louis Castell. Andy is 17. Louis is 20. Louis is the one that drove Richard Roja to the car wash. He drove him there in a car that was owned by a young lady by the name of Maxine Hernand. She was the girlfriend of Louis, had been the girlfriend of Richard. As they were driving past the car wash, someone in the car mentioned, hey, that's a nice ride. He turns the car around, parks the car north of the car wash so they're not seen. There's another girl in the car, her name is Stephanie Martin. She's 15 years of age. She also was Louis' girlfriend. She stays in the car while the three guys get out: Richard Roja, Andy Aria, and Louis Castell. They stand to the back of the car, and while she's dozing, Louis and Andy disappear over the wall which adjoins the car wash. Richard sneaks around the front, and that's where he sneaks up on Michael Fro and encounters him. Michael's down. He chases Amy down out in the front of the parking lot near what we call the vacuum cleaner bays. He catches up to her. He grabs her by the shirt. As she turns, he fires a shot. She's got an entry wound to the back of the head. She goes down. He stands above her. He fires again. Richard goes back to the car. Louis has been able to get the wallet and the keys. He gets the keys, he gets in the car, the Lincoln parked in the third bay. He gets in the car and he's trying to get the car started, but he can't find the right key. And he's fiddling around, and the gun goes off, and the gun goes right out the window. Andy's standing around, and the bullet strikes the wall in the car wash bay. He has a nick on his finger. Louis and Andy take off. Richard stays in the car momentarily, still can't find the key, and finally bales. As he bales out of the car, he runs from the car wash. Here comes Louis and Andy in the Kia with Stephanie. He runs, he hops into the car and they drive off. They drive to a Red Roof Inn there where they meet up with Angela, who is Stephanie's sister, and a guy by the name of P.J. Torre, and they park at the motel.

Ladies and gentlemen, that's a real brief synopsis of the facts that we have in this case. Michael Fro, age 24, the limo driver sustained three gunshot wounds to the head. He didn't die. As responding officers arrived, they found Michael Fro. He was going into convulsions at the scene. He was transported to St. Joseph's Hospital via ambulance, and he succumed to his wounds later on that day. Amy was dead when officers first arrived. She received two gunshot wounds to the head.

Ladies and gentlemen, the charges in this case that have been read to you, and you heard a lot of information in a very short period of time, I'd like to go through it very quickly, if I could.

(NOW THE COUNTY ATTORNEY EXPLAINED IN DETAIL TO THE JURY WHY THERE WERE FIVE DIFFERENT CHARGES AGAINST RICHARD ROJA, WHAT HE INTENDED TO PROVE AND HOW HE WAS GOING TO DO IT. NEXT HE INTRODUCED HIS ROSTER OF WITNESSES:)

Let me give you a brief synopsis of these witnesses. Evangelina Ballester, she's traveling southbound on 59th Avenue. She lives in the Glen Apartments. She's going to work. She's getting into the left turn lane. She sees something over to her left. She hears the gunshots. She sees this guy run up and grab Amy Hopp, and she sees him shoot her. She sees him shoot from above. She thinks she hears three shots.

In any event, ladies and gentlemen, she goes through this traumatic event. She's upset; she's excited; she's scared. She's turning left. She runs the light. As she is turning left, she gets a glimpse of the fellow, and she heads toward her place of business.

Christine Can drove by just moments before the shooting. When she drives by just moments before, her attention is drawn to the business which is just north of the car wash. It's an automotive business, a repair shop. What Christina Can sees is a car in that repair shop. It has some lights on. She doesn't notice anything about the car wash. She can tell you there's one person in that car, and the car is facing the westbound direction, it's 3:55 a.m, so she saw that.

Daniel Henders lives in a trailer across the street from the car wash. When he hears the noises, the sounds, he stands up in his trailer and he looks out the window, and he's able to see some activity in the front of the car wash. He's going to describe to you what he saw.

John Steve lives in the trailer park just to the east. John Steve overhears the shots. He's going to tell you what he heard.

Stephanie Martin, you heard me mention Stephanie Martin. She is the 15-year-old girlfriend of Louis Castell. She's sitting in the car. It's a 1996 Kia. As the three guys stand to the rear of the car, she can't hear what they're saying, she's been drinking, she's dozing, she knows they're at the back of the car. They disappear. She dozes, she hears what sounds like a gunshot. She wakes up. She sees Louis and Andy coming back to the car. They get in the car first. And then about a minute later or so, Richard gets in the car. They go and meet Angela at the Red Roof Inn. Angela and Pete. That's P.J. Torr.

Ursula Ocan, she's also the girlfriend of Louis. Then we have Sandra Martin. That's Louis' sister and Richard's aunt. She will tell you that Richard stayed with her in California, that her live-in boyfriend at that time was Jose Mercad. He had a .45 caliber gun.

We will call Steven Cam from California. Steven Cam is going to tell you that he sold the .45 caliber Browning semiautomatic handgun to Jose Mercad. He sold it to Jose because he was on probation and he wasn't supposed to be in possession of a weapon.

Criminalist Bill Morr is going to tell you, ladies and gentlemen, the bullets that were found at the car wash and the bullets that were removed at autopsy were .45 caliber bullets, with a left twist, six lands and six grooves. He took measurements of those lands and grooves. What that is are markings on the bullet that come from the barrel of the gun, identifying marks that an examiner who is trained to examine that can look at and draw conclusions from. A Chief Medical Examiner will tell you that Michael sustained three gunshot wounds to the head, and that Amy sustained two gunshot wounds to the head. He's going to say that the cause of death was gunshot wounds to the head on both.

Monica Muno is the defendant's aunt, Louis' sister. She's going to tell you that Tenise Roja, Richard Roja and Louis used the middle bedroom at a place called the Ranch Apartments. That house, that's where Richard and Louis and Tenise had access to the middle bedroom. In the middle bedroom is a magazine that's found by Sergeant Brad when a search warrant is executed on that house. The search warrant is executed on March 12th, 2003. He finds on the shelf of the closet a magazine with .45 caliber ammunition. That's the same kind of ammunition that we have from the car wash. But do you know what else? It's got the same headstamp, the same manufacturer of the ammunition from the car wash.

Maxine Hernand, she's the owner of the Kia. She is the girlfriend of Richard and Louis, and she loaned that 1996 Kia to Richard and Louis. She waited for them to return because they were supposed to go get something to eat. They took it March 3rd. They didn't come back until March 4th. She's holed up in Mary Mungar's house. She didn't have any transportation other than her Kia, so she's waiting for them to return. They don't return during the evening, so she goes to sleep. That's at Ranch Apartments, apartment number 2046. What you will notice, ladies and gentlemen, at the Ranch Apartments, apartment 2046 is one of those northern most apartments in the complex. It's directly across the wall from Amy Hopp's complex. Her complex is what we call the Glen, and it was a second story apartment. It had kind of like a little porch area out front.

And while Maxine Hernand was staying at that apartment that night, sometime during the night Richard came back up to the apartment unbeknownst to Maxine. Richard, Louis, Andy and Stephanie came back in the car. Louis, Andy and Stephanie waited downstairs in the car. Richard apparently came back up to the apartment. Maxine was asleep. When she woke up the next morning, they came back. Louis, Richard and Andy came back and Louis is carrying a wallet. He sits down on the couch, he opens up the wallet. She sees photographs, one or more of some kids, or a kid. Louis cuts up the wallet, cuts up the pictures, throws them in a little barbecue kettle that's out there on the porch, and they burn the wallet. Cuts up the keys that he's got. She says she overheard Richard say that he shot two people. She saw some unusual activity over the course of the next couple of days. After that morning as soon as she leaves, she doesn't return that night. It's another day or two before she returns. And she sees Richard, Andy and Louis, apparently their attention is focusing on the T.V. reports about the car wash and what happened there.

Criminalist Howard Birn from the Department of Public Safety, he's going to appear and testify. When the police executed a search warrant, in fact, sometime later, after they found out some information, they went back, they looked at the kettle, they scraped the ashes out of the kettle and submitted it to Howard Birn. He examined it. There were a couple of chunks of burned plastic in that barbecue and he examined that burned plastic. And do you know what? He found one of those pieces of burned plastic was consistent to a Mohave County library card. What does that have to do with anything? Michael Fro was from Mohave County. His mother is going to tell you that he had a library card of Mohave County. Also, he found evidence of what he was able to conclude was a Safeway card. He's going to be able to tell you the bar code, it's got numbers on it. He's going to be able to tell you the numbers. Not all of them, but he's going to be able to tell you those numbers. And we're going to call the records custodian from Safeway. She's going to be able to tell you that Michael Fro did, in fact, have an account with Safeway. And she is going to be able to give you the numbers as we go on through.

Donna Fro is going to tell you that Michael had keys, a wallet, and photos in his wallet. We're going to call Mary Mungar. She rented the apartment at the Ranch Apartments. She had an open-door policy with regards to Tony Mo and his friends. How did she meet with Richard? How did that come about? Tony Mo befriended Tenise. Tenise became Tony Mo's girlfriend. When Richard came from California, he started hanging out at the apartment. He was an invited guest of Mary Mungar. Then after Richard began hanging out, Louis began hanging out. Louis was Richard's uncle. And then near the end, Andy started hanging out at the apartment as well. Following the shooting, Richard confessed to Mary that he shot and killed two people, a guy and a girl, at the car wash.

(THEN THE COUNTY ATTORNEY IDENTIFIED THE DETECTIVES WHO WOULD BE TESTIFYING AND WRAPPED UP HIS PRESENTATION BY STATING THAT HE WOULD PROVE RICHARD ROJA KILLED MICHAEL FRO AND AMY HOPP. NOW MR. MILL, THE PUBLIC DEFENDER, MADE HIS OPENING REMARKS. HE DESCRIBED THE CONFUSING SITUATION WITH SO MANY PEOPLE OCCUPYING THE ONE-BEDROOM, ONE-BATH APARTMENT AT THE RANCH APARTMENTS. NOW HIS DEFENSE BEGAN:)

Richard Roja has been saying since the moment of his arrest that he is not responsible for this double homicide at the car wash, and he has gone on saying that for what is now the better part of two years. Simply, he was not there at the car wash. And he's been waiting now for almost two years for the government to come up with scientific proof that he was there, that he's responsible for the shooting that Mr. Barr is pointing his finger at Mr. Roja for doing. Mr. Roja's tennis shoes were taken from his feet right at the time of the arrest, the police took a lot of pictures of shoe impressions, footwear impressions, what I like to call just footprints at the scene of this car wash, and they compared them to Richard Roja's shoes. And what the comparison shows and you'll hear about is, who knows? Can't make a match. The shell casings found at the scene were .45 caliber. And I guess the government is saying that Richard took a gun that was a .45 caliber from California. There won't be any proof that he did so. Period. And those shell casings that were found at the scene were collected and compared. They were compared to a .45 magazine that was found in a closet at Mary's house along with a whole bunch of other junk, a magazine goes into a gun so it can be fired. They took that magazine, and the government has tried to demonstrate that that's Richard Roja's magazine. There's no proof of it. And they take fingerprints off of it. Nothing. Nothing to show that it's Richard Roja's magazine. And there's a whole bunch of people that stayed at the house, too. And so they take the shell casings from the car wash and then they compare it to the magazine, and the comparison results are, who knows? We just don't know.

And they, the police lift a whole bunch of fingerprints off of that white Lincoln that's in the car wash bay, Mr. Fro's limousine, because Richard Roja got in that limousine, according to the government, fumbled with keys, tried to start the car, couldn't find the right key, had his mitts everywhere, and we anxiously await for two years the results on those fingerprints. Not Richard's. Not Richard's. And there's blood found at the scene, hair, things of that nature, not Mr. Roja's. Here's what the government has and here's what we are left with. Richard Roja is said to have confessed to Mary and Maxine, and that Stephanie's a witness to all of this. So you've got these three women who are going to come in and testify that Richard Roja is a gunman. That's what you're going to be left with. Those are the people who link Richard Roja to this homicide. And I'm going to pull out their statements because during pretrial procedures the question, on a number of occasions they conflict with one another. If you pull out one of them and just isolate Stephanie and look at her statements over the last two years, each of those statements conflicts horribly. And then if you even just take one statement from one woman like Stephanie, even within that statement you'll be dazzled and unimpressed with all of the inconsistencies within a single statement.

There is one eye witness to this event that has no ax to grind that is not a part of the apartment. And she is the Spanish speaker, Evangelina Ballester. She's the one driving by, and she gets a good look at the gunman, at the killer. As he is chasing down Ms. Hopp, she is struck by the gunman's hair. That's really what she is struck by. It's longer hair and it's combed back. And this is one of those self-service car washes where there's a lot of light, a lot of fluorescent tubes out there. And so she becomes a real quick focus of the detectives, and she's shown Richard Roja's picture, and a bunch of pictures, actually, and she does not identify Richard Roja as the gunman.

But here's what she does. She, Evangelina Ballester, sits down the day of the double homicide, with a civilian employee who is one of these experts in drawing, and a composite drawing is done of Evangelina's description of the gunman. The civilian employee draws the gunman's face. She looks at the composite drawing, she says that looks like the guy. That composite drawing does not look like Richard Roja. For a good reason. But do you want to know who it looks like? It's remarkably similar to one person. Mary's son. The gunman looks just like Mary's son Andy.

(WHILE A SLIGHTLY CONFUSED JURY TRIED TO WRESTLE WITH THE CAST OF CHARACTERS, THE COUNTY ATTORNEY SUMMONED HIS FIRST WITNESS, POLICE OFFICER DONALD LABRA, WHO WAS THE FIRST ONE CALLED TO THE CRIME SCENE WHEN SHOTS WERE REPORTED. HE DESCRIBED THE SCENE—THE FEMALE DEAD AND THE MALE CONVULSING—AND HOW HE SECURED THE AREA AND MARKED THE LOCATIONS OF THE SHELL CASINGS AND OTHER POTENTIAL CLUES. HE ARRIVED AT THE SCENE AT 3:59 A.M. AND THE 24-HOUR CAR WASH WAS WELL LIGHTED. HIS LENGTHY TESTIMONY CONTINUED INTO THE AFTERNOON SESSION WHEN HE IDENTIFIED NUMEROUS PHOTOS TAKEN AT THE CRIME SCENE BEFORE THE PARAMEDICS ARRIVED. WHEN OFFICER LABRA COMPLETED HIS TESTIMONY, THE DEFENSE DECLINED TO CROSS-EXAMINE HIM AND HE WAS EXCUSED. THE NEXT WITNESS TO BE CALLED—EVANGELINA BALLESTER—NEEDED AN INTERPRETER WHO SAT NEXT TO HER IN THE WITNESS BOX. SHE TESTIFIED THAT ON THE MORNING OF MARCH 4, 2003, SHE WAS ON HER WAY TO WORK—WHERE SHE STARTED AT FOUR A.M.—AND DROVE BY THE CAR WASH. THE TESTIMONY CONTINUED:)

Q. And was your attention at some point drawn over to the car wash located at the northeast corner?
A. Yes.
Q. Could you describe to us what drew your attention to the car wash?
A. When I heard the gunshots.
Q. And you used the word "gunshots" as in plural.
A. Yes.
Q. Could you tell us how many you heard?
A. First I heard two.
Q. As you drove by, were your windows rolled up or were they rolled down?
A. Up, yes.
Q. And did you have any music or any radio playing?
A. The radio softly.
Q. So were you stopped at a red light at that time?
A. Yes, but I stayed there listening and looking.

Q. Now, when your attention was drawn to the car wash, could you describe to me what you saw?

A. Well, just when I looked, that was when he was chasing after the girl.

Q. And could you describe to me how it was you were able to conclude that the guy was chasing the girl? What did you see?

A. I thought that they were playing, because they were hiding from one side to another side, and then they ran.

Q. What was the girl doing to make you believe that she was hiding?

A. When I saw the girl running, she was running from the side over where the vacuum cleaners are. When she was running over, I was stopped there on 59th, and she ran over to one side by 59th. And the guy ran and he grabbed her, and the girl had a small towel in her hand.

Q. Ms. Ballester, I will have you take a look at an aerial blow-up. Do you recognize the location of the car wash on the aerial blow-up?

A. Uh-huh.

Q. Now, when you said that you saw the guy run up to the girl and grab her, could you show us where in terms of the aerial photograph, where the guy was and where the girl was?

A. It was by this wall that he was playing, he was like looking for her. So when the girl ran, when she ran towards the front where the soda machines are, that was when he grabbed her. And he shot her twice. I heard two shots.

Q. Now, when you heard the two shots involving the girl, was that two more shots than what you had heard?

A. When the girl fell, he also fired at her on the ground.

Q. So he shot the girl three times?

A. More or less. I was scared. Not any more. Not any more.

Q. And did you see the male, what he was doing just prior to shooting the girl?

A. Yes, I saw when he was following her.

Q. Could you describe the girl for us, please?

A. Well, I saw her wearing a little lilac colored suit, and her hair was kind of longish and light colored.

Q. What about the guy, did you notice what he was wearing?

A. The one who killed her?

Q. The one who shot at her, yes, ma'am.

A. He was wearing one of those white undershirts without sleeves, and Levis.

Q. Do you know the color of the Levis?

A. They were, I don't know whether they were blue or black, but they were dark.

Q. What about the shoes?

A. Black.

Q. The guy, did he look in your direction or was he looking toward the girl?

A. Well, I was there at almost the same direction, looking, and when he fired at her, I got really scared. And when she fell, I left.

Q. Did you run a red light to leave the area?

A. Yes. I got to my work, and when I got to my work, I was really a wreck. And the security officer saw that and he went to that place to look and he told the detectives.

Q. The male, could you describe to me what the male looked like?

A. Short in height, he was not tall. Black hair.

Q. Was he wearing any glasses?

A. No.

Q. Did he have any, like, a baseball hat or anything on his head?

A. No.

Q. Did you hear him say any words?

A. No.

Q. Could you describe in terms of his racial make-up, please?

A. Well, he looked kind of like a home boy.

Q. Did he appear to be Hispanic, Anglo or something other than that?

A. Well, I don't know. He was neither dark nor light skinned. I don't know whether he might have been Chicano or Hispanic.

Q. Now, the hair, could you describe to me how the hair was situated on his head?

A. He had it—it was really flat, flat. It was all pushed back, real, really small. It was all combed towards the back, it looked to me.

Q. Did you see what the man did after shooting the girl?

A. Yes.

Q. What did he do?

A. Well, he looked all around, and then he ran towards the back of the car wash.

Q. Now, you said the guy wasn't very tall. Do you remember that?

A. Yes.

Q. Could you estimate for me his height?

A. Well, a little bit taller than me. He was short.

Q. How tall are you, ma'am?

A. I don't know.

Q. Ma'am, if you would, could you show me how the man grabbed the woman and shot her.

A. Well, I saw when he grabbed her from here at her blouse. I saw when he caught up to her.

Q. Did he shoot her while he still had ahold of her?

A. He just grabbed her and shot her.

Q. Could you tell where he shot—

A. And the girl fell backwards.

Q. After the male shot the woman, did you see what he did with the gun?

A. He took it with him. Well, I saw that he ran with the gun.

Q. When you observed the male shoot the female, could you tell where the gun was pointing?

A. I don't remember if it was here or here, here or in the head.

Q. You're pointing to either your upper chest area or your head; is that correct?

A. Uh-huh.

Q. And in terms of the male versus the female, which one of them was taller?

A. They looked more or less the same.

Q. After you reported to work that morning, did you have some contact with police officers?

A. Yes. The detectives went to my job immediately.

Q. Did you have a chance to talk to the detectives shortly after this happened?

A. Yes, in the lunchroom at the workplace.

Q. Was it the same morning?

A. Yes.

Q. Did you have an opportunity at a later time, the next day or thereafter, to talk to other detectives about what happened?

A. That same day in the morning they took me to the police station.

Q. Did you try to assist the detectives in putting together a picture or a drawing of what the guy looked like?

A. Yes.

Q. Did the detectives at any point show you a photo lineup to take a look at?

A. Yes.

Q. Were you able to identify anyone in the photo lineup as being the person in the car wash?

A. Well, very few details.

Q. When you say very few details, what do you mean?

A. Well, in the characteristics of the hair and height, and all that.

(NOW THE WITNESS DESCRIBED HER DIFFICULTIES IN PICKING THE KILLER OUT OF A GROUP OF PHOTOS, OTHER THAN REPEATING HE HAD HIS BLACK HAIR COMBED BACK AND HIS FACE WAS A LITTLE MORE ROUND. THE QUESTIONING RETURNED TO THE GUN SHOTS:)

Q. Now, Ms. Ballester, when you talked about looking over at the car wash after hearing those gunshots, was it after you heard the two gunshots that you saw the girl?

A. It was afterwards.

Q. Could you describe to me in terms of how those gunshots sounded in terms of, were they close together? Were they apart? Was there some time in between the gunshots?

A. They sounded right close together.

Q. How much time after you heard the first couple of gunshots did you first notice the girl?

A. It wouldn't have been even three minutes.

Q. How much time entirely were you stopped waiting at the light looking to your left at the car wash?

A. I was there about four or five minutes, I think, since I heard the first shots.

Q. Before you heard the second series of gunshots with the girl, did you hear her scream at all?

A. No, I didn't hear her scream. My windows were closed.

Q. Ms. Ballester, could you tell me how many shots all total that you heard?

A. I heard around four shots.

Q. While you were stopped at the light to turn left and you looked over at the car wash, did you see the Lincoln in the third bay?

A. Yes.

Q. Did you see any activity by the car?

A. I saw when the guy ran. The girl ran, and then he ran behind her.

Q. Ma'am, did you see any other individuals, any other men in the area of the car when you were beginning to focus on the girl?

A. No.

(THE PUBLIC DEFENDER TOOK OVER AT THIS POINT AND SHOWED THE WITNESS DIFFERENT PHOTOGRAPHS SO SHE COULD PINPOINT THE PLACES IN THE CAR WASH WHERE SHE FIRST SAW THE MURDERER BEST AND WHERE HE SHOT THE GIRL. THEN HE QUESTIONED HER ABOUT THE KILLER'S HAIR LENGTH AND STYLE, AND HIS HEIGHT AND AGE.)

Q. What is your best estimate then of the age of the man you saw?

A. More or less between 25 and 28.

Q. And the man that you saw was about your height; is that correct?

A. A little bit taller.

Q. The man that you saw do the shooting had one hand on the woman and a gun in his other hand; is that true?

A. Yes.

Q. Did the man who did the shooting ever have two hands on the gun?

A. When he grabbed the girl here and he pointed the gun at her, but I didn't notice if he grabbed it with both hands or not.

Q. Ms. Ballester, you don't know how tall you are?

A. I don't remember.

Q. With your permission, when you're testifying today, would you mind if my investigator measured you?

A. No.

Q. This is him here, all right? I don't mean to embarrass you, but we'd like that information, okay?

A. That's fine.

MR. MILL: That's all I have, Your Honor.

THE COURT: Any redirect?

MR. BARR: Your Honor, may we approach?

THE COURT: Yes.

(Whereupon, the following proceedings were heard at the bench out of the hearing of the jury:)

MR. BARR: Your Honor, I want to ask to have the defendant stand up and ask the witness if the individual's taller or shorter than the defendant.

MR. MILL: No, that's very suggestive. You can ask how tall she thought he was in comparison to her, and you can do it a bunch of different ways other than to have my client stand there in front of her. Do it with me.

THE COURT: The defendant can stand and be identified. She can compare him and she can say whether he's taller or shorter. If you want to make a record on this later, we can.

(Whereupon, the following proceedings occurred in open court in the presence of the jury:)

THE COURT: Go ahead, Mr. Barr.

MR. BARR: Thank you, Judge. May it please the Court, can we have the defendant stand up in this case, please?

THE COURT: Mr. Roja, will you please stand. Go ahead.

BY MR. BARR:
Q. Ms. Ballester, I will ask you to take a look at the defendant in this case. Did the individual that was in the parking lot of the car wash, did he appear to be taller or shorter than the man that's now standing?
A. More, a little bit shorter.
Q. When you say a little bit shorter, could you tell me how much? A half inch? An inch?
A. Just a little bit, a little bit was all. A little bit shorter.
Q. Mr. Roja, you can sit down. And when you say that the man that you saw in the car wash on March the 4th, that man did not have a shaved head; is that correct?

MR. MILL: Objection. Leading.

THE COURT: I think he's reiterating the testimony that's already been elicited. She can answer.

THE WITNESS: No, his head wasn't shaved.

Q. Is the individual that's seated here in the courtroom, the defendant in this case, is his hair similar in appearance color-wise to the hair that you saw on the individual in the car wash?
A. Well, it looked darker to me.
Q. It looks darker now, or it looked darker then?
A. In the car wash.
Q. And so you were making your observations based upon the lighting that you had in the car wash?
A. Yes.
Q. And there were areas of the car wash that were better lit than other areas?
MR. MILL: Objection. Leading.

THE COURT: She can answer if she knows.

THE WITNESS: Yes.

Q. Ma'am, I'm going to present to you the six photographs depicted in Exhibit Number 139 and ask if you recognize any of the individuals in that series of photos as being here in court today.

MR. MILL: Objection. Irrelevant.

THE COURT: Overruled. She can look at them.

MR. MILL: Your Honor, I'd like to be heard on that?

THE COURT: I made my ruling. You can supplement my ruling outside of the presence of the jury. Go ahead.

Q. Do you recognize anyone that's depicted in those photographs as being here in court today?
A. He looks different to me. Maybe it was the hair.
Q. When you say he looks different to you, are you talking about he looks different to you from the fellow at the car wash, or he looks different to you from the fellow that's seated here in the courtroom?

A. He looks different to me because his hair wasn't like that.

Q. Ms. Ballester, when you talked to the detectives the first time, did you describe to the detective that you thought the guy was 22 to 23 years old?

A. I remember, yes, more or less.

Q. Now, Ms. Ballester, we've seen the photograph of the car wash. We have an idea of your position at the stoplight.

MR. BARR: May it please the Court, can she step out and demonstrate for me the positions of the girl and the guy at the time that he shot her?

MR. MILL: I object.

THE COURT: What is the objection?

MR. MILL: Beyond the scope of redirect.

THE COURT: She can step out.

Q. Ms. Ballester, if your car was over here and you were going to turn left and you were looking toward the car wash in the direction that I'm now facing?

A. Yes, I was looking like this. I was like this, and I was looking over towards there.

Q. Can you demonstrate for me, using me and using yourself, how you saw the guy grab the girl and then shoot her, how he was positioned and how she was positioned?

A. He was coming from over there to here. I was like this, looking over there when I saw the guy run behind the girl. When the girl stopped, like this, with the towel, he came out from the other side of the wall. So I saw when he grabbed her like that. He grabbed her and shot her.

Q. Did you have a front view of the man or a back view of the man, or a side view?

A. I saw him when he came running to grab the girl.

Q. When he came running to grab the girl, was he facing in your direction?

A. No; no.

Q. After the man shot the girl did you see him do anything, move the body at all?

A. When he killed her, he just looked in all directions and then ran.

Q. Ma'am, in this photograph there appears to be a body that's covered with white linen.

A. Yes.

Q. Could you be mistaken as to the actual location of where the girl was at the time that she was shot?

MR. MILL: Objection. Beyond the scope; asked and answered; and also leading this witness.

THE COURT: She can answer if she knows.

THE WITNESS: I saw that it was right in front of the soda machine.

MR. BARR: I have no further questions of this witness. Thank you.

(AT THIS POINT THE COURT RECEIVED TWO QUESTIONS WRITTEN BY TWO MEMBERS OF THE JURY.)

(Whereupon, the following proceedings were heard at the bench out of the hearing of the jury:)

THE COURT: The first question.

MR. MILL: I think the answer may spark some discussion about gangs, and so I would object.

THE COURT: How about asking if she knows if the defendant is any specific ethnic background?

MR. MILL: Okay.

THE COURT: How about the second one, is that okay?

MR. MILL: Yes.

(Whereupon, the following proceedings occurred in open court in the presence of the jury:)

THE COURT: Ms. Ballester, the first question posed by one of the jurors is, if you recall or if you know, was the gun in the right hand or the left hand of the person that shot the woman?

THE WITNESS: I don't remember that.

THE COURT: All right. And do you know what the ethnicity of the person who shot the woman was?

THE WITNESS: The race? He looked Chicano.

THE COURT: Thank you. Any other questions? Can this witness be excused, Mr. Barr?

MR. Barr: Yes, Judge.

THE COURT: Ms. Ballester, as you're walking out, could you have Mr. Mill's investigator measure your height for the record, all right?

THE WITNESS: Yes.

THE COURT: Thank you.

(NEXT THE COUNTY ATTORNEY CALLED A NEW WITNESS WHO MADE EARLY MORNING NEWSPAPER DELIVERIES AND HAD DRIVEN BY THE CAR WASH AT APPROXIMATELY FOUR A.M. ON THE MORNING OF THE MURDER. SHE TESTIFIED THAT THERE WAS A CAR PARKED ADJACENT TO THE CAR WASH IN FRONT OF AN AUTO REPAIR SHOP WITH ITS HEADLIGHTS ON. SHE SAID A MAN WAS SITTING IN THE DRIVER'S SEAT, BUT COULDN'T GIVE ANY BETTER IDENTIFICATION OF THE MAN OR THE CAR. WHEN SHE READ ABOUT THE CAR WASH MURDERS, SHE FELT IT HER DUTY TO REPORT TO THE AUTHORITIES WHAT SHE SAW THAT MORNING. SHE DIDN'T SHED MUCH LIGHT ON THE MURDERS, BUT SHE DID INTRODUCE THE POSSIBILITY THAT THE MURDERER HAD AN ACCOMPLICE. WHEN HER TESTIMONY CONCLUDED, THE COURT RECESSED UNTIL THE FOLLOWING DAY. AFTER THE COURTROOM CLEARED, THE FOLLOWING PROCEEDINGS WERE HELD:)

THE COURT: Did we get Ms. Ballester's height?

MR. MILL: Yes. Would you like to know it?

THE COURT: I'm guessing five foot one.

MR. MILL: Five foot and three-quarters of one inch.

THE COURT: That's pretty good.

MR. BARR: That was pretty good, Judge.

THE COURT: Do you want to just tell the jury that tomorrow.

MR. BARR: I have no problem stipulating to that. Five foot and three-quarters of an inch.

MR. MILL: I have no more record to make on the objections I made at the bench.

THE COURT: Are you sure?

MR. MILL: Yeah. Given the answer, I'm okay.

THE COURT: Okay. All right, we will see you back here tomorrow. How are we coming, Mr. Barr? Are we on schedule here?

MR. Barr: We're moving right along. I've got two officers. I'll talk to Mr. Mill, maybe we can stipulate to some of their material.

THE COURT: That will be great.

(Whereupon, the trial was adjourned until Tuesday, January 23, 2005, at 10:15 a.m.)

SECOND DAY, JANUARY 23, 2005
MORNING SESSION

(THE FIRST PROSECUTION WITNESS WAS A 27 YEAR OLD GENTLEMAN WHO LIVED IN A MOBILE HOME ACROSS THE STREET FROM THE CAR WASH. AFTER ESTABLISHING HIS LOCATION AND OTHER PERTINENT DATA, THE EXAMINATION CONTINUED:)

Q. In the early morning hours of March 4th at about 3:55 a.m, what were you doing?
A. I got up due to back pain, and I asked my fiance to rub it out because I had to go to work at 5:00 that morning.
Q. And did something happen during the course of the next several minutes that drew your attention to something outside of the mobile home that you were staying in?
A. Yes, sir. At that time I heard a scream, so I opened up the drapes and I looked outside the window, and I was trying to figure out where the screaming was coming from.
Q. Where did it sound like the screaming was coming from?
A. Sounded like it was coming from a distance, and then I finally identified it was coming from across the street at the car wash.
Q. And in terms of your viewpoint, could you see the car wash as you're looking out your window?
A. Yes, sir.
Q. Could you describe the lighting conditions over at the car wash?
A. Around the base it was heavily lighted, but anything around it, around 15, 20 feet is all dark.
Q. Prior to hearing the girl screaming, did you hear the sound of gunshots?

A. Yes, sir.
Q. Could you describe to me how many gunshots you heard? A. I heard three.
Q. Could you describe to me the manner in which you heard those gunshots? In other words, were they in rapid succession, was there some delay between the gunshots, and if there was some delay could you describe to me how long?
A. There would probably have been a half a second delay.
Q. You said you heard three shots?
A. Yes, sir.
Q. Then you heard screaming?
A. Yes, sir.
Q. Did the screaming take place immediately after that third shot, or was there some delay between the shots and the screaming?
A. There was no delay in between the shots and the screaming.
Q. When you looked out and you looked over toward the car wash, could you describe to me what you saw?
A. When I identified where the screaming was coming from, I seen a blond lady, they were—they were in the lighting, and I seen a Mexican, or Hispanic I should say. The lady, she kept backing up, yelling at this guy, and he kept approaching her.
Q. Did you make out what the lady was saying?
A. No.
Q. Now, as she is backing up and this guy's approaching her, could you tell me with respect to the car wash where she was?
A. She was on—she started out on the third bay, and then she got backed up all the way back out to the fourth bay to where her vehicle was.
Q. Now, when you saw the Hispanic male approaching the female, and you heard the yelling, could you describe to me what happened next?
A. She dropped out of sight, or I couldn't see her any more. And then all of a sudden he went out of sight, and then all of a sudden the screaming stopped.
Q. Did you hear any additional gunshots?
A. That's when I heard the three gunshots, is when they both dropped out of sight.
Q. So did you hear the screaming before the three gunshots or afterwards?
A. Before the gunshots.
Q. The Hispanic male that you mentioned that was in the parking lot approaching the girl, did you see what he did or where he went?
A. I did not see what he did except just kept pushing her back toward the fourth bay. And that was basically it.
Q. Now, were you close enough to view the Hispanic male, be able to make any kind of identification?
A. The only identification I could make out was his clothing.
Q. Could you describe the clothing for me, please?
A. His clothing was a white and black striped shirt, black running pants, and he wore a baseball cap backwards. And that's all I could describe.

Q. Now, the guy, after you heard the third shot, could you describe to me where he went?

A. After the shots were fired, he started running back toward the car.

Q. From your vantage point was the car to the left of the car wash or was it to the right of the car wash? By that I mean, was it north of the bays or was it south of the bays?

A. It was south of the bays.

Q. When you say that he ran toward the car, did you see him get into the car?

A. Yes, sir.

Q. Could you describe the car for me?

A. What I told the dispatcher, it looked like a silver or a beige Corsica or Toyota.

Q. A Toyota, is that kind of like a small foreign car?

A. A little compact car.

Q. Do you know if it had two doors or four doors?

A. It looked like a two door.

Q. What makes you say it looked like a two door?

A. Somebody had to get out of the vehicle at that point in time to let him in. And then after he got in, the other person got in.

Q. Did you notice anything about the car other than the color and the approximate size?

A. As it was leaving, I noticed that it had a dent under the passenger door panel.

Q. Did the car at any point approach your position at the mobile home?

A. No, sir. What it did, it did a circle around in the parking lot, came back and headed northbound.

Q. You said the girl that you saw had blond hair?

A. Yes, sir.

Q. Could you describe her apparent physical size and shape?

A. She was blond haired, pretty heavy-set, and she wore white pants. And that's all pretty much I could describe.

Q. Did you see this male get into the car you said looked kind of like a Toyota or something?

A. Yes, sir.

Q. Could you describe what side of the car he got in on?

A. He got in on the driver's side.

Q. You mentioned earlier that you thought the car was a two door car because somebody got out of the car?

A. Yes, sir.

Q. Was it the driver, or was it somebody else in the car, or could you tell?

A. It looked like somebody else was in the car, because he got out, came out of the back seat area, and as soon as he got in the car, he got in the back seat.

Q. You said it appeared as though somebody else got out of the back seat area of the car; is that correct?

A. Yes, sir.

Q. To apparently let this Hispanic male into the car?

A. Yes, sir.

Q. Did you ever get any kind of a view or vantage of the person that got out of the car?

A. No, sir.

Q. Could you tell whether it was a male or female?

A. Not really.

Q. In terms of the Hispanic male, you gave us kind of a clothing description of this guy. Could you give us kind of a physical description?

A. He was medium build, approximately about five-six.

Q. After the last shots that you heard, what did you do?

A. I told the dispatcher. She said, yeah, we called the police already. There should be a detective over there, an officer will come by and see you.

Q. So you called 911?

A. Yes, sir.

Q. Were you talking to the 911 dispatcher when you were seeing the shooting or seeing what was happening at the car wash, or was that afterwards?

A. No, I was describing to it to her as it was happening.

Q. Were there any obstructions between your vantage point and the car wash?

A. No, sir.

(NOW THE PROSECUTOR BROUGHT OUT MORE PHOTOGRAPHS—AERIAL AND GROUND PHOTOS—TO RE-ESTABLISH THE LOCATION OF THE WITNESS' MOBILE HOME AND THE CAR WASH. HE CONTINUED:)

Q. Could you tell me what kind of business was north of the car wash?

A. That was a little tire repair place, or electronics.

Q. Some kind of automotive place?

A. Yes, sir.

Q. Did you indicate that you opened the window?

A. I opened the shades.

Q. And is that window tinted or is it clear?

A. No, it's clear.

Q. You wouldn't be able to see the automotive shop out of your window?

A. Right.

Q. Prior to seeing the Hispanic male get into the car, did you see the car move at all?

A. Not from that point. After all the shots and everything were done, he got in and took off, and that was the only part I saw.

Q. Did you have an opportunity to talk to a responding police officer?

A. Yes, sir.

Q. Did they take you someplace nearby to have you take a look to see if you could identify someone?

A. Yes, sir.

Q. And were you able to identify that person as being the person at the car wash?

A. No, sir.

Q. Now, did you see the Hispanic male at the car wash with a gun?

A. I seen him pointing something. Whatever he had, he had it turned to the side.

Q. When you said he had it turned to the side, what do you mean?

A. Pretty much gangster style with the chamber pointing sideways instead of straight up and down.

Q. Did you ever see what he did with his hand after you heard the shots?

A. As he was running back toward the car, he shoved something down the front of his pants.

Q. Could you tell what it was that he shoved down the front of his pants?

A. No, sir, I couldn't.

(NOW THE PUBLIC DEFENDER CROSS-EXAMINED THE WITNESS ABOUT THE DESCRIPTION OF THE CAR HE SAW, AND THE FACT THAT AN UNIDENTIFIED BACK-SEAT PERSON GOT OUT TO LET THE HISPANIC MALE INTO THE CAR. THE WITNESS ALSO CONFIRMED THAT HE DIDN'T ACTUALLY SEE THE SHOOTING.)

Q. You saw the woman back up, you heard shots, you heard a scream?

A. Yes, sir.

Q. Or did you see the woman back up, you heard a scream, then you heard shots?

A. I seen the woman backing up, screaming at the guy, and then I heard the shots.

Q. You did not see her fall?

A. No, sir.

Q. The yell was loud enough that you could hear it from your trailer, correct?

A. Yes, sir.

Q. Was it a panicked kind of yell?

A. Yes, sir.

Q. You were previously awake because your back hurt?

A. Yes, sir.

Q. Is that what took you to the window to open the drapes, the scream?

A. Yes, sir.

Q. You provided the police a description of the Hispanic male, correct?

A. Just his clothing. Not facial.

Q. It's true that if the guy was not black, he was Hispanic?

A. He was Hispanic.

Q. And you never told the police it was a black male?

A. No, sir.

(THE COUNTY ATTORNEY IN HIS REDIRECT EXAMINATION TRIED TO RECONCILE THE DIFFERENCES BETWEEN THE TESTIMONY THE WITNESS GAVE TO POLICE OFFICERS ON THE DAY OF THE MURDER AND HIS TESTIMONY HERE IN COURT.)

Q. Was your memory better shortly after the incident took place, or is it better today?
A. It's pretty much better today.
Q. It's better today. All right. And you don't remember saying to the detective that you saw the car in the business north of the car wash?
A. No, sir.
Q. If the detective had placed that in the report that he prepared concerning an interview that he conducted with you, would that be inaccurate or false?

MR. MILL: Objection. Calls for speculation. How should he know whether it's inaccurate or false what another detective does.

THE COURT: He can answer.

Q. Would that be inaccurate?
A. I basically wouldn't know what to expect from either one of them. All I can do is just tell what I saw.
Q. In the report where it says the car drove into the car wash parking lot from north to south, do you recall now that the car did that?

MR. MILL: Objection. Asked and answered.

THE COURT: He can answer.

THE WITNESS: No. I don't remember the car driving into the car wash. I know it did turn around in the car wash heading northbound.

Q. If I understand your description of what took place, you went to the window after hearing the screams; is that correct?
A. Yes, sir.
Q. And you're looking out—are you looking out the window at the time that you hear the gunshots?
A. Yes, sir.
Q. That's when you hear three gunshots?
A. Three.
Q. Prior to hearing the girl scream, could you describe to me what you were doing?
A. I was just watching and describing to the dispatcher what was going on.

MR. BAR: I have no further questions of this witness at this time. Thank you, Judge.

(NOW THE COURT ASKED THE JURORS IF THEY HAD ANY QUESTIONS OF THIS WITNESS. THREE JURORS HANDED IN THEIR QUESTIONS, AND THE COURT DEEMED THAT TWO OF THE QUESTIONS COULD BE ASKED:)

THE COURT: The first question submitted by the jury, did the car that you saw have its lights on?

THE WITNESS: Yes, sir.

THE COURT: Just to follow-up, could you tell which lights were on?

THE WITNESS: The headlights were on at the time.

THE COURT: And, secondarily, could the witness, that's you, use a photo of the car wash to show how the gunman backed the female up as you've testified? The jury would like to see the placement of both the gunman and the blond-headed woman that you saw. Do you have such a photo, Mr. Barr?

MR. BARR: I can use the one that we used yesterday.

THE COURT: Perhaps the witness can demonstrate how he saw the two backing up.

MR. BARR: In terms of this particular photograph, could you point out to us please where it was that you saw the young lady, the blond-headed lady, backing up, and where you saw the male?

THE WITNESS: Okay. Let's say this trash can is the blond-headed lady, the male was here, basically, holding the gun like this toward her, backing her right up. She's got her hand over her mouth screaming. She's backing up toward this car. When she got about halfway in this car area, that's when I lost visual sight.

THE COURT: And also there's a second part to that question. Where was the car when the person got in? I guess that's what the question refers to.

THE WITNESS: The car was over on this side. It was way in the dark area over here. A little more.

THE COURT: Okay. Mr. Barr, any follow-up questions to any of the questions asked by the jurors?

MR. BARR: Yes, Judge. I do have a couple of brief follow-up questions.

Q. In terms of this particular photo, the photo does reflect that there's a vehicle in one of the car wash bays; is that correct?
A. Yes, sir.
Q. Was that vehicle in the car wash bay when you looked out?
A. Yes, sir.
Q. Could you tell what type of vehicle it was?
A. I told her it looked like a Lincoln.

(THE COUNTY ATTORNEY CLEARED UP A FEW FACTS THAT HAD ALREADY BEEN STATED, AND THE WITNESS WAS EXCUSED. THE NEXT WITNESS, MR. STEVE, ALSO LIVED IN AN ADJACENT MOBILE HOME PARK, AND HE, TOO, HEARD THE GUNSHOTS AND THE GIRL SCREAMING:)

Q. Now, I'd like to take you back to March 4th of 2003 in the morning hours. It was still dark. Were you sleeping?
A. Yes, I was asleep, yes.
Q. Were you awakened by some noise?
A. Yes, I was.
Q. And after you awoke, what did you hear?
A. Well, after gaining my consciousness, I realized that they were actually gunshots that I was listening to. That's what woke me up. I heard two rapports. There's a lot of gunshots in the area. So I opened the bedroom window to get a sense of direction, and I heard two more rapports, and there was a slight pause and there was another weapon fired. And it isn't like the standard drive-by, empty a clip and keep on going.
Q. What made these different?
A. The drive-by shootings are a rapid fire, empty clip, and they're out of the neighborhood. This one was more deliberate, like they were taking the time to give a direction to where they were shooting to.
Q. So there was some time between the shots?
A. Yes, sir.
Q. Now, in terms of the morning of March 4th, 2003, you indicated that you heard two shots, correct?
A. Yes.
Q. And then you heard a third shot; is that correct?
A. Right.
Q. Was there a pause between the first two shots and the third shot?
A. Yes, there was. It was only momentary, maybe a couple of seconds, three seconds.

Q. Now, you mentioned that you went to the window?

A. Right.

Q. After you opened the window, what did you hear?

A. I heard, there was a woman or somebody, there was a lot of voices, but then there was a woman screaming. I couldn't distinguish what she was saying, but I could hear her voice. It was a sense of panic anyway. There were two shots that followed that, two rapid fired shots, and then there was a pause for a second, and then there was another deliberate shot. I told my wife to call 911. I said somebody got hurt this time.

Q. You said you heard some voices and then you heard the screaming?

A. Right.

Q. You couldn't identify what she was saying?

A. I couldn't understand anything that they were saying, no.

Q. Could you tell how many different voices you heard out there?

A. Not really. It was just kind of chaotic. There was a couple of voices, and then I heard the scream, and then the two rapid fired shots.

Q. And then you indicated there was a pause before you heard the last shot?

A. Right. The last shot to me was deliberate. There was no question about it.

Q. Now, did you have an opportunity then to leave your mobile home and go over to the crime scene?

A. Yes, I did.

Q. And approximately how long did it take you to get over there?

A. Maybe a minute, minute and a half. I had to put my pants and a jacket on and then walk over there.

Q. When you arrived, could you describe what you saw?

A. There was one police car on the scene already, and you could hear others arriving because of the sirens. As I walked over to the patrol car, I saw the body of a female laying on the ground, and it was a few minutes later as I was walking back and forth in the area that I saw the body of the man.

Q. Mr. Steve, you indicated that you often hear random gun fire in your neighborhood?

A. Every couple of weeks, Friday, Saturday nights you will have a drive-by.

Q. This gun fire sounded different?

A. Definitely.

Q. Could you make out any type of caliber in terms of the gun fire that you heard?

A. I've been firing weapons for many, many years, and I would say that it had to be at least a .38 or a nine millimeter.

Q. Is that a large caliber weapon?

A. It would be a large caliber handgun, yes.

Q. Would you consider a .45 caliber to be a large caliber handgun?

A. Oh, yeah.

MR. MILL: I'm not sure he's qualified to give his opinions. Objection. Lack of qualification.

MR. BARR: I will lay additional foundation.

THE COURT: All right.

BY MR. BARR:

Q. Mr. Steve, you have indicated that you have been firing weapons for a number of years?

A. Yes, sir.

MR. MILL: Objection, Your Honor. I haven't been notified of this person being called as an expert witnesses, just a fact witness.

THE COURT: Did you interview this witness?

MR. MILL: My office did, but under the Rules they must tell me who is their experts.

THE COURT: I'm going to overrule the objection. I don't believe that he's testifying as an expert, at least at this point he's not. But why don't you keep laying the foundation and I'll make any further ruling if I feel that I have to. Go ahead.

BY MR. BARR:

Q. Mr. Steve, you have indicated you have been firing weapons for a number of years; is that correct?

A. Yes, sir.

Q. And that firing weapons, is that a hobby of yours?

A. Pretty much, yes.

Q. Do you fire weapons at a firing range?

A. Yeah. We go to firing ranges or else back out in the hills.

Q. Do you have a personal weapon?

A. Oh, yes.

Q. Have you received training in the use of weapons?

A. Yes. I spent seven years in the military and four years as a reserve officer.

Q. And in the four years as a reserve officer, then, did you become familiar with the sounds of large caliber versus small caliber weapons?

A. Most of the weapons you carried were either .38, 357 or nine millimeter.

(AFTER MORE DISCUSSIONS BY BOTH ATTORNEYS REGARDING THE LOCATION OF HIS MOBILE HOME, THE WITNESS WAS DISMISSED.

THE NEXT WITNESS WAS POLICE OFFICER VALENZ, WHO WAS THE SECOND OFFICER TO ARRIVE AT THE CRIME SCENE.)

Q. Could you describe to me what you saw when you arrived at that location?

A. When I arrived at that location, the victim was in front of the Lincoln Town Car off to the passenger side and in a pool of blood.

Q. Could you describe his overall condition at that time?

A. He was breathing and going through convulsions.

Q. Did you take any actions to do any type of medical intervention with the victim at that time?

A. Because of the amount of blood and the victim's still breathing, I got back on the radio with dispatch and let them know that they needed to call fire because we still had a victim possibly still alive.

Q. You come back on the radio and requested fire. Could you describe to me how much time elapsed before fire arrived?

A. It was a matter of a couple of minutes.

Q. Was there anything that you could do to assist the male victim in his condition at that time?

A. At that point I didn't want to move him because the amount of blood that was coming out from the head area, I didn't want to do any movement of his body.

Q. Was the fire department then allowed in to treat the victim?

A. Yes. The truck stayed out of the crime scene. Approximately four to five firemen came in with a gurney and started to work on the subject.

Q. And did they eventually transport the victim from the scene?

A. Yes, they did.

(NOW THE PROSECUTOR CALLED DAVID CRAVE, A CRIME SCENE TECHNICIAN WITH THE POLICE DEPARTMENT. HE DESCRIBED HIS DUTIES, EXPERIENCE AND BACKGROUND. HE DETAILED A FEW OF HIS DUTIES:)

Q. You said fingerprint processing. What do you mean fingerprint processing? What do you do?

A. When we have people arrested, the detention facility fingerprints the suspect, and so the fingerprints come up to our division via printer. We have an AFIS computer, which is a fingerprint computer. We put the cards through.

Q. Do you also go out to crime scenes and process latent prints?

A. Yes, we do.

Q. Is there a difference between, for instance, the prints that you talked about that you get from an individual in person, versus the type of fingerprint that you would find, for instance, at a crime scene?

A. Yes.

Q. Could you describe, what's the difference?

A. The difference is, we have a known print, we have ten prints, we have ten fingers on a card that we can use for comparisons versus if we go to a crime seen we may only have one fingerprint. And so we enter that fingerprint in the computer and ask it to do a latent search. Latent means hidden. And it has to be processed with chemicals or dye processing. As soon as we get the latent print, we stick it in the computer and ask it to look for matches on template cards.

Q. Could you describe to me the scene as it existed upon your arrival?

A. It was basically taped off and there was a white Lincoln Town Car in the wash bay. There were officers who were outside of the taped area making sure nobody came into the crime scene.

Q. And then could you describe to me what you did upon arrival at the scene?

A. Myself and my ID supervisor, we talked to Tom Clay at the scene. He gave us a briefing and told us what was found, and basically I was told one victim was transported and was on life support with a through-and-through gunshot wound to the head. I was told there was four shell casings and one slug that were found, and that there was a bullet hole found in the vehicle that was in the wash bay.

Q. Is that the normal procedure when you arrive at the scene, that you get some sort of briefing from the detective?

A. Yes.

Q. Could you describe to me what your duties would normally be?

A. There are several tasks, and my supervisor had me photograph the scene. She said, you're the main ID tech on this case, start photographing.

Q. Moving from the outside in, could you describe to me what you did in respect to this scene at the car wash?

A. I photographed the outside of the scene. It was night so I used flash photography. I did some time exposures, and then I waited to daylight, then I photographed the outside of the scene using daylight.

Q. You indicated that you went to an area where apparently a witness had made some observations; is that correct?

A. Correct.

Q. Did you subsequently take photographs after being advised as to the location of that witness?

A. Yes, I did.

Q. Now, with respect to the photographs that were taken from the vantage point of that trailer, did you use any particular type of lenses?

A. I used the standard 50 millimeter lens.

Q. Could you give me a general description of your activities at the crime scene?

A. I basically photographed, I believe there was hair found on the Lincoln Town Car, and I collected the hair from there. I also collected some blood that was found near a fence on the east side of the car wash.

A presumptive blood test was done by one of my co-workers and she came up with positive results, so I collected that.

Q. In terms of upon your arrival, was the male victim still located at the car wash or had he already been transported?
A. The male victim was transported.
Q. The female victim, she was still present?
A. That is correct.
Q. Could you describe to me what activity you took with respect to the female victim?
A. Yes. When the Medical Examiner arrived, we had other officers assisting blocking view from the public, and I photographed the body at the scene. Once the photographs were complete, the Medical Examiner put the body in a stretcher and covered the body up. I took her thumbprint, I believe it was the left thumb, and I sent that back with a detective to give to a co-worker.
Q. Was that for the purpose of attempting to identify the body?
A. Yes.
Q. In terms of shell casings, did you take any steps to record the location of the shell casings?
A. Yes.
Q. How about portions of bullets?
A. Yes.
Q. Could you tell me, for instance, in terms of the shell casings, the type of steps that you took to record the actual location of those shell casings?
A. First I photographed wherever the shell casings were, then I moved in closer and took individual shots of each casing.
Q. Could you describe to me, for instance, the bays that you photographed, the general lay-out?
A. There were five wash bays, and I believe the one furthest south I placed a marker by it and photographed it as being E. The next one I put a marker by it and put marker F, and went from E to I.
Q. So you used letters to label the bays?
A. Correct.
Q. When you labeled the bays, what is the purpose in labeling those?
A. So we go back later on and determine what bay we collected evidence from, so when we mark our evidence, we can mark it wherever the number is.
Q. In terms of the bays at the car wash, could you describe to me what you found starting from the bay, I believe you described it as bay labeled E, could you describe to me what you found in bay E?
A. I didn't find anything in bay E.

Q. Could you move northward of those bays and describe to us what you located, for instance, in bay F?

A. I don't believe I found anything in bay F either.

Q. Moving northward to bay G?

A. Bay G was where the Lincoln Town Car was located.

Q. Would you describe the condition of the Lincoln Town Car?

A. It had a bullet hole in the driver's side window, there was blood to the front passenger side on the ground, there was a bullet strike on the north wall, there were several shell casings, and I believe there was some slugs found, and there was hair on the front driver's side fender.

Q. When you say that you didn't find any items of evidence located in, for instance, bay F or bay E, is that absent footprints?

A. Yes. I didn't search for shoe impressions. That wasn't part of my task.

Q. That was because it was your supervisor that was involved with recording the shoe impressions?

A. That is correct.

Q. In terms of moving northward then from the bay where the car was situated, bay G, could you describe to me what you located in the bay after G, bay H?

A. I believe there was a Pepsi can found in one of the bays. I don't recollect if it was H or I.

THE COURT: Mr. Barr, let's take our noon recess at this time.

AFTERNOON SESSION

(AT THE START OF THE P.M. SESSION, MR. CRAVE WAS ASKED TO IDENTIFY NUMEROUS PHOTOGRAPHS HE HAD TAKEN, SUCH AS THE POSITION OF THE FEMALE VICTIM'S BODY, THE TYPE OF AUTOMOTIVE BUSINESS NEXT DOOR, AND THE WALL THAT SEPARATED IT FROM THE CAR WASH, VARIOUS SHELL CASINGS AND SLUGS SHOWN WITH A RULER TO INDICATE THEIR SIZE AND SCALE, A HOLE IN THE DRIVER'S SIDE WINDOW OF THE LINCOLN CAR, A SHELL CASING FOUND INSIDE THE CAR, AND MANY OTHER VIEWS OF THE CRIME SCENE. THE JURORS WERE BECOMING "SEDATED" WITH ALL THIS MINUTAE, SO THE COUNTY ATTORNEY APPROACHED THE JUDGE.)

(Whereupon, the following proceedings were heard at the bench out of the hearing of the jury:)

MR. BARR: It would be my intention to call this witness back to have him testify about some additional examinations that he did in this case as well as fingerprint evidence at a later time, and I've asked counsel if he has any objection.

MR. MILL: Could we go off the record?

THE COURT: We will tell the jury that Mr. Crave is going to be excused and he's subject to recall, he will be recalled.

MR. BARR: Right.

(Whereupon, the following proceedings occurred in open court in the presence of the jury:)

THE COURT: After a bench conference with counsel, it's the State's intention to excuse Mr. Crave at this time subject to being recalled. He will be recalled at a later time for further testimony. And Mr. Mill is reserving his cross-examination of Mr. Crave at such time as Mr. Crave is recalled by the State; is that correct?

MR. MILL: Yes.

MR. BARR: That's correct, Judge.

THE COURT: Thank you, sir. You're excused.

(Witness excused, subject to recall.)

THE COURT: Please call your next witness.

(THE STATE CALLED ITS NEXT WITNESS, MS. URSULA OCAN, A NEIGHBOR OF THE VICTIM AMY HOPP IN THE GLEN APARTMENT COMPLEX. SHE EXPLAINED THAT THE GLEN COMPLEX WAS SEPARATED BY A SHORT BRICK WALL FROM THE RANCH APARTMENT COMPLEX WHERE THE DEFENDANT RICHARD ROJA AND HIS COUSIN LOUIS CASTELL LIVED WITH TONY MO. THE LAST TIME SHE TALKED TO THE DECEDENT WAS TWO DAYS BEFORE HER MURDER:)

Q. Could you describe to me your last contact with Amy Hopp?
A. She drove up in front of my apartment just to talk about her new boyfriend.
Q. When you say she drove up, could you describe what she drove up in?
A. A Lincoln Town Car.
Q. Could you describe the color?
A. White.
Q. Have you ever seen her in that vehicle before?
A. No.

Q. Did you have a conversation with Amy at that time?

A. Yes.

Q. With respect to Amy, what did she do?

A. She sat on top of the hood.

Q. Of the white Lincoln?

A. Yes.

Q. And how long did this conversation last?

A. About 15 minutes.

Q. And this conversation that you had with Amy with her on the hood of the car, was it out in the open and in plain view?

A. Yes.

Q. Do you recognize the automobile that's depicted in this photograph?

A. That was Amy's boyfriend's car, a white Lincoln.

Q. Do you know a person by the name of Louis Castell?

A. Yes.

Q. Could you describe to me how you came to know him?

A. He approached me.

Q. Did he approach you at the Glen Apartments?

A. He was at Ranch and then he came over to the Glen Apartments.

Q. Are you familiar with the Ranch apartment complex?

A. Not really.

Q. Do you ever walk through the Ranch apartment complex?

A. Yes.

Q. How often do you walk through the Ranch apartment complex?

A. I used to walk through there Monday through Friday to take my kids to the school bus.

Q. Were you familiar with a person by the name of Tony Mo?

A. Yes.

Q. Were you familiar with where Tony Mo lived?

A. Yes.

Q. Now, you said you had met Louis Castell; is that correct?

A. Yes.

Q. Did you and Louis Castell begin dating?

A. Yes.

Q. And approximately over what period of time?

A. About two months.

Q. Over that period of time, at one point were you introduced to a person by the name of Richard Roja?

A. Yes.

Q. Who introduced you?

A. He introduced himself.

Q. Where did that introduction take place?

A. When Louis jumped over the wall to approach me.

Q. When you say he jumped over the wall, are you saying that he jumped over the wall that separated the Glen from the Ranch Apartments?

A. Yes.

Q. What about Mr. Richard Roja, did he approach you at that time?

A. Yes.

Q. Did he do the same thing?

A. Yes.

Q. He jumped over the wall into the Glen Apartments?

A. Yes.

Q. Now, I'll ask you if Richard Roja identified his relationship to you with reference to Louis Castell?

A. Louis did.

Q. And what did Louis tell you?

A. That it was his cousin.

Q. And could you describe to me in terms of the frequency that you would see Louis Castell in the area of the Glen or the Ranch Apartments?

A. Every day.

Q. Could you describe to me how often you would see Richard Roja in the area of the Ranch Apartments?

MR. MILL: My objection is foundation as to when.

THE COURT: Well, the question was how often, so it wasn't a when question. So she can answer if she can.

THE WITNESS: Every day.

BY MR. BARR:

Q. And when you talked about seeing Richard Roja, are those in the weeks just preceding the death of Amy Hopp?

A. Yes.

Q. And you indicated that you were dating Louis during that period of time; is that correct?

A. Yes.

Q. Were you familiar with the vehicle that Louis drove during that period of time?

A. Yes.

Q. Could you describe the vehicle for us?

A. It was a light brown Kia.

Q. Did you ever ride in the vehicle?

A. Yes.

Q. And in terms of that vehicle, how frequently would you see the Kia automobile let's say the last couple of weeks before Amy's death?

A. Not that frequently.

Q. Can you identify for us, please, what car is depicted in the photographs marked 110 through 113?

A. The brown Kia, Louis' car.

Q. In terms of the brown Kia, can you describe to me the general condition of that car?

A. It was in good condition except it had some dents.

Q. Could you describe to me where the dents were?

A. On the driver's side, I believe. All along the side panel towards the back and in front.

Q. And in terms of the Kia that you've identified, did that Kia have tinted windows?

A. Yes.

Q. In terms of Richard Roja, when you came into court this afternoon did you have any difficulty in recognizing him?

A. Yes.

Q. Could you describe to us why.

MR. MILL: Objection. Relevancy.

THE COURT: Overruled. She can answer.

THE WITNESS: He looks more business type.

Q. The last time you saw Richard Roja, was he wearing glasses?

A. No.

MR. MILL: Objection. Relevancy.

THE COURT: Overruled.

MR. MILL: Ask that the answer be struck.

THE COURT: Overruled.

Q. Could you describe to me in terms of your testimony this afternoon, does this photograph show us the area of the Ranch apartments as it applies to the person you've said is Tony Mo?

A. Yes.

Q. Does it depict the location of the apartment of Tony Mo?

A. Yes.

Q. You have indicated that that's a second story apartment; is that correct?

A. Yes.

Q. Did that second story apartment have a balcony?

A. Yes.

Q. With respect to where Amy resided, could you tell us where you recall Amy living shortly before her death on March 4th of 1999?

A. On the second story, the balcony.

Q. You told me that you dated Louis and that you had been introduced to Richard, and you saw them on just about a daily basis; is that correct?

A. Yes.

Q. Were you familiar with where they resided in the apartment complex, the Ranch apartment complex?

A. They stayed with Tony Mo.

Q. Now, in terms of photographic exhibit, you mentioned I believe that Tony's apartment was a second story apartment; is that correct?

A. Yes. Right there. That's the balcony.

Q. Did you see Louis and others out on the balcony of that apartment?

A. Yeah.

Q. How frequently would you see them out on the balcony?

A. About every other day.

Q. What about Richard, did you see Richard at that apartment as well?

A. Yes, I did.

Q. Now, when you met with Amy and she sat up on the hood of that Lincoln a couple of days before her death, did you see Richard and Louis in the general vicinity at that time?

MR. MILL: Objection. Leading.

THE COURT: She can answer. Overruled.

THE WITNESS: Yes.

Q. Ma'am, could you tell us where you saw Richard while you were out talking to Amy while she sat on the hood of that Lincoln?

A. On the sidewalk just below their apartment.

Q. And when you talk about being on the sidewalk, was it strictly just Richard or were there other people out there as well?

A. There was other people out there.

Q. And in terms of what they were doing at that time, were they conversing? Were they standing still? What were they doing?

A. They were all huddled together talking real loud.

Q. Could you overhear the conversation that was taking place?
A. They were loud enough so that I could hear them talking, but I couldn't understand what they were saying.
Q. And the conversation that you were having with Amy, could you describe the conversation.
A. Just that she had met a guy and she was happy.
Q. She was happy, she recently met a guy?
A. Yes.
Q. Did she describe where the car came from?
A. It was his.
Q. In terms of Amy, could you describe, you said you knew her for about three or so years, maybe a little bit more. Could you describe her type of personality for us, please.

MR. MILL: Relevancy objection.

THE COURT: I'm going to sustain the objection. I don't see—unless you could give me any reason why, I'm going to sustain it. If you want to tie it up outside the jury's presence, you can do that at a later time.

MR. BARR: All right. May we approach then?

THE COURT: All right.

(Whereupon, the following proceedings were heard at the bench out of the hearing of the jury:)

THE COURT: What's personality got to do with it?

MR. BARR: She's aware that Amy had a very outgoing personality and always talked to people in the apartment complex. She's also aware that Amy talked to the guys over at Tony's Mo's apartment. That's what she can tell us, she was put on notice by Amy that she knew those guys.

THE COURT: But she can testify that she observed Amy where she was.

MR. BARR: No, that's not—

THE COURT: I'm still not seeing—

MR. BARR: That's the reason why I was going to talk about the personality and the fact that she's very outgoing and very talkative.

THE COURT: She didn't talk to the guys, did she?

MR. BARR: Not on that occasion.

THE COURT: What about on a prior occasion?

MR. BARR: Yeah, she was aware that Amy knew these guys based on the fact that she had seen them in conversation before.

THE COURT: She can testify that she observed them, the defendant, talking on a prior occasion. The victim's personality, I don't think that matters whether she was introverted, or whatever.

MR. BARR: I didn't want to go into that detail.

THE COURT: Why don't you focus on that, she observed the victim and that person talking on prior occasions.

MR. BARR: Okay.

(Whereupon, the following proceedings were held in the presence of the jury:)

THE COURT: Go ahead, Mr. Barr.

MR. BARR: Thank you.

BY MR. BARR:
Q. Ms. Ocan, did you observe Amy previously have any communication with the fellows that stayed at Tony Mo's apartment?
A. Yes.

MR. BARR: Your Honor I don't have any additional questions for this witness at this time.

THE COURT: Mr. Mill?

CROSS-EXAMINATION
BY MR. MILL:
Q. Good afternoon, Ms. Ocan. You have met Richard Roja, my client, in the past, correct?
A. Yes.

Q. You see him today, right?
A. Yes.
Q. And you see his hair today?
A. Yes.
Q. He's more business-like, you say?
A. Yes.
Q. And is now wearing glasses?
A. Yes.

(NOW A LENGTHY DISCUSSION ENSUED BETWEEN THE WITNESS AND THE PUBLIC DEFENDER ABOUT THE LENGTH OF RICHARD ROJA'S HAIR AND THE DISPARITY IN SEVERAL OF HER DESCRIPTIONS OF IT. IT ALMOST BECAME A HEATED DISCUSSION UNTIL MR. BARR OBJECTED TO IT AS BEING ARGUMENTATIVE, AND THE COURT SUSTAINED THE OBJECTION. THE PUBLIC DEFENDER CONTINUED:)

Q. Ms. Ocan, two days before Amy's death she pulled up in that Lincoln and sat on the hood, right?
A. Yes.
Q. The guys just to the south of you were on the sidewalk, correct?
A. Yes.
Q. There was a huddle, right?
A. Yes.
Q. There was Richard, right?
A. Uh-huh, yeah.
Q. And Louis, correct?
A. Yes.
Q. How many others?
A. About six altogether.
Q. And were they pointing over to the car?
A. No. They were just all huddled up talking.
Q. Talking loudly?
A. Yes.
Q. Well, Ms. Ocan, did you hear Richard say, got to have that car?
A. No.
Q. Did you hear Louis say that?
A. No.
Q. Did you hear him say anything about a car?
A. No.
Q. Let's make that clear, they start to huddle and look over to that car?
A. No.

Q. You're not suggesting that there was some sort of agreement over there to get this car, were you?

A. No.

MR. MILL: Nothing further.

THE COURT: Any redirect?

MR. BARR: Yes.

REDIRECT EXAMINATION
BY MR. BARR:

Q. Ms. Ocan, in terms of Richard Roja, you talked about his head being shaved. Did you normally see Richard with his head shaved?

A. He always had a hat on. I'm sure it was shaved.

Q. Well, what do you mean when you say he always had a hat on?

A. He always had a hat on.

Q. What kind of hat?

A. It was just a white hat, I remember.

Q. Was it like a cowboy hat?

A. No, like a baseball cap.

Q. How would he wear the baseball hat?

A. Backwards.

(THE NEXT WITNESS CALLED BY THE STATE WAS 21-YEAR-OLD ANGELA MARTIN. AFTER A LENGTHY INTRODUCTORY EXAMINATION, THE COUNTY ATTORNEY GOT TO THE MEAT OF THE INTERROGATION.)

Q. Do you have any sisters?

A. Stephanie and Isabel.

Q. How old is Stephanie?

A. Seventeen.

Q. How old is Isabel?

A. Five.

Q. Ms. Martin, do you know an individual named Richard Roja?

A. Yes.

Q. How do you know him?

A. Through Louis.

Q. What's Louis' last name?

A. Castell.

Q. When did you first meet Richard Roja?

A. Just, March 3rd.

Q. And what year was that?

A. '03.

Q. That was the day before the car wash incident; is that correct?

A. Yes.

Q. Let's talk about March 3rd, 2003. Where were you at approximately 9:30 p.m. on March 3rd, 2003?

A. I was at home.

Q. And where were you living at that time?

A. At my grandmother's house.

Q. Who else lived there with you at your grandmother's house?

A. My cousin Pete, and my sister Stephanie, and my aunt and uncle.

Q. Your aunt and uncle lived with you at that residence. Who was there at 9:30 p.m. on March 3rd of 2003? Who else was there with you?

A. We were outside, me and Pete, and I don't know who was there that day.

Q. While you and Pete were outside, did you have any visitors?

A. Yes.

Q. Who drove up, or who came up to see you?

A. Richard, Louis, Stephanie, and Andy.

Q. Do you know Andy's last name?

A. Aria.

Q. How did those people arrive at your grandmother's house?

A. In a car. In a tan Kia.

Q. Did you know at that time whose car that was?

A. No.

Q. So when your sister Stephanie and Mr. Castell, Mr. Roja, and Andy showed up, what did they want?

A. They came back because they were down the street at a friend's house, my sister's friend's house.

Q. How long did you stay with those people at your grandmother's house?

A. I took off with them when they came.

Q. Where did you go from your grandmother's house?

A. We went to the Ranch Apartments.

Q. How did you get over there? Who went, and in what vehicles?

A. We all went in the tan Kia.

Q. Who all went in the tan Kia?

A. Me, Richard, Louis, Stephanie and Andy.

Q. What did Pete do?

A. Pete stayed behind.

Q. And so you went to the Ranch apartments. Did you go into any apartments there?

A. No. We stayed outside.

Q. And how long did you stay at the Ranch apartments?

A. Like, maybe 20 minutes.

Q. So you stayed there about 20 minutes, and where did you go next?

A. Went back to my grandmother's house.

Q. And what did you do at your grandmother's house?

A. Stayed outside for a while, and then Louis said that his friends had to get a room and, I was the one that had ID.

Q. When you said a room, what kind of a room?

A. A motel.

Q. So you agreed, since you had ID, to rent the motel room?

A. Yes.

Q. What motel did you go to?

A. Red Roof Inn.

Q. What time was it when you rented the room at the Red Roof Inn?

A. It had to have been like eleven.

Q. Eleven o'clock on the night of March 3rd?

A. Yes.

Q. Who all went from your grandmother's house down to the Red Roof Inn?

A. I went with my cousin Pete in his car, and my sister, Richard, Andy and Louis went in the tan Kia.

Q. So you arrived, you rent the motel room at the Red Roof Inn. How long do you stay?

A. Until like approximately two o'clock in the morning. I stayed there.

Q. What were you doing?

A. Just kicking back.

Q. And at about two in the morning, where did you go?

A. Went back to the Ranch apartment.

Q. How long do you think you were at the Ranch this time?

A. About 10 minutes, 15 minutes.

Q. So you left to go there at about two in the morning, and you went to the Ranch and you stayed there for about ten minutes or so; is that about right?

A. Yeah.

Q. Where did you go next?

A. Went back to the motel room.

Q. And who was in what cars as you went back to the hotel room from the Ranch Apartments?

A. I went with my cousin Pete, and the other car followed.

Q. Who was in the Kia that was supposed to follow you?

A. My sister Stephanie, Richard, Louis and Andy.

Q. When you and Pete arrived at the Red Roof Inn, were Stephanie, Richard Roja, Louis Castell, and Andy, were they right behind you?

A. No.

Q. How long did you wait at the Red Roof Inn for them?

A. About ten minutes.

Q. Were you able to get into the motel room?

A. No.

Q. Why not?

A. Because I didn't have the key.

Q. Did you think you had the key when you left?

A. Yes.

Q. You waited at the Red Roof Inn and the other four people hadn't shown up, what did you and Pete do?

A. We went to go put gas in.

Q. To put gas in Pete's car?

A. Yes.

Q. And where did you go from the gas station?

A. We waited there for a while because we were trying to see if they went down 51st. So we went back to 51st.

Q. Why did you take that route back that's different than the one you had taken?

A. That's the one we always went up because we live by 51st.

Q. Did you think there was a good chance that you might see those guys on that route?

A. Yes.

Q. As you were driving up 51st, did you see anything unusual?

A. Yes.

Q. What did you see?

A. I seen the lights at the car wash.

Q. What kind of lights?

A. Like police lights and T.V. station lights.

Q. After you and Pete saw those, what did you do?

A. Back to the room.

Q. Back to the Red Roof Inn?

A. Yes.

Q. When you got back to the Red Roof Inn, what did you do?

A. My cousin turned up his radio so that they could hear, and my sister came down to let us up there because you had to have a key to get in from the bottom.

Q. You had to have the key to get into the grounds of the hotel?

A. Yeah.

Q. Okay. So Stephanie let you in, and did you go up to the room that you had rented?

A. Yes.

Q. Who was in the room when you arrived?

A. Louis, Richard, Andy, and Stephanie.

Q. During the entire time that we have been talking about from 9:30 p.m. on March 3rd when you were at your grandmother's house until you arrived back at the Red Roof Inn, after you had seen the police cars and whatnot, was Tony Mo with you at any time during all of this?

A. No.

Q. Was Tony Mo in the car that you were able to observe with Stephanie, Louis, Richard and Andy?

A. No, he wasn't.

Q. Okay. During this same period of time, did you see any weapons?

A. Yes.

Q. What weapons did you see?

A. I seen a shotgun in the trunk.

Q. The trunk of which car?

A. The tan Kia.

Q. When did you see that, do you remember?

A. They left it in the trunk when we went to the motel.

Q. And what other weapons did you see?

A. I saw a handgun.

Q. Where did you see the handgun?

A. On Richard.

Q. So when you say on Richard, it was on his person?

A. He had it tucked in his belt.

Q. In the front or in the back?

A. In the front.

Q. What part of the gun were you able to see?

A. Just the handle.

Q. What color was the handle of it?

A. Black.

Q. After you got back to the hotel, did you ever hear Richard say anything about the incident at the car wash?

A. No.

Q. We talked before, I asked you if you had talked to Detective Clay about this case before and you said that you had?

A. Yes.

Q. And the first time that you spoke to Detective Clay, did you tell him everything in a truthful fashion?

A. No.

Q. What part of what you told him was not the truth?

A. That my sister wasn't in the car with Louis, Richard and Andy.

Q. Did you say that she was in the car with you and Pete?
A. Yes.
Q. Was that true?
A. No.
Q. And the next time that you spoke to Detective Clay, did you tell him the truth about everything?
A. Yes.
Q. Ms. Martin, I just have a couple more questions for you. Do you recall what Mr. Roja was wearing that evening?
A. No.
Q. Do you recall who was driving the Kia and where people were sitting?
A. No, I don't recall.

(THE PUBLIC DEFENDER TOOK OVER THE CROSS-EXAMINATION OF THE WITNESS MS. MARTIN.)

Q. Stephanie is your little sister?
A. Yes.
Q. She was 15 at the time?
A. Yes.
Q. Was Stephanie going to school at the time?
A. Yes.
Q. And Stephanie was in your charge that night, wasn't she, Angela?
A. Yes.
Q. And what you decided to do with your 15-year-old sister was go rent a room with some guys, right?
A. Yes.
Q. That was Richard and Louis?
A. Yes.
Q. Richard was 15, too?
A. Yes.
Q. You were going there just to rent them a room and then go home?
A. No.
Q. So you went back there to kick back with them?
A. Yes.
Q. And kick back means what?
A. Hanging out with them.
Q. Just staying in a hotel room?
A. Yeah.
Q. Watch T.V?
A. We were there playing cards, me and my sister.

Q. Drugs?

A. No.

Q. Alcohol?

A. No. My sister was drinking.

Q. Your 15-year-old sister?

A. Yes.

Q. Did you get her the alcohol?

A. No. I wasn't old enough to purchase alcohol at the time.

Q. Where did she get the alcohol?

A. I don't know. She didn't have the alcohol in the motel.

Q. Did you see her drink?

A. No.

Q. The whole night you did not see her drink?

A. I didn't—I knew she was kind of buzzing because she didn't look right.

Q. You could tell by looking at her that she was intoxicated?

A. Yes.

Q. Angela, wasn't she passing out?

A. She was passed out in the car.

Q. Was she passing out in the room that you could see?

A. I don't remember.

Q. Was she losing control of her bladder?

A. I don't remember.

Q. Was she losing control of her other bodily functions, Angela?

A. I don't remember.

Q. Were you allowing her to be intoxicated in that room?

A. She was not drinking in the room. I don't know if they gave her alcohol when I wasn't with her. I wasn't in the car with her when she was gone.

Q. And what you did, Angela, after the homicide—you knew there was a homicide, right?

A. Yes.

Q. At the car wash, correct?

A. Yes.

Q. And you knew Richard had a gun that night, right?

A. Yes.

Q. And Stephanie, your sister, was in that car, right?

A. Yes.

Q. And so what you did, Angela, is, you got on the phone that night, March 4th, and you called the police, didn't you?

A. No.

Q. You didn't call the police, did you?

A. No.

Q. You didn't call them the next day either, did you?

A. No.

Q. You didn't call them at all, did you, Angela?

A. No.

Q. Okay. Now, Angela, what date was it that you went to talk to Detective Clay for the first time?

A. I don't remember the date I went.

Q. Does it sound like March 15th?

A. Maybe, yeah.

Q. They came out and got you, right?

A. No.

Q. They came out and got your sister?

A. Yes.

Q. And then you came, correct?

A. No.

Q. Here's what happened, Angela. Correct me if I'm wrong. You and Stephanie talked about her being in that Kia that night, correct?

A. Yes.

Q. And you did so before you talked to Clay for the first time, right?

A. I don't remember.

Q. When you walked in to talk to Detective Clay that first day, you said, Stephanie was with me, right?

A. Yes.

Q. And you were aware that your sister was saying the same thing to Detective Clay, weren't you?

A. Yes.

Q. And that's because you got together and talked about it, right?

A. Yes.

Q. So that you could protect your little sister, correct?

A. Yes.

Q. And it's real important that you tell the truth, don't you agree?

A. Yes. Like I told him, I didn't tell them the true story the first time.

Q. Did you think it was important to tell the truth the first time?

A. I don't know how to explain it: I don't know how to put it. I just didn't want my sister to get in trouble, that's why I told them that story that she was with me in Pete's car.

Q. And it was made up, correct?

A. Yes.

Q. My question is, how much other testimony today is a story?

A. None.

Q. Everything else is the truth, right?

A. Yes.

Q. Just that one part was made up?

A. Yes.

Q. Now, during your second interview with Detective Clay, did you tell Detective Clay at one time that you wanted to stop the interview and have a private conversation with your sister?

A. I don't remember.

Q. Did you tell Detective Clay that Stephanie was never in that Kia?

A. I don't remember.

Q. Did you tell Detective Clay the first interview that when you went and rented the room, you traveled with Stephanie in your car?

A. I don't remember.

Q. But that's not true, is it?

A. I don't remember.

Q. Did you tell Detective Clay during the first interview that from your drive from Red Roof to Ranch you had Stephanie in your car?

A. I don't remember.

Q. Did you tell Detective Clay that Stephanie was in your car when you went to get gas at 51st Avenue?

A. I don't remember.

Q. Do you recall Detective Clay saying during the second interview that he pulled the gas station videotape and checked it?

A. Yes.

Q. And do you recall Detective Clay saying Stephanie's not with you and P.J?

A. Yes.

Q. Do you recall you, at that point, telling Detective Clay that you wanted a time out?

A. No, I don't remember that.

Q. So, Angela, is that the point where Detective Clay mentioned the videotape at the gas station that you change your story about Stephanie?

A. No. I came out with the truth to him.

Q. At the point where he talks about a videotape?

A. Yes.

Q. So Detective Clay has to have physical proof in his hand before you tell him a different version, correct?

A. Yes.

(IN HIS REDIRECT EXAMINATION, THE COUNTY ATTORNEY TRIED TO ESTABLISH THE CONDITION OF MS. MARTIN'S SISTER STEPHANIE.)

Q. Ms. Martin, there were a number of questions asked of you on cross-examination regarding what condition your sister was in, and I want to clear that up a little bit. The hotel room that you rented at the Red Roof Inn, was that on the first floor, second floor, or what floor was it on?

A. I don't remember.

Q. Do you remember how far it was from the hotel room at Red Roof to the gate where you were let in?

A. You had to get let in, and then there was an elevator. I know it was upstairs.

Q. When you went back to that hotel after you had seen the police lights and everything at about four in the morning on March 4, 2003, who was it that came out to the gate and let you in?

A. Stephanie.

Q. And did she drive to the gate to let you in?

A. No. She walked.

Q. She walked to the gate. Did she walk back with you to the Red Roof?

A. Yes.

Q. Did you carry her back?

A. No.

Q. Did P. J. carry her back?

A. No.

Q. She walked under her own power?

A. Yes.

Q. Okay. Ms. Martin, do you love your sister?

A. Yes.

Q. And would it be fair to say you don't want to see your sister get in any trouble?

A. Yes.

Q. And would that be the reason why you didn't call the police when you saw the homicide incident?

MR. MILL: Objection. Leading.

THE COURT: She can answer.

THE WITNESS: Yes.

(COURT WAS ADJOURNED UNTIL THE FOLLOWING DAY.)

THIRD DAY, JANUARY 24, 2005
MORNING SESSION

(NOW THE FIREWORKS BEGAN. THE STATE'S OPENING WITNESS WAS STEPHANIE MARTIN, SISTER OF THE PREVIOUS WITNESS WHO HAD LIED TO HIDE HER WHEREABOUTS ON THE NIGHT OF THE CAR WASH MURDERS TWO YEARS BEFORE. STEPHANIE WAS NOW 17 YEARS OLD AND HAD DROPPED OUT OF SCHOOL IN HER FRESHMAN HIGH SCHOOL YEAR. THE COUNTY ATTORNEY ESTABLISHED THAT STEPHANIE LIVED IN HER GRANDPARENTS HOUSE WITH HER SISTER

ANGELA AND OLDER COUSIN PETE (P.J.) SHE STATED SHE AND HER SISTER WERE VERY CLOSE.)

Q. How did you come to meet Louis Castell?
A. We were taking evening walks, me and a friend and I had met him.
Q. Where did you meet him?
A. At a friend's house.
Q. With respect to March the 4th, which is the morning of the shooting, could you tell me how much time before then it was that you met with Louis?
A. Maybe a week or two.
Q. Could you describe to me Louis, please. How old was he?
A. He was 20 at the time.
Q. Were you attracted to Louis?
A. Yeah.
Q. Did you attempt to develop a relationship with Louis?
A. Yeah.
Q. And did you and Louis begin to date?
A. Yes.
Q. And this is all prior to the morning of the shooting; is that true?
A. Yes.
Q. Now, were you aware that Louis had recently been released from prison?
A. Yes, I was.
Q. Was Louis aware of your age?
A. Yes, he was.
Q. And in spite of your age, he continued to date you; is that correct?
A. Yes.
Q. Now, through Louis, did you come to meet a fellow by the name of Richard Roja?
A. Yes, I did.
Q. Could you tell me the circumstances under which you met Richard Roja?
A. Louis had came over for a visit, and Richard happened to be with him and I asked him who he was.
Q. And was he introduced as a relative of Louis?
A. Yes, he was.
Q. What was the relationship in the introduction that you were advised between Louis Castell and Richard Roja?
A. They said they were brothers.
Q. Now, over the course of the next several times that you met Louis, did you see Richard?
A. Yes, I did.
Q. Would you describe Richard for me, please?
A. He was about maybe five-six, five-five, and about 200 pounds, maybe.

Q. So in terms of size, was he smaller than Louis?

A. Yes, he was.

Q. You mentioned height, was he shorter?

A. Yeah.

Q. And in terms of weight, was he less weight than Louis?

A. Yes, he was.

Q. Anyway, when you saw Richard, could you tell me up until the time of the shooting about how many times you saw Richard?

A. Maybe two, three times.

Q. When you saw Richard those two or three occasions, was he with Louis?

A. Yes, he was.

Q. Did you ever talk to Richard individually?

A. Sometimes.

Q. Now, were you aware of what Richard's age was?

A. Yeah. He was right around my age.

Q. Now, in terms of Richard, could you describe to me, for instance, what he looked like?

A. Brown eyes, shaved head, they looked alike, both of them. They looked the same.

Q. Now, when you saw Richard and Louis on these occasions, did Richard or Louis drive?

A. I seen both of them drive.

Q. And did you see what kind of car they drove?

A. They drove a brown Kia.

Q. Now, did you come to meet a fellow by the name of Andy Aria?

A. Yes, I did.

Q. Could you tell me with respect to the date of the shooting, when it was that you first met Andy Aria?

A. Maybe about a couple of days before.

Q. Could you describe Andy Aria for me, please?

A. Maybe about five-four. He was about 250, maybe.

Q. You said he was about five-four?

A. Yeah. He was short. I don't know about how high, but he was short.

Q. Was Andy a lot bigger than the other two?

A. In weight, yes.

Q. And you said you met Andy you believe a couple of days before?

A. Yeah.

Q. Do you remember the circumstances?

A. Louis had dropped by and Andy happened to be with him, and I asked him who he was and he said he was a friend.

Q. Could you describe Andy's appearance for me, please?

A. Brown eyes, bald head.

Q. On the day preceding the morning of the shooting, could you describe to me what you did that day?

A. The day before?

Q. Yes, ma'am.

A. Wednesday morning I had got up and got ready for school.

Q. Did you go to school that day?

A. Yes, I did.

Q. Did you have an opportunity to meet with Louis that day?

A. Yes, I did.

Q. Could you describe to me where it was that you met with Louis?

A. He came over to the house, my grandparents house.

Q. When did he come over to the house?

A. About, maybe about 7:00 a.m., before I left to school.

Q. And did you make any plans with Louis at that time?

A. I had just told him to stop by later if he wanted to.

Q. Did you have an opportunity to see Louis again that day?

A. Yes, later on that evening.

Q. After you got back from school?

A. Yes.

Q. And when you saw him later in the day, was it at your grandparents house?

A. Yes, it was.

Q. When he came back and you saw him later that evening, was he alone?

A. No. He was with Richard and Andy.

Q. And when they showed up that day, how did they come to show up?

A. They drove.

Q. What kind of car were they in?

A. A brown Kia.

Q. And who was driving the car?

A. Louis was at the time.

Q. Did you make any plans as to future activities for that evening?

A. I believe so.

Q. What plans did you make?

A. Just to kickback and hang out together.

Q. Did Louis and Richard and Andy stay there at your grandparents house?

A. No. They left for a brief time.

Q. Did they return?

A. Yes, they did.

Q. Were they still driving the Kia?

A. Yes.

Q. Was Louis driving?

A. Yes, he was.

Q. Were plans made, future plans made about what your activities were going to be that evening when they returned?

A. As it got later, there was plans made.

Q. When you say as it got later, what was the plan?

A. We planned to go rent a motel and kick back.

Q. When you say kick back, what do you mean?

A. Just hang out, kick back, talk.

Q. Did Angela become involved in the plan?

A. Yes, she did.

Q. In what way?

A. They asked if she would rent the motel room because she had ID.

Q. When you say they asked, who asked?

A. Louis.

Q. And did you go and rent the motel room?

A. Yes.

Q. Where did you go?

A. Went to Red Roof Inn.

Q. Could you tell me who went to the motel?

A. Angela and P.J. went in P.J.'s car. Me, Richard and Louis and Andy went in the brown Kia.

Q. And in terms of the motel, did you rent a ground floor room or was it a second, third, or fourth story room, or do you recall?

A. It had to be a room between the second and fourth floor. We had to get an elevator.

Q. Who provided the money to rent the motel room?

A. Louis.

Q. And when you arrived at the motel room, what did you do?

A. I believe we went back to the apartment.

Q. Did you go back to the apartment early the next morning?

A. Yes.

Q. And when you say you went back to the apartment, what apartment are you referring to?

A. To Tony Mo's apartment in the Ranch complex.

Q. How did you know Tony Mo?

A. I had met him about a day or two before.

Q. Did you meet him by himself, or was he with someone else?

A. He was with Louis.

Q. Had you been to Tony Mo's apartment before that evening?

A. About once or twice maybe, yes.

Q. Why were you going from the motel to Tony Mo's apartment?

A. I believe they needed to pick up something. I'm not sure. Talk to somebody or something.

Q. So who left to go to Tony Mo's apartment?

A. Me, Louis, Richard and Andy.

Q. Did you go in the Kia?

A. Yes, we did.

Q. What about P.J. and Angela?

A. They were supposed to follow us over there also in their car.

Q. And what happened then when you got over to Tony Mo's Ranch apartment complex?

A. We had pulled to the side, I believe we pulled up and, just, Richard got off.

Q. When you say Richard got off, what do you mean?

A. He ran upstairs real quick, and that was it.

Q. How long was he gone?

A. About three to five minutes.

Q. Could you describe to me what the seating arrangements were like in the Kia at that point?

A. Louis was driving, I was in the back seat, and Andy was in the back seat also.

Q. And what about P.J. and Angela, did they show up at Tony Mo's Ranch Apartment complex?

A. They were supposed to follow us there, but I didn't see them. They might have stayed behind.

Q. When Richard returned to the car, what happened?

A. He just got in the car and we left.

Q. Where did he sit?

A. In the passenger side.

Q. And you remained in the back seat?

A. Yes.

Q. And in terms of the back seat, which side of the car were you sitting on?

A. The driver's side.

Q. So you were directly behind Louis?

A. Yes.

Q. And Andy was to the right?

A. Yes.

Q. As you began leaving the Ranch Apartment complex, where were you going?

A. Back to the motel.

Q. Did you pass by the Guys Car Wash?

A. Yes.

Q. Could you describe to me as you passed the car wash, was anything said inside the car? Was something said inside the car by one of the occupants?

A. I believe so.

Q. You believe so, or you know?

A. Yes.

Q. Okay. And was the statement, was it coming from Andy? Was it coming from Richard? Was it coming from Louis?

A. I'm not sure who it was from.

Q. Was it loud enough for you to hear?

A. Yes.

Q. Was it loud enough for Louis and Richard to hear?

A. Yes.

Q. What was the statement that was made as you passed by the car wash?

A. "Look at that car."

Q. "Look at that car?" Did someone comment about it being a nice car?

A. I think so.

Q. You guess so, or you know so?

A. I guess so. I'm not sure.

Q. Was there some conversation about the car?

A. There was whispers. I didn't hear the whole conversation.

Q. Whispers between who?

A. Louis and Richard, I think.

Q. You think?

A. Yeah.

Q. Now, after the person mentioned about the car at the car wash, and you heard whispering coming from up front between Richard and Louis, could you make out what words they were saying?

A. No.

Q. Could you tell me what the reaction was, or the interaction was between Richard and Louis?

A. Interaction?

Q. Yes. They were looking at each other?

A. Yeah.

Q. What about Andy, what was Andy doing?

A. I believe he made a statement about the car.

Q. What kind of statement about the car?

A. He just said what kind of car it was.

Q. Was it loud enough for you to overhear?

A. Well, he was sitting right next to me, so, yes.

Q. Was it loud enough for Richard and Louis to hear?

A. Yes.

Q. Tell me what the statement was about the car. Just go ahead and tell me.

A. I think it was a Continental. He said, it's a Continental, or something like that.

Q. He said it was a Lincoln Continental or something like that, is that what you said?

A. Yes.

Q. And then the statement about the kind of car, what kind of car it was, then you saw the whispering going on between Richard and Louis and these two guys looking at each other, did Louis take any actions with respect to the Kia?

A. Yes. I believe a U-turn was made.

Q. When you say, I believe a U-turn was made, was a U-turn made?

A. Yes.

Q. Why don't you describe to me about how far down the roadway past the car wash Louis had gone before turning around.

A. Maybe about a little bit more than a half a mile.

Q. A little bit more than a half a mile after the initial statement was made?

A. Yeah.

Q. With respect to where Louis turned the car around, could you describe?

A. By the Jack-in-the-Box.

Q. When Louis turned the car around, did you ask Louis anything about where they were going?

MR. MILL: Objection. Leading.

THE COURT: She can answer.

THE WITNESS: I don't remember.

BY MR. BARR:

Q. After Louis turned the car around, could you describe to me where he went?

A. He had drove going back.

Q. When you say he went back was he heading back toward the area of the car wash?

A. Yes, he was.

Q. And what happened when he got to the area of the car wash?

A. A right turn was made.

Q. Could you describe the car wash for me?

A. Describe it? How?

Q. Well, is it a self-serve type car wash?

A. Yes, it is. This is a self-service.

Q. When you said Louis turned right, where did he turn right?

A. In a tire shop.

Q. Now, when Louis pulled the car into the tire shop, could you tell me where he parked?

A. I believe he pulled in kind of towards the back and parked by a bush, a big bush.

Q. Who else was in the car at that time?

A. Louis, Richard, and Andy.

Q. As you passed by the car wash, did you see any cars in the car wash?

A. I don't remember seeing the car myself.

Q. Pardon me?

A. I don't remember looking, even bothering to look at the car.

Q. Were the lights on in the car wash or were they off?

A. They were on.

Q. When you pulled into the tire shop parking lot, could you describe to me, were there lights on in the tire shop parking lot?

A. No, there wasn't.

Q. So in terms of the lighting conditions of the tire shop parking lot, could you describe to me what they were?

A. It was dark.

Q. You said Louis stopped the car there by a bush; is that correct?

A. Yes.

(NOW THE WITNESS WAS ASKED TO IDENTIFY PHOTOS OF THE BROWN KIA SHE WAS RIDING IN AND SHOW WHERE LOUIS, THE DRIVER, HAD PULLED THE CAR INTO THE DARKENED TIRE SHOP PARKING LOT FACING THE WALL THAT SEPARATED IT FROM THE WELL-LIT CAR WASH.)

Q. Could you describe to me what happened after Louis stopped the car?

A. The three guys got out.

Q. And where did they go?

A. They were standing at the rear of the car.

Q. And what were they doing at the rear of the car?

A. I don't know.

Q. Did they appear to be engaging in discussion?

MR. MILL: Objection. Leading.

THE COURT: She can answer, if she saw.

THE WITNESS: I don't know. They appeared to be.

Q. When you say they appeared to be, did they appear to be talking to each other?

MR. MILL: Objection. Leading.

THE COURT: She can answer.

THE WITNESS: Yeah.

Q. How long were they standing at the rear of the car?
A. I'm not sure.
Q. Was it more than a minute?
A. Yeah, I think so.
Q. Stephanie, they were standing there for more than a minute, did the three of them, remain at the rear of the car or did they leave?
A. They left.
Q. Would you describe to me who left and where they went?
A. They just disappeared.
Q. Where did Richard go?
A. I believe he walked off towards the side.
Q. When you say you believe he walked off towards the side, toward what side?
A. Towards the right-hand side.
Q. Did he walk toward the front of the car wash?
A. Yes.
Q. What about Louis and Andy, did they walk in the same direction, or did they go somewhere else?
A. They went somewhere else.
Q. Could you describe to me where they went, please?
A. I think they jumped the wall.
Q. When you say you think they jumped the wall, are you talking about the wall between the car wash and the tire shop?
A. Yes.
Q. And then what were you doing after they jumped the wall? Did you stay in the car?
A. Yes, I did.
Q. Could you tell me how long they were gone?
A. I don't remember.
Q. Were they gone just a matter of seconds, or was it more than that?
A. I don't know.
Q. Did you doze while you were in the car?
A. Yes, I did.
Q. Did you start to drop off to sleep?

MR. MILL: Objection. Leading.

THE COURT: She can answer.

MR. MILL: Your Honor, may I be heard?

THE COURT: No. She can answer. You can make a record later, Mr. Mill.

MR. MILL: Thank you.

THE WITNESS: Yes.

Q. Is that what you were doing in the car at that time?
A. Yes.
Q. Did something wake you up?
A. It was a loud noise.
Q. What did it sound like?
A. Like a shotgun—a gunshot.
Q. Where did it sound like it was coming from?
A. I don't know. It sounded like—I don't know. I just remember it was real loud.
Q. Just a real loud noise?
A. Yes.
Q. After you heard the real loud noise, did you sit up to see what was going on?
A. When I heard the noise, Louis and Andy were already back at the car.
Q. Between the time that Andy and Louis left the car area and the time that they returned, did it seem to you to be a long period of time or a short period of time?
A. A short period of time.
Q. After Louis and Andy got back to the car, what happened?
A. The car started, and Richard had already got back to the car by then.
Q. All right. When Louis and Andy got back to the car, did they get in the car?
A. Yes.
Q. Had Louis left the keys in the car?
A. I don't know.
Q. Did he leave the car running or did he start the car?
A. No, the car was off.
Q. So when Louis got back in the car, did he get in the driver's seat?
A. Yes, he did.
Q. Where did Andy get into?
A. The back seat.
Q. Next to you?
A. Yes.
Q. After Louis and Andy got back to the car, did you hear any more gunshots?
A. No.
Q. After Louis and Andy got back to the car and they got in, where was Richard?
A. I don't know.

Q. Where was Richard the next time that you saw him?

A. Getting in the car.

Q. Where was he coming from?

A. I didn't see where he came from.

Q. When you say he was getting in the car what side of the car was he getting into?

A. The passenger side.

Q. And somebody opened the door for Richard to get in?

A. No.

Q. When Richard got into the car, was the car already running?

A. Yes, it was.

Q. After Richard got in the car, where did you go?

A. On our way back to the motel.

Q. When you pulled out of the tire shop parking lot, did you pull into the car wash? Where did you go, Stephanie?

A. We pulled into the car wash, I think.

Q. When you pulled into the car wash, did Louis just continue driving, or did he stop the car?

MR. MILL: Objection. Leading.

THE COURT: She can answer.

THE WITNESS: He kept driving.

BY MR. BARR:

Q. When you say you pulled into the car wash, did you see a car other than a Kia in the parking lot of the car wash?

A. Yes.

Q. The other car, could you describe it for me, please?

A. It was a white car.

Q. The type of car?

A. A Lincoln Continental.

Q. Could you describe to me where it was?

A. Under one of the car wash stalls.

Q. After driving through the car wash parking lot, could you describe to us where you went?

A. After the car wash parking lot?

Q. Yes, ma'am.

A. We turned on that street right there.

Q. And did you drive, then, back to the hotel?

A. Yes.

Q. After Richard got back in the car, did he make any statements just before Louis left?

A. I don't remember if it was Richard or Louis who said it.

Q. Was Richard present when the statement was made?

A. Yes, he was.

Q. What statement was made?

A. Something about, shot himself or shot something.

Q. Shot himself or shot something?

A. Just shot yourself, or something.

Q. Did Richard make any statements about seeing anything inside the other car?

A. He said he seen something, but he didn't know—a device or something. I don't know if he knew what it was. I don't remember hearing if he said what it was. Something.

Q. He saw something in the other car?

A. Yes.

Q. And you don't recall what it was he said?

A. No.

Q. But this is coming from Richard?

A. Yes.

Q. This is after he gets back in the Kia?

A. Yes.

Q. In terms of seeing something inside the car, from the statement that was made, were you lead to believe that it had something to do with an object that was inside the car? What type of object was it?

A. I don't know what it's called. I don't remember the word he used.

Q. Well, you don't remember the word he used, but do you remember based on the words what you thought he was talking about?

A. Yeah.

Q. What was it?

A. Some—I think he said it was a scanner or something.

Q. Well, would you describe to me then what the seating arrangements were in the car as you headed back to the hotel?

A. Louis was driving, Richard was in the passenger side, and me and Andy were in the back.

Q. And did you return, go directly back to the Red Roof Inn?

A. Yes.

Q. When you got back to the Red Roof Inn, was Angela and P.J. there?

A. Yes, they were.

Q. Did you go up to the motel room?

A. Yes, we did.

Q. Did you spend the rest of the morning there at the Red Roof Inn?

A. Yes, we did.

Q. Could you describe to me who was there?

A. Myself, Louis, Andy, Richard, Angela, P.J.

Q. During that entire time you talked about the time when you first got to the Red Roof Inn, you talked about earlier in the evening, you talked about going to Tony Mo's apartment, you talked about going by the car wash and then the Red Roof Inn, did you ever see Tony Mo with any of these guys?

A. No.

Q. And could you describe to me what the activities were like at the Red Roof Inn after you got back there following the car wash?

A. Louis had been laying down, Andy and Richard were like, Andy was kind of like paranoid or something. I don't know.

Q. Could you describe Richard's demeanor for me, please?

A. Richard was just sitting down.

Q. Were you playing cards that morning?

A. Yes.

Q. Were you participating in playing cards?

A. Yes, I was.

Q. How about Angela?

A. Yes.

Q. How about Richard?

A. He watched us.

Q. Were you watching the T.V?

A. Yeah.

Q. Did you see anything on the T.V. that morning, anything out of the ordinary?

A. No.

Q. Did you happen to watch the news while you were at the motel room?

A. No.

Q. After you got back to the motel and you met with Angela, did you talk to Angela about what had happened?

A. I don't remember.

Q. When you left the hotel that morning, where did you go?

A. I went home.

Q. About what time was it that you left the motel?

A. About 6:30 a.m.

Q. Who took you home?

A. P.J. and Angela.

Q. During the time period following the car wash, could you describe to me in terms of Andy, did you notice any injuries on Andy?

A. Yes, I did.

Q. Would you describe it for me, please?

A. He had a cut or scrape, something on his hand.

Q. Did you notice this while you were in the car or back at the motel?

A. I noticed he was holding his hand at the car.

Q. Did you go to school that day?

A. Yes, I did.

Q. Did you meet up with Louis and Richard and Andy sometime later that day?

A. In the evening later on, yes.

Q. Would you describe to me where it was?

A. I don't remember.

Q. That night, that following night, did you go to Mary Mungar's apartment?

A. Yeah. Yeah, we did.

Q. Could you describe to me where you stayed over the course of let's say the next week or so?

A. I think I spent two or three nights at Mary's, and the rest I spent with Louis at his mom's.

Q. Did you continue to associate with Louis and Richard and Andy over the course of the next week?

A. Yes, I did.

Q. Now, during that time, did you see Andy and Louis and Richard hanging out together?

MR. MILL: Objection. Leading.

THE COURT: She can answer that.

THE WITNESS: Yes, I did.

Q. When you saw Louis, did you see Richard with him?

A. Sometimes.

Q. And how about Andy?

A. Sometimes.

Q. And did you also—you said you spent at least two or three nights or so over at Mary Mungar's apartment; is that correct?

A. Yes.

Q. Is Mary Mungar Tony Mo's mom?

A. Yes.

Q. Now, you became aware that Andy and Richard and Louis were arrested; is that correct?

A. Yes.

Q. And that took place approximately a week or so later; is that correct?

A. Yes.

Q. Did you continue to associate with these three guys up until that time?

A. Yes.

Q. After the car wash shooting, did your relationship with Louis become even more intimate?

A. Yes, it did.

Q. When you went by the car wash, after you heard the noise and you saw Andy and Louis get in the car, and then you saw Richard get in the car, when you went by the car wash you said you pulled out on that one street. Do you remember that?

A. Yes.

Q. Could you describe to us in terms of the manner in which Louis drove, did he drive in a slow pace, leisure pace?

A. Regular.

Q. Away from the car wash?

A. Yes.

(NOW THE COUNTY ATTORNEY SHOWED THE WITNESS PHOTOS OF THE INTERIOR OF THE BROWN KIA AUTOMOBILE AND DETERMINED THAT AFTER THE SHOOTING, LOUIS WAS IN THE DRIVER'S SEAT, RICHARD SAT IN THE PASSENGER SEAT, AND ANDY SAT IN THE BACK SEAT BEHIND THE PASSENGER SEAT, AND STEPHANIE REMAINED IN THE SEAT BEHIND THE DRIVER.)

Q. Ma'am, you said that you saw the white car in the bay of the car wash as you went through the parking lot. Do you remember that?

A. Yes.

Q. Did you see any bodies as you sped through the parking lot?

A. No.

Q. Now, did you continue to converse with Louis after his arrest?

A. Yes, I did.

Q. And, in fact, did you continue to converse with Louis on almost a daily basis?

A. Yes, I did.

Q. Would you describe to me what your relationship with Louis was at that time? How did you feel about him?

A. I loved him.

Q. Now, at some point were you contacted by detectives in this case, Detective Clay, on or about March the 15th of 2003?

A. Yes.

Q. And did you meet with Detective Clay down at the police station?

A. Yes.

Q. When you met with Detective Clay on March 15th, 2003, did you admit that you were in the car at the time of the car wash shooting back on March 4th, 2003?

MR. MILL: Objection. Leading; improper impeachment.

THE COURT: Overruled.

Q. In your first interview with Detective Clay, did you admit to Detective Clay that you were in the car?

A. No.

Q. Did you deny that you were in the car?

A. Yeah.

Q. Was it your intention to mislead Detective Clay in terms of your being in the car at the time of the car wash shooting?

A. Yes.

Q. Now, when you met with Detective Clay, did you meet with Detective Clay a second time?

A. Yes, I did.

Q. Did it take place approximately a week later?

A. Yeah.

Q. Did you continue to tell Detective Clay at that time that you were not in the car?

A. No.

Q. When you showed up for that second interview with Detective Clay on March 23rd, 2003, did you just go right in there and tell Detective Clay that you were in the car?

A. No.

Q. So you denied to Detective Clay at the beginning of that interview that you were than in the car, still?

MR. MILL: Objection. Leading.

THE COURT: Well, it's been asked and answered. She's already answered that, so let's ask the next question.

Q. During the course of that interview that you had with Detective Clay on March 23rd, did he confront you about having a tape or something that he had from the gas station showing that you weren't in P.J. and Angela's car?

A. Yes, he did.

Q. And after he confronted you about having a tape showing you not being in the car, did you tell Detective Clay that you were in the Kia?

A. Yes, I did.

Q. And then did you describe to Detective Clay in detail about what had happened?

A. Yes, I did.

Q. Now, when you described that in detail to Detective Clay, did you tell Detective Clay the details as best as you remembered them at that time?

A. Yes, I did.

Q. And was your memory fresher then, than it is today?

A. Yes, it was.

Q. When you met with Detective Clay on those two occasions, either on the 15th or on the 23rd, was your aunt present during those interviews?

A. During the second interview she was.

THE COURT: Mr. Barr, what is the aunt's name, for the record, that you're referring to?

BY MR. BARR:

Q. Could you describe to us the name of your aunt, please?

A. Yolanda Telle.

Q. Does she have a relationship to P.J?

A. Yes, she does. She's Pete's mother.

THE COURT: We will take our noon recess at this time, ladies and gentlemen. We will start up at 1:30. The admonition is still in effect.

(Whereupon, the following proceedings were held out of the presence of the jury:)

THE COURT: Ms. Martin, you can get off the stand. Just be back here at 1:30, all right?

THE WITNESS: Yes.

THE COURT: Thank you. Mr. Mill, you wanted to make a record, you wanted to approach and the Court denied that, so this is your opportunity to make any type of record.

MR. MILL: Thank you. Actually, let me make a motion at this time, my first motion for a mistrial. This is a very critical witness, Stephanie Martin. I would say that 90 percent of the words that have been spoken with her on the witness stand have come from Mr. Barr rather than Ms. Martin.

What Mr. Barr should have done is questions like, tell us what happened at this car wash. Instead, he lead her step by step through this testimony. I objected as frequently as I dared. I think this now takes us to constitutional dimensions where there is a 14th Amendment violation of due process and fair trial rights to my client because this critical witness' testimony has come from Mr. Barr, not from the witness stand.

THE COURT: The motion for mistrial is denied. We will see you back here at 1:30.

AFTERNOON SESSION

THE COURT: When we left off, Ms. Martin was still on the stand under direct examination. Please continue.

BY MR. BARR:

Q. Ms. Martin, can you describe to us the events that took place during the evening hours and the early morning hours of March 4th. During that period of time had you been drinking?

A. Yes.

Q. And when did you start drinking that day?

A. About a couple of hours after school.

Q. What were you drinking?

A. I had been drinking a mixture.

Q. What kind of mixed drink?

A. A mixture of mixed drinks, like LaClub Margarita, it comes made, and some Tequila Sunrise. I don't remember what other stuff.

Q. Also during that period of time, did you see Richard Roja at any time that evening with a gun?

A. No.

Q. You mentioned earlier on direct examination that Andy had some sort of cut on his finger; is that correct?

A. Yes.

Q. Did you have an opportunity to take a look at it?

A. Back at the motel room, yes.

Q. Was it the kind of cut that would bleed?

A. It bled a little.

Q. In terms of that cut on the finger, did he have that cut before you went to the car wash?

A. No, he didn't.

Q. Also, Stephanie, you've spent a considerable amount of time talking to us about what happened March 3rd and March 4th; is that correct?

A. Yes.

Q. You've also admitted to us that you initially denied to Detective Clay about what happened; is that correct?

A. Yes.

Q. Have you told us the truth here this morning?

MR. MILL: Objection. Vouching.

THE COURT: She can answer.

THE WITNESS: Yes.

MR. BARR: I have no further questions. Thank you, Judge.

THE COURT: Mr. Mill.

CROSS-EXAMINATION

BY MR. MILL:

Q. Good afternoon, Ms. Martin. When you were first introduced to Richard, it was Louis doing the introduction; is that correct?

A. Yes.

Q. And that was at your house; is that right?

A. Yes.

Q. And you testified this morning that Louis introduced Richard as his brother; is that right?

A. Yes.

Q. And that's not true, because they're nephew and uncle; is that right?

A. Yes.

Q. Let me ask you, Ms. Martin, you have been provided with transcripts by the prosecution; isn't that true?

A. Yes.

Q. Of every time that you've been interviewed; is that right?

A. Yes.

Q. You've been provided a transcript of your first interview with Detective Clay on March 15th, correct?

A. Yes.

Q. You have been provided with your second interview with Detective Clay on March 23rd, correct?

A. Yes.

Q. You testified under oath in front of a grand jury in this case on September 10th; is that correct?

A. Yes.

Q. You've been provided with that as well?

A. Yes.

Q. Have you looked at them?

A. Yes.

Q. Studied them?

A. Yes.

Q. Gone over them with the prosecution?

A. Yes.

Q. Got gone over them with the prosecution yesterday after court?

A. Yeah.

Q. And gone over those transcripts with the prosecution today?

A. Yeah.

Q. Did you get up early this morning and come in to meet with the prosecution?

A. Yes.

Q. Were you talked to at all by the prosecution over the lunch hour?

A. For, like, two minutes.

Q. And when you testified this morning, Stephanie, that you were at one time in love with Louis, do you recall saying that?

A. Yes.

Q. You're not in love with him any more?

A. Not in love with him? I'll always love him. He treated me good.

Q. And you kept seeing him even after the car wash murder, right?

A. Yes.

Q. You're not suggesting, Stephanie, that Louis told you to lie about this case, did he?

A. No.

Q. Or that you lied for him, did you?

A. No.

Q. When you went in on March 15th, were you?

A. No.

Q. Because you're your own woman?

A. Yep.

Q. And you told that to Detective Clay a number of times, didn't you?

A. Yes.

Q. And Detective Clay said he didn't believe you a whole bunch of times?

A. Yes.

Q. And suggested to you that it was Louis that was making you lie, didn't Detective Clay basically do that?

A. Yeah.

Q. And told you that you're lying just to protect this man you love?

A. Yeah.

Q. And you told him that's not right?

A. That's right.

Q. Because you're your own woman, that's what you told him?

A. Yep.

Q. You have given descriptions this morning, you gave physical descriptions of these three guys, right?

A. Yes.

Q. You forgot to give us a clothing description of Richard, would you mind doing that, on the night of the shooting?

A. He had white shorts on and—and I don't remember what kind of shirt he was wearing.

Q. No hat?

A. No.

Q. And a bald head?

A. Yes.

Q. Shaven down to the nub on March 4, 2003, correct?

A. Yes.

Q. Now, this morning you testified, Ms. Martin, that you were in the back seat of that car the whole time; is that true?

A. Yes.

Q. When you met with Clay the second time, you told him you were in the front seat until you got to Ranch Apartments; is that true?

A. I could have. I don't remember.

Q. You just don't remember?

A. Yeah.

Q. All right. Now, Stephanie, you were drunk the night of the shooting, weren't you?

A. Yeah.

Q. You had at least four wine coolers, correct?

A. Uh-huh.

Q. And two Tequila Sunrises out of the bottle, right?

A. Yeah.

Q. And the four wine coolers, got you buzzed?

A. Yeah.

Q. And then the two Tequila Sunrise bottles put you over the edge, didn't they?

A. Yeah.

Q. You were so intoxicated, Stephanie, that you were losing consciousness that night, weren't you?

A. Yeah.

Q. You were so intoxicated that you were throwing up, correct?

A. Yeah.

Q. You were so intoxicated, Stephanie, that you were in your own world; is that correct?

A. Somewhat.

Q. And in your perspective, were you as intoxicated as if you're so drunk that your perspective is limited to just a few feet in front of you?

A. Not really.

Q. So that what occurs even just beyond a few feet in front of you is just all blurry?

A. Some of the night it was like that.

Q. Were you so intoxicated that you just don't recall things?

A. Yeah.

Q. Stephanie, you testified that you were sitting on the other side of that block wall, correct?

A. Yeah.

Q. And all you saw or heard that went down at the car wash was perhaps the last shot, right?

A. Yes.

Q. Stephanie, did you hear a bang, bang, bang, a long pause, and then a scream, a real loud scream, and then three more bangs?

A. I don't recall any of that.

Q. You didn't hear any sounds that were so loud they could be heard blocks away?

A. I don't recall any of that.

Q. Well, I'm not asking you if you recall now. I'm just asking if you heard that?

A. No.

Q. And was that because you were so drunk, Stephanie?

A. I had dozed off.

Q. You passed out, Stephanie, isn't that a fair characteristic?

A. It's the same thing.

Q. But you're very, very certain about the people that were in the car and what their positions were in the car; is that true?

A. Yeah, because I was wide awake after I heard that last shot.

Q. And, Stephanie, after you heard that last shot, people got in your car, talked about a scanner, you knew the very next day that a homicide had taken place there, didn't you?

A. Yes.

Q. You saw it on the news, correct?

A. Yes.

Q. Did you get on the phone and call the police?

A. No, I didn't.

Q. You waited until they came to your house on March 15th, right?

A. Yeah.

Q. To handcuff you and take you down, right?

A. Yeah.

Q. And that's when you sat down and you had your first conversation with Detective Clay, correct?

A. Yeah.

Q. March 15th, you and Detective Clay in a little video room, right?

A. Yeah.

Q. You didn't know it was being recorded, did you?

A. No.

Q. Have you watched the video?

A. No, I haven't.

Q. And when you first started talking to Detective Clay, you didn't tell him anything about a hotel or a motel, did you?

A. No, I didn't.

Q. You told him that you just went with Louis and Richard to Ranch and then back home, right?

A. Yes.

Q. You didn't even mention Andy, did you?

A. I don't know.

Q. It was just you and Louis and Richard; is that true?

A. Yeah, I guess.

Q. And when they took you home late that night, you kicked back until about three a.m, and you just went to bed. Is that what you told Detective Clay?

A. Yeah.

Q. And then the next morning Louis returned, and you talked about why you didn't go out the night before; is that true?

A. Yeah.

Q. And then Detective Clay asked you a little bit about the Red Roof Inn. Do you remember that?

A. Yeah.

Q. You didn't volunteer it, did you?

A. No, I didn't.

Q. And Detective Clay said to you, let's not tap dance around, you know what happened. Do you recall that, Stephanie?

A. Yeah.

Q. Do you recall saying, I don't know what happened?

A. Yeah.

Q. And do you recall Clay then saying, you were in the car wash when they stopped?

A. Yes.

Q. And your response was, no, I wasn't, I was at home. Do you recall that?

A. Yeah.

Q. What you said then, Stephanie, was when you were confronted with the Red Roof Inn and you knew they had the receipt, correct?

A. Yeah.

Q. And you knew that that receipt showed your sister Angela renting that room, right?

A. Yeah.

Q. And so you knew that you had to tell them something about the hotel at that point, correct?

A. Yes.

Q. You still didn't tell them the truth about the hotel, did you?
A. No.
Q. You said that you went to bed and you got paged by Louis at about five a.m. Remember that?
A. Yeah.
Q. And on the pager was the telephone number of the Red Roof Inn. Do you remember that?
A. Yes.
Q. And you recognize the telephone number of the Red Roof Inn because you'd go there to kick back anyway, right?
A. Yeah.
Q. So the clue was at five a.m. you're sleeping, and you get the pager with the Red Roof Inn number, that's your prompt to go to the Red Roof Inn, right?
A. Uh-huh.
Q. Is that what you told the detective?
A. I don't know.
Q. You don't remember that?
A. Uh-uh.
Q. And then you told the detective, so at five a.m. you went to the Red Roof Inn, hung out a little bit, and went home at 6:30; do you recall that?
A. Yeah.
Q. And then Detective Clay follows up on the Red Roof pager story and says to you, how would you know what room to go to at the Red Roof Inn. Do you remember that?
A. Yes.
Q. And your response was, they would put that in at the end of the number so you could see it on the pager. Do you remember that?
A. Yes.
Q. All of that is false, right?
A. Yes.
Q. We are not done, Stephanie, because didn't you tell Detective Clay that there was another way that you were going to know which room it was. Do you remember telling him you would just go to the parking lot, turn the stereo system up loud until the boys looked out the window?
A. Yes.
Q. Is that true?
A. No.
Q. Do you remember when Detective Snel came in the room and had the Red Roof Inn receipt in his hands?
A. Yes.

Q. And he sort of set it on the corner of the table away from you; do you remember that?

A. I don't remember.

Q. Do you remember, Stephanie, saying, let me see that?

A. Yeah.

Q. Because you wanted to see if Angela's name was on it and the time was on it, right?

A. No.

Q. Once you saw the receipt, Stephanie, then you admitted to Detective Clay you actually went to the Red Roof Inn, correct?

A. Yes.

Q. And what you did was, you told him you went there, kicked back a little bit, and went home, correct?

A. Yes.

Q. Nothing about a car wash, was there?

A. No.

Q. And then you went to school, right?

A. Yep.

Q. And you continued to deny the car wash even when you showed up the second time with Detective Clay; is that true?

A. Yes.

Q. March 23rd, you still told him, I don't know what you're talking about; is that true?

A. Yeah.

Q. I wasn't in the car; is that true?

A. Yes.

Q. Shooting? What shooting? I was with my sister. Did you tell him that?

A. Yeah.

Q. Oh, yeah, we drove around and went to a gas station; right?

A. Yeah.

Q. And it wasn't until the gas station videotape is mentioned that you decided you were going to tell another version; is that true?

A. Yes.

Q. Another version that's going to put Richard Roja at the car wash, right?

A. Yes.

Q. For the first time, correct?

A. Yes.

Q. And now we are almost three weeks posthomicide, correct?

A. Yes.

Q. Now, your testimony is, Stephanie, that you heard some talk about a Lincoln, correct?

A. Yes.

Q. Hey, there's a car there; do you remember that?

A. No.

Q. You said that this morning, right?

A. I said somebody. I don't know.

Q. You don't know who said that, true?

A. Yes.

Q. And you can't say that Richard said that or Louis said that, can you?

A. No.

Q. Or Andy said that, right?

A. No.

Q. But after that conversation, there was a U-turn, correct?

A. Yes.

Q. All right. Now, you testified this morning that you all parked in that automotive lot just north of the car wash, true?

A. Yes.

Q. Isn't it true, Stephanie, that in the past you weren't certain where you did park?

A. Yes.

Q. And isn't it true that at one time you thought you may have even parked at the car wash?

A. I don't recall that.

Q. That you just turned into a place, but you didn't know where? Do you remember that, Stephanie?

A. I may have.

MR. BARR: The State's going to object along this line of questioning.

THE COURT: What is the objection?

MR. BARR: The objection is hearsay.

THE COURT: Counsel, approach the bench.

(Whereupon, the following proceedings were heard at the bench out of the hearing of the jury:)

THE COURT: What is the specific hearsay objection?

MR. BARR: Doesn't she go on and tell us it's the tire shop?

MR. MILL: I believe she does. May I ask the question again?

THE COURT: Yes.

(Whereupon, the following proceedings were held in the presence of the jury:)

BY MR. MILL:

Q. Stephanie, do you recall this exchange. Question: Okay, so a U-turn is made. What happens? Next answer: We pulled into the—I'm not sure if it was the car wash or if it was the place next to it. Do you recall that?

A. Yes.

Q. Question: Why aren't you sure?
Answer: Because I don't remember.
Do you remember that?

A. Yes.

Q. Question: You don't remember because you were drunk?
Answer: I was. Yeah, I was. I remember turning into a place. Do you remember that?

A. Yes.

Q. And then later on you believed it could have been the car wash, right?

A. Yes.

Q. Well, Stephanie, you have testified this morning that you're certain it was the place north of the car wash, right?

A. Yes.

Q. Now, but a few months ago you didn't know. It could have been the car wash, true?

A. True, it can be, possibly.

Q. As you sit here right now, are you sure that you parked in the place north of the car wash?

A. Yes.

Q. What has happened between October of 2004 and today to firm up your opinion?

A. I don't know. I wasn't sure back then. I'm pretty sure now.

Q. Now, Stephanie, you testified this morning that you believed Louis and Andy went over that wall, right?

A. Yes.

Q. Under oath to the grand jury you said in September that you don't know what they did after you heard voices from the trunk, correct?

A. Yes.

Q. And then you told the grand jury that a little bit later on, perhaps you did see them after they talked at the trunk. Do you recall that?

A. Perhaps. See them what?

Q. Did you tell them that you didn't see anything because there was a big old bush?

A. Yes.

Q. But, Stephanie, you figured they went over the wall because you didn't hear any running. Do you remember telling the grand jury that?

A. Yes.

Q. So, Stephanie, you didn't see anybody go over that wall, did you?

A. Yes.

Q. You saw Louis and Andy go over that wall?

A. Yes.

Q. With your own eyes?

A. It's blurry, but, yes.

Q. Blurry because of your intoxication?

A. Yes.

Q. When you told the grand jury you thought you saw somebody go over the wall, was that a truthful statement?

A. Yes.

Q. Why didn't you tell the grand jury that you saw two men, those two guys, go over the wall with your own eyes?

A. Because I wasn't sure of what I seen then.

Q. What has happened between September and today that has firmed up your memory?

A. I don't know.

Q. Help me out. Did you testify this morning that you did not drive into the car wash to pick up Richard?

A. Yes.

Q. That the car remained where it was in that auto lot until Richard came running out, right?

A. Yes.

Q. Now, during your second interview with Clay, you told him just the opposite, didn't you, Stephanie?

A. I don't remember.

Q. That you drove into the car wash to go get Richard. Do you remember telling him that?

A. No, I don't.

Q. Let me refer you to page 7 of 3/23.

Question by Detective Clay: Okay, who gets back to the car first?

Answer: Andy and Louis.

Question by Clay: Then what happened.

Answer: Richard wasn't with them.

Question: How did you get Richard?

Answer: They drove into the car wash because they didn't know where Richard was at.

Question: So they pull out here and go in? Do you remember that?

A. I don't remember that.

Q. And then Richard gets in; do you recall that?

A. I don't recall it.

Q. Well, which is it, Stephanie, did you drive in to get Richard, or did he come running back to the car?

A. He got in the car.

Q. At the automotive?

A. Yes.

Q. Did you ever drive that Kia into the car wash area?

A. No.

Q. Did the wheels of that Kia ever touch the car wash lot?

A. Yes.

Q. Okay. Was that to pick up Richard?

A. No.

Q. That was later, right?

A. Yes.

Q. Now, you testified this morning that you actually heard words coming out of Richard's mouth when he got back in the car. Do you recall that?

A. No. I said I didn't know if it was Richard or Louis who said it.

Q. Thank you. And there was talk about a scanner, right?

A. Yes.

Q. And some talk about shooting myself or shooting yourself. Do you recall that?

A. Yes.

Q. But you're not sure what was said?

A. Yes.

Q. And you're not sure who said it?

A. Yes.

Q. At the grand jury, do you recall this question and answer.

Question: Was there any discussion after the return to the car about what had happened at the car wash?

Answer: No, I don't recall any. Did you give that answer?

A. Yes.

Q. Today you're testifying that you did hear some conversation, correct?

A. Yes.

Q. What has happened between September in the grand jury and today that triggered a memory of conversation?

A. I don't know.

Q. When you got to the Red Roof Inn, Stephanie, had P.J. and Angela already been there?

A. Yes.

Q. You didn't get there before your sister Angela, did you?

A. No.

Q. And so you didn't go downstairs to unlatch the door to let your sister Angela in, did you?

A. Not that I recall that, no.

Q. So what you did, Stephanie, is, you were so drunk that you had to be carried in; is that true?

A. No. I had to be helped in.

Q. Louis had to help you in?

A. Yeah.

Q. Because you couldn't walk?

A. No, I could walk. I just needed help.

Q. So that you wouldn't fall over?

A. Yeah.

Q. How old were you at the time, 15?

A. Yes.

Q. After Louis was arrested, did you continue to talk with him?

A. Yes.

Q. Did you go see him in jail?

A. Yes.

Q. You didn't see Richard, right?

A. No.

Q. Your relationship with Louis really got off the ground after the car wash, right?

A. Yeah.

Q. That's when you started to be intimate with him?

A. Yes.

Q. And actually Detective Clay questioned you about your sexual life with Louis, didn't he?

A. Yes.

Q. And do you recall, Stephanie, that you were concerned that Louis was going to get in trouble because you were just 15?

A. Yes.

Q. And that was one of your concerns that you didn't want to talk about, right?

A. Yes.

Q. You didn't want to hurt Louis?

A. Yes.

Q. How old was he at the time?

A. Twenty.

Q. So, Stephanie, what do you do when you get home from this whole night at about 6:00 or 6:30 in the morning?

A. I get ready for school. I went to school.

Q. Did you tell grandma about what happened that night?

A. No.

Q. And you just went to junior high school?
A. Yes.
Q. What grade?
A. Eighth.
Q. Now, when you're in the car driving away from this car wash scene, you say Richard's in there, too, right?
A. Yes.
Q. And able to hear conversations of everybody, right?
A. I said I heard some talking; I don't remember what was being said.
Q. Do you recall Louis saying, I'm sorry?
A. Yes, I do.
Q. To you?
A. Yes.
Q. In front of everybody?
A. No. That was when him and Andy were in the car.
Q. Was that leaving the car wash?
A. I'm not sure if it was leaving the car wash, but I remember him saying it.

MR. MILL: That's all I have, Your Honor. No further questions.

THE COURT: Redirect.

REDIRECT EXAMINATION
BY MR. BARR:

Q. Ms. Martin, when you were asked some questions a little while ago concerning Richard and Louis, did you explain to us this morning during your direct examination that when you saw Richard, he was always with Louis?
A. Yes.
Q. Is that accurate, every time you saw Louis you saw Richard, too?
A. At first, yeah. It wasn't until after I got to know Louis that he was sometimes by himself.
Q. So later as your interest and your relationship with Louis got stronger, there were times that you didn't see Richard with Louis; is that correct?
A. Yes.
Q. Was Tony Mo at any time with you and Richard and Louis and Andy that day?
A. No.
Q. Now, Stephanie, you've described that you were intoxicated, that you had been drinking, correct?
A. Yes.

Q. And, in fact, after you had denied being in the car with Detective Clay at the second interview that you had with him on March the 23rd, you proceeded to explain to Detective Clay that you were in the car, but that you were intoxicated?

A. Yes.

Q. When you got back to the motel, you got sick, correct?

A. Yes.

Q. And was that illness not only attributed to the alcohol that you had which you had been drinking, but was it also attributed to what happened?

A. It could have been.

Q. Were you scared?

A. Not scared. Kind of shocked.

Q. And when Louis was telling you that he was sorry, was that because after what happened with the car wash, you started to get a little upset and emotional?

A. He may have.

Q. When you tell us what you saw at the car wash, have you ever at any time described seeing Richard Roja doing the shooting at the car wash?

A. No.

Q. Does the fact that you had been drinking, does that affect some of your memory?

A. Yes, it does.

Q. In spite of the fact that you had been drinking, is what you testified to today what you observed from the Kia?

A. Yes.

Q. On the March 23rd interview after you were confronted by Detective Clay about the gas station videotape, do you remember that?

A. Yeah.

Q. Is that when you basically broke down and told Detective Clay what happened?

A. Yes.

Q. Now, through that time, you were maintaining to Detective Clay that you weren't in the car, correct? Up until that point.

A. Yes.

Q. You were trying to mislead him?

A. Yes.

Q. And why were you doing that?

A. I didn't want none of them to get in trouble.

Q. You didn't want none of them to get in trouble?

A. (Nods head in the affirmative.)

Q. Now, after a while your relationship with Louis cooled; is that correct?

A. Yes.

Q. In fact, at some point you broke off your relationship with Louis; is that true?
A. Yes.
Q. And now you moved on, and you are now married, correct?
A. Yes.
Q. And you don't have any association with Louis any more?
A. No.

MR. BARR: No additional questions. Thank you.

THE COURT: Do any jurors have a question of this witness?

(Whereupon, the following proceedings were heard at the bench out of the hearing of the jury:)

THE COURT: I think this question was asked already.

MR. BARR: It was asked.

MR. MILL: It was asked, but you can ask it again. I don't care.

THE COURT: Do you want me to ask it again?

MR. BARR: I don't have any objection. It was asked.

THE COURT: The next question is, did Stephanie see any weapons at all that night.

MR. MILL: Okay.

THE COURT: Did Stephanie see any weapons that night? If so, who had them?

MR. BARR: That was asked.

THE COURT: Do you want me to ask her?

MR. BARR: You can ask her again.

THE COURT: Okay. Next question, when they went from the Red Roof Inn to Tony Mo's apartment, did they pass the car wash and did they see the Lincoln at that point in time? Do you know what they got at the apartment?

MR. MILL: Okay.

MR. BARR: Okay.

THE COURT: And at any time at the car wash or at the auto parking lot did you ask why are we here? Did you ask the three males when they got back in the car what they had been doing? If you did ask them, what did they tell you? It assumes that somebody said something.

MR. BARR: I didn't hear all that.

THE COURT: Do you want to read it.

MR. MILL: I don't object to any of those questions.

THE COURT: Is it okay?

MR. BARR: Yes.

THE COURT: Okay.

(Whereupon, the following proceedings occurred in open court in the presence of the jury:)

THE COURT: Ms. Martin, if you can, I'm going to ask you a number of questions that the jurors have submitted. At any time at the car wash or at the auto parts parking lot did you ask, why are we here?

THE WITNESS: No, I don't believe I did.

THE COURT: Did you ask the three males once they got back in the car what they had been doing?

THE WITNESS: No.

THE COURT: When you went from the Red Roof Inn to Tony Mo's apartment, did you pass the car wash when you went north?

THE WITNESS: Yes, we did.

THE COURT: And did you see the Lincoln at that point in time?

THE WITNESS: I didn't, no.

THE COURT: Do you know what they got at the apartment?

THE WITNESS: No, I don't.

THE COURT: Did you see any weapons at all that night?

THE WITNESS: No, I didn't.

THE COURT: Do you recall what Richard Roja was wearing the night of the shooting?

THE WITNESS: I believe he had white pants on.

THE COURT: Do you recall if he had a hat or a cap on?

THE WITNESS: No, he didn't.

THE COURT: What about Louis and Andy, did they have a hat or cap on, if you recall?

THE WITNESS: No, they didn't.

THE COURT: Mr. Barr, any follow-up questions to any of those questions I asked?

MR. BARR: Yes, Your Honor. I just have a couple.

BY MR. BARR:
Q. In terms of the weapons, you said that you had not seen any weapons, correct?
A. Correct.
Q. Had you previously advised Louis and Richard that you didn't like guns?
A. Yes.
Q. When Richard got back in the car, do I understand what you said is that Richard was the last one to get there?
A. Yes.

MR. BARR: I have no further questions. Thank you, Judge.

THE COURT: Mr. Mill, any follow-up to any of those questions?

MR. MILL: No.

THE COURT: Thank you, ma'am. You're excused.

(Witness excused.)

THE COURT: We're going to take our afternoon recess at this time. Let's take about 15 minutes, ladies and gentlemen.

(Whereupon, the following proceedings were held out of the presence of the jury:)

THE COURT: Anything I need to take up with either counsel?

MR. MILL: No.

THE COURT: Mr. Barr, what do you have lined up?

MR. BARR: I was just talking to Detective Clay. I have four short witnesses. I was wondering if I need to call a fifth.

THE COURT: If we take off early today, that's fine.

MR. BARR: Okay.

(Whereupon, a recess was taken, after which the following proceedings were held in the presence of the jury:)

MR. BARR: Your Honor, the State would call Monica Muno.

(MONICA IS DEFENDANT RICHARD ROJA'S AUNT. RICHARD AND HIS SISTER LIVED WITH HER IN A THREE BEDROOM HOME NOT FAR FROM THE CAR WASH, ALONG WITH MONICA'S THREE SONS, HER MOTHER, AND HER BROTHER, LOUIS CASTELL. SHE TESTIFIED THAT LOUIS, RICHARD AND SISTER TENI SHARED THE MIDDLE BEDROOM IN THIS CROWDED HOME. SHE SAID "WHOEVER GOT TO THE ROOM FIRST SLEPT IN THERE FIRST." SHE ADMITTED SHE KICKED RICHARD AND LOUIS OUT OF HER HOUSE A FEW DAYS BEFORE THE CAR WASH MURDERS BECAUSE THEY HAD AN ARGUMENT WITH HER MOM. MONICA DIDN'T KNOW WHERE THEY WENT, ONLY THAT THEY STAYED WITH "FRIENDS." THE PUBLIC DEFENDER CROSS-EXAMINED MONICA BY TRYING TO CLEAR UP THE RAFT OF RELATIVES LIVING IN VARIOUS BEDROOMS, AND THEN ASKED IF SHE KNEW OF ANY AMMUNITION CLIP IN THE CLOSET OF THE MIDDLE BEDROOM,

AND SHE DENIED ANY KNOWLEDGE. SHE ALSO TESTIFIED THAT AT THE TIME OF THE MURDERS, RICHARD DIDN'T HAVE MUCH HAIR. THE COUNTY ATTORNEY'S REDIRECT EXAMINATION GOT MONICA TO STATE THAT SHE DIDN'T REMEMBER RICHARD EVER WEARING A BASEBALL CAP, AFTER WHICH SHE WAS EXCUSED. THE NEXT WITNESS WAS SANDRA MARTIN WHO WAS THE SISTER OF MONICA MUNO. SANDRA WAS 26 YEARS OLD AND LIVED IN CALIFORNIA WITH HER HUSBAND, SEVEN CHILDREN AND HER NEPHEW RICHARD ROJA. SHE WAS RICHARD'S FAVORITE AUNT. TESTIMONY CONTINUED:)

Q. While Richard was living with you in California, did your husband Jose purchase any weapons?

A. Yes.

Q. What kind of weapons did he purchase?

A. It was a handgun.

Q. What color was it?

A. It was black.

Q. How many times did you see that gun after your husband got it?

A. About two or three.

Q. Where did he keep that weapon?

A. Out in the garage.

Q. Were you able to go out there and have access to that weapon whenever you wanted to?

A. No.

Q. Why not?

A. He kept it locked.

Q. And you didn't go out there to the garage?

A. He was the only one with the key.

Q. And at some point that weapon turned up missing; is that correct?

A. Yes.

Q. And was that approximately the middle of February of 2003? You told Detective Clay when he came to your house to speak to you that the weapon that your husband had purchased turned up missing one or two days prior to the day that Richard went to Phoenix, correct?

A. No, that was the last time that I had seen it.

Q. Okay. And are you currently living with Jose?

A. No, I'm not.

Q. Why not?

A. I'm separated from him about a year ago.

Q. To the best of your knowledge where is Jose now?

A. Incarcerated.

Q. Do you know where at?
A. In northern California somewhere.
Q. Do you know an individual named Louis Castell?
A. Yes, I do. He's my brother.
Q. Who is taller between Louis and Richard?
A. I don't know. I haven't seen them together lately.

(NOW THE PUBLIC DEFENDER CROSS-EXAMINED SANDRA TO BRING OUT THE FACT THAT HER SOON-TO-BE-DIVORCED HUSBAND JOSE WAS A DRUG DEALER OUT OF THEIR GARAGE AND HAD A LOT OF SHADY PEOPLE COMING TO THE GARAGE, ANY ONE OF WHOM COULD HAVE STOLEN THE MISSING GUN. THE COUNTY ATTORNEY IN HIS REDIRECT EXAMINATION GOT DOWN TO BRASS TACKS:)

Q. Isn't it true that what you said to the detective was, you believe the weapon was missing one or two days prior to Richard Roja leaving town?
A. No.
Q. So there were lots of people that were living in your garage?
A. Not living. They were always there.
Q. So the door wouldn't be locked when these people who were always there were going in and out?
A. No. My husband told them lock it behind them.
Q. Isn't it true that Jose told you that he felt that Richard had taken his gun, correct?
A. Yes.

MR. MILL: Objection. Hearsay.

THE COURT: Overruled. She can answer. She's answered.

COUNTY ATTORNEY: I have no further questions, Your Honor.

THE COURT: Can counsel approach the bench?

(Whereupon, the following proceedings were heard at the bench out of the hearing of the jury:)

MR. MILL: Can we stay on the record for a minute?

THE COURT: Go ahead.

MR. MILL: What is the last question? What was your last question?

COUNTY ATTORNEY: Whether she was told by her husband that her husband thought Richard took the gun.

MR. MILL: And she said what?

COUNTY ATTORNEY: She said, yes, she was told that.

MR. MILL: That's terrible, Judge. I'd ask that you reconsider that and sustain my objection, and instruct the jury not to consider that answer.

THE COURT: Why don't we argue that outside the presence of the jury.

MR. MILL: Okay.

(Whereupon, the following proceedings occurred in open court in the presence of the jury:)

THE COURT: All right, ma'am, did you say Richard Roja, when he was living with you, wore glasses all the time, or not all the time, or some of the time, or what was your answer if you recall?

THE WITNESS: I said some of the time.

THE COURT: Some of the time?

THE WITNESS: Not all the time.

(THE COUNTY ATTORNEY CALLED TO THE STAND THE REPRESENTATIVES OF THE LIMO TAXI SERVICE THAT THE DECEDENT MICHAEL FRO WORKED FOR. HE IDENTIFIED MICHAEL AS BEING A DRIVER FOR THE FIRM AND DRIVING THE WHITE LINCOLN TOWN CAR SHOWN IN A PHOTO EXHIBIT. HE STATED THAT WHEN HE PICKED UP THE CAR FROM THE POLICE DEPARTMENT AFTER MICHAEL'S MURDER, THE DRIVER'S SIDE WINDOW HAD BEEN SHATTERED BY A BULLET HOLE. THE PUBLIC DEFENDER DECLINED TO CROSS-EXAMINE THIS GENTLEMAN, AND THE COUNTY ATTORNEY CALLED HIS NEXT WITNESS, POLICE DETECTIVE RICH BRAD, WHO SEARCHED THE MIDDLE BEDROOM OF RICHARD ROJA'S AUNT MONICA—THE BUSY BEDROOM:)

Q. While you were searching the middle bedroom of that residence and you were looking for items, were you looking for items that were associated with weapons?

A. Yes, sir.

Q. And while you were searching the middle bedroom of that residence and went to the closet area, did you discover an item that you associated with weapons?

A. Yes.

Q. Could you describe, please?

A. It was a magazine that had some ammunition in it, and the ammunition was a .45 caliber.

Q. Did you seize that magazine?

A. Yes, sir.

Q. And where in terms of that middle bedroom did you locate that magazine?

A. As depicted in the documentation from the actual search warrant site, it was found in the middle bedroom, about the middle of the closet, on the shelf inside of the closet.

Q. Now, Sergeant, could you describe to us what a magazine is?

A. Sure. A magazine is where the bullets are actually held in a semiautomatic weapon. You would slide this up into the weapon, and it's spring-loaded, so as you fire the round, the round is extracted from the handgun, another round is automatically inserted into the weapon. In that semiautomatic weapon they call them a magazine, where if you heard the term a clip, that's usually associated with a fully automatic handgun.

Q. So the magazine is the device that actually feeds or stores the rounds so they could be fed into the weapon automatically?

A. Yes, sir.

CROSS-EXAMINATION

BY MR. MILL:

Q. Was the magazine hidden from view when you found it?

A. Right, at least partially out of view.

Q. Sergeant, also found in that middle bedroom was a black nylon wallet with identification belonging to Jonathan Andy Aria; is that true?

A. Yes, sir, it was.

MR. MILL: Nothing further.

THE COURT: Redirect.

MR. BARR: I just have one additional question.

Q. Sergeant, photographic Exhibit Number 158, does that show us the magazine in the location that you found it?

A. Yes, sir.

Q. Based upon reviewing the photograph, you can testify today that it appears that it was under some other items on the shelf in the closet?

A. Yes, sir.

MR. BARR: No further questions. Thank you, Judge.

THE COURT: Thank you. You're excused.

THE COURT: Ladies and gentlemen, I'm going to excuse you a little bit early. Let's start tomorrow at 10:15.

(Whereupon, the following proceedings were held out of the presence of the jury:)

THE COURT: Everybody can be seated. I stated at the bench conference that we would make a record outside the jury's presence. Mr. Mill objected to the answer that Ms. Martin gave. And to tell you the truth, I'm not sure I know specifically what the question was. I know her answer was yes. Do we need that read back, the specific question?

COUNTY ATTORNEY: I can tell the Court the question. The question, as I recall, was, did your husband Jose tell you that he believed that Richard had taken the gun.

THE COURT: And the answer was yes. There was an objection, and the objection was hearsay.

MR. MILL: Correct.

THE COURT: Why don't you tell me, in my reconsidering it why don't you tell me what exception to the hearsay rule that falls under.

COUNTY ATTORNEY: Your Honor, first of all, the State would submit to the Court that it's not hearsay. I was not using it to show that Richard took the weapon. I was using it to rebut Sandra's testimony on cross-examination that Richard didn't have any access to the weapon, that the weapon was locked in the garage, and that the only person that had a key to the garage was Jose.

I was introducing that statement to show that the person who controlled access to the garage thought that Richard did have access and had taken the gun, that's different than trying to use the statement for the purpose of Richard took the gun, it's to rebut Sandra's testimony. And since it's not being used for the truth of the matter asserted, it's not hearsay.

THE COURT: Mr. Mill?

MR. MILL: Whether you use it for case in chief or in rebuttal, the question is, what is it trying to prove, not that the State gets automatic hearsay things in for rebuttal. It's just, what is he trying to prove? He's trying to prove that Richard stole the gun in the opinion of Jose, and that's exactly what the statement is. So it is hearsay.

THE COURT: The Court, in reconsidering it's rule regarding Ms. Martin's answer, the Court does find that it was hearsay. I don't really believe that there's an exception. Given the importance of the answer and given the totality of the facts surrounding this case, I'm going to sustain the objection. And the defendant's move to strike, is it your wish, Mr. Mill, for the Court to instruct the jury to disregard the answer given.

MR. MILL: Yes.

THE COURT: Okay. So when they come back tomorrow, I'll just tell the jury that to—I won't underline the whole the question and the answer, I'll just—rather than do that, I think that may be underlying the whole of what was said. I can just tell the jury that the Court reconsidered its ruling regarding Ms. Martin's answer to the question as to whether her husband believed that the defendant stole the gun, and the Court would sustain the defendant's objection and motion to strike, and I would instruct the jury to disregard the answer given by that witness.

MR. MILL: Okay.

THE COURT: Anything else on that?

MR. MILL: Can I just have one moment. Nothing more. Your Honor, there is a exhibit that I need to redact that we talked about, if I could do that with your clerk.

THE COURT: That's fine. Are you going to just use white-out?

MR. MILL: Could we re-Zerox it?

MR. BARR: That's fine with me, Judge.

THE COURT: And how are we looking for tomorrow? Have you got your witnesses lined up?

MR. BARR: I have enough witnesses lined up for tomorrow. A couple of cancellations, but I will have the day full of witnesses. I'm moving them around so that we fill up the time. I apologize to the Court, I thought with the witnesses that I had left we would be getting closer to 4:30. I had another witness that I thought was going to be another hour.

THE COURT: That's fine.

MR. BARR: We're pretty much on schedule.

THE COURT: That's fine. That's all I wanted to tell the jury. I didn't want them to think that we're just sitting around.

FOURTH DAY, JANUARY 25, 2005
MORNING SESSION

(THE MORNING STARTED WITH A FEW LARGE LEGAL HASSLES OUT OF THE HEARING OF THE DEFENDANT AND THE JURY. THE PUBLIC DEFENDER REQUESTED A MISTRIAL BASED ON THE PREVIOUS DAY'S HEARSAY TESTIMONY WHEN SANDRA MARTIN SAID HER HUSBAND CLAIMED RICHARD ROJA STOLE HIS GUN. HE DID AN EXCELLENT JOB OF PRESENTING HIS CASE, BUT THE JUDGE DENIED HIS MOTION FOR A MISTRIAL. NEXT THE PUBLIC DEFENDER DISCUSSED A WITNESS—MAXINE HERNAND—WHO WAS SLATED TO BE EXAMINED LATER THAT MORNING. MAXINE HAD ORIGINALLY REPORTED IN HER AFFIDAVIT THAT TONY MO HAD PARTICIPATED IN THE CAR WASH MURDERS, AND LATER CHANGED HER TESTIMONY AND SAID TONY MO WASN'T WITH THE OTHER MEN THAT NIGHT AFTER ALL. SHE SAID SHE WAS CONFUSED ABOUT ANOTHER PENDING CASE CONCERNING TONY MO. THE PUBLIC DEFENDER WANTED TO BRING THIS OUT IN HIS REDIRECT EXAMINATION, BUT THE JUDGE DENIED HIS REQUEST, SAYING THAT MAXINE HERNAND SIMPLY MADE AN HONEST MISTAKE. THE JURY RETURNED, AND THE FIRST WITNESS WAS A LIBRARIAN WHO IDENTIFIED MICHAEL FRO'S LIBRARY CARD. THE NEXT WITNESS WAS 22-YEAR-OLD MAXINE HERNAND. SHE STATED THAT SHE KNEW RICHARD ROJA AND HAD DATED HIM

BEFORE HE MOVED TO CALIFORNIA, AND WHEN HE RETURNED FROM CALIFORNIA SHE WAS SERIOUSLY DATING HIS UNCLE, LOUIS CASTELL. SHE TESTIFIED SHE OWNED THE BROWN KIA CAR AND LOANED IT TO LOUIS THE EVENING OF THE MURDERS. SHE DIDN'T SEE HIM AGAIN UNTIL SIX A.M. THE FOLLOWING MORNING WHEN HE RETURNED TO THE RANCH APARTMENT WITH RICHARD AND ANDY. HER TESTIMONY CONTINUED:)

Q. Now, you said that when Louis, Richard and Andy returned to the apartment, what did Louis do?

A. He came in and sat down next to me with a towel.

Q. And in terms of what Richard was doing when he sat on the couch, could you describe?

A. Richard was standing against the balcony door looking out.

Q. In terms of Louis, you said he sat on the couch. What was he doing when he sat on the couch?

A. He opened up the towel.

Q. Could you describe the towel for me, please?

A. It was a white towel with blood spots on it.

Q. What did he have inside the towel?

A. Keys and a wallet.

Q. Could you describe the wallet for us?

A. It was a brown leather wallet.

Q. What about the keys?

A. It was a bunch of keys together.

Q. Now, what did Louis proceed to do with the wallet?

A. He started looking through it to see if there was anything he could take from it.

Q. Was Richard and Andy still in the same living room as Louis is going through the wallet?

A. Yes.

Q. When Louis was describing to you where the wallet had come from, could you describe to me his demeanor, how he told you about it?

A. Bragging about it.

Q. Pardon me?

A. Bragging.

Q. And when he was talking about it, was it loud enough for others in the room to hear what he was saying?

MR. MILL: Objection. Leading.

THE COURT: Well, she can testify she doesn't know if the others could hear it or not, so she can testify that it was loud enough for her to hear it. If she has any indication whether or not the others heard it, she can testify to that. So, in other words, I'm sustaining the objection.

MR. MILL: Thank you.

BY MR. BARR:

Q. Ms. Hernand, when Louis was making the statements to you reference the wallet, was Richard in the room?
A. Yes.
Q. Was Richard participating in that conversation at that time?
A. No.
Q. What was in the wallet?
A. Social security card and different cards that were in there.
Q. Did he leave the cards in the wallet, or did he take them out?
A. He left them in the wallet.
Q. And could you describe to me what he did with the wallet?
A. He got scissors and cut it up.
Q. Who got the scissors?
A. Louis.
Q. And does he just cut the wallet up in pieces?
A. Yes.
Q. Describe what Louis did for us, would you?
A. He sat down next to me, grabbed the scissors, and started cutting the wallet to pieces.
Q. Any money? Did you see any cash?
A. None.
Q. Did he make any statements about no cash?
A. No.
Q. What did Louis do with the wallet after it was cut up?
A. He asked Tony if they could burn it, if they had a grill.
Q. Ms. Hernand, did you see what Louis did with the parts of the wallet that he cut up?
A. Yes.
Q. What did he do?
A. Threw them in the barbecue grill.
Q. Did he just throw them in the grill and leave them there, or did he do something with the barbecue?
A. He burned them.
Q. How about the keys, do you know what he did with the keys?
A. He got wire cutters and cut them up to pieces.
Q. Did he cut them up at the table in the living room?
A. At the coffee table.

Q. Do you know what he did with them after he cut them up?

A. No.

Q. What Louis was doing at the coffee table, was that in plain view of the other people that were in the living room at that time?

A. Yes.

Q. After you saw Louis burn the parts in the barbecue, did you stay there at the residence?

A. Yes.

Q. For how long?

A. For another two hours.

Q. Did you eventually go to work that day?

A. Yes.

Q. About what time did you leave the apartment?

A. Around eight a.m.

Q. And where did you go?

A. To Jack-in-the-Box to get something to eat.

Q. Did you see what was happening down on 59th Avenue as you went down toward Jack-in-the-Box?

A. Yes.

Q. What could you see?

A. Police cars that were there at the car wash.

Q. Before the time that you saw Louis cutting up the wallet, before that time and let's say from the time that Richard returned from California, did you ever see Richard with a gun?

A. Yes.

Q. Would you describe to me on how many occasions you saw him with a gun?

A. Twice.

Q. Can you describe the gun for me?

A. It was a .45 caliber black automatic.

Q. How did Richard carry the gun?

A. He had it always tucked underneath his shirt.

Q. Now, you said it was a .45 caliber?

A. Yes.

Q. How did you know it was a .45 caliber?

A. Because he told Louis it was.

Q. Were you present when he was telling Louis?

A. Yes.

Q. Ms. Hernand, in terms of this conversation about the gun, you said you knew it was a .45 because of what you overheard?

A. Yes.

Q. Now, the day that you saw Louis cutting up the parts of the wallet, that day, with respect to that day, how much time before that are we talking about when the conversation takes place between Richard and Louis about the gun? Are we talking about a week? Are we talking about days?

A. It was a few days before.

Q. When Richard was talking to Louis about the gun, were you able to see the gun?

A. Yes.

Q. And how was Richard handling the gun at that time?

A. He always kept it underneath his shirt.

Q. Did you have an opportunity to see the gun out in the open?

A. Yes.

Q. Now, while you overheard the conversation between Louis and Richard, did you ever hear Richard—

MR. MILL: Objection. Leading.

THE COURT: Well, I haven't heard the end of the question, Mr. Mill, so I'm not going to rule on the objection. Why don't you finish the question.

MR. MILL: May we approach?

THE COURT: Yes.

(Whereupon, the following proceedings were heard at the bench out of the hearing of the jury:)

MR. MILL: Well, the objection is leading because he's about to tell her what to say.

MR. BARR: Richard described as to where he got the gun.

THE COURT: Why can't he ask, do you know where Richard got the gun?

MR. MILL: Because there's a real issue as to whether Louis told her or Richard told her. And I've got her in the transcript saying it's from Louis. And it's hearsay, so I don't want him to lead her through this.

THE COURT: Here's what we will do. Let's break for lunch and we can handle the issue.

(Whereupon, the following proceedings occurred in open court in the presence of the jury:)

THE COURT: Ladies and gentlemen, rather than do this at the bench, I want to take care of a couple of issues outside of your presence, so let's break a little early for lunch. We will resume at 1:30.

(Whereupon, the following proceedings were held out of the presence of the jury:)

THE COURT: Ms. Hernand, you are to be back here at 1:30. All right?

THE WITNESS: Okay.

(Whereupon, the witness was excused until 1:30 p.m.)

THE COURT: Let's take up the issue. Mr. Mill, you objected. You said there was lack of foundation. The witness testified that it looked like the gun that she saw the defendant have. I didn't know, is that the actual gun?

MR. BARR: No. We never recovered the gun.

THE COURT: Is there a criminalist that's going to testify to what type of gun that is?

MR. BARR: That's correct. The situation is this. I'm going to lay additional testimony concerning the gun that disappeared. You heard yesterday the State's position that the gun disappeared from California. The statement that's about to come from the witness is that she overheard a conversation between Louis and Richard about where the gun came from.

THE COURT: Mr. Mill's objection is that there is at least a discrepancy as to who originated that conversation, or where the conversation came from.

MR. MILL: Right. The way I understood it from my independent view of this witness, Louis told this witness the gun came from California and that Richard took it from his uncle, and that Richard was not adopting that statement, or that the State was going to have trouble making that foundation that Richard adopted it. Things are getting a little clearer today. I have not heard this exchange between Richard and Louis. This is the first time I'm hearing it.

THE COURT: Which exchange?

MR. MILL: This witness saying that it's Richard and Louis talking about the gun. Before it was my understanding it was just Louis.

THE COURT: And, Mr. Barr, I guess my question to you would be, if the witness' answer would be that she heard this from Mr. Castell, would that not be hearsay?

MR. BARR: It's not hearsay if Richard's there participating in the conversation.

THE COURT: I don't know what the conversation consisted of. Can you make an offer of proof what the conversation consisted of?

MR. BARR: I will. During the latest interview the defense counsel did in this case with Ms. Hernand, she's asked by Rick Mill, do you know he carried it loaded? Ms. Hernand, yeah, most of the time. Next question by Mr. Mill: Did he tell you or did you ask where he got it from?

THE COURT: And she's referring to who in that conversation?

MR. BARR: She's referring to Richard.

THE COURT: Okay.

MR. BARR: She follows up with, him and Louis were talking about it and he had got it from California.

THE COURT: Okay. Mr. Mill, do you have any other information that she makes that assumption based on what Mr. Castell told her?

MR. BARR: If I could read further.

THE COURT: I'm sorry, go ahead.

MR. BARR: Rick Mill: How do you know.

Maxine: From his uncle.

Rick Mill: Who said that?

Maxine: Louis and Richard. They were both talking and I was there.

Rick Mill: Louis asked where he got the gun?

Maxine: No. Richard was telling Louis.

Rick Mill: He got it from his uncle in California? Yeah. That's the exchange dealing with the gun that I was about to get into.

THE COURT: And my ruling is that Mr. Barr can elicit that from the witness. Also, on the gun, I guess you're going to have a criminalist testify that that is a .45 caliber semiautomatic?

MR. BARR: Yes.

THE COURT: Because she can't testify to it.

MR. BARR: She can at least tell us that appears similar to the gun that she saw.

THE COURT: I understand that, but you're going to have your criminalist look and say, yes, that's a .45 caliber; is that right?

MR. BARR: That's correct.

THE COURT: Until that time, I'll withhold my ruling.

MR. BARR: All right. You asked earlier were we going to present the gun. We never recovered the gun.

THE COURT: I understand that. Anything else?

MR. MILL: I wanted to find what he was referring to. Do you want me to do that later?

THE COURT: Unless you think that Mr. Barr was taking that out of context and that there's more to this than I heard already, then I made my ruling.

MR. MILL: Okay. If I'm not dreaming this up.

MR. BARR: Counsel is right, she is asked a question at some point, where did you hear that the gun came from California. Initially she says Louis.

THE COURT: But at some point she is going to testify that she heard it from this defendant?

MR. BARR: That's correct.

MR. MILL: Well, fine. I would like Mr. Barr not to lead her through that and let's see what she has to say on her own.

THE COURT: Well, if she didn't have any recollection of the conversation, I guess she could refresh her memory, or he can help her out like that if she says I don't know or I don't remember. I don't know what she's going to say.

MR. MILL: I don't know either, but if past testimony is an indication of what is going to happen in the future, here's going to be the question, isn't it true that Richard told you that he got his gun from his uncle in California? Objection. Leading. Sustained. And then you'll go on. Mr. Barr will go on to say, what did Mr. Roja say about where he got the gun? And the witness will say, oh, let me tell you.

THE COURT: I don't know what Mr. Barr is going to ask, or how he's going to ask it, but it seems to me the better practice will be to ask her if she ever had any indication of where the gun came from.

MR. BARR: I can ask her that, Judge. My last question to the witness as far as I remember is, did you ever overhear a description, and I started to get into where the gun came from. That was my question as far as I recollect. I was going to have her describe that, and that's when I was cut off.

THE COURT: Okay. I don't remember exactly how you asked it, but I think we have discussed this and I think everybody knows what has to be done. If you find something else on this that you want to bring to my attention, just let me know.

MR. MILL: Thanks.

THE COURT: Court's at recess.

(A luncheon recess was taken until 1:30 p.m., after which the following proceedings were held in the presence of the jury:)

AFTERNOON SESSION

(CONTINUING DIRECT EXAMINATION OF MAXINE HERNAND)

BY MR. BARR:
Q. When we left off, we were talking about conversation that you overheard reference the gun. Do you remember that?
A. Yeah.
Q. Can you tell me, first of all, when did that conversation take place with relation to the car wash shooting?
A. A few days later.

Q. Was it after the car wash shooting or before the car wash shooting?

A. Before.

Q. Can you tell me in terms of the number of days before the shooting that you heard the conversation?

A. Three or four days before.

Q. Why don't you go ahead and describe to me what was happening in the room at the time that you overheard the conversation.

A. We were sitting down on the couch.

Q. When you say "we were sitting down on the couch," who was sitting down?

A. Me and Louis were sitting on the couch, and Richard on the other couch.

Q. And could you describe to me, was Richard and Louis having a conversation?

A. Yes.

Q. Okay. Did you have any trouble hearing the conversation?

A. No.

Q. Were they talking back and forth to each other, or was it one person talking and then the other?

A. Back and forth talking.

Q. In terms of the conversation that's taking place, was it about the gun?

A. Yes.

Q. Could you describe to me what Richard said about the gun?

A. He was telling Louis that it was a .45.

Q. Was there a conversation at that point about where the .45 came from?

A. Yes.

Q. Who was describing where the .45 came from?

A. Richard.

Q. Would you describe to me what Richard said?

A. That the .45 came from his uncle in California.

Q. Now, you told us that you saw the gun and that Richard carried the gun on his waist?

A. Yes.

Q. When you were overhearing this conversation, did he have the gun out or was it still in his waist?

A. In his waist.

Q. You said you saw the gun a couple of times?

A. Yes.

Q. Did you see Richard with the gun out so you could see the type of gun that it was?

A. Yes.

Q. Could you describe to me, was that before or after the car wash shooting?

A. Before.

Q. And did that take place at the Ranch Apartment?

A. Yes.

Q. Was anyone else present at the time that that happened?

A. Yes.

Q. Who?

A. Louis.

Q. With respect to the conversation that we just talked about, the conversation about the uncle in California, when did you see Richard openly display the gun?

A. It was three or four days before the shooting.

Q. After the shooting, did you ever see Richard carrying that .45?

A. No.

Q. During this period of time when you were seeing Richard over at the Ranch Apartments after he returned from California, do you recall the type of shoes that he wore?

A. He would wear white K-Swiss.

Q. How do you know that it was K-Swiss kind of shoes?

A. Because it has a label on the back of the shoe.

Q. Now, you said that you left and you went to work that day; is that correct?

A. Yes.

Q. Did you ever come back to the Mungar apartment at the Ranch?

A. A day or two later.

Q. When you came back to the Mungar apartment, did you ever have a conversation with Richard about the car wash?

A. No.

Q. Did Richard Roja ever make any statements to you about the car wash?

A. No.

Q. Did you overhear Richard Roja describe at some point what had happened at the car wash?

A. Yes.

Q. Could you tell me where you were when you overheard him describe what happened at the car wash?

A. In the living room.

Q. Now, and this was how many days after the car wash?

A. About two days later.

Q. And who was Richard talking to when you heard him describe what happened at the car wash?

A. To Louis.

Q. What did you hear Richard say?

A. That he couldn't believe what he had done at the car wash.

Q. Did he go on and further describe about the shooting?

A. Yes.

Q. What did he say about the shooting?

A. That he had shot the lady two times in the head.

Q. Did he say anything about why he shot the lady in the head?
A. Because she was running.
Q. Did he say anything about anyone else at the car wash?
A. Her boyfriend.
Q. Did he say that he did anything with regard to the boyfriend?
A. Yes.
Q. What did he say?
A. That he shot him in the head, too.
Q. When he made those statements, did he follow-up and make any further description about what happened at the car wash?
A. No.
Q. After the shooting at the car wash, I'd like to talk a little bit about Andy, okay? Did you know Andy?
A. A little bit. Not really.
Q. Had you met him before the day of the car wash?
A. Yeah.
Q. And where did you meet him?
A. At the apartment.
Q. And about how many times did you see Andy before the car wash?
A. A few times.
Q. And you said that Andy left with Louis and Richard that night, do you remember that?
A. Yes.
Q. Now, when they came back, did you notice anything about Andy in terms of whether he had any kind of injuries?
A. Yes.
Q. What did you notice about Andy?
A. He had a cut on his finger.
Q. After you overheard the conversation between Richard and Louis two or three days after the car wash shooting, did Richard ever make any statements to you directly about the killing?
A. No.
Q. Did you ever see what happened to the .45 caliber gun?
A. No.
Q. Ms. Hernand, after you overheard the conversation between Richard and Louis, did you call the police?
A. No.
Q. Ms. Hernand, why didn't you call the police?
A. I didn't.

(NOW THE PROSECUTING ATTORNEY ASKED MAXINE IF SHE COULD IDENTIFY PHOTOS OF RICHARD, ANDY AND LOUIS AS THEY

APPEARED IN MARCH OF 2003, AND SHE RECOGNIZED EACH OF THEM. THEN HE ASKED HER TO POINT OUT RICHARD ROJA IN THE COURTROOM, WHICH SHE DID. SHE ALSO TESTIFIED THAT SHE NEVER SAW HIM WEARING GLASSES. HE CONTINUED:)

Q. Ms. Hernand, there came a time when you became aware that some arrests were made in this case, correct?

A. Yes.

Q. And you had contact with police detectives from the police department; is that true?

A. Yes.

Q. The first time that you talked to the detectives, did you provide them with the information that you have testified to today?

A. Yes.

Q. Ms. Hernand, I'll have you take a look at what's been marked Exhibit Number 165. Do you recognize the shoe that's depicted in that photograph?

A. Yes.

Q. Ms. Hernand, when you look at the shoe that's depicted in photographic Exhibit Number 165, does that appear to be the same type of shoe that Richard Roja had?

A. I don't know, but it's a K-Swiss shoe.

Q. In looking at that shoe, does that appear to be a similar shoe to what Richard Roja was wearing?

A. Yes.

MR. BARR: I don't have any additional questions. Thank you.

THE COURT: Mr. Mill.

CROSS-EXAMINATION
BY MR. MILL:

Q. Ms. Hernand, you, too, have had every single transcript in this case. Every time you have made a statement in this case that has been taken down, you have taken those transcripts home, haven't you?

A. No.

Q. Do you have copies of those transcripts?

A. Yes.

Q. Have you looked at them?

A. Yes.

Q. Have they been provided to you by the State?

A. Yes.

Q. Have you read through them?

A. Yes.

Q. In preparation for your testimony today?

A. Yes.

Q. Ms. Hernand, you saw Richard Roja leave with a group of guys the night of the homicide shooting; is that your testimony?

A. Yes.

Q. Could you tell me what Richard Roja was wearing?

A. No.

Q. Could you tell me what Louis was wearing?

A. No.

Q. Could you tell me what Andy Aria was wearing?

A. No.

Q. Could you tell me what Tony Mo was wearing?

A. No.

Q. Can you tell me if Richard Roja had a gun when he left that night?

A. No.

Q. Did he have the gun that you saw, the .45 caliber?

A. Probably.

Q. You think he did?

A. Probably.

Q. Okay. And you're saying that because you saw that on his person that night, is that why you're saying that?

THE COURT: Hold it. Mr. Mill, before you ask your next question, why don't you let her finish answering the last one.

MR. MILL: I'm sorry. I get excited.

THE COURT: Ask your next question.

Q. Did you see the gun on Mr. Roja with your own eyes, Ms. Hernand?

A. No.

Q. The night that you say Richard Roja left with those guys at the homicide, did you see the gun on him?

A. He always carried it on him.

Q. Did you see the gun on him?

A. No.

Q. You saw this gun on Richard Roja when he had two conversations with Louis; is that your testimony?

A. Yes.

Q. Both those conversations were before the homicide at the car wash; is that your testimony?

A. Yes.

Q. And they were both in the living room?
A. Yes.
Q. At Mary Mungar's apartment?
A. Yes.
Q. While one was on one couch and the other was on the other couch?
A. Yes.
Q. One time Richard actually pulled out that gun, correct?
A. Yes.
Q. Both times Richard talked about that gun, right?
A. Yes.
Q. And you heard both those conversations?
A. Yes.
Q. And you saw it with your own eyes, correct?
A. Yes.
Q. Louis was there, you were there, and Richard was there, correct?
A. Yes.
Q. Mary was not there?
A. No.
Q. Ms. Hernand, during those couple of weeks leading up to the homicide, you saw a lot of people in the Mary Mungar apartment, didn't you?
A. Yes.
Q. You saw Richard there, Andy there, Louis there, right?
A. Yes.
Q. You, yourself, were there?
A. Yes.
Q. Mary was there at times, right?
A. Yes.
Q. Tenise was there?
A. Yes.
Q. That's Richard's sister, right?
A. Yes.
Q. Tony Mo, the son of Mary, was there, right?
A. Yes.
Q. Stephanie was there, right?
A. Yes.
Q. Okay. And Angela, her sister, was there, right?
A. Yes.
Q. Lots of people in and out of that place, right?
A. Yes.
Q. People could wake up in the middle of the night and you'd have to step over people, correct?
A. Yes.

Q. And you slept there with all of them, right?

A. Not all the time.

Q. About two or three times?

A. Yes.

Q. How many people, Ms. Hernand, were in the room when Richard pulled out the gun when you saw it?

A. Only me, Richard and Louis.

Q. How many people, Ms. Hernand, were in the room when you heard Richard talk about that gun the second time?

A. The same people.

Q. And you met Richard about two years before this car wash shooting, right?

A. Yes.

Q. You were about 19 at the time, correct?

A. Yes.

Q. Richard was 13?

A. Yes.

Q. But he told you he was 17?

A. Yes.

Q. And you believed him?

A. Yes.

Q. Ms. Hernand, when you went to the mall with Richard, how would you get there?

A. My friend Priscilla.

Q. Who would drive you guys to the mall?

A. Priscilla.

Q. Who would drive you to go to the movies?

A. Priscilla.

Q. Did Richard ever drive?

A. No.

Q. Because he was under age, right?

A. Yes.

Q. He never told you that he was 13?

A. No.

Q. Now, let me ask you about this wallet cutting up. Ms. Hernand, was Richard cutting up that wallet?

A. No.

Q. Was Richard going to get the scissors?

A. No.

Q. Did Richard get wire cutters?

A. No.

Q. Did Richard just stand there?

A. Yes.

Q. Looking out the window?

A. Yes.

Q. Not even looking towards the table where all that stuff was, was he?

A. No.

Q. Just looking out the window?

A. Yes.

Q. Was he saying, get rid of the stuff, Louis?

A. No.

Q. Was he saying, get the barbecue going, Louis?

A. No.

Q. Just stood there; is that right?

A. Yeah.

Q. Now, Ms. Hernand, you have testified a little bit ago that Richard and Louis were always together. Do you recall that?

A. Yes.

Q. When you were dating Richard, was Louis always there?

A. Yes.

Q. When you started dating uncle Louis, was Richard always there?

A. No.

Q. When you went out on a date with Louis, did Richard go along?

A. No.

Q. In fact, you were only at the Mungar apartment a few times, right?

A. Yes.

Q. Can you tell this jury all the times that you weren't there at the Mungar apartment, was Richard always with his uncle?

A. Yes.

Q. And you knew that because?

A. They were always together.

Q. March 12th, the day of the arrest, let me take you there, okay, Maxine? All right? Police are outside in the parking lot, correct?

A. Yes.

Q. You walk out of the Ranch apartment?

A. Yes.

Q. You walked downstairs onto the asphalt and there's a police officer there, correct?

A. Yes.

Q. They were there getting ready to take down the apartment; you're aware of that?

A. Yes.

Q. And you had just come from the apartment, so you knew who was there, right?

A. Yes.

Q. And you knew Andy was there?

A. Yes.

Q. And you knew Louis was there, right?

A. Yes.

Q. And what you did, Maxine, is that you walked into the police officer downstairs and he asked you where you lived; do you recall that?

A. No.

Q. Did you tell that police officer, I live at 2046?

A. No.

Q. That's my residence?

A. No.

Q. Did the police officer ask you, is anybody else up there?

A. No.

Q. And do you recall telling the officer, Andy's not home?

A. No.

Q. Ms. Hernand, you spent the night at 2046 the night of the car wash homicide, right?

A. Yes.

Q. You didn't arrive there just the next morning after it happened, did you?

A. No.

Q. What you did, Ms. Hernand, is, the first time you talked to Detective Clay, you told him you weren't there that night, didn't you?

A. No.

Q. And you told Detective Clay that you didn't get over to that apartment until ten that morning, didn't you?

A. I don't remember.

Q. Let me ask you, was it March 12th that you were first interviewed by Detective Clay?

A. Yes.

Q. All right. Let me ask you if you remember this give and take with you and him. Detective Clay says, there was a double murder at the car wash.

Your answer: Last Thursday? I was there in the morning before I went to work.

Question: In the morning? Thursday morning you were at the apartment?

Answer: Uh-huh.

Question: Okay, what time did you get up?

Answer: Because I go to work, like, about 11.

MR. BARR: Your Honor, I'm going to object along this line of impeachment. May we approach?

THE COURT: Yes.

(Whereupon, the following proceedings were heard at the bench out of the hearing of the jury:)

MR. BARR: That's exactly what she's testified to.

MR. MILL: No, I just asked her if she spent the night there. She's going to say she spent the night there. She says in the transcript, I didn't spend the night there.

MR. BARR: But your misconstruing what she said. The homicide takes place on Wednesday night before Thursday morning. They're going back a week, and you're talking Thursday. She didn't spend Thursday night there.

MR. MILL: Then it's your job to clear it up.

THE COURT: Let's try to be specific about the dates if she's confused.

MR. MILL: I will do my best.

THE COURT: Thank you.

(Whereupon, the following proceedings occurred in open court in the presence of the jury:)

THE COURT: Go ahead.

MR. MILL: Thank you.

BY MR. MILL:
Q. Ms. Hernand, did you then tell Detective Clay, "I went to visit Louis around ten in the morning. I only stayed there for, like, 10 or 15 minutes because I had to go to work." Did you say that?
A. Yes.
Q. You told Detective Clay that you weren't even there the night of the homicide, didn't you?
A. No.
Q. Did you say that statement that I just read?
A. Yes.
Q. Were you talking about a different day?
A. That was a long time ago. I can't remember that far back.
Q. You don't remember the interview with Detective Clay?
A. No.

Q. Have you gone over it before today, your transcript?

A. No.

Q. Do you recall at page 60 the same issue, whether you spent the night there, telling Detective Clay the following:

Question: Did you stay the night there?

Answer: Uh-uh.

Question: Wednesday night, Thursday morning, where did you sleep?

Answer: I slept at home. I was at home when I got to sleep.

Do you recall that?

A. No.

Q. You don't recall giving that answer to Detective Clay?

A. That was—I don't remember.

Q. Do you recall telling Detective Clay that you weren't even at the Mungar house the night that this homicide occurred?

MR. BARR: Objection. May we approach?

THE COURT: Okay.

(Whereupon, the following proceedings were heard at the bench out of the hearing of the jury:)

MR. BARR: She's talking about the car wash.

MR. MILL: Look, this is my cross-examination. If you want to clear something up, you can. I'm trying not to mislead anybody. But, Mark, you are breaking up my rhythm and I don't appreciate it. I need some time with her and I don't appreciate you coming up to the bench.

THE COURT: I want to make sure we are not getting into that area that I precluded.

MR. BARR: The reason why I approached, in my book I see Andy—

MR. MILL: That's screwed up.

THE COURT: Let's make sure.

MR. BARR: That's the reason why I was asking.

THE COURT: Make sure you guys are on the same page on this if you're going to approach with something.

MR. MILL: This is the second time this is happening. I'm not sure why this is happening.

THE COURT: Do you want to do it during the break.

MR. MILL: No. I'd rather keep going with her.

THE COURT: You need to make sure that he knows what you're talking about.

MR. BARR: Are we on the same transcript?

MR. MILL: Right.

THE COURT: Okay.

(Whereupon, the following proceedings occurred in open court in the presence of the jury:)

THE COURT: Go ahead.

MR. MILL: Thank you.

Q. Now, Maxine, you had indicated that a few days before the homicide Richard told Louis he got the .45 from an uncle in California, correct?

A. Yes.

Q. Now, have you ever told the police that it was actually Louis who said that gun, he got it from California?

A. No.

Q. Did you tell Detective Clay that on March 16th?

A. No.

Q. And, Ms. Hernand, your testimony is that you did not hear directly from Richard what happened at the car wash, right?

A. Yes.

Q. Richard did not speak to you face-to-face, right?

A. Yes.

Q. You overheard it?

A. Yes.

Q. Because he was talking to Louis, right?

A. Yes.

Q. The first time, page 9, that you talked to Detective Clay on March 12th, did you tell him that Richard didn't say anything?

A. Yes.

Q. And then did you go on to say that you might have overheard some things because the guys talk?

A. Yes.

Q. And you made clear to Detective Clay that they always talk in another room, right?

A. Yes.

Q. And that the conversations you would just overhear, correct?

A. Yes.

Q. That you would eavesdrop upon them, right?

A. Yes.

Q. The conversations wouldn't be in the same room, correct?

A. Not all the time.

Q. Well, you told him that they would always go in Mary's bedroom and close the door, right?

A. Yes.

Q. And this was just the guys acting like guys, correct?

A. Yes.

Q. Now, Detective Low isn't here, but you know who he is?

A. Yes.

Q. Did he then come in to talk to you after Detective Clay?

A. He talked to me before Detective Clay.

Q. And do you recall telling him actually you didn't eavesdrop, you talked directly to Andy and Louis and Richard about these things?

A. No.

Q. And on March 16th, four days later, do you recall telling Detective Clay, I didn't eavesdrop. Richard flat out told me these things?

A. No.

Q. You don't recall saying that?

A. No.

Q. And your memory today, then, is that actually you just overheard these conversations, right?

A. Yes.

Q. Did you hear it directly from Richard, or did you overhear it?

A. Overhear.

Q. And on March 12th, I'm referencing the barbecue now, Ms. Hernand, you were asked on March 12th by Detective Clay: Did they return with anything? And do you recall what your answer was?

A. No.

Q. Do you recall telling Detective Clay, they returned with nothing?

A. No, I don't remember.

Q. Page 9. Question: What time did they show up?

Answer by you: Almost 7:00 in the morning.

Question: What did they have?

Answer: They had nothing with them.

Do you recall those questions and your answers?

A. No.

Q. Now, it's your testimony now, Ms. Hernand, that you did spend the night, the night of the car wash shooting, at Mary's, true?

A. Yes.

Q. And that Tony couldn't have gone because Tony was at the apartment, too, right?

A. Yes.

Q. And Tony was with Tenise, right?

A. Yes.

Q. And that you were up all night watching Tony and Tenise inside that apartment?

A. No.

Q. You were asleep, weren't you?

A. Yes.

Q. And you slept from about one a.m. to about six or seven the next morning, correct?

A. Yes.

Q. Maxine, how many times did Richard say that he shot the guy at the car wash?

A. Once.

Q. How many shots?

A. Three.

Q. And you heard that one time?

A. Yes.

Q. Do you recall telling the detective your first time out that you overheard Richard say he shot the guy five times?

A. No.

Q. Do you recall telling Detective Low the same day, Ms. Hernand, that Richard said three or four times?

A. No, I don't remember.

Q. And you testified before the grand jury in September of '03, right?

A. I don't remember.

Q. And do you recall telling the grand jury that you heard Richard say he shot the guy three times?

A. I don't remember.

Q. Is it five? Is it three or four? Or is it three, Maxine?

A. I don't know.

Q. And do you recall the first time out with Detective Clay saying Richard said he shot the girl three times?

A. No.

Q. Do you recall telling the grand jury you overheard Richard say he shot the girl two times?

A. No.

Q. And today, is it your testimony that you overheard him say twice with the female victim?

A. No.

Q. Is it three times?

A. No, I don't remember.

Q. You don't remember how many times Richard said he shot the female victim?

A. No.

Q. In fact, you don't remember how many times he shot the male victim, do you?

A. It was a long time ago. How am I supposed to remember?

Q. Well, you're here providing testimony for the government, aren't you?

A. Yes.

Q. Okay. Has your memory faded since this all happened?

A. No.

Q. Maxine, did you overhear Richard say why he shot the guy?

A. Yes.

Q. Is it your testimony because the guy wouldn't furnish anything other than money and keys?

A. No.

Q. What is your testimony?

A. They were trying to steal a car.

Q. You overheard Richard say he shot the guy because the guy wouldn't turn over the money and keys.

A. Yes.

Q. September of '03, did you tell under oath the grand jury you heard Richard say he shot the guy because the guy was trying to run?

A. Yes.

Q. So is it your testimony today that you overheard Richard say he shot the guy because he was trying to run, because he wanted his wallet and keys, or because he wanted to steal the car?

A. Because he wanted to steal the car and the money and keys.

Q. And Richard said all of that, correct?

A. Yes.

Q. And when you testified this morning, you just said one of them, right?

A. Yes.

Q. And now you're remembering more, correct?

A. Yes.

Q. Because I'm reminding you; is that right?

A. Yes.

Q. Ms. Hernand, do you know how Andy got shot from Richard?

A. No.

Q. Did you overhear Richard say anything about Andy getting shot?

A. Yes.

Q. Did you overhear Richard say that Andy got shot when Andy was trying to block the girl from running?

A. Yes.

Q. And that's what you told Detective Clay on March 16th?

A. Yes.

Q. So that what you overheard was this big guy, Andy, got shot when he was trying to block that female victim from running?

A. He got in the way.

Q. And what you understood was that Richard was saying that he was shooting the girl, shot the girl and the bullet then hit Andy; is that what you heard?

A. Yes.

Q. You never saw Richard with glasses before; is that what you testified to?

A. No.

Q. Did he ever wear contacts?

A. No.

Q. Do you know if those are prescription glasses?

A. No.

Q. He always shaved his head when you knew him, right?

A. Yes.

Q. And he shaved it every couple of days, correct?

A. Yes.

MR. MILL: There is one topic I'd like to discuss with the Court. We can do it at the bench or at a recess.

THE COURT: Does it concern this witness?

MR. MILL: Yes, it does.

THE COURT: Would that finish your questioning?

MR. MILL: That would.

THE COURT: Why don't we have redirect, then we will address it. And then if it's something that we need to have further testimony of this witness, we can always do that also. Okay?

MR. MILL: Yes.

THE COURT: Go ahead, Mr. Barr.

MR. BARR: Thank you, Judge.

REDIRECT EXAMINATION
BY MR. BARR:
Q. Ms. Hernand, the relationship between Louis and Richard, what did you notice about the relationship between the two?
A. They were close.
Q. And in that relationship that you saw between Louis and Richard, did Louis appear to be protective of Richard?
A. Yes.
Q. And you were asked a number of questions about when you first started having contact with the police after the arrest in this case; do you remember that?
A. Yes.
Q. Actually, on March the 12th, the arrest had not yet taken place; is that true, when you were standing outside the apartment?
A. Yeah.
Q. And you became aware that Richard and Andy and Louis were arrested later that day; is that correct?
A. Yes.
Q. The things that you've said from the witness stand about what you overheard Richard say, are you telling that to us because that's what you heard?
A. Yes.
Q. When you tell us about the gun and you talk about the gun that you saw on Richard, are you telling us that because that's what you remember seeing?
A. Yes.
Q. And do you have a specific memory of Richard talking about what kind of gun it was?
A. Yes.
Q. You were asked some questions about conversations, about making a statement to one of the detectives early on about hearing some information about the gun. Do you remember being asked that a couple of minutes ago on cross-examination?
A. Yes.

Q. Do you remember overhearing additional information from Louis about what was going to happen with Richard because of the gun?

A. Yes.

Q. Ms. Hernand, you talked about not being engaged directly in the conversation with Richard Roja when he said that he shot the girl at the car wash then shot the guy; do you remember that?

A. Yes.

Q. Is it your testimony today that you overheard those statements?

A. Yes.

Q. Could you describe for us the manner in which that conversation is taking place?

A. He's saying it to Louis.

Q. Is he saying it in a loud voice so you could overhear?

A. Yes.

Q. Is he saying it in response to any questions that Louis is asking him?

A. No.

Q. You testified earlier that Richard said he shot the girl two times, correct?

A. Yes.

Q. In terms of the shooting of the guy, you were asked a question by Mr. Mill about saying that it was three times, possibly four times, and then three times, and then three times. Do you recall how many times specifically?

A. More than once.

Q. On the early morning when Richard and Louis and Andy came back to the house, where was Tony when they arrived?

A. He was there in the kitchen.

Q. The last time that you saw Tony, where was he?

A. In the kitchen with Tenise.

Q. The last time you saw Tony before you went to sleep that night, where was he?

A. In the kitchen with Tenise.

Q. Ms. Hernand, when you tell us that you heard Richard talking about stealing a car, do you remember what you talked about on cross-examination?

A. Yes.

Q. Did you overhear that in the conversation that he was having with Louis, or was that some other time?

A. In the conversation with Louis.

Q. And was that the only time they talked about it, or was this going on for some period of time?

A. For some period of time.

Q. Could you describe to us who those conversations were between?

A. With Andy, Richard, Louis and Tony.

Q. Did you overhear portions of those conversations?
A. Yes.
Q. You were asked questions about Andy in terms of Andy and the wound that you saw, you were asked some questions by the defense counsel whether you overheard Richard talking about how Andy got shot; do you remember that?
A. Yes.
Q. Is that a conversation that you overheard, or is that something that Richard told you directly?
A. Overheard.
Q. Where was Richard when you overheard the conversation about how Andy got shot?
A. In the living room.
Q. And was Andy standing there at the same time?
A. Yes.
Q. Did you see an injury on Andy at that time?
A. Yes.

THE COURT: Before you go, let me ask the jury if they have any questions of this witness.

(Whereupon, the following proceedings were heard at the bench out of the hearing of the jury:)

THE COURT: See if there's an objection.

MR. MILL: Okay.

MR. BARR: Okay.

THE COURT: How about number two?

MR. MILL: That's okay.

MR. BARR: Okay, no problem.

THE COURT: How about number three? Did she ask Louis a number of questions, I think you can ask if she asked him that, but I think Louis' answer to any questions might be considered hearsay.

MR. MILL: Okay.

THE COURT: I think these are okay. Number four.

MR. MILL: Okay.

MR. BARR: That's fine.

(Whereupon, the following proceedings occurred in open court in the presence of the jury:)

THE COURT: Ms. Hernand, I'm going to now ask you a number of questions that were submitted by the jurors. Do you need any water?

THE WITNESS: No.

THE COURT: The first question, when did you overhear Mr. Roja admit to the killing? Was it the day of the car wash shooting?

THE WITNESS: It was two days later.

THE COURT: Did Richard Roja come back to the apartment at any time during the night before he returned at six a.m. with Louis and Andy? And the following: Is it possible that he came in while you were sleeping on the couch and you would not have awakened?

THE WITNESS: No, he didn't come back.

THE COURT: To the best of your knowledge, they did not?

THE WITNESS: No.

THE COURT: Did you notice anything different with the passenger side of the Kia when you got back in the next morning and went to the Jack-in-the-Box or any time later that day?

THE WITNESS: No.

THE COURT: Did you wonder about the bloody white towel, wallet and keys? Did you ask Louis anything about them?

THE WITNESS: No.

THE COURT: This is to clarify the last question. When Louis opened the towel with the blood on it, did you ask him why there was blood on the towel?

THE WITNESS: No.

THE COURT: Did you at any time ask Louis why he was cutting the keys, or the wallet?

THE WITNESS: No.

THE COURT: Around the date of the shooting, did you know of Louis' relationship with Stephanie?

THE WITNESS: No.

THE COURT: Was Mary present when Louis was cutting up and burning the wallet?

THE WITNESS: She was asleep.

THE COURT: She was asleep in the bedroom?

THE WITNESS: Yes.

THE COURT: Mr. Barr, any follow up questions to any of the questions or answers that were given?

MR. BARR: Yes, I do have a couple of follow-up questions.
Q. Ms. Hernand, did you intend to spend the night there that night?
A. No.
Q. Were you there that night and did you sleep at the house that night because you were waiting for your car?
A. Yes.
Q. And to your knowledge Richard or Louis or Andy didn't come back during the night?
A. No.
Q. When Louis came in with the bloody towel and the wallet, and he put that on the coffee table, was he making statements about where he got them?
A. No.
Q. Had he made statements to you before he started cutting up the wallet?
A. No.
Q. Did you have any knowledge when he was cutting up the wallet as to where the wallet came from?
A. No.

Q. Maxine, why didn't you ask Louis where he got the wallet or where it came from?

A. Because I didn't want to know.

MR. BARR: No further questions. Thank you, Judge.

THE COURT: Any follow-up questions, Mr. Mill?

MR. MILL: Yes.

RECROSS-EXAMINATION
BY MR. MILL:
Q. Louis came in with a bloody towel, right?
A. Yes.
Q. Did you say, Louis, my friend, where did you get that bloody towel?
A. No.
Q. Did you say, Louis, where did that wallet come from?
A. No.
Q. Or the keys?
A. No.

MR. MILL: Nothing further.

(THE NEXT WITNESS CALLED WAS 19-YEAR-OLD TABATHA TACKE, WHO WAS AMY HOPP'S ROOMMATE AT THE GLEN APARTMENTS. SHE RECALLED THAT THE MEN INVOLVED IN THE CAR WASH MURDERS HAD ON SEVERAL OCCASIONS WHISTLED AT BOTH WOMEN FROM THEIR RANCH APARTMENT NEXT DOOR, AND INVITED THE WOMEN TO COME OVER AND "PARTY." SHE DESCRIBED THE LINCOLN CAR AS BEING IN GOOD CONDITION, AND SAID IT HAD OFTEN BEEN PARKED IN FRONT OF AMY'S APARTMENT, NEXT TO THE LOW WALL SEPARATING IT FROM THE RANCH APARTMENTS. SHE WAS FOLLOWED ON THE STAND BY A WOMAN FROM SAFEWAY FOOD STORES WHO EXPLAINED WHAT A SAFEWAY CLUB MEMBER CARD LOOKED LIKE, AND TESTIFIED THAT THE DECEASED MICHAEL FRO HAD A MEMBERSHIP CARD. NEXT CAME HOWARD BIRN, A FORENSIC DOCUMENT EXAMINER FOR THE DEPARTMENT OF PUBLIC SAFETY. AFTER DESCRIBING HIS EDUCATION AND JOB EXPERIENCE, HE WAS ASKED HOW HE HAPPENED TO BE INVOLVED IN THE CAR WASH MURDERS:)

A. Detective Clay from the police department submitted some debris that apparently had been recovered from a burn site. Specifically, there were a couple of pieces of plastic that appeared to be melted, and there was a request made to try and identify what those pieces of plastic might have at one point in time been.

Q. Did you examine those pieces of plastic?

A. I did, yes.

Q. How did you go about conducting an examination of burned pieces of plastic?

A. I first began just, like, looking at the material visually with the unaided eye to see if there was anything that could be deciphered. I was able to see some letters and numerals that appeared to be decipherable. I then used a hand magnifier, which gives me the opportunity to magnify it about five times so that I could more clearly see what was there.

And then the final part of the examination was sticking it under what's called a stereo zoom microscope that allows me to get to about 30 times magnification. With that microscope and light directed down into some of the creases where the material had melted onto itself, I was able to decipher certain text and numerals from that material.

(AFTER A LENGTHY DISCUSSION OF THE BURNED DEBRIS, THE DETECTIVE IDENTIFIED TWO PIECES OF PLASTIC AS BEING A LIBRARY CARD AND A SAFEWAY CLUB MEMBER CARD. HE WAS FOLLOWED ON THE STAND BY A POLICE OFFICER WHO TESTIFIED THAT HE WAS THE ONE WHO RECOVERED THESE PIECES OF PLASTIC CARDS FROM THE BARBEQUE ON MARY MUNGAR'S PATIO. NEXT CAME THE DECEDENT MICHAEL FRO'S MOTHER, DONNA. SHE LAST SAW HER SON ON MARCH 3, 2003, THE DAY BEFORE THE MURDER WHEN HE VISITED HER IN HER HOME. SHE DESCRIBED HIS WALLET AND MENTIONED THAT HE HAD $200 IN IT TO PAY SOME BILLS. SHE ALSO KNEW THAT HE HAD A LOCAL LIBRARY CARD. AT THE CONCLUSION OF HER BRIEF TESTIMONY, THE COURT WAS ADJOURNED UNTIL MONDAY.)

FIFTH DAY, JANUARY 29, 2005
MORNING SESSION

(THE FIRST WITNESS WAS DR. PHILLIP KEE, THE COUNTY'S CHIEF MEDICAL EXAMINER. HE DESCRIBED HIS WORK IN PERFORMING AUTOPSIES AND SAID HE HAS PERFORMED MORE THAN 9,000 AUTOPSIES PERSONALLY. HE IDENTIFIED MICHAEL FRO AS A SUBJECT

EXAMINED BY HIS DEPARTMENT, AND STATED THAT HE HAD THREE GUNSHOT WOUNDS THAT EXITED THROUGH HIS BODY, GIVING HIM SIX BULLET WOUNDS. USING A SERIES OF GRUESOME PHOTOS, HE IDENTIFIED EACH WOUND AND DETERMINED THE SHOTS WERE AT CLOSE RANGE. THEN HE DESCRIBED HIS AUTOPSY FINDINGS FOR AMY HOPP. SHE WAS SHOT TWICE: ONCE AT VERY CLOSE RANGE. BOTH SHOTS EXITED HER BODY, LEAVING FOUR WOUNDS. AS WITH MICHAEL, BOTH WOUNDS WERE CAUSED BY A .45 CALIBER HANDGUN. THE PUBLIC DEFENDER HAD A VERY BRIEF CROSS-EXAMINATION, AND THIS LENGTHY TESTIMONY CONCLUDED IN TIME FOR LUNCH RECESS. WHEREUPON, THE FOLLOWING PROCEEDINGS WERE HELD OUT OF THE PRESENCE OF THE JURY:)

THE COURT: Anything before we come back at 1:30?

MR. MILL: No, thank you.

MR. BARR: There is one thing. I have Marco Hernand. Marco was the young fellow that overheard the statement about jacking the car, and you indicated in your order on the 404(b) that if I could attribute or associate that statement to the defendant, if I could prove it by clear and convincing evidence. I have him coming in this afternoon at 3:00 as well as two officers on that incident. I'd like to be able to present that evidence to the Court for the Court to make a decision concerning whether my evidence appears to be clear and convincing. Could we do that later on this afternoon?

THE COURT: That's fine.

MR: BARR: Otherwise for this afternoon I have Mr. Steve Cam who is coming from California, I have Bill Morr, and I also have an additional witness prior to those witnesses.

THE COURT: Mr. Mill indicated to my judicial assistant that we may be able to wrap this case up this week. Are you that optimistic? MR. BARR: I'm optimistic that we can do that. I might be a little bit behind today but not very much. And all I've got is a series of approximately six witnesses left. Substantial witnesses would be Mary Mungar and Detective Clay. I think those can pretty much be done in a day. I think we can wrap it up this week.

THE COURT: With that thought in mind, maybe if you could start thinking about the jury instructions. I've gotten some from Mr. Mill already. All right?

MR. BARR: Yes, but I think we may be able to complete the evidence presentation this week.

THE COURT: All right. I'm sure the jury will be glad to hear that. All right, we will be at recess.

AFTERNOON SESSION

(THE FIRST WITNESS TO TESTIFY WAS STEVEN CAM FROM CALIFORNIA. HE HAD PREVIOUSLY OWNED THE .45 CALIBER HANDGUN, BUT HAD SOLD IT IN JANUARY, 2003, TO JOSE MERCAD, RICHARD ROJA'S UNCLE. HE IDENTIFIED THE GUN AND ITS MAGAZINE (CLIP) AND SAID HE SOLD IT TO JOSE FOR $300. THE PUBLIC DEFENDER OBJECTED TO THIS GUN BEING INTRODUCED AS EVIDENCE SINCE IT HAD NOT BEEN CONNECTED TO THE CASE, BUT THE JUDGE OVERRULED HIM. SOME INTERESTING TID-BITS EMERGED IN THE CROSS-EXAMINATION BY THE PUBLIC DEFENDER:)

Q. And you're on probation at this time?
A. Yes, I am.
Q. For a drug offense?
A. Yes.
Q. Out of California?
A. Yes.
Q. Is that a felony?
A. Yes.
Q. For how long are you on probation?
A. For three years.
Q. When were you placed on probation?
A. November of '03.
Q. I'm sorry, that would be then after you sold a gun to Mr. Mercad?
A. I was on probation out of Ventura County as well. That was November of '02, I was placed on that probation.
Q. Mr. Barr, the prosecutor, asked you if you had any other felonies and you told him no. Do you recall that a minute ago?
A. He asked me if I had any prior felonies before the January of '03, and I said no.
Q. So November of '03 you've got your drug felony, right?
A. Yes. That was my second one.
Q. What's out of Ventura County?
A. Possession.
Q. Also a felony drug offense?
A. Yes.

Q. So you were on probation when you had this gun, correct?
A. Correct.
Q. How long did you have this gun before you decided to get rid of it?
A. Approximately three months?
Q. Okay. And then you sold it to Jose Mercad?
A. Correct.
Q. Where did that transaction take place?
A. In Jose's garage.
Q. You went to jail after you sold him the gun, correct?
A. Correct.
Q. Were you and Jose involved in a drug trade?
A. Yeah, probably a couple of times.
Q. Did you buy drugs from him?
A. Yes.
Q. Jose dealt with you, a felon, is that correct?
A. Correct, yes.
Q. Did you ever fire the gun?
A. No, I did not.
Q. Did you ever put the magazine into it?
A. Yes, I did.
Q. Do you know if you had to use two hands to fire that weapon?
A. I never fired it.
Q. And you do not know what happened to that weapon; is that right?
A. No, I don't.
Q. Thank you. That's all I have.

THE COURT: Any redirect?

REDIRECT EXAMINATION
BY MR. BARR:
Q. Mr. Cam, you indicated that you now have two felony convictions; is that correct?
A. Yes.
Q. And you're still on probation?
A. Correct.
Q. Mr. Cam, in terms of the weapon, did you note any problems with the weapon?
A. No, I did not.
Q. Anything that would indicate to you that this weapon in any way, shape or form would malfunction?
A. No.

Q. Are you familiar with handguns?

A. Yes, I am.

MR. BARR: I don't have any further questions.

(THE NEXT WITNESS CALLED WAS WILLIAM MORR, A CRIMINALIST WITH THE POLICE DEPARTMENT. AMONG OTHER THINGS HE SPECIALIZED AS A FIREARMS EXAMINER. HE EXPLAINED IN DETAIL HOW A SEMIAUTOMATIC GUN AND A REVOLVER DIFFER IN HOW THE BULLETS ARE FED TO THE CHAMBER AND HOW THEIR CARTRIDGES EJECT. THE PROSECUTOR CONTINUED:)

Q. In terms of the field of firearms identification, Mr. Morr, is there a way to examine shell casings or bullets and link them to a weapon?

A. Yes, sir.

Q. Could you describe to me, first of all, in terms of shell casings, how you go about doing that?

A. We know that each firearm during its manufacture acquires what we call tool marks. These are marks that are placed on the different parts of the firearm from its manufacturing operations. Some of these marks can be transferred to a cartridge case for a bullet. In the case of a cartridge case, we have what we call breach face marks. These are marks that are stamped into the head of the cartridge. We can have chambering marks which are found on the side of the cartridge. When the cartridge expands and is pulled out of the firearm, it scrapes on the inside of the chamber. The ejector, which causes the cartridge case to be thrown out of the firearm, can leave a mark. The firing pin impression, the firing pin, strikes and makes a crater in the cartridge or in the primer. That can also leave markings. These markings are individual to a firearm and can serve to link a cartridge case back to a firearm.

Q. Now, you mentioned that you look for certain identifiable marks on the casing. Why don't you describe to me what a cartridge case is, please.

A. A cartridge case is the housing for a cartridge which is a loaded unit of ammunition that's placed in the firearm. The cartridge case is this brass, sometimes steel, sometimes aluminum box. And in it, all of the other components are placed.

Q. It contains not only the bullet but the case, as well as the primer?

A. And the gunpowder, yes, sir.

Q. And how do you go about examining shell casings? What do you look for?

A. We use an instrument called a comparison microscope, which is two microscopes hooked together so we can place one cartridge case on one stage, another cartridge case on the other stage, and we view them simultaneously. What we're looking for are the marks that I previously described that are left on a cartridge case when it's fired through a particular gun.

(NOW THE CRIMINALIST IDENTIFIED THE SIX SHELL CASINGS FOUND AT THE CRIME SCENE IN A RATHER LENGTHY SEQUENCE. HE EVEN IDENTIFIED THE MANUFACTURER OF THE BULLETS AND THE DATE OF MANUFACTURE, INDICATING WHAT A "SCIENCE" THE BUSINESS OF CRIMINAL INVESTIGATION HAS BECOME. HE TESTIFIED THAT ALL SIX SHELL CASINGS ALSO CAME FROM THE SAME GUN. HE ALSO IDENTIFIED THE BULLETS AND BULLET FRAGMENTS TAKEN FROM THE CRIME SCENE AS BEING FIRED FROM THE SAME .45 CALIBER HANDGUN. THE PUBLIC DEFENDER ON CROSS-EXAMINATION ESTABLISHED THAT THE MAGAZINE CLIP IN QUESTION COULD FIT INTO A VARIETY OF NINE DIFFERENT HANDGUNS. NOW THE PROSECUTOR CALLED HIS NEXT WITNESS, DIANA MOLIN, AN EVIDENCE TECHNICIAN WITH THE LOCAL POLICE DEPARTMENT. SHE EXAMINED THE CRIME SCENE FOR FOOTPRINTS OR SHOE IMPRESSIONS:)

Q. On T.V. sometimes we see technicians trying to preserve shoe impressions by using a plaster cast or something like that. Why didn't you use something like a plaster cast in this case?

A. Shoe impressions, there's different types. You have to take into account what you're collecting that shoe impression off of. As for an example in a door kick, sometimes there's been residue left from dirt on that door, an electrostatic dust lifter is a piece of equipment that uses a piece of mylar which looks a lot like window tinting sheets. You put the sheet over the impression, you put a static charge to it, so the dust adheres to that sheet. Once it's done, that's taken back to the lab and photographed. That's done with dust impressions. Other types of impressions like the floor out in the hallway, they're very smooth, hard floor. We have all left possibly our shoe impressions before we walked in here. One way to do that would be to scan across the floor. It could be done with an electrostatic dust lifter, or it could be done with black powder, with a light dusting of the black powder, and a lift may be done of it a lot like we do with our latent prints.

Q. In terms of the shoe impression that's reflected in the car wash photograph, how is that preserved? Is that a black powder shoe impression, or is that a natural shoe impression, a cast impression, or is that using the electrostatic dust collector?

A. This was taken through photography alone. We have a shoe impression that there had been water there. We have a water residue impression left behind. An impression left in dirt is photographed with light at a slight angle.

Q. What do you mean it's photographed at a slight angle?

A. It's photographed with a slight lighted angle because the impression is a three dimensional print left in dirt. In order to see the impression detail, by giving it side lighting it helps to illuminate the impression in order to do a comparison at a later time. It brings out more detail within the shoe impression.

(DETECTIVE MOLIN SPENT A CONSIDERABLE TIME IDENTIFYING SHOE IMPRESSIONS OBTAINED BY ALL OF THESE METHODS AS THE COURT DAY ENDED. A RECESS WAS CALLED UNTIL THE MORNING, AND THE FOLLOWING PROCEEDINGS WERE HELD OUT OF THE PRESENCE OF THE JURY:)

THE COURT: Mr. Marc Hern, is he here?

MR. BARR: Yes, sir, he's here. Would you like me to call him in?

THE COURT: If you would.

MR. MILL: Your Honor, could I run to the facilities?

THE COURT: Sure.

(Whereupon, there was a pause in the proceedings.)

THE COURT: This is the time set for the Court to conduct a hearing concerning Mr. Marc Hern's potential testimony. Mr. Hern, could you come forward, please. Let's just focus on this narrow piece of testimony rather than go through the whole examination of Mr. Hern, all right?

MR. BARR: Yes, Judge.

THE COURT: Go ahead.

BY MR. BARR:
Q. Sir, would you state your name for the record.
A. Marc Hern.
Q. How old are you?
A. Twenty-one.
Q. Back in March of 2003, did you live in an area of the Ranch Apartments?
A. Yes.
Q. Back on March the 2nd of 2003, were you at the Ranch Apartments?
A. Yes.
Q. And were you there when an incident took place involving other persons at the Ranch Apartments?
A. Yes.
Q. Would you describe for us what took place, please?
A. I came from my apartment and proceeded to walk west towards my friend's apartment that lived in another complex behind me. I noticed there was three

people on top of the balcony up there. Proceeded to keep walking, then I overheard somebody say, "jack that car," and I just ignored them. And then they said it again. I looked up, and then just ignored them.

Then I heard, "Why don't you take that stick out of your ass?" And I turned around and I said, "What?" They said, "Why don't you take that stick out of your ass?" And then I just proceeded to ignore them. And I guess somebody got mad and started to come down. The female that was up on the balcony said, "You better start running, he's going to come down there and shoot you." I said, "yeah, yeah."

Q. How many people were up on the second landing?

A. Three.

Q. Do you know what the apartment number was?

A. 2046.

Q. And you indicated there were three people?

A. Yes.

Q. Males and/or females?

A. Two males and a female.

Q. Now, you indicated as you were walking by, the first statement that you apparently heard was something about jacking a car?

A. Yes.

Q. Were you able to attribute who said or who made that statement?

A. Not by looking, but when I turned around and the person who said, take that stick out of your ass, his voice was different.

Q. You indicated that the female also made some statements; is that correct?

A. Yes.

Q. And after the female made some statements, what did you do?

A. I didn't believe what she was saying at the time until I saw the gentleman coming down the stairs.

Q. And when they began coming down the stairs, who began coming down the stairs?

A. It looked like the person there.

Q. Are you talking about the gentleman seated to my left?

A. Yes.

Q. Do you recognize anyone here in the courtroom as being at the Ranch Apartment complex on March the 2nd, 2003?

A. Yes.

Q. Could you please point him out and briefly describe what he's wearing?

A. He's wearing glasses. He's sitting right there.

MR. BARR: May the record reflect identification.

THE COURT: Yes.

BY MR. BARR:

Q. Now, Mr. Hern, the individual that you've identified in the courtroom today, could you attribute any of the two statements that you have described coming from the second floor balcony to that man?

A. No, not personally I can't.

Q. Let's see if you understand my question. You said one of them said, take that stick out of your ass, and the other one apparently said, jack that car?

A. Uh-huh.

Q. Is that correct?

A. Yes.

Q. After these three, the two males and female, came down the stairs, what did you do?

A. I proceeded to run towards my friend's apartment.

Q. At any time while you were proceeding to run from the area, did you see any of the individuals with a gun?

A. Yes.

Q. Would you describe who had a gun?

A. The gentleman that I pointed out before.

Q. Could you describe to me what he was doing with the gun?

A. He had the gun in his possession. The other male and female followed behind him, and it was pretty much—I ran to the door, and then my friend came out, and then we came back out to the apartment complex, to the parking lot itself because I wanted to see where he was going to go so I could then call somebody. I didn't want to run back into them again.

Q. Now, as you were walking by the second floor apartment and you heard the words about jacking that car, were there any cars in the parking lot, the northern parking lot area of the Ranch Apartments?

A. Yes.

Q. Could you describe any type of vehicles that you observed in that parking lot?

A. A 1980 four-door Caprice with chrome spoked wheels.

Q. From your position on the sidewalk on the north area of the Ranch Apartments could you see if there were any vehicles to the apartment complex directly north?

A. On the other side of the wall?

Q. Yes, sir, the Glen Apartments.

A. You could see vehicles parked there, but I couldn't tell what—

Q. When the individual made the statement about jacking the car, could you tell in what general direction he was looking?

A. No.

Q. After you fled that area and these three individuals ran after you, did you at some point report what happened to the police?

A. Yes.

Q. Would you describe how that came about, please?

A. After I came back from the apartment that I ran to, I found out what direction they went to, I walked to the office, the front office there, and called the cops.

Q. Now, during your dealings with the three individuals, the two males and the female, did either or any of those individuals ever point a gun directly at you?

A. No.

Q. And in terms of the gun that was displayed, could you describe how it appeared, please?

A. Black, small handgun.

Q. Could you tell whether the gun was a semiautomatic or a revolver?

A. It was a semiautomatic.

Q. Were any statements made in reference to the gun that you overheard?

A. Yes.

Q. Could you describe the statements, please?

A. The female proceeded to tell the gentleman to shoot me, to shoot me, and then to give it to her and then it was given—she wanted it to be given to her. Then it was given to the other male, and that male kept making a gesture to come back and forth like he wanted to point it at me, and walked away, like he was confused, he didn't know what to do. That was about it.

Q. Now, in terms of your contact with the police officers, did you describe to the responding police officers what had taken place?

A. Yes.

Q. Were you able to articulate the statements that you overheard while those statements were still fresh in your mind?

A. Yes.

Q. And how soon after this incident was it that you had contact with the police officers?

A. About five minutes afterwards.

Q. After the police officers responded and you provided them with a description of what had occurred, were you subsequently able to identify the suspects?

A. Yes.

Q. How did you go about doing that?

A. They walked me to an area in the complex and then the other officers proceeded to pull each of them out one by one.

Q. Were you able in your description to the responding officer to attribute the statements of each of those individuals to the person that you were able to identify?

A. Yes.

Q. Were you able to describe to the responding officer which one said what?
A. Yes.
Q. While the matter was still fresh in your mind?
A. Yes.
Q. And this afternoon just prior to taking the witness stand to testify in this case, did you have contact with a detective Tom Clay of the police department?
A. Yes.
Q. Did he show you a series of photographs?
A. Yes.
Q. Two groups of six photographs each?
A. Yes.
Q. And did you examine those photographs and attempt to identify the persons reflected in those photographs with respect to the incident that took place at your apartment complex in 2003?
A. Yes.
Q. When you identified the individual in the courtroom here today, is that the individual that said to you, or made the statement about jacking the car?
A. I couldn't tell you.
Q. At least in terms of the two males that were present on that occasion, the individual that you pointed to here today, was he one of the males that were present?
A. Yes.
Q. In terms of the statements that were made, jack that car versus take that stick out of your ass, was it the same male making the statements?
A. No.
Q. Were you able to distinguish between the voices of the two males?
A. Yes.

MR. BARR: I don't believe I have any additional questions of this witness at this time. Thank you.

THE COURT: Mr. Mill.

BY MR. MILL:
Q. When this person said, jack the car, what are the words that you recall exactly?
A. "Why don't you jack that car?"
Q. Was this a male that said it?
A. Yes.
Q. Was the male saying it to you or to his friends?

MR. BARR: Objection. Calls for speculation on the part of the witness.

THE COURT: Well, if he knows he can answer who they were saying it to. This is just an evidentiary hearing.

THE WITNESS: I wasn't looking in the direction, so I don't know if he was saying it to me or looking at his friends saying it.

BY MR. MILL:
Q. When the person said, why don't you jack that car, you didn't see whose mouth that came out of?
A. No.
Q. Did you see if that person was pointing at anything?
A. No.
Q. Was there a white '96 Lincoln around the area?
A. Not by my memory, I couldn't see a Lincoln in that parking lot.

MR. MILL: I have nothing further.

THE COURT: Anything else, Mr. Barr?

Q. Were you able to distinguish between the two voices, the two male voices because of the differing sounds?
A. Yes.
Q. Were you able to attribute one statement dealing with, take that stick out of your ass, versus the other statement which was, why don't you jack that car?
A. Yes. Each male made one of those statements.

MR. BARR: I don't believe I have any additional questions.

THE COURT: Mr. Barr, I didn't know if either counsel are going to ask the witness or if he even knows the time that this was said in relationship—the date that this was said in relationship to the incident in this case. That hasn't been brought out.

MR. BARR: Thank you, Judge.

BY MR. BARR:
Q. Mr. Hern, could you describe to me when this incident took place, the approximate time of day?
A. Three in the afternoon.
Q. What were the lighting conditions like when the statements were made?
A. It was daylight.

Q. When you heard the statement, take that stick out of your ass, did you see the male that made that statement?

A. No.

Q. Were you subsequently able to identify the voices and attribute those voices to the individual males based upon additional statements that they made?

A. Yes.

Q. And were those statements made to you after they chased after you?

A. In the parking lot.

MR. BARR: I have no further questions of this witness at this time. Thank you.

THE COURT: Let me ask him a question, just trying to cut to the chase here. Mr. Hern, did you at some time become aware that there was a shooting at a car wash nearby, two people were killed, did you ever become aware of that?

THE WITNESS: Yes.

THE COURT: This incident that we're talking about today, are you able to say when this occurred in relationship to that shooting?

THE WITNESS: Yes.

THE COURT: When? Was it after it? Was it before it? How many days before it, if you know?

THE WITNESS: Before it.

THE COURT: And do you know how much before it?

THE WITNESS: No.

THE COURT: Was it days? Was it weeks? Was it months? Or do you have any concept of the time?

THE WITNESS: I'd be lying to you if I tried to make an assumption.

THE COURT: That would be bad. We wouldn't want you to lie. I'm just trying to get an idea. But some time after this happened you became aware of what I will refer to as the car wash incident; is that right?

THE WITNESS: Yes.

THE COURT: Was that through the newspapers or just word of mouth?

THE WITNESS: Word of mouth.

THE COURT: All right. Do either counsel have any questions pursuant to the questions I just asked?

MR. MILL: No.

MR. BARR: No, Your Honor.

THE COURT: Thank you. Anything else?

MR. BARR: Not from this witness at this time.

THE COURT: Thank you, Mr. Hern.

(Witness excused.)

THE COURT: Do you want him to wait outside or no?

MR. BARR: Yes, Your Honor, if he could.

MR. BARR: The State will call Officer Bill Scheck.

BY MR. BARR:
Q. As part of your duties as a patrol officer, did you respond to an area of the Ranch Apartments approximately 3:00 in the afternoon on March 2, 2003?
A. Yes.
Q. Would you describe the purpose of your response, please?
A. I received a call of a subject with a gun.
Q. Were you the first officer on scene or the second?
A. The second officer.
Q. Would you describe to me what you observed when you arrived, please?
A. When I arrived, I was towards the north center of the complex and I observed Officer Hors speaking with a subject later identified as the victim, Marc Hern, and another witness at that location.
Q. And in terms of your actions at the scene, did you conduct an interview with the victim?
A. Yes.

Q. Would you describe to me where that interview took place?

A. It would have been like on the sidewalk area between two apartment buildings just south of where we later found the suspects.

Q. In terms of the suspects, could you identify the suspects for me, please?

A. Richard Roja, Tony Mo, and Tenise Roja.

Q. And were those people contacted at the apartment?

A. Right outside.

Q. Would you describe to me what happened, please?

A. Well, myself and Officer Hors went around the corner and saw them standing there, and since there was information about one of them having a gun, we ordered them down at gunpoint, and where Mr. Roja and Mr. Mo were detained in handcuffs.

Q. Now, were you able to identify Mr. Roja?

A. Yes, I was.

Q. And how did you go about identifying him?

A. Obtaining his name and information and description of him, physical characteristics.

Q. Did he have any individual identifying characteristics?

A. Yes, he did.

Q. What did he have?

A. He had a tattoo, I believe it said Roja on his left arm, as indicated in my report.

Q. In terms of your interview with the victim, was the victim able to articulate to you information concerning statements that these individuals had made?

A. Yes, he did.

Q. While he was making those statements to you describing what those individuals had said, were you taking down notes of what he said?

A. Yes, I was.

Q. Were you able to incorporate by way of quotations into your report the actual statements that the witness attributed to those individuals?

A. Yes, I was.

Q. What did the witness tell you with reference to the actual statement, the first quoted statement that he overheard as he walked in the parking lot?

A. The first statement that he heard was, give it to me; give it to me.

Q. Did he describe a statement in reference to jacking a car?

A. Yes, he did.

Q. What did he tell you?

A. He said that he heard the statement, "why don't you jack the car now."

Q. Was that incorporated into your report as quoted information?

A. Yes, sir, it is.

Q. And could you describe to me in terms of your arrival at the scene, what was the approximate time of your arrival?

A. Probably a couple of minutes. I believe it was a hot call, an emergency call, so I believe it was probably a couple of minutes after it was dispatched.

Q. You indicated that you had contact with these individuals, Richard Roja, Tony Mo, and the female; is that correct?

A. That's correct, sir.

Q. And was any type of identification procedure conducted with reference to the victim Mr. Hern?

A. Yes, it was.

Q. Could you describe to me what that was, please?

A. Well, as I recall, again, we had brought them down the stairs and detained them in handcuffs, and I believe Officer Hors stood by with them while I recontacted Mr. Hern around the corner and had him walk around and look at all of the people that we had detained there, and he positively identified as all the parties that were involved.

Q. Was he able to positively identify and attribute the statement that he provided to you to the individual suspects?

A. Yes, most of them.

Q. In terms of, why don't you jack that car now, was he able to attribute who made that statement?

A. Yes, he was.

Q. And who did he indicate to you made that statement?

A. Mr. Roja.

Q. In terms of the statement, give it to me; give it to me, was he able to attribute which of the two males made that statement?

A. Yes.

Q. Who did he ascribe that statement to?

A. Mr. Roja.

Q. Finally, did Mr. Hern describe to you an additional statement concerning a stick?

A. Yes, he did.

Q. And was this also attributed as quoted information in your report?

A. Yes.

Q. What was the direct quote?

A. "Why don't you get that stick out of your ass?" But he wasn't sure who had stated that.

Q. Now, in terms of the identification procedures, did Mr. Hern have any difficulty attributing the two previous statements of, give it to me; give it to me, and, why don't you jack that car now, attributing those statements to Richard Roja?

A. I don't recall him having any difficulty.

Q. And is Richard Roja present in the courtroom today?
A. He's sitting in the blue shirt next to defense counsel, with the glasses.
Q. Did Mr. Hern also describe to you having observed a gun?
A. Yes, he did.
Q. Did he describe to you who was holding the gun?
A. I believe he told me it was Mr. Mo, in his waistband. He said he could see something that looked like a black handgun in the front waistband of Mr. Mo.

MR. BARR: I don't believe I have any additional questions of this witness at this time. Thank you.

THE COURT: Mr. Mill?

BY MR. MILL:
Q. Mo was holding the gun according to Marc Hern?
A. In his waistband.
Q. And not Roja?
A. That's correct.
Q. And did Marc tell you out there at the scene that he saw Richard as he spoke the words, why don't we jack that car?
A. Well, I believe I was asking him which person was saying what when I was speaking with him.
Q. Did he tell you, I only heard the person or persons speaking, rather than see them?
A. I don't recall him saying that because, as indicated in my report, they're particular statements to Mr. Roja, and then in reference to the statement about getting the stick out of your ass, he wasn't sure who said that.
Q. But he was sure Roja said the jack statement?
A. That's correct.

MR. MILL: That's all I have.

THE COURT: Officer Scheck, I have a question. The statement made reference the jacking of the car, did Mr. Hern ever attribute, or were you able to ever attribute that reference to any particular car?

THE WITNESS: No, because Mr. Hern had told me at the time when the statements were being made that he didn't know. He heard that, making the statement, but he didn't know why they were making the statement. He didn't know what they were talking about.

THE COURT: The car that was involved in this incident, the Lincoln Town Car, I don't know if you're aware of it, but that's a white Lincoln Town Car involved, was there any talk about a white Lincoln Town Car as far as you know?

THE WITNESS: No, Your Honor, because this was I believe two days prior, and I don't think there was—

THE COURT: I guess the better question would have been, did you see a white Lincoln Town Car in the vicinity when you did your investigation?

THE WITNESS: Not that I recall. I didn't really become involved in that part of the investigation at the time because nothing really involved a car.

THE COURT: Okay.

THE WITNESS: Other than that statement.

THE COURT: Do either counsel have a question based on my questions?

MR. MILL: No.

THE COURT: Thank you, sir. You can step down.

THE WITNESS: Thank you.

THE COURT: Anything else on this issue, Mr. Barr?

MR. BARR: Yes, Judge. I have one last witness. I call Detective Tom Clay.

THE COURT: Have a seat. Is this going to be very long, this witness?

MR. BARR: No, Your Honor. Brief.

BY MR. BARR:
Q. Detective Clay, as a follow-up today did you have contact with Marc Hern?
A. Yes.
Q. Did you attempt to present to Marc Hern a photo lineup?
A. Yes.
Q. Would you describe to me what you did?
A. I had a photo lineup with six photos containing a picture of Richard Roja and a photo lineup with six photos containing a picture of Tony Mo. I had him look at each lineup individually, and he was not able to identify anyone.

Q. In either of the lineups?
A. That's correct.

MR. BARR: I have no further questions.

MR. MILL: No questions.

THE COURT: Anything else on this issue?

MR. BARR: No, Your Honor.

THE COURT: Given the testimony, the Court finds that there is not clear and convincing evidence to allow the testimony concerning this, why don't you jack that car now, allegedly heard by Marc Hern, that somebody said at the apartment in question. Court's at recess. We will see you at 10:15.

SIXTH DAY, JANUARY 30, 2005
MORNING SESSION

(THE MORNING BEGAN WITH A CONTINUATION OF THE TESTIMONY OF POLICE INVESTIGATOR DIANA MOLIN. SHE SAID SHE WAS UNABLE TO CONNECT ANY OF THE SHOE IMPRESSIONS WITH THE SHOES OF EITHER OF THE ACCUSED PERPETRATORS. THEN SHE DESCRIBED HER EFFORTS TO LIFT LATENT FINGERPRINTS FROM THE LINCOLN TOWN CAR)

Q. In terms of the white Lincoln Town Car, you said you went ahead and processed it for latent prints. Why don't you describe to me what you mean by a latent print?
A. What happens, when our friction ridge on the palms of our hands come in contact with the surface, we deposit a residue perspiration and amino acids in possibly oils that we derive from our skin or hair. It's deposited upon the surface, leaving an outline of the ridge detail of the hands. Also, it could be a foreign substance, maybe oil or some type of foreign substance that comes in contact with the hand. When the hand touches a surface, it leaves an outline of all the ridges. And what we try to do in the latent processing is try to develop those unseen fingerprints that are left behind on a surface. And with the white Lincoln Town Car, being that it's a hard smooth surface, a powder processing was applied to develop those latents.
Q. Based upon your training and experience are there factors involved in a person's ability, for instance, to leave a fingerprint?
A. In leaving a fingerprint behind, there must be some type of a substance, either perspiration oils or some type of foreign substance, that's on those ridges that

will leave a latent print behind. It is possible not to leave a latent print behind being that there is no substance on the hands maybe due to no perspiration, maybe very drying of the hands, maybe peeling of the hands, there's nothing on the surface of the hand to leave behind as an impression when it comes in contact with a surface.

(AFTER FURTHER LENGTHY IDENTIFICATION OF EXHIBITS, DETECTIVE MOLIN STATED THAT THE ONLY LATENT FINGERPRINTS SHE WAS ABLE TO RECOVER BELONGED TO THE TWO MURDER VICTIMS—AMY HOPP AND MICHAEL FRO. THE CROSS-EXAMINATION BY THE PUBLIC DEFENDER CONCERNED EXHIBITS OF MOSTLY PARTIAL FINGERPRINTS THAT WERE MEANINGLESS FOR THE MOST PART, AND THE PROSECUTOR TOOK OVER ON HIS REDIRECT EXAMINATION BUT WASN'T ABLE TO CONNECT ANY OF HER INVESTIGATION TO THE SUSPECTS. NOW THE PROSECUTOR CALLED MARY MUNGAR TO THE STAND. SHE'S THE 42-YEAR-OLD MOTHER OF TONY MO, AND IT WAS IN HER CROWDED APARTMENT THAT RICHARD ROJA STAYED. AFTER INTRODUCTORY REMARKS, THE COUNTY ATTORNEY CONTINUED:)

Q. When had you met Tenise Roja?
A. It was right at the end of October. Probably around Halloween.
Q. How did you come to know Tenise Roja?
A. She was Tony's girlfriend.
Q. How long did you know Tenise before she moved in with you?
A. Just a few days. We'd been talking, and she just gradually started staying there.
Q. Now, I guess I'll use the term moved in, but you said she gradually started to stay there. Can you describe what you mean by that?
A. She didn't move in per se. She would stay there, talk with me, she'd go home to change her clothes, sometimes she would go home, but she stayed with me a lot.
Q. Was there another place that she stayed?
A. At her grandmother's house.
Q. Do you know who she stayed with at that house?
A. I knew her grandmother lived there, and I think her aunt.
Q. And you mentioned that another individual named Clint lived with you. What was Clint's last name?
A. Knight.
Q. How did you know Clint?
A. He used to live at the Ranch apartments, and he got evicted and he asked if he could stay at my house.
Q. And you allowed him to do that?
A. Yes, sir.

Q. How old was Tony when he started dating Tenise?
A. Seventeen.
Q. How old was Tenise at that time?
A. Sixteen.
Q. How did you get along with Tenise Roja?
A. Good.
Q. Now, at some point, did other people start staying at the apartment with you?
A. Later. In February, 2003.
Q. And in February of 2003, who started staying at the apartment with you?
A. Richard Roja came from California.
Q. How did it come to be that Richard Roja started staying with you at the Ranch apartments?
A. He came from California. Tony asked if they could stay there until their mom came from California.
Q. How long did you think it was going to be before Richard and Tenise's mother arrived from California?
A. They said two weeks.
Q. At the time Richard came, how many nights per week was Tenise staying over at your apartment?
A. Most—I mean, all the time.
Q. I want to talk briefly about the apartment. Can you describe, what type of apartment was it?
A. It was a small one bedroom. It had a bedroom with a bathroom in the bedroom, and a dining room, kitchen and front room.
Q. What floor of the apartment complex was it on?
A. On the second floor.
Q. Can you describe what were the sleeping arrangements right before Richard started to stay with you. When there was Tony, Tenise, you and Clint, what were the sleeping arrangements?
A. I'd sleep in my room, Tony and Tenise would sleep on the floor in the front room, and Clint would take the couch.
Q. After Richard started to stay with you in the middle of February, where did he sleep?
A. Just wherever there was room. Tony and Tenise always slept on the floor, and they just slept where there was room.
Q. How did you meet Louis Castell?
A. He came to my house the day before Richard came.
Q. And how were you introduced to Louis?
A. Tony said that's Louis, and that's about it.
Q. Okay. And what relationship did Louis have to Tony or to anybody that you knew?
A. He was Tenise's uncle.

Q. And did Louis start staying with you?

A. Not right away.

Q. After Richard started staying with you or about the time when he first moved in, did you observe what he brought with him when he came to stay at your place?

A. Yes, sir.

Q. Can you describe what he brought with him?

A. Like a duffel bag.

Q. Did you ever have an opportunity to see him unload things out of the duffel bag?

A. Yeah.

Q. And did you ever see him unload a weapon out of the duffel bag?

A. Yes, sir.

Q. When did that happen in relationship to when he first moved in?

A. It was right away. He was talking in the other room.

Q. When you say the other room, which room of the apartment are you talking about?

A. In the bedroom.

Q. Who was in the bedroom with him?

A. Louis.

Q. And where were you?

A. I was in the front room, and I had walked by and looked in and saw him with the gun, with it in his hand.

Q. Was it a handgun?

A. Yes, sir.

Q. Do you know what color it was?

A. Black.

Q. When you saw Richard had this gun, did you say anything to him?

A. No, sir.

Q. Why not?

A. He wasn't, I mean, waving it. He put it back into the bag. I didn't think I needed to say anything.

Q. Were you worried that it might be dangerous to have a gun in the apartment?

A. No.

Q. Did your opinion regarding that ever change?

A. Yes.

Q. Can you tell me why your opinion changed?

A. I was leaning across my bed one time to reach something, and my hand went underneath the blanket and I put my hand right on the gun, on the trigger, and it scared me.

Q. As a result of the incident that you just described, what did you do?

A. I told him to get the guns out of the house. I didn't want that gun in there.

Q. Who did you tell that to?

A. Everybody. I just said it loud, get those guns out of here.

Q. When you say everybody, can you tell me specifically the names of the people that you were talking to?

A. Louis, Richard, Andy and Tony.

Q. Andy is not a name that you have talked about so far in your testimony. Do you know Andy's last name?

A. Aria.

Q. How did you know Andy?

A. He came with Louis.

Q. Now, after you told everyone you wanted the guns out of the house, did you think that that order was obeyed?

A. Yes, sir.

Q. Why did you think that?

A. I didn't see them any more.

Q. Had you seen any other weapons in the apartment before you had kind of issued this get-them-out-of-here order?

A. The shotgun once.

Q. When you say the shotgun, what shotgun are you talking about?

A. I don't know where it came from, but it was a shotgun.

Q. Where did you see that in the house?

A. It was under the couch.

Q. Did you ever find out whose shotgun it was?

A. No.

Q. Who all was in the apartment when you saw the shotgun under the couch?

A. Nobody. I was there by myself. I lifted the couch up, and it was there.

Q. What did you do after you saw it there?

A. I told my son that whoever that is, to get it out of here.

Q. Okay. So as far as you knew, after you had told the kids no more guns in the house, they were all gone?

A. Yes, sir.

Q. At the time on March 3rd and March 4th of 2003, were you employed?

A. Yes, sir.

Q. What were your hours of employment at that time?

A. 7:00 to 3:30.

Q. How would you get to work every morning?

A. A man would give me a ride to work that I worked with.

Q. Why did you have a man giving you a ride to work?

A. I didn't know how to drive, and I didn't have a car.

Q. What time would you wake up in the morning to get ready for work?

A. Between 5:00 and 5:30.

Q. What time would this man come and pick you up?

A. Between 6:15 and 6:30.

Q. Was that a regular schedule every day of the week?

A. Yes, sir.

Q. And what time did you usually come home from work?

A. Between—well, I got off at 3:30, so I'd get home between 4:00 and 4:30.

Q. How would you get home from work?

A. People gave me rides or I'd take the bus.

Q. And what did you do that night when you got home the night of March 3rd?

A. I went in my room and watched the news.

Q. Do you remember what time you went to bed?

A. I normally went between nine and ten.

Q. Were there nights when you went to bed after that time?

A. Yes, sir.

Q. Under what circumstances, what would keep you up where you wouldn't go to bed at your normal time?

A. Doing methamphetamine.

Q. So, during the period of time that we are talking about, did you use drugs?

A. Yes, sir.

Q. And you mentioned methamphetamine. Was there any other drug that you used?

A. Marijuana.

Q. And when you would use the methamphetamine, what would one of the affects be of that?

A. Stay up all night.

Q. And the night before the car wash incident you recall that you did sleep?

A. Yes, sir.

Q. And would that also lead you to believe that you hadn't used any methamphetamine that night?

A. Right.

Q. So you went to bed. Do you recall who was in your apartment when you went to bed that night?

A. I know for sure Tony and Tenise were asleep on the floor, Clint was on one couch, and there was a body on the other couch. I saw some hair sticking out.

Q. After you went to bed between nine and ten or so, did you ever wake up at any time in the evening?

A. Yeah. I got some water.

Q. Do you recall what time that was?

A. No, I don't.

Q. When you got up to get your water, were you able to again observe who was in the apartment sleeping?

A. I saw Tony and Tenise on the floor, and as long as he was home it didn't matter who else was there.

Q. That was kind of your primary focus was whether Tony was home or not?
A. Yes, sir.
Q. Did it appear to be the same people that you had observed when you went to bed?
A. Yes, sir.
Q. So you got your drink of water, you went back to bed. Did you wake up again before you got up for work in the morning?
A. Not that I know of.
Q. Did anything the remainder of that evening cause you to wake up? Did you hear any noises?
A. No. They were always quiet.
Q. Did you wake up for work at your normal time, which I think you have told us is around 5:30?
A. Yes, sir.
Q. Did the person that gives you a ride to work, did he come by at his normal time?
A. Yes, but I had to—I couldn't find my shoes.
Q. So when you were searching for your shoes, where did you look for them?
A. There's bags all over the house, because the kids had all their bags. I said, Tony, where's my shoes? He felt around, found them, and handed them to me.
Q. So during the course of looking for your shoes, you learned that Tony was there?
A. Yes, sir.
Q. And were you able to see who else was there at that time? Well, Clint was on the little couch.
Q. Did you see Richard there?
A. No, sir.
Q. Did you see Andy Aria there?
A. No, sir.
Q. Did you see Louis there?
A. No, sir.
Q. Did you see Stephanie Martin there?
A. No, sir.
Q. After you found your shoes, did you go to work?
A. Yes, sir.
Q. What route did you take?
A. We'd go south on 59th Avenue.
Q. As you went south on 59th Avenue, did you see anything unusual?
A. Yes, sir. I saw some flashing lights which caught my eye. I saw some officers, men in suits, and then I looked over and I saw a body laying there.
Q. Where did you see this body?
A. In the parking lot of the car wash.

Q. And when you saw these things, what did you do?

A. I must have screamed. I felt an ugly feeling. I was scared for the boys.

Q. Why were you scared for the boys?

A. I thought maybe it was one of them.

Q. You thought maybe one of them had gotten hurt?

A. Yes, sir.

Q. What did you do after that?

A. I said, I have to go back, we have to go back, and he turned around and went back.

Q. Why were you concerned that it might be one of the boys? When you say one of the boys, are you talking—

A. I meant Louis, Richard or Andy, because they weren't there.

Q. Why did you think something might have happened to them?

A. Well, people would mess with them, like they'd see them and start throwing gang signs, or whatever. Problems can start like that very easily.

Q. What did you see when you went back there?

A. I saw a body laying there, and I saw a foot sticking out from under the sheet, and I saw the sheet wasn't all the way up and I saw there was blond hair.

Q. When you saw the blond hair, how did you feel?

A. Relieved, but not better.

Q. And where did you go after that?

A. We turned around and went back to work.

Q. Did you go home after your work?

A. Yes, sir.

Q. When you arrived at home, what did you do?

A. I went and watch the news.

Q. And was there anything on the news about what you had seen earlier that day at the car wash?

A. Yes, sir.

Q. Now, when you heard that story, who was all in the apartment at that point?

A. The boys were in the front room; I was in my bedroom.

Q. When you say the boys, who are you talking about?

A. I can't remember everybody. I mean, I know Richard and Louis and Andy were there. I'm not sure about Tony and Tenise.

Q. Did the kids join you in watching the news usually?

A. No.

Q. When the story about the car wash came on, did the other kids in the apartment, did they watch that story?

A. I heard them run towards the T.V.

Q. Did that seem unusual to you?

A. Yeah.

Q. Was there any discussion after the story appeared on T.V. that you were able to hear?
A. A discussion directly to me?
Q. Right.
A. With Louis.
Q. So you had a discussion with Louis. Was it before or after the news story?
A. After.
Q. So you had a conversation with Louis. How did you feel after you had that conversation?
A. Scared.
Q. Did you talk to anyone else about what you talked to Louis about?
A. Yes, sir.
Q. Who was that?
A. Richard.
Q. And what did Richard talk to you about?
A. The car wash.
Q. And who else was present when you had this conversation with Richard?
A. The bedroom door was open, but it was just me and Richard.
Q. Who was in the front room?
A. I know Louis and Andy were. I don't remember if Tony and Tenise were there.
Q. What did Richard tell you about the car wash?
A. I had asked him how he was feeling, and he said he felt bad. I asked him what was he thinking.
Q. What did he tell you?
A. He said that—he was like shocked—in shock.
Q. What was he in shock about?
A. The whole situation. He had told me that when he shot the gun, shot the man, that the water thing from the car wash was running and the blood from the man was coming out and mixing with the water and going down the drain. And that stunned him. It affected him.
Q. What else did he tell you about shooting a man?
A. Just that he was mad. He had a lot of anger.
Q. Did he directly tell you that he had shot the man?
A. Yes, sir.
Q. Did he tell you who had shot the lady?
A. He said he did.
Q. Tell me what he told you about shooting the lady.
A. Well, she had run off screaming, and he said that she was screaming and screaming and he had to shut her up, and he shot her.
Q. Did he tell you anything else?
A. Yeah. Just that he felt bad.

Q. Did he tell you why he felt bad or what caused him to feel bad about it?

A. The whole situation. He had said that he was going through the wallet and found a picture of a kid with a baby.

Q. Did he tell you what he did with that picture?

A. He said he threw it out the window.

Q. After Richard told you these things, what did you do?

A. I was scared. I didn't know what to do.

Q. Did you call the police?

A. No, sir.

Q. Why didn't you call the police and tell them what you had heard?

A. Because I didn't think they would protect us. You know, snitch.

Q. After the car wash incident on the 4th, did things change around your apartment?

A. Yes, sir.

Q. Can you tell me how they changed?

A. Louis and Andy stayed there constantly. We weren't left alone. Somebody was always with either my son or myself. They would pick me up from work every day.

Q. When you say "they," who do you mean?

A. Richard, Andy and Louis.

Q. Was that different than had been done prior to the car wash shooting?

A. Yes, sir.

Q. And after the car wash shooting, was it an every day thing?

A. Yes, sir.

Q. What else changed around your apartment after the car wash shooting?

A. As far as, I mean, we were—I was scared.

Q. Did Louis and Andy spend more time at your apartment before the car wash shooting or after the car wash shooting?

A. After.

Q. Did they actually stay overnight at your apartment after the shooting?

A. Yes, sir.

THE COURT: We will resume again at 1:30, ladies and gentlemen.

(A luncheon recess was taken until 1:30 p.m., after which the following proceedings were heard in the presence of the jury:)

AFTERNOON SESSION
CONTINUING DIRECT EXAMINATION

Q. Ms. Mungar, you've already testified that shortly after the incident at the car wash occurred, that you saw some news coverage of that; is that correct?

A. Yes, sir.

Q. Was there ever a time when on the news coverage that there was a composite drawing shown of the people that were suspected of doing the crime?

A. I saw one.

Q. Where were you when you saw that?

A. At the house.

Q. Who else was in the house with you?

A. I don't remember exactly who. Some of the boys.

Q. Were the people that were there at the house with you, were they right next to you when you saw this?

A. Yes.

Q. When you saw the composite, did any of the people that you were in the room with make any comments about the composite?

A. Yes, sir.

Q. What comments were made and by whom?

A. Tenise.

Q. At the time Tenise made a comment that you heard, was Richard in the room?

A. Yes, sir.

Q. Where was Richard located compared to where you and Tenise were?

A. We were all right there on the couch.

Q. What did Tenise say about the composite?

A. She said it doesn't look like him.

Q. Who was the "him" she was referring to?

A. Richard.

Q. Now, I want to talk about March 12th of 2003. Did you go to work that day?

A. Yes, sir.

Q. And were you contacted at work by someone?

A. Yes, sir.

Q. Who was that?

A. A detective.

Q. What did he say to you?

A. He told me to come straight home.

Q. Did you go straight home?

A. No, sir.

Q. Why not?

A. I was scared.

Q. What were you scared about?

A. I didn't know what was going to happen or what I was going to find when I got there.

Q. And so where did you go instead of going straight home?

A. I went to Tenise's grandmother's house.

Q. Why did you go there?

A. I wanted to see what was going on at my house.

Q. Were you looking for anybody in particular?

A. Just to see if one of the boys were there or Tenise was there.

Q. Okay. And who was there at the grandmother's house?

A. Tenise and Richard.

Q. And did you speak to them about the call that you had received from Detective Forem?

A. I talked to Tenise about it.

Q. After you spoke to Tenise, what did you do?

A. I went home.

Q. When you arrived at your residence, what did you find?

A. As I was coming up the stairs, I saw rubber gloves, and I thought somebody had gotten hurt and I was scared. A uniformed officer came out of nowhere and shoved me outside. And that's where I stayed the rest of the time. The detective was in the house searching. He had a uniformed officer with me outside.

Q. That officer, do you remember where he took you?

A. To the police department.

Q. What happened after that?

A. We sat—I sat in my interrogation room, I guess you would call it, and they questioned me.

Q. What did you think was going to happen at that point?

A. I didn't know. I was scared. I was afraid of the police, and both sides.

Q. What were you afraid was going to happen to you?

A. Retaliation if I said something.

Q. So you were worried about being a snitch?

A. Yes.

Q. So did the officers ask you questions about what you knew about the car wash?

A. Yes, sir.

Q. Did you tell them what you knew?

A. No.

Q. Why didn't you?

A. I didn't want to say anything. I was afraid.

Q. What did you tell the officers about the car wash?

A. That I didn't know anything.

Q. Was that the truth?

A. No.

Q. After you told the officers that, were you allowed to leave?

A. About 1:00 in the morning.

Q. Between March 12th, 2003, and March 30th of 2003, did you ever feel an urge to tell somebody what you knew?

A. I wanted to, but I was afraid.

Q. Why were you afraid?

A. If I snitched, that they would come after me or my son.

Q. That was the reason why you didn't want to tell what happened. Why did you want to tell what happened?

A. I didn't want anybody else to get hurt, and it was the right thing to do.

Q. Did anybody contact you about what you had said?

A. Detective Clay.

Q. And how did Detective Clay contact you?

A. He called me—or I called. I don't remember, but we spoke on the phone.

Q. And after you spoke to him on the phone, did you eventually meet with him?

A. Yes, sir.

Q. Where did you meet with Detective Clay?

A. At a Circle K by my house.

Q. Why didn't you meet at your house?

A. I didn't want anybody to see me getting in the car with him.

Q. So after you met him at the Circle K, where did you go with him?

A. To the police department.

Q. And did you tell Detective Clay what you knew about the car wash murder?

A. Yes, sir.

Q. Did you tell him everything you remembered?

A. Yes, sir.

Q. Ms. Mungar, do you recall at your apartment, did you have a barbecue at that apartment?

A. Yes, sir.

Q. What kind of barbecue was it?

A. Like those little round ones with the round lid, the miniature version of the smokers.

Q. You said you gave a full statement to Detective Clay. You've testified that you used drugs before; is that correct?

A. Yes, sir.

Q. Were you using drugs on either March 3rd or March 4th of 2003?

A. Yes, sir.

Q. What about March 4th, the day of the incident?

A. Yes, sir, I did.

Q. When did you do that?

A. After I had gotten home.

Q. What kind of drugs did you use?

A. Methamphetamine and marijuana.

Q. And were the kids around when you did that?

A. Yes, sir.

Q. Can you given me the names of people you remember being there?

A. Louis, Richard, Andy, Tony and Tenise.

Q. Was that something that happened frequently?

A. Yes, sir.

Q. The people that you've named, were they the people that you usually did drugs with at that time, around that time?

A. Yes, sir.

Q. How would you get the drugs?

A. One of them would bring it.

Q. Did you ever buy drugs yourself?

A. For my own use.

Q. Did you ever go out and procure drugs for the other people?

A. No, sir.

Q. Did they ever provide you with drugs?

A. Yes, sir.

Q. And then you would do the drugs with those people?

A. Yes, sir.

Q. Ms. Mungar, are you currently using drugs?

A. No, sir.

Q. When is the last time that you used drugs of any kind?

A. The end of last year, like November.

Q. At this point I have no further questions, Your Honor.

THE COURT: Mr. Mill.

CROSS-EXAMINATION
BY MR. MILL:

Q. You've been off drugs since November of the year 2004; is that right?

A. Yes, sir.

Q. What was your drug of choice around the time the car wash happened?

A. Marijuana always, but speed when I had it.

Q. And you wouldn't buy drugs for these other kids who were living in your house, would you?

A. I bought my own.

Q. Because when you bought drugs, it was just for you; is that right?

A. Yes.

Q. And you would buy marijuana just for you, right?

A. They would smoke it with me.

Q. So you would buy marijuana and allow these kids to smoke it with you?

A. Yes, sir.

Q. You would buy methamphetamine as well, right?

A. I had bought the methamphetamine for myself.

Q. You would share it with the kids?

A. Not the methamphetamine. Not the speed.

Q. Keep you up for days at a time, wouldn't it, Mary?

A. I didn't have that much money to do it that long.

Q. Did it ever keep you up for days at a time?

A. If I had enough, I would.

Q. And sometimes the people in your house would supply you with your speed, right?

A. Yes, sir.

Q. Would you take it in your nose?

A. We smoked it.

Q. Would you smoke it with the 15-year-old, Richard Roja?

A. Yes, sir.

Q. Would you smoke it with the 16-year-old, Tenise Roja?

A. Yes, sir.

Q. Would you smoke it with your son?

A. Yes, sir.

Q. Would you smoke it with Louis and Andy?

A. Yes, sir.

Q. How old are you now?

A. Forty-two.

Q. And you were 40 at the time?

A. Yes, sir.

Q. And, in fact, that's why they were living with you, so that you could have your access to speed; is that right?

A. I got my own. Theirs was extra.

Q. Well, they brought you some, didn't they?

A. Yeah, but I wouldn't count on it.

Q. There was an unwritten agreement that they could stay there rent free because they would supply you with your dope; is that true?

A. No.

Q. Mary, do you remember me interviewing you last year?

A. Yes, sir.

Q. Have you had a chance to look at that transcript?

A. I didn't study it. I glanced at it.

Q. Was that August 23rd of 2004, Mary?

A. I guess.

Q. Do you remember me asking you this question, Mary? Did any of them pay you rent?

Answer: No.

Was there an understanding that instead of paying you rent, they would supply you with the drugs?

Answer: It was not spoken.

Do you remember saying that?

A. No.

Q. Did you say that to me?

A. Yes, I did.

Q. Question: Just an understanding that was not spoken?

Answer, by you, Mary: Right.

"He," meaning Louis, would give it to me when he had it. He would say, make sure mom's getting high first. Do you recall saying that?

A. Yes.

Q. So there was an unwritten rule that you would get the dope in exchange for them living rent free?

A. No. I mean, if they didn't give it to me, it's not like they couldn't stay there, because they didn't have it all the time.

Q. Did Louis call you "mom"?

A. Yes.

Q. Did everybody call you "mom"?

A. Some of them did.

Q. And would Louis say, make sure that mom's getting high first?

A. Yes, sir.

Q. They wanted to keep you high, right?

A. Yes, sir.

Q. And you would get so high on this speed, that at times you'd stay up the entire night, right?

A. Yes, sir.

Q. At your apartment when Richard came to live with you, that's the time frame that you used to get so high on meth and stay up all night?

A. After they came I did it more.

Q. What methamphetamine did to you, it would make you start to hallucinate?

A. I know what hallucinations are. It never made me hallucinate.

Q. Is it your testimony, Mary, that you saw Richard unpack a gun?

A. Yes, sir. I saw him take it out of the bag and put it back in.

Q. That was right after he started staying at your place?

A. Yes, sir.

Q. Did you go up to him and say, hey, Richard, no guns in my house?

A. No, sir.

Q. Did you get on the phone and call the police?

A. No, sir.

Q. Because you don't trust the police either, do you?

A. I didn't.

Q. Did you say, Richard, this gun has got to be removed from my house?

A. No, sir.

Q. Did you approach him at all on that subject?

A. No, sir.

Q. Did you simply let him take the gun and put it back in his bag?

A. He didn't wave it around. He just had it in his bag.

Q. Had he waved it around, that's the point in time you would have asked him to get it out?

A. Yes, sir.

Q. Or had he waved it around, that's when you would have called the police?

A. I wouldn't have called the police. I would have dealt with it myself.

Q. Just told him to get it out, right?

A. Yes, sir. I would probably see what was bothering him to make him wave it around.

Q. You testified there came a point in time when you told the boys to get the guns out of the house; do you recall that?

A. Yes, sir.

Q. So you were referring to this gun that Richard pulled out, right?

A. Anything that was there.

Q. And you saw Richard's gun, right?

A. I just saw him put it into the bag.

Q. Now, on a typical morning when you had to go to work, Mary, you would be the first one up, right?

A. Yes, sir.

Q. And there would be a lot of people on your floor, on the couches, in the living room, right?

A. It varied.

Q. People could sleep under blankets and you don't know who's who under those blankets?

A. I didn't check beds.

Q. And on any typical morning as you're trying to get out, you'd see heads and hair and shoes and clothes and bags, right?

A. Yes, sir.

Q. And a lot of blankets, true?

A. Yes, sir.

Q. And the first time that you're talked to by the police on March 12th, you tell them that Tony and Tenise were sleeping in your living room, right?

A. Yes, sir.

Q. And on one occasion, Mary, you actually felt a gun that was underneath the blanket; is that true?

A. Yes, sir.

Q. And that was in your living room, right?

A. It was in the bedroom.

Q. So you could actually see it on top?

A. No, it was under a blanket.

Q. And did you take a look at that gun?

A. No. I told them get the guns out of there at that point.

Q. And this was after you saw Richard with a gun?

A. Yes, sir.

Q. I'd like to ask you, who was home at the time you went to sleep the night of the car wash, all right? You've testified that the night you went to sleep, who was home?

A. I can't exactly remember everybody that was there. I know Clint was on the little couch, Tony and Tenise were asleep on the floor, and hair was sticking out of the blanket.

Q. How about Richard, was he there?

A. No.

Q. How about Andy and Louis, were they there?

A. No.

Q. How high were you on March 3rd when you went to bed?

A. I didn't have anything.

Q. The same interview, did you say in your interview with me in August, I thought Richard, Andy and Louis, as far as they—okay, there was Tony and Tenise, and there was Clint; do you recall saying that?

A. Yes, sir.

Q. Then, question: I'm counting now. Six kids?

Answer: Yeah.

Question: And they were all there when you went to bed?

Answer: As far as I know, I don't know if they left before or after I went to bed. But the night before they had all been there, but I don't know what times they left.

Did you say that?

A. Yes, sir.

Q. So who was home the night that you went to bed? Do you know?

A. At one point they all were, but it wasn't a remarkable night. I didn't pay attention when the other boys left. My son was there, and that's all that mattered.

Q. Do you recall this question: Were you pretty high when you went to bed?

Answer: Well, I was loaded. I wasn't on speed.

A. Right.

Q. Question: What were you loaded on? Marijuana?

Answer: We had—yeah.

Do you recall that?

A. Yes, sir. But that was the norm for me.

Q. So when I asked if you were high the night you went to bed, what you meant was you weren't speeding, you were just on marijuana?

A. Right.

Q. And the day that Richard Roja told you that he's responsible for this killing was on March 4, 2003?

A. Yes, sir.

Q. And what you did not do on 3/4 is get on the phone and start calling the police, did you?

A. No, sir.

Q. And what you didn't do is look at Richard and say, my God, young man, I need to take you to the police, did you?

A. No, sir.

Q. Or did you call his mamma?

A. No, sir, I didn't.

Q. Did you call her when you saw the gun in his hands?

A. No.

Q. Did you call her when you smoked speed with him?

A. She wouldn't have been surprised.

Q. Did you not call the police all this time because you were scared or because you don't like police officers?

A. I was afraid to snitch.

(NOW THE PUBLIC DEFENDER REMINDED MARY MUNGAR THAT SHE HAD BEEN CALLED ON MARCH 12TH BY DETECTIVE FOREM TO GIVE HIM A STATEMENT ABOUT WHAT SHE KNEW OF THE CRIME:)

Q. So, Mary, the situation is, you have a confession from Richard Roja to a double homicide in your head at this time, don't you?

A. Yes, sir.

Q. And you're face-to-face with a police officer, aren't you?

A. Yes.

Q. And do you pull him aside and say, I got to tell you something?

A. No, I didn't.

Q. And then Forem told you, didn't he, Mary, that we have had you under surveillance. Do you recall that?

A. I don't remember.

Q. Do you recall him asking you if they could expand the search at your apartment from drugs to the car wash homicide?

A. My house was destroyed.

Q. Do you recall them asking you that?

A. No, sir.

Q. What kind of shoes did Tony wear back then?

A. Tennis shoes.

Q. Did the boys, meaning Louis, Andy and Tony, trade shoes back then?

A. Tony had size 14 feet. They couldn't fit in his shoes.

Q. Did you tell Detective Clay at that time that the boys traded shoes?

A. Not Tony. The other boys switched shoes between themselves.

Q. Did you tell Detective Clay that Richard told you about the blood and water mixing and going down the drain?

A. I did, but I don't remember what day.

Q. And on April 15th you never told Detective Clay that Richard felt bad because he looked at the wallet and saw a child's photo, did you?

A. I don't remember if I told him that day or not.

Q. And the first time that you said that, Ms. Mungar, is when I interviewed you in August, about a year later; is that true?

A. I don't know.

Q. What you've told the police and this jury is that Richard Roja was responsible for that car wash homicide, correct?

A. Yes, sir.

Q. Because he told you he was, right?

A. Among others, yes.

Q. And he told you, and you told the police that your son is not responsible for that car wash homicide, correct?

A. Yes, sir.

Q. Because you were present and saw your son at home that whole night, right?

A. He gave me my shoes in the morning.

Q. 3/12, the first interview with the police, did you say the following: Is there anything I can do to help? Do you recall that?

A. I don't remember. I was out of my mind that day.

Q. Do you recall then on the 15th of April talking to Detective Clay about the car wash and the other crimes that your son is charged with; do you recall that?

A. Yes, sir.

Q. And do you recall telling Detective Clay after you told him everything, I just hope to God this helps my son?

A. I wanted him protected.

Q. Ms. Mungar, what you hope is that your testimony today is going to help your son; is that true?

A. No, sir.

MR. MILL: I have nothing further.

THE COURT: Redirect.

REDIRECT EXAMINATION

Q. Ms. Mungar, the statement that defense attorney asked you about in terms of you hope that it helps your son, first of all, how did you mean, you hope that it helps your son?

A. I wanted him protected.

Q. On the night of March 3rd, you've testified that at some point you got up to get a drink of water?

A. Yes, sir.

Q. Did you see your son when you got up to get that drink?

A. Yes, sir.

Q. When was the next time that you saw your son that evening?

A. In the morning when I told him where's my shoes, and he sat up and got them for me.

Q. Is that why you believe your son was not involved in the car wash shooting?

A. Yes, sir.

Q. And the defense attorney asked you if you believed that Mr. Roja was involved in the car wash shooting based on what he had told you?

A. Yes, sir.

Q. Is that the only reason you think he was involved in the car wash shooting?

A. No, sir.

Q. There are other reasons as well?

A. Someone else told me—

MR. MILL: I move to strike the last answer.

THE COURT: All right, the answer will be stricken.

Q. Ms. Mungar, you testified on cross-examination that when you were going back to your apartment on the 12th after you had been contacted by Detective Forem, that you were afraid because you had heard somebody say they were going to go out running and gunning. What did you take that to mean?

A. That they weren't going to go willingly. They were going to shoot when the police came.

Q. Was that one of the reasons why you were afraid to go back to your apartment?

A. Yes, sir.

Q. Ms. Mungar, what did you think the penalty was for snitching on Louis Castell or Richard Roja or Andy Aria?

A. That he'd kill me or my son.

Q. Did you base that feeling on things that you had heard?

A. Yes, sir.

Q. To the best of your knowledge, has your son been given any deals or made any promises regarding another case in exchange for your testimony here today?

A. No, sir.

COURT: Do any members of the jury have a question of this witness?

(Whereupon, the following proceedings were heard at the bench out of the hearing of the jury:)

THE COURT: I don't believe I can ask this.

MR. MILL: I don't think you can.

THE COURT: I think that you should ask number two to clear this up, because it's Louis that's making the running and gunning statement, not Richard. But one and three I think are objectionable.

(Whereupon, the following proceedings occurred in open court in the presence of the jury:)

THE COURT: The Court, after discussing the submitted questions with counsel, believes that the following questions can be asked. During cross-examination you said something to the effect they were going out running and gunning. Do you recall who said this to you?

THE WITNESS: Louis.

THE COURT: And have threats been directed at you or your son that you've been privy to, that you've heard?

THE WITNESS: Yes, sir.

THE COURT: Beside not being able to sleep, are there any other side effects of methamphetamine? For example, either confusion or delirium, or any other side effects that you've seen that you suffer from when you've taken that in the past?

THE WITNESS: I never had enough money at one time to get that bad.

(NEXT THE PROSECUTOR RECALLED DAVID CRAVE, THE CRIME SCENE INVESTIGATOR, FROM THE PREVIOUS WEEK. HE DISCUSSED HIS ATTEMPTS TO CONNECT FOOTPRINT IMPRESSIONS WITH

ACTUAL FOOTWEAR. IN A VERY LENGTHY DESCRIPTION OF HOW HE PROCEEDS AND WHY HE DOES THINGS, THE RESULTS OF HIS FINDINGS CAN BEST BE SUMMED UP IN THE PUBLIC DEFENDER'S VERY SHORT CROSS-EXAMINATION:)

Q. Did Richard Roja's two K-Swiss shoes make the car wash impressions? Yes, no, or I don't know.
A. I don't know.

MR. MILL: Nothing further.

THE COURT: Any questions by any of the jurors for this witness?

(Whereupon, counsel for the respective parties approached the bench and conferred with the Court out of the hearing of the jury.)

THE COURT: I wonder why neither of you asked this question. Can I ask him these questions?

MR. BARR: No. He can answer this question.

MR. MILL: But you can ask it.

MR. BARR: Sure, you can.

THE COURT: Tell me, he can't answer the size of the shoe?

MR. BARR: No. He was looking at the tread patterns.

THE COURT: Can he explain that, why he's not able to ascertain that? Can he answer who did the Fila shoes belong to? I can ask him that any way. He can say he doesn't know.

MR. MILL: Yes.

THE COURT: Because that seems to be the same question.

MR. BARR: Detective Clay will be able to answer those questions in terms of size.

THE COURT: These are all the same questions. Okay. What about me telling the jury that some of these questions are able to be answered by a later witness at another time?

MR. BARR: That's fine.

MR. MILL: Okay.

(Whereupon, the following proceedings occurred in open court in the presence of the jury:)

THE COURT: Ladies and gentlemen, obviously some of you were thinking alike because a lot of these are duplicate questions. So I'll only ask it one time to this witness. It's obviously the same question. Mr. Crave, do you know the size of any of those shoes that you examined?

THE WITNESS: I did not document any of the sizes. The sizes are kind of irrelevant when you're looking at the one-on-one and the overlay. If there was a different size, the overlay would definitely be bigger or smaller.

THE COURT: I guess the follow-up question to that, are you able to ascertain from the overlay or the pattern what the size of the shoe is?

THE WITNESS: No.

THE COURT: And so was there, or do you know if there was a size 14 shoe in any of the ones that you examined?

THE WITNESS: No.

THE COURT: Did you know who the Fila shoes belonged to?

THE WITNESS: I only know what I was told who they belonged to.

THE COURT: Ladies and gentlemen, some of these questions I have been told by the attorneys are going to be able to be answered by a future witness, and Mr. Crave is not in a position to answer these questions, as he said. All right. Ladies and gentlemen, we will take our evening recess. Let's start at 10:15 tomorrow. I didn't remind you last night about the admonition. I usually do that. I know you're aware of it, but I do just remind the jurors about the admonition I talked about. Thank you. Have a good evening.

(Whereupon, the following proceedings were held out of the presence of the jury:)

THE COURT: In talking to counsel, Detective Clay is going to be the first witness tomorrow?

MR. BARR: That's correct.

THE COURT: And then after him, you have one other witness, or is he your witness?

MR. BARR: I anticipate at least at this time Detective Clay would be my last witness.

THE COURT: I'm just trying to get a handle on jury instructions that I have been working on.

MR. BARR: Excuse me, I do have one other witness to lay the foundation on the one pair of shoes, so I'll be calling him, too.

THE COURT: Okay. Mr. Mill, you're not sure exactly what your case is going to consist of yet, I take it? I'm just trying to get a time. Do you think we will go through tomorrow and then maybe argue on Thursday, or do you think tomorrow is a day that we're going to be arguing? I don't know how long any of that is going to take.

MR. MILL: I think probably Thursday for argument.

THE COURT: Would you agree with that, Mr. Barr?

MR. BARR: Yes.

THE COURT: That will give you a chance for jury instructions. With that in mind, maybe the State is going to make some sort of decisions as far as what the instructions are going to be.

MR. BARR: Yes, sir.

THE COURT: And any additional ones, Mr. Mill, that you want to get based upon I guess the evidence that we've heard so far. I don't know if there's any additional ones, but if there are, let me know.

MR. MILL: Okay. I don't think so. Judge, tomorrow they're going to play this jail tape, the! Redacted? One?

THE COURT: Yes. Have you listened to it?

MR. MILL: No, but they have circled what they're going—I'm too tired to deal with it right now, but there is an objection I would want to make.

THE COURT: When is it going to be? Is it going to be played through Detective Clay?

MR. BARR: Yes. Before I finish my case we will be playing that tape.

THE COURT: I'm just trying to get an idea when Mr. Mill can make his objection to whatever it is. It's not going to be early in the testimony, is it?

MR. BARR: No, Your Honor.

THE COURT: Do you think we can make it before noon tomorrow? I mean, does that give you enough time to—I'm just trying to get a feel for how long Detective Clay is going to be on before you get to that point.

MR. BARR: What time are we coming back in the morning?

THE COURT: 10:15.

MR. BARR: We may get to a point just before noon where we would hear the tape.

THE COURT: Before you get to it, maybe you can give us about ten or fifteen minutes before so that we have a discussion before noon, that we can talk about this outside of the jury's presence.

MR. BARR: Yes, sir.

THE COURT: Okay, we will see you tomorrow.

SEVENTH DAY, JANUARY 31, 2005
MORNING SESSION

(THE FIRST WITNESS CALLED WAS DETECTIVE TOM CLAY OF THE LOCAL POLICE DEPARTMENT. THE PROSECUTOR STARTED OFF WITH HIS USUAL IDENTIFICATION QUESTIONS, DESCRIBING HIS EXPERIENCE AND QUALIFICATIONS. HE STATED AS A HOMICIDE DETECTIVE HE WORKS DEATH INVESTIGATIONS, SUICIDES, OFFICER-INVOLVED SHOOTINGS AND HOMICIDES. HE DESCRIBED THE SCENE OF THE CAR WASH MURDERS WHEN HE ARRIVED AT 4:45 A.M. ON MARCH 4, 2003, AND IDENTIFIED NUMEROUS EXHIBITS THE COUNTY ATTORNEY PRESENTED. DURING THIS VERY LENGTHY EXAMINATION, THE JUDGE INTERRUPTED WITH "WE HAVE GONE

THROUGH THIS ALREADY. LET'S NOT BELABOR IT, PLEASE," AS THE
COUNTY ATTORNEY REHASHED THE AUTOPSY. HE QUICKLY MOVED
TO A NEW AREA OF THE INVESTIGATION:)

Q. Could you describe to us what events occurred on 3/9 please?
A. I received a call from a caller who had only given the first name Ursula about
a Kia.
Q. Is that the first time that a Kia was mentioned in your investigation?
A. Yes, sir.
Q. In terms of the Kia, did you have any additional information as to where to
locate that Kia at that time?
A. No.
Q. Detective, in terms of your significant developments in this investigation, did
some additional significant development occur on March 12th of 2003?
A. Yes.
Q. Could you describe to me, on March the 12th of 2003, were you provided
information from another law enforcement agency on that date reference a
brown Kia?
A. Yes, I was.
Q. Were you provided with the names of Louis Castell and Maxine Hernand and
a license plate number to the vehicle?
A. Yes.
Q. And did you take any actions with respect to that license plate number?
A. Yes.
Q. What did you do?
A. With the license plate, we researched it and ran a registration check.
Q. Were you able to determine the registered owner?
A. Yes.
Q. And then what did you do?
A. I made contact with Rita Brow, who is the manager of the Ranch
Apartments.
Q. What was your purpose in doing that?
A. To speak with her about information I had received.
Q. Did you have contact later that day with law enforcement officers from the
police department reference that vehicle?
A. Yes.
Q. Would you describe to me approximately what time you're dealing with now?
A. On 3/12/03 about 12:30 p.m. I received a page from Sergeant Beck who told
me the Kia had been observed in the parking lot of the Ranch Apartments and
officers were currently out with two or three subjects.
Q. Did you proceed to the area of the Ranch Apartments?
A. Yes.

Q. What time did you get there?

A. 12:45, 12:50.

Q. Would you describe to me what you observed upon arrival, please?

A. Sergeant Anders was there. He had several patrol officers with him. And there were three individuals separated seated in the rear of patrol cars. They weren't handcuffed that I recall. And a couple of them I recall the windows being down. Basically, the subjects were separated and seated in the back of the patrol cars.

Q. Were they three males or males and females?

A. There were two males and a female.

Q. Could you describe to me who those people were, please?

A. They were identified as Maxine Hernand, Richard Roja and Tony Mo.

Q. Did you have any contact with Maxine Hernand at that time?

A. I had brief contact with her.

Q. What was the purpose of making contact with her at that time?

A. To look in the Kia.

Q. Did she agree to allow you to look at the car?

A. Yes.

Q. And did you make contact with Mr. Roja at that time?

A. Yes.

Q. Where was he?

A. He was seated in the back of a patrol car.

Q. What was your purpose for contacting him?

A. Just to see who he was and to determine if anyone else was in the apartment.

Q. Did he identify himself to you?

A. Yes.

Q. Were you able to determine if anyone else was in the apartment?

A. Yes.

Q. Were you provided with a name of the person that was in the apartment?

A. Yes.

Q. What name?

A. He said his sister Tenise was there.

Q. Did he describe anyone else?

A. No.

Q. So what did you do?

A. I was uncomfortable with people being in the apartment, which was the upper level and me on the lower level. I took another detective and we went upstairs to make contact to see who was in the apartment and ask them if they would step out. We also wanted to obtain photographs of the people associated with the Kia.

Q. So you went upstairs. Did you make contact at the apartment?

A. Yes, I did.

Q. Would you describe what happened, please?

A. A female opened the door. She invited us in. As she opened the door, a rather large male individual was stepping out of the bedroom, and he made it a point to close the door behind him.

Q. Were you able to identify the female?

A. Yes.

Q. Who was that?

A. Tenise Roja.

Q. And did she identify herself to you?

A. Yes, she did.

Q. What did you notice when you entered into the apartment?

A. It smelled of burning marijuana. I also noticed as you walk in the door, immediately to your right there was a small entertainment center with a T.V. and there was a crack pipe on the top of it. A small glass pipe.

Q. So then what did you do?

A. I asked them if they would be willing to step down so we could take their pictures. I asked the male subject for his name.

Q. Did he provide you with a name?

A. He provided me with a name, yes, sir.

Q. What name did he provide you?

A. I believe it was like Juan Sot.

Q. Would you describe this individual? You said he was a rather large individual. Would you describe this individual in terms of physical stature, please?

A. Yes. He was about six foot, six foot one, 250, 280 pounds, shaved head, and darker complexion.

Q. With reference to that individual, what did you do?

A. We obtained his photograph and determined he had given us a false name.

Q. You said that you obtained his photograph. Did you ask him to go on down below to be photographed?

A. Yes.

Q. Was he willing?

A. Yes.

Q. What about Tenise Roja, did she accompany you downstairs, too?

A. Yes, she did.

Q. And at some point did you return back up to the apartment?

A. Yes.

Q. Would you explain why?

A. The subject who identified himself as Mr. Sot said he had a wallet in the apartment and that it was Tenise's apartment, so I asked her if we could go up and look for it. She accompanied me back to the apartment where she allowed me go in and do a cursory look around for the wallet.

Q. Why were you in need of locating the wallet?

A. From the subject's—the information he was providing, I felt like he was giving a false name, and it was a way to call his bluff, if you would, to see if there was a wallet with his name that would solve the problem.

Q. And so when you went back upstairs, what happened?

A. Ms. Roja let me go into the apartment. She walked with me. I kind of walked through the living room into the bedroom. There was a closet door in the bedroom that was opened. I kind of glanced looking for a wallet, and I didn't see one and I left.

Q. Did you observe anyone else in the apartment?

A. No.

Q. Would that be the same apartment that Mary Mungar described as being her residence?

A. Yes.

Q. And then what did you do, Detective?

A. Based on what I observed in the apartment, we decided to write a search warrant for the marijuana and drug paraphernalia. So I went to the station. I was going to go to the station to write the warrant, and then we released the subjects after we obtained photographs and identification.

Q. When you say you released the subjects, who are you referring to?

A. Tony Mo, Maxine Hernand, Richard Roja and Mr. Sot, who we misidentified as Jonathan Aria.

Q. Did you return to the apartment that day?

A. Yes.

Q. In the interim period, was that apartment maintained and secured?

A. Yes.

Q. Would you describe how, please?

A. Two detectives and patrol officers remained there. They were outside the apartment.

Q. When you returned to the apartment, could you provide me with the approximate time?

A. I want to say the area of 2:30 roughly.

Q. And would you describe what was happening when you returned?

A. Once I had a warrant signed, I called Sergeant Beck and told him I had a signed warrant which would authorize them to begin the search, and then I immediately drove out there. As I go in, they started yelling at me as they're bringing a subject out of the bedroom.

Q. What did you see?

A. They had a subject that they had handcuffed that they brought out of the bedroom, and we obtained a name from him.

Q. What was the name?

A. He gave us a name, Louis Castell.

Q. Detective, I'll hand you what's been marked and admitted as Exhibit Number 126. Those are the Fila tennis shoes that were located on the patio of 2046 during the execution of a search warrant on March the 12th of 2003.

A. Yes.

Q. First of all in terms of the shoes located on the patio, with respect to the patio of that apartment, could you describe where it exists, please?

A. It's the area labeled balcony. It's probably eight feet long by six or eight feet wide. The Arcadia door, the glass door basically runs the entire length of the balcony.

Q. Did you have an opportunity to contact Maxine Hernand again that day?

A. Yes.

Q. Would you describe to me the circumstances of that contact, please?

A. Detective Low, Detective Forem and I were in the apartment searching when a patrol officer came back, or came upstairs, and told us Maxine Hernand was back at the scene.

Q. And so did you go down and make contact with her?

A. Detective Low and I went down. He talked to her. I kind of stood by.

Q. Was she there by herself at that time?

A. Yes, she was.

Q. Was she driving the Kia?

A. Yes.

Q. With respect to Maxine Hernand, what did she do?

A. She agreed to come to the police station and talk to us in further detail.

Q. What was your intention in having Maxine Hernand go to the station?

A. To speak with her about this case, to determine information she had, and we wanted to have her at the station so we could audio and video record her.

Q. Why didn't you just interview her out there in front of the apartment?

A. Well, when you have witnesses that seem to be reluctant and have indicated they don't want to talk to you there with people around, later on they might deny that they made a statement. And so the purpose of a video or audio interview is to record it and document what they say.

Q. Was Maxine Hernand, then, was she interviewed at length on that day?

A. Yes.

Q. Who conducted the interview?

A. I spoke with her and Detective Low also spoke with her.

Q. Could you describe to us her demeanor back at the police department?

A. She seemed tired, fatigued.

Q. And was this just a 20, 30 minute interview, or what was it?

A. Probably over the course of the evening it was, you know, probably an hour, hour and a half total, with some breaks. She told us things that caused other things to happen, so there was times where she just sat in the interview room alone.

Q. Now, the information that you obtained from Maxine Hernand, was that the first time that you obtained information concerning the actual identity of the persons involved in the car wash shooting?

A. Yes.

Q. And did Maxine Hernand, at that time provide you with a description of what she had overheard at the apartment?

A. Yes.

Q. Would you describe to me in terms of Ms. Hernand, was she cooperative with you at the police station?

A. Yes.

Q. Did she provide you with an address for her future contact with you?

A. Yes.

Q. At the station on that date, then, was she subsequently permitted then to return or leave the station that day?

A. We arranged to take her home, because at that point we needed to keep the Kia.

Q. Did you subsequently conduct a search of the Kia?

A. Yes.

Q. Now, you indicated that there was contact made with Louis Castell on that date; is that correct?

A. Yes, sir.

Q. Could you describe to me, first of all, Louis Castell and basically his physical description, please?

A. He was probably five-ten, five-eleven, 170, 180 pounds, basically a shaved head. There was little hair. That's about it.

Q. I present to you what's been marked Exhibit Number 157. Is that a photograph of Louis Fernando Castell that was taken on or about March the 12th.

MR. MILL: Your Honor, I object to 404.

THE COURT: The objection is overruled.

BY MR. BARR:

Q. Was that photograph taken on or about March the 12th of 2003?

A. Yes.

Q. Detective, with respect to Louis Castell, did you have an opportunity to seize his shoes?

A. Yes.

Q. Detective, did you have contact on that date not only with Louis Castell, but did you also have contact on that date with Andy Aria?

A. Yes.

Q. Did you have contact on that date then with Richard Roja?
A. Yes.
Q. Did you also seize his shoes?
A. Yes.
Q. Finally, did you have contact on that date with Tony Mo?
A. Yes.
Q. Did you seize his shoes?
A. Yes.
Q. Now, while we are on the shoes, could you describe to me the pair of shoes that you seized from Louis Castell?
A. It's a pair of Reebok.
Q. You seized a shoe from Andy Aria on that date as well; is that correct?
A. Yes, sir. It's a dark blue Nike.

THE COURT: We're going to take our noon recess at this time, ladies and gentlemen. Again, we will start up at 1:30.

(Whereupon, the following proceedings were held out of the presence of the jury:)

THE COURT: I've been working on the jury instructions. I have a working model here. I haven't received Mr. Barr's yet, but hopefully that will happen.

MR. BARR: I apologize. I stayed last night and I listed the standard jury instructions and also the statutory, and I didn't bring my printout with me here this morning. But I will have that this afternoon when I come back.

THE COURT: Okay. Mr. Mill has made what has been termed a second motion regarding the jail tapes concerning the inaudible portions. The Court's inclined to listen to the tapes over the noon hour so I can make an intelligent ruling on them hopefully. If you have copies of the tapes that I can look at.

THE COURT: Okay. He can just give them to me. Mr. Mill, you don't have any objection, I take it, to me listening to the tapes?

MR. MILL: No. It's just the one redacted thing.

THE COURT: I take it you're going to finish with Detective Clay, Mr. Barr, and then rest, or do you have another short witness?

MR. BARR: I do have an area that I intend to go into on direct, and that would be the statements of Andy Aria that I want to bring to the Court's attention.

MR. MILL: This is new to me. He's going to bring in statements of Andy? I have been given a lot of materials over the weeks by the State, and this is blindsiding me. I did not know that we were going to go into Andy's statements. I'm hearing it for the first time. The government had told you at that time it was not going to present the statements of Andy Aria. I don't have that with me. I think that's been settled.

THE COURT: Well, I've got all the motions here. I've got your motion here. Let me make sure. Motion included jail calls, Roja police interview, other acts motion, shoe impressions, gun magazine, marijuana and gang reference.

MR. MILL: Let me say, Judge, when I started this trial, I talked to Mr. Barr about if we're going to get into these statements, and I was never told that we were. I was lead to believe Andy Aria's statements were not to be brought in, in this case. That's why we severed this case, at least one of the reasons. If the State wanted to tell me this and give me the transcript and all this, they should have done it before opening statements.

THE COURT: You're not telling me that you never saw the Andy Aria interview transcripts that were attached to all the motions?

MR. MILL: Of course not. I have read the transcript, but the government has lead me to believe, or this is the assumption I'm under, that they could not get into this subject. We are now changing the rules at the very end of this trial and I'm being blind-sided, Your Honor. And if you would like briefing on this, then we need to spend the weekend briefing this.

THE COURT: We are not going to spend the weekend briefing this.

MR. MILL: It's that important.

THE COURT: You're saying that you were told specifically that the State would not present any statements by Andy Aria; is that correct? That just takes a yes or no.

MR. MILL: I don't want to mislead you. That's what I believe I was told, Judge. That was the impression that I was under starting this trial. I'm trying to be candid with you.

THE COURT: What is the prejudice to your client concerning the Andy Aria statements?

MR. MILL: Because now here's the State's closing, even Andy Aria who I have never cross-examined admits to being in that car and participating in this shooting.

Therefore, Maxine and all the other women are telling the truth. They have now corroborated a huge part of their case having never given me the opportunity to get Mr. Andy Aria on the witness stand to impeach him, to ask him about everything he's done, ask him why he lied about his name, why he was hanging out in that apartment, on and on and on. That's what they're doing with this. If I could, Your Honor, it's a real back-handed way to implicate my client in this crime.

THE COURT: So are you saying the solution is to get Mr. Aria up here to take the Fifth, which I believe he'd do with his attorney?

MR. MILL: I'm saying the solution is to exclude whatever the government is trying to do right now.

THE COURT: I'm going to take the lunch hour to research it.

(A luncheon recess was taken until 1:30 p.m., after which the following proceedings were heard outside the presence of the jury:)

AFTERNOON SESSION

THE COURT: First of all, with regards to the proposed tapes which were termed the jail tapes, I've reviewed those, and the Court is not going to preclude the tapes from being played. I don't think that they're inaudible. I was able to hear what was said. Anything else on that subject?

MR. MILL: No.

MR. BARR: Your Honor, the State has prepared copies of the transcripts of the portion that's on the tape and has enough copies to provide to the jurors when the tape is played.

MR. MILL: Objection.

THE COURT: You're objecting to what? To the transcripts?

MR. MILL: Yes.

THE COURT: And what is the basis of that?

MR. MILL: I don't think it's accurate. I don't think it says what the State has typed up it's saying. I'd ask that the jury make that determination without the help from the prosecution on that.

THE COURT: Well, I'm just going to throw out a suggestion. I listened to it. I don't know what you're referring to that's not accurate. If you can be more specific.

MR. MILL: It's the italicized language. I'd like the jury to decide what's being said rather than them reading along with what the State thinks is being said.

THE COURT: Anything else on that?

MR. MILL: No.

THE COURT: I'm going to permit the transcription, but I'm going to tell the jury that this is the State's rendition of what's on the tape. They are the sole judges of the facts, and it's up to them to decide what is actually said on the tape. Next, let's go to the Aria statement. Mr. Mill, I don't see any reason that the Court has to preclude the statements coming in, or at least certain statements. That said, I did look at the transcript of Mr. Aria's statements to Detective Clay. I do have some problems with—at least the case law says they should be clearly inculpatory statements. There are some here, at least I don't know what was going to be introduced, but I marked on here a couple of statements which I think are troublesome to me, and those appear on page 2. And maybe we could deal with this at a later time. Also, I believe that before these can be introduced, at least Mr. Aria has to—we have to have some indication that he does intend to take the Fifth Amendment either by him outside the presence of the jury telling us that—

MR. BARR: I agree, Your Honor. We took the liberty of contacting Mr. Aria's attorney and asked him if his client would be willing to take the stand and testify in this matter if we called him. He said he would not. He said his client would invoke his Fifth Amendment privilege to remain silent if he was called to testify.

THE COURT: Mr. Mill, just on that aspect of the unavailability, not conceding any other part of your motion, do you believe that's sufficient at least to show unavailability?

MR. MILL: No.

THE COURT: Are you requesting that Mr. Aria be brought to court and he take the Fifth?

MR. MILL: Yes. I would like the State to ask him these questions and let him take the Fifth.

THE COURT: Which questions?

MR. MILL: The questions that are in the subject matter of the transcript: Is it true that you did that? Is it true that you said that?

THE COURT: We are not going to do that. If he takes the Fifth, I'm not going to waste the Court's time with asking him all those questions. We can have him come, but it will be outside the presence of the jury. If he tells me he intends to take the Fifth Amendment, then that will be the end of it unless you can show me some case law or some rule that I need to elicit all those other questions.

MR. MILL: I'd love to have the time to do that, Judge, but I don't. May I make a record on your ruling?

THE COURT: My judicial assistant has indicated Mr. Aria can be up here tomorrow morning. We can have him brought up here.

MR. MILL: That's fine, however we need to do it. But we need to see if he will talk about this.

THE COURT: What do you mean talk about it? If he says—I hate to repeat myself, but if he says he doesn't want to, then he wants to invoke his Fifth Amendment right, to me that's him saying he doesn't want to talk about it.

MR. MILL: Okay.

THE COURT: And what I'm inclined to do, I'm trying to get a idea how we're doing on time. How much more time do you have with Detective Clay, Mr. Barr, would you say?

MR. BARR: Judge, I believe we will be done by 2:15.

THE COURT: Mr. Mill, are you going to spend a lot of time with Detective Clay?

MR. MILL: Judge, I don't know. I wasn't planning on it. I had about 20 minutes, 15 or 20 minutes worth of material.

THE COURT: Here's what I'm getting at, that I would give you until tomorrow morning before we have Detective Clay testify on the Aria statements, so you'll have an opportunity to make a response. And what we will do is have him complete his testimony, and then subject to recall, then after you're done with him, then the State is going to rest, then you can put on any witnesses today that you want to put on.

MR. MILL: Okay. That's fine. We can proceed that way, but I do need to make a record on what you're doing, if I could.

THE COURT: Yes, sir. That's why I'm giving you until tomorrow to do that. You can make your record now, then we won't bother with it tomorrow. So you tell me what you want to do. I was giving you until tomorrow. You said you didn't have an opportunity to research it, but if you want to make your record now and not make it tomorrow, then so be it.

MR. MILL: We can proceed that way and do it tomorrow. That's fine. I will put it in writing and give it to you. But at this juncture I'm moving for at least a week's continuance of this trial.

THE COURT: That's denied.

MR. MILL: And the opportunity to research factually any impeaching material that I might have on Mr. Aria who is now an out-of-court declarant. And at this time I'm entitled to do that, at least I think I am, because now I need to impeach the credibility of a person who is not even speaking in court. I need some time to do that, and I need to get my investigator working on that. You're giving me overnight. That's all I have.

THE COURT: It's not like this just came up. This was out there, these statements. The case law was out there, too, and the Rule was out there. I don't know what transpired between you and the State, and all I know is what the Rules says, what the cases say, and what I'm reading from in the transcript at this juncture.

MR. MILL: It did just come up. For the State to take this case right to the very end and then risk injecting error in it I think is appalling. But you made your ruling and I will supplement my record with constitutional references for tomorrow.

THE COURT: Okay. Well, you can see if you can come up with some compromise on this. But I will say that on page 2 there are certain aspects of this where Mr. Aria is referring to the defendant. I don't want to keep the jury waiting, but I will discuss it in detail after we finish the testimony today. We will go over it very specifically, because I want to make a specific ruling as to what Detective Clay can and cannot testify to. Why don't we bring the jury in and we will get started.

(NOW THE DETECTIVE IDENTIFIED THE SHOE SIZES OF THE VARIOUS ALLEGED PERPETRATORS. ARIA'S NIKE SHOES WERE SIZE 13, LOUIS CASTELL'S REEBOK SHOES WERE SIZE 10, TONY MO'S SHOES WERE SIZE 13, AND RICHARD ROJA'S K-SWISS SHOE SIZE WASN'T

DESCRIBED FOR SOME UNKNOWN REASON. NOW THE COUNTY ATTORNEY SWITCHED DIRECTION:)

Q. In terms of your continued investigation, did you have contact on March the 15th with Stephanie Martin?

A. Yes.

Q. What were the circumstances surrounding your contact with her on that date?

A. Received some information that she might have been in the car on the night of the car wash murder, and so she was picked up to talk to.

Q. And would you describe her demeanor for us on March 15th of 2003.

A. Uncooperative.

Q. In terms of the interview, was she interviewed?

A. Yes.

Q. The approximate length of the interview?

A. Probably an hour, hour and a half.

Q. In terms of the information that you obtained, did she deny being in the car?

MR. MILL: Objection. Hearsay; impeaching his own witness.

THE COURT: Sustained.

BY MR. BARR:

Q. Let me put it this way, Detective. Did she admit to being in the car?

MR. MILL: The same objection.

THE COURT: The same ruling.

BY MR. BARR:

Q. On March 15th did you confront her about her statements about the car?

A. Yes.

Q. Did she continue to be uncooperative?

MR. MILL: Hearsay objection.

THE COURT: That goes to demeanor, being uncooperative. He can answer that.

THE WITNESS: Yes.

BY MR. BARR:

Q. Now, Detective, after you completed the 3/15 interview with Stephanie Martin, did you have an opportunity to conduct a reinterview of Maxine Hernand?

A. Yes.

Q. And when was that reinterview conducted?

A. On 3/15.

Q. What was the purpose of conducting a reinterview of Maxine Hernand?

A. To see if she had any additional information we hadn't discussed in the first interview, and we were going to release her car back to her.

Q. Was she cooperative?

A. Yes.

Q. Did she provide additional information to you?

A. Yes.

Q. Was Louis Castell in custody at that time?

A. Yes.

Q. Detective, you indicated that a reinterview of Maxine Hernand was done. You indicated your purpose was to ask her about any other areas. Were you able to ask her about those other areas that you were referring to?

MR. MILL: Objection. Hearsay.

THE COURT: Well, he can answer that question. He hasn't asked a question that would require a hearsay answer yet. He can answer the question as far as were you able to ask her.

THE WITNESS: Yes.

BY MR. BARR:

Q. After Maxine Hernand's interview, Detective, did you take any actions?

A. I contacted detectives and directed them to Mary Mungar's apartment to check the barbecue grill.

Q. Detective, is that the first time that you had information concerning a barbecue?

A. Yes.

Q. Detective, in terms of the barbecue, did you receive the property, the materials that were seized from the barbecue?

A. I checked them out of property.

Q. Detective, on March the 23rd did you have an opportunity to reinterview Stephanie Martin?

A. Yes.

Q. Would you describe her demeanor for us on March 23rd?
A. She was more cooperative, more talkative.
Q. As you conducted the interview with Stephanie Martin on March 23rd, was she able to provide you additional detailed information?

MR. MILL: Objection. Calls for hearsay.

THE COURT: He can answer whether she was. But the specifics, that remains for the next ruling. So you can answer that question.

THE WITNESS: Yes.

BY MR. BARR:

Q. Was she able to answer or provide to you specific details of events which had occurred on March 12th—pardon me.

MR. MILL: Objection. Hearsay.

THE COURT: I'm going to sustain the objection.

BY MR. BARR:

Q. Detective, at that interview with Stephanie Martin, was she able to describe to you the location where the car was parked?

MR. MILL: Hearsay. Ask that we be able to approach the bench.

THE COURT: I'm going to sustain the objection. Let's ask the next question.

BY MR. BARR:

Q. Detective, you were in the courtroom the other day when Ms. Martin was asked a question about a Dan Ray interview. Do you remember that, about a statement she apparently made during the course of that interview?
A. Yes.
Q. About where they parked; is that correct?
A. Yes.
Q. Did she ever tell you during the course of your interviews with her the location of where the car was parked?

MR. MILL: Objection, hearsay, to this witness.

THE COURT: Why don't counsel approach, please.

(Whereupon, the following proceedings were heard at the bench out of the hearing of the jury:)

THE COURT: You're referring to when she talked about the parking? I can't remember if she said she didn't remember.

MR. BARR: She was impeached by Mr. Mill about a statement that she made in a Dan Ray interview where she says, I'm not sure if we were down in the south area down on the street or the parking lot. She's never said that to the detective or us before. And this is a prior consistent statement.

THE COURT: What's the objection?

MR. MILL: It is a prior consistent statement which is out-of-court and is hearsay. It's hearsay. Anything that Ms. Martin may have said in court that there's an inconsistent prior statement about and she was given the opportunity to explain it, which I usually did, then we can bring up the inconsistent prior out-of-court statement to impeach her. Otherwise, we can't. Mr. Barr is not going through the right steps. He's trying to relive her hearsay through this detective.

MR. BARR: That's inaccurate. What Mr. Mill did was try to insinuate that Ms. Martin was now changing her stories. And a prior consistent statement does come in if it's prior to the motive to lie, and that's what he was doing was suggesting that she was lying here on the witness stand the other day. The prior consistent statement should come in.

THE COURT: Okay.

(Whereupon, the following proceedings occurred in open court in the presence of the jury:)

THE COURT: I'm going to overrule the objection. Ask your next question.

BY MR. BARR:

Q. Detective, did Stephanie Martin ever describe to you that they parked on the street or parked anywhere else other than the business to the north?
A. No.
Q. On March 24 of 2003 did you take a trip out of state?

A. Yes.
Q. What did you do?
A. Flew to Santa Anna, California.
Q. What was your purpose in doing that?
A. To contact Jose Mercad.
Q. Were you successful in doing that at that time?
A. No.
Q. And what was your purpose in going to contact Jose Mercad?

MR. MILL: Objection. Calls for hearsay. It's going to call for hearsay.

THE COURT: What his purpose is?

MR. MILL: It will.

THE COURT: Can counsel approach the bench.

(Whereupon, the following proceedings were heard at the bench out of the hearing of the jury:)

THE COURT: What is his answer going to be to this question?

MR. BARR: The answer is going to be he's trying to track down the origin of the gun.

THE COURT: How is that a hearsay?

MR. MILL: Is he going to say that Sandra told me on the phone or Jose told me on the phone before that Richard stole my gun.

MR. BARR: That wasn't my intention. My intention was—

THE COURT: I just want to make sure he doesn't answer it the other way. His purpose was to track down the gun, that's the answer. Okay.

(Whereupon, the folowing proceedings occurred in open court in the presence of the jury:)

BY MR. BARR:

Q. Detective, was your purpose in going to Santa Anna on that occasion, was it your purpose to track down the origin of the gun?
A. Yes.

Q. Now, Detective, we talked a little bit earlier about the barbecue. What did you do with the materials that were submitted from the barbecue?

A. They were submitted to the Department of Public Safety Crime Lab so they could analyze them and see what they could find.

(NOW DETECTIVE CLAY DESCRIBED THE CHARRED PIECES RECOVERED FROM THE BARBECUE PIT AND BASICALLY REPEATED WHAT MR. BIRN HAD TESTIFIED TO PREVIOUSLY, THAT THEY WERE PART OF A LIBRARY CARD AND A SAFEWAY CLUB CARD. HE ALSO REPEATED PREVIOUS TESTIMONY ABOUT THE SHELL CASINGS, THE MAGAZINE (CLIP) AND THE FACT THAT HE VISITED MR. DANIEL HENDERS' MOBILE HOME TO SEE FOR HIMSELF THAT HE HAD AN UNOBSTRUCTED VIEW OF THE CAR WASH DURING THE MURDER NIGHT. THEN THE FIESTY PUBLIC DEFENDER CROSS-EXAMINED DETECTIVE CLAY:)

Q. The Reebok shoes were not traced to any of the impressions at the car wash, were they?

A. No, they weren't.

Q. The Fila shoes were not traced to any of the impressions, right?

A. The Fila had impressions from the car wash that were similar.

Q. But not identified, correct?

A. No.

Q. The other pairs that you seized were not identified either to this car wash scene, correct?

A. That's correct.

Q. The gun that was used to kill Amy Hopp and Michael Fro was never found, right?

A. That's correct.

Q. Mr. Barr asked you if you went to California to talk to Stephen Cam about tracing the origins of the gun; is that true?

A. He asked if I talked to Cam, yes.

Q. Did you ever find the origin of the gun?

A. Yes.

Q. Do you know if the Sig Sauer was used in this case?

A. Without a weapon, I cannot say positively which weapon was used.

Q. How many weapons did Mr. Morr tell you could have been used in this case?

A. I believe there were nine on the list.

Q. Did you take any photographs of any other of the nine, other than the one that you showed in court? You took a description down in your police report of Richard Roja the day of his arrest; isn't that true?

A. Yes.

Q. Five foot nine?

A. Yes.

Q. 170 pounds?

A. Yes.

Q. Age 15?

A. Yes.

Q. Who did the Fila shoes belong to that are in evidence?

A. Someone that wears a size ten.

Q. Do you have a person in mind to connect to the Fila shoes?

A. Yeah.

Q. Do you know who wore those shoes?

A. Positively, no.

Q. You found them at Ranch along with a whole bunch of other shoes?

A. I found them in Mary Mungar's apartment.

Q. How far is Ms. Evangelina Ballester's view as she described it to the scene of the shooting?

A. Probably 120 feet.

Q. How far is Mr. Henders' view from the trailer to the scene of the shooting?

A. An estimate, I didn't measure it, it's probably about 350, 400 feet.

Q. And who had the superior view?

A. I won't say either one had a superior view. I think from the different position each one had a view.

Q. Well, Ms. Ballester's view would be about two-thirds closer than Mr. Hender's?

A. She would be closer and at a different angle.

Q. Did you have any doubt that Ms. Ballester's description was accurate, Detective?

A. I believe her description was accurate for what she recollected she saw.

Q. Did you show her a photographic lineup?

A. Yes.

Q. Did you show her a photographic lineup with Richard Roja's picture in it?

A. Yes.

Q. When she got to Richard Roja's photograph, did she say he was the shooter?

A. She didn't identify him in any manner.

Q. Didn't identify him in any manner. Did the fire department come on-scene?

A. Based on reports, they did, yes.

Q. And does your record list then the people who entered and exited the crime scene?

A. Yes.

Q. Does it include six members of the fire department as getting on the scene?

A. I don't remember the number, but a number of people.

Q. Did Technician Diana Molin eliminate those?

A. Not from what I have seen.

Q. Did you ask her to go to eliminate those shoe prints?
A. At the time I thought it was covered, yes.
Q. But it was not?
A. It doesn't appear to be.
Q. Did this man, Richard Roja, give you blood when you wanted it?
A. I'm not sure how to answer that.
Q. To your knowledge did he ever resist that?
A. I believe they were taken under virtue of a warrant, and he didn't resist the warrant, no.
Q. Did you talk to Richard Roja about what happened at the car wash?

MR. BARR: Objection, Your Honor. Calls for hearsay.

MR. MILL: Calls for yes or no.

THE COURT: He can answer if he talked.

THE WITNESS: Yes.

BY MR. MILL:

Q. Was that on March 12th?
A. Yes.
Q. Did Richard Roja cooperate with you in every way?
A. Yes.
Q. Did Richard Roja give you a false name?
A. No.
Q. Did he answer all your questions?
A. Yes.
Q. And Andy Aria told you he was Mr. Sot, right?
A. Initially, yes.
Q. And Uncle Louis Castell gave you a name that you didn't think was quite right; isn't that true?
A. That was initially, it was something that didn't quite click. But once we got on the same page, we figured it out.
Q. When you got out to Ranch on March 12th, was Richard Roja running from the scene?
A. When I got there he was in the back of a patrol car.
Q. Was he sitting quietly?
A. Yes.
Q. Was he cooperating with you folks?
A. Somewhat.

Q. Was he yelling, screaming, saying, no, I'm not going to answer your questions?
A. No.
Q. He just sat there, right?
A. Yes.
Q. And then you let him go, right?
A. That's correct.
Q. And later on when the police came to arrest him, did he take off running?
A. No.
Q. Did he cooperate?
A. Yes.
Q. Did he hide in a closet?
A. Well, I was outside the house walking away.
Q. But when you guys were outside of Ranch securing it for the time that it took you to get that warrant, one guy was still up there, right?
A. Yes, sir.
Q. You didn't know that, right?
A. That's correct.
Q. And that was Louis Castell, correct?
A. Yes, sir.
Q. And for hours he hid in a closet, right?
A. I don't know if he was in the closet the entire time. He was in the apartment.
Q. And then you have to serve the search warrant, open the closet and, surprise. There he is, correct?
A. He was found in a closet, yes.
Q. Was he hiding behind clothing?
A. Yes, he was.
Q. Detective Clay, there's been a lot of testimony concerning Amy Hopp's apartment as it related to Mary Mungar's. You have been present for that, correct?
A. Yes, sir.
Q. In your investigation, have you come across any proof that Richard Roja was staking out Amy Hopp?

MR. BARR: Objection.

THE COURT: He can answer.

THE WITNESS: I guess it depends on what you mean by staking out.

BY MR. MILL:

Q. Did you see him, did you come across any witnesses that indicated that he was watching her?

A. That he knew her and might have talked to her.

Q. Okay. That he wanted her dead?

A. If he recognized her at the car wash, he may well have wanted her dead.

Q. And that's a theory on the police department's part, correct?

A. It's a good possibility, yes, sir.

Q. And it's nothing but a theory; isn't that correct?

A. I guess that's for the jury to decide.

Q. Do you have any proof of that?

A. The testimony of Tabatha Tack, Amy's roommate.

Q. Tabatha Tack, who said that anybody who walked by the apartment who was female got whistled at, right?

A. Yes.

Q. You knew, Detective, when you got to that crime scene that somebody had probably been inside that Lincoln, correct?

A. Yes.

Q. And you knew that because the keys were gone, a wallet was gone, and the window was shot out, right?

A. Yes.

Q. And you knew that there was a possibility that someone may have touched the inside of that car, correct?

A. Yes.

Q. The person who touched the inside of this car may be responsible in one way or another for the deaths of two people, correct?

A. Yes.

Q. And you did not direct Diana Molin to do a sophisticated method of fingerprinting on the inside of that car, correct?

A. We don't super glue cars.

Q. And the reason you don't super glue cars is because you might have to do some damage to the car, right?

A. There's no "might" about it. The prints off a seat, when you look—when I get into a car, I don't touch the seat. Most of the people touch the dash, the steering wheel, the windows. It's not a likely area that a suspect would necessarily leave a print.

Q. So it is then your assumption that the person didn't leave a fingerprint, and that caused you to not request the super glue test?

A. It's my belief there were much better areas in the car that we could get prints from than to destroy the car and to do super glue.

Q. Is it also your belief that you should do everything humanly possible if there were fingerprints inside that car?

A. Within reason.

Q. Were the seats taken out of the car so the rest of the car wouldn't be ruined?

A. No.

Q. Now, it's your belief, Detective, that that magazine that was found in the middle bedroom was used in this case; is that correct?

A. No.

Q. You just don't know one way or another, do you?

A. I know that magazine from Mr. Morr's testing came from a Colt. A Colt is also a weapon on the short list of weapons that could have fired it, and that the gun that belongs to that magazine or the gun missing from California could have, either one, been the weapon.

Q. Detective, how did Andy Aria's wallet get into the middle bedroom where that magazine was?

A. I have no idea. He was friends with Louis and Richard. He may have stayed there.

Q. When you first got those K-Swiss, Richard Roja's shoes, you thought there was blood on the heels?

A. Yes.

Q. You submitted them to he lab for that purpose?

A. That's correct.

Q. No blood, correct?

A. That's correct.

Q. That blue barrel that was next to the wall, did you check that for blood?

A. I visually checked it for blood, yes.

Q. Was any presumptive test done on that barrel?

A. There was nothing visible to test.

Q. Was the barrel fingerprinted for fingerprints?

A. No. It's a very rough surface.

Q. Did you attempt to have the barrel fingerprinted?

A. No.

Q. Was there any blood on the wall that divided the auto business from the car wash?

A. No, there wasn't.

Q. There was a blood spot in the car wash bay E that was not collected; is that correct?

A. Yes, in one of the bays there was some blood not collected, that's correct.

Q. Did you ever tell the technicians not to collect that spot?

A. No.

Q. Do you know why it wasn't picked up?

A. I believe it's probably just an oversight.

Q. You testified on direct that there was some misting spatter on one of the bumpers, right?

A. On the front bumper, yes.

Q. Was that tested for blood?

A. No.

Q. Was it collected for testing later on?

A. No.

Q. Your interview with Maxine on 3/12, she told you or you asked her if she was even at the apartment the night of the shooting; is that true?

A. Yes.

Q. And in the beginning of her interview did she tell you she was not?

A. Yes.

Q. And did she tell you that she didn't even get to that apartment until the next day?

A. Yes.

Q. Your interview with Angela was on 3/15, correct?

A. The first one, yes.

Q. When you told her that you had people who could put Stephanie in the car, was her response, they're lying?

A. No.

Q. Stephanie, when you interviewed her on 3/23, did she express that she was afraid that she was going to be arrested?

A. There was some discussion about the possibility she could have a liability in it.

Q. Did you make it clear to her that she was going to walk out of there that night as long as she wasn't a participant?

A. I made it clear she was going to walk out no matter what she said, whether we determined she had liability or not.

MR. MILL: That's all I have, Your Honor. Thank you.

REDIRECT EXAMINATION
BY MR. BARR:

Q. Detective, in terms of the interview of Stephanie, after you confronted her about the fact that you had a statement from Angela and you advised her that she was going to be walking out of there no matter what she said, did she then begin to provide you with details of what she observed on 3/4 of 2003?

A. Once we allowed her aunt to be present.

Q. Detective, you talked about the magazine being a style that goes into a Colt; is that correct?

A. Yes.

Q. Did you have any information to indicate any other type of weapon was used?

A. No.

Q. Now, you contacted Richard Roja outside the apartment on March the 12th, correct?

A. Yes, sir.

Q. And when you asked him about the apartment upstairs, what did you ask him?

A. If anyone else was in the apartment.

Q. What did he tell you?

A. My sister Tenise.

Q. Did he say anything to you about Louis Castell being up there?

MR. MILL: Objection. Asked and answered; leading.

THE COURT: He can answer it.

THE WITNESS: No.

BY MR. BARR:

Q. Did he say anything about Juan Sot or Andy Aria being up there?

A. No.

Q. Detective, in terms of on-duty fire department personnel, have you observed them to be wearing tennis shoes when they respond to a scene?

A. No.

Q. Detective, in terms of the shoes that you received in this case, if I understand correctly, you've got two pairs of shoes that correlate with shoe prints from the scene; is that correct?

A. Yes, sir.

Q. And one pair of shoes would be this pair of Fila, correct?

A. That's correct.

Q. Those shoes were found on the patio of Mary Mungar's apartment?

A. Yes.

Q. We also have the K-Swiss shoes that were seized from Richard Roja; is that correct?

A. Yes, sir.

Q. Out of all those shoes, the only two pairs that correlate to what Mr. Crave undertook were those two pairs, correct?

A. That's correct.

Q. Now, Detective, in terms of the other pairs of shoes that were seized, you have a pair here from Andy Aria that's a size 13?

A. Yes, sir.

Q. And a pair from Tony Mo. Is that a size 13?

A. Yes, sir.

MR. MILL: Your Honor, haven't we plowed these fields before?

Objection. Cumulative.

MR. BARR: This is redirect. He's opened these doors on cross.

THE COURT: He can answer. I'm going to overrule the objection.

BY MR. BARR:

Q. In terms of the Fila being a size ten and the Reebok, what size?
A. Ten.
Q. Those were seized from Louis Castell, the Reeboks?
A. Yes.
Q. Detective, would you describe for me Richard Roja's demeanor at the time that he was contacted at the police department, please.

MR. MILL: Objection. Relevancy.

THE COURT: He can answer.

THE WITNESS: Defiant comes to mind.

MR. BARR: No further questions of this witness at this time.

Thank you.

THE COURT: Any Members of the Jury have a question?

(Whereupon, the following proceedings were heard at the bench out of the hearing of the jury:)

MR. MILL: I think they're both objectionable.

THE COURT: Wait a second.

MR. MILL: It's objectionable and it's going to call for hearsay. Number two, his opinion why they were not released is not relevant.

MR. BARR: Obviously the juror's confused in terms of this question. None of them were under arrest at the time.

THE COURT: Okay. How about the first question?

MR. BARR: Judge, in terms of the first question, I don't think we should get into the first question, and that's the reason why I structured my questions.

THE COURT: Okay, thank you.

(Whereupon, the following proceedings occurred in open court in the presence of the jury:)

THE COURT: The question that the Court can ask, Detective, did you ask Steve Cam to identify the magazine from the gun, or if he could identify the magazine from the gun?

THE WITNESS: Mr. Cam's never seen that magazine.

THE COURT: Why were Maxine, Tony and Richard released after the arrest, if that in fact took place?

THE WITNESS: When the officer initially made contact at the Ranch Apartments on 3/12 at 12:30, they were not under arrest. The Kia information had come up as a possible lead. That was it. We did not have enough to make an arrest at that time. When Maxine returned to the scene and went to the station to talk to us, information elicited from her then allowed us to make arrests and to serve additional warrants.

THE COURT: Thank you. Mr. Barr, do you have any questions based upon the questions asked?

MR. BARR: I do.

BY MR. BARR:

Q. In terms of Mr. Cam and the magazine, did Mr. Cam describe a magazine with more holes in it than the magazine that we have here in court?
A. No.
Q. In fact, did Mr. Cam describe that you had a hole for every one of the rounds in the magazine?
A. Yes.

MR. BARR: No further questions.

THE COURT: Mr. Mill, any questions?

MR. MILL: No.

THE COURT: Thank you.

(Witness excused.)

THE COURT: Can I have counsel approach the bench.

(Whereupon, the following proceedings were heard at the bench out of the hearing of the jury:)

THE COURT: How are you going to present the telephone tapes?

MR. BARR: Mr. Mill had originally stipulated to the foundation for the tapes, but he just told us on his last break that he's withdrawing the stipulation. So we will have to call a foundation witness to do it.

THE COURT: What about the Aria testimony, are we going to wait until tomorrow for that?

MR. BARR: The way I understood the Aria testimony is, he still wanted to have an opportunity to make his statements and objections in the record, so I was reserving that.

THE COURT: Do you want to rest now with the understanding that you'll be reopening, and start your case and put your witnesses on?

MR. MILL: Is the State resting?

MR. BARR: With the exception of those areas, the State will rest.

MR. MILL: Okay.

THE COURT: Are you ready to go?

MR. MILL: Yes.

THE COURT: Who are you putting on? Your investigator? How many witnesses do you have lined up?

MR. MILL: No, Judge. I would rather wait until the State rests before I put my witnesses on. I have two.

THE COURT: The investigator and who is the other one?

MR. MILL: Detective Low.

THE COURT: Is he here right now?

MR. MILL: Yes.

THE COURT: They're resting with the understanding I'm going to permit them to reopen to present the other evidence, so we are at an impasse now.

(Whereupon, the following proceedings occurred in open court in the presence of the jury:)

THE COURT: Ladies and gentlemen, let's take our afternoon recess at this time. We will take 15 minutes.

(Whereupon, the following proceedings were held out of the presence of the jury:)

THE COURT: Pursuant to the bench conference we had, my understanding is that the jail tape, there was previously a stipulation concerning the foundation. That's been withdrawn, or there is no stipulation. And the State needs another witness to lay the foundation; is that correct?

MR. BARR: Actually, the State needs two witnesses to lay that foundation. Deputy Hawk and the custodian of records from the jail. So we can have them available tomorrow hopefully. I haven't talked to them yet. We just found this out on the break, but we will take care of it. I would also let the Court know that defense counsel also informed me that he's going to request that the entire 3/24 jail tape be played for the jury and be admitted into evidence if we establish a foundation; is that correct?

MR. MILL: That's correct.

THE COURT: All right. Have you looked at the transcript, Mr. Mill? There was one part here that I do have some concern about as far as your client is concerned, on the third page. But since you've looked at it, I guess you don't have the same concerns I might have. He said, "You made me cry, fool. I can't believe it. I fucking carry your ass for you to go over there and do shit like that." Your client answers, "I know, fool. Yeah, it's not even funny, dog."

MR. MILL: I don't even know what they're saying.

THE COURT: Well, you may not know what they're saying, but that could be characterized as some sort of tacit admission by your client. I'm just pointing that out to you so you're aware of it and the record is aware of it.

MR. MILL: You're right. It should be taken out.

MR. BARR: So the record can be clear and the Court can understand, the State intends to introduce the portions that have already been ruled on as being admissible. That's the only part of the tape the State wants to play. Any additional portion of the tape, Mr. Mill can cue up on his own. That's all we intend to play.

THE COURT: There's another part that I think, Mr. Mill, I don't deem to tell you how to do your job, but on page 4, the bottom of page 4, there's another part of the conversation that I would be concerned about if you really intend to play the whole tape. So why don't you redact what you believe should be redacted. You can give your copy to Mr. Barr, and then you can make a decision whether or not there needs to be any further rulings by the Court. But my prior ruling still stands concerning the top of page 1 and the top of page 2.

MR. MILL: Okay.

THE COURT: When do you think you're going to have that redacted, what you need redacted? Will you have that by tomorrow?

MR. MILL: I can. Do you expect us to argue tomorrow, Judge?

THE COURT: No. Based on what has been happening today, I think we will end up arguing it on Monday. But I think we're going to need tomorrow to hammer out these other issues.

MR. MILL: All right.

THE COURT: If you want to consider that, I don't know if you're set on introducing that entire tape.

MR. MILL: Well, let me go over it with my client. My problem is getting those two small excerpts out. And the jury reading the transcripts, they're going to make more out of what those words are than I think what they really mean. And so let me work on it with my client to see if there's more that we want to put in, to put it into context.

THE COURT: I'm going to rethink the transcript issue. The jury is going to have the tape and they can play it as many times as they want. I'm not sure there's any case law or rule that permits me or mandates me giving them a transcript of the tape since that's the jury's determination what is said on the tape. I'll consider that, and we can talk about it tomorrow.

Let me put that aside for a second and let's talk about the Aria admissions. Mr. Storr and Mr. Aria will be here tomorrow morning, is my understanding. Mr. Aria will take the Fifth Amendment and then we will go forward.

MR. BARR: I have additional copies of the transcript made and prepared for everybody with the parts that the State was intending to proceed on.

THE COURT: I'm looking at what's been red lined by you. I've got concerns based upon my reading of the Williamson case, Williamson specifically talks about inculpatory statements, not exculpatory, not implicating other people. And what you have red lined, at least on page 2 where it says they came back and told me they had a hotel, starting there, I've got a problem with that.

(HERE THE JUDGE AND THE ATTORNEYS DISCUSSED PROBLEMS THE JUDGE HAD WITH PRIOR PRECEDENCE, SETTING CASES AND RULINGS, EVEN BRINGING IN SUPREME COURT JUSTICE O'CONNOR'S OPINION. IN A LENGTHY DISCUSSION HE EXHAUSTED ALL POSSIBILITIES OF HIS CASE LOSING IN AN APPEAL TO HIGHER COURTS BECAUSE, AS HE SAID, "UNFORTUNATELY, WE WILL BE DOING THIS AGAIN WITH OTHER PARTICIPANTS, MAYBE TWO MORE TIMES," REFERRING TO POSSIBLE FORTHCOMING TRIALS OF ANDY ARIA AND LOUIS CASTELL. THE PRESSURE ON THE JUDGE MOUNTED AS HE READ PARTS OF THE TAPE TRANSCRIPTS THAT HE THOUGHT SHOULD BE DELETED IN ALL FAIRNESS TO THE DEFENDANT—MAYBE MORE FAIRNESS THAN HE DESERVED. SOME OF THE PARTS OF THE TAPES HE QUESTIONED THAT WERE SPOKEN BY ANDY ARIA WERE:)

THE COURT: "They came back and told me they had a hotel, and me and Louis, Richard, and, you know what I'm saying, we had went, we were going back to the hotel." And, "I seen them, they looked at the car wash and seen the white Lincoln." "Figured we could get that car, do you know what I'm saying, and cruise around in that car." Detective Clay asks, "So you guys stay at the motel," referring to the other guys. "They were going to try and take the car," reference to the other individuals, not him. So that should be out. That's all I found that was clearly objectionable. I'm not saying that I didn't miss anything. Mr. Mill, if you want to go over that maybe a little bit closer, and if you have anything else on that I'll certainly hear that. We could take that up tomorrow.

MR. MILL: Could I state a general objection.

THE COURT: Sure. Specific or general, we listen to all of them here.

MR. MILL: I have expressed this to you before lunch. This has caught me by surprise, and I would have tried this case probably differently. I probably would have asked some of these people who were taking the witness stand what they thought of Tony's or Andy's ability to tell the truth, whether they thought he was the type to curry favor with the police in order to extract himself from the situation he's in. You know, I'm being caught flat-footed because I think I would have tried this case differently. And to the extent that I had been given this, the State's intention in this transcript at the very last minute, my client, who I'm trying to do a real good job for, is not going to get a fair trial. I move for a mistrial based on the Fourteenth Amendment, due process clause. Also, because to the extent that I think everybody is looking at me, Rick Mill, as being a person who should have anticipated this, should have planned for it, should have cleared it up perhaps with the prosecution early on, shouldn't have just assumed, although I have a different interpretation, that this wasn't going to come in. I question whether Mr. Roja has been given a good lawyer that has at least met or exceeded minimum community standards of lawyering in a case like this.

THE COURT: Mr. Mill, you still have your case to put on. You can put on what witnesses you want. I don't know if any of these people would have been able to testify as to Mr. Aria's veracity or whether he would cover himself or to curry favor. I'm not sure, given the statements, that he was currying any favor or doing himself a favor. Given the fact that he's facing a capital first-degree murder trial. So that argument I'm not sure holds any water.

MR. MILL: Judge, how would you like to go through a trial like this, like Mr. Roja, and learn at the last minute that this is going to happen to you and not have your attorney know this throughout so that he could craft his questions around it. That's not right. And that's where I think we come into some problems for Mr. Roja.

THE COURT: Well, I don't understand your consternation given the context of everything that I have heard in this case. However, as I said, you still have your case to put on. I'm giving you some additional time if need be. I understand that you want either a mistrial or a lengthy continuance, and I'm not about to give it to you.

MR. MILL: I'm not done.

THE COURT: I thought you were.

MR. MILL: I'm sorry. That's the due process claim. And I've stated that and the Sixth Amendment claim. There's another issue here, and that is that I believe you're depriving Mr. Roja of the ability to confront and cross-examine Mr. Aria, who is now going to be one of his accusers in a way. We are making an attempt to redact that which points the finger at Mr. Roja, but this jury now has been exposed to four women who talk about different events that occurred at the car wash. When you redact things and then read about what Mr. Aria says is happening at the car wash, Mr. Aria now becomes bigger than life, and it is as if he is pointing the finger at Roja. It's as if when these statements come in, that Aria is saying Mr. Roja figures in a dotted line, and it's really for the jury to fill that line in, Judge. You're taking out some of the "we's" and the "they's" and I appreciate that, but even when Aria is on these pages saying, what I did, I was at the car wash, I did this and I did that, Aria is speaking, it's implicating him because it's bolstering all of the other witnesses that the State has called in this case. And that's really the reason they want to do it. So there are confrontation issues here.

THE COURT: Anything else?

MR. MILL: Yes. There is a real issue as to whether Aria is saying this to save himself or to get himself out of this case. Whether he's actually implicating himself or exculpating himself. I don't think Aria understood the concepts of like conspiracy and accomplice liability when he's making the statement. He's making this statement to say he's not the shooter and he was just there doing stuff. So he's really trying to curry favor with the police and dump it all on Mr. Roja. But if Aria is trying to get his rear-end out of this by pointing the finger, then Sandra O'Connor will tell you it's not reliable, there are Sixth Amendment implications here, Rick Mill should have the opportunity to go after Mr. Aria and try and chew him up on cross-examination and shed light on what he has to say. That's my read on Aria's statements, and I think that Sandra O'Connor wouldn't let this in. But what am I? I'm just the defense attorney in all this.

THE COURT: And I'm not Sandra O'Connor, obviously. But, you know, just an observation, Mr. Aria could very well have said he wasn't there as well as what he did say. And he didn't say that. So it was a statement against his interest. He implicated himself as being there. And my read on this is at least he's admitted the one element or one of the counts that he's charged with. Okay, anything else?

(NOW THE ATMOSPHERE BECAME TESTY. THE PUBLIC DEFENDER ACCUSED THE PROSECUTION OF SHANGHAIING HIM AND EXCHANGED NASTY WORDS WITH HIS ASSISTANT. MR. MILL ALSO MADE A MOTION FOR A MISTRIAL DUE TO LACK OF NOTICE AND DUE PROCESS. IT WAS A VERY TENSE SITUATION AND SHOWED THE DEDICATION THE PUBLIC DEFENDER HAD FOR HIS JOB OF DEFENDING A CLIENT. AFTER A LENGTHY, OFTEN VITUPUROUS DISCUSSION, THE JUDGE STEPPED IN AND COOLED DOWN THE SITUATION:)

THE COURT: All right. There was a motion for a mistrial. I'm going to deny it. Let's talk about where we are as far as the mechanics or the logistics in this trial. Detective Clay has ended his testimony. I told Mr. Mill that he could do some more research on this Aria issue. What do you want to do about the rest of the afternoon? Mr. Barr, what is your inclination?

MR. BARR: I have indicated to the Court that I'm pretty much completed with the testimony that I intend to present with the exception of the Aria statements and the tape. So that's where the State is. And we will rest with the understanding I can bring that evidence in.

THE COURT: Mr. Mill, what do you want to do?

MR. MILL: Judge, whatever you'd like me to do. If you'd like me to put on some of my case, that's fine. I could put on my whole case in about 20 minutes to a half hour.

THE COURT: Why don't we do this then. Why don't you rest, Mr. Barr, with the understanding that I can tell the jury that there is some more evidence and it will be taken out of context, but the State is resting except for that testimony, which will not be lengthy.

MR. BARR: All right.

THE COURT: Do you want to take a little break and then we will bring the jury back in.

(Whereupon, a recess was taken, after which the following proceedings were held in the presence of the jury:)

MR. BARR: Your Honor, subject to the limitations that we have discussed, the State will rest.

THE COURT: The State is now going to rest with the understanding that they are going to reopen their case tomorrow because some witnesses are not here today. But the State is resting, and they're going to have a couple more witnesses. I don't think it's going to be anything lengthy. Just so you understand that. All right, Mr. Mill.

(THE DEFENSE CALLED ITS FIRST WITNESS, DETECTIVE BRUCE LOW, OF THE LOCAL POLICE DEPARTMENT, AND IN A VERY SHORT DIRECT EXAMINATION DETERMINED THAT IN HIS INTERVIEW OF MAXINE HERNAND ON MARCH 12, 2003, SHE STATED, "THEY DIDN'T GET NOTHING FROM THE CAR." SURPRISINGLY, THAT ENDED HIS DIRECT EXAMINATION OF THE DETECTIVE. NOW THE PROSECUTOR CONDUCTED HIS CROSS-EXAMINATION OF THE DETECTIVE.)

BY MR. BARR:

Q. Detective Low, in terms of the interviewing process with Maxine Hernand, you had some contact with her on March 12th out at the Ranch; is that correct?
A. Correct.
Q. Why was it that you proceeded to take her back to the police department from the Ranch apartment complex?
A. She told me when I contacted her that she had information that she would like to talk to me about, was very afraid of talking at that location, and wanted to go back to somewhere where she could not be seen to talk to me about it.
Q. So when you took her down to the police department, did you conduct a lengthy interview with her?
A. Yes.
Q. And to your knowledge was she subsequently interviewed further on another date?
A. Yes.
Q. By Detective Clay?
A. Yes.
Q. Would you describe her demeanor during the course of the interview at the police department on March 12th?
A. She was cooperative, appeared to give the information as she knew it.

MR. BARR: No further questions of this witness. Thank you.

THE COURT: Mr. Mill, any redirect?

MR. MILL: No.

(NEXT THE PUBLIC DEFENDER CALLED ON TERRY HORRA, AN INVESTIGATOR FOR THE COUNTY LEGAL DEFENDER'S OFFICE AND, IN EFFECT, THE PUBLIC DEFENDER'S ASSISTANT. HE DESCRIBED HIS IMPRESSIVE EXPERIENCE IN LAW ENFORCEMENT AND ALSO HIS FAMILIARITY WITH HANDGUNS, ESPECIALLY .45 CALIBER GUNS. THE DIRECT EXAMINATION CONTINUED:)

Q. Mr. Horra, at my request did you go out to the Hender's trailer park?
A. Yes, I did.
Q. Did you take measurements from Hender's trailer to where the car wash was?
A. Yes.
Q. Did you measure it then as the crow flies or in a different way?
A. I measured it line of sight.
Q. So you went to the middle car wash bay?
A. Yes.
Q. Is that your understanding where the Lincoln was parked?
A. Yes, sir.
Q. How many feet from the middle car wash bay to the wall where Hender's trailer was?
A. 544 feet.
Q. Did you do that in the daytime or the nighttime?
A. That was daytime.
Q. While you were standing looking at the car wash, were you able to see any people there?
A. There were several people at the car wash at that time.
Q. Tell me what kind of view you had and what sort of detail you could see.
A. I could make out gender based on clothing and hair styles, or guess at it. I couldn't be positive. In fact, I was wrong on one occasion. I went over to the car wash and checked. You could make out race if it was very distinct. Other than that, there wasn't much else you could determine.
Q. Could you tell whether someone was raising their arms or lowering their arms?
A. You could tell arm movements.
Q. How about anything in a person's hands?
A. I couldn't tell what their hands were doing. I guess if they had been holding something large, I would have known that.
Q. Mr. Horra, at my request did you investigate how common Winchester .45 auto bullets are?
A. Yes, I did.

(NOW THE PUBLIC DEFENDER WENT INTO A LENGTHY DISCUSSION OF .45 CALIBER GUNS AND BULLETS AND HAD MR. HORRA IDENTIFY

NUMEROUS MODELS AND TYPES. WHEN THE PROSECUTOR CROSS-
EXAMINED HIM, HE CONTINUED THE RATHER BORING DISCUSSION
OF BULLETS AND .45 CALIBER GUNS TO TRY TO DESTROY MR. HORRA'S
CREDIBILITY. FINALLY, HE CHANGED THE SUBJECT:)

Q. You indicated that you went out to Mr. Henders' trailer park, correct?
A. The park where Mr. Hender's trailer was.
Q. You went out to the position of his trailer, correct?
A. Yes.
Q. You talked about how you measured to where the middle bay was, correct?
A. Yes, sir.
Q. Now, between the time that you took those measurements and now, Mr. Horra, did you ever go back and try to make an observation as to what Mr. Henders could see in the lighting of that car wash?
A. I have not been out there at night, no.
Q. So you can't tell us really, Mr. Horra, the ability to see a figure under lights shining from that car wash, can you?
A. I could not tell you what you could see at night with the lights.
Q. What time of day was it that you went out there and looked?
A. I believe about two or three in the afternoon.
Q. Was it a cloudy day or a sunny day?
A. It was a bright, clear day. No clouds.
Q. Did you have anybody hold a dark, black object?
A. No, I didn't.
Q. And so then you can't tell us whether you could identify whether somebody who would have a black or dark object in their hand and then put it in their waistband?
A. I did not do that. From what I could see, I don't know that that would be possible.
Q. You didn't try it?
A. I did not try it.

MR. BARR: I have no further questions of this witness. Thank you.

THE COURT: Redirect?

MR. MILL: No redirect, Your Honor. We rest.

THE COURT: Ladies and gentlemen, we're going to recess for the evening. I've got some issues that I need to take up with counsel tomorrow morning and I'm going to have you come back at 1:30 tomorrow afternoon.

And I'll just give you a preview. We will finish all the testimony tomorrow, and we will begin the closing arguments then on Monday. And then I anticipate the jury getting the case for a decision on Monday. So I guess that's good news. We're ending earlier than we had anticipated. So if you could come back tomorrow at 1:30. We will see you then. Have a nice evening.

(Whereupon, the following proceedings were held out of the presence of the jury:)

THE COURT: With regards to tomorrow, I'd ask you to come back at 10:15. Mr. Storr will be here, at least from my understanding, and Mr. Aria about 10:30, and then we can handle that aspect of the case. I made some notes, I just wanted to make sure of a few things. We talked about a stipulation as far as the jail tape. Did we come to any conclusion? I can't remember, did they say this is being taped, or something to that effect?

MR. BARR: Judge, the initial stipulation that I thought that we had in this case was the stipulation that said that the recording was legally authorized to be recorded, the telephone conversation of March 24, 2003. That was my understanding as to what we were going to be agreeing on.

THE COURT: Okay.

MR. BARR: And then both parties of the conversation were advised that the conversation was being recorded.

MR. MILL: Could we approach or just go off the record?

THE COURT: Sure.

(Whereupon, an off-the-record discussion was held.)

THE COURT: We have been talking at the bench about the stipulation concerning the jail tapes. The parties are going to try to work out a stipulation regarding that, regarding the preliminaries, the foundation. Hopefully you can. If you can't, then Mr. Barr knows that he needs to have his witnesses here at 1:30.

What I've done on the Aria tapes, I've underlined in red the areas that I believe were not proper, and I would ask that, Mr. Barr, you take this copy, show it to Detective Clay so he's aware of it. Also, with the understanding that Mr. Mill will get an opportunity to research this issue tomorrow. If there's any more or less that you want in, we can talk about it at 10:15 tomorrow.

So, Mr. Mill, if you can come up with something on Mr. Aria that you want to present to the Court and have considered for impeachment, let me know and I'll consider it. I understand your position but—pardon me?

MR. MILL: Was he on probation? I think he was on juvenile probation.

THE COURT: I have no idea. Maybe you can talk to Mr. Barr about that and then we can talk about that tomorrow. That's why we have all morning tomorrow to talk about it. Okay?

MR. MILL: Okay.

THE COURT: All right. We will be at recess.

(Whereupon, the trial was adjourned until Thursday, February 1, 2001, at 10:30 a.m.)

EIGHTH DAY, FEBRUARY 1, 2001

MORNING SESSION
(Whereupon, the following proceedings were held out of the presence of the jury:)

THE COURT: The record will reflect the presence of counsel and the defendant. We're here to discuss some of the matters we had yesterday that were in controversy, namely what I'll term the Aria's statements. It's my understanding that the State is going to withdraw it's request to present those statements; is that correct?

MR. BARR: Your Honor, the State has reviewed the State's request to do so, and we are going to withdraw our request to use those statements.

THE COURT: Other than what you filed this morning, Mr. Mill, anything else on that issue?

MR. MILL: No.

THE COURT: Secondly, the stipulation concerning the jailhouse phone call statements, have you come up with something?

MR. BARR: I believe we have reached an agreement on that.

THE COURT: So what we're going to do when the jury comes back at 1:30 is, I take it we're going to read that stipulation to them?

MR. BARR: Yes, Judge.

THE COURT: And play that tape. It will be entered into evidence at that time, correct?

MR. BARR: That's correct.

THE COURT: And you talked yesterday about possibly calling Detective Lowe?

MR. BARR: Yes, sir.

THE COURT: Is that still going to happen?

MR. BARR: Yes, it's still going to happen. There's something I need to correct in terms of one of the witnesses early on.

MR. MILL: Could I have a heads-up as to what that is?

MR. BARR: It's on Mr. Henders.

THE COURT: That was the man that was in the trailer observing the events?

MR. BARR: Yes, Judge.

THE COURT: And after Detective Low testifies, will the State then finally rest?

MR. BARR: Yes, sir.

THE COURT: Mr. Mill, you have indicated you're not going to have any surrebuttal; is that correct?

MR. MILL: Yes, that's true.

THE COURT: And then we're going to argue the case on Monday morning; is that right?

MR. BARR: That's correct, Judge.

THE COURT: Okay. Can we turn now to the jury instructions.

(THE JUDGE ALSO MENTIONED THAT THEY WOULD NOT BE GIVING PRINTED TRANSCRIPTS OF THE ARIA TAPES TO THE JURY, AND THEN

THEY GOT DOWN TO THE JURY INSTRUCTIONS, A DAUNTING AND QUITE BORING TASK. HOWEVER, WE FINALLY GOT A CHANCE TO HEAR RICHARD ROJA SPEAK:)

MR. MILL: I have talked at length with my client about his testifying. It has run hot and cold even throughout the trial, but he chooses not to testify and that is on my advice.

THE COURT: Mr. Roja, you've heard what Mr. Mill just said. You understand you do have a right to testify. On the other hand, you have a right to invoke your Fifth Amendment rights and not to testify. And the Court will advise the jury if you choose not to testify that they're not to consider your not testifying in making their decision. I take it you've considered that?

THE DEFENDANT: Yes, I have considered what he's saying. I'm going to go along with not testifying.

THE COURT: All right. Thank you.

(THEY CONTINUED TO NIT-PIK THE INSTRUCTIONS TO THE JURY WORD FOR WORD FOR HOURS UNTIL THEY WERE INTERRUPTED BY THE JUDGE'S JUDICIAL ASSISTANT.)

THE COURT: My JA has just informed me that juror number two has called and has asked to be excused because he just got laid off from work. That's all he told my judicial assistant, so I don't know what that means. Any comment by either counsel?

MR. MILL: I think we should bring him in. There's a law you can't do that, employers can't lay you off because of jury duty.

THE COURT: My judicial assistant is telling me it was not because of the jury service. There's a lot of lay-offs going on, so I'm not surprised if somebody gets laid off of work any more. I can't picture in my mind which juror that is. It's the number two juror.

MR. MILL: Man or woman?

THE COURT: It's a man. He's got dark hair, a little heavy-set. He was I think a computer engineer. He was sitting in the second chair. I can have him come in. We can interview him on the record outside of the presence of the other members of the jury. On the other hand, I can just excuse him. We have 14 jurors left. If I excused him, we'd have 13 left, so we'd still have one alternate.

MR. BARR: I'd recommend you bring him in. It's a little different story. The juror that we had the other day was sick. And I certainly understand that, but in this situation, for the record, we ought to do that.

THE COURT: All right. I imagine—well, he may tell us he's very stressed, that he just doesn't feel that he could give this a good—he can't track what's going on. I'm going to have him come in.

(A luncheon recess was taken until 1:30 p.m., after which the following proceedings were heard outside the presence of the jury:)

AFTERNOON SESSION

THE COURT: We are in chambers. The record will reflect the presence of counsel. Mr. Mill's waived his client's presence. I have juror number two here.

(JUROR NUMBER TWO EXPLAINED THAT HE HAD BEEN LAID OFF LAST NIGHT DUE TO THE CLOSING OF HIS OFFICE. HE STATED HE WAS THE SOLE SUPPORT OF HIS FAMILY AND IT WAS AFFECTING HIS CONCENTRATION, THINKING ABOUT HUNTING FOR A NEW JOB. THE COURT AND THE ATTORNEYS AGREED THAT HE SHOULD BE DISMISSED, AND HE WAS.)

(Whereupon, the following proceedings occurred in open court in the presence of the jury:)

THE COURT: The record will reflect the presence of the jury, counsel, and the defendant. Ladies and gentlemen, as you see, we have another empty chair today. Juror number two had a personal situation that he felt he had to attend to. And after speaking to him and counsel, we felt that it was something that he should attend to, and so I dismissed him as a juror. So we have 13 jurors. Obviously, now you see why we had 15 to start with. And we will continue. At this time the State had previously rested with the understanding that they would reopen their case at a later time. And at this time they will present some further evidence. Go ahead, Mr. Barr.

MR. BARR: Thank you, Judge. The defense and the State have entered into a stipulation.

THE COURT: I received a stipulation from the parties, and I'll read the stipulation to you at this time. The State and defense have agreed to the following:

1. The tape is a legally authorized recording made by detectives of a telephonic conversation on March 24, 2003.

2. The defendant was a party to the conversation and was advised that the call was being recorded. That's the stipulation, and I will include that in the record. Just so the jury understands, since it's in evidence, it's going to be played now for you one time, but you'll have an opportunity—if the jury wishes to listen to it again, we will supply you with these devices: The speakers, the recording device, et cetera.

(Whereupon, a tape recording was played.)

THE COURT: Mr. Barr?

MR. BARR: In rebuttal, the State would call Detective Bruce Low.

MR. MILL: Your Honor, does the State then rest its case?

THE COURT: So the State's rested, and this is rebuttal evidence?

MR. BARR: That is correct, Judge.

MR. MILL: I'm urging the motion which I filed.

THE COURT: Go ahead, Mr. Barr.

DIRECT EXAMINATION
BY MR. BARR:

Q. Detective Low, I believe we covered yesterday that you responded to the scene of the car wash shooting on March 4th, 2003; is that correct?
A. Yes.
Q. Would you describe to me what your activities were upon your responding there.
A. When I got there, I was assigned to speak to several people who said that they witnessed something involving the incident.
Q. Did you have an opportunity to talk to a Mr. Daniel Henders?
A. Yes.

Q. Could you describe to me when and where you talked to Mr. Henders?

A. It was around 5:45, 6:00 in the morning. I went over to his house and spoke to him there inside of the home.

Q. Was he able to provide you with details of his observations of activity that had occurred over at the car wash?

A. Yes.

Q. Detective Low, have you had an opportunity on listen to the 911 tape as it applies to Mr. Henders?

A. Yes.

Q. Could you describe to me, does Mr. Henders on the 911 tape appear to be describing the events as they occurred?

A. It did not sound that way to me, no.

Q. Does it appear on the 911 tape that he's describing what he's observed immediately after?

A. Yes.

Q. Now, when you're talking to Mr. Henders, did you have an opportunity to look from the area from which he made his observations of the car wash?

A. Yes. I had him point out the window and describe the actions as he was seeing them from the window.

Q. And as he is relating to you what he observed, did you have any difficulty in making those observations or seeing the activity at the car wash at that time?

A. No.

Q. As you continued to speak to Mr. Henders, what did he point out?

(NOW DETECTIVE LOW BASICALLY REPEATED MR. HENDERS' PREVIOUS TESTIMONY, DESCRIBING HOW THE KIA LEFT THE SCENE OF THE CRIME, AND HOW A MALE SUBJECT GOT INTO THE CAR AS IT DROVE AWAY. HIS TESTIMONY WAS SUDDENLY INTERRUPTED BY THE PUBLIC DEFENDER.)

MR. MILL: I'm sorry, my objection is beyond the scope of rebuttal. What is it from my case that this witness is rebutting?

THE COURT: Could I have counsel approach the bench, please.

(Whereupon, the following proceedings were heard at the bench out of the hearing of the jury:)

MR. MILL: This witness is just rehashing what Henders told him out there. I presented two witnesses: Low, not for this purpose, and my investigator, T.J, who described the view from Henders' trailer. That's it. I haven't opened up the door to bringing what Henders said on a previous occasion. That should have been gone into on the State's case after Henders testified. So it's beyond the scope of rebuttal.

MR. BARR: I disagree. I agree that it is proper in terms of Mr. Henders. I also feel an obligation, number one, to bring out the information concerning the tape. After we got that jury instruction yesterday, I wanted to make sure that they're clear. Also, in terms of the information, I believe I can impeach Mr. Henders in the statements that he made. That's what we're talking about here. He's put Mr. Henders' credibility on the line.

(Whereupon, the following proceedings occurred in open court in the presence of the jury:)

THE COURT: The Court's going to overrule the objection. Go ahead, Mr. Barr.

Q. Detective Low, I left off with Mr. Henders describe to you that the car was doing a circle, or circles in the parking lot of the car wash.
A. He never used the word "circles." He said the car turned around and then went southbound.

MR. BARR: I don't believe I have any additional questions of this witness. Thank you.

THE COURT: Mr. Barr?

MR. BARR: The State would rest. Thank you.

THE COURT: Anything else from the defense, Mr. Mill?

MR. MILL: No, Your Honor.

THE COURT: Ladies and gentlemen, that concludes the testimonial part of our trial. I'm sorry that you had to return today for a short time, but look at the bright side. You have the rest of the afternoon off.

What we're going to do is try to settle the jury instructions this afternoon and any other issues we might have, and then, as I said yesterday, we will come back on Monday and both parties will have an opportunity to make their closing arguments to you on Monday, and the jury will get the case for a decision. So let's start up again at 10:15 on Monday morning. And everybody have a safe weekend, and hopefully nobody gets ill or has anything go wrong, because we need you here on Monday.

(Whereupon, the following proceedings were held out of the presence of the jury:)

THE COURT: Mr. Mill, you subsequently made another motion.

MR. MILL: Yes.

THE COURT: The Court's going to deny the defendant's motion at this time. The Court believes that there is substantial evidence to go to the jury on all counts.

(NOW THE JUDGE AND THE ATTORNEYS AGAIN TACKLED THE WORDING OF THE JURY INSTRUCTIONS, MENTIONING NUMEROUS PRIOR TRIALS AS GUIDELINES, AND REVIEWING DOZENS OF PAGES OF WORDING SUGGESTIONS. WHEREUPON, THE TRIAL WAS ADJOURNED UNTIL MONDAY, FEBRUARY 5TH, 2005, AT 10:15 A.M.)

NINTH DAY, FEBRUARY 5, 2005
MORNING SESSION

(BEFORE THE JURY WAS BROUGHT IN, THE JUDGE, THE ATTORNEYS AND THE DEFENDANT GATHERED IN THE COURTROOM TO REVIEW THE FINAL INSTRUCTIONS TO THE JURY, AND ALL CONCURRED. THE JURY WAS THEN CALLED IN.)

THE COURT: Ladies and gentlemen, you have been passed out copies of the final instructions of law. What I'm going to do is read all but the last two pages, which are instructions and suggestions on how to conduct your deliberations. After I read that initial portion, the attorneys are going to have an opportunity to make their final arguments to you. We probably will not go beyond the lunch hour, so we will be taking a break at the noon hour. So if you would please follow along with me.

It is your duty as a juror to decide this case by applying these jury distributions to the facts as you determine them. You must follow these jury instructions. They are the rules you should use to decide this case. It is your duty to determine what the facts are in the case by determining what actually happened. Determine the facts only from the evidence produced in court. When I say evidence, I mean the testimony of witnesses and exhibits introduced in court. You should not guess about any fact. You must not be influenced by sympathy or prejudice. You, as jurors, are the sole judges of what happened. You must consider all these instructions. Do not pick out one instruction or part of one and ignore the others. As you determine the facts, however, you may find that some instructions no longer apply. You must then consider the instructions that do apply, together with the facts as you have determined them.

In their opening statements and closing arguments the lawyers have talked to you and will talk to you about the law and the evidence. What the lawyers said and will say is not evidence, but it may help you to understand the law and the evidence. The lawyers are permitted to stipulate that certain facts exist. This means that both sides agree those facts do exist and are part of the evidence.

You are to determine what the facts in the case are from the evidence produced in court. If the Court sustained an objection to a lawyer's question, you must disregard it and any answer given. Any testimony stricken from the court record must not be considered.

The State has the burden of proving the defendant guilty beyond a reasonable doubt. In criminal cases such as this, the State's proof must be more powerful than that. It must be beyond a reasonable doubt. Proof beyond a reasonable doubt is proof that leaves you firmly convinced of the defendant's guilt. There are very few things in this world that we know with absolute certainty, and in criminal cases the law does not require proof that overcomes every doubt. If, based on your consideration of the evidence, you are firmly convinced that the defendant is guilty of the crime charged, you must find him guilty. If, on the other hand, you think there is a real possibility that he is not guilty, you must give him the benefit of the doubt and find him not guilty.

You must start with the presumption that the defendant is innocent. The State must then prove the defendant guilty beyond a reasonable doubt. This means the State must prove each element of the charges beyond a reasonable doubt. If you conclude that the State has not met its burden of proof beyond a reasonable doubt, then you must find the defendant not guilty of those charges.

You must decide whether the defendant is guilty or not guilty by determining what the facts in the case are and applying these jury instructions. You must not consider the possible punishment when deciding on guilt. Punishment is left to the judge. The only matter for you to determine is whether the State has proven Richard Roja guilty beyond a reasonable doubt. The defendant's guilt or innocence is not affected by the fact that another person or persons might have participated or cooperated in the crime and is not on trial now. You should not guess about the reason any other person is absent from the courtroom.

The State must prove guilt beyond a reasonable doubt with its own evidence. You must not conclude that the defendant is likely to be guilty because the defendant did not testify. The defendant is not required to testify. The decision on whether or not to testify is left to the defendant acting with the advice of his attorney. You must not let this choice affect your deliberations in any way.

In determining the evidence, you must decide whether or not to believe the witnesses and their testimony. As you do this, you should consider the testimony in light of all the other evidence in the case. This means you may consider such things as the witnesses' ability and opportunity to observe, their manner and memory while testifying, any motive or prejudice they might have, and any inconsistent statements they may have made.

The testimony of a law enforcement officer is not entitled to any greater or lesser importance or believability merely because of the fact that the witness is a law enforcement officer. You are to consider the testimony of a police officer just as you would the testimony of any other witness.

The State has charged the defendant with five separate offenses. A charge is not evidence against a defendant. You must not think the defendant is guilty just because of a charge. The defendant has plead not guilty to each charge. His plea of not guilty means that the State must prove each element of the charges beyond a reasonable doubt.

Evidence may be direct or circumstantial. Direct evidence is the testimony of a witness who saw, heard, or otherwise observed an event. Circumstantial evidence is the proof of a fact or facts from which you may find another fact. The law makes no distinction between direct and circumstantial evidence. It is for you to determine the importance to be given to the evidence, regardless of whether it is direct or circumstantial.

(THE JUDGE CONTINUED WITH HIS LENGTHY INSTRUCTIONS REGARDING FAIRNESS TO THE DEFENDANT, AND HE DESCRIBED THE CHARGES AGAINST RICHARD ROJA AND EXPLAINED EACH. NOW HE MOVED TO THE CLOSING ARGUMENTS.)

THE COURT: Mr. Barr, are you prepared to make your closing argument at this time?

MR. BARR: I am, Your Honor.

THE COURT: Please proceed.

MR. BARR: Good morning, ladies and gentlemen. We now come to the close of the case. The last two weeks, ladies and gentlemen, we have been rebuilding that block-constructed house created by Richard Roja. It's a house filled with conspiracy, with armed robbery and murder. And what we have been doing through presentation of these witnesses is rebuilding this house block by block by block. This is why we spent two weeks presenting this evidence and presenting the various types of evidence throughout the course of this case.

Now, ladies and gentlemen, when we started this case, we told you the basic facts: Date; time; location. We talked to you about the charges, first of all, dealing with conspiracy to commit armed robbery. We talked about the fact that we were dealing with a discussion, however brief, in the Kia, concerning that nice car, that nice ride, the Lincoln. And we talked about how in this case the defendant was successful along with his accomplices, Louis Castell and Andy Aria, in obtaining the wallet and the keys, and the object of the conspiracy was to jack that Lincoln, to steal that car. But it was a failed attempt to get the car.

Ladies and gentlemen, we are dealing with two victims here on the armed robbery counts. We are also dealing with two victims on the murder counts as well.

In armed robbery, we had to show it was a robbery with a gun or firearm, taking property from another person's immediate presence and against their will. The murder we talked about, premeditation, looked for the opportunity to reflect. Felony murder, in the course of and in furtherance of the armed robbery. We explained to you the differences between direct evidence versus circumstantial evidence. Remember the example is, it's not snowing when you go to bed, it's cold. You go to bed and there's no snow on the ground, but when you wake up the next morning there is snow on the ground. Circumstantial evidence that it snowed during the night.

We told you we were going to have eye witnesses, we were going to have fact witnesses, that we were going to introduce exhibits which included shell casings, bullets, fragments, and photographs and diagrams and shoe prints, and burnt cards.

Ladies and gentlemen, we advised you we weren't calling the witnesses in order, that we had the responding officers to deal with, Labra and Valenz.

Evangelina Ballester, Christine Can, Daniel Henders, Jon Steve, Stephanie Martin, and we explained to you who she was, and Angela, Ursula Ocan, Sandra Martin, and who she was, Jose Mercad, Steven Cam, Mr. Bill Morr, D.P.S, Dr. Phillip Kee being the Chief Medical Examiner, Monica Munoz, the defendant's aunt, Sergeant Bradshaw who searched and obtained that magazine.

We talked about calling Maxine Hernand and how she was the owner of the Kia and the girlfriend of Richard and Louis and loaned the 2000 Kia four-door car to Louis and Richard and waited for them to return with the car on March 3rd and 4th. She stayed at the Mary Mungar apartment, that's the Ranch Apartments, and when

Richard and Louis and Andy returned, Louis was carrying a wallet and some keys that were wrapped in a towel. She described to you what she observed. We told you what she was going to tell you, that she observed this going into the barbecue, and that we are dealing with some pictures of kids, that they were cut up and burned. She said she overheard Richard say that he shot two people.

Criminalist Howard Birn, D.P.S. examined the burned plastic residue. He found it consistent with the County Library card and also with the Safeway card.

We talked about Donna Fro and how she had the opportunity to observe that wallet just the day before Michael was killed, the keys, the wallet, the photos. We talked about the custodian of records from the County Library and the Safeway records. And we talked about Mary Mungar and who she was. We talked about Detective Forem, how he executed the search warrant on March 12, 2003. If you recall, ladies and gentlemen, we estimated that the shoes that were obtained from the patio were, in fact, seized by Detective Forem on March 12th.

Detective Low, he was involved in the apprehension of Louis Castell. Tabatha Tack, she knew Andy Aria. She also was able to identify Richard Roja. And we talked about Detective Tom Clay, how he was the case agent in this case. He did the scene, that he gathered the evidence that was submitted in the case, and he contacts the major witnesses.

I'd like to go through those witnesses as they have testified before you over the course of the last two weeks. Officer Labra was the very first responding officer. He was the first officer that came to the scene. He responded at 3:59 a.m. He stopped at the northeast corner of the car wash, parked his car right there. As he entered into the lot, the first thing he sees is that male victim.

He says he's got his gun drawn. Remember, he's responding to a shots fired call. When he gets there, the first thing he does as he's approaching, he sees that a victim is laying there on the north side in the car wash. He says he clears those bays, as he moves up, as he's going through, and what is he looking for? He's looking for suspects. He's looking for other victims. Who's with him? No one. He's there by himself. He's looking for more victims and more suspects. He does see the other victim. He sees Amy lying out in front. She's by the vacuums. He says the male victim, he's on the ground, he's by the white Lincoln. He says he's still alive. He says he's going into convulsions at the time. He went back to check on the second victim. He said she was deceased. She was a female. He talks about the male victim and how he had a gunshot wound to the head. He graphically described what he observed about the matter and the blood. He talks about the female victim and the gunshot wound that she sustained to the head. He said Officer Valenz arrives. When he arrived, he secured the scene. He said the fire department was en route for the male victim. The fire department appeared and rendered aid to the male victim. They found shell casings and described the location of those shell casings.

Ladies and gentlemen, we move on to Evangelina Ballester. She was going to work about 4:00 a.m. She was southbound in the left turn lane. She said she waited for the red light. She heard two shots. She looks over and she sees a guy chasing a girl. She first sees the guy. And she said she thought they were playing, kind of like hide and seek, or something.

She says the girl was trying to hide, the guy ran up and grabbed her "here." Do you remember what she said? The girl had a towel, and she said she heard two shots. Maybe shot three times, she wasn't sure. And she got scared when the girl fell. She said the guy was Hispanic or Chicano. He was taller than the girl by a little bit. And he just grabbed her and shot her. The gun, she said it was square, more or less. She didn't recall the color, didn't know too much about guns. She said from the witness stand it looked like a .45 and she didn't know anything about guns, but that's what she said. She said she heard no screaming, and she heard a total of four shots. She spent about four or five minutes at the red light, and then she ran the red light. She ran the red light because she got scared. She got scared and drove off. She said there were about three minutes between the first set of shots and the second set of shots. And she said she saw a car in the bay.

On redirect she was not able to identify the defendant as the man at the car wash. She said the gunman was a little shorter. She said the defendant's hair was similar in color, but she believed it was a little darker at the car wash, and she believed that the hair was combed back flat on the head. She said the man didn't have any glasses on. Mary Mungar told us something, ladies and gentlemen, the defendant, Richard Roja, ran to watch the news. This is after the shooting. This is in Mary Mungar's residence. This is out in her living room. And you remember she talked about how they were all seated on the couch with Tenise. Tony was there and the defendant was there, and she overheard Tenise say when the composite came up that that didn't look like him. And she was referring to Richard Roja. And that's the composite. No, it doesn't look like him, at least not with the hair. Ladies and gentlemen, we called Christina Can. She was there just before 4:00 a.m. because she had to deliver papers on the paper route. She saw some lights on at the car wash. She didn't notice any cars in the car wash, but she did notice that there was a car with its lights on in the parking lot of the business to the north of the car wash. And she said she saw one person in the car on the driver's side, and she thought it was a man. She couldn't give a description. The car was small. It was gold or tan. She called the police later on when she heard about the shooting. She said she saw the car.

Ladies and gentlemen, what we are dealing with are snippets in time. People that are driving by at 35 miles per hour that see a little snippet of time, a little observation. And that's what we are presenting to you.

We called Daniel Henders. Daniel Henders was in his mobile home across the street. He heard shots. And he looked out, and he said he heard screaming. He says he looked in the car wash, there was more screaming and more shots. He said he saw a blond lady backing up. She was backing up in the lights, and she was yelling, saying something. He said the guy approached her back toward the fourth bay. He says he heard three gunshots. And after firing the shots, the guy, he described as an Hispanic male, ran to the car. He said the girl was blond, heavy-set, had pants on. As he ran to the car, he said, he put something dark in his pants. The Hispanic male, he said, got in the driver's side. That's how he concluded it was a two-door car, because he got on the driver's side and somebody got out of the car and he got in.

He said the Hispanic male was medium build, about five foot six. He saw the car do a U-turn in the lot and go southbound. He told Detective Low that that car came from the auto business north of the car wash when Detective Low talked to him on March the 4th within just an hour and a half of what happened. Obviously, he's mistaken. When he comes in and testifies to you on the witness stand, he's mistaken in terms of, he's got the car now south. That's not what he told Detective Low right after it happened. He told him the car was in the auto business north, that the car exited that auto business and drove southbound into the car wash parking lot, and it drove the wrong way on the street and then exited the lot and drove southbound. On cross-examination he denied seeing the car parked in the north lot and denied seeing the car go into the wash from north. He said the guy got in the back seat, because he knows the other guy got out. He said he saw an Hispanic male, he thought he had a ball cap on turned backwards. He said it was too far to see emblems on the hat. This seems kind of unusual. I asked him which is better, is memory better now than it was shortly after the incident occurred? And he said his memory was better now.

Ladies and gentlemen, use your common sense and apply that to the facts of this case. He also said that the car had its headlights on, that he also was able to see the Lincoln in the bay, and he also said he believed he was talking to the 911 operator and describing what was going on at the time.

Now, we called Detective Low to make sure that we cleared that up. He wasn't talking to the 911 operator at that time. He was talking to her shortly thereafter. We called Jon Steve. Jon Steve is not a visual witness but he's a hearing witness. He lives in Glen Mobile Homes. His bedroom faces north. He woke up to the sound of gunshots. He said, I heard a couple of voices. He talks about where he's located inside that trailer park.

He says he woke up to the sound of gunshots. He said he heard a couple of voices, he couldn't identify what they were saying, he said he heard a scream and then a rapid fire. He said there was a pause, and then there was the last shot. He said it sounded like definite shots. He said he got to the scene about one minute to one and a half minutes later. Time frame: He walked from all the way over where his mobile home was. He told you the first thing he does is call 9-1-1. He then gets dressed, then he goes out, and he walks over to the scene, and he says that's about a minute, minute and a half.

Ladies and gentlemen, that's beyond the bounds of common sense. It's difficult to do that in a minute or a minute and a half. It probably took a little longer. Now, he says when he gets here, he sees one police officer on scene. He sees the other one arriving. Between the first shots and the screams, he said he heard additional shots.

Officer Valenz, the second unit to arrive, says he's there within a few seconds. Officer Labra is already on scene. Fire is there within two minutes. He said his job was to stand by the male. He says that the male's injuries were beyond what he could deal with. This is something for a medic. The male was breathing and convulsing. He said Officer Blan was taking photographs. He says that the victim was transported from the scene, and he was able to assist in securing the scene.

Ladies and gentlemen, I bring this up again because Officer Valenz, he's there within just a few seconds. Well, obviously, he's not there within a few seconds. It depends on which witness we're dealing with. If we're dealing with a witness that's going through fear and trauma, Officer Labra, he said it was eight to ten minutes before the fire department got there. Valenz said it's just a couple of minutes. So when people are making observations of something that's a fairly traumatic experience, that time lengthens out. When people are just hearing something, they're not visually seeing that trauma, that kind of condenses. And I use that to demonstrate the difference between Jon Steve and, let's say, Evangelina Ballester. She says she's there five minutes, probably shorter than that. Jon Steve, probably a little longer than one half minutes to get his clothes on and get to the scene. Officer Valenz, probably not a few seconds, probably a couple of minutes. In any event, they're there fairly quickly.

We called identification technician David Crave. He described for us the layout of the car wash. When he arrived, he said, the female victim was still present at the scene. He said he works from the outside to the inside to take photos. They identify the location of the items by putting placards next to them so that we can see where they were in the photos, we can identify where those photos of evidence are located. He described the Lincoln for us. He said there was a hole in the driver's window, it looked like it was coming from the inside out. He said there was also blood on the front passenger side fender, and he said there was a bullet strike on the wall above the window. We interrupted Mr. Crave's testimony and called him back later on in the case to talk about the shoe evidence. Ursula Ocan. She knew the victim. She had seen the victim, Amy Hopp, just a couple of days before her death. And Ursula lived in the Glen Apartments. She also knew that Amy had a boyfriend who owned the Lincoln Town Car and that it was white. She said Amy and I talked a couple of days before, Amy sat on the hood of that car out there in plain view. She said she saw Louis and Richard outside with the others just across the wall.

Ladies and gentlemen, in terms of what we are dealing with, it is just a short distance between the Glen Apartments on the outside across the driveway, a couple of parking spaces, a black wall, parking spaces on the north side of Ranch, a driveway, and that second story balcony apartment of Tony Mo. When she sees this, she says they're outside on the ground level. She says she heard them, they were out there, they were huddled together with the others, but she said she knew that Louis and Richard lived in Tony's second floor apartment in the Ranch, and that was directly south and across the brick wall. Ursula lived in Glen but walked through the Ranch daily. That's how she knew Louis. And she walked by there daily because she was taking her kids to the bus stop. She was introduced to Richard by Louis, and he identified him as a cousin. She indicated that Louis drove around in that Kia, so she'd been in the Kia. She identified Richard Roja here in court for us. She said he was difficult to recognize, he's bigger and now has glasses. Richard was with Louis, and she often saw the guys on the second floor balcony. She cannot say that Richard saw Amy on the car that day, although Richard and Louis and others were outside. And on cross-examination she was asked if Richard's head was shaved and she said, I think so. But she also described on redirect when she saw Richard, she only saw the sides of his head, that it was close cut. She said he wore a hat backwards.

Angela Martin. Angela Martin knew Richard Roja through Louis. She met Richard on 3/1 of '03. She described Richard, Louis and Stephanie, her sister, her younger sister, and how they arrived with Andy in a Kia. Angela had identification, so she was the one that rented the room at the Red Roof Inn. And how Louis paid and they were going there to kick back, to hang out in the room, Angela and her cousin Pete. And they got there about 11:00. About 2:00 a.m. or so they went back to the Ranch Apartment. Her and Pete drove in the one car. She thinks Louis went up to the apartment. She said in the Kia was Richard, Louis, Andy, and Stephanie. She said they drove back to the hotel. She said the Kia didn't return, so Angela and Pete waited, then they go back, they went to a gas station, got some gas, and went back looking for the Kia.

They drove by the car wash, saw some news camera activity, and she said they went back to the Red Roof Inn. She didn't have a key. Stephanie came down to take them back up to the room, and they rode in an elevator. Back at the room, Richard, Louis, Andy, Stephanie, and now it's Pete and Angela.

And note, ladies and gentlemen, she didn't see Tony at all that evening. She saw Richard Roja, she said. She saw Richard Roja with a black handgun that evening. And he had it, and he had it tucked in his pants. She said it was in the front, and she saw the handle that night. She was asked if Stephanie was drinking that night. She said she was. She said, but she didn't see her drinking. She knows that she was buzzing because of what Stephanie was telling her. She tried to keep her sister out of it when she talked to Detective Clay. On cross-examination she agreed she did not call police when she saw Richard with the gun that night, and she agreed she tried to protect her sister by saying that she, Stephanie, was with her and Pete when they talked to the law enforcement officers, Detective Clay. Ladies and gentlemen, remember that when Angela and Pete got back to the Red Roof Inn, Louis, Richard, Andy and Stephanie were already there. She described earlier that she saw a shotgun in the trunk of the Kia. She didn't hear any talk about the car wash when she got back to the hotel.

We called Stephanie Martin, ladies and gentlemen. She is now 17 years old. She was 15 at the time. She was going to school. Angela is her older sister, but she didn't necessarily do what Angela tells her. She said she met Louis Castell about two weeks before this happened. She developed a relationship with him. She knew he had been to prison. She was 15. Her relationship turned intimate after the car wash shooting. She was introduced to Richard Roja by Louis. He was introduced as a relative. She described Richard Roja as five foot five inches, 200 pounds. She was able to identify him here in court. We submit it's obviously a mistake. Richard was shorter than Louis and had less weight. She saw Richard two to three times before the night of the shooting. She said when she saw Richard, he was always with Louis. She met Andy a couple of days before the car wash. She described Andy as five foot four, 250 pounds. Heavier than the others. We submit that's in error as well.

Louis introduced Andy as a friend. The day prior to the car wash, she saw Louis later on that evening. Louis was with Richard and Andy, and they drove up in the brown Kia and Louis was driving. Later she says Angela rented the room at the Red Roof Inn, and they went there to hang out.

Early the next morning, they went back to the Ranch. She said she had been there before, Tony's apartment at Ranch. She knew Tony through Louis before the car wash incident. Stephanie said Louis drove to Ranch. She said Richard got out, and Richard got back in the car going back to the hotel. She said they made a right turn on 59th Avenue. They're going southbound. They're going past the car wash. She said something was said, but she's not sure which person said it. "Look at that car." Some kind of comment about a nice car. Then there were whispers. Remember what she described, there were whispers. She said there were whispers between Louis and them, Andy and Richard.

In the car you've got Louis, Andy, Richard, and Stephanie. She said she didn't hear the whole conversation. She said there was interaction between Louis and Richard. They were also looking at each other. She said Andy made a statement about, "It was a Lincoln Continental," and they were looking at each other.

Louis was driving. Richard's in the passenger seat. Andy and Stephanie are in the back seat. She says Louis makes a U-turn by the Jack-in-the-Box, and drove back to the car wash. They passed the car wash, pulled into the business north of the car wash described as a tire shop. They parked in the dark area of the tire shop in the back by the bush. She said the lights were on in the car wash, but it was dark in that parking lot. She said Louis parked the car, and he parked the car facing the wall.

She said Louis, Richard and Andy got out of the car and they stood by the back of the car. They appeared to be talking. She couldn't hear what they were saying. She said they stood there for more than a minute and then, she said, they disappeared. Richard went one way; Andy and Louis went the other way. She said Richard goes on the right side out near the front of the car wash, and Andy jump the wall. She said she stayed in the car. She dozed. She doesn't know how long that was. She woke up to a noise. Louis and Andy were back to the car first. Louis started the car, and Richard came back to the car later after they did. About how much time? Maybe a minute. Louis was the driver of the car. Andy was in the back seat. She doesn't know if the car moved before Richard got in. She said Louis drove from the tire shop into the car wash parking lot.

She said that Stephanie saw the white car in the wash bay. She denied seeing the victim, Amy Hopp, laying out there. After Richard got back in the car, she said something was said about nearly shooting himself, or something like that. She's not sure if it was Richard or Louis who made the statement. She said Richard talked about a device in the car, and when pressed, she said Richard wasn't talking about the Kia. He was obviously talking about the other car, something about a scanner, but she wasn't sure what word Richard was saying to describe it. She said Louis drove back to the motel. Andy was paranoid at the hotel. She said, we sat down and played cards at the hotel. Richard watched T.V. Andy had an injury to his hand after the car wash, she noticed. She said she went to school the next day, left about 6:30 a.m. She described that she'd been drinking that evening, and she also described what she had to drink. She said she continued her relationship with Louis. In fact, they had gotten more involved and intimate after the car wash, and she saw Louis daily until he was arrested. That would have been on March 12th. Stephanie loved Louis at the time. She met with Detective Clay on March 15th of 2003, and she admitted that she denied being in the car. She denied seeing Richard with a gun that night.

On cross-examination Stephanie said she moved from the front seat to the back seat. She admitted to drinking that night, admitted some of the night was blurry and doesn't recall everything. That may be due to the alcohol. She agreed she may have heard only the last shot. Louis walked her up to the room. She didn't remember going down to get Angela, and she remembered talk of almost shooting himself, but she wasn't sure who said that. She said whenever she saw Richard, he was with Louis. She said she never saw Tony that night.

We called Monica Muno. That was Richard's aunt's. She described the relationship and how Richard came from California. And she described the layout of the house. Monica said that Richard, Tenise and Louis shared the middle bedroom, and their stuff was in the middle bedroom. She said she heard about the car wash shooting. She knew Richard and Louis were not home because they had been kicked out of the house a day or so before. She was worried about them. Why did we call Monica Muno? Because Monica established for us who was in that middle bedroom.

We called Sandra Martin. She said she was Richard's favorite aunt. She said back at this time she lived in California at the time of the car wash shooting. Her husband was Jose Mercad. And she said Jose was currently in prison. She identified Richard Roja. She looked at the glasses. I don't know if you caught her, ladies and gentlemen, but her chuckle on the witness stand when she looked at Richard and went ahead to say, well, she had seen Richard with glasses before.

Ladies and gentlemen, she said Richard stayed with her and Jose in California. She said that Jose bought a gun, it was a blue/black handgun, and she said she saw it two or three times after he bought it. She said Richard left California around Valentine's Day. If you look at this time sequence that we are dealing with, ladies and gentlemen, Jose's gun she said turned up missing, the last time she saw the gun was a couple, two or three days before Richard left, but she said she didn't believe Richard took it because the gun was kept in the garage where Jose dealt with all his drug people, so it was locked up there and she didn't believe that Richard took the gun.

We called Daniel Khaz. He said that Michael was in possession of a leased 1996 Lincoln, that he worked for his service, that he gets calls to pick up people. He said there was also a dispatching radio, kind of like a scanner type radio. But it's connected to his dispatchers. We called Detective Brad. He executed part of the search warrant. He told us that he found the magazine with the bullets in the middle bedroom closet on the shelf.

We called Maxine Hernand. She said she met Richard Roja while riding with a friend. Richard said he was 17 years of age. She said she was 19 years of age. She met Richard about three years ago. She was friends with Richard. They used to go to the malls together. It lasted for about six months. She said Richard then moved to California. She did not learn Richard's true age until after his arrest. She said Richard came back from California in February of 2003. She was seeing Richard when he got back. She said he stopped the relationship because he wanted to see other girls. She said she had no interest in Louis at first, but then they got together. She said she took precautions of doing this in front of Richard. And she said she met Mary and son Tony. She said Tony was thin, taller than Richard, had thick black hair. And she said that Mary had a one bedroom apartment. She slept in that bedroom. She said that Tony's girlfriend was Tenise, and she said she often loaned her car to Louis, her Kia. She described the Kia for us. She loaned the car to Louis the evening before the car wash. She said Richard and Andy went with Louis. She said she stayed at the apartment and watched T.V. She said Tony and Tenise were on the computer. She said Louis, Andy and Richard did not return, and she went to bed. She went to sleep on the coach at about 1:00. She said Mary was in the bedroom asleep. She did not see anyone return until the next morning about 6:00 a.m. Louis, Richard and Andy returned to the apartment together the next morning. She said Louis sat down on the couch next to her in front of the coffee table. When he sits down on the couch, he's carrying that white towel. He's got bloodstains on it. He opens it up. It's got some keys; it's got a wallet in there. She described it as a brown leather wallet. She said the keys are just a bunch of keys. She said Richard stood over by the door, and Louis was looking through the wallet. She said Maxine saw some kind of identification in the wallet, and she also saw a picture of a little girl, maybe a Social Security card. She said Louis appeared to be bragging about it. She said Louis got scissors from the kitchen and cut up the wallet. She did not see the cash in the wallet. Louis puts the pieces in the barbecue and burns them. And, she said, Richard was right by the door when this happens. She said she stayed about two hours after they got home, and left about 8:00 a.m, she went to the Jack-in-the-Box to get food, she saw police at the car wash as she drove by. Maxine saw Richard two times with a black handgun before the car wash shooting. She did not see him with the gun after the car wash shooting. She said she overheard Richard talking to Louis about his gun when he came from his uncle in California. She overheard him say it was a .45 handgun. She said she saw the gun one time in Richard's waist. She said he always carried it. She saw the gun before the car wash shooting. Do you remember her description about Louis and Richard being in the room when this was going on? She also described for us the type of shoes that Richard was wearing, that he had K-Swiss shoes, because it has a label

582 Linda L. Russo, RPR with George B. Blake

on. Richard said he couldn't believe what he had done at the car wash. He said he shot the lady two times in the head because she was running. He talked about her boyfriend, and said he shot him in the head, too. She said the comments weren't directly said to Maxine. They were directed at Louis. Maxine noticed that Andy had a cut on his hand after the car wash. She never called the police. She identified Richard for us. She said she never seen him in glasses before. On cross-examination she said she was not sure of the number of shots Richard said he shot the guy. She told the police Richard got the gun a few days before the shooting from his uncle. She described before that, that Richard shot the guy because he tried to run, and wanted money and car keys. And also described she overheard Richard say Andy got shot trying to block the girl from running. She described Louis and Richard as close. And when we asked her about her behavior, remember what she said from the witness stand, "I'm stuck in the middle. That's why I'm here." She identified Richard for us. She identified Richard's shoes. She heard Richard talking two days later. Maxine said she didn't want to know.

We called Detective Byrn. He was the detective that was contacted by Detective Clay following that interview on 3/15. Detective Byrn goes to the apartment, the Ranch Apartment, after Maxine's 3/15/03 interview. He finds plastic and ashes in the barbecue on the balcony of the second story apartment. He said it was out on the balcony barbecue he impounded the materials.

We called Bonnie Camp. She was the Custodian of Records at the County Library. She identified Michael Fro as having a County library card. She described to us what the County Library card looked like. We showed you that, ladies and gentlemen, because if you will recall, Mr. Birn comes in and he's able to give us a slice of that card that's recovered from the ashes. Kara Glove talked about a Safeway card, and we showed you what the Safeway card looks like. She said that Michael Fro did have a Safeway card, and that he used the card before 3/4/03. She gave us the number. And the number she gave us was 420 0354 6810. Why is that important? Because you recall that Mr. Birn, when he goes through his analysis, that's what he's able to obtain from that card.

We called Donna Fro. She said she last saw Michael with Amy on March 3rd. Saw Michael's wallet. She held it. It was a brown wallet. She gave it back to Michael. The wallet had pictures of children in it, and there was about $200 in the wallet. She said Michael had keys on a keyring with a clip, and she said there were about ten keys.

Howard Birn said he received the materials, the burned plastic pieces and ash. He examined them. He said the one was consistent with the County Library card. He looked at it. We showed it to you on the monitor. There was writing on it. He also identified seven numbers that he was able to identify from the Safeway card, bar code. Those are the seven numbers. They were consistent, consistent with the card being a County Library card, consistent with being a Safeway card. We encourage you to take a look at that evidence.

We called Dr. Kee. He talked about the autopsy performed on 3/5/03. He said Michael died from multiple gunshot wounds. He said he observed swelling of the face and the eyes.

Gunshot wound number one was a non-contact, or intermediate wound. He said it was a distant shot, meaning that it's beyond two or three feet.

The second gunshot wound entered the right side of Michael's head. He cuts across the brain and exits out the temporal bone on the left side.

Gunshot wound number three, he described that as a lethal wound. Gunshot wound number three entered the back of the head on the left side, exited out the forehead, comes out the eyebrow. He said the cause of death to Michael Fro was multiple gunshot wounds to the head. The manner was homicide. There were three distinct wounds, and all three wounds were through-and-through.

Amy Hopp, he described her as a Caucasian female, appeared to be stated age of 21 years. She sustained two gunshots wounds. Wound number one entered the back of the head. Gunshot wound two was to the left cheek, chin area. Cause of death for Amy was multiple gunshot wounds to the head. He said about the wounds that they were large caliber bullets.

We called Tabatha Tackt. She lived in the Glen Apartments where Amy lived. She described where Amy lived. She also was aware of the second-story apartment where the guys hung out at Ranch. The guys at Ranch invited Amy up to their apartment. Tabatha knew Andy from school. She said she looked at the photo of Richard and said, yeah, when they invited us up, he was also there. She couldn't say that Louis was there at the time that the invitation to her and Amy was made. She couldn't say this man was there, but she could say that Richard was there and Andy was there. She said it happened shortly before Amy was killed. She said Amy's boyfriend drove a Lincoln Continental. It was parked at the apartment almost every night.

(NOW THE PROSECUTOR REMINDED THE JURY OF THE CARTRIDGES FOUND AT THE CRIME SCENE, THE BULLETS, THE BULLET FRAGMENTS AND THE MAGAZINE CLIP FOUND IN THE MIDDLE BEDROOM. IT WAS A VERY LENGTHY RECAPITULATION OF PREVIOUS LENGTHY TESTIMONY, BUT THE PROSECUTOR INTRODUCED A NEW SLANT ON THE MAGAZINE CLIP SITUATION:)

You remember we asked him about the magazine, and he said that magazine doesn't fit the gun. Ladies and gentlemen, we suggest to you, the State's position is not that that magazine fit that gun, or that that magazine was used on March 4th. What that magazine shows you, ladies and gentlemen, is that the people that had that middle bedroom also had access to those types of bullets. That's what it shows you. The same bullet, the same manufacturer, the same caliber. It could have been used as a back-up magazine.

But we submit to you, ladies and gentlemen, because of the manner in which Steve Cam talked about that gun and the condition of that gun, he said his father passed this gun on to him. It was a Browning .45 caliber, semiautomatic handgun, with a Sig Sauer system. He said it was black in color. He said it was in good condition. He knows. He took it apart. He put it back together. It was in operational condition. It was working properly, and it was kept in good condition. We never recovered the weapon from the defendant. He got rid of the gun. We didn't get the gun, but we have the next best thing, the Browning .45 caliber semiautomatic handgun with the Sig Sauer System, identified by Steven Cam.

Ladies and gentlemen, we went on to call Mary Mungar. She lived at the Ranch Apartments, apartment 2046. It was a one bedroom apartment. She met Tenise through Tony. They were boyfriend and girlfriend. Tony was 17; she was 16.

In February of 2003, people started to stay at the Ranch apartment. Richard came from California. Tony asked if he could stay because his mom was coming in about two weeks, so she okayed the deal, and they slept on the floor. She said, I slept in my bedroom. She said when Richard arrived, he brought a backpack and a suitcase with him. When he was unloading the suitcase, she saw him talking to Louis and he had a gun in his hand. It was a black handgun. She is not able to tell you it was a .45 caliber semiautomatic with a Sig Sauer System, but what she can tell you is that it's a black handgun. She said what she was concerned about was the dangerous aspect of the gun. He wasn't waving it around or anything. But she said the second time she saw that gun, she was reaching on her bed under the covers, she said her finger hits the trigger, and she said, that's it. The gun's out of this apartment. And she tells the boys she didn't want this gun in the apartment any more.

On 3/3/03 she was picked up by Tenise and Maxine from work. She said she sometimes stayed up all night. She did smoke marijuana, she did do speed, also known as methamphetamine, but not this night. She said she went to bed, and speed keeps you up. She said she had to go to work in the morning. She said Tony and Tenise were there, and she's not sure if she saw Maxine. She said Tony and Tenise were on the floor. When she went up to get her coffee, they were there. She also says that she couldn't find her shoes. She asked Tony where her shoes were. Richard or

Andy or Louis before work, she didn't see them. She did not see Stephanie, either. She said she drove by the car wash and saw police. She was worried; she was afraid for the boys. It could be one of them. Then she saw the blond hair sticking out and realized it wasn't them.

She called home and had a conversation with Louis. She said in terms of the unusual activity, she said the guys, after the news would come on, would run to the T.V. She said afterwards she talked to Louis. She said Richard then comes into the bedroom. She says the doors open, and this is after Louis, and she said Richard walked in and he talked about feeling bad and how his anger just came out, and that he was still in shock. And talked about the guy and talked about the shooting. He said in this description here that she gives us from the witness stand, she said he was seeing the blood, he was describing seeing the blood go down the drain and mixing with the water.

Ladies and gentlemen, the photos of that car wash depict that. This is not something you could see from the street. This is something that shortly after this has occurred, this young man is removed from the scene, so Richard said he was mad and he chased after the girl and she ran off screaming. Richard said he had to shut her up, and he ran off after her and he shot her.

Mary said she was afraid after this. She didn't want to be a snitch. She was afraid to call the police. She was afraid they could not protect her.

After that, Richard, Andy and Louis would continuously pick her up from work, and she said they stayed at the apartment. And after the car wash, things changed. She was not alone. She said Richard said he saw the blood flowing and mixing with the water. And that's a very compelling statement. Mary remembers the composite shown on T.V. and how the others were there, how Richard and Tenise and Tony were on the couch. And she recalls Tenise saying, it doesn't look like him, referring to Richard.

She went to work. She continued to go to work. On 3/12/03 she was called at work. The detective at her home told her to come right home, and she returned to the apartment. She told the police she doesn't know anything. She said she feared for her and her son. Sometime later, around the end of March, she talked to a guy from church and then Detective Clay. She talked to Detective Clay. She wouldn't meet him at her work. She wouldn't get into his car because she was afraid. She met him at a prearranged place, at a Circle K. She said she didn't want anybody see her get into the car with Detective Clay. She recalled the barbecue at the apartment. It was a smoker type, and it was out on the patio. Mary admitted to using drugs, but she didn't believe that they impacted her ability to see and observe and hear what had taken place.

On cross-examination, of course, she was cross-examined about the use of those drugs, and the fact that others at the apartment smoked marijuana. She said she didn't call the police when she saw Richard unpack the gun. She said the night of the car wash she said she didn't have drugs. The night of the car wash, she went to bed. Clint was on the couch, Tony and Tenise were on the floor. She said Richard talked about the killings on 3/4/03, but she did not call the police.

Diana Molin was called. She talked about responding to the scene. At first she went to the fire department and police personnel, took photos of the shoe prints at the scene. She processed the Lincoln for prints. She described how you leave a print. One thing I hope you take away from this trial is that a fingerprint is a chance impression. Just because you touch an object doesn't mean you leave a fingerprint. What you have is a chance impression. It depends on a lot of things. First, it depends on the oil on the skin and what's been on the skin. Next it depends on the surface condition; it depends on weather conditions; whether the surface is rusty or smooth; whether it's fabric or whether it's leather; whether it's cold, wet or damp. She said damp metal is not conducive to leaving ridge detail. The only prints in the car she said she was able to identify, one to Michael Fro. Michael Fro is the one who leases the car, yet she's only able to get one out of that car. Amy's prints were on a cigarette wrapper inside the car. She didn't have any fingerprint from Louis, Richard or Andy identified to the car. But she described fingerprints, in the process she described it as a chance impression. She processed the Kia as well. She got seven partials, but out of any of those partials she was not able to identify Richard, Louis or Andy's fingerprints to that Kia. Why? We know they were in the Kia. We know Louis drove the Kia. Fingerprints are a chance impression. Sometimes you get them; sometimes you don't.

Louis borrowed that car, and drove Maxine's car on a regular basis. Richard and Andy rode in Maxine's car. She describe the black powder process and the way to look for prints. She said car fingerprint may stay on the car even though it's washed. She said it depends on what's in the oils at the time that the fingerprint impression was made.

The bottom line is, you can touch something and not leave a print. David Crave examined the shoes submitted by Detective Clay. He did adhesive overlay of the shoe impressions—of the shoe. He did a one-on-one photo enlargement of prints. He went through and described the process for you so that you could sit here and take a look at what we have. He did not see any random characteristics on the shoes, the K-Swiss and the Fila. He says they were not unique to be able to identify the shoe. He said there's no significant wear pattern; he said there's no unusual marks. This shoe just had normal tread patterns. He said the relative size and same pattern type of shoe is what you see. He was able to tell you that it's consistent with the

K-SWISS. He said he did see the wear pattern, he said, but the shoe had good tread, not enough wear pattern to be able to make an identification.

Finally, we called Detective Clay. Detective Clay was the case agent. He knows the case. He responded to the scene on 3/4/03. He talks about the lighting conditions in the car wash, the lighting conditions in that business north. He noticed that the bay was still wet when he got there. He described the process of collecting the photos. We have already seen the photos. He describe the items of evidence, the location, how he impounded them. He gives a little more detailed description about the car in terms of the bullet hole in the window coming from the inside going out, the driver's side from the inside out. No, he didn't do gunshot residue from the inside of the car. You could see that the gun was fired inside the car. He noted the bullet strike on the wall at the car wash bay, and he also noted the crumbs of paint and plaster on the hood of the Lincoln. He saw what was high velocity mist blood spatter on the passenger front fender just out by the bumper area. He said he noticed that when the car was about to be towed. He said there was no wallet found in the car. He said they searched the car. He said the car was dusted for prints using a black powder method. No, they didn't use Super Glue because that destroys the vehicle. He said he couldn't locate Michael Fro's wallet. He called people, he met with people, he talked to Donna Fro. They couldn't recover the wallet. They couldn't find where that wallet went to, nor the keys to the Lincoln, because the keys to the Lincoln weren't there.

On 3/9 he had contact with Ursula, the first time the Kia is mentioned. On 3/12, the next significant development, Maxine Hernand and Louis Castell spotted at the Ranch Apartments. Detective Clay went to the scene. Maxine, Richard and Tony were detained in the cars, and he said he goes up to Richard and asked Richard who was in the apartment. He said Tenise. He doesn't say anything about Louis; doesn't say anything about Andy.

He said he goes up to the apartment. Tenise and a guy who gives him a false name were there. He says, I go and get a search warrant and then I return about an hour later, and Louis is being taken out of the apartment from the closet by Detective, Sergeant Becker and Bruce Low. He says after he returned and after Louis is taken out, he says Maxine comes back in the Kia. She's by herself. She talks about Detective Low. She didn't want to talk to him, she was willing to talk to him at the police station. She goes down to the police station. He says Maxine is cooperative, appears tired, but she gives the car for him to process.

He speaks to Maxine again on 3/15, and she gave more details. And he also says that on that date, he says he has contact with Richard Roja, Louis Castell, Andy

Aria. He also describes to us the shoes that he takes from these individuals. He has contact also with Tony Mo and gets his shoe and his shoe size. He talks about an interview with Stephanie Martin he did and how she denied being in the car. This is on 3/15/03. He interviews Maxine on 3/15/03. She's cooperative. She calls after the interview, called Detective Byrn to go and take a look at that barbecue. They find the materials in that barbecue, and that's subsequently submitted. He submitted the remainder of the bullets, fragments and shell casings. He followed up with Howard Birn on the plastic. Originally they thought it might have been one card. He obtained shoes from the search warrant at the apartment, submitted those for examination with David Crave, and did the follow-up on the gun. On 3/12/03, telephone call to Jose Mercad, and later we flew to California, had contact with Sandra Martin. And he said the gun was never found.

Now, let's talk about the elements of the conspiracy here. The judge has read you the instructions. First of all, in terms of what the State has to prove in terms of the conspiracy, you've got the instruction written out for you. It talks about an agreement with one or more persons to engage in certain conduct. That the defendant intended to promote or assist in the commission of the conduct, and that the intended conduct would constitute the crime, whether known or unknown by the defendant. Let's talk about that.

Ladies and gentlemen, the State is not required to prove certain things. What we have to show in terms of the existence of a conspiracy, the State doesn't have to show the making of an express or formal agreement, nor need the State prove that all the means set forth in the indictment were agreed upon, nor that all the means agreed upon were actually used.

Use your common sense. Apply it to the facts and the inferences that are logically applied thereto. The mentioning of the Lincoln, the nice ride. Stephanie gives us the whispers, the looking, the U-turn, the parking in the dark, the standing by the trunk. She gives us the conspiracy. The intent to promote or assist, Richard's disappearance around the front of the car wash, and then Louis and Andy over the wall. Where were they going? See the shoe prints; see the shell casings. Richard, Jose, Steve Cam's father's gun. That's what we have. The intended conduct would be armed robbery. Richard knew that using a gun to get the Lincoln or to jack the Lincoln was an armed robbery.

How do we know that? Richard got rid of the gun afterwards. And note that Mary or Maxine, neither one of them saw Richard with the gun afterward. Just because they act in similar manners, does not alone prove conspiracy. That's what the judge's instruction was. Just because they associate, doesn't mean conspiracy.

But in this case, ladies and gentlemen, Richard, Andy and Louis approached the victim in a dissimilar manner. Remember, the two went over the wall and the one went around the front. They were not together. They weren't just hanging around together. As one approached, they split up.

Now, the instruction, ladies and gentlemen: First determine if there's is a conspiracy. That is, an agreement by conduct, and conduct existed. Was Richard Roja a knowing member?

The instruction: It is not necessary for the State to prove the conspiracy succeeded. In this case, the conspiracy to jack the Lincoln. He didn't get the Lincoln. It was a failed attempt. We don't have to prove to you that it succeeded for it to be a conspiracy. He was unsuccessful in getting the Lincoln.

The instruction: We must show that he aided. Ladies and gentlemen, examine Mary's statement of what Richard said, examine what Maxine told us Richard said, and then examine Stephanie's description and the footprint evidence.

The conspiracy, ladies and gentlemen, is a separate charge from the armed robbery. We ask you to examine the accomplice instruction, that the defendant is held accountable for the conduct of another if an accomplice, with the intent to promote, aids, agrees or attempts to aid another in the planning of or committing of the offense. In terms of what Louis and Andy are doing, just as long as they have the state of mind, with the intent of the defendant to do that. Stephanie talks about the meeting and the discussion, then the disappearance. We've seen the shoe prints. And we also know that Richard was the last one to get back to the car. He was working with his accomplices, Louis and Andy, to commit this robbery. The robbery instruction, ladies and gentlemen, requires four things:

Took another person's property. In this case keys, wallet.

The defendant attempted to take the Lincoln.
The taking was against their will.
And the defendant threatened or used force with the intent to coerce surrender of the property. It was Michael's property, but he was taking it from both Amy and Michael.

Ladies and gentlemen, we suggest to you that through the course of this testimony and the evidence that you have seen, the layout of the two apartments, that Richard Roja knew Amy. That she could identify him. She had seen him on previous occasions. And, ladies and gentlemen, that's one of the reasons Richard Roja chased after Amy and shot her. He had to stop her.

Ladies and gentlemen, the instruction on committing a robbery, taking property by force while the defendant or an accomplice is armed with a firearm. In this case, ladies and gentlemen, the firearm is a .45 caliber semiautomatic handgun. The display of the firearm is sufficient. In this case, the weapon was used on both victims.

You have been given an instruction concerning first-degree murder. The fact that we were dealing with two types of first-degree murder: Premeditated and felony. There are alternate theories on the premeditated murder. It has a leg for a lesser included instruction of second-degree murder. What that means, ladies and gentlemen, is that you could find one or both, or either.

The two types, the felony murder, does not have any lesser included involved in it. In other words, felony murder is first-degree murder. You look at the felony murder, was an armed robbery committed? Yes, it was. There's felony murder committed in the course of and in furtherance of that armed robbery. That's felony murder. That's first-degree. It's also charged premeditated murder, because the premeditation involved in shooting Michael Fro and in tracking down and shooting Amy Hopp is premeditated murder as well. What does that mean? If you feel the State has not sufficiently proven premeditation beyond a reasonable doubt, then that's second-degree murder. But only if you make your decision regarding the felony murder. Premeditated murder requires any length of time to permit reflection.

In Michael Fro's case, did Richard Roja have the opportunity to reflect? He had the opportunity to reflect, ladies and gentlemen. Did he plan it out? No, he didn't sit down and plan it out. But did he have that opportunity to reflect? How much time do you have to have? It's as brief as successive thoughts in the mind. Just an opportunity to reflect.

In this case he did reflect. He left the car with the weapon. He left the car with the weapon and he approached the rear of that 1996 Lincoln, and he approached from the rear. He drew his gun and he raised his gun to shoot, and he raised his gun to shoot Michael Fro. And he squeezed that trigger. Remember what Bill Morr told you about the gun. You have to squeeze the trigger to make it go. Now, the victim, he's down-range. Remember the testimony of Dr. Kee. He says he's talking about three head shots. We are not talking about a shot to the torso. We are talking three head shots. He's got to have the victim down range, and he has to take the time to make sure he has the weapon aimed in his direction. He wants to fire, and that's what he does. So he has the time to reflect about what he's doing.

He has the victim down-range, and then he squeezes off the second shot. He gets him again. He gets the victim down range again and he squeezes off the third shot. Now, the second and third shots are lethal wounds. And note the blood spatter of the victim on the lower portion of the passenger side in front of the car. There's more than intent. There's premeditation here, ladies and gentlemen. We remind you to recall that we are dealing with all three are head shots. We are not talking about body shots, a shot to the torso. This is his premeditated planning to kill the victim. How about Amy? What about premeditation on Amy? What are we dealing with? Richard heard a girl scream. Richard ran after Amy. Richard grabbed Amy by the shirt. He grabbed her by the shirt and he pointed the gun at Amy. Remember that's what Evangelina Ballester tells us. And then he squeezes off the first shot, because the gun doesn't go off automatically. You have to squeeze that trigger to make it go. And then the victim starts to go down. He positions the gun at her again. We're dealing with another head shot, so he has to position that gun to where he can get that shot off, and then he squeezes off the trigger for a second round. Remember what Mary Mungar told us. Richard said he ran after Amy to shut her up. And, ladies and gentlemen, we submit that Richard, by the evidence, did see Amy present and he knew who Amy was. If you find that the State has not proven premeditation beyond a reasonable doubt, or cannot agree, then you look at felony murder.

Ladies and gentlemen, we submit to you that this case is a felony murder case, and the judge has read to you an instruction about felony murder. We also have two under first-degree murder. That the defendant has been charged with first-degree murder, and you have been given two definitions of first-degree murder: Premeditated murder and/or felony murder. Both constitute first-degree murder.

In order to find the defendant guilty of first-degree murder, all 12 of you must agree that the State has proven beyond a reasonable doubt that the defendant committed first-degree murder. However, your verdict need not be unanimous as to whether it's premeditated or felony. Just as long as you all agree it's first-degree. That's what that means.

Felony murder, we talked to you about what it was. Look at the instruction. It's acting alone or with one or more other persons, and in the course of and in furtherance of this crime or immediate flight from that crime, the defendant or another person caused the death of another person. In this case, Amy Hopp and Michael Fro.

When you read the instruction when it says "the defendant or another person caused the death of any person," we are talking in this case about intended victims. We are not talking about any person. We are talking Michael Fro and Amy Hopp.

Finally, the evidence that we presented has dealt with gun evidence, the car wash, the shell casings, that .45 caliber with the WCC headstamp, the identifiable bullets, the full metal jacketed bullet, that's consistent with what we later found in the magazine, .45

caliber. It's the same gun and no other. We don't have a shotgun. We're not dealing with another type of weapon. We are dealing with one weapon here.

The car wash, the shell casings by both bodies. We are dealing with one shooter. That's all consistent with what the evidence is. We have one shooter here, not two. The same gun shell casing inside the Lincoln. Again, we know that the person who has that gun gets inside the Lincoln because that's where the shell casing is found that's responsible for the bullet hole coming out the window. Richard was seen with a gun in his waistband by Angela. He was seen a couple of times by Maxine. And Mr. Henders, looking across the street, says he sees the guy putting something in his waist as he's leaving the scene. Richard was seen with the gun after coming from California. Maxine heard Richard say he got it from his uncle in California. The gun was a .45 caliber. Richard's uncle had a black gun. We brought in Stephen Cam to tell you what kind of gun it was. Mary saw the gun in Richard's luggage.

The tape recorded telephone call. Why did we have this tape recorded telephone call? Basically, ladies and gentlemen, we stipulated that this was a legally authorized call that was made, a recorded call made by the detectives. And Richard knew it was recorded. That was part of the stipulation. What is said here, ladies and gentlemen, the first thing Richard Roja says is, "Hey, Fool, it wasn't even me, fool. I was just at the wrong place at the wrong time when my homeboys got arrested." And then the unidentified caller says, "Uh-huh." And Richard Roja says, "I was right there by the car and the car links me to everything and they're trying to throw crazy ass charges on my ass." And then the unidentified caller says, "Hey, what do you call it. Hey, how did they find out it was Jose's gun?"

Listen to it. You got to listen to it intently to hear that, but you'll hear him say that. Listen to the call. Richard Roja, "Hey, Fool, this shit's recorded, dog. Naw, that's what they're trying to say. They said that somebody's uncle and shit."

Unidentified caller, there's some kind of talk. Richard Roja, "My uncle, yeah, and I was like what the blank, and I'm sure like what. I don't know." Then there's another inaudible from the unidentified caller. Richard Roja, "Somebody's being a snitch." That's what he called it on the phone, a "snitch." He said, "Somebody's sending rumors, they're trying to lock me up forever, fool." He says, "They didn't even find it." They didn't even find what? "They didn't even find it, but, yeah, they got my—they got my nana's pad over here." There's an additional portion of the tape recording that you're going to hear. Unidentified caller says, "You have three. We just—I called that, think on, you got three open charges." Richard says, "Three open?" He says, "Yeah." Unidentified caller says, "Yeah." And they agree. And the unidentified caller says, "It says the one they're holding you on right now is, I think 'cause you were there." Richard, "Yeah." Unidentified caller, "Fucking conspiracy.

I mean, first-degree murder." Richard Roja, "Yeah." Unidentified caller, "Because you were there, that's why." Richard Roja, "Exactly. And if they can't prove it, Dog, I'm gonna get out." And that's where the tape cuts.

THE COURT: Mr. Barr, how much more time do you have left?

MR. BARR: I have the tape, and then about ten more minutes.

THE COURT: Why don't we take our noon recess. We've been going at it for two hours. Why don't we take our break now. We will come back at 1:30 and Mr. Barr will finish his closing argument.

AFTERNOON SESSION

THE COURT: The record will reflect the presence of counsel and the defendant. It was my understanding, Mr. Mill, that you wanted to bring something to the Court's attention?

MR. MILL: I do, regarding the audiotape that's about to be played.

THE COURT: Okay.

MR. MILL: What Mr. Barr did was write down the transcript verbatim, which is what the Court precluded the State from doing, showing the jury a transcript which would indicate what the State thinks is said on that tape. And I would ask that that handwritten transcript that's up here on the board not be shown to the jury when they're about to play the tape, otherwise they're doing exactly what the Court has ordered them not to do.

THE COURT: Mr. Barr?

MR. BARR: Yes, Judge. We are in middle of closing argument, and that's the State position as to what's being said. If Mr. Mill disagrees with what's being said, of course he will have an opportunity to counteract that and show his own version of what he thinks that tape says. I don't think the State should be in any way precluded from pointing out to the jury what we believe is being said on that tape.

THE COURT: Anything else on this issue?

MR. MILL: The State is not portraying this as what it believes is being said. It is saying this is what is on the tape. So it's misleading.

THE COURT: All right. I think this is argument, and you can certainly make an argument to the contrary if you believe it's appropriate. So it is ordered denying the defendant's motion. Can we bring the jury in now?

MR. MILL: Yes.

(Whereupon, the following proceedings were held in the presence of the jury:)

THE COURT: Ladies and gentlemen, when we left off, the State was in their initial closing argument by Mr. Barr. Go ahead, Mr. Barr.

MR. BARR: Thank you, Judge.

Ladies and gentlemen, before we left off we were talking about the gun evidence, we described the shell casings and the bullets, what was observed and taken from the car wash. We also pointed out the statements that the defendant made to Maxine Hernand and Mary Mungar, as well as the fact that the defendant returned to the vehicle with Stephanie Martin.

In any event, we described to you a tape recorded telephone call that was taken on or about March 24th. And on March 24th it was a legally authorized call that was legally authorized to be recorded. And Richard Roja is one of the individuals on the call. The other voice is unknown. Unidentified. But Richard Roja is certainly speaking on that recorded call. And, ladies and gentlemen, he knew that that call was being recorded.

I'd like to go ahead and play that tape for you at this time. I want you to be aware, ladies and gentlemen, that there's an area there where he talks about, "Hey, how did they find out it was Jose's gun?" I want you to listen to that. You can hear that.

(Whereupon, a tape recording was played.)

MR. BARR: It's a very brief tape. However, ladies and gentlemen, when you play that tape, you can hear the unidentified caller talking about Jose's gun. That's Jose Mercad. Jose Mercad, the person that Steve Cam sold the gun to.

Ladies and gentlemen, we talked a little bit about the physical evidence. I'd like to review some of that physical evidence with you. The physical evidence that we have in this case would be the cut up wallet contents, the County Library card, the Safeway card. We talked a little bit about the shoe print evidence from the scene, shoe print evidence that was illustrated by Mr. David Crave. The physical evidence of the actual shoes, the K-Swiss. You can take a look at these. You can compare them to the acetate and the actual one-on-one photo blow-ups that we have in this case. You will have an opportunity to do that all. That's in the evidence. You'll have an opportunity to see that. And that came from this shoe, the K-Swiss. You'll also have the Fila shoes.

Well, here's Louis' shoe. Here's the Fila shoe. You can look at the sizes inside. Comparable size tennis shoes. Let me get to these boats that Andy was wearing and Tony was wearing, obviously a radical difference in terms of sizes.

Ladies and gentlemen, we've taken the liberty of having numerous photographs of these shoes entered into evidence so that there's no question who was wearing which shoe at what time. You have photos, so there's no question about what shoe we're talking about and which shoe was taken off each individual. That's the shoe print evidence.

Ladies and gentlemen, finally, you've got Richard's statements to Maxine about how he shot the guy and then shot the girl, and the number of times. Maxine, she's not a perfect witness because she didn't remember everything 100 percent all the time. She's a person. She says she knows he shot him more than once. She can't tell you specifically how many times he shot them, but she knows he shot them more than once. And you know that's consistent with the scene, the physical evidence. That's consistent with what we have in terms of the shell casings, the bullets. And here you'll have a chance to take a look at them. It's consistent with what Richard says to Mary Mungar when he says he saw the guy's blood mixing with the water. You've seen the photo. We're not going to show that photo again. He had to be there. He had to be there, and he had to see it. You know it; you feel it; it's right there. He told Mary that he ran after the girl to shut her up.

Evangelina Ballester tells us about how the guy approaches the girl, and so does Daniel Henders talk about the guy approaching the girl. We know that happened. That's what the evidence shows us. He shot the girl. And then she also saw the kid's photo in the wallet. Well, you heard Mrs. Fro talk about how he had childrens photos in the wallet. The bottom line is, ladies and gentlemen, also in terms of Stephanie, how he came back to the car, and the description about how he almost shot himself. Well, Stephanie wasn't perfect. She couldn't tell you it was Richard that said that, but it was somebody in the car who almost shot himself.

Well, ladies and gentlemen, that's the same person who had the .45 caliber semiautomatic handgun that shot and killed Michael Fro and then shot and killed Amy Hopp, he got in that car and discharged that weapon and blew that hole into that car window. So, ladies and gentlemen, those are the statements that we are talking about. We encourage you to use your common sense in looking at this evidence.

And that reminds me of my old house. We told you that we spent the last couple of weeks here reconstructing the blocks, the building blocks to this old house.

Ladies and gentlemen, it's Richard Roja's house. It's Richard Roja's house from back in March of 2003. This is Richard Roja as of March the 12th of 2003, and that's what he looked like. And we had several people throughout the course of this proceeding tell you that, yeah, that's how Richard Roja appeared back in March of 2003.

Ladies and gentlemen, what we've shown you in terms of the building blocks in this case, we have shown you the evidence, we have shown you the statements. And, you know, it's not perfect. It's a simple house. You can look into the windows of the house and you see it's fraught with conspiracy, it's fraught with armed robbery, and you see it's fraught with murder. That's the house. It's a simple house. Some of the blocks may be a little out of kilter, maybe missing a block here, but you can still see it.

It's a house that's the State's case, ladies and gentlemen. It's Richard Roja as he was back on March the 3rd and March the 4th of 2003. And, do you know what? He's standing right at the door of that house and he's got that .45 caliber semiautomatic handgun in his hand. He may have had a hat on his head, we don't know, but he's standing right there at that door. In fact, we've got his shoe prints leading up to the door.

Ladies and gentlemen, review the evidence, examine the State's case, look at the photographs. Return a guilty verdict of all counts. We thank you very much for your time.

THE COURT: All right. Mr. Mill, please begin when you're ready.

MR. MILL: Good afternoon, ladies and gentlemen. I want to start not with the four women: Maxine, Angela, Stephanie, and Mary, which might be a logical place to start, but I do want to begin with a guy who in my judgment epitomizes everything that is wrong with the prosecutor's case, and in a real sense, everything that's right about our short case that we presented to you.

That guy is Daniel Henders. He's the trailer park guy, and he came to court and he took the witness stand under oath and he told you all about certain things, including that that car, the Kia, he didn't know it was a Kia, was not in the auto bay dark lot, the business. And he told you that the shooter then ran to the small car. And Mr. Henders, told you that he was replaying this contemporaneously to 9-1-1 as it was being said, and he told you that the small car then went northbound, made a U-turn. And after he's done telling you all this, he's real early on in the trial, the prosecution calls Detective Low to say when Henders was first interviewed that he saw the car in the dark auto lot, he was not on 9-1-1 contemporaneously. Low said, I listened to the 9-1-1 tapes and it was obvious that Henders' called 9-1-1 shortly afterwards, which is probably just like every 9-1-1 call. You see an event and you go to the phone and you call. And Detective Low told you that the car was not near Missouri, it was in the auto lot. And that it was southbound and not northbound. And on and on and on. And so you folks are looking for somebody to give you a consistent version of what is happening, and this is what you're getting.

The State is calling its own witness, putting him on the witness stand to say one thing, and then impeaching its own witness with a police officer because he said something else, and you're left with two different stories from one witness. And this is the theme of the State's case. It's hard enough to follow one story from one guy, and you all have to follow more than one story from one guy, and here's what we counter with.

From my office, investigator T.J. Horra is called as a factual witness, and he simply tells you, I went out to the Henders' trailer area, and by the fence I measured it. And T.J. said, I couldn't get inside here, so I just measured it from the fence, so add another ten feet. But from here, you have to go all the way across the field. And T.J. had two different measurements: One to the car wash bay, and one on the middle, where Amy Hopp probably was lying. And he told you 560 feet roughly, add another ten gets you to about 570 feet, or just shy of two football fields.

Now, has anybody ever sat in the end zone and tried to watch the action on the other side of the field? You know what you can see and you know what you can't see. And you double that in this case, and you have almost two football fields. And T.J. said he did this in the daytime. Admittedly, I could see peoples silhouettes, perhaps what their section was by what they were wearing, but could you see what was in their hands? Probably not. And then Mr. Barr goes after him. Did you recreate it? Did you put something in the hands? Did you do this? Did you do that? And Mr. Horra is trying to give you an idea of what you can see from the Henders' trailer.

Here's the problem. Early on, here's what the State needs Mr. Henders to say. That the shooter that he saw was wearing a baseball cap backwards, and that the shooter was shooting like this, a gangster style shooting. They need him to say that because there's one woman who was a heck of a lot closer, a lovely lady who spoke only Spanish, who got a heck of a good look at this and saw clear in here, if nothing else was clear, height, weight, all that other stuff.

And as this composite is drawn, and it's drawn from her mouth, and it's shown to her, she says it's pretty good. Chubbier maybe, but the hairline, that's the hair. Combed back, that's the hair. The one thing she said is, that's the hair.

So Mr. Henders must give you one piece of information that's important, the baseball cap. Because from all the way across the field, a baseball cap looks like the hair that Evangelina Ballester saw, and is flat out wrong.

Well, there was another approach the State tried to use to counter, to soften the blow of Evangelina. It's Ursula Ocan. She was called early on. She had hair, like, down to her waist, I think. And she gets on the witness stand, and I cross-examine her, and I ask her, didn't you just say outside that Richard was shaved down to the nub? And did you see her twist? Did I say that? Yes, I did say that. But did you say outside that he was shaved down to the nub around the time of the car wash shooting? Yes, but I just saw the sides. He always wore a cap and he also wore it backwards. And the State is really into that. And, see, on redirect, they ask her the question, and the color of the hat, Ms. Ocan, was what? White. That didn't fit. Plus, she's the only one, Ms. Ocan, to say that perhaps Richard didn't have a shaved head. Every single other witness, be it aunt, be it the other aunt, everybody else says that Richard looked like this the day of the shooting. And it's really uncontroverted. And they need the baseball cap to put hair on this guy, because hair looks like a baseball cap.

Look, cross-examine of Ms. Ocan probably wasn't fun. Cross-examination is probably not a pleasant experience for anybody. But it's under the Constitution, and I've got a job to do, to defend this guy. And I hope I'm not offending anybody, but you just can't come to court, tell your story and not be tested and challenged. So here's what we are left with. Ms. Ballester is mistaken on the hair, according to the government. But believe Mr. Henders from across the field. And when I had her make the "X" on this photo, 34, she made two "X's" but I believe the way it came down was that this "X" represented her view.

And so Ms. Ballester is on the street, and that's a pretty darn good view. And she said it lasted three to five minutes. Mr. Barr says that's extended. It probably is. It lasted at least one cycle of a light, at least long enough for her to see everything and see the guy look around. You could tell a baseball cap from here. And this is the view, this is a picture taken the morning of the shooting from the fence line at the Henders trailer.

So here's what you're getting from the government. Instead of Mr. Henders was just too darn far, and just too darn inconsistent, what the State should be telling you is, forget about Henders. Just forget about him totally. He's all over the place, and he's too darn far. And that's really just a fair assessment of Mr. Henders. But they can't do that because they need that ball cap, they need something on Richard's head to look like hair. And that's how thin the State is spread.

Now, here's the other slim evidence. At that time the State wanted you to accept as the gospel from Mr. Henders the gangster style of the holding of the weapon. Here's what, now in closing argument, Mr. Barr is telling you, that the magazine probably wasn't used in this homicide, that this magazine has been featured since day one by the State as if it was used in this homicide, and it wasn't. Until somebody from this jury, posed a question to Detective Clay on the witness stand: Detective Clay, did you ask Mr. Cam whether this very magazine was his? He said, no, that's not mine. And so the government gave up on the magazine, but there was a long period of time there that this was the feature, right down to Mr. Morr talking about little scratches, a little scratch made only by European style weaponry on the latch, right down to the latch looking like that of a European style weapon. This was it, until just recently. And that's why the State asked Mr. Henders about this and then put Mr. Morr on the stand to say, did you try to fire the weapon? Because the State knew that this magazine, when inserted in the Sig Sauer, just didn't work. It could get the first round off if you stuck your finger in it, or if you held it with your thumb in it, but after that it would jam unless you continued to put pressure up to close that gap at the very top, to close that gap. And so it was important to have Mr. Morr, the expert, say when you turn the gun like this, boom boom, boom. It closes the gap and you can fire that weapon. It is now operable. So Morr was asked that question, and he spit the bit. No, I didn't try it that way. I asked him, well, why not? I wasn't asked to.

And then we asked Detective Clay, did you ask him to do it? No. He's the expert. I just give the gun to him. That's why when I say that Henders epitomizes everything that's wrong with the State's case, I mean it. You all are asked to make a pretty heavy decision here whether my client is guilty of murder, two first-degree murders, and what you're given is people like Henders. And to make matters worse, what the State should do with Mr. Henders is just dismiss him and say believe some of it, but not all of it, and not impeach their own witness. Let me move on to the scientific evidence. And I want to be as brief as I can with you all, and I will not cover everything because it's really hard to sit and listen to all this. But the scientific evidence, what you've learned that's really important is, really, there are three levels of proof in scientific cases:

1. We cannot make an identification.
2. We make an identification, i.e. 100 percent match; or
3. That big old middle ground similarities between tread size, similarities between tread design, things like that, it's a gray area.

And I think you have to kind of pocket that.

But you know Richard Roja has, and I said this in my opening, been waiting the better part of two years to have the government come up with some sort of physical evidence to say he is responsible for that homicide, and it just hasn't happened. And it doesn't matter how many pictures the State puts into evidence of shoes, how many angles it puts into evidence of tennis shoes, how many acetates it sticks up on that board, when it gets down to it, there is just one thing relevant, and it is my one and single question to Mr. Crave after two times on the witness stand and burning about eight hours of time up here. And that question was: Did Richard's shoes make the impressions at the car wash? Yes, no, or I don't know. Mr. Crave's answer: I don't know. This isn't a civil case. And the Judge has instructed you on that. The burden of proof here is the highest. It's far above a civil case. In a civil case it's probabilities. In a civil case it's 51 percent and you get the money. That's all you have to show. But this is proof beyond a reasonable doubt. This is proof that has to leave you folks sitting on the jury not just a little bit convinced, not saying he's possibly guilty, probably guilty, likely guilty, could be guilty. Similarities, things of that nature. This is proof that leaves you, the Judge's words, "firmly convinced." You feel good about convicting him because you're now "firmly convinced" that he's the responsible party for taking two lives on March 4th. And do you get the feeling that the State now believes that it can simply present a whole bunch of iffy weak evidence in order to build its house because it believes that if they put a whole bunch of weak evidence together you get a strong case? And that's simply not true. You put a whole bunch of weak evidence together and you still have a weak case. You go to school and you get a C in every single class, your average is a C.

And just because you stretch probably one hour's worth of testimony into a couple of days on shoe impressions does not mean it's any better evidence, does not mean that the final conclusion is anything other than, I don't know. It is not a situation where quantity is going to win out over quality.

The State flew in Mr. Cam from California. Two-time felon. Drug dealer. He told you that. Convicted in Ventura County and Orange County, 2002, 2003, of dope transactions. And the gun that he got from his dad was sold, he says, to Mr. Jose Mercad, but really the situation was more of a pawn situation. When he got out of jail and off probation he was going to take that gun back. And that gun transaction took place in the garage where Mercad did his dope deals. We know that because Richard's aunt came in and testified to that. And if you believe for one moment that in a drug infested place like that dealing with felonies, that Richard Roja is the only possibility of taking that gun just because he disappeared around that time, then you'll believe a lot. And what you should ask the State is, would you please, would you please give us some good, hard facts that Richard Roja stole that gun, that he left with that gun, a Sig Sauer Browning around Valentine's Day. And instead you get Mr. Cam. But it must be true, according to the government, because they give you a scratchy tape that they've played here, and you have to sit there and listen, and some unknown person is talking to Richard on this tape. It's two years, and this is what they're coming up with, a scratchy tape, where it sounds sort of like some unknown person is talking about Jose's gun, and it sounds like this person has information about the case just like all these women do who testified, and they're discussing the evidence. And what you hope to get on that tape is a statement by Richard Roja, I shot the man; I shot the woman; the blood and the water mixed; I was angry. I don't know. But you don't get any of that on the tape.

You get Richard saying this is the kind of evidence that they have against me, Dude, or what's the language they use? "Fool." Or "Dog." Everything is punctuated like that. And you get things like Richard saying they're trying to say that he was involved. They're linking me to the crime basically, because at the time of the arrest, at the time of the arrest on 3/12, not the day of the homicide on 3/4, that I guess is in this tape, they found Richard in the car. We know that to be true because Detectives Clay and Forem and Low all found Richard and Maxine and—well, Louis was in the closet—down by that car when they were arrested. So that's what Richard is apparently saying in this tape.

You know, if those bullets that were found in the middle bedroom closet were some sort of rare bullet, you might say, hallelujah. But this is a March of 2003 crime, and the headstamps were 2002. Now, how many bullets do you think Winchester, one of the most popular companies out there, according to the testimony, produced in 2002? Fifteen million? It sounds like a little bit of smoke from where the State is coming from. But there's no fire here.

T.J. Horra from my office said you can buy the Winchester headstamp, 2002, at any Wal-Mart. He checked, and that's about how popular it is. So if you all can come up with some rare bullet to link Richard Roja to this crime, fine. Otherwise, what you're dealing with is Winchester, which have been making the .45 auto cartridges since the year, according to Mr. Morr, 2003.

So the shooter gets in the car, has a gun in his hand, because we know that because the window was shot out. And let me say this. There is no doubt that a latent fingerprint is a chance impression. It certainly is. And just because I touch a surface, although a nice shiny surface is good, it doesn't mean I'm going to leave a fingerprint, because of oils and all that. And I may just touch it and smear it. And there's a whole bunch of different reasons.

Look at those seats and tell me that a guy with a gun who's getting into in car, who fires the gun, who is fumbling with keys and trying to get them in there, isn't going to leave his paw prints somewhere, perhaps on the seats. I'm not 100 percent sure

I can't tell you that. It could be just chance. But what is important here is how the State treated this whole issue of fingerprints. Richard Roja on trial for his life is told that these are just chance prints. Therefore, we don't do the Superglue method. Therefore, we don't give you the chance that your prints may not be there. Or, what if they did that and his prints were there? It would be a run up the flagpole, just as sure as I'm standing here. So what it is, is Richard, if we found your prints in the car, you'd be guilty. Richard, because we can't find your prints in the car, well, you're still guilty.

The failure to do the extra test highlights a couple of things:

Number one, they never ran the prints against Tony Mo's known prints. Mr. Barr, on direct with the witnesses, did you run the prints found in the car—this is with Diana Molin—found in and on the car against the three other guys? Yes. And that was it. Nothing against Mo.

And, number two, doesn't this really just highlight the State's cavalier attitude towards taking those prints in the first place?
Mr. Barr: Diana Molin, can you get prints off a wet piece of metal like a car?
That would be very difficult, Mr. Barr.

Well, she did. She got a couple of fingerprints off the wet metal on the outside. Didn't match anybody but Mr. Fro or Ms. Hopp, but she did. And I asked her on cross-examination, can you let it dry? Oh, yes, I can let it dry. And after you let it dry, is that when you did the fingerprinting? Yes. And is that when you found prints? Yes. Why didn't you Superglue the seats, Diana Molin? I wasn't asked. I don't do it anyway.

Detective Clay: I probably wouldn't consider that. In the first place, that's a biohazard. We have to buy the car.

Look, this isn't a car theft case. This is a murder case. The State must go the extra mile. It is their burden to do so. Their failure to do so be used against them and it should not be used against my client. Moving on to the topic of the wall, the wall between the apartment complexes has become a focal point of a number of witnesses. And you heard from Ursula, and you heard from Tabatha on that, that Amy Hopp would be on the hood of that car, this is Ursula, and the boys would huddle, and the boys would look over at us, including Amy, and they'd do things like whistle.

And I think you're supposed to get a cold chill because the appearance is that days before this homicide Richard Roja and the boys had scoped out that car, had liked it, and they knew what they were going to do. The feeling is that because they eyeballed each other over that wall, Richard Roja was now conspiring to kill, or at least take that car days before it happened.

And yet when Mr. Barr asked the crucial question, did you hear Richard Roja say anything to Amy? The answer was, no. And when I asked Tabatha, did the boys whistle at any female that walked by? The answer was, yes. And this sort of weird inclination that there was going to be something more, some sort of conspiracy going back that far just turned out to be absolutely nothing.

Let me get to the women. Here's what the State has. There are four women: Stephanie: Richard was at the car wash. Maxine and Mary: Richard confessed to killing two people. And, finally, Angela: Richard was with the group.

So, where is Rick Mill coming from on this? And here's what the State is going to say. Why, why on God's green earth would the four women lie about what they knew about Richard? Why would they do that? Is there some sort of weird conspiracy here to get Richard? And, if so, Rick Mill has got to come up with a reason.

Well, listen, that is your real situation out there. You've probably never even heard the likes of the way these people were living, including Richard. A 40-year-old woman smoking dope with her son; the one bedroom junior apartment that they all lived in; 15-year-olds sleeping with 15-years-olds; a 15-year-old sleeping with a 21-year-old; the speed; the marijuana; the sex. And this apartment was, I can just imagine waking up, it's all blankets and hair and shoes and guns and everything all over the place. And Louis, who gets all the women in the world, he's got Ursula, he's got Maxine, he's got Stephanie, and they're all talking together. From the car wash homicide to the arrest, eight solid days, they're all there. Don't expect Rick Mill to instill some method to that madness out there or some sense in the absolutely senseless.

Why did they all lie to get Richard? I don't have a clue. I cannot answer that question. Why did all four women lie to the police? That's one consistency in this case, I guess. All four of those women told the police a version that differs from what they came in and told you at trial.

Why did Stephanie Martin lie to the grand jury September 10th, 2003? Why does a mother smoke speed with her son? Why does a grown woman say she wasn't high on March 4th? I wasn't high. You weren't high? I wasn't high because I didn't smoke speed that night. I just smoked pot. They're living in their own worlds, folks. Here's how the State handled the four women, and they did so in each case.

Step 1: Get them to tell their story. That took the bulk of the testimony of each of these women. The car wash, the shooting, the confessions from Richard, and all of that.

Step 2: Confess that you were lying to the police early on; and

Step 3: Give each woman—I say "women," but, I mean, Stephanie was 15 at the time. Give each of them the opportunity to hug some sort of emotion as an excuse for their lying to the police. I was scared. I was nervous. I was shy. I made that one up. I was indifferent.

Stephanie: I didn't want to get in the middle of this stuff.

Indifference. Mary: I felt scared that the boys were hovering around me, running and gunning, until one of the jurors had the wherewithal to ask a question.

Mary, who said they were running and gunning, it wasn't Richard, it was Louis. How about, I don't trust the police. I have unknown fears.

Mary: I didn't want to go to my apartment because I didn't know what I might find.

The State asked Angela, were you dishonest with Detective Clay? Her answer was, yes, the first time. And then the following question: And were you dishonest during your second meeting with Detective Clay, too? And she was supposed to say yes, but she said oh, no. And it came out that Angela was dishonest the first meeting and Angela was dishonest the second meeting, because she said Stephanie was with me and P.J. all night long, she wasn't even at the car wash.

And what really happened was, the State pitched her a softball. She's supposed to hit it and say I'm sorry. And it was a swing and a miss. It didn't go according to plan. Maxine, did you approach the detectives and volunteer the information? Answer: Yes. Oops. Question again: Did you approach the detectives and volunteer information? Oh, yes, she said. Missed it again, because she didn't. Because her version to the detective was different than her version here in court. And there were times when Maxine forgot her lines altogether.

Mr. Barr: Maxine, you overheard a conversation about a gun with Richard and Louis? Yes. When did that occur in relationship to the car wash? The correct answer was "before" because, remember, Richard has gotten rid of that gun after, so she would have seen it and had the conversation. When did that occur in relation to the car wash? After. After the car wash? Yes. You heard Richard talk about the gun before the car wash? Yes. So was it before the car wash or after the car wash? Before. And then she went on later on: After. Before. Step three was a visible failure at times as well. Do you remember Mary? She couldn't tell the truth to the police early on because she was scared because the boys were hovering around her from March 4th all the way to I guess April 15th when she was recorded by the police. Who was hovering? Well, they started getting closer and closer, hanging around me more and more, Louis and Andy. The implications here are that Louis and Andy are some kind of Godfather's looking at Mary. She's got information, we need to hang with her so that Mary doesn't talk. And the implication was 24/7, Louis and Andy were suppressing her from giving truthful material to the police department.

Number 3, the emotion. I was scared. And what really happened with Mary? She went to work every day. She was driven to work by other people. Somebody came and picked her up in the morning. When she drove by the car wash and screamed, it was with another person unnamed. Nobody went to work and sat in her office. Nobody made her not call the police. Maxine and Tenise would pick her up from work, and this whole thing, this whole cocoon of danger because the boys were hanging on her just fails miserably.

She was at her office; she had a phone; she could call. She could call the police any time she wanted to. And in her head, since March 4th, she had horrible, horrible statements from Richard that he killed two people because he was angry, and he watched as the blood mixed with the water. This is what she knows. From March 4th to April 15th she says nothing. She was scared. That's what the State is asking you to believe.

So what does Mary do? On March 12th she's called at work by Detective Forem, would you please come straight to your house. Oh, yes, Detective. She gets to Ranch, and Detective Forem says, did you come straight here? Yes, I did. Did you stop anywhere on the way? No, I did not.

In court she tells you, I lied. Step two. I lied. I wasn't truthful with the police. I was scared. But now I speak the truth. And when Rick Mill is asked why all these women would conspire to tell lies to implicate Richard, you don't have to walk very far to get to that point with this girl. So she finally gets to Ranch, and she's face-to-face with the police officer. And they're searching her apartment. There's a lot of police officers there. Clay is there off and on. And she's finally at a point where she can tell somebody of this horrible confession. Nobody is hovering around her any more. There's no reason to be scared. And what does she do? She looks at Forem in the eye and lies. And she continued on the stand. Why didn't you tell the police earlier about Richard? Scared.

Here are a few more for you. I didn't think the police would protect me and my son. I was distraught. Distraught? I was afraid of the police. I was afraid of the boys. I was worried. I was worried about snitching. She didn't talk to the police until April 15th for a reason, and that was to protect her boy. And every lull in the testimony when she was up on the witness stand, every lull, during numerous lulls in her testimony when there was a pause, she would add, but Tony was home. But Tony was with his girlfriend Tenise. Tony and Tenise always slept in the middle of that floor. I reached for Tony's shoes. I tried to find my shoes, and Tony was home. Tony was home; Tony was home; Tony was home. And the final straw was when I asked her, did you tell the police that you were doing this to help your son? And what she told the police was, I can't believe I'm telling you this; I hope to God this helps my son.

There are minor inconsistencies in this case and there are major ones. People who tell the truth and have to retell it a number of times may suffer from some minor inconsistencies. Nobody can be perfect. I agree. Because you're retelling the event as you perceived it rather than making it up, and having to remember what your previous lies were so that you can retell the story every time. And people who make stuff up, they faulter, and they don't faulter with minor inconsistencies. They faulter big time with the big events. Not, this tie was blue, and it turned out to be aqua. Something really, really significant. Major inconsistencies. And let me point to just a few. Maxine, at trial, she takes the stand and tells you, I spent the night at Ranch. I was there all night. And she talks about Tenise and Tony being there and playing on the computer, and the boys leaving, and the boys coming home. The next morning she was there.

Maxine. March 12th with Detective Low, question: Did you stay the night on Wednesday/Thursday? Answer: No. I slept at home. And I asked Maxine on the stand, did you tell Low that? No. Yes. I don't know. I don't remember. That's a major inconsistency, and you've got to ask yourselves what on earth is going on with Maxine? Maxine, at trial, there was the barbecue, and you all heard the testimony. Okay. With Detective Low back in March of 2003: When Louis came home, he had nothing. Louis got nothing from the car. Wallet, towel, keys, picture, nothing, she said to Detective Low. And that's why I called her to establish that. And one of the jurors asked Maxine, did you ask Louis about the towel and keys, and all that stuff? No. Did you get the feeling that she was awfully mechanical, that she did real well when the government was leading her through her testimony asking her questions that would require just a yes or no response. But when she had the stepping stones set out in front of her, she did a pretty good job of stepping on them. Did you see Richard with a gun? Yes. Did you hear him talk about the gun? Yes. Did he say where he got the gun? Yes. Did it come from California? Yes. Yes. Yes. But when you ask her to go it on her own and you ask her to ski outside the wave, things just fell apart. I mean, talk about major inconsistencies. Stephanie, who tells you this story about the hotel, the Red Roof Inn and the big bang, and waking up, and all that, when she first meets with Detective Clay, no hotel, no car wash. I went to sleep. Then Clay, they go and get this Red Roof bill and they show it to her. Oh, well, yeah, we did go to that hotel, but it was at 6:00 in the morning, or 5:00 in the morning, because they paged us. And no car wash, or nothing like that, but I went to the hotel just before going to school.

And then at trial, the Kia was parked in that dark auto lot. But to the grand jury September of 2003, I don't know where we parked. We may have parked in the car wash, we may have parked in that auto lot. I don't know. Under oath. Today she's firm. A couple of years ago she doesn't know. And I asked her what happened between then and now to firm up her opinion, or I asked her it a number of different ways, or to change your opinion. What's happened? Something has got to happen. I don't know. And one of you asked in written form of Stephanie, did you ask the guys why they pulled into this dark business? No. Do you remember what Richard Roja was wearing? Yes. White pants, no hat. Why did she tell all these inconsistencies? She's scared. And when the State asked her the one question, was Tony with you at all that night? Did you count the seconds before she answered? Was Tony with you at all that night, Stephanie? No. I'd like you to push aside these four women who are all over the board. You shake it, it's gone, and you draw anew. Push it aside. And what are you left with? Not Henders. He's so way out there. But you're left with Evangelina Ballester, the most solid eye witness that you've got. What she wanted to tell you was, she looked at this photo lineup of Richard Roja, who wasn't one of the guys she picked out. Well, actually, the State did kind of a bizarre lineup here. They said, do you recognize anybody in this courtroom in this set of pictures? Richard was one of them. Like we're supposed to be identifying people in the courtroom rather than at the crime scene. But here's what the State wanted. No, I don't see anybody in the courtroom that matches these six pictures. Because then they could argue, she's just really out there, she's not a real good identifier. The guy was right in front of her. Oh, I recognize this person here as being that person there. That was the end of that. But when it came to the photograph of the person who did the killing, and Richard was shown to her, she did not recognize him. What she recognized over and over again was one thing that she was so clear on from her pretty good vantage point was the hair on that guy.

In summing, Richard's been chased across two years, and they've come up with no prints and no hair. No hair, no blood, no guns. They've have given you a scratchy tape and an inconclusive shoe impression where the expert says, I don't know. If you're convinced of Richard's guilt firmly, firmly convinced of Richard Roja's guilt on that evidence, convict him. You're duty-bound to do so. But the evidence that you have been given is miles and miles apart from that. Any doubt that you have should be resolved in Richard's favor. And I'd ask that you find him not guilty. Thank you, Judge.

(NEXT THE COURT CALLED ON THE ASSISTANT PROSECUTOR TO GIVE HIS SUMMATION TO THE JURY. HE MADE A VALIANT EFFORT TO UNDERMINE THE DAMAGE TO THE STATE'S CASE DONE BY THE PUBLIC DEFENDER:)

Ladies and gentlemen, this is the State's opportunity to respond to what has just been argued to you. And upon listening to it, basically the gist of it is to disregard the testimony of basically all of the State's witnesses.

Ladies and gentlemen, you know after hearing Detective Clay speak, you know certainly by the mountains and mountains of exhibits that you have been shown over the past two weeks, that Detective Clay and the police and State don't necessarily take each and every witness at face value. When they're told the story, they go back, they check those details and the facts and see if those facts can be corroborated by other evidence.

I want to give you an example of that. An example is the testimony of Maxine Hernand. The defense counsel spent a great deal of time telling you why you should throw that testimony out, that it didn't mean anything, that she is inconsistent, that she lied to the police. And because of these things, that she wasn't sincere. She was scared of somebody who she thinks shot two people, that you should throw her testimony out for that reason.

Ladies and gentlemen, Maxine Hernand said that there was a barbecue at Mary Mungar's apartment, and that Louis Castell had burned the things that he had taken back from the robbery in that barbecue. So what do the police do? They check it out. They see whether or not that story holds water, whether or not there are things to corroborate what she says. Just because somebody tells us something, we don't always believe it. We check it out. We see whether it makes sense. We do that. And what did we find? We went to the barbecue, because the police investigated the contents of the barbecue, and what do they find in this barbecue? Two pieces of plastic. Not just any two pieces of plastic, but a County Library card melted at the bottom of the barbecue, and a Safeway card. That Safeway card has 11 digits on it, seven of them were detectable after the fire, and all seven of them consistent with the Safeway card that belonged to Michael Fro. Now that's a story checking out to the last digit. So he doesn't want you to believe Maxine Hernand. It gets better. He doesn't want you to believe Maxine Hernand because she tells you the truth when she heard Richard Roja say that he killed those two people. That's a story that checks out. But that's not all, ladies and gentlemen. Let's look at Maxine's statement regarding the K-Swiss shoes. She makes a statement, she sees Richard Roja wearing K-Swiss shoes. And what do they find? They find when they arrest Richard Roja they have K-Swiss shoes. He's wearing K-Swiss shoes. And not just any K-Swiss shoes, ladies and gentlemen, but K-Swiss with the exact same tread type, with the exact same size dimensions as the imprints that were found at the car wash bays at the murder. What are the odds of that happening by sheer circumstance?

No, ladies and gentlemen, Richard Roja stood at that car wash bay in his K-Swiss shoes, leaving impressions. And when Mary Mungar testified that Richard told her that he had watched Michael Fro's blood leave his body and roll down into that drain, that part of her story is backed up. It's backed up from what you saw at that scene.

And, see, when the defense counsel says throw Mary Mungar's testimony out because it doesn't make any sense, well, it does, ladies and gentlemen. And it was checked out and it was investigated. Mary Mungar wasn't at that car wash. How would she have known what that picture looked like? How would she have known that? She knew it because Richard Roja told her, as he had told Maxine Hernand.

Finally, ladies and gentlemen, let's go back to Maxine Hernand's testimony again. Let's check it a third time. It's checked out the first two times with the barbecue contents and the K-Swiss. Let's check it again. She says to the police, Richard said that he got the gun from his uncle in California. So, did the police just accept that at face value? No. They looked into it. They checked it out. And, guess what? They find out that Richard Roja has an uncle in California named Jose Mercad. They find out that Jose Mercad was sold a weapon that fired the same kind of ammunition that was found at the scene, .45 caliber ammunition, that it's the similar type gun to that type of gun that fired that ammunition. And that Jose Mercad just happens to have that gun at the same window in time that Richard Roja is living with him, what are the odds of that again just being a coincidence, just being a happenstance? Long odds, indeed, ladies and gentlemen. Long odds, indeed.

When you heard the tape, when you heard one of Mr. Roja's own acquaintances asking the question, how did they know it was Jose's gun? That had to be a surprise. Ladies and gentlemen, that had to be a surprise, because when you try to eliminate a trail like Richard Roja did, when you kill both victims, when you go and chase down Amy Hopp, a person that you know has seen you and can ID you, and to make sure to clean that trail up, you shoot her in the head again, you think that ought to do it. And when you have the evidence burned up in the barbecue, you think that ought to do it. You think you've covered your trail.

When you think the fear of what you might do to your witnesses will keep them quiet, and it seems to at first, you think you've done it, but what you don't know can hurt you. And in this case he didn't know about shoe impressions, he didn't know that these detectives would bust their butt and go get the contents out of that barbecue so an expert could find out what was on there. The police would go that extra yard. They would find that evidence.

Ladies and gentlemen, a lot was made out of Daniel Hender's testimony that maybe it couldn't have been very accurate given how far away he was. But, again, ladies and gentlemen, did the police take that testimony at face value, or did they test it? They tested it. They took pictures from where his vantage point was. Should you throw out everything that Daniel Henders said? Should you say, we should just ignore him? No, ladies and gentlemen. You consider all the evidence. When Evangelina Ballester puts an "X" where she thought she saw the girl fall, and you can tell from just looking at the photo where the body is, you know that's wrong. Does that mean that she wasn't trying to do her best on the stand? No, that doesn't mean that at all. Daniel Henders called 9-1-1 because that's what he felt citizens should do when they hear things, when they hear gunshots. And he's right. That's what you should do. And you should endeavor to do your best.

Was Daniel Henders right when he said his memory was better now than it was two years ago? Probably not. So people can be sincere and be mistaken about certain details. I believe, the State believes that applies to both Daniel Henders and Evangelina Ballester. Sometimes you're not prepared for things you see and hear, and you do the best that you can to remember it. People focus on different things. Some people may focus on clothing, other people may focus on actions. That's part of common sense, and you know how to judge when people are telling the truth and when they're not. The best way to do that, I believe page 4 in your jury instructions says, you evaluate witnesses' testimony in the context of all the other evidence that's in the case. And that's pretty much how you do it in your daily life. You kick the tires, you open the hood, you check out what people say to you, and you see if it makes sense in light of all the other things that you know. And in this case, ladies and gentlemen, you know that this man told two people that he did the shootings. You know that his own acquaintance believes that he had Uncle Jose's gun. You know that gun was no longer in California. You know the contents at the barbecue of the Ranch Apartments that just coincidentally happened to have the County Library and Safeway cards matching Michael Fro's. You know that the kind of shoes this man wears and wore at the time were K-Swiss, that they had a unique tread pattern on them. You look at the tread pattern. What does it look like? Is it the same size and shape as the shoe imprints that were left at that scene and left by that bay door? You know that. So when it comes down to all those things that you know, when you use that to judge the witnesses' testimony, these women turned out to be pretty right-on. Their stories hold up. They have been checked out, cross-checked, checked three times in the case of Maxine Hernand, and in each case they have not been found lying. The proof that was gathered after the statement substantiated the statement that had been made. There's been some talk about trying to create another defendant in this case, trying to say that Tony Mo did this. Ladies and gentlemen, we asked every single witness, not just Mary Mungar but every single witness whether Tony Mo was with those people or not. Angela Martin, Stephanie Martin, Maxine Hernand, we asked those people and none of them said that Tony Mo was there.

All of the evidence points at Richard Roja. Not one scrap of evidence that's been brought in, other than this allegation by the defense that somehow Evangelina Ballester picked out Tony Mo is false. She didn't pick him out. When you have all the evidence that the State has, all the evidence that I have gone through with you, that Mr. Barr has gone through with you, when you have all the physical evidence and it all points in only one direction, you don't need to worry, you don't need to hide anything, you don't need to omit anything, and you don't need to do anything else. You just put your proof in front of you people and have the decision be made. Ladies and gentlemen, the State will ask that you find Mr. Roja guilty on all charges. Thank you.

(IT'S DECISION TIME! THE JUDGE AGAIN REMINDED THE JURORS OF THEIR DUTY AND RESPONSIBILITIES, AND OUTLINED THE VARIOUS CHARGES AGAINST RICHARD ROJA. THEN AT 3:00 P.M., THE JURY RETIRED TO DELIBERATE THEIR VERDICT.)

TENTH DAY, FEBRUARY 6, 2005
MORNING SESSION

(THE MORNING STARTED OFF WITH A QUESTION FROM THE JURY TO CLARIFY THE DEFINITION OF ONE OF THE CHARGES. THE JUDGE SET UP A TELEPHONE CONFERENCE CALL WITH THE COUNTY ATTORNEY AND THE PUBLIC DEFENDER. NOTICE HOW MUCH FRIENDLIER EACH PERSON IS NOW THAT THE BATTLE IS OVER. THE TELEPHONE CONVERSATION CONTINUED:)

THE COURT: Clarification of point two of first-degree felony murder. If two people commit armed robbery and only one of them shoots and kills, are both people liable or responsible for first-degree felony murder?

Mark, any comment on the question, or any type of answer that you think should be given? I think the answer to that is, of course, yes. Rick?

MR. MILL: The answer is yes, if they're both committing the felony. But I think that to say yes to the jury would just highlight one instruction over the others. I will waive my client's presence on this issue and ask that the jury just be told to reread the instructions.

THE COURT: Yes, that's always my inclination. I think if you give any sort of specific answer, you start getting in trouble, because I think the answer is in the instructions.

MR. MILL: It is, and it's in the accomplice liability instructions, too, and the definition of felony murder.

MR. BARR: Right.

THE COURT: So my inclination is just to tell the jury, please refer to the rest of your instructions for the answer to this question.

MR. MILL: That's fine.

THE COURT: Mark?

MR. BARR: Judge, you're not going to refer to the accomplice instruction?

THE COURT: Well, it's in there.

MR. BARR: I ask that you not.

MR. MILL: I ask that you not highlight any one instruction.

MR. BARR: It sounds to me in order to assist the jury when they come back with a question such as this, that we need to point to the instructions. And I assume we don't have any objection to instructing the jury that they need to reread the instructions, but I think we can inform the jury that there is an instruction that deals with accomplice and liability for an accomplice.

THE COURT: All right. I'm at a disadvantage because I don't have all the instructions here in front of me. Since it's noontime, I'm inclined to just let them go to lunch and have the bailiff tell them that I'll answer the question after lunch. What I'll do is call you guys back up about 1:00 or so, so I can look at it, research it, and I'll come up with an answer.

MR. MILL: Okay.

MR. BARR: Okay.

(Thereupon, a recess was taken.)

THE COURT: Hello. Mr. Mill, Mr. Barr, I'm back in chambers. I have had time to review the question as well as the instructions. I have also had an opportunity to do some research on this issue. The question, just to reiterate it, clarification of point two of first-degree felony murder. So what we're asking, if two people commit armed robbery and only one of them shoots and kills, are both people liable or responsible for first-degree felony murder? That's the question.

I've had both your inputs on this. My answer to them will be as follows: Please refer to your instructions reference accomplice liability on page 6, as well as the elements of felony murder on page 12. Also refer to the instruction on page 3 reference absence of any other persons, as well as all the other instructions. And I'm going to send this back to them as soon as they get here. I'll let you both know if anything else happens. All right?

MR. BARR: Okay.

THE COURT: Thank you.

MR. MILL: Thank you.

MR. BARR: Thank you.

(Whereupon, a recess was taken, and then the following proceedings were held in the presence of the jury:)

THE COURT: The record will reflect the presence of the jury, counsel, and the defendant. Ladies and gentlemen, has the jury reached a verdict?

THE FOREPERSON: Yes.

THE COURT: Can you hand all forms of verdict to the bailiff, please. The clerk may now read and record the verdicts.

THE CLERK: State of Arizona versus Richard A. Roja.

Count 1: Conspiracy to commit armed robbery.
We, the jury, do find the defendant, Richard A. Roja, as to
Count 1: Guilty.
Do you further find this to be a dangerous offense? Yes.
Count 2: Armed robbery, Michael Fro.
We, the jury, do find the defendant, Richard A. Roja, as to
Count 2: Guilty.
Do you further find this to be a dangerous offense? Yes.
Count 3: Armed robbery, Amy Hopp.
We, the jury, do find the defendant, Richard A. Roja, as to
Count 3: Not guilty.
Do you find this to be dangerous? No.
Count 4: First-degree murder, Michael Fro.
We, the jury, do find the defendant, Richard A. Roja, as to
Count 4: Guilty.
Count 5: First-degree murder, Amy Hopp.
We, the jury, do find the defendant, Richard A. Roja, as to
Count 5: Guilty.
Are these your true verdicts, so say you one and all?

THE JURY PANEL: Yes.

(NOW THE CLERK POLLED EACH OF THE 12 JURORS TO DETERMINE
IF THIS WAS INDEED THEIR VERDICTS, AND ALL ANSWERED
AFFIRMATIVELY. THE JUDGE THANKED THE JURY FOR THEIR SERVICE
TO THE COMMUNITY, AND REMANDED RICHARD ROJA TO CUSTODY
WITHOUT BAIL. THEN HE SET UP A DATE FOR THE SENTENCING.)

ELEVENTH DAY, MAY 4, 2005
MORNING SESSION

(THE PROCEEDINGS BEGAN WITH THE JUDGE, THE PUBLIC
DEFENDER AND THE PROSECUTOR IN COURT, AS A HANDCUFFED
AND CHAINED RICHARD ROJA WAS BROUGHT INTO THE COURTROOM.
THE PUBLIC DEFENDER, IN ATTEMPTING TO INTRODUCE
MITIGATING CIRCUMSTANCES TO INFLUENCE THE JUDGE, CALLED
ON RICHARD'S MOTHER, FRANCIS ROJA:)

MRS. ROJA: Francis M. Roja. I just wanted to state that I understand what Richard
is facing. And I know that not everyone knows Richard, but for the most part

Richard is a smart kid and a good boy, and we hope that the Court will take into consideration that he's never been in trouble with the law in any way, shape, or form prior to this incident. And I would hope, Judge, that you would please consider my son's background. And I know that's asking a lot, but considering his young life, that's our future. I would just hope that we look at all aspects involved in this circumstance. And that's it.

THE COURT: Thank you, ma'am. Anybody else, Mr. Mill?

MR. MILL: Patsy Martin is the grandmother of my client.

THE COURT: Go ahead and make any statement you would like to make, ma'am.

MRS. MARTIN: I'm Patsy Martin. I'm Richard's grandmother. Richard has always, always been, I mean, a good kid. I mean, I don't know what happened in this situation. I mean, he's never hurt anybody. And I know this is all like a big, bad dream to all of us. The thing is, I was just hoping and praying that the Court would find leniency in the sentencing. And I'm really sorry for the victims. If there was any way I could change things. All I ask, I know Richard is a very intelligent boy. I mean, I love him. I'll always love him no matter what, but I'm just hoping that the Court will find leniency in his sentencing.

THE COURT: Thank you, ma'am. Anybody else, Mr. Mill?

MR. MILL: No, thank you, Your Honor.

THE COURT: Mr. Barr, is there anything you'd like to say on the State's behalf?

MR. BARR: Have you had an opportunity to review my sentencing memorandum?

THE COURT: Yes.

MR. BARR: How about the letters from the victims that I brought in this matter?

THE COURT: I reviewed all the letters that have been submitted to the Court.

MR. BARR: Thank you, Judge. May it please the Court, can I at least point out to the Court some areas of the letter from Mrs. Fro that I'd like the Court to pay special attention to?

THE COURT: That's fine.

MR. BARR: When Richard Roja murdered her son, Michael, and his girlfriend, he took away their chances to experience joy and sorrow, a full life cycle, the intimacy of marriage, the pride of marriage and raising their children and succeeding in business. Since Michael was a loving and affectionate son, I know that he would have been the same with his children. And the letter goes on and describes how this has devastated and destroyed her life.

What was not expressed in this letter is something that unfortunately she brought to my attention on a number of occasions, and that is that the defendant and his uncle and others involved in this offense would be laughing and joking and smiling while they were on the chain, that was particularly offensive to her, on more than one occasion. It appears to me perhaps the seriousness of the devastating loss of life really hasn't sunk into this defendant. His age has been considered and the fact the State did not seek the death penalty in this matter, and that his age is not much different than the victims 21 and 24.

Looking at the letter provided by the sister, what she spells out, which she talks about in terms of Michael, how he would frequently call her, cheer her up and talk to her sometimes several times a day by telephone. This defendant is going to have that opportunity with his family. He's alive, and he will be in prison, he'll have that opportunity to communicate and discuss things with his family, to laugh, to joke if he wants to. But Michael Fro and Amy Hopp will never have that opportunity again.

As set forth, the aggravating factors that the State believes are applicable in this case, perhaps the most shockingly evil thing about this crime is where and when it occurred and how it occurred that two such young people minding their own business, doing one of those functions in society that we do on occasion, that's washing a car.

I'd ask this Court to sentence the defendant to the maximum available term, consecutive on all counts, that the defendant never have an opportunity to take a gun and shoot another individual. Thank you.

THE COURT: Mr. Mill, do you want to come forward with your client.

MR. MILL: Sure.

THE COURT: Is your true name Richard A. Roja?

THE DEFENDANT: Yes.

THE COURT: Mr. Roja, is your date of birth December 4th, 1987?

THE DEFENDANT: Yes.

THE COURT: Mr. Roja, pursuant to a verdict by a jury, it is the judgment of the Court that you are guilty of Count 1, conspiracy to commit armed robbery, a class two dangerous felony; Count 2, armed robbery, a class two dangerous felony; Count 4, first-degree murder, a class one dangerous felony; and Count 5, first-degree murder, a class one dangerous felony.

I have read the presentence report, its recommendation, I reviewed the letters that have been submitted by the victims and the victims' family, I have reviewed the two sentencing memorandums submitted by both parties, and I heard the evidence at trial. Anything else?

MR. BARR: Yes, Judge. The State, in its presentence memorandum, mentions an approximate value of the vehicle as well from $600 to $700 damage.

THE COURT: The Court will retain jurisdiction over the restitution issues.

MR. BARR: Yes, Judge.

THE COURT: Mr. Mill.

MR. MILL: Your Honor, I've submitted what I have to say in writing. The records from Orange County Foster Care should become a part of the record somehow because they speak volumes to at least this five year important period of my client's life. The time when most kids are enjoying things like Cub Scouts, he's going to foster care review hearings. I do not offer this as some sort of excuse for what he did, but this is time for mitigation. And when I compare Richard Roja to kids who were raised in healthy normal families that I see all the time, I can tell you that after reading through those two volumes of materials, it's not difficult to predict what would have happened to Richard Roja. It is not a defense to what he did, but it certainly provides mitigation.

The only other comment I'd like to make is the presentence report reflects a lack of remorse and a lack of caring for the surviving people. That's at my direction, and I've told Richard Roja not to talk to the presentence officer, that he's got to clam up when it comes time to expressing things like remorse. And that's at my direction.

Finally, I, too, on occasion observed Richard Roja to be laughing on the chain over the year and a half or so that it took this case to get to trial. But I don't think we should forget that he was 15 and 16 or 17 at the time, that he's on this chain and he cannot be in tears every time that he's making a public appearance. I don't think that's demonstrative that he doesn't respect the Court or respect the victims. I believe it's just an indication that he's a young guy. That's all I have.

THE COURT: Mr. Roja, anything you'd like to say?

THE DEFENDANT: This whole case, do you know what I mean, has been based on nothing but hearsay. The State over there, they keep saying "he did it." Nobody came up in trial and said "he shot him." They had an eye witness, and the girl said it wasn't me. She couldn't identify me. Do you know what I mean? I figure it's conspiracy. I thought I was set up. They work together, the detectives over there, side-by-side through the whole way. There's been rumors they were being paid. Not them, but the witnesses. And they all lied under oath, committing perjury. They lied sometimes in my trial and they lied from before the grand jury. They switched the story totally. And about me not having remorse, I just didn't talk to the lady. She was trying to ask me questions. I told her I didn't want to talk about the case. By me laughing on the chain, do you know what I mean, I could see my uncle once in a while. Me and him are close. When I see him, this is the only time we get to talk right here. That's the only way. I never disrespected nobody. Do you know what I mean? I know two innocent people died, but maybe, you know, that girl said that we were there, you know. She said that we were there, whatever, but nobody said that I shot them. Nobody seen me shoot them. The lady that seen it said it wasn't me. If you can't see that, where's it at? And they're saying the victims' family. Look at my family. There's two other co-defendants in this. Look at the mother of my other co-defendant in the next case, Tony Mo. She's a drug addict. She was on drugs. She tried to commit suicide December of 2004. I don't know how you—how the jury could believe people like that. I still stand with my innocence. I did not shoot those people. I know innocent people died. I feel bad for that, but I didn't shoot them. And that's it.

THE COURT: Anything else?

MR. MILL: No.

THE COURT: All right. Mr. Roja, I heard the evidence in this case and so did 12 people. Those 12 people found you guilty. In my view, the evidence was overwhelming that you were the person that shot those two people. And you know it and I believe you know it. And I can understand that for whatever purpose you're denying it at this time. This was a heinous crime. Mr. Fro, you shot him three times. The last time he was still alive. And then as Amy Hopp ran away screaming, you shot her twice in the head. And you were there, Mr. Roja, and you know exactly what you did. This was two murders for absolutely no reason. These people were washing their car. And I'm not sure exactly why you did it, if you were high on drugs. That's inconsequential.

I did read all the papers, the documents from Orange County. Yes, you had a miserable childhood, but, you know, there's a lot of people out there that have had worse childhoods than you and they don't go out and commit double homicide. It's unfortunate that your mother and your grandmother are hurt by this, but the only person that you can blame for them being hurt is yourself for getting involved in this. As was stated, they can visit you in the Department of Corrections. The families of the two victims will never see them again, never speak to them again.

I have considered the aggravating and mitigating circumstances. The mitigating circumstances being your age and no prior felony convictions. The aggravating circumstances being multiple victims of multiple perpetrators, the fact that it was done for pecuniary gain, the effect on the families. And also the manner of the killing, the terror. The witnesses testified to the screaming of Amy Hopp as she tried to run away from you before you shot her. Based upon that, the Court believes: As to Count 4, first-degree murder, a class one dangerous felony, the Court sentences the defendant to natural life imprisonment. That will run consecutive to Count 5, first-degree murder, a class one dangerous felony, also consecutive natural life imprisonment. Those two counts will run concurrent with Count 1, conspiracy to commit armed robbery, a class two dangerous felony. The Court finds the aggravating circumstances outweigh the mitigating.

It is ordered sentencing the defendant to 18 years in the Department of Corrections on Count 1 and on Count 2. Also 18 years in the Department of Corrections. These two counts will run concurrent with Counts 4 and 5. The defendant is given credit for 792 days of presentence incarceration.

Mr. Roja, you do have a right of appeal. You need to file your notice of appeal within 20 days of today's date. If you cannot afford a lawyer or the transcripts, they will be provided for you free of charge. Please sign off on your appeal rights.

(SO ANOTHER TRIAL ENDS WITH THE MURDERER PLEADING INNOCENCE AND THE STATE REQUIRED TO PAY FOR HIS UPKEEP FOR AT LEAST THE NEXT 36 YEARS—LESS CREDIT FOR 792 DAYS ALREADY SPENT IN PRISON.)